Donald Warhol

Blind

6-25-63

INTERPRETING
RELIGION

PRENTICE-HALL INTERNATIONAL, INC., *London*
PRENTICE-HALL OF AUSTRALIA, PTY., LTD., *Sydney*
PRENTICE-HALL OF CANADA, LTD., *Toronto*
PRENTICE-HALL FRANCE, S.A.R.L., *Paris*
PRENTICE-HALL OF JAPAN, INC., *Tokyo*
PRENTICE-HALL DE MEXICO, S.A., *Mexico City*

INTERPRETING RELIGION

DONALD WALHOUT

Aratus Kent Professor
of Philosophy and Religion

Rockford College

PRENTICE-HALL, INC.
Englewood Cliffs, N.J.
1963

To

Dr. Samuel J. Harrison
and
Dr. Howard W. Alexander

Après dix ans, mais un peu plus

PREFACE

This book is devoted to the examination of problems in religious thought. It combines text and readings in the proportion of about forty per cent to sixty per cent, respectively. The text is not merely a gloss or introduction to the readings, but rather an independent, continuous development of thought throughout the chapters. Two readings are supplied for each chapter, so that the reader is confronted with three contrasting discussions on each subject. It is hoped that this feature will overcome the difficulties commonly felt when each approach is taken separately, namely, the lack of unity in a book of readings, and the lack of diversity in a one-man performance.

Although the contributors to this volume differ widely in their views, all take a sympathetic, constructive approach to religion. In a complete philosophy of religion it is necessary to give due place to skeptical and hostile attacks as well. But this book is directed to the need for people to be challenged by what thoughtful intellectuals who take religion seriously are saying. One does not learn much about Shakespeare from those who think his plays are not worth reading or attending. So it is with religion. If there is dissent or skepticism in the end, at least it should not be based upon the misconceptions of childhood or of unconcerned opponents.

The readings chosen are all by recent twentieth century writers. Thus, while the book follows basically a problems approach, it may also be viewed as a partial survey of contemporary religious thought.

Although *Interpreting Religion* is predominantly Protestant in outlook, it may be used successfully by all who are interested in the common ground of philosophy and religion.

A personal word may be mentioned. The author is neither a theologian nor a clergyman, but a philosopher, whose interest in religious thought lies mainly, but not exclusively, in its philosophical side and in the relationships between religions, especially Christianity and other religons. Accordingly the book is for the most part on the border area between philosophy and theology. I call it "Religious Interpretation," which I venture to suggest is a distinctive sort of enterprise.

A few technical points about the book are also in order: the footnotes for the writer's own text are printed at the back of the book, whereas the footnotes for the reading selections are printed at the bottom of the page. For all but two of the reading selections the titles are those of the authors themselves or else slight modifications using the authors' own words. In the cases of Gilson and Carnell, separation from original context meant that titles had to be supplied. The two readings for each chapter are placed chronologically. The Biblical quotations in the selections by Thompson and Carnell and the New Testament quotations in the writer's own text are from the Revised Standard Version of *The Holy Bible* (copyright 1946, 1952) and are reprinted by permission of the Division of Christian Education of the National Council of Churches of Christ in America.

I wish to thank my wife Justine for handling many miscellaneous tasks connected with the book and for her encouragement. I would also like to thank Rockford College for a semester's leave of absence, which, though given for the study of Oriental philosophy at the University of Hawaii, nevertheless afforded some time for progress on this book. Acknowledgment is gratefully extended to the writers represented in the volume, some of whom also supplied biographical information; to the Photoduplication Department of the University of Chicago Library; and to three Rockford College students, Anne Peterson, Florence Coleman, and David Ishizaki.

D. W.

Rockford, Ill.

CONTENTS

Part Two · *Problems of Theistic Religion*

INTERPRETING
RELIGION

INTRODUCTION

PURPOSE

The purpose of this book is to usher the reader into the discussion of some of the lively issues which are at the forefront of contemporary religious thought. To accomplish this it will be necessary to formulate questions with precision and to explain and sometimes debate possible viewpoints on these questions. Both the text and the readings are designed to do these things. Beyond this, however, the goal is for the reader to begin to share in the discussion—in his own situation and at his own level—and to clarify his own religious convictions. The measure to which the reader achieves this goal will be the measure of the success of this book.

Since this is the purpose of the book, the reader should be warned at the outset that it is not a book of factual material to be merely learned or memorized. The study of religion has its factual sides—comparative religion, the sociology of religion, Biblical history, and so forth—and the reader would do well to consult works in these areas when more information is needed. But the writings in this volume are all interpretations of questions whose controversial character makes other interpretations possible; therefore, they need to be examined critically. Naturally if they are to be beneficial they must be read thoroughly and comprehended; not merely learned, but evaluated. There must be a peculiar combination of due respect for the authors and their viewpoints and a ready willingness to criticize wherever criticism seems appropriate.

The purpose in view means that there are some things which the book is not intended to do. The aim is not, for example, to present a full-fledged philosophy of religion or systematic theology in the technical sense of these terms; it is not to present a survey of the world's religions; it is not to give an analysis of the current religious situation in America or in the world; it is not to formulate a distinctive religious message for our times or to advocate how religion should be applied to various practical situations. These kinds of inquiries are necessary to the most comprehensive understanding of religion and would form natural sequels to the present study. The present study itself, however, is concerned with the analysis and interpretation of some of the intellectual questions which thoughtful students are bound to face when they begin to think seriously about religion. It is an introduction to problems of religion for a student audience that is often eager, sometimes confused, always alert.

PROCEDURE

The approach to the questions discussed in the text portion of this book is an approach that will be called religious interpretation. It may be defined as the approach which interprets the meaning and significance of religious beliefs and practices from the standpoint of religion itself rather than from some other standpoint such as philosophy or history. Since the term "religious interpretation" is not in common use, although the procedure itself is, it may be helpful to contrast the approach with two other disciplines: philosophy of religion, and theology.

In the traditional sense, philosophy of religion is generally taken to be an examination of religion from the standpoint of critical reason with the aim of determining what is true or false in religious beliefs and what is of value in religious phenomena. An exception to this view is found in modern linguistic analysis. But according to a typical traditional account, philosophy of religion requires a person "to abstract for the time being from such religious beliefs as he personally may have, and to consider without initial partiality the beliefs, practices, and teachings of all religions. . . ." Thus "philosophical curiosity, as directed upon religion, demands that one examine such evidence as there may be, whether demonstrative or only probable, of the truth or falsity of the dogmas of the various religions."[1]

Religious interpretation, as here conceived, differs from philosophy of religion, first of all, in proceeding from a sympathetic, internal standpoint in relation to religion rather than from the objective, external standpoint of philosophy. A second difference is that religious interpretation begins with certain preliminary assumptions about religion, whereas philosophy of religion does not, or at least has as one of its goals the examination of all assumptions. The principal assumptions of religious interpretation are these: that religion is something distinct and not reducible to the categories of some other discipline such as science; that religion is an avenue to truth; that religion has value and importance in some nonemotive sense; and that religion can to some extent be understood and expressed rationally. In accepting these assumptions the intention is not to say that they should not be critically examined, but rather that any particular subject must begin with some premises in order to get started. All particular disciplines, like mathematics or biology, start with some assumed ideas about their field without first stopping to ask and answer all of the philosophical questions that could be raised about the field. Religious interpretation is like these particular disciplines, while philosophy of religion is an overview concerned with total examination.

Theology is the formal presentation and explanation of the doctrinal beliefs and requirements of a particular religion. A typical definition runs: "Theology is the methodological explanation of the contents of the Christian faith."[2]

Religious interpretation, as here conceived, is like theology in that both begin with assumed starting points. But two differences may be noted. One is that religious interpretation is wider in scope. It may be concerned with dimensions of religion that are wider than those which pertain to a single religion. One may, for example, try to explain appreciatively the teachings of a religion different from one's own, and this would be religious interpretation rather than theology. Or he may elucidate a belief held by several religions, such as monotheism, or even a factor pertinent to all religions, such as the need for religion, and this would be religious interpretation rather than theology. The other difference is that, even within a particular religion like Christianity, religious interpretation has a somewhat broader compass than theology. Theology is largely concerned with formal exposition of basic doctrines and requirements, whereas religious interpretation is directed to the over-all spirit and meaning of the religion and may employ less formal ways of illuminating its nature. The books of C. S. Lewis, for instance, are not generally regarded as theology in the technical sense; but they are concerned with clarifying and interpreting the meaning of Christianity and can therefore be regarded as religious interpretation. Radhakrishnan's *The Hindu View of Life* would be another example. Theology is, of course, religious interpretation also, but a special case of it.

Another term which needs to be clarified in the present connection is philosophical theology. This term is somewhat ambiguous. Sometimes it is used as a synonym for philosophy of religion, with the possible qualification that it is more concerned with beliefs relating to God and man than with the entire scope of religious life. At other times it appears to be thought of as more like theology than philosophy, namely, the kind of theology which employs philosophical categories and relates itself consciously and explicitly to secular modes of thought. In this case it is often contrasted with systematic theology.[3] Now depending on whether philosophical theology is regarded primarily as philosophy of religion or as theology, religious interpretation would have the same relation to it as it has to the associated discipline, as already explained.

Of course in any discussion it is quite impossible to separate completely one discipline or procedure from the others. The ensuing chapters certainly raise philosophical questions and contain philosophical elements, and therefore some readers might prefer to call the work philosophy of religion in the broadest sense in which that term is used today. There are also theological elements, especially in Part Three, and therefore some readers might prefer to call the book theology in the broadest sense in which that term is used today. The writer thinks, however, that in the technical senses of these terms neither term is fully adequate and that religious interpretation is a more fitting description of the approach.

There is one field in which religious interpretation is very commonly employed today, and that is in the field of comparative religion when the aim is to expound sympathetically the teachings of the various religions as seen from the perspectives of those religions themselves.[4] Religious interpretation is, in fact, a very frequent procedure in expositions of religion. It is any attempt to explain and interpret any religious idea or practice from any general or particular religious standpoint. Here we are only giving a name to this very common approach. In this book we shall be applying it to the domain of religious problems.

The justification for adopting this approach is that, if we are to understand or judge religion with any degree of fairness and adequacy, we ought to base our understanding or judgment upon knowledge drawn from religion's own view of itself and not merely upon knowledge drawn from external, disinterested accounts of it. This point will be defended in Chapter I, where the idea of external and internal standpoints is elaborated.

PERSPECTIVE

Religious interpretation cannot proceed apart from some perspective on the part of the interpreter. No one can expound religious ideas from a completely positionless, convictionless island of pure thought. There is always a dominant milieu within which religious interpretation takes place. The milieu of the present volume is a Protestant one. This means that the writer's convictions are Protestant, and that this fact influences the selection of topics, the treatment given, and the conclusions reached. A writer should always strive for methodological fairness and impartiality, and he may hope that his presentation will not appear unduly biased. Yet it is well to acknowledge his convictional perspective from the beginning so that the reader may be aware of it.

Merely to indicate a Protestant perspective may not seem to be specific enough for some readers. Therefore the writer wishes to register his support for the growing movement which seeks conciliation among the various theological camps. Despite genuine differences there appears to be an overt attempt in all groups, or at least by some of the leaders in all groups, to find more common ground than has been evident in the past. There seems to be an increasing awareness that the problems which confront world Christianity are more important than some of the doctrinal differences that have impeded concerted effort in the past. The writer also expresses sympathy with the attempt to find new descriptive labels, if labels are inevitable, to communicate this irenic endeavor. He is attracted by what Professor William Hordern calls in one book "modern orthodoxy"[5] and in another book "a new Reformation theology,"[6] both of which in their context convey dissatisfaction with the customary labels that have been wielded so easily in recent decades. The writer is opposed, however, to the tendency in this type of movement to discount any form of natural or rational theology—a tendency which he personally regards as a somewhat irrationalist tendency. A scientist recently asked, "Don't you think that most thinking people today want to gain the truth they can find in all of the theological factions without aligning themselves rigidly with one?" The writer takes this as a good expression of the spirit he hopes will prevail in this book.

The Protestant milieu of the book also means that it is oriented toward, and will doubtless be most profitable to, an audience predominantly influenced by Protestant culture. This does not mean that the reader is presupposed to have definite convictions or affiliations. On the contrary, most college classes in religion, except in restrictive religious schools, include a wide variety of student opinion, both as to content and clarity. It is this heterogeneous type of classroom situation which the writer has had primarily in mind. However, it is hoped that this book may be suitable for more homogeneous situations as well, for, common to all the presupposed classroom situations is the belief in freedom of thought, the need for knowledge of varying views, and the right of individual interpretation on religious matters. This emphasis is an important part of the Protestant milieu directing the book's design.

PLAN

The topics treated in the book are arranged in three major parts. Part One, comprising Chapters I-V, includes questions which are relevant to all religion, and are therefore likely to be of interest to any person concerned with religion. Part Two, Chapters VI-X, deals with problems relating especially to theistic religion, that is, problems which are peculiarly relevant to religion based explicitly on belief in God. The third part, Chapters XI-XVI, is devoted specifically to problems connected with the understanding of Christianity. These three divisions may be called, respectively, general religious interpretation, theistic interpretation, and Christian interpretation.

This threefold classification of problems has been developed from a suggestion contained in an article by Professor John C. Bennett of Union Theological Seminary.[7] In the article, entitled "Are there Tests of Revelation?," Dr. Bennett suggests that there are two wider circles of faith to which a Christian belongs in addition to that of his own circle of faith. These wider circles are, first, the circle of faith itself, which would include all those who have a positive response to life, who have a serious religious concern; and second, the circle of theistic faith, which would include all those who trust in one personal God. This classification is not elaborated in the article, which has a different theme, and naturally Dr. Bennett is not responsible for the use here made of the idea, or for the content of this book, but it can readily be seen how the suggestion lends itself to a format for an extended survey of religious questions: we shall first discuss some questions of mutual interest to everyone in the broadest circle of faith, then certain questions of significance for the circle of theistic faith, and finally some problems of vital concern to the circle of Christian faith.

The adoption of this classification should not be interpreted in a theoretical way as implying a progression from religion in general as the most important stage of religion, to theistic religion as a mere illustration of general religion, to Christianity as a mere illustration of the previous two stages. Christians would generally regard the order of ascendency to be the reverse, with Christian faith being viewed as the completion of religious and theistic experience. The plan is not designed to be a dialectical development from general religion to specific religion; it is simply a recognition that people of differing persuasions can discuss many things of mutual interest before they turn to matters of special concern within their own circle of faith. Thus the plan is not so much an argument as an invitation; it is not a deduction but a decision. The writer feels, however, that the plan of organization corresponds to two interests of most people—an interest in the universal questionings of man, and an interest in their own religious situation.

Another possible misunderstanding should be dealt with. It may be thought that our intention is to set forth in Part One only those conclusions which represent the common agreement of all religion, in Part Two only those conclusions which have the agreement of all theism, and in Part Three only the beliefs which are accepted by all of Christianity. This is not the intention. There would be a thin diet of thought to express if we had to confine ourselves in the three parts to the few general points which could command the acceptance, respectively, of all religious persons, of all theists, and of all Christians. Much of the value of dialogue among different interpreters would be lost if each one tried merely to express the common agreements of everybody. An interpreter must go beyond this, just as in a good classroom discussion the conscientious student will go beyond merely making statements that everybody in the class would agree to. Parts One and Two, being of a wider scope than the specific treatment of Christian thought in Part Three, will necessarily contain conclusions of a more generalized order. But there is a difference between conclusions of a general order and statements which are unexceptionable generalities. So in all of the parts it is fitting, not to say inevitable, for an expositor to handle the subject from his own announced perspective. Thus the reader may expect to find *throughout the book* some statements which might be accepted by everyone, some statements which are acceptable only to theists, some only to certain theists, some only to Christians, some only to Protestants, some only to certain Protestants, perhaps some to nobody, etc. This is a consequence of writing in a Protestant milieu—to some people its weakness, to others its strength.

It may be argued by some that one's own outlook is so dominating, so distorting, that it is a meaningless and misleading gesture to try to discuss questions of a general religious nature or questions concerning theism as such. The only intelligent course to follow, they may say, is to set forth immediately the primary Protestant convictions and then recognize frankly that any further discussion is an apologetic expression of this bias. The writer believes, on the contrary, that on this matter of objectivity the truth lies somewhere between two extreme views—the one which says we can step outside of our immediate standpoint entirely and judge questions with thorough objectivity, as some philosophers have claimed, and the other which maintains that we cannot judge anything at all except through the thoroughly distorting medium of our own standpoint.[8] Moreover, there is a danger in making academic work in religious philosophy appear to be more like deduction than dialogue, more like proclamation than inquiry. The plan of the book is designed to overcome this danger. Yet there is nothing binding in the arrangement of parts and chapters that would prevent a different sequence from being used to suit a different approach.

Now in the chapters that follow, each topic is first discussed by the writer, and then two reading selections from contemporary authors are presented on the same topic. The reader is thus confronted with three analyses of each subject. Sometimes the readings give viewpoints which represent alternative interpretations to that of the writer or to each other, and sometimes they examine additional aspects of the topic without necessarily implying conflict. The criterion for the selection of the readings has been a conjecture of what would be likely to prove provocative to the kind of audience held in mind. Most of the readings turn out to be from Protestant pens, reflecting the milieu of the book. The number of Catholic and Jewish writers included may not, I fear, sufficiently suggest the degree of profit which Protestant thinkers today find in the writings of other traditions. The readings are confined to contemporary authors not out of scorn for the past but because contemporary thought on the persistent questions of life is what people tend to seek first for their personal guidance and growth.

PART ONE

COMMON QUESTIONS IN A COMMON QUEST

I · THE NATURE OF RELIGION

Our study begins with a consideration of the general nature of religion, but first some preliminary questions regarding our standpoint in the discussion and the very possibility of our undertaking must be dealt with.

EXTERNAL AND INTERNAL VIEWPOINTS

The first thing we must decide upon in determining the definition of religion is the standpoint from which we shall make our judgment. One viewpoint is that of the person who is not immersed in the experience of religion, who is disinterested and detached, who tries to describe it from the outside. The other perspective is that of the person who is enlivened by the spirit of religion, who is absorbed and involved in it, who tries to portray it from the inside. These two approaches have been called the external and internal standpoints. One is that of the nonparticipant in religion, the other is that of the participant. Both approaches have much to contribute to a full understanding of religion. But when the question is one of discovering the essence of religion, we can hardly expect the nonparticipant to be of much assistance. No matter how obvious its social and physical aspects may be, religion springs from the needs of individual personalities; it is called into existence through man's inner longings and aspirations. The focal point is the experience in which these aspirations are fulfilled; all else is derivative. Consequently, unless we know something of the meaning of religion in the inner life of the individual, we are not equipped for the job of understanding it. And we can only obtain the credentials by being participants ourselves. In this respect religion is like many other spheres of life. We could hardly acquire, for instance, a complete understanding of music or science if we had only learned about them through the descriptions of others, and had never entered into the experience of musical performances or scientific experimentation ourselves.

It would be a prolific project to review even a small portion of the interpretations of religion which have been given by those who regard themselves as nonparticipants.[1] Fortunately, such a task will be unnecessary if we can detect what is wrong in principle with this method of approach. Let us do so by asking ourselves what our own natural tendency would be in describing activities in which we have no personal concern or experience. It may be put forward as a reasonable hypothesis that in such cases our inclinations would move us almost invariably in one or both of two directions: description of externals, and explanation by origins. Consider baseball or politics as examples. In the one direction, if we are nonparticipants, baseball usually means the throwing of balls, the swinging of bats, and the running of players. Politics is likely to mean election speeches, taxes, graft, and vague hero worship. In the other direction, we may be inclined to explain baseball by how the thing got started and what could possibly lead people to play it; while in politics we may judge a candidate by his geographical origin, an issue by its sponsors, and a practice by its goodness or badness in the past. We must also add that such opinions are sometimes made by people who are not ignorant in other fields. Unfortunately, our views are not always rendered less naive by our being learned. But how different are all such descriptions from those of a man who plays a sport with interest and knowledge, or a man who has dedicated his life to the cause of wise government.

In religious interpretation we can notice the same twofold tendency. In the first place, without participation, we cannot examine religion through our own experience of it, but can only describe how other people's experiences and actions appear to us. The inevitable outcome of such an approach is a definition of religion as comprising institutions, ceremonials, creeds, cultural inheritance, and the like. All these external aspects of religion have been momentous in the history of civilization, and for many purposes it is useful to restrict our attention to a sociological definition of this sort, but at the same time we must recognize that these things would not have come into being apart from the dramatic experiences of individuals and communities. These outward features, therefore, are properly regarded as by-products. They are important buttresses to the sanctuary of religion, but do not provide its foundation.

Likewise, in studying the origin of religion, we may, without participation, be misled into confusing the origination of it with what it is. There are several ways of approaching the origin of religion which would be useful to distinguish at this point.

The least rewarding of these approaches is the etymological one. Very often the origin of a word can shed much light on our understanding of the reality which the word designates. But in the present case it is not so. The origin of our word religion from the Latin *religio* is obscure. According to A. C. Bouquet, the word may have had an *l-e-g* origin, so that it meant " 'to take up, gather, count, or observe', i.e., 'to observe the signs of a divine communication'."[2] This origin, associating religion with divination, he regards as more probable. Another alternative is that the word has an *l-i-g* origin, which he interprets as signifying " 'to bind', so that 'religio' meant 'a relationship', i.e., 'a communion between the human and the superhuman'."[3] This latter meaning of the word tends to give

religion a wider scope than just its primitive forms. However, the word
religio, with the latter origin, has also been interpreted as meaning "taboo,
restraint."[4] Thus the weight of the etymological emphasis seems to be
markedly on the side of the superstitious and restrictive forms of religion,
while its freeing and integrating character, as manifested in higher forms,
is not disclosed. This approach is therefore inadequate, for, quite apart
from the obscurity of the matter, any definition which is confined to so
narrow a plane can do little more than call our attention to some aspects
of some religions. It cannot bring us to the heart of all religion.

The historical approach to the origin of religion is more common and
more productive. Its chief value lies in providing necessary data to be
taken into account in a general definition, rather than in disclosing by itself the essence of religion. There is a factual difficulty which attends any
investigation of this kind, namely, that there is no way of verifying
directly what the origin of religion really was. Consequently a number of
theories have been proposed, none of which has gained universal acceptance. Some investigators find the origin of religion in magic, some in
animism, some in *mana*, still others in ancestor worship, others in the "high
god" concept, others in reactions to biological events, and so forth.[5] But
this is not the main point which needs to be made here. Our question is
whether we could infer the essence of religion from a knowledge of its
origin, even if it could be ascertained more exactly how religion had its
beginning. One sound objection against such an inference is always the
reminder that the origin of something ages ago does not tell us what that
phenomenon is like now. But a further objection is often neglected,
namely, that a purely factual account of the beginning of religion is not
even capable of telling us what the essence of religion was then. The
reason is that the scientific historian, like the sociologist, must approach
his particular problem of beginnings with the eyes of an outer sentinel,
and is therefore restricted, through this self-imposed duty, to the outward
evidences of religion, without entering its inner bastion.

The origin of religion can also be approached from a psychological point
of view. Here the aim is not to uncover the first signs of religion in the past,
but to determine what factors in the human self gave birth to religion.
This approach to religion appears to be the most promising of all those
external approaches mentioned so far, since it directs us to the personal
springs of religion—which after all must have been the source of religion
in the past too—and since it brings us to an area more open to verification.
Yet a nonparticipating psychologist is no different from other external
observers. He is in the same position as the sociologist, the etymologist,
and the historian; he differs only in his subject matter. The mere fact that
a psychologist deals with the human self as his subject is not by itself a
sufficient qualification for understanding religion. Freud's conception of
religion as an illusion "born of the need to make tolerable the helplessness

of man and built out of the material offered by memories of the helplessness of his own childhood and the childhood of the human race"[6] surely
reflects the standpoint of an alien observer and not one who knows
mature religion from the inside. Thus as nonparticipants we are bound, in
this field too, to concentrate on the outer religious behavior of the self,
the outer results of religion. Even when this limitation is overcome by
internal understanding, we still cannot say, of course, that the genesis of
something is the same thing as its essence. But we can say that a knowledge of the psychic roots of religion, internally grasped, may be the best
clues to understanding its essence.

If it is true that nonparticipants are prone to dwell upon externals and
origins, we should be encouraged to realize the importance of participating in the experience of religion, not only for its own intrinsic value, but
even in order to understand what it means. This does not mean that no
one can judge religion who does not already approve of it, or who does
not accept the tenets of some particular religion. But it does mean that no
one who has not at some time participated wholeheartedly in the experience of religion is equipped for the task of understanding it. Our
standpoint, then, must be that of a participant, drawing upon our own
experience, upon the experience of the community of faith to which we
may belong, and upon the experience of other persons and communities
so far as we can place ourselves sympathetically within their framework
of meaning.

ON DEFINING RELIGION

We need next to consider two objections, one theoretical and one
practical, to the very attempt to define religion, and then give some
positive reasons why the attempt is worthwhile.

The theoretical objection, voiced by Prof. G. H. Clark,[7] is that there
is no essence of religion to define. Every religion is unique in itself and
not a mere illustration of a common thread running through all of them.
What we mean by religion, therefore, can only be given by indicating
Christianity, Islam, Hinduism, etc., and not by pointing out an underlying
essence within them all.

The first point to be made in reply to this objection is that there must
be some common features in these religions in order for us even to think
of them as religions. Without some common factors there would be no
basis for thinking of them together or classifying them as we do under
the same term. This was one of the elementary lessons of thought taught
by Plato at the very beginning of Western philosophy. People know in a
general way what is meant when religion is referred to; yet they could
not do so unless there were something in common, some essence, in religion.

But the objection may not rest on so elementary an error; so we should look for a more subtle confusion. Such a confusion often results because there are two things that might be meant when one speaks of the essence of anything. In one sense essence may mean merely the common features or characteristics of a group of things, without implying that those common features are good or bad or that they are more important than the particular instances in the group. In this sense the statement of the essence of anything is value-neutral; it may be called the factual essence. In the other sense the essence of anything means the ideal form of it, the perfect, qualitative character which that thing can have. In this sense there is a value judgment involved; the meaning here may be called the ideal essence. Now the confusion arises when someone thinks we are trying to give the ideal essence of something when we are only trying to give its factual essence, i.e., a plain description.

Thus the confusion in the present objection is this: the objection wrongly supposes that when we offer a factual definition of religion we are suggesting that this common essence is the most important thing about religion and that particular religions have the status of mere examples of some ideal type which is universally present in all of them. The uniqueness of individual religions would thus be surrendered to an unreal religion-in-general. But that is not our intention. There is nothing in the attempt to formulate the factual essence of religion which requires us to say that there is a perfect type running through all religions or to reject as meaningless the claim of any particular religion to be supreme. To use an analogy, we may give a factual definition of what planets are without suggesting that all planets are equally capable of maintaining life. It may be that several planets are able to sustain life and it may be that only one is capable of doing so; the definition itself does not determine this point. The same may be said in the case of religion.

This objection may also involve a fear that one's own religion will be somehow tainted, somehow degraded, if similarities are pointed out between it and other religions. This is a fear which needs to be overcome, for similarities there certainly are. Moreover, the pointing out of similarities need not detract from one's own faith.

The practical objection to defining religion is that religious phenomena are so voluminous and so diverse that it is impossible to see any unifying factors. So many have been the attempts, and yet so conflicting the conclusions, that the endeavor has little hope of reaching any general agreement.

In reply to this objection, several things must first be kept in mind about the multiplicity of definitions. For one thing, there is often more agreement than is evident on the surface. Many writers, who appear to be giving different definitions, are really bringing out the same basic concepts, even though they express them in different words. Again, some of

the definitions would be viewed by practically everyone as being obviously one-sided. For example, Matthew Arnold's famous definition of
religion as morality touched by emotion[8] can easily be seen to be incomplete and superficial if it is meant to cover all of actual religion. Further,
many definitions can be seen to be not so much wrong as only partial,
correct in what they say but leaving out something important.

But an adequate reply to this objection must not seek merely to soften
the divergency; it must present positive reasons why the task of general
description is significant despite inevitable divergency. Four such reasons
may be offered.

First, the attempt to define religion is a duty which the student, and
any other person who is going to deal with religion intellectually, has to
himself and other people. That is, if he is interested in religion, he thinks
about it, speaks about it, uses the term frequently. It would seem to be
obligatory, therefore, for him to try to clarify what he means by the
term and how he is going to use it, so that he does not merely throw the
term around loosely.

Second, to understand religion may be a way of coming to understand
people, which is a priceless quality to have. Religions are not abstract
entities; they are ways of life pursued by people. Therefore in understanding religion we understand more about people. It could even be
argued that religious beliefs are the primary things that make people what
they are, that constitute their personal selves. In penetrating what is common in these convictions of people, we may see more clearly our affinities
with other human beings—our common plights and aspirations. A bare
definition, of course, will not do this. But a definition which is accompanied by continuous study, and which is open to re-examination, may be
a useful vehicle in this direction.

Third, we should not minimize the theoretical value attaching to an
effort like this. The endeavor to understand something more adequately
than one has before is of value in itself. If there were to result a conception which did gain general acceptance, this would be a contribution
to knowledge, and hence a good in itself. And if the prospects are not
bright for ideas in this field to receive general acceptance, this is no reason
to discard the value to be found in intellectual undertakings.

Fourth, the understanding of the nature of actual religion may be helpful in enabling us to clarify and express the particular religion or kind of
religion that we consider ideal. This may be done by assisting us to see
more knowingly how our own conception of the ideal may be regarded
as the fulfillment of the religious quest of man. In referring to ideal religion here, we do not mean to suggest that there is an ideal religion-in-
general present, or potentially present, in all religions. The ideal may very
well be conceived to be a particular religion. The definition alone does not

settle this question. The only point here is that by knowing some of the common features of man's religions we may be able to relate our conception of true religion more effectively to religious tendencies in general and to indicate more meaningfully how it completes and answers those tendencies. If this is so, we have another worthy reason for pursuing the definition of religion.

A DEFINITION PROPOSED

We cannot take space to review and criticize even a selection of the numerous definitions of religion that have been proposed.[9] Instead we shall move directly to a definition which seems to us accurate and comprehensive.

Religion, then, as defined here, means *ultimate commitments and endeavors concerning reconciliation*. It will be noted that there are four major concepts in the definition. Religion involves, first, a quality of ultimacy or extremity; second, the commitments or dedication of the whole personality; third, resultant endeavors or activities; and finally, some sort of reconciliation as the object or end. It may be helpful to give immediately a fuller form of the definition which expands these four points but still stays within the compass of a single sentence. A brief discussion will then be added on each of the points separately. The longer definition is as follows: religion designates *the most deeply gripping and most persistently governing attitudes, beliefs, and endeavors of a person or a group in response to the yearning for reconciliation with that reality, or else an ideal situation, which is regarded as bringing the highest fulfillment because it is regarded as the highest value.*

It will be convenient to take up the four key terms in reverse order. The concept of reconciliation points to the object or goal of religion. This is a factor which is sometimes neglected in definitions that stress inner feelings and attitudes. Yet outer circumstances are just as influential in initiating religion as inner ones. The two, in fact, are inseparable. Thus it may be suggested that in all religions there is to be found a recognition, or an intimation, of a situation that is disrupted and demands healing. The call to religion is a situation in which there is some incompleteness, disharmony, brokenness, or alienation—a situation where things need to be set right. In a world of perfect unity and harmony we would be beyond the distinction between religion and nonreligion. There might, of course, be religion in an entirely different sense from ours. But our religion is born in a world disturbed and severed. A religious person usually feels this incompleteness or alienation most intensely in his own case. He finds himself confronted with life situations which require amelioration or unification before he can attain self-fulfillment. For this reason we must look for the personal roots of religion in deep-seated needs rather than in fear or some other psychological tendency. But a person is not always concerned solely with his own reconciliation; he might be vitally concerned for others'. Hence it is a mistake to think of religion exclusively as a search for individual salvation. In any case the point here is that there is always a disrupted whole which the religious person longs to have completed, for such unification will allow everyone concerned to realize his highest fulfillment. Such fulfillment is looked upon as the intrinsic good of the personality; and it is so regarded because it is based upon right relationship with the object of highest value in the universe. That is, reconciliation ultimately means right relationship with the object of highest value. Thus the idea of reconciliation includes the idea of value which is frequently employed in definitions of religion. But it does so by placing primary focus on the central problem of religion, namely, reconciliation, and not by lifting out one aspect of the total situation. The goal of religion, then, we may conclude, is that of reconciliation, either effecting it where it does not exist or maintaining it where it does exist.[10]

In order to effect or maintain the desired reconciliation, the religious person naturally does something about it; appropriate activities are carried on. Hence we must not stress the importance of beliefs and attitudes in religion at the expense of actions. The term "endeavors" instead of "actions" is used in the definition because the word "actions" usually denotes observable, physical performances, whereas in some religions the only prescribed activity may be an inner cultivation or contemplation. This last is true, for instance, in some forms of mystical religion. The term "endeavors" is wide enough to include both outwardly visible actions and inwardly practiced strivings. We should also note in this connection the fact that concern for final reconciliation often generates hosts of particular actions which, taken by themselves, are not usually thought of as religious in the popular sense, but which, if derived from the final aim, are properly regarded as religious acts. For instance, in a number of religions the concept of the ideal state of reconciliation generates many little acts of kindness which may seem to have little bearing on the lofty ideal; nevertheless, they are religious acts in so far as they are dictated by and done for the sake of the ideal. Thus the phrase "endeavors concerning reconciliation" includes not only endeavors directly promoting the final reconciliation in any religion, but also many little acts of reconciliation derivatively related to it.

The term "commitment" is aptly suited for our definition because, unlike alternative words, it unites several significant connotations relevant to religion. The core of commitment is dedication or devotedness. To be committed is to give one's allegiance to some value, some cause, some loyalty. The religious person is one who has pledged his allegiance to the cause of reconciliation. He is not undecided, wavering, or wayward in his loyalties, for he has made up his attitudes, has hammered them out in a definite direction, and is prepared to sustain them. Furthermore, "commitment" can also be used to cover the case where what we are devoted to might not always be a matter of explicit awareness on our part. We may publicly announce one set of principles, but actually be committed, consciously or unconsciously, to another set. In a word, commitment may signify those deeply buried allegiances which can actually govern our thought and behavior, but of which we are not fully aware.

Still another ingredient in commitment is faith. Faith is certainly a fundamental element in all religion. To commit oneself always involves some measure of risk; it is to venture out in a direction not fully charted by intellectual certainty. To commit oneself also means having trust and confidence in the eventual realization of reconciliation and in the agencies making for such realization.

A final connotation of "commitment" is that of implicit belief. Religion includes beliefs, and religion which draws out the whole personality will assign a large role to consciously articulated belief. Yet beliefs are not always explicitly stated, even though they are implied in the other facets of religion. Hence we had better say that belief is present in all religion, but sometimes implicitly. The term "commitment" seems best adapted to allow for this minimum meaning as well as to include more elaborate creeds and intellectual systems. Belief and faith will be discussed in the chapters immediately following. Meanwhile we note only that the idea of commitment conveys something of their pre-eminence in religion.

The last term to be discussed, but appearing first in the definition, is "ultimate." The quality of ultimacy in religion is one of its most marked characteristics. Ultimacy means, first of all, that religion summons all parts of the personality into its service. It affects the whole being, intellectual, emotional, volitional, physical. Religion is not a partial, fainthearted salute to duty: it is a total response. We may call this phase ultimacy in breadth. But religion is also characterized by ultimacy in depth. This means that religion is the most gripping and most permeating of life's responses. We have many temporary, changing commitments in the ordinary affairs of life, but a religious commitment is supreme over all others. The concern for reconciliation is an "ultimate concern"[11] and takes precedence over all other concerns. Religious endeavors, in turn, are those patterns of activity most demandingly called forth by the supreme commitment to reconciliation. Thus in breadth and in depth of response, religion is ultimate.

The question now arises: if religion means ultimate commitments and endeavors concerning reconciliation, is everyone religious? Some interpreters have thought of religion in such a way as to characterize every-body as religious by definition. But this seems an unwise procedure, notwithstanding its attractiveness. It does not clarify the issue to define religion so that it ceases to have a real opposite, so that nonreligion becomes meaningless and impossible. Both our language patterns and our general feeling tend to support this contention. In popular language there is certainly a distinction between the religious and the irreligious, implying that it is possible for people not to be religious. But even more important, there is a common feeling that religion involves something a little more zealous, a little more absorbing, a little more strenuous than what is conveyed by the concept of merely living, and that therefore we are not religious just through the sole fact of existing. This fact is illustrated in such an expression as, "He does that with almost a religious zeal." But if we cannot say everyone is religious by definition, we must also avoid another extreme, that of confining the scope of the religious to one type of religion, for example, monotheism. Our definition satisfactorily avoids this latter tendency. As for the former extreme, the definition does not beg the question as to whether everyone is religious or not. It may very well be that everyone is religious; but if so, it is a matter of finding out, and not one of definition. It is very instructive for some purposes to assume as a postulate that everyone is religious, and this is possible with our definition. Generally speaking, however, it may be more plausible to assume the possibility that some people have no ultimate commitments at all, have no concern for reconciliation, and are therefore nonreligious. This is not necessarily a negative value judgment, since in some cases it might be better to have no religion than to embrace certain of the religions of mankind. The assumption about the extent of religion can be, in either case, no more than an assumption, since no one is in a position, geographical or religious, to judge all human beings. We wish simply to point out the difference between the question of defining religion and the question of determining whether everyone is religious.

MARKS OF RELIGION

Partly by way of summary and partly by way of extension, we shall conclude this brief characterization of religion with an enumeration of some of its salient components. While not in every case dominant or ubiquitous, these may at least be said to be commonly or frequently part of what we designate as religion. No claim to exhaustiveness is made for the list.

SUPREME OBJECT OF LOYALTY. This is perhaps the most characteristic mark of religion. Usually the supreme object is taken to be an actual being, either a personal creator or an impersonal ground of existence, or in some cases even a human being. But in some humanistic religions it may only be an ideal type of life that is anticipated and striven for, often within the future of man on the earth. It is this supreme object which directs and integrates the loyalties of religious adherents.

FAITH. The religious life is one that is lived in and by faith. This quality should not be thought of merely as the regrettable consequence of the fact that scientific and logical proof of religious beliefs is unattainable. Rather religion finds a positive value in the trust and confidence that is called faith, and with it a personal incentive which can transcend that of the strictly intellectual affirmations in life. Such faith is exhibited in many and various life situations.

REVELATION. This term, to be refined later, when taken in its broadest and nontechnical sense, suggests another characteristic aspect of religion, namely, the fact that there is some intuitive source, some experience of immediacy, through which the beliefs and values that are accepted are made known, or at least suggested. Not every experience in life is equally cognitive: certain kinds of experience are specially illuminating for the religious consciousness.

BELIEFS. Religions vary in the emphasis they place upon rationally for-mulated doctrines. Those which are not theologically-minded may seem to have little emphasis at all. But when we recognize that beliefs may be implicit as well as overt, we can see that they are associated with every religion. There is always some conception about the universe and about man's life and destiny. Then, of course, in some religions, like Buddhism, Islam, and Christianity, adherence to certain beliefs is fundamental.

PATTERNS OF DEVOTION. Being concrete rather than abstract, religion does not stop short with the acknowledgment of, the belief about, or even the faith in, a supreme object of loyalty. Ways of physical and mental response toward the supreme object are established and regularly re-peated. In these patterns of devotion the believer expresses his allegiance and praise to the supreme object, dedicates his efforts to its ends, and re-news his own resources.

FELT MORAL DEMANDS. Morality may or may not occur without reli-gion; but religion does not exist without a moral dimension. So pervasive is religion in the lives of its adherents that it has relevance to their deci-sions in practical affairs. There are some things which, due directly to their religious persuasion, religious persons feel they ought to do or ought not to do. These moral demands are felt to be part of their religion.

APPROPRIATE ACTIONS. But a still more distinctive aspect of religion is the fact that it gives impulsion, motivation, to carry out these moral de-mands in action. Religion energizes people to exercise their moral obligations in the world, often at great personal risk.[12] It may be argued that some religions, like Pietism or mystical Taoism, show a more passive, submissive character. But it may be replied that there is here a different kind of moral understanding leading to different patterns of action. We may say in any case that religion prescribes appropriate actions for its felt moral demands and impels these to be carried out, even though there is sometimes failure to do so.

INTIMATIONS OF FINAL ATTAINMENT. Religion does not generally say that the ultimate fruition of what it seeks is found in the present unredeemed moment. Indeed a transformation is generally needed, so that reconciliation is possible only after certain actions have been undergone or certain events accomplished. Yet some awareness of what this final attainment would mean is possible even now, as manifested in certain experiences, trends, or signs. Thus religion contains intimations of final fruition even in the present.

THE IDEA OF THE HOLY

RUDOLF OTTO

Rudolf Otto (1869-1937) was a German theologian and philosopher whose interest in religion carried him into systematic theology, comparative religion, the psychology of religion, and philosophy. He studied at Erlangen and Göttingen and taught at Göttingen, Breslau, and then chiefly at Marburg. In addition to his work, The Idea of the Holy, *his works include* Religion and Naturalism *(1905),* Religious Essays *(1931), and* Mysticism East and West *(1932). In the following selection, he presents his well-known interpretation of religion as being essentially nonrational in character.*

I. THE RATIONAL AND THE NON-RATIONAL

It is essential to every theistic conception of God, and most of all to the Christian, that it designates and precisely characterizes deity by the attributes spirit, reason, purpose, good will, supreme power, unity, self-

From Rudolf Otto, *The Idea of the Holy*, trans. John W. Harvey (New York: Oxford University Press, Inc., Galaxy Books, 1958), pp. 1-11. Reprinted by permission.

hood. The nature of God is thus thought of by analogy with our human nature of reason and personality; only, whereas in ourselves we are aware of this as qualified by restriction and limitation, as applied to God the attributes we use are "completed," i.e. thought as absolute and unqualified. Now all these attributes constitute clear and definite *concepts:* they can be grasped by the intellect; they can be analysed by thought; they even admit of definition. An object that can thus be thought conceptually may be termed *rational.* The nature of deity described in the attributes above mentioned is, then, a rational nature; and a religion which recognizes and maintains such a view of God is in so far a "rational" religion. Only on such terms is *belief* possible in contrast to mere *feeling.* And of Christianity at least it is false that "feeling is all, the name but sound and smoke";[1]—where "name" stands for conception or thought. Rather we count this the very mark and criterion of a religion's high rank and superior value—that it should have no lack of *conceptions* about God; that it should admit knowledge—the knowledge that comes by faith—of the transcendent in terms of conceptual thought, whether those already mentioned or others which continue and develop them. Christianity not only possesses such conceptions but possesses them in unique clarity and abundance, and this is, though not the sole or even the chief, yet a very real sign of its superiority over religions of other forms and at other levels. This must be asserted at the outset and with the most positive emphasis.

But, when this is granted, we have to be on our guard against an error which would lead to a wrong and one-sided interpretation of religion. This is the view that the essence of deity can be given completely and exhaustively in such "rational" attributions as have been referred to above and in others like them. It is not an unnatural misconception. We are prompted to it by the traditional language of edification, with its characteristic phraseology and ideas; by the learned treatment of religious themes in sermon and theological instruction; and further even by our Holy Scriptures themselves. In all these cases the "rational" element occupies the foreground, and often nothing else seems to be present at all. But this is after all to be expected. All language, in so far as it consists of words, purports to convey ideas or concepts;—that is what language means;—and the more clearly and unequivocally it does so, the better the language. And hence expositions of religious truth in language inevitably tend to stress the "rational" attributes of God.

But though the above mistake is thus a natural one enough, it is none the less seriously misleading. For so far are these "rational" attributes from exhausting the idea of deity, that they in fact imply a non-rational or supra-rational Subject of which they are predicates. They are "essential" (and not merely "accidental") attributes of that subject, but they are

---

[1] Goethe, *Faust.*

also, it is important to notice, *synthetic* essential attributes. That is to say, we have to predicate them of a subject which they qualify, but which in its deeper essence is not, nor indeed can be, comprehended in them; which rather requires comprehension of a quite different kind. Yet, though it eludes the conceptual way of understanding, it must be in some way or other within our grasp, else absolutely nothing could be asserted of it. And even mysticism, in speaking of it as τὸ ἄρρητον, the ineffable, does not really mean to imply that absolutely nothing can be asserted of the object of the religious consciousness; otherwise, mysticism could exist only in unbroken silence, whereas what has generally been a characteristic of the mystics is their copious eloquence.

Here for the first time we come up against the contrast between rationalism and profounder religion, and with this contrast and its signs we shall be repeatedly concerned in what follows. We have here in fact the first and most distinctive mark of rationalism, with which all the rest are bound up. It is not that which is commonly asserted, that rationalism is the denial, and its opposite the affirmation, of the miraculous. That is manifestly a wrong or at least a very superficial distinction. For the traditional theory of the miraculous as the occasional breach in the causal nexus in nature by a Being who himself instituted and must therefore be master of it—this theory is itself as massively "rational" as it is possible to be. Rationalists have often enough acquiesced in the possibility of the miraculous in this sense; they have even themselves contributed to frame a theory of it;—whereas anti-rationalists have been often indifferent to the whole controversy about miracles. The difference between rationalism and its opposite is to be found elsewhere. It resolves itself rather into a peculiar difference of *quality* in the mental attitude and emotional content of the religious life itself. All depends upon this: in our idea of God is the non-rational overborne, even perhaps wholly excluded, by the rational? Or conversely, does the non-rational itself preponderate over the rational? Looking at the matter thus, we see that the common dictum, that orthodoxy itself has been the mother of rationalism, is in some measure well founded. It is not simply that orthodoxy was preoccupied with doctrine and the framing of dogma, for these have been no less a concern of the wildest mystics. It is rather that orthodoxy found in the construction of dogma and doctrine no way to do justice to the nonrational aspect of its subject. So far from keeping the nonrational element in religion alive in the heart of the religious experience, orthodox Christianity manifestly failed to recognize its value, and by this failure gave to the idea of God a one-sidedly intellectualistic and rationalistic interpretation.

This bias to rationalization still prevails, not only in theology but in the science of comparative religion in general, and from top to bottom of it. The modern students of mythology, and those who pursue research into the religion of "primitive man" and attempt to construct the "bases" or "sources" of religion, are all victims to it. Men do not, of course, in these cases employ those lofty "rational" concepts which we took as our point of departure; but they tend to take these concepts and their gradual "evolution" as setting the main problem of their inquiry, and fashion ideas and notions of lower value, which they regard as paving the way for them. It is always in terms of concepts and ideas that the subject is pursued, "natural" ones, moreover, such as have a place in the general sphere of man's ideational life, and are not specifically "religious." And then with a resolution and cunning which one can hardly help admiring, men shut their eyes to that which is quite unique in the religious experience, even in its most primitive manifestations. But it is rather a matter for astonishment than for admiration! For if there be any single domain of human experience that presents us with something unmistakably specific and unique, peculiar to itself, assuredly it is that of the religious life. In truth the enemy has often a keener vision in this matter than either the champion of religion or the neutral and professedly impartial theorist. For the adversaries on their side know very well that the entire "pother about mysticism" has nothing to do with "reason" and "rationality."

And so it is salutary that we should be incited to notice that religion is not exclusively contained and exhaustively comprised in any series of "rational" assertions; and it is well worth while to attempt to bring the relation of the different "moments" of religion to one another clearly before the mind, so that its nature may become more manifest.

This attempt we are now to make with respect to the quite distinctive category of the holy or sacred.

II. "NUMEN" AND THE "NUMINOUS"

"Holiness"—"the holy"—is a category of interpretation and valuation peculiar to the sphere of religion. It is, indeed, applied by transference to another sphere—that of ethics—but it is not itself derived from this. While it is complex, it contains a quite specific element or "moment," which sets it apart from "the rational" in the meaning we gave to that word above, and which remains inexpressible—an ἄρρητον or *ineffabile*—in the sense that it completely eludes apprehension in terms of concepts. The same thing is true (to take a quite different region of experience) of the category of the beautiful.

Now these statements would be untrue from the outset if "the holy" were merely what is meant by the word, not only in common parlance, but in philosophical, and generally even in theological usage. The fact is we have come to use the words "holy," "sacred" (*heilig*) in an entirely derivative sense, quite different from that which they originally bore. We generally take "holy" as meaning "completely good"; it is the absolute moral attribute, denoting the consummation of moral goodness. In this sense Kant calls the will which remains unwaveringly obedient to the moral law from the motive of duty a "holy" will; here clearly we have simply the *perfectly moral* will. In the same way we may speak of the holiness or sanctity of duty or law, meaning merely that they are imperative upon conduct and universally obligatory.

But this common usage of the term is inaccurate. It is true that all this moral significance is contained in the word "holy," but it includes in addition—as even we cannot but feel—a clear overplus of meaning, and this it is now our task to isolate. Nor is this merely a later or acquired meaning; rather, "holy," or at least the equivalent words in Latin and Greek, in Semitic and other ancient languages, denoted first and foremost *only* this overplus: if the ethical element was present at all, at any rate it was not original and never constituted the whole meaning of the word. Any one who uses it to-day does undoubtedly always feel "the morally good" to be implied in "holy"; and accordingly in our inquiry into that element which is separate and peculiar to the idea of the holy it will be useful, at least for the temporary purpose of the investigation, to invent a special term to stand for "the holy" *minus* its moral factor or "moment," and, as we can now add, minus its "rational" aspect altogether.

It will be our endeavour to suggest this unnamed Something to the reader as far as we may, so that he may himself feel it. There is no religion in which it does not live as the real innermost core, and without it no religion would be worthy of the name. It is pre-eminently a living force in the Semitic religions, and of these again in none has it such vigour as in that of the Bible. Here, too, it has a name of its own, viz. the Hebrew *qādôsh*, to which the Greek ἅγιος and the Latin *sanctus*, and, more accurately still, *sacer*, are the corresponding terms. It is not, of course, disputed that these terms in all three languages connote, as part of their meaning, *good, absolute goodness*, when, that is, the notion has ripened and reached the highest stage in its development. And we then use the word "holy" to translate them. But this "holy" then represents the gradual shaping and filling in with ethical meaning, or what we shall call the "schematization," of what was a unique original feeling-response, which can be in itself ethically neutral and claims consideration in its own right. And when this moment or element first emerges and begins its long development, all those expressions (*qādôsh*, ἅγιος, *sacer*, &c.) mean beyond all question something quite other than "the good." This is universally agreed by contemporary criticism, which rightly explains the rendering of *qādôsh* by "good" as a mistranslation and unwarranted "rationalization" or "moralization" of the term.

Accordingly, it is worth while, as we have said, to find a word to stand for this element in isolation, this "extra" in the meaning of "holy" above and beyond the meaning of goodness. By means of a special term we shall the better be able, first, to keep the meaning clearly apart and distinct, and second, to apprehend and classify connectedly whatever subordinate forms or stages of development it may show. For this purpose I adopt a word coined from the Latin *numen. Omen* has given us "ominous," and there is no reason why from *numen* we should not similarly form a word "numinous." I shall speak, then, of a unique "numinous" category of value and of a definitely "numinous" state of mind, which is always found wherever the category is applied. This mental state is perfectly *sui generis* and irreducible to any other; and therefore, like every absolutely primary and elementary datum, while it admits of being discussed, it cannot be strictly defined. There is only one way to help another to an understanding of it. He must be guided and led on by consideration and discussion of the matter through the ways of his own mind, until he reach the point at which "the numinous" in him perforce begins to stir, to start into life and into consciousness. We can co-operate in this process by bringing before his notice all that can be found in other regions of the mind, already known and familiar, to resemble, or again to afford some special contrast to, the particular experience we wish to elucidate. Then we must add: "This X of ours is not precisely *this* experience, but akin to this one and the opposite of that other. Cannot you now realize for yourself what it is?" In other words our X cannot, strictly speaking, be taught, it can only be evoked, awakened in the mind; as everything that comes "of the spirit" must be awakened.

III. THE ELEMENTS IN THE "NUMINOUS"

Creature-Feeling

The reader is invited to direct his mind to a moment of deeply-felt religious experience, as little as possible qualified by other forms of consciousness. Whoever cannot do this, whoever knows no such moments in his experience, is requested to read no farther; for it is not easy to discuss questions of religious psychology with one who can recollect the emotions of his adolescence, the discomforts of indigestion, or, say, social feelings, but cannot recall any intrinsically religious feelings. We do not blame such an one, when he tries for himself to advance as far as he can with the help of such principles of explanation as he knows, interpreting "aesthetics" in terms of sensuous pleasure, and "religion" as a function of the gregarious instinct and social standards, or as something more primitive still. But the artist, who for his part has an intimate personal knowledge of the distinctive element in the aesthetic experience, will decline his theories with thanks, and the religious man will reject them even more uncompromisingly.

Next, in the probing and analysis of such states of the soul as that of solemn worship, it will be well if regard be paid to what is unique in them rather than to what they have in common with other similar states. To be *rapt* in worship is one thing; to be morally *uplifted* by the contemplation of a good deed is another; and it is not to their common features, but to those elements of emotional content peculiar to the first that we would have attention directed as precisely as possible. As Christians we undoubtedly here first meet with feelings familiar enough in a weaker form in other departments of experience, such as feelings of gratitude, trust, love, reliance, humble submission, and dedication. But this does not by any means exhaust the content of religious worship. Not in any of these have we got the special features of the quite unique and incomparable experience of solemn worship. In what does this consist?

Schleiermacher has the credit of isolating a very important element in such an experience. This is the "feeling of dependence." But this important discovery of Schleiermacher is open to criticism in more than one respect.

In the first place, the feeling or emotion which he really has in mind in this phrase is in its specific quality not a "feeling of dependence" in the "natural" sense of the word. As such, other domains of life and other regions of experience than the religious occasion the feeling, as a sense of personal insufficiency and impotence, a consciousness of being determined by circumstances and environment. The feeling of which Schleiermacher wrote has an undeniable analogy with these states of mind: they serve as an indication to it, and its nature may be elucidated by them, so that, by following the direction in which they point, the feeling itself may be spontaneously felt. But the feeling is at the same time also qualitatively different from such analogous states of mind. Schleiermacher himself, in a way, recognizes this by distinguishing the feeling of pious or religious dependence from all other feelings of the dependence. His mistake is in making the distinction merely that between "absolute" and "relative" dependence, and therefore a difference of degree and not of intrinsic quality. What he overlooks is that, in giving the feeling the name "feeling of dependence" at all, we are really employing what is no more than a very close analogy. Anyone who compares and contrasts the two states of mind introspectively will find out, I think, what I mean. It cannot be expressed by means of anything else, just because it is so primary and elementary a datum in our psychical life, and therefore only definable through itself. It may perhaps help him if I cite a well-known example, in which the precise "moment" or element of religious feeling of which we are speaking is most actively present. When Abraham ventures to plead with God for the men of Sodom, he says (Gen. xviii. 27): "Behold now,

I have taken upon me to speak unto the Lord, which am but dust and ashes." There you have a self-confessed "feeling of dependence," which is yet at the same time far more than, and something other than, *merely* a feeling of dependence. Desiring to give it a name of its own, I propose to call it "creature-consciousness" or creature-feeling. It is the emotion of a creature, submerged and overwhelmed by its own nothingness in contrast to that which is supreme above all creatures.

It is easily seen that, once again, this phrase, whatever it is, is not a *conceptual* explanation of the matter. All that this new term, "creature-feeling," can express, is the note of submergence into nothingness before an overpowering, absolute might of some kind; whereas everything turns upon the *character* of this overpowering might, a character which cannot be expressed verbally, and can only be suggested indirectly through the tone and content of a man's feeling-response to it. And this response must be directly experienced in oneself to be understood.

We have now to note a second defect in the formulation of Schleiermacher's principle. The religious category discovered by him, by whose means he professes to determine the real content of the religious emotion, is merely a category of *self*-valuation, in the sense of self-depreciation. According to him the religious emotion would be directly and primarily a sort of *self*-consciousness, a feeling concerning oneself in a special, determined relation, viz. one's dependence. Thus, according to Schleiermacher, I can only come upon the very fact of God as the result of an inference, that is, by reasoning to a cause beyond myself to account for my "feeling of dependence." But this is entirely opposed to the psychological facts of the case. Rather, the "creature-feeling" is itself a first subjective concomitant and effect of another feeling-element, which casts it like a shadow, but which in itself indubitably has immediate and primary reference to an object outside the self.[2]

---

[2] This is so manifestly borne out by experience that it must be about the first thing to force itself upon the notice of psychologists analysing the facts of religion. There is a certain naïveté in the following passage from William James's *Varieties of Religious Experience* (p. 58), where, alluding to the origin of the Grecian representations of the gods, he says: "As regards the origin of the Greek gods, we need not at present seek an opinion. But the whole array of our instances leads to a conclusion something like this: It is as if there were in the human consciousness a *sense of reality*, *a feeling of objective presence, a perception* of what we may call '*something there*', more deep and more general than any of the special and particular 'senses' by which the current psychology supposes existent realities to be originally revealed." (The italics are James's own.) James is debarred by his empiricist and pragmatist standpoint from coming to a recognition of faculties of knowledge and potentialities of thought in the spirit itself, and he is therefore obliged to have recourse to somewhat singular and mysterious hypotheses to explain this fact. But he grasps the fact itself clearly enough and is sufficient of a realist not to explain it away. But this "feeling of reality", the feeling of a "numinous" *object* objectively given, must be posited as a primary immediate datum of consciousness, and the "feeling of dependence" is then a consequence, following very closely upon it, viz. a depreciation of the *subject* in his own eyes. The latter presupposes the former.

Now this object is just what we have already spoken of as "the numinous." For the "creature-feeling" and the sense of dependence to raise in the mind the "numen" must be experienced as present, a *numen praesens*, as is in the case of Abraham. There must be felt a something "numinous," something bearing the character of a "numen," to which the mind turns spontaneously; or (which is the same thing in other words) these feelings can only arise in the mind as accompanying emotions when the category of "the numinous" is called into play.

The numinous is thus felt as objective and outside the self. We have now to inquire more closely into its nature and the modes of its manifestation.

IS CHRISTIANITY UNIQUE?

GORDON H. CLARK

Gordon H. Clark (1902–) was educated at the University of Pennsylvania and has taught philosophy there and at Wheaton College and Butler University. He has written on the history of philosophy, e.g., Thales to Dewey *(1957), and also on religious subjects, e.g.,* A Christian View of Men and Things *(1952), and* Religion, Reason, and Revelation *(1961). In this selection he presents his argument that there is no common essence in religion at all.*

Religious leaders who are not strongly attached to biblical Christianity have on occasion recommended a so-called "universal" religion synthesized from elements of all the world religions. This proposal can be buttressed by the allegation that Christianity itself is a synthesis of borrowings from earlier systems of worship. The idea of the Virgin Birth, it is said, has been copied from the story of Buddha's birth or from Greek mythology, and the doctrines of Paul are explained as adaptations from the Greek mysteries. Macchioro even asserts that Paul was an initiate to the pagan rites. Conservative Christians, on the other hand, maintain that Christianity is unique.

For example, J. Gresham Machen in his monumental work, *The Virgin*

From Gordon H. Clark, "Is Christianity Unique?," *Christianity Today*, Vol. IV, No. 6 (Dec. 21, 1959), 24-25. Reprinted by permission.

Birth of Christ, produces evidence to show that the original account of Buddha's birth contains no extraordinary factor, and that only after Christianity had come on the scene were those stories altered in the direction of a virgin birth. The same author in *The Origin of Paul's Religion*, and other authors as well, explode the theory that Paul borrowed from the pagan mysteries. Thus Christianity has been defended as unique.

Such studies are all to the good. Christianity would be compromised if it could be shown to be a mosaic of borrowings. Yet, the fact that Christianity is unique is subject to an exaggerated evaluation. For, when one analyzes the situation, it will be discovered that every religion is unique— Buddhism and Islam as well as Christianity. In fact, failure to recognize this results both in a misunderstanding of Christianity and in a false philosophy of religion as well.

THE ERROR OF SYNCRETISM

Nearly all volumes on the philosophy of religion assume that there is a common, universal phenomenon, religion, which may be the subject matter of a single science. William E. Hocking in *Living Religions and a World Faith* commences by asserting—"In its nature religion is universal and one." The same author in a later volume, *The Coming World Civilization* (p. 149), emphasizes and elaborates the same idea. Other authors are in essential agreement on this point.

The unity of religion is sometimes sought in an experience of conversion, an integration of personality, or some sort of emotion. The present article cannot discuss extensively this point of view except to say that it is entirely too broad a definition of religion. Any selected emotional experience (abstracted from intellectual or doctrinal content) can be found in politics, marriage, business success, and in aesthetic experience as often as in religion. Here the topic must be restricted to religious *ideas*.

TRUTH: THE DECISIVE CRITERION

The reason every religion is unique is that each one is a particular complex, and the several factors are interdependent. If it were not so technical, a comparison might be drawn with Euclidean and noneuclidean geometries, or even with plane and spherical geometry. They may all use the word *triangle*, but the word does not mean the same thing in the several cases. In plane geometry a triangle is a figure that necessarily contains 180 degrees. A spherical triangle must contain more. Both triangles are bounded by straight lines, but "straight lines" do not mean the same thing. So it is in religion, and even more so: a common word may be used in two or more religions, but not a common idea. For example, Christianity, Islam, and orthodox Judaism all talk about God. Indeed, they all talk about the God of Abraham, Isaac, and Jacob. Notwithstanding this striking identity in phraseology, the three religions do not mean the same thing. Obviously the triune God, whose second Person is Jesus Christ, is not the God of Judaism or Islam. The disparity is still more obvious if one analyzes the ideas of sin, salvation, or the future life. Each of these ideas is formed in relation to each of the others within a single religion. Clearly *heaven* is not the same in all. When further we add Buddhism to this list of religions, the situation becomes still more complex—or, rather, still more clear and simple. Nirvana and heaven (either the Christian one or the Mohammedan) are not the same thing at all. One form of Buddhism, possibly it is the purer form, is definitely atheistic. All plausibility therefore that heaven, or God, or any other idea is the common definitive element in a universal religion is lost. And it is virtually rubbing an author's nose into it to ask: Is communism a religion? Does one say that communism is antireligious? If so, it is none the less zealously and religiously so.

From a systematic point of view the inductive attempt to find a common element in all religions involves a hysteron-proteron; that is, it requires at the outset the knowledge it professes to obtain in the end. Let us take a parallel case. If Lewis Carroll tells Alice to examine all Snarks to find their common nature, Alice, at least in her waking moments, would not know whether all the objects before her were snarks or even whether any of them were. The philosophy of religion is in the same perplexity with Alice. The objects before it are Christianity, Buddhism, Confucianism, and so on. Are they religions or are they not? This question could be answered only after we knew the common element in all religions—only after a list of religions had been drawn up. But to draw up the list requires the knowledge that induction from the list is supposed to provide. Thus it is that so many volumes on the philosophy of religion or on comparative religions proceed on an impossible foundation.

The attempt to consider religion as a common, universal phenomenon ought really to be abandoned. There are religions, but there is no religion. Christianity is unique. Neither the Virgin Birth nor the Pauline theology was borrowed from other religions, and to try to merge these ideas in some syncretistic religion is to destroy Christianity. There would remain neither sin, heaven, nor Jesus Christ. But of course Islam is unique too and would equally be destroyed in a merger. The more important question therefore is not whether Christianity is unique, but whether Christianity is true.

SUGGESTED BOOKS

Bergson, Henri, *The Two Sources of Morality and Religion*, trans. R. Ashley Audra and Cloudesley Brereton. New York: Holt, Reinhart & Winston, Inc., 1935. Contrasts static and dynamic religion and interprets the latter as essentially mysticism.

Finnegan, Jack, *Youth Asks about Religion*. New York: Association Press, 1949. Designed as answers to questions frequently asked by young people. The book is elementary, but the author is a recognized scholar.

Fromm, Erich, *Psychoanalysis and Religion*. New Haven: Yale University Press, 1950. Defends humanistic religion as opposed to what the author (a psychoanalyst) regards as authoritarian religion.

Hutchison, John A. and James A. Martin, *Ways of Faith*, second edition. New York: The Ronald Press Company, 1960. An introduction to religion, Eastern and Western, with major emphasis on the West.

James, William, *The Varieties of Religious Experience*. New York: Longmans, Green & Co., 1902. A pioneer study in the psychology of religious experience by a well-known American psychologist and philosopher.

King, Winston L., *Introduction to Religion*. New York: Harper & Row, Publishers, 1954. A comprehensive survey of general features of religion—psychological, sociological, practical, and intellectual.

Noss, John B., *Man's Religions*, revised edition. New York: The Macmillan Company, 1956. An extensive work in the history of past and present religions.

Spiegelberg, Frederic, *Living Religions of the World*. Englewood Cliffs, N.J.: Prentice-Hall, Inc., 1956. A survey of contemporary religions, with a special interest in the nature and development of the religious impulse itself.

II · TRUTH IN RELIGION

The problem of truth in religion is one of the most difficult and most crucial questions to be faced in interpreting religion. It is of general religious concern because people of any faith are inclined to regard the plausibility of a religion as a requisite for its acceptability. That is, while a few people might say that even if religion is false it is justifiable if it brings satisfying emotional results, the vast majority would doubtless judge such a view to be intellectually dishonest and would follow their own religion only so long as they could honestly believe that it contains the truth or part of the truth. Certainly the latter view is dominant in the organized religions of the world. A problem for any religion, then, is that of rendering plausible whatever claims to truth it may make.

The problem may be awakened in an alert person in a rather shocking form. He may suddenly reflect and ask himself: are my own religious beliefs true? Of all the beliefs current in the world, are these which I have been reared in, or which I have come to cherish otherwise, really justifiable? Perplexity over this question will naturally suggest the more general question: can any religious beliefs be justified, and if so, how can it be done? A still more ultimate question is whether truth and falsity can be said to apply to religion at all. These questions are closely related and together constitute the problem of religious truth. Another way of stating it is to say that such questions raise the problem of the cognitive significance of religion, as contrasted with its personal, social, or other significance. In this chapter we shall explore these questions, dealing first with some necessary definitions of terms, then with the extent of knowledge, next with the religious attitude toward truth in religion, and finally with the source and criterion of religious truth.

BELIEF, KNOWLEDGE, AND TRUTH

Since our problem is to determine how we can *know* whether *beliefs* are *true*, we will be aided greatly if we begin with some considerations concerning the meaning of these central terms—knowledge, belief, and truth. Each of these terms has many ramifications which we cannot examine in detail. Nevertheless, it will be useful for our discussion to understand at the outset what is widely accepted as the basic meaning of these terms.

We begin, for convenience, with belief. The basic meaning of belief seems to be, in brief, the conviction that a statement is true. The word has other auras of association in addition to this simple, literal meaning, but they need not detain us long. Thus, for example, belief sometimes has an association of inferiority, especially when it is contrasted with knowledge. In fact, belief is sometimes set in opposition to knowledge, belief being but an uncertain conjecture, or "mere belief," as the saying goes, while knowledge is certain, tried, trustworthy. We would do better, however, to use opinion in such cases, and to contrast knowledge with opinion instead of with belief, since knowledge always includes belief, albeit something more. On the other hand, belief may also have an aura of superiority, especially when contrasted with unbelief or disbelief. When thus used, as in religion, for instance, it usually connotes something of deeply vital significance to the holder of the belief, something which the person who is unable to believe is missing. But we can fairly say that religious beliefs have this extra value quality not just because they are beliefs, but because they are *religious* beliefs. The same may be said for value beliefs generally. In any case this value quality is a special association not generally attached to the term belief.[1] Again, belief is sometimes taken as a synonym for statement or proposition. In this sense belief would not depend on anyone's holding the belief, as when someone speaks about the beliefs in a creed. Yet it seems that the subjective element of affirmation is more usually intended in belief. So when all is said and done, we may settle on the simplest and clearest definition of belief, namely, the conviction that a statement is true.

Turning now to knowledge, we shall notice two principal connotations of the term. The most usual connotation is that of common, public knowledge, and we shall deal with it first.

What we *know* to be so we also *believe* to be so; hence, knowledge includes belief. But it includes something more. First, knowledge requires a high degree of confirmation by whatever methods are appropriate to the type of knowledge in question. Scientific knowledge, for example, must be verified by observation and experiment; mathematical knowledge must be proved by rigorous logical demonstration, and so on. This requirement might be called a qualitative factor—intensity of confirmation. But there is also a quantitative requirement for public knowledge. In order to rank as knowledge, a belief must be generally accepted by all those persons who are capable of understanding the belief and have followed the test of verification. If experts or authorities disagree, the belief is regarded as a theory but not as knowledge. One other characteristic of knowledge must be mentioned, namely, that knowledge is not only believed to be true but *is* true. We do not say a person has knowledge (except perhaps as a figure of speech, as in the phrase "ancient knowledge"), when his belief is false.

The first meaning of knowledge, then, which is probably dominant in philosophical and scientific usage, can be approximated in the following definition: knowledge consists of beliefs which are confirmed beyond reasonable doubt, accepted by qualified persons, and true. This definition refers, as already indicated, to public or objective knowledge. It may be called the knowledge of public agreement.

But there is another sense of knowledge which is also in common usage and which is, as we shall see, more relevant to religion. This knowledge is considered true and highly confirmed but lacking in general public agreement. It may be illustrated by a person's awareness of his own headache, or of his own state of envy, or of the depth of another person's friendship for him. These are feelings which cannot be known but only guessed at by observing someone's outward behavior. Yet they are commonly regarded as examples of knowing, even though in the nature of the case they are not publicly verified. The only way of fitting this sense of knowledge into our previous definition would be to say that all the characteristics of knowledge are present, except that in this case other people are not qualified to judge. In one sense this is true, of course, but it sounds a bit awkward to state the matter thus. It seems better to say that we have here a somewhat different, though commonly recognized, meaning of knowledge. Knowledge in this sense means beliefs which are true and highly confirmed, but which are not open to the usual methods of public testing. We shall call this the knowledge of personal awareness. If the former meaning of knowledge is dominant in philosophy and science, the second meaning is more frequent in references to art, morality, and religion. We shall therefore have occasion to use the term in this second sense as well as in the first, for it is in common usage right along with the meaning of knowledge as public agreement.

Next we consider the term truth. No attempt will be made here to examine the various theories about the nature of truth or about the tests of truth. For our purpose it will only be necessary to state the basic meaning of the term truth which all these theories are attempting to explain. The main difference between truth, on the one hand, and belief and knowledge, on the other, is that the latter both include an element of subjective affirmation, whereas truth does not. We can say that we *believe* something and that we *know* something, but there is no corresponding act in which we *true* something. Truth is the objective attribute which is grasped in belief and knowledge. There would still be truth without belief and knowledge, for there are truths which no one knows or yet believes. Thus truth refers primarily to statements or propositions[2] rather than to human acts of apprehending. Truth is a relation between a statement and reality. A statement is true if it affirms what is so of reality or else denies what is not so of it. Truth, in a word, is that property of a statement whereby the statement records accurately what is so or not so of reality. An important thing to remember is that statements of truth or falsity, i.e., propositions, are not the same as verbal expressions. Truth need not be put into ordinary human language in order to be true. If it did, it would depend on human speaking and writing. But truth does not depend on human acts at all. This difference between propositions and verbal expressions is mentioned in order to make room for the claim that in some experiences, such as those of art and religion, there may be a grasp of truth which cannot be translated into a linguistic medium.

This discussion of truth gives a conception of truth regarded as objective and not as merely pragmatic.[3] That is, it implies that there is a real distinction between truth and falsity quite apart from human feelings and actions, and that truth cannot be defined as whatever ideas happen to work for man. In giving this conception, I believe I have recorded correctly the overwhelming conviction of religious thinkers, certainly those within the major religious traditions of the world. It is true that many religions have held to the finite character of all human knowledge, which may seem to imply that all religious beliefs have a purely pragmatic justification. But this is different from saying that ultimate truth is itself pragmatic, different from saying that the very meaning of truth lies in the effects of a belief, e.g., in the contentment it brings. Despite misleading utterances in both East and West, the intended view of the religions stressing relativism has doubtless been that human ideas are relative, not that ultimate truth itself is an illusion.

Some religious writers today tend to speak of truth as if it characterized private religious experiences as well as propositions. Following Sören Kierkegaard,[4] they distinguish between subjective truth and objective truth. The distinction intended here is a plausible one; but it refers properly not to the meaning of truth but to the manner of apprehending it. We should speak of subjective and objective modes of discovering truth, rather than of subjective and objective truth. The basic meaning of truth could then be kept uniform.

RELIGION'S CLAIM TO KNOWLEDGE

With these definitions in mind, we may approach the central question of religious knowledge—whether religion is or can be a path to truth. We shall break in upon this question by asking: is there religious knowledge? There are religious beliefs in abundance, but, as knowledge has been defined, is there religious knowledge?

A still more basic question would be to ask whether we possess any knowledge at all of any kind. The claim that no knowledge is possible has occasionally been defended. But in the common meaning of the term which has been indicated, it is more frequent, and surely more accurate, to maintain that we do possess a certain amount of knowledge. It is difficult to ascertain the extent of that knowledge, since the border-line between knowledge and opinion is not entirely precise. Yet examples come readily to mind. Our knowledge that living things die, or that objects thrown from windows fall to the ground, or that twice two is four, would quickly qualify. Science, too, has produced knowledge. Even though there is a wide difference in the degree of confirmation among its theories, and even though every scientific belief is, in the technical sense, a theory, still some beliefs have been confirmed so often that further tests are not considered significant, and these are rightly called scientific knowledge. Of course, if beliefs, in order to count as knowledge, had to be confirmed with absolute certainty, with no further clarification or confirmation conceivable, we should be forced to say that there is no knowledge, for that would be imposing a condition upon knowledge which is beyond the human mind. But since this extreme connotation is not customary, we need not hesitate in affirming that we do have a limited body of knowledge, a small quantity of well-authenticated, generally accepted truths.

But do we possess any religious knowledge? That is our question. On the qualitative side, exponents of religious beliefs maintain that their beliefs are very strongly confirmed by the means appropriate to religion. So intense is the confirmation, in fact, that religious beliefs are matters of ultimate commitment and concern. But on the quantitative side, religious beliefs cannot claim the kind of uniform agreement which characterizes the familiar examples of public knowledge, e.g., scientific or mathematical knowledge. Religious beliefs are legion, and there is no unanimity concerning them, even among the most learned and serious of religious persons. Hence it must be recognized that in the ordinary meaning of objective, public knowledge, religion has not afforded knowledge of this sort. If there were a body of religious knowledge in this sense, we could simply consult an "encyclopedia of religious knowledge" and find out the truth about God, man, and other religious questions by looking them up. But encyclopedias contain largely historical information, and religious knowledge can hardly be equated with this. If there is knowledge through religion, then, it is the knowledge of personal awareness.

It can thus be seen how the problem of religious truth becomes especially acute. Religious beliefs are not subject to the ordinary tests of observation, science, and logic, and there is therefore no body of public knowledge in religion. Yet religion claims to be a way to knowing—knowing through personal awareness—and religious beliefs claim to be true. How, then, can the claim be vindicated?

RELIGION'S CONCERN FOR TRUTH

In face of this problem, it may seem advisable to some people for religion to replace its concern with truth by a more vigorous interest in other values. As long as religion brings power into personal life and stability into society, they may argue, what does it matter whether truth is claimed or not? Or again, since the multitudinous religious beliefs cannot be tested by ordinary public means, why not regard all of them as neither true nor false but as more or less helpful for the individuals who hold them? Inasmuch as this attitude appears to be a prevalent one in society and on the college campus, it may be well to try to state more adequately why religion is concerned with truth and why, if it gives up this interest, it gives up its soul.

Without a concern for truth religion could not, in the first place, make any effective judgments upon human existence as it is, for those judgments could just as well be regarded as inaccurate or inapplicable. In Chapter I we suggested that religion arises in situations which are out of joint, broken, and in need of reconciliation. In these situations religion makes analyses, judgments, even proclamations, as to what needs to be mended, eliminated, or transcended. Occasionally these utterances become deeply stirring and profoundly prophetic. Yet if they were not accompanied by the belief that they were in fact true, such judgments would lose their force and possibly their relevance. The denials of these judgments would have to be asserted to be equally plausible with the judgments themselves, and this would make the judgments lose their point. Can we imagine Moses, for example, raising Israel from tribal customs to a high ethical monotheism by first giving his people the ten commandments and then turning around and telling them that they could just as well regard the ten commandments as false, as far as he was concerned, so long as they were willing to go along with them? Human nature does not respond to a religious system which puts forward teachings and then says they might as well be considered false teachings since truth is not important to religion.

The point here is that without a concern for truth one is logically committed to opening the floodgates for all sorts of opposing claims to be just as valid as one's own, including claims that may foster superstition, indifference, and moral reversion, the very things one may be seeking to overcome through his religion. The only antidote to this is a healthy concern for, and an honest attempt to state, what is true in religion.

But religion not only addresses itself to that in human life which needs to be overcome; it also brings us positive doctrines about the nature of the overcoming. It claims to lead us toward that reality, or perhaps an ideal situation, where reconciliation is to be found. But if there is no sense that these doctrines are true, no claim that the prescribed response brings us into truth, one is virtually saying that it does not matter whether we drift into illusion. Now to live consciously in illusion, or even to be indifferent to the possibility of it, is not only psychologically harmful but religiously sterile. No ultimate commitments and endeavors will be likely to result from such an attitude. The real consequence of such an attitude would be that religion, instead of bringing us to that reality where reconciliation is to be found, would be keeping us from it. In the words of a noted Indian scholar: "Religious consciousness firmly believes in the existence of its object, in an ontological sense. There is an ultimate and independently existing reality. . . . Ultimately, nothing can be religiously valuable unless it is logically true."[5]

Still we shall be reminded that all this does not diminish the multiplicity of beliefs and does not advise us how to select the truth from amid the multiple claims. The point is a fair one and must not be ignored. But in this section we are dealing only with the very concern for truth. And on this point it is plainly preferable to seek truth with patience than to foment illusion through indifference. It is better to have the uneasy tension of truth and claims contending than to have the easy truce of illusions embracing. If this be acknowledged, we can approach the problem of religious truth with more sympathy and personal interest.

SOURCES OF KNOWLEDGE

Our next step, then, is to try to be more specific about the source and criterion of religious truth. We shall approach this task by first identifying the principal sources or types of human knowledge in general, and then by seeing how the knowledge-claims of religion fit into this picture. We shall then be prepared to suggest what criteria are possible.

The classification of types of knowledge to be presented is an elaboration of the two meanings of knowledge defined earlier. These two meanings, the knowledge of public agreement and the knowledge of personal awareness, can be further subdivided, depending on which factor in consciousness happens to be predominant. In this classification we can see that the claim to religious knowledge fits into a familiar outline of types of knowledge. It should not be inferred from this, as many liberal theologians formerly did, that religion is not unique or that religious knowledge is just another kind of empirical or rational knowledge. We wish only to suggest that the claim to religious knowledge cannot be regarded as meaningless or occult, since it has affinities with other forms of human knowledge. It should also be added that in speaking of the sources of knowledge in this section we are referring to what philosophers call the epistemological sources of knowledge, i.e., the vindicating foundations of knowledge within human consciousness, and not to external sources or transmitters of knowledge, e.g., archaeological finds, scriptural texts, or church traditions. This does not mean that religious knowledge is more subjective than objective when its total origination is considered; it means that the confirmation of religious belief occurs in conscious experience rather than in unconscious factors.

If we ask, then, what aspect of consciousness is predominant in our human knowledge, we can readily see that the knowledge of public agreement can be divided into knowledge in which the senses are predominant and knowledge in which reason is predominant. Sensory knowledge includes both the ordinary, publicly confirmable observations of daily life, for example, that it is raining outside, and the more sophisticated knowledge of science, for example, that the earth follows an orbit around the sun. All knowledge probably requires some intellectual recognition and a certain amount of reasoning, and science involves a great deal of intellectuality in the formulation of hypotheses, the deduction of consequences, and the framing of experiments. But in the end both ordinary observation and science are based on the good auspices of the senses. On its confirmatory side at least, science is an extension of the senses. Rational knowledge includes both the self-evident principles of logic and mathematics, for example, the so-called law of contradiction, which says that a thing cannot both exist and not exist at the same time, and the logical inferences made from such principles. In such cases the source of knowledge is reason itself and not the senses.

It is more difficult to subdivide the knowledge of personal awareness on this basis. But several distinguishable types stand out. There is, first of all, a person's awareness of his own self-consciousness. It would be impossible to say, however, that one factor is predominant in this awareness; a total complex of factors is present. Then there is the awareness of one's own sensations, for example, that this fish is oily to one's own taste. Here the senses are predominant. In another sort of awareness we can recognize the feelings as predominant. These may be more private in character, for example, one's awareness that he feels hopeful a certain event will occur; or they may be of a more interpersonal nature, for example, one's awareness that a bond of friendship exists between another person and himself. Finally, we may distinguish the kind of knowing awareness we have in value situations. The most familiar examples of such awareness are esthetic appreciation—that this music is beautiful; moral understanding—that human beings have certain rights; and religious experience—that God is real. Again it is difficult to say which factor of consciousness is predominant in such awarenesses. But perhaps it would be fair to say at least that intellectual and sensory elements do not appear to be as dominant as the moving experiences of emotion and will. It will be questioned by skeptics whether such awareness should be classified as knowledge. Yet, on the other hand, there is widespread recognition that there is beauty in some sense, that there are ethical principles of some sort, and that there is cognitive significance in religion. In any case religion itself maintains that knowledge is possible through this source. The problem is to make explicit the truth contained therein.

All these types of knowledge are exhibited in the following table:

I. Knowledge of Public Agreement
   A. Sensory knowledge
      1. Ordinary public observations
      2. Science
   B. Rational knowledge
      1. Self-evident principles
      2. Logical inferences
II. Knowledge of Personal Awareness
   A. One's own self-consciousness
   B. One's own sensations
   C. Feelings, individual or interpersonal
   D. Value intuitions
      1. Esthetic appreciation
      2. Moral understanding
      3. Religious experience

There is another source of knowledge which some may wish to classify separately, namely, acceptance of an authority. Upon analysis it can be seen that in our classification authority can be more conveniently classified as a derivative form of one of the other types of knowledge. When we talk about acquiring knowledge through the authority of an expert mathematician, for example, or news information through the authority of a correspondent, it is plain that the real source of such knowledge, epistemologically, is rational thought in the one case and sensory observation in the other. Authority here is the means of transmitting knowledge rather than the source of it. When we speak more particularly of authority in the religious sense, e.g., a scripture or a person, it is clear that, in order for the authority to be regarded as an actual giver of truth, there must be an original personal conviction on our part, a faith-judgment, that the authority is a genuine one. Apart from this prior conviction of faith, there is no experimental or rational way of proving whether an authority is in fact a source of knowledge, unless of course there is some obvious contradiction of publicly known facts. For us, therefore, the primary factor is the intuitive experience which leads to the acceptance of an authority. Furthermore, the truth which the authority possesses must first have been given in some revelatory experience; so again we are led back to personal consciousness as the real source. Thus it can be seen that in either case authority is best classified under our very broad second division of knowledge.

Let us emphasize once more, then, that from the viewpoint of religion itself, the gateway to religious truth is to be found in those peculiarly intimate and incisive experiences called, in the philosophical sense, intuitive, and in the religious sense, revelatory. Religion does not live and move on the plane of sensory observation or rational analysis but in the dimension of experience we have delineated as personal awareness, or in religious language, personal encounter. Within this dimension some have claimed that there is knowledge which is direct and immediate, and in religion this is called mysticism. Others maintain that ultimate reality is never totally revealed in such experience and that truth is therefore partly hidden as well as partly disclosed. This kind of religious experience is generally called faith. In Chapter III we shall discuss faith as the more typical and universal religious response, the claim to mysticism being confined in any tradition to a relatively few.

It is not to our point to discuss the psychology of religious experience. It is relevant, however, to point out that, with respect to its epistemological source, the claim to religious knowledge is not entirely unlike other types of knowledge commonly recognized. This alone does not justify the claim, but at least it should entitle the claim to serious consideration, even by the skeptical.

THE CRITERION OF RELIGIOUS TRUTH

An intuitive source of religious truth must not mean pure subjectiveness. If it did, there could be no claim to truth, for by definition truth is not true for this or that individual. Hence there is a legitimate demand that religious truth-claims be shown to be objectively plausible. Apart from such plausibility there is no obvious differentiation of these claims from private feelings or whims. Apparently we must maintain both sides of a very delicate paradox, pointed up forcefully by two sentences from John Baillie which were written in close proximity: "The most important of all verities is a verity that cannot be argued." And yet: "A religion that refuses to exhibit its own reasonableness is fellow to a political regime that refuses to submit to a free referendum. . . ."[6] Thus religion must necessarily engage in the task of taking that which is given in the life of personal encounter, and showing that the truth-claims based upon it have a certain reasonableness.[7] This is religion's criterion of religious truth. It may be said to consist in two parts: confirmation in the deepest inner experience of personal life, and the offering of good reasons why the world-outlook based on such experience is justified. This criterion is, of course, that employed by religion when it speaks at the level of rational vindication. Some religions claim in addition, or perhaps exclusively, a self-authenticating revelation which cannot be and need not be vindicated by reason. And both of these sorts of internal criteria must be distinguished from the external criteria that philosophy may use in its work. We might say that the criterion I have indicated is the criterion of religious interpretation; self-authenticating revelation is the criterion of theology; and rational standards alone are the criteria of philosophy.

Proceeding with the discussion of the stated criterion, we need to ask what sorts of reasons can be given to justify a religious outlook. In what ways can religion show its reasonableness? We shall list some of the ways that seem most fruitful for the task.

RELIGION CAN APPEAL TO FELLOW WITNESSES. The fact that people have at many times and in different manners come to the same conclusions as we ourselves, lends a note of credibility which private feelings alone would not possess. In Christianity, for example, the testimony of the continuing historical community of the church is an important counterbalance to individual experience. While the notion of proof is out of the question here, truth-claims do gain in reasonableness if there are witnesses to their validity.

RELIGION CAN TRY TO DEMONSTRATE THAT IT MEETS HUMAN NEED. While the meeting of human needs is not *ipso facto* a proof of religious beliefs, still we should expect of a true religion that it would in fact meet human needs. Therefore, if a religion does awaken, stir, and fulfill the deep unsettledness in the soul of man and thereby leads to positive fruitions in the individual and in the world, this can be taken as evidence that truth has been sounded.

RELIGION CAN HARMONIZE ITSELF WITH SCIENCE. One of the greatest blocks to the acceptance of religion has been the espousal by some forms of religion, either through ignorance or through arrogance, of views which needlessly oppose the findings of scientists who were honest in their researches and may have had no other motive besides the discovery of empirical truth. When religion learns that it is not a rival of science, and instead incorporates the discoveries of science, it makes a great stride toward its own reasonableness.[8]

RELIGION CAN ATTEMPT TO SHOW ITS ADEQUACY TO THE FACTS OF MAN AND HISTORY. The record of human behavior is full of a vast number of things, heroic and barbaric, humane and insane, good and evil. Explanations of it often fail through a one-sided selection of facts. The religion that can render this historical drama comprehensible, do justice to its complexity, make sense out of both the sensible and the senseless, will have high priority in its claim to truth.

RELIGION CAN ENTER INTO DIALOGUE WITH SECULAR THOUGHT. One easy way for religion to acquire a reputation of irrationality is to remain in dogmatic seclusion from secular challenges and the alternatives to religion. While some may scorn such dialogue on the ground that it requires us to adopt secular standards, this attitude does more harm than good by leaving the impression of escapism and refusal to face criticism. If there is truth, let it speak to all.

RELIGION CAN REMOVE MISCONCEPTIONS OF ITSELF. It is perhaps no exaggeration to guess that nine-tenths of the refutations of other views are based on interpretations of those views which would not be acceptable to the holders of those views themselves. If this is so, one of the most forceful things we can do is clear away misinterpretations of our own beliefs and thus remove misguided objections to them.

RELIGION CAN APPROPRIATE THE POSITIVE RESULTS OF PHILOSOPHY. To do its job well, philosophy must serve no ulterior cause but must appeal only to independent rational criticism. But if there really is truth in religion, as religion believes, it should not fear the philosophy of religion but should welcome whatever clarifications or demonstrations it can offer. Philosophy may be an ally in helping to make explicit the truth in religion.

RELIGION CAN FACILITATE INTERNAL PARTICIPATION IN ITS PRACTICE. If religious knowledge has its source in personal awareness, the impression should not be conveyed that external, rational analysis is sufficient to grasp it. If there is any point to the old adage about trying something to find out for oneself, a religion can enhance its reasonableness by making the opportunity for participation in its practice accessible, intelligently conceived, and responsible.

In these ways religion can start from its base in personal awareness or faith and by reason give an account of its plausibility. In these ways it moves from subjectivity to objectivity, a movement never finished but always demanded.

THE TEST OF RELIGIOUS TRUTH

SAMUEL THOMPSON

Samuel M. Thompson (1902–) received his degrees from Monmouth College and Princeton University and has spent his career in philosophy at his alma mater. He is a contributor to the volume, The Heritage of Kant *(1939), and the author of an introductory textbook,* The Nature of Philosophy *(1961). The present selection is taken from his major work in the philosophy of religion. In the selection he clarifies the problem of religious truth and makes some useful distinctions pertinent to a solution.*

RELIGION'S OWN TEST OF TRUTH

Claims of religious truth may be examined at two levels. They may be tested within the limits of a particular religious faith, and by criteria which that religion specifies. Such tests assume the truth of the religion within which they are used, and so this level of test is a matter of inner consistency. A religion is bound to reject what is inconsistent with its own principles in so far as the inconsistency is recognized and its principles are adhered to, unless the conflicts are considered non-essential. If there were only one true religion it would contain in itself the tests of truth for all religions, but it seems quite plain that a claim to be the only true religion cannot be warranted by any test of truth within that religion itself.

This suggests the other level at which a claim of religious truth may be tested. It is the test of the primary principles of the religion itself. We refer here not to particular beliefs within a religion, to be examined in the light of the standards which that religion sets up; we refer rather to the truth of those standards themselves. This presents a special problem which we shall return to later in the chapter; it is, in fact, the central problem for a philosophy of religion. At this point, however, we shall look at some of the internal tests of truth which are used by actual religions. One reason for this is to see something of the great differences there can be in tests of religious truth.

From Samuel M. Thompson, *A Modern Philosophy of Religion* (Chicago: Henry Regnery Company, 1955), 137-49. Reprinted by permission.

If the beliefs of a religion are fantastic so also are likely to be its tests of truth. There is a religious sect, active recently in this country, which uses as a test the bite of poisonous snakes. To survive the bite of such a creature, presumably while under the spell of some strong religious emotion, is supposed to be the way in which God identifies those who are to be His authentic spokesmen. This, of course, is sheer savagery. Again, some piteous creatures so interpret the written oracles of their faith that they allow their own children to die rather than permit blood-transfusions. Here ignorance and arrogance go hand in hand.

Sometimes striking qualities of physique and personality are accepted as true signs of religious authority. Where people expect that a message from God, or from their gods, will be distinctive and will carry something of the mystery of its source in its content and in its mode of transmission, pathological behavior and unrestrained emotional frenzy may be looked upon as indications of religious truth. In religions with well established traditions and a highly organized priesthood, the very occupancy of a religious office will carry authority with it, especially if it is supposed that the occupant is in some way chosen by God.

Some of these tests have been used in the two higher religions of our own culture, Judaism and Christianity. But in both of these the supreme test of truth is moral and spiritual. It is in certain qualities of attitude, attitudes reflected in thought and practice, that the difference between the true and false is to be found. When we say that a religion, such as one of these, is true, we mean that he who has the faith to perform the acts which it prescribes in the attitudes which it enjoins will find the presence of God and will do the will of God. Truth here is existential truth, and its standards are existential standards. An attitude is an existing fact, it is the fusion of motive and feeling and expectation and evaluation in which action takes place. Mood alone is not enough, nor is feeling alone.

It is true that feeling alone is often taken to be the true test. Much of conventional religious worship seems intended to produce certain states of feeling. The presence of the desired feeling is taken to be the test of the success of the religious act. Anything which can be done in the presence of the feeling induced by the religious exercise is thought to be warranted by it. But since people are able to have intense and vivid religious feelings together with hate for others, and since few persecutions can match the vicious cruelty of some which have been blessed in the name of God under the guidance of such feelings, this test seems defective. It is the other way, in the teachings of the higher religions: the test of a religious feeling or emotion is the attitude it evokes. Religious feeling may be dangerous if it is not subjected to this test.

Micah, the prophet, saw the fundamental importance of attitude, and he set it forth in vivid contrast to conventional ideas of man's relation to

God—and in contrast to traditional ceremonies which evoked intense emotions of awe and adoration.

> With what shall I come before the LORD,
> and bow myself before God on high?
> Shall I come before him with burnt offerings,
> with calves a year old?
> Will the Lord be pleased with thousands of rams,
> with ten thousands of rivers of oil?
> Shall I give my first-born for my transgression,
> the fruit of my body for the sin of my soul?
> He has showed you, O man, what is good;
> and what does the LORD require of you
> But to do justice, and to love kindness,
> and to walk humbly with your God?[1]

It is in our desire to do justice and in our love of kindness and in our humility before God that we find God.

What brings human blessedness? One answer is given in the Sermon on the Mount. It is to be poor in spirit, to accept suffering and persecution, to be meek and merciful, to hunger and thirst for righteousness, to be pure in heart (that is, sincere) and to be peacemakers.[2] Over and over again Paul echoes this theme. "Put on then, as God's chosen ones, holy and beloved, compassion, kindness, lowliness, meekness, and patience, forbearing one another and, if one has a complaint against another, for-giving each other; as the Lord has forgiven you, so you also must forgive. And above all these put on love, which binds everything together in perfect harmony. . . . And be thankful."[3] Paul's supreme expression of this attitude is in his incomparable celebration of love. To speak in the tongues of angels, to have prophetic powers, to understand all mysteries and have all knowledge, to have all faith—even faith that will remove mountains—these are nothing without love. What are the signs of love? They are patience and kindness, absence of jealousy and boasting and arrogance and rudeness; they are the refusal to insist on one's rights, freedom from irritableness and resentment, the refusal to rejoice at wrong and the willingness to rejoice in the right.[4]

In Christianity the supreme test of truth is not agreement with dogma or theological correctness. Doctrine does not test belief; rather the tests of doctrine are in the fruits of belief as they are found in attitude and deed. What does your religious belief lead you to do and what are the attitudes it induces in you? What leads, says Paul, to "immorality, im-

---

[1] *Micah*, Chapter 6, verses 6-8.
[2] *Matthew*, Chapter 5, verses 3-12.
[3] *Colossians*, Chapter 3, verses 12-15. See also *II Corinthians*, Chapter 6, verses 4-7.
[4] *I Corinthians*, Chapter 13.

purity, licentiousness, idolatry, sorcery, enmity, strife, jealousy, anger, selfishness, dissension, party spirit, envy, drunkenness, carousing, and the like" is false.[5] These are the "works of the flesh," the consequences of man's attempt to live without God and of his pretense to self-sufficiency. How can we tell that it is God's presence in us which guides us, and that "our sufficiency is from God"?[6] Paul's answer is, by the "fruit of the Spirit." The "fruit of the Spirit is love, joy, peace, patience, kindness, goodness, faithfulness, gentleness, self-control,"[7] And Paul adds, "If we live by the Spirit, let us also walk by the Spirit. Let us have no self-conceit, no provoking of one another, no envy of one another."[8]

THE SPECIAL PROBLEM OF RELIGIOUS TRUTH

Religious truth is existential. If religion is true it brings us into the appropriate relationship with its object. Its object, by whatever name it is called, is thought to be in some sense the final reality or at least it is that to which man owes his final devotion. If the object of religion is God, as the higher theistic religions assert, then a true religion opens our awareness to the presence of God and so makes accessible to us the fruits of that awareness. But religion does not bring us an understanding of the nature of its object. If its object is God then we must go to theology and philosophy if we seek some understanding of God's nature, and if it has some other object then we must go to the science which studies the nature of that object. Yet the study of theology or the philosophy of religion or a special science is not a religious exercise; it is no more a religious act than the study of nutrition is nutritious.

The religions which center upon God, especially the higher of the monotheistic religions, are faced with a special difficulty. One aspect of the difficulty is found in the fact that although such a religion does not provide any adequate understanding of the nature of God, the people who profess that religion do engage in acts and ceremonies which express some definite ideas about God. These ceremonies may include, for example, such acts as adoration, petition, confession and repentance, and the services of love. They could not be performed meaningfully in the absence of some ideas about God, ideas which enable the worshipper to think of God as the appropriate object of such acts. Yet we could not expect those ideas about God to be at all adequate, for no theistic religion restricts these acts to those who have demonstrated their theological or philosophical competence.

---

[5] *Galatians*, Chapter 5, verses 19-21.
[6] *See II Corinthians*, Chapter 3, verse 5.
[7] *Galatians*, Chapter 5, verses 22-23.
[8] *Galatians*, Chapter 5, verses 25-26.

The ideas about God involved in the practice of religion do not provide, by themselves, a conceptual understanding of God's nature. They apply to God, as we shall see later, as metaphors or analogies. They express something about the nature of God, but they do not express it directly; they express it in terms of other things, of things which come within the range of man's direct experience. God is described, for example, as a father, and this familiar human relationship of father and child is thought to tell us something of what God is like. If an analogy does succeed in expressing the nature of God in terms of something else then it is true, but it is true as an analogy and not as a concept adequate to its object.[9] So the problem of existence is especially acute when we are concerned with the existence of God. Not only are we unable to verify the existence of God directly, we are unable even to say what it is whose existence we cannot verify directly except as we refer to it in analogy with something else.

A religion like some varieties of Humanism, or like the religion of Marxist Communism, does not have the same difficulty which confronts theism. For a religion which worships Humanity worships something whose specific instances, at least, can be examined directly. A religion which finds its ultimates in a social goal, such as the classless society of Marxism, is not troubled by the possible disparity between its ideas about that society and reality; for its society is not actual, it is not yet in existence, so its nature can be dictated by dogma. In neither of these religions is the existence of the object or the nature of the object a problem. The only basic problem of the one is whether its object is worthy of worship, and of the other whether the attainment of its ideal is the ultimate fulfilment of existence. The special problem of religious truth which concerns us here is one which presses hardest upon the theistic religions, and we shall discuss it with reference to them.

Religious forms and creeds do not themselves guarantee truth. They are like the labels on packages, for whether a package is full or empty does not show on the label, and sometimes the label's description of the contents is misleading. So religious forms may be used without effect, just as one may read a label and fail to use what is in the package.

If we are going to apply the test of truth which one of the higher theistic religions provides then we need some assurance that the religion which supplies this test is itself true. Suppose that what Paul calls the "fruit of the Spirit" is in truth the fruit of weakness. How can we tell? What are the credentials of the criterion Paul offers us? Paul himself would insist, perhaps, that this criterion is the obvious implication of the nature of God as He shows Himself to us. We may well grant that the

---

[9] The doctrine of analogy will be discussed in Chapter XXIII, "Knowledge by Analogy." [In *A Modern Philosophy of Religion.*]

THE TEST OF RELIGIOUS TRUTH

values implicit in this criterion will show their superiority on comparison with any rival set, but how can we trust them to take us to God unless we know there is a God for them to take us to? If we *believe* that God exists, and if our belief is true, well and good; but not even Paul asks us to accept the existence of God on faith. "Ever since the creation of the world his invisible nature, namely, his eternal power and deity, has been clearly perceived in the things that have been made."[10]

It would be a simple matter to test the truth of religion if we could use the common tests of existential truth. For the usual tests are simply the presence or absence of the objects to which the statements apply. We are seldom left in uncertainty about the existence of something we see with our own eyes or hear with our own ears or touch with our own hands. But the problem is a more difficult one if the existence in question cannot be confirmed in this straightforward way. Of course we can be fooled by our senses, but still we have ways of avoiding this which work quite well in most cases. But when we are concerned with a supposed existent with which, even if it does exist, we cannot make direct and unequivocal contact our problem is exceedingly difficult. This is the special problem of religious truth. Religion requires the existence of its object, unless it is a kind of religion which does not claim existence for its object. But the existence to which religion promises to take us cannot be found in the direct experience which provides the ordinary tests of existential truth. How, then, is religious truth to be tested?

In raising this problem we do not mean to say that even if God exists we can have no direct contacts with God. We mean rather that if the existence of God is problematical then it is also problematical that our contacts are contacts with God. There may be no question about our having the experience which we interpret as contact with God; the question concerns our interpretation of the experience. Perhaps I have a most complete confidence in the existence of God because I have experiences which seem to me to make sense only if I understand them as contacts with God. But I may be mistaken, not about having the experiences but about the kind of interpretation which makes sense.

At one time, for example, physicists thought that the transfer of heat from a hot to a cold body could be understood only as the passage of some invisible material fluid, which they called "caloric" or "phlogiston," from the hot to the cold body. So when I conclude that God is present, and conclude this on the ground that my experience makes sense only on that supposition, I may be quite mistaken. Perhaps I rule out too quickly and too uncritically other plausible explanations. Or perhaps I am simply ignorant and do not know of the other explanations.

We well know how prone man is to give a religious interpretation

---

[10] *Romans*, Chapter 1, verse 20.

to the things he does not understand and which yet seem important to him. Thus has man long interpreted matters of chance and mystery. Before the causes of disease were known disease was thought to be an act of God. Storms, earthquakes, and all kinds of natural disasters were understood in the same way. No doubt there is much today in the beliefs of even the more advanced religions which mistakes mystery for value and takes ignorance to be a sign of religious truth. It is this fact which puts us on our guard against a too easy acceptance of claims which are made in the name of religion.

So it is that when we try to apply the ordinary tests of existential truth to the special case of religious truth we find ourselves in trouble. For the object of religious belief does not confront us in the unequivocable fashion of the more familiar physical objects. The strongest and most persistent of all religious doubts are those which question the existence of the objects of religion. Religion claims truth, and the truth it claims is existential truth; but the very objects to which religion claims to take us are those things whose existence is questioned. How then can we apply the test of existential truth to religious truth?

It is no answer to our problem to appeal to the assurance of faith. It is the case that faith's sureness of the presence of God is sometimes stronger than our ordinary confidence in our senses, but such assurance is not itself a test of truth. If strength of belief alone were a test of truth then the truest beliefs would be those of delusion, for nowhere is belief held more strongly or more implacably or more fiercely in the face of contrary evidence than in the delusions of paranoia.

THE RATIONAL TEST OF RELIGIOUS TRUTH

If we cannot test religious truth directly then our test must be indirect. Of course if it is a test of existential truth the test must involve some direct reference to existence; but in the test of religious truth the existence which primarily concerns us, such as the existence of God, may not be something to which we can refer directly. Even so, our difficulty may seem easy to resolve, for I may establish indirectly the existence of one thing (A) by confirming directly the existence of something else (B), provided B could not exist if it were not for the existence of A. My argument, then, would be:

  (1) The existence of B requires the existence of A.
  (2) B does exit (a fact which I verify directly).
  (3) Therefore, A exists.

We follow here in principle the same line of reasoning which a farmer may use in reaching the conclusion that a fox robbed his hen roost. He did not see the fox there, but he has reason to think that there are foxes in the area. He knows that they take chickens. He knows that his chickens have been taken by an animal rather than by a human thief, for he finds telltale signs. Among these are prints which he is sure can be made only by a fox, and these prints lead to and from the chicken house. The inference is plain; all the signs point to a fact which, although not verified directly, is the only plausible explanation of the signs themselves.

We have here the application of a general principle of verification which applies to claims of existential truth. When we find changes in existing things, and we can account plausibly for those changes only by reference to the existence of something else which is not directly present to us, then those changes we observe are signs of the existence of something else.

This kind of inference is so common and familiar that we apply it often without any clear awareness of our mode of thinking. Robinson Crusoe's sight of the footprint in the sand led directly to his awareness of the existence of another person on his island. For here he found a physical fact, something in actual existence, and he knew without question that the existence of this fact required the existence of another fact. He knew it because he knew that human footprints in the sand do not form themselves, and because he knew that in those circumstances the print could have been made only by another human foot. He assumed, of course, that everything which happens makes sense; and this we must assume in any inquiry.

Perhaps the test of religious truth is the same in principle. We have certain experiences in which we encounter actual existence. If the only plausible explanation of the existence of these things we find is the existence of the object of religious belief, and if the rule of inference we apply in the ordinary affairs of life is sound, we can hardly avoid the conclusion that the object of religious belief does exist. The matter seems to be quite obvious. The test of existence in the case of religious truth is the same in principle as the test we use in our everyday encounters with existence. It is the same principle by which a letter implies a writer, a sonata a composer, a house a builder, and so on throughout the whole range of our contacts with our world. This applies not alone to human contacts either; for coal deposits, oil pools, certain arrangements of geological strata, growth rings of trees—all are signs of certain definite existing situations in the past.

But is the matter so simple after all? We have neglected one important difference between the examples we have used and the use of the same indirect method in establishing, say, the existence of God. The difference is in the fact that when we infer that a fox has been in the hen house we already know that foxes exist, and it is only the recent presence here of *a* fox which our argument establishes. Robinson Crusoe already knew that other human beings existed, it was only the recent presence of one at that place which the footprint showed. We might very well use this same kind of argument to establish that God was present and acting in some specific situation if we already knew the existence of God. But how can we use this argument to establish God's existence itself?

The indirect argument, as we ordinarily use it, enables us to infer existence from existence. But in these familiar uses of it we go from one existence in our world to some other existence in that same world. Our inference rests on what we know of things in this world, and of the conditions under which they occur. But how can we use such a principle of inference to go from the existence of something in our world to the existence of God?

One thing we must recognize. The encounter with some unexplained natural fact does not itself justify an inference of the existence of something beyond the natural world, *in so far as it is possible that this so far unexplained fact has an explanation in terms of other facts of nature.* In so far as that possibility, as a possibility, is intelligible we must content ourselves to wait for our explanation until we have a more adequate understanding of our own world. So far as this is the case, any interpretation we may make of the fact which attributes to it anything but a natural significance is an interpretation which rests on faith and not on reason. Such interpretations may be justified in certain circumstances; we must not pre-judge them. But their justification does not furnish rational evidence of religious truth.

There are only two circumstances which justify our use of the indirect argument to establish the existence of something which is not itself a part of our world of nature. One circumstance is our discovery of something in our world which nothing else in our world could possibly account for. The other circumstance would be the discovery that this world of nature itself requires something else to account for its existence. Within these restrictions the test of existential truth may be used as a test of religious truth, provided the basic principle of the test is sound. If we can infer soundly from existence to existence in the natural order then the use of the same principle to establish religious truth is sound provided its use is limited by the restrictions we have pointed out.

The restrictions which hedge our use of the argument from existence to existence when we apply it to religion can be seen also from a different approach. For somewhat similar restrictions apply to any sound use of the principle. Suppose we admit that the indirect argument is sound in principle, how can we be sure we have applied it correctly? The assurance it gives is not absolute, for many errors can arise in our use of the principle. If I argue: "B exists, and if B exists than A exists, therefore A exists" there are several points at which I may be in error. The argument itself is logically valid, but this means only that if the premises are true the conclusion is true. But are the premises true? Suppose we grant that B does exist, still the second premise, that if B exists then A exists, may be false.

The problem this raises is important enough to merit our careful attention, for it is misunderstanding on this point which has led some to dismiss religion's claims of truth and has led others to offer a faulty justification of those claims. When we say that if B exists (e.g., the footprint in the sand) then A exists (the earlier presence of another human being at that place), we argue that A was the cause of B. But we go further than this, for we rest our case on the conviction that *only* A could cause B. In Robinson Crusoe's case the argument was quite convincing. He had been confident that he was the only person on the island, and he knew of no way a footprint could get into the sand except by the pressure of a human foot, and he knew it was not his own foot that made it. His assurance rested on these two foundations: footprints do not bring themselves into existence, and this footprint in this set of circumstances could have been made only by a human being and by someone other than himself.

The argument from the existence of B to the existence of A is inconclusive just to the extent that there are other possible causes of B. Before the argument is conclusive we have to narrow down the possibilities to A alone. Crusoe did this by means of the positive knowledge he had of footprints, the island he was on, and other physical facts. We must also narrow down the possibilities, and as successfully, when we use this principle to test claims of religious truth.

It is not enough, as a test of religious truth, that we encounter something in existence for which we can find no explanation in the world of nature. We are not warranted in carrying our inference from natural fact to God for the reason merely that there is something in nature which we do not understand. If we were justified in such a course then the greater our ignorance the greater our evidence of God's existence and action; and it is just this kind of error which religious obscurantism so often makes when it discourages and even actively opposes the study of nature for fear something will be taken away from God. We cannot argue from ignorance; our argument needs a positive basis in evidence if it is to have any rational strength. Its positive basis, the only sound positive basis, is not the existence of something we are unable to account for in terms of nature, it is rather the positive evidence we have that the existence in question is one for which no process of nature or natural cause could possibly account. Our evidence must show that no matter how much more complete man's knowledge of nature may become he still will never be able to find in nature the explanation of some of the existence he actually encounters.

We must not assume that there is general agreement on this method of solving our problem. For many reasons men have often hesitated to apply this principle to the objects of religious faith. Their objections we shall consider when we come to examine more directly the way in which this principle applies to the existence of God. At this present point in our discussion, however, we may note one peculiar fact, that most of those who attempt to discredit the indirect test when it is applied to the existence of God find themselves forced finally to reject its application to all other things as well. For often their criticism turns from a special application of the principle to the principle itself, and they find themselves drawing the somewhat disturbing conclusion that nothing which exists testifies to the existence of anything else. Although many have announced that this is their conclusion no one yet has provided a demonstration of how it can be put into practice.

ARE THERE TESTS OF REVELATION?

JOHN C. BENNETT

John C. Bennett (1902–), a leading Protestant spokesman on social issues, studied at Williams College, Oxford University, and Union Theological Seminary. He has taught at Auburn Theological Seminary, Pacific School of Religion, and Union Theological Seminary, recently becoming at the latter institution the Dean of the Faculty and the first appointee to the Reinhold Niebuhr Chair of Christian Ethics. His books include Christian Ethics and Social Policy *(1946),* Christians and the State *(1958), and* Christianity and Communism Today *(1960). In this selection Dean Bennett asks whether, with all the recent emphasis on subjectivity, there are any objective standards for what we accept as religious truth.*

Let us grant much of what is said about the circle of faith, about the relativistic predicament. Yet, are there no objective checks upon our faith? Are there no approaches to faith which can be recommended to those outside the circle? I believe that those questions can be answered in

From John C. Bennett, "Are There Tests of Revelation?", *Theology Today*, Vol. XII, No. 1 (April 1955), 73-84. Reprinted by permission.

the affirmative and the remainder of this paper will be devoted to my attempt to give affirmative answers.

There are three general characteristics of our minds and of our relationships which must be mentioned first very briefly.

The first is that awareness of the relativistic predicament does enable us to begin to transcend it. This is an essential condition for self-criticism.

The second is that we are capable of entering into other circles of faith and thought and life imaginatively to a considerable extent. There is a vast difference between the closed minded person who never even respects anyone who differs from him and the person who tries to be fair to others, to see the world as they see it, to try out imaginatively and experimentally the convictions of those who live in another circle. Sympathetic historical scholarship tries to reconstruct the thought and life of another period in this way. It is not without success even though there are limits to possible success. We are able to criticize our own circle from this outside vantage point. This is an aspect of our self-transcendence which Reinhold Niebuhr following Augustine emphasizes so much.

This is possible, also, because we do not always remain at the same level of conscious intensity in our own commitment. Sometimes the relation of faith to apologetics or to criticism is presented as though faith were always the same in intensity. Paul Tillich's discussion of the relationship of faith to estimates of probability is an illustration of what I mean. There are moments of sure commitment when probable evidence is irrelevant. But there may also be long periods between those moments and whether or not the moments recur may depend upon how much confirmation based on probable evidence we may encounter in the meantime. What we think about our own circle of faith after various imaginative excursions into other circles may be extremely important either as a source of correction or as a source of confirmation, perhaps of both at the same time.

My third suggestion concerning the nature of our minds and of our relationships has to do with the way in which there is actual interaction between our circle and other circles, between our circle and many forces which have some independence of it, which may have wholly independent origins. Think how Christianity has been able to have relationships with many different philosophical traditions, to ally itself with them for a time, to be corrupted by them to some extent, to use them, to disentangle itself from them, to outlive them so far as their period of real vitality is concerned. Perhaps at a later time Christianity will rediscover one or more of these traditions and use it differently. We might say that one acid test of the intellectual adequacy of a religion, of the truth of what is claimed to be revelation, is this kind of capacity to relate itself to movements of thought, illumine them and to be illumined by them and yet always to transcend them and to do this not with one official Christian philosophy but to do it again and again with many philosophies. This has been put vividly by Professor Robert Fitch. He wrote in his book *A Certain Blind Man:*

> Thus it is that we note in the history of Christianity—in contrast to the history of some other religions—an extraordinary talent for getting into trouble and an equally extraordinary talent for extracting from that trouble some fresh insight into truth, some device of spiritual discipline, that shall illuminate the mind and elevate the soul of man. To be specific, I believe it is accurate to say that no other great historic religion has been tested against such a diversity of social, political and economic institutions, has had to compete so continuously with independent and secular systems of ethics and philosophy; and has had to bear up under such a frontal attack from science and from the technology of an industrialized society. Christianity has meddled with all of these things, and all of these things have meddled with Christianity (pp. 50-51).

My comment on this passage is that it is a good description of the kind of objective tests to which any circle of faith and thought and life must be subjected. It is possible that more than one such circle will survive such a test and that may leave us always with a decision—perhaps the decision—as Whitehead and Toynbee both say—between Christianity and Buddhism. All right—let it be so but it is not unimportant to have the real alternatives limited in this way.

What I shall now do is to suggest some facts of our experience, some pervasive realities which cannot be ignored by those who belong to any circle of faith. Doubtless they can be interpreted in quite different ways from the point of view of different circles of faith and yet they have a stubbornness about them which is likely to cause them to modify the assumptions held within any circle. There is no neutral standpoint from which they can be surveyed and yet they can be expected to have a decisive influence on all standpoints. They can be expected to be the rocks on which many faiths and philosophies will sooner or later be wrecked.

One of these realities which any circle of faith and thought and life cannot ignore is the existence of a constantly growing body of tested knowledge which the various sciences have contributed to our experience. The boundaries of this tested knowledge may be much debated in detail but such debate provides no escape from the necessity to come to terms with the results of this whole scientific process. World views with the authority of religious faith can be shattered by it and only those faiths can stand indefinitely which can be constructively reinterpreted in the light of this growing body of knowledge. Scientific methods have been applied to the religious traditions themselves, as we all know so well, and surely one objective test of the truth of any faith is its capacity to absorb the results of these investigations. This scientific knowledge has become embodied in technological changes which profoundly affect the conditions under which people in all circles of faith must continue to believe and to reflect upon their beliefs. Here I may be moving too fast, but I think that any circle of faith which is purely negative in relation to all of these technological changes is open to serious doubt. That is admittedly a Christian judgment which rests in part on a basically affirmative attitude toward God's creation, for all such technological changes are, in a sense, an elaboration of creation. One test of a circle of faith is whether or not it can be demythologized without being destroyed. That does not mean that we must accept Bultmann's particular ideas concerning what the myths are or his particular conclusions concerning what is left after this demythologizing process has been carried through.

My other suggestions concerning the realities which test all circles of faith will be given, not in the order of some inevitable logical priority but in the order of their striking power against the pretensions of any circle of faith which attempts to ignore them. Also these are only examples to illustrate a possible method.

1. The first is the universality of death. Traditional religions have usually taken death seriously and have attempted to give meaning to it, to prepare believers to face it with courage, and to comfort those who are bereaved by it. As between the traditional religions it would be difficult to think of death by itself as a factor which would provide an objective test of their adequacy because each prepares people to face death in the light of its view of life. The Christian expectation of an ultimate fulfillment which safeguards the meaning of personal existence and announces the coming of God's kingdom as the symbol of God's victory over all human history—this will be more convincing to Christians than to Buddhists who do not start with the same concern about the individuality of the person or about history as the sphere of the rule of God. In this context one can hardly escape from religious relativism. Yet the fact of death can bring to nought faiths and philosophies which ignore it. It is the surest mark of human finiteness. It deflates optimistic or progressivistic humanisms which concentrate so much attention on the future of society that they find it possible almost to overlook the end of the individual person.

Today the deflation of these optimistic faiths has helped us all to see how far we live in a world of death. The curious optimism of Communist naturalism is able to leap over the fact of death. This may be because Communism after the early Marxist influence had passed developed an indifference to the individual person. There may be deep meaning in Malenkov's statement that an atomic war would threaten the existence even of a Communist civilization. There is here a recognition of a possible defeat of the dialectic of history by a factor which had been previously unrecognized by Communist theory. The fact of death, especially if it means that there may be no institution or community remaining to preserve the results of one's work, and no man and no God to remember that one ever lived or that anything ever existed, can lead men to raise the religious question again even though they have been thoroughly indoctrinated with an optimistic atheism. When the clearly recognized real alternatives are an atheism of despair or an atheism disguised by a grim Stoicism on the one hand and a transcendental faith on the other the whole spiritual situation may change.

2. A second reality which is a test of faith is the many-sided fact of evil. I have not here included death under evil because it is surely no unmixed evil. Death gives a sad and often tragic finality to many forms of evil as far as our experience goes. Premature death may be a tragic loss that is evil in itself but as the world is constituted, if there were no death, as Professor Hocking has said so well, life would lose shape and history would become rigid. But that is an aside.

Evil which is the result of human choice, with all possible degrees of responsibility for the choice, raises the hardest questions for any circle of faith. Again the traditional religions all have ways of dealing with this and the only surprise blow that evil can strike is against the modern faiths. It is the optimistic faiths such as liberal progressivism and Communism which are most threatened. Absolute idealism as a total view of life has already been quite well deflated by the evil which it too easily explained. As for Communism, its superficial conception of the origin of evil in economic institutions and its lack of preparation for post-revolutionary evil will surely bring disillusionment in the end.

One of the remarkable facts about Christianity is that, while the problem of evil is its greatest theoretical problem, the experience of evil often leads men to accept it. I think that the reason for this can be seen if one puts together four elements of the Christian strategy in dealing with evil. The first is the realistic facing of evil as seen in the emphasis on sin and in the centrality of the cross. The second is the partial explanation of evil in the freedom of persons to resist God. We can see the significance of this explanation if we were to imagine the intellectual and spiritual burden involved in any absolute monism according to which God is the only effective doer. The third is the moral imperative to remove the evil that can be removed, to forego either the indifference of fatalism or the complacency of a deterministic faith. The fourth is the resources for personal redemption from or victory over the evil that cannot be removed.

This total Christian approach to evil may be able to break through into other circles of faith, especially those controlled by the various kinds of secular optimism to which I have referred. One aspect of Christian teaching about human nature proves sometimes to be the entering wedge: the recognition that sin is often most destructive on the higher levels of human development—where spiritual pride and idealistic rationalizations combine with new forms of power to create the corporate destructive forces which haunt us most. The things that have happened in recent years threatening the characteristic faiths of modern men can be understood in the light of the Christian diagnosis of the human situation. The real question is how far the acceptance of this diagnosis will open minds to Christian revelation as the promise of redemption.

3. A third reality is the pressure upon us of a real moral order which can be discerned apart from revelation. I realize that every way of stating this idea has been challenged by a combination of Barthian theology and ethical positivism or cultural relativism. There are justified attacks on a conception of natural law which fails to take account of the unique moral situations to which law is applied. Natural law as a Catholic doctrine can be criticized in this way. The revolt of legal positivists against natural law has enabled judges to recognize quite new social realities and to bring to them a more humane understanding of justice. I live in circles where one of the chief targets is "moralism." I think that these attacks on moralism are chiefly attacks on too great confidence in moral exhortations or moral discipline as contrasted with the need for an inner change which is a gift of grace and is prepared for by receptivity rather than by moral effort. They are also attacks on self-righteousness in those who seem to be morally successful. But when all of these things have been said—the moral order remains. And at the center of this moral order is the human need for love.

I am deeply impressed by the evidence from psycho-therapy that without love we are destroyed, that hostility is one of the clearest symptoms of sickness. Eros as the love of those who are most loveable is not enough. There is no redemption of a person unless that person is lovingly accepted as he is by parents or friends, in his sickness and in spite of his own incapacity to love in return. There is a moral problem here because we are asked to accept the person in spite of moral criticism. On the other hand there can be no real healing unless there is honest facing of reality and deliverance from blind egocentricity and hostility. The psycho-therapist, however, is usually limited in his emphasis upon love to the more intimate personal relations.

When we approach the moral needs of society at large there must be a wise balancing of interests and a wise balancing of power in a frame of law. Also, there are many things called for which create bitter problems

for love, as in the case of the policies that seem necessary to restrain agres-
sion. And yet it has never been as plain as it is today that there can be no
security against universal destruction without the development of world
community. One essential ingredient of the life of such a world community is a widespread caring for the dignity and the welfare of people
which crosses all boundaries. Perhaps we can get through the immediate
East-West conflict on the basis of the much emphasized power to deter,
but this cannot by itself provide even relative security for long. It will be
necessary to have something like a world community, based upon many
mutual interests, upon the universal need for order and justice, and yet inspired by something more—by the presence in many hearts of this caring
for the dignity and welfare of neighbors at a distance. It may be a sign of
much bitter experience that I use what to some readers may seem minimum terms. But this is a minimum, and without it years of glaring with
fear at one another beside our stockpiles of bombs with the assumption
that to annihilate or to be annihilated is both a technical and a *moral*
possibility will produce a callousness incompatible with the most elementary human decency.

We are often told that we live in a time of moral disintegration and
chaos. I am not sure of that, but even if it is true the moral order shows
through in many ways. The very success of the Communists in their
propaganda, especially in Asia, comes from the fact that vast populations
see the possibility of a new status of dignity and justice unheard of before
in most of the world. We have seen the most desperate crimes the modern
world has ever known committed because of race prejudice, and yet at
this very time every form of racial discrimination is on the defensive as
never before. We see the institutions of family life and the traditional
standards of sexual morality greatly threatened, but one factor in all of
this is more equal justice than ever before in the relations of men and
women. Also there is the possibility of the development of standards
which give more emphasis than has been usual in the past to honest and
sensitive personal relations in the family. Remember that all that I am
suggesting is that signs of a moral order shine through the deep and bitter
moral problems of our time. These signs can be better understood, the
Christian thinks, from the standpoint of the Christian revelation, but they
can be seen from other standpoints.

4. I shall mention one more example of the realities by which any circle
of faith must be tested. Probably this one is the most western, and those
brought up in an entirely different tradition will be less likely to be convinced by it than by the others. I call it "the depth of the personal self."
I speak of it here because we have seen in recent years a new emphasis
upon the depth of the self against dominant philosophies and psychologies,
against political collectivism, and against cultural tendencies to lose the

self in the impersonal human mass. The revolt in behalf of the self has come on soil prepared by Christian faith and yet it has often come in non-Christian forms. The excesses of existentialist trends in philosophy seem to be the revenge of the human self on theories and cultural tendencies which have neglected it. Atheistic existentialism seems to teach a wild freedom of the self with very little structure conditioning that freedom. Perhaps it is one of the signs of this wild freedom that Sartre, the chief prophet of the movement, can become a supporter of Communist policies. The Kierkegaardian preoccupation with subjectivity, to which I referred earlier, came as a protest against the neglect of the individual person in the depth of his being. Kierkegaard in a wonderfully prophetic passage in the *Concluding Unscientific Postscript* says this: "In the midst of all our exultation over the achievements of the age and the nineteenth century, there sounds a note of poorly conceived contempt for the individual man; in the midst of the self-importance of the contemporary generation there is revealed a sense of despair over being human. Everything must attach itself so as to be part of some movement; men are determined to lose themselves in the totality of things, in world history, fascinated by a magic witchery; and no one wants to be an individual human being" (p. 317).

When I refer to the self I mean exactly that which modern empirical philosophies have tried to explain away: an enduring center of personal experience, deeper than the stream of consciousness, with genuine freedom and responsibility, transcending all social groups, knowing an ultimate aloneness. In recent years the self has been rediscovered because it hurt and could not be ignored, because it hurt with all of the familiar symptoms of anxiety and guilt. The very efforts of political collectivisms to break the self by their ingenious terror have helped to call attention to its existence, especially when it refused to be broken. I think that Christian teaching about the self, about its depth and its transcendence may win response in some other circles of faith very much as Christian realism about human nature has done in recent years. It is so hard for our contemporaries, even when they have rediscovered the personal self, to do justice to both the individual person and the community.

The Christian sees the self, not as a substance with fixed boundaries but as an active center that is endlessly involved in relations. The self is always in community but it belongs wholly to no community because it is ultimately responsible to God and yet this responsibility to God includes responsibility for the communities of which it is a member.

In the space which remains let me indicate two more steps that can be taken, though each of them should be the subject of many books.

The first is a mere speculation. When we ask about the chief alternative to the Christian view of life which might well survive the various tests which I have mentioned: the most likely answer would be a traditional mystical faith such as Buddhism or a reformed Hinduism. The faiths which are most vulnerable to these tests are those which are the product of the wisdom of modern man. I only want to raise this question: will the mystical type of religion which has very little interest in time and history be forced to accommodate itself to the rising historical consciousness of Asia? Nationalism and Communism have certainly created a new climate. The Indian mystic may not be much concerned about the world of time, but the Indian people were much interested in the timetable of the British government in giving them freedom and today the pressures of a threatening historical situation upon them have produced new temporal urgencies. Is all of this on a very superficial level, unlikely to affect the spirituality of the East? The fact that most intellectuals in the Asian countries are studying natural science and technology, that those interested in social science are attracted by such a history-centered faith as Marxism must have some meaning. Does it mean that the non-historical type of spirituality will be so modified that there will be a greater openness to the Christian revelation? That is a possibility. I have said that the tests of circles of faith narrow the alternatives. Perhaps for most people in both East and West the alternatives will be narrowed by the impact of the consciousness of history upon the East. And yet for a very long time, even if this happens, we can expect the development of syncretistic alternatives. For example, Gandhism is an adaptation of Hinduism to meet this new situation.

My more serious step is to suggest the existence of concentric or at least overlapping circles. The Christian circle may be regarded as a part of a larger circle of faith. Indeed, I believe that there may be three such circles in this relationship to each other. The widest would be the circle of faith which is a reverent and loyal response rather than a negative response to whatever is regarded as ultimate. I wonder if one reason for the wide appeal of the theology of Paul Tillich is not that it rests upon an elaboration of this affirmative response. Long before he comes to the content of Christian revelation, he has presented a prior and more inclusive faith that life has positive meaning, that our dependence upon the ultimate is the source of courage rather than of despair.

His "principle of correlation" may disguise the fact that he comes to the Christian revelation not only with questions but with preliminary answers as well, answers which are given in the language of a philosophy but which are quite clearly expressions of a religious faith which is prior to the Christian faith.

I believe that there is another circle between this widest circle and the Christian circle. It may seem old fashioned to use the word but I call it the theistic circle. The weakness of theistic philosophy has often been that it has failed to recognize that it was the spelling out of a faith and not the development of rational arguments which are self-sufficient. The classical arguments for belief in God should be rejected if they are regarded as "proofs," but they are true and important if seen in this context of a religious faith which supports and need not rival the Christian faith. Perhaps what I am saying is no different from the common assertion that *general revelation* rather than *natural theology* is the sounder concept to be used in connection with this belief in God, which has a broader foundation than the Christian revelation.

Let me put side by side two statements from two Christian philosophical theologians who differed profoundly in spirit and method but who finally came to the same point where "the leap of faith" separated them both from a naturalism which accepts the world of experience but asks no ultimate questions about it. F. R. Tennant wrote, "Further back than a creative spirit it is neither needful nor possible to go. But further back from the world we can and must go . . ." (*Philosophical Theology*, vol. II, p. 113). William Temple wrote "the principle of personality is adequate [as an explanation] for it supplies a ground of explanation which calls for no further explanation, thus delivering us from the infinite regress" (*Nature, Man and God*, pp. 262-263).

Perhaps we can bring the latter statement up to date if we say not "the principle of personality" but the principle that we should be related to the ultimate reality as "thou" and not "it."

I have said much about circles in this paper, and now we have come full circle, back to our starting point. The Christian philosopher of religion who begins with the grounds for theism may in fact in his own spiritual life be controlled by his Christian presuppositions.

We must distinguish between his spiritual biography and the real relationship between the various levels of his thought. We may agree with Temple and others that theism needs to be fulfilled by the discovery that the God to whom it points has acted to reveal himself and to redeem men from the evil which is the chief obstacle to belief in him. We may also realize that a vague theism is the material for idolatry especially if it becomes fused with the idea of an almighty who is on our side as a nation. And yet this theistic faith which needs both fulfillment and correction from the Christian revelation does have a basis that is in part independent of that revelation and can give some support to it. It does provide pointers to the truth of Christian faith which can be seen, dimly perhaps, apart from Christian faith. Such pointers may be of no interest to the person who sees God in Christ with unchanging assurance. I only ask such a person to withhold his theological scorn from those of us, of whom I am one, whose assurance is less unchanging and who are grateful for every glimpse of truth which is available outside the Christian circle.

SUGGESTED BOOKS

Abernethy, George L. and Thomas A. Langford, eds., *Philosophy of Religion*. New York: The Macmillan Company, 1962. A book of readings arranged topically and including both classical and modern writers.

Carnell, Edward J., *An Introduction to Christian Apologetics*. Grand Rapids: Wm. B. Eerdmans Publishing Company, 1948. An investigation of problems of truth as they bear upon the defense of conservative Christianity.

Frank, Erich, *Philosophical Understanding and Religious Truth*. New York: Oxford University Press, 1945. Six lectures in the philosophy of religion, suggesting there is truth by imagination in religion.

Hook, Sidney, ed., *Religious Experience and Truth*. New York: New York University Press, 1961. Papers by contemporary philosophers and theologians on religious symbolism, the nature of faith, and meaning and truth in theology.

Kaufman, Gordon D., *Relativism, Knowledge, and Faith*. Chicago: University of Chicago Press, 1960. The author argues that if man is understood historically, the relativism of human thought can be accepted without undercutting all truth or requiring the thinker to except himself.

Lyman, Eugene W., *The Meaning and Truth of Religion*. New York: Charles Scribner's Sons, 1933. Attempts to show how faith and intuition are sources of truth and lead to a conception of religion based on ethical theism.

Mitchell, Basil, ed., *Faith and Logic*. Boston: The Beacon Press, 1957. Essays by eight Anglicans sympathetic to linguistic analysis on questions of meaning and truth in theology.

Wieman, Henry N., *Intellectual Foundation of Faith*. New York: Philosophical Library, Inc., 1961. A critique of some contemporary answers to the question of faith from the standpoint of naturalistic religion which relates faith to creativity.

III · FAITH

Because of the centrality of faith in religion, and because of common misinterpretations to which it is subject, faith deserves a separate analysis. We shall first consider some of these misinterpretations, then attempt to clarify the meaning, value, and objects of faith, and conclude by relating the concept of faith to those of reason and certainty. In this general treatment it will be impossible to convey all of the richness and specificity which faith connotes for particular religious groups or viewpoints. But this handling of the subject should not be taken to mean that there is some general feeling of faith which is somehow more valuable than faith within a specific context or community. It only means that there are some significant questions about faith that need to be discussed and can be discussed in common discourse. It is to these questions that we shall confine ourselves in this chapter.

THE LOCUS OF FAITH

Among the various misinterpretations of faith there are two which are perhaps most frequent. Our purpose in beginning the discussion with these is to direct attention to the real province of faith, i.e., the aspect of man's experience that is meant when we speak of faith. If we employ the familiar classification of man's experience into emotion, intellect, and will —a classification inadequate for technical purposes but still useful for more popular expositions—we may say that the misinterpretations mentioned consist in overemphasizing emotion, on the one hand, and intellect, on the other. In contrast, it seems more appropriate to say that faith refers primarily to the volitional side of experience, and still more appropriate to say that all aspects of a man's personality enter into his faith, with the factor of will being pivotal.

According to the first of these misinterpretations, faith is thought of as irrational credulity. Faith is taken to mean the blind acceptance of some belief or some authority, or the blind obedience to some command or rule. Faith becomes almost a synonym for gullibility, the response of uninformed and unintelligent feeling with no support from theoretical understanding or practical reason. Even educated people today can still be heard to speak of faith in this way, without pausing to reflect that, if this were all there is to faith, religion could never have the appeal it has for people of high intellect and societies of high morality.

Such a misconception of faith may result from concentrating too exclusively on the actual irrationalities of man, which, unfortunately, are not hard to find. Slavish followers do succumb to political rabblerousers; unthinking publics do fall for propaganda pressures; comfort-seeking people do give themselves to irrational promises. But the lesson to be learned from these incidents is not a real definition of faith, but rather a realization of how easy it is for a noble potentiality in man to be corrupted. The very fact that we make negative appraisals on such incidents of attachment would seem to suggest that these are all perversions of a capacity which, if properly reasoned and directed, would be an appropriate and valuable part of experience. Meanwhile the world does show us other kinds of examples—the faith of a Ghandi or of a Schweitzer, for instance. Let us not, therefore, add to the sum of blind faith by continuing the uncritical assumption that all faith must be of the irrational sort. Faith is not irrational credulity.

The second of these misinterpretations regards faith as a special mode of directly acquiring objective truths. Faith is taken to mean the act of apprehending and accepting given truths which are proposed to the mind by some authority—church, scripture, personage, or perhaps God directly. Such knowledge may concern either the natural or the supernatural order. In this view faith is made primarily intellectual in character, or at least significant primarily for its intellectual content. This is the view which prevailed in Scholasticism, but it is by no means confined to that tradition.[1]

Since there is a wide difference between faith and the ordinary workings of reason—a difference which cannot be denied—this view is compelled, like all views, to contrast faith in some way with reason; but it does so by considering them as different ways of reaching the same end, namely, the attainment of guaranteed knowledge. The relation may be stated as follows: man's faculty for obtaining knowledge is his cognitive function, and this has two divisions, reason and faith. Reason is the means of understanding truth through the natural powers of the mind, while faith is the means of grasping truth through the supernatural deliverance of propositions. Faith is thus the cognition of revelation regarded as a body of objective knowledge.

This view is not to be lightly disregarded, for it is held by eminent defenders. Moreover, we ourselves insisted in the previous chapter that the religious experience of faith is not devoid of cognitive elements, but is on the contrary an avenue to religious truth. The difference between these views may not seem great, but it cannot be overlooked. If faith is a mode of apprehending given truths, then the center of faith is merely the obedient assent to these truths on pain of contradiction. But that seems quite remote from what faith is in the religious experience of life situations. If, on the other hand, faith is primarily personal encounter with reality, which it appears to be in life, then the truth involved is not already presented in the form of propositions, requiring only assent, but is implicit and unformulated until it is elaborated by accompanying reason. In the one case faith is merely acceptance of proposed statements. In the other case it is a response to reality from which statements of belief need yet to be worked out, subject to the demand for reasonableness. In the one case faith is explicitly intellectual; in the other it has latent intellectual content. Both views recognize that there are some beliefs which, if they are to be accepted at all, must be accepted through faith. But in the one case these are given propositions, in the other later elaborations. In the one case they are like the rational certainties of intellect; in the other they are the practical certainties of life. We can only suggest that attention to the actual faith experience of people will show the latter view to be more accurate and the former view to be but a pale, over-intellectualized abstraction from the reality of this experience.

If we are right in these assertions, we shall find the locus of faith not so much in the attachments of feeling or the accumulations of knowledge as in that part of our personality which concerns decision-making, attitude, and character, the domain of life broadly called will. Emotion and intellect are always present in faith, for we cannot isolate portions of our personality. But a person's faith is essentially the basic orientation of his will which sets the inclination of his character, the tone of his purposes, the direction of his decisions and actions. This means that faith is always something which, to some extent, we can choose to accept into the structure of our personality, or reject. It also means that faith, when chosen, forms a steady, enduring disposition as the volitional background for day to day actions.

THE MEANING AND VALUE OF FAITH

Faith, like other human experiences, reveals two sides, inner and outer, subjective and objective. On the one hand there are attitudes or dispositions of the will, and on the other there are objects toward which faith is directed, objects in which, as we say, one has faith. A psychologist may pay greater attention to the inner side of the experience, as illustrated by Erich Fromm's distinction between rational and irrational faith.[2] A theologian may place greater emphasis on the outer objects, as illustrated by Martin Buber's distinction between faith in a person and faith in a doctrine.[3] All would doubtless agree that both sides must be considered in a complete account. Here we shall discuss the inner aspect first and then turn to the objects.

The basic element in faith appears to be the attitude of trust and loyalty.

These two terms differ in nuance of meaning, yet seem to belong together in this context. Both convey the sense of devotion to something or someone regarded as intrinsically reliable, even if that reliability has not been intellectually ascertained or completely understood. Both suggest confidence in the object's worthiness to be trusted. The term trust points more to the inward assurance and conviction of the reliability of the object, while the term loyalty points more to the dedication and determination to serve the object of faith. Both qualities are foci of faith. To have faith is to be trustfully loyal.

A second element that is prominent may be called, if the term is not too open to misunderstanding, the spirit of self-abandonment. This word has a double connotation. It suggests first of all a person's willingness to venture forth in the cause he has chosen, to throw himself adventurously into life's fray, to risk something for the end he serves. This is the opposite of a staid, withdrawn, frozen quality of life. The other connotation is that of readiness to give up something of one's own, to surrender preoccupation with self, to lose oneself in the service of some worthy goal. This is the opposite of a calculating, self-centered, what's-in-it-for-me quality of life. With the spirit of self-abandonment man voyages to new worlds for freedom, works patiently with nature's complexity for knowledge, builds hospitals and businesses for human well-being, brings comfort to an orphan for the orphan's sake.

Already implied in the two previous elements, but worthy of separate emphasis, is what we may call the courage to act. This means the predisposed preparation of a person to move into action on behalf of a cause without harmful stalling and indecision. We may have the attitude of trust and loyalty and the spirit of self-abandonment, but if we do not possess that lively readiness, that permanent penchant, to act whenever and wherever our cause demands, our faith is not complete. There is then an element of courageousness in all genuine faith. This courageousness is not reckless, for it knows when to act, when not to act, and when action is impossible. But when action is possible and required, it heeds the summons.

These elements of faith must be thought of as forming a pattern of life which endures through daily vicissitudes. Faith has a persistence about it which differentiates it from feelings and emotions that come and go. Thus, while faith may show itself in short-lived actions, these are but projections of a more permanent orientation of the self. Just as the factor of persistence makes one of the differences between happiness and pleasure, so it makes one of the differences between the attitude of faith and momentary acts of heroism. In moral faith, for instance, persistence makes the difference between the businessman who occasionally contributes to charity and one who is continually concerned about the state of his employees, or the difference between the student who crams at key times in order to be free to relax most of the time and the student who studies most of the time in order to be free to relax at key times.

This account of faith refers to all significant manifestations of it. The peculiarly religious dimension of faith is present when faith becomes a matter of ultimate commitments and concern, when it relates an individual intimately to the objective reality, or else the ideal value, that he regards as supreme. We speak of faith, and rightly so, in many contexts of life, not all of them directly religious, but it is probable that the peculiarly religious aspect is not entirely absent from any genuine experience of faith.

To sum up, we have stressed three principal elements in the experience of faith. These may be brought together in a definition by saying that faith is a persistently governing disposition of the self, composed essentially of trust and loyalty, a spirit of self-abandonment, and courage to act, all in relation to a chosen object or end.

To define faith in this way is almost tantamount to indicating its value for man's life. But a few words may be added on this point. In doing so we do not mean to suggest that the human value of faith is necessarily its most important attribute, or to dissociate the value of faith from the significance of faith as adoration and service to the ultimate religious reality, which in theistic religion means God.

For human beings, then, faith, when purified of irrational attachments and addressed to objects of real worth, is of paramount importance. Genuine faith frees man from frustrating impediments and releases him for creative living or even heroic dying. It enables him to meet the unknown, or the partly known, inventively, hopefully, sometimes joyfully. It allows him to affirm other people in their dignity and their rights in spite of their peculiarities or their lapses. It assists him in the unification of his divided self by giving him confidence in the processes that will unite it. But beyond all this is the great paradox that a religious faith makes it possible for man to lose his self, i.e., to give up what he took to be his self, and to find himself anew in a way he did not expect. Thus faith is a factor in the discovery and fulfillment of man's self, for until he devotes himself by decision to some cause, some supreme object, he does not know what is required to be a self.

To summarize, faith helps man psychologically in the integrating of personality and religiously in the practicing of ultimate commitments and endeavors.

OBJECTS OF FAITH

The outer side of faith means the objects or goals to which faith is directed. Ultimately the meaning and importance of faith cannot be separated from its objects, for there are debilitating causes to which man gives himself as well as ennobling ones. Let us consider, therefore, some of the objects in which reasonable people have faith, and in fact must have faith in order to live productively. We shall do this primarily to complete by examples the discussion of the meaning and value of faith. But there is another aim, namely, to offset the common misunderstanding that faith is something which applies to a special sphere of life, a religious sphere, different from ordinary life. The examples come from ordinary life and show that faith is necessary there. Whether they are all religious in character is a matter of perspective: they are not generally spoken of as religious, but from a true religious standpoint, wherever there is genuine faith there is a religious element. In any case they show the relevance of faith to life.

The most obvious example of faith in ordinary life is that of faith in other persons. This is the fundamental faith relationship, the prototype by which other relationships of faith are to be comprehended. It is the most vivid and direct way in which individuals come to know the meaning of faith. There are many relations to other people that demand faith. The most revealing is that of the personal trust we need to have toward our intimates—a friend, a parent, a spouse, a colleague. But there are others. We need to have faith in the candidates we elect to represent us, in the professional people who serve us, in the motorists who fill the streets, in all who make us promises, in all whose advice we follow, in all whose goods we buy. Social life could not continue long without some measure of faith. The real question for choice concerns not the need for it but the character and the extent of it. And in this connection experience tends to show that the most satisfying personal life is one which includes the capacity for deeply-felt and extensive faith-relationships.

By derivation from these person to person relationships it can easily be seen how faith is needed in the wider phases of civilized society. The groups to which we belong or whose causes we support are not machines grinding out assured results; they are collections of people working with limitations for common ends. We cannot demonstrate their integrity; we cannot know in advance the outcome of their efforts. Yet to remain noncommittal, to refrain from giving our support to movements working for social justice or individual well-being, would be disastrous for the life of society and for ourselves. The only solution is a willing faith in whatever private or public institutions we judge to be working for a more humane way of life.

Another example that comes readily to mind is faith in moral principles and moral causes. This of course is implicit in the faith we have in social movements and organizations. But it may also be in existence even if it has not found embodiment in institutions. We may arrive at the principles we accept by intellectual means, but the capacity to act upon these principles unflinchingly as the right ones requires a degree of conviction that can only be called faith. The same is true regarding any particular practices that we may follow, or perhaps generate, as appropriate expressions of these moral principles.

Closely related to this type of faith is the faith that people have in the eventual triumph of moral causes, or in what has been termed the friendliness of the universe. If there were no conviction that moral endeavors had a chance of realizing their ends, there would be little likelihood that they would be undertaken at all; yet, this conviction cannot be logically demonstrated to be warranted; it is a postulate of moral faith.

Still another example may be found in man's attitude toward the order and intelligibility in the world. It is generally acknowledged that an implicit trust in the regularity of natural law is indispensable even for the ordinary performances of daily life. But a deeper level of faith is seen in the presupposition which all human inquiry, scientific or otherwise, makes when it sets about to investigate the universe.[4] There would be no use in trying to explain the natural world if there were no conviction of fundamental orderliness. It would not be possible to persist in an inquiry, experiment after experiment, year after year, through failures and false leads, without an abiding faith that in the end the world is more than chaos, in the end intelligible to rational thought.

Correlative to this faith in the orderliness of the world is another example which may seem paradoxical at first. It is the faith in reason itself. If rational inquiry is to proceed at all, there must be a confidence that reason can make some headway. Except in pure deduction perhaps, reason addresses itself to what is not known or only partly known. By its very nature it does not know and therefore cannot guarantee any conclusions in advance. So, the belief that its researches are worthwhile and may culminate in success is an act of faith. This is why the familiar formula to the effect that reason can go so far and then faith takes over is so inadequate. Faith is present at the beginning of reason's inquiry, and, we may hope, reason is not absent at the end of faith's affirmations. Reason, in short, gets its impetus in a context of faith.

At this point in our discussion of objects of faith we come to an important junction. The humanist will maintain that the highest objects of faith are those human ideals already mentioned as objects of faith. The theist, on the other hand, will declare with Luther: "Faith is a living, well-founded confidence in the grace of God, so perfectly certain that it would die a thousand times rather than surrender its conviction."[5] For the theist, all other faith derives its significance by relation to this final faith. The Christian will be even more specific and identify final faith with God as seen in Christ. So we come to a parting of the ways in our religious companionship, the theist from the non-theist, and the Christian from other theistic communities. We shall discuss these other contexts of faith in Parts Two and Three; meanwhile, we have seen some examples of the indispensability of faith in our common life, and our need to strengthen it.

FAITH AND REASON

Several questions are frequently raised when faith is thought of in relation to reason. One of these is whether there is a different subject matter for faith and for reason. The answer to this question must be yes *and* no, depending on what aspect of reason is meant. If reason is thought of as the faculty for obtaining verified truths, or what we earlier called public knowledge, then it is clear that there is a limited domain, notably the natural world, in which this is possible. And there are other matters which, if we have beliefs concerning them at all, are largely matters of faith. Examples have been given in the previous section. In this sense there are different subject matters for faith and for reason. But if reason be taken to mean any use of our intellectual capacity—the faculty for forming concepts, making judgments, and relating propositions—then it is clear that there is no subject matter to which reason is entirely irrelevant. We cannot divide up our personality and say reason will be left out of this or that area. Likewise faith, as part of our personality, enters into all spheres of life. In this sense faith and reason are interrelated in all areas. The one may be predominant in a certain region and the other in another. But there are no exclusive areas from which one or the other is barred.

Another question is whether faith and reason can conflict. A reasonable reply to this question would seem to require three statements simultaneously rather than a single, simple answer. First, there can be no conflict between faith as such and reason as such, because faith, unlike reason, does not form and validate propositions, but is primarily an orientation of character and will. Second, there can, however, be conflicts, serious conflicts, when the implicit intellectual content of faith is drawn out and compared with some conclusions claimed for reason. In other words, conflict may occur between the beliefs which some people accept on faith and the beliefs which other people claim for reason. The controversy between theists and non-theists is often of this sort. But third, since truth is one and does not contradict itself, there can be no ultimate conflict between ideal faith and correct reason. So the conflicts must always be viewed as stemming from some imperfection in the kind of faith we hold or the kind of reasoning we employ.

Finally, there is the ever-present question of the priority of faith or reason. We have already intimated that in ordinary life there is no separation of faith and reason, which suggests that there is no exclusive ascendency of one over the other but rather an interrelatedness of the two, with perhaps one or the other being more prominent at different times. But we are here concerned more particularly with the question of priority in relation to religious beliefs. When the question is one of the justification for religious beliefs, which is prior in that justification, faith or reason?

There are four positions which are most frequently adopted on this question, namely:[6]

1. Reason prior, excluding faith;
2. Reason prior, with faith subordinate;
3. Faith prior, excluding reason;
4. Faith prior, with reason subordinate.

Of these the second and fourth are most commonly held today.

Before we can adopt one of these positions, however, we must distinguish what realm of discourse we have in mind. As far as religion itself is concerned, regarded as a way of orienting our practical life, faith is prior to reason as the basis for accepting beliefs. Religion does not wait for the systematic deliberations and attempted proofs of reason before being lived. In theology, there is a greater and more conscientious use of reason than there is in practical religion. But its basis is still in faith. It begins with certain beliefs of faith, often called dogmas, and then by reason works out and systematizes, elaborates and defends, the further doctrines and applications which the faith implies. The famous phrase of St. Augustine, *credo ut intelligam*, is frequently cited to describe this approach of theology. In philosophy, however, it is the overwhelming opinion of thinkers that philosophy is a rational activity, a work of intellect.[7] There are differences as to what philosophy can do and what it ought to do, but there is general agreement that what it does do is done by reason, however much or little that may be. Philosophy may include faith as data, but its own work is that of reason.

Thus, when different realms of discourse are considered, the only conclusion is that sometimes faith and sometimes reason is prior, depending on the context. Yet there is a continuing controversy as to which is really superior, theology or philosophy. Which is the higher court of appeal? Some thinkers maintain that theology is the head of all sciences and supersedes philosophy.[8] Others hold that philosophy is the last court of appeal and must test the utterances of theology.[9] But from the viewpoint of religion it is not obvious why such a battle needs to rage. Both enterprises are important and both have needed functions to perform. Theology is necessary for a mature faith, and philosophy is necessary for our life as rational men. There need be no exclusive or universal priority. If we accept this view, we must make room for a fifth position besides those mentioned above. We may call its main contention the principle of variable priority, in contrast to the common contention of the other four positions, all of which maintain some kind of uniform priority. We shall thus accept a position which is consistent both for ordinary life and for the realm of thought, namely, the thorough interrelatedness of faith and reason, with sometimes the one and sometimes the other predominant, depending on the context.

FAITH AND CERTAINTY

We shall conclude with some remarks on the question of whether faith can give certainty. If religious beliefs are beyond strict demonstration and are accepted on faith, must we then live in uncertainty? To answer this question we must distinguish several meanings which the term certainty can have and see how faith is related to these.

One meaning of certainty is that of logical necessity. When a conclusion follows validly from its premises, we say that it is logically necessary. Such conclusions may sometimes be called logical certainties. The model examples are found in mathematics and formal logic. It is plain that religious beliefs accepted on faith are not certainties in this sense, since faith is not a kind of rational deduction.

Another meaning of certainty is that of extremely high probability. When we say we are certain the sun will rise tomorrow, or the Mississippi flows into the Gulf of Mexico, what we mean is that these phenomena have occurred so often without exception in the past that to question them now would be unreasonable. Religious beliefs are not certainties in this sense either, for faith is not essentially a matter of empirical observation and probability.

Again, there is certainty in the sense of psychological certitude. This kind of certainty is entirely a subjective state of mind and has nothing to do with the nature of the belief held, as do the two previous meanings. In this sense, it is true, of course, that religious beliefs have given a great deal of certainty to people. That is, men at all times have felt psychologically certain of all kinds of beliefs, including those that are irrational and fantastic. Despite the strength of such feelings, however, this kind of certainty is something which should arouse caution. The mere fact of being subjectively convinced of a belief, apart from theological or philosophical scrutiny, is at best an incomplete warrant for its acceptance.

There is a final meaning of certainty which may be called practical assurance. This is the assurance which comes when beliefs are lived out in practice and known by personal conviction to be worthy of acceptance. This certainty differs from psychological certitude in that it affects and fulfills the total personality. It is total existential concern. Furthermore, it does not fear rational scrutiny, but welcomes it for whatever clarification it can bring. This is the kind of certainty which faith can yield and which is also commendable. From the strictly intellectual point of view, religious beliefs are not certainties; faith is not the same thing as rational certainty. But if faith is not rational certainty, neither is it an intellectual inquiry to be judged solely by intellectual standards. It is the living of life by conviction. And in that living there can be practical certainty which is more vital than the others because it is deeper in man's being.

FAITH AS KNOWLEDGE

ÉTIENNE GILSON

Étienne Gilson (1884–) has been one of the foremost historians of medieval philosophy and expositors of St. Thomas. He studied chiefly at the University of Paris and the Sorbonne and has taught at the universities of Lille, Strasbourg, Paris, Harvard, and Toronto. His many writings include The Unity of Philosophical Experience *(1937),* God and Philosophy *(1941), and* History of Christian Philosophy in the Middle Ages *(1955). In this selection he presents the Thomistic conception of faith as a form of knowledge.*

In order to clear up the difficulty, let us begin by defining the proper nature of religious faith. To have faith is to assent to something because it is revealed by God. And now, what is it to have science? It is to assent to something which we perceive as true in the natural light of reason. The essential difference between these two distinct orders of assent should be carefully kept in mind by anybody dealing with the relations of Reason and Revelation. I know by reason that something is true because *I see* that it is true; but I believe that something is true because *God has said it.* In those two cases the cause of my assent is specifically different, consequently science and faith should be held as two specifically different kinds of assent.

If they are two distinct species of knowledge, we should never ask one of them to fulfill what is the proper function of the other. We should never do it for the simple reason that, since they are specifically distinct, one of them cannot possibly be the other one. For instance, I cannot pos-

Reprinted with the permission of Charles Scribner's Sons from *Reason and Revelation in the Middle Ages*, pp. 72-78, by Étienne Gilson. Copyright 1938 Charles Scribner's Sons.

sibly ask you to believe that I am here; you cannot believe it, because
you see it. On the other hand, I cannot cause you to see that I am now
interpreting for you the fifth article of the second section of the second
Part of the *Summa Theologica* of Saint Thomas Aquinas. I can only ask
you to believe it. Later on, if you check up my reference, you will see
whether I was right or wrong in quoting it; and then you will know
whether I was right or wrong, but it will become impossible for you to
believe it. Now the same distinction should apply to the problem of reason and Revelation. According to its very definition, faith implies assent
of the intellect to that which the intellect does not see to be true, either as
one of the first principles, or as one of their necessary conclusions. Consequently, an act of faith cannot be caused by a rational evidence, but entails an intervention of the will. On the contrary, in scientific knowledge,
my assent is sufficiently and completely determined by its very object.
Whence there follows that, in Thomas Aquinas' own words, since "it is
impossible that one and the same thing should be believed and seen by the
same person, . . . it is equally impossible for one and the same thing to
be an object of science and of belief for the same person." In short, one
and the same thing cannot be at one and the same time both an object of
science and an object of faith.

When we read those lines, what they say seems to be pretty obvious;
and, in a way, it was; yet those simple statements are a landmark in the
history of Western thought. By taking such a stand, Thomas Aquinas was
challenging the distinction more or less confusedly implied in so many
theologies, between the simple faith of common people, and the enlightened faith of the *meliores*, who add to faith its understanding.[1] It is typical of Saint Thomas Aquinas that he could not tolerate even the shadow
of such a confusion: "that which is proposed to be believed equally by all
is unknown by all as an object of science: such are the things which are
of faith simply." Consequently, if we are dealing with those things which
are essentially of faith, it becomes absurd to draw any distinction between

---

[1] The Gnostic distinction between Faith, considered as an inferior type of religious
knowledge, and the Gnosis, considered as an intellectual experience of religious truth,
has never been accepted by any Father of the Church or medieval theologian; to
them, there was but one Catholic faith, the same for all Christians, and one to which
the assent of the most learned theologians was just as strictly bound as that of the
most illiterate people. Yet, Clement of Alexandria, for instance, certainly admitted of
a hierarchy, if not of beliefs, at least of believers. His "Christian Gnostic" believes the
same things as all the other Christians, but his own faith is crowned by a religious
"knowledge" which is refused to common believers (see the texts collected in G.
Bardy, *Clément d'Alexandrie*, J. Gabalda, Paris, 1926; pp. 246-312). A slight touch of
that aristocratic religious feeling can still be detected in an early text of Saint Augustine: "nam et a *melioribus* etiam dum has terras incolunt, et certe a bonis et piis
omnibus post hanc vitam . . ." (*De libero arbitrio*, II, 2, 6). All good and pious men
(*omnes*) will see God in future life, but the *meliores* can already *know* something
about Him.

the mass of the simple believers and the aristocracy of those who add to the same faith its understanding. As believers, all Christians are in the same predicament, for all of them agree as to what they believe, and none of them has any scientific knowledge of it.

What then should we answer, when great theologians, who sometimes are also great saints, enjoin us to accept their reasons as necessary demonstrations of what we hold as true by faith? Simply that it cannot be done. The authority of so high a saint and of so great a theologian as Saint Anselm himself has absolutely nothing to do with the question. In fact, "the reasons employed by holy men to prove things that are of faith are not demonstrations." And why? Because they cannot be. If that which they pretend to demonstrate were really demonstrated, it would become scientifically known and therefore could no longer be believed.[2]

Saint Thomas did not content himself with a mere abstract statement of his general answer to the question, he applied it to the solution of many particular problems. And no wonder, for in all thoses cases the very nature of Revelation, of faith and of theology itself was at stake. In its own way, theology itself is a science, whose conclusions necessarily follow from their principles; but those principles are articles of faith, and faith itself is an assent to the word of God accepted as word of God. Were we to say, on the contrary, that there are necessary demonstrations of the revealed truth, we could no longer believe in it, there would be no articles of faith, no principles of theological reasoning, no theology conceived as a distinct order of knowledge. In other words, revealed theology, or the theology of Revelation, would disappear as religious knowledge; what would be left in its place would be natural theology, that is to say, metaphysics.

Such was the fundamental reason why Saint Thomas Aquinas never failed to stress the transcendent nature and incomparable dignity of the word of God every time he could find some appropriate occasion to do it. If it is of the essence of an article of faith to rest upon divine authority alone, its would-be demonstrations cannot possibly be necessary demonstrations. Now our faith in Revelation should not be a merely natural assent to some rational probability. When something is rationally probable, its contrary also is rationally probable. It is but an opinion, Religious faith is not an opinion. It is the unshakable certitude that God has spoken, and that what God has said is true, even though we do not understand it. Hence Thomas Aquinas' repeated warnings not to overrate the value of such probabilities, lest, as he himself says, "the Catholic faith seem to be founded on empty reasonings, and not, as it is, on the most solid teaching

---

[2] THOMAS AQUINAS, *Summa Theologica*, Pt. IIa-IIae, qu. I, art. 5; transl. by the Fathers of the English Dominican Province, pp. 10-13.

of God.["3] And again: "And it is useful to consider this, lest anyone, pre-
suming to demonstrate what is of faith, should bring forward reasons that
are not cogent, so as to give occasion to unbelievers to laugh, and to think
that such are the grounds on which we believe things that are of faith."[4]

By thus excluding from theology all necessary demonstrations of purely
rational nature, Thomas Aquinas was cutting loose from the theologism
of the early Middle Ages. From now on, and up to our own days, there
have always been men to maintain that Revelation is a self-sufficient and
self-contained order of truth, whose ultimate foundation is divine authority alone and not the natural light of reason. This, however, should
immediately be added, that the specific distinction introduced by Thomas
Aquinas between faith and rational knowledge was not understood by
him as a separation, still less as an Averroistic opposition.

ABSOLUTE FAITH
AND THE COURAGE TO BE

PAUL TILLICH

*Paul Tillich (1886–) is known internationally as a prominent and
controversial Protestant theologian. Born in Germany, he studied
at Berlin, Tubingen, Breslau, and Halle. He taught at Berlin, Marburg, Dresden, and Leipzig, he was at Frankfurt when the Nazis
came to power. In protest he left and came to the United States
in 1933. Here he was a professor of theology at Union Theological Seminary until 1955, then a University Professor at Harvard
until 1962 when he took a position at the University of Chicago.
His works include* The Interpretation of History *(1936),* The
Protestant Era *(1948),* Systematic Theology *(1951, 1957), and
numerous shorter books. His interpretation of faith as the ultimate
concern of personality is presented here.*

We have avoided the concept of faith in our description of the
courage to be which is based on mystical union with the ground of being
as well as in our description of the courage to be which is based on the

From Paul Tillich, *The Courage to Be* (New Haven: Yale University
Press, 1952), pp. 171-78. Reprinted by permission.

---

[3] THOMAS AQUINAS, *Summa contra Gentiles*, Bk. II, Ch. 38; same transl. p. 83. Cf.
Bk. I, Ch. 8; p. 15.
[4] THOMAS AQUINAS, *Summa Theologica*, Pt. I, qu. 46, art. 2, Answer; same transl., p.
250.

personal encounter with God. This is partly because the concept of faith has lost its genuine meaning and has received the connotation of "belief in something unbelievable." But this is not the only reason for the use of terms other than faith. The decisive reason is that I do not think either mystical union or personal encounter fulfills the idea of faith. Certainly there is faith in the elevation of the soul above the finite to the infinite, leading to its union with the ground of being. But more than this is included in the concept of faith. And there is faith in the personal encounter with the personal God. But more than this is included in the concept of faith. Faith is the state of being grasped by the power of being-itself. The courage to be is an expression of faith and what "faith" means must be understood through the courage to be. We have defined courage as the self-affirmation of being in spite of non-being. The power of this self-affirmation is the power of being which is effective in every act of courage. Faith is the experience of this power.

But it is an experience which has a paradoxical character, the character of accepting acceptance. Being-itself transcends every finite being infinitely; God in the divine-human encounter transcends man unconditionally. Faith bridges this infinite gap by accepting the fact that in spite of it the power of being is present, that he who is separated is accepted. Faith accepts "in spite of"; and out of the "in spite of" of faith the "in spite of" of courage is born. Faith is not a theoretical affirmation of something uncertain, it is the existential acceptance of something transcending ordinary experience. Faith is not an opinion but a state. It is the state of being grasped by the power of being which transcends everything that is and in which everything that is participates. He who is grasped by this power is able to affirm himself because he knows that he is affirmed by the power of being-itself. In this point mystical experience and personal encounter are identical. In both of them faith is the basis of the courage to be.

This is decisive for a period in which, as in our own, the anxiety of doubt and meaninglessness is dominant. Certainly the anxiety of fate and death is not lacking in our time. The anxiety of fate has increased with the degree to which the schizophrenic split of our world has removed the last remnants of former security. And the anxiety of guilt and condemnation is not lacking either. It is surprising how much anxiety of guilt comes to the surface in psychoanalysis and personal counseling. The centuries of puritan and bourgeois repression of vital strivings have produced almost as many guilt feelings as the preaching of hell and purgatory in the Middle Ages.

But in spite of these restricting considerations one must say that the anxiety which determines our period is the anxiety of doubt and meaninglessness. One is afraid of having lost or of having to lose the meaning of one's existence. The expression of this situation is the Existentialism of today.

Which courage is able to take nonbeing into itself in the form of doubt and meaninglessness? This is the most important and most disturbing question in the quest for the courage to be. For the anxiety of meaninglessness undermines what is still unshaken in the anxiety of fate and death and of guilt and condemnation. In the anxiety of guilt and condemnation doubt has not yet undermined the certainty of an ultimate responsibility. We are threatened but we are not destroyed. If, however, doubt and meaninglessness prevail one experiences an abyss in which the meaning of life and the truth of ultimate responsibility disappear. Both the Stoic who conquers the anxiety of fate with the Socratic courage of wisdom and the Christian who conquers the anxiety of guilt with the Protestant courage of accepting forgiveness are in a different situation. Even in the despair of having to die and the despair of self-condemnation meaning is affirmed and certitude preserved. But in the despair of doubt and meaninglessness both are swallowed by nonbeing.

The question then is this: Is there a courage which can conquer the anxiety of meaninglessness and doubt? Or in other words, can the faith which accepts acceptance resist the power of nonbeing in its most radical form? Can faith resist meaninglessness? Is there a kind of faith which can exist together with doubt and meaninglessness? These questions lead to the last aspect of the problem discussed in these lectures and the one most relevant to our time: How is the courage to be possible if all the ways to create it are barred by the experience of their ultimate insufficiency? If life is as meaningless as death, if guilt is as questionable as perfection, if being is no more meaningful than nonbeing, on what can one base the courage to be?

There is an inclination in some Existentialists to answer these questions by a leap from doubt to dogmatic certitude, from meaninglessness to a set of symbols in which the meaning of a special ecclesiastical or political group is embodied. This leap can be interpreted in different ways. It may be the expression of a desire for safety; it may be as arbitrary as, according to Existentialist principles, every decision is; it may be the feeling that the Christian message is the answer to the questions raised by an analysis of human existence; it may be a genuine conversion, independent of the theoretical situation. In any case it is not a solution of the problem of radical doubt. It gives the courage to be to those who are converted but it does not answer the question as to how such a courage is possible in itself. The answer must accept, as its precondition, the state of meaninglessness. It is not an answer if it demands the removal of this state; for that is just what cannot be done. He who is in the grip of doubt and meaninglessness cannot liberate himself from this grip; but he asks for an answer which is valid within and not outside the situation of his despair. He asks for the ultimate foundation of what we have called the "courage of despair." There is only one possible answer, if one does not try to escape the question: namely that the acceptance of despair is in itself faith and on the boundary line of the courage to be. In this situation the meaning of life is reduced to despair about the meaning of life. But as long as this despair is an act of life it is positive in its negativity. Cynically speaking, one could say that it is true to life to be cynical about it. Religiously speaking, one would say that one accepts oneself as accepted in spite of one's despair about the meaning of this acceptance. The paradox of every radical negativity, as long as it is an active negativity, is that it must affirm itself in order to be able to negate itself. No actual negation can be without an implicit affirmation. The hidden pleasure produced by despair witnesses to the paradoxical character of self-negation. The negative lives from the positive it negates.

The faith which makes the courage of despair possible is the acceptance of the power of being, even in the grip of nonbeing. Even in the despair about meaning being affirms itself through us. The act of accepting meaninglessness is in itself a meaningful act. It is an act of faith. We have seen that he who has the courage to affirm his being in spite of fate and guilt has not removed them. He remains threatened and hit by them. But he accepts his acceptance by the power of being-itself in which he participates and which gives him the courage to take the anxieties of fate and guilt upon himself. The same is true of doubt and meaninglessness. The faith which creates the courage to take them into itself has no special content. It is simply faith, undirected, absolute. It is undefinable, since everything defined is dissolved by doubt and meaninglessness. Nevertheless, even absolute faith is not an eruption of subjective emotions or a mood without objective foundation.

An analysis of the nature of absolute faith reveals the following elements in it. The first is the experience of the power of being which is present even in face of the most radical manifestation of nonbeing. If one says that in this experience vitality resists despair one must add that vitality in man is proportional to intentionality. The vitality that can stand the abyss of meaninglessness is aware of a hidden meaning within the destruction of meaning. The second element in absolute faith is the dependence of the experience of nonbeing on the experience of being and the dependence of the experience of meaninglessness on the experience of meaning. Even in the state of despair one has enough being to make despair possible. There is a third element in absolute faith, the acceptance of being accepted. Of course, in the state of despair there is nobody and nothing that accepts. But there is the power of acceptance itself which is experienced. Meaninglessness, as long as it is experienced, includes an ex-

perience of the "power of acceptance." To accept this power of acceptance consciously is the religious answer of absolute faith, of a faith which
has been deprived by doubt of any concrete content, which nevertheless
is faith and the source of the most paradoxical manifestation of the courage to be.

This faith transcends both the mystical experience and the divine-
human encounter. The mystical experience seems to be nearer to absolute
faith but it is not. Absolute faith includes an element of skepticism which
one cannot find in the mystical experience. Certainly mysticism also
transcends all specific contents, but not because it doubts them or has
found them meaningless; rather it deems them to be preliminary. Mysticism uses the specific contents as grades, stepping on them after having
used them. The experience of meaninglessness, however, denies them (and
everything that goes with them) without having used them. The experience of meaninglessness is more radical than mysticism. Therefore it transcends the mystical experience.

Absolute faith also transcends the divine-human encounter. In this encounter the subject-object scheme is valid: a definite subject (man) meets
a definite object (God). One can reverse this statement and say that a
definite subject (God) meets a definite object (man). But in both cases
the attack of doubt undercuts the subject-object structure. The theologians who speak so strongly and with such self-certainty about the divine-
human encounter should be aware of a situation in which this encounter
is prevented by radical doubt and nothing is left but absolute faith. The
acceptance of such a situation as religiously valid has, however, the consequence that the concrete contents of ordinary faith must be subjected to
criticism and transformation. The courage to be in its radical form is a key
to an idea of God which transcends both mysticism and the person-to-
person encounter.

SUGGESTED BOOKS

Buber, Martin, *Two Types of Faith*, trans. Norman P. Goldhawk. London:
    Routledge & Kegan Paul, Ltd., 1951. A comparative study of the doc-
    trinal faith of early Christianity and the trustful faith of Israel.
Dewey, John, *A Common Faith*. New Haven: Yale University Press, 1934.
    A pragmatic reconception of faith as a quality of life devoid of super-
    natural reference.
Hick, John, *Faith and Knowledge*. Ithaca: Cornell University Press, 1957. An
    analysis of traditional conceptions of faith and a reinterpretation by a
    British philosopher friendly to both analytic philosophy and Barthian
    theology.
Kroner, Richard, *The Primacy of Faith*. New York: The Macmillan Com-
    pany, 1943. A German-born theologian and philosopher expounds a neo-
    Reformationist position on the faith-reason issue.

Meland, Bernard E., *Faith and Culture*. New York: Oxford University Press, 1953. The meaning of faith for modern times interpreted according to a reconstructed liberalism.

Pegis, Anton C., ed., *Basic Writings of St. Thomas Aquinas*, Vol. II, pp. 1055-1121. New York: Random House, Inc., 1945. St. Thomas's account of faith in *Summa Theologica*, II-II, Qq. 1-7.

Tillich, Paul, *Dynamics of Faith*. New York: Harper & Row, Publishers, 1957. After criticism of what faith is not, faith is analyzed as man's ultimate concern pervading his whole personality.

IV · RELIGION AND SCIENCE

In its organized forms, religion is much older than science, never having been absent from man's life. But though science is of a more recent origin, modern life and thought are thoroughly infused with the spirit, the benefits, and the effects of science. Professor Kusch, a Nobel Prize winner and Chairman of the Department of Physics at Columbia University, speaking before the American Association for the Advancement of Science in December 1960, stated:

> Every facet of our lives has been, in one way or another, fashioned or modified by science and by a derivative technology. Without some perceptive understanding of science it is impossible to live successfully in the modern world and to contribute to the growth of our society. It is essential to the existence of a world in which the human spirit may grow and flourish, for all members of our society to have an increased awareness of the nature of science, of its historic role in changing the course of our civilization, of its content, of its power and of its limitations.[1]

This impact of science is a fact with which any discussion of the relationship between religion and science must begin. Two historical stages in this relationship have passed and are not likely to return—that in which religion existed without science, and that in which religion controlled science as a submissive subordinate. Two further stages have now reached ascendency—that in which religion and science vie independently for man's attention, and that in which religion is servile to science in the sense that only a religion which can square itself with the finality of mechanical explanations is considered acceptable. A final stage, the qualitative ideal from religion's point of view, would be a harmonious synthesis of religion and science. But whether that will be possible in actual history is not yet apparent.

Our purpose here, however, is not historical but systematic. In this chapter we shall examine some of the current types of tension between religion and science and then offer some observations on the subject of synthesis.

We shall not take space for an extended discussion of what science is or of scientific methods.[2] It will be enough to propose that science has its present meaning from three principal meanings of the term: a certain method of inquiry, a group of exact disciplines, and the capacity to predict from known data. Combining these into a single statement, we may say that science means the pursuit of natural knowledge which relies primarily on hypothesis, observation, and crucial experiment, which is able to use present knowledge for the prediction and often the control of future events, and which is found with greatest precision in physics, chemistry, biology, and related fields. Beyond this the familiarity with science and scientific methods already possessed by the average reader is all we need to presume here, so we may move directly to our main business.

FACTUAL CONFLICTS

It would be better if we could concentrate on the idea of a constructive synthesis of religion and science. However, quite apart from the difficulty of discovering the clues to such a synthesis, the reality of tensions between the two still looms so large that we must deal with that part of the subject first.

The most widely heralded type of tension concerns factual conflicts. A factual conflict occurs when one person or group defends, on religious grounds, a certain statement about the world of nature, and another person or group maintains, on scientific grounds, a contradictory statement about the world of nature. The examples of the Copernican revolution, the discoveries of Galileo, Darwin's theory of evolution, and discoveries about the age of the earth all illustrate how science and religion have conflicted at the factual level. This type of tension is not, in an informed view of religion and science, a reasonable one. Nevertheless, such factual conflicts have received the widest attention, and the reasons for this are quite understandable. These conflicts are the most obvious ones; they are more explicit and open; they can be easily stated; they can be written down and understood by everybody; and finally, in our Western history at least, they penetrated what was taken to be the very foundation of religion and so were of great concern and anguish. In view of this widespread concern, we should begin by making our attitude toward factual conflicts clear.

It is impossible and unnecessary to consider factual conflicts here one by one. Aside from the endlessness of such a task, many of the extreme controversies have subsided.[3] What is needed, therefore, is not a piecemeal analysis, but a set of deductions from our view of religion and science that will give us a single over-all perspective. Such a perspective should enable us to see that there is no reason for the beliefs of religion and the verified factual statements of science to conflict.

From the side of religion, one of the greatest sources of controversy has been the tendency to give a religious character to certain factual matters. That is, it has been regarded as a religious matter to believe that the natural world exists in one way rather than another, for example, that the cosmos was created in six literal days, that the planets were arranged in a certain pattern around a fixed earth, or that man arose in a certain way. Answers to such questions of fact were thought to be part of religion itself, so that it was a religious duty to believe one way rather than another on these matters. This was not because it was inconceivable that God should have made the world otherwise, but because it was believed that God directly revealed these factual descriptions of the natural world. Revelation was taken to include scientific truths as well as other truths of a religious nature. But if we conceive of revelation as consisting essentially of divine self-disclosures instead of factual statements, the source of the controversy ought logically to be reduced. It is then the province of science to describe the processes that occur in the natural world, and its findings ought not to conflict with the real nature of religion.

This does not mean that the judgments of science and the judgments of religion refer to different worlds. It is certainly no solution to the problem to say that science refers to one world, the natural, while religion refers to another world, the supernatural, and therefore they do not conflict. Both kinds of statements may, in fact, refer to the same objects. For instance, to say that there are a certain number of people in the world is to make a scientific statement capable, in principle, of accurate verification through observation and counting, but to say that all people have immeasurable value to a supreme being is to make a religious judgment capable of certification only by intuitive experiences. Yet the two assertions refer to the same objects, human beings. It must be added immediately that scientific judgments and religious judgments do not *always* refer to the same objects. There can be objects of religious judgments, such as God, which are not within the scope of science, and there are also scientific objects with which religion is generally unconcerned. The point is that the difference between the two kinds of statement is not a difference in worlds referred to, but rather a difference in the characteristics or aspects of any object that might be referred to. Scientific statements refer to objects in their aspects of observability and measurability, while religious statements refer to objects in their aspects of value and of relevance for entering into our ultimate commitments. This being so, religion and science ought not to conflict because their beliefs do not refer to the same content. Thus we see that the nature of revelation, on the one hand, and also the content of religious beliefs, on the other hand, both lead to the deduction that religion and science cannot be contradictory but only compatible and complementary.

From the side of science, there seems to be a corresponding source of controversy. If some religionists have given a religious hue to certain questions which belong more properly in the domain of science, some scientists have given a scientific hue to certain questions which are more properly regarded as religious. Thus, Freudians have claimed that the existence of God is an illusion on the ground that it is merely a psychological projection of a protective father image. If such a statement is put forward as scientific, it is certainly not like any statements of science according to any common conception of science, for it is not open to any of the usual tests of observation and experimentation. What the statement shows at most is the role which the idea of God plays in some neurotic cases. Even there, moreover, the facts cited cannot be said to disprove the existence of God, because they may only point up the distortions to which the idea of God is subject. The belief in God, therefore, is not a scientific hypothesis open to confirmation or disconfirmation by the methods of science. It is a religious tenet subject to the religious test of the meaning of God in spiritually sensitive human experience. There is no attempt here to suggest a curtailment of science, as if anyone could say that science should go only up to a certain fixed point and no further. Educated persons will want *bona fide* science and its methods to expand in any realm where it can have fruitful results. But we must be sure that we understand the nature of science. And if the nature of science means that it must be related, however indirectly, to what can be observed and measured, it is not reasonable for us to expect science to do something which by its very nature it cannot do. Our attempt should be not to limit science from the outside, but only to understand its inherent nature, including its inherent limitations. If these limitations be understood, the source of controversy between religion and science ought logically to be reduced.

Let us now apply these ideas on religion and science to two instances of factual conflict, one from the past and a possible one from the future.

The instance from the past is the occurrence of miracles. Many religious persons have held that if certain miracles did not factually occur in the past, belief in God would be undermined and hence their religion destroyed. Likewise many scientific persons have held that if certain miraculous events did occur in the past, belief in natural law would be undermined and hence their science destroyed. Both attitudes seem inappropriate to the nature of religion and of science. If religion lives in the realm of value, commitment, and endeavors after reconciliation, the meaningfulness of religion need not be destroyed if many miraculous events could be shown not to have occurred exactly as they were reported.[4] Similarly, if science lives in the realm of probable and present observation, it is clearly not in a position to pronounce on the factual validity of every report about the past. It seems scientifically wise, therefore, not to hold a conception of natural law which precludes by definition the occurrence of unusual and unpredictable events. Mutual receptivity and openness to reinterpretation may go a long way toward overcoming factual conflicts in this area.[5]

The possible future instance is the artificial production of life. There seems to be a distinct possibility, in the scientific sense, that at some future time living entities may be produced from certain nonliving protein molecules.[6] In such an eventuality, the religious beliefs of many persons might be shaken, because the discovery would shatter their belief that life originates only from God; however, it would strengthen the theory that life arose from chance combinations of matter. But there is no reason why the religious position of theism need be weakened at all by such a discovery. In the first place, the present distinction between the living and the nonliving is not necessarily final. It may be that the smaller entities and particles are themselves characterized by life of some sort not yet understood or studied. In that case the artificially produced living things would still arise from life, and the discovery would only push the question of the origin of life one step lower. Secondly, the discovery would shed no light on the question of the origin and dependence of the contingent world of matter. Thirdly, such a discovery, being the result of man's *purpose*, would be a poor argument to use in support of a belief in *chance*. If anything, it might tend to confirm the view that the original impetus bringing matter into life, as well as the whole course of evolution, must have been in some sense purposeful. Finally, a contribution to our knowledge of how life can arise would not affect the value of life. The religious valuations we make of the entire universe, and of its component parts, including living things, would not be settled for us by a factual discovery of this type. It is important for us to think on these things, if possible, before discoveries are made, so that we do not expect science to prove or disprove nonscientific beliefs, and so that religion will not, as in the past, find itself first attacking science and then making *post hoc* apologies.

OTHER TYPES OF TENSION

Let us realize, then, that factual conflicts between religion and science are out of order. Does this mean, then, that there are no tensions between the two? Many interested persons like to think so. Once the particular battles over factual questions have been resolved, it is thought, peace and harmony reign. Science has its own realm and religion has another; they cannot conflict, so there is an end to the matter.

But to perceptive thinkers, such as A. N. Whitehead,[7] the tensions do not disappear with the resolution of factual controversies. There are more subtle, less definable tensions which show up more sensitively when not overshadowed by the historically dramatic factual struggles. One reason for such tensions, as mentioned before, is that religion and science do not refer exclusively to different realms of objects. Another reason is that both science and religion are human phenomena, and the same person is called upon to be both scientific and religious. For these reasons tensions result with respect to governing presuppositions, personal attitudes, and cultural values. We shall refer briefly to each of these types of tension, mostly to become aware of them and realize the problems involved in them. Solutions cannot be found in these areas as easily as in the case of factual conflicts; the solutions are not as uniform and generalizable. This is because these tensions are not so objective; they are more individual, fluid, elusive.

The first of these tensions is what we may call presuppositional tension. This means that while there may be no factual conflicts between religion and science, still they each function with working postulates which carry them in opposite directions. As examples of religious presuppositions we may mention the following beliefs: man partially transcends nature; man is capable of responding with freedom in his environment; awareness of God is necessary for fulfillment of personality. Some examples of scientific presuppositions, on the other hand, would be the postulate of uniform and universal laws of cause and effect, as in physical science; the postulate that knowledge of the individual must come through the study of his behavior, as in psychological science; and the postulate that man is the product of his natural and cultural environment, as in social science. If these scientific presuppositions are ultimately and literally true, it is clear that a far different conception of the universe would result from the one assumed by the religious presuppositions. Thus while nothing but compatibility and harmony may be actually intended, the net result may be that these different working postulates, each justifiable in its own sphere, lead to different goals and hence to divisions and tensions. Religion and science may be like two friends who plan to stick together for life, but because of different professions and callings, are carried away into different places, duties, and disciplines. When they meet again, things are somehow not the same any more.

Of course the parting of the ways may not always be as reluctant as this analogy suggests. A common opinion in scientific circles seems to be describable somewhat as follows: "Very well, let us be friends. We will admit that there is no factual conflict between us. We will even admit that religious hypotheses have led to some good things. We recognize that our scientific postulates are only assumptions and not proven facts; they constitute, if you will, a scientific philosophy. But we think they are the only legitimate ones for reasonable men to hold. Just wait and see: science will prove itself to be capable of finding all necessary explanations, thus leaving religion by the wayside." There is thus a significant group of scientists who hold that, in the words of John Dewey, "the advance of culture and science has completely discredited the supernatural and with it all religions that were allied with belief in it."[8] Similarly, religion has sometimes defined its principles in such a way as to make scientific principles a farce. There are some religionists who are just as scornful of scientific assumptions as some scientists are of religious hypotheses.

In this type of tension, we ought not to hold our religious beliefs in so crude a form as to render scientific work insignificant. We ought to ask ourselves continually whether our scientific postulates in any given form are really so unmodifiable as they may appear to be. The closer we can bring our presuppositions together, the closer we will move toward integration of thought and knowledge.

Another type of tension is that which occurs within an individual person. Presuppositional tension is more of an external thing; it can be viewed as a tension between a set of scientific beliefs and a set of religious beliefs, between science as a way to truth and religion as a way to truth. But the kind of tension we shall now expose dwells in the inner life of an individual, in his attitudes, motives, and decisions. Sometimes this personal tension is caused when presuppositional tension burrows its way into one's private life instead of confining itself to an opposition between one person and another, one group and another, or one organization and another. This may be especially true for people who are actively engaged in both science and religion, and who therefore come into contact with the conflicting presuppositions more directly. The danger here is that a person may follow contradictory sets of beliefs, one scientific and one religious, in different circumstances and spheres of his life. Such a situation is not uncommon among students who accept their religious background without thinking, and are now beginning to learn science.

But this is not all that should be included under the heading of personal tensions. In addition to reconciling our inner beliefs, there is the really difficult task of cultivating the scientific attitude and the religious attitude at the same time. This problem is not one that exists just for professionals in science and religion, for if both of these have value, all of us ought to cultivate and extend the scientific way and the religious way in our individual lives. The danger is that we will become so engrossed in one that we will neglect and even scorn the other. Unwittingly, the scientific Darwin became a hater of Shakespeare and a neutral on religion, and the intuitive Bergson became a minimizer of science. The difficulty is that these two attitudes involve contrasting ingredients and call for contrasting qualities. On the one hand, we must be analytical, skeptical, objective, experimental, anchored to the observable, persuaded only by stubborn fact. On the other hand, we must be subjective, involved, valuing, committed, living in faith beyond facts. This does not mean that both science and religion could not benefit by incorporating the other's typical attitudes into itself. Rather, that is in a way the ideal. But these two groups of attitudes are extremely difficult to combine in the same breast. Here precisely is the problem. There will be no final solution, for it is not even a stable problem in the ordinary sense. It is an existential hazard to be confronted at all times and to be resolved in the inner man of each individual.

The last type of tension to be noted is what might be called cultural tension. This is the conflict that occurs when science or religion as a whole is called into question in the name of the other. The very value of either science or religion may be repudiated on behalf of the other's cause. It has been reported that some Oriental thinkers have, in support of religious values, taken a negative view of Western science because it has played the leading role in producing our mechanized, materialistic civilization. Whether this report is true or not, and if so, how extensive the feeling is, is immaterial, for the same opinion has been voiced in the West itself. On the other side, scientifically minded persons have, in support of scientific values, denounced religion as a restricting influence in human affairs. It is not enough to say, against this latter contention, that it is not a scientific statement (which it is not), and that it really represents another religion, a religion of science. The point is that the judgment, however regarded, is still made on behalf of science in opposition to religion. Thus another tension results because of what science is and does, and what religion is and does. It is doubtful whether anyone would advocate the total abolition of either of these activities, even if it could be imagined how that could be done. But there are certainly those who advocate a drastic curtailment of the role that one or the other plays in modern culture, and hence there is a conflict of values of no small magnitude.

In such a situation, where there is still no universal acceptance of both science and religion, we must seek with great earnestness, historically and systematically, to discover what things are essential in each activity and what things are distortions. It may be that the source of the opposition of one to the other stems solely from the distortions to which each has been put. The fault would then lie in human delinquency rather than at the doorstep of either science or religion. The problem basically is whether either science or religion, even broadly conceived, can take over the function of the other. Both possibilities have at times been held as ideals in the human mind, meaning in the one case the unending extension of science, and in the other the total authority of religion. But both ideals must ever fail. Religion does not discover the facts and laws of the natural world, and science does not save us.[9] Yet man by his very nature needs both knowledge and salvation, and we must therefore look not for the eclipse of science or religion but for their rightful position in civilization.

TOWARD SYNTHESIS

We have called attention to factual, presuppositional, personal, and cultural conflicts. But we should not leave the impression that tension between religion and science is the only important relationship between them to be found in the past or to be anticipated in the future. There has been much harmony in the past. And as far as the future is concerned, just as a flower may be the last but yet the most brilliant part of the plant that has borne it, so the flowering synthesis of science and religion may be the last but yet the most fruitful effect of the historical developments that have produced them.

There seem to be two ways in which science and religion can and should draw nigh to each other. One is in the realm of attitude and method, and the other is in the realm of content. Borrowing Kant's words, these two parts of the synthesis may be called the regulative ideal and the constitutive ideal. That is, in any such synthesis, both science and religion would, in the first place, be influenced and regulated to some extent by each other's characteristic attitudes, motivations, and ways of proceeding; and, in the second place, each pursuit would, as far as possible, make use of the other's beliefs in constituting and organizing its own body of teaching. The task is a tremendous one, and I do not know the way in which it might be worked out. Admittedly it is an ideal, and not something which simply requires an exposition. But there do seem to be a few suggestions to be made.

Most of us are on terrain that is at least approachable when we contemplate the first aspect of the synthesis. Here we are concerned with the transference of one mode of response to a different kind of human pursuit from the one where it is normally found. There have been examples of this in the past, as there are today. Certainly the motivation of many pioneer scientists in the past was a religious one. They were unlocking the mysteries of nature which God had entrusted to them. It was not so much science for science's sake as it was science for religion's sake— science pursued in order that one might be creative and express one's divinely given endowments, science pursued in order to discover the truth about God's universe, science pursued in order to control nature where it could be brought more effectively into an ethical-religious service. If many scientists have lost a religious motivation and have thereby assisted unwittingly in allowing science to drift into the service of mechanization, gadgetry, and dehumanization, there is certainly nothing inherent in science to make such a result the inevitable outcome of scientific history. Indeed, the proper scientific spirit would be—for the sake of science itself if nothing else—an active opposition to such perverted uses of science. A contemporary example of the impact of religion on science occurs when various groups of scientists band together to make common declarations on important public questions, such as denunciation of further tests of hydrogen bombs[10] or repudiation of biological claims of racial superiority. For many scientists the motivation in these pronouncements is undoubtedly religious.

Examples of the reverse influence, that of science upon religion, are also available, although they have generally been more recent in date and sometimes more reluctantly accepted. The scientific, historical study of the Bible is now generally regarded as a valuable ally in the discovery of Biblical truth. The scientific study of mental health and the phychology of religion are doing much to guide the thinking of religious people in their conception of religious personality, religious activities, religious counseling, and religious instruction. The scientific study of comparative social customs and religions is now taken seriously into account in our discussions of the relation between the religion we hold and the religions of other groups and cultures. These are examples of the appreciation and acceptance by religion of the scientific way of approaching things. They show the helpful influence which scientific methods and motivations can have in the formulation of religious beliefs and practices.

These few examples illustrate the influence of religious attitudes upon people working in science, and of scientific attitudes upon people working in religion. This influence upon the persons involved is where we must look for any synthesis of method and attitude. Is such synthesis widespread? Unfortunately, it is not. It is far from universal even among the educated people we call scientific or religious, and it is less apparent among the population as a whole, where it would have to be achieved in order to have a genuine synthesis. But at least the examples we can find make it easier to see what synthesis means at this level. When scientists are motivated and inspired by religious values, and when religious people do not shy away from, but rather incorporate scientific objectivity and procedure in their lives and work wherever they can, there is the kind of rapprochement we seek.

When we come to the idea of synthesis in content, however, we are in a less luminous region. For one thing, the idea of synthesis in content may arouse the image of a chemical synthesis in which different elements lose their unique properties and unite into a new compound with new properties. This we cannot expect. The belief in God and the belief in man's dignity are not the subjects studied by physics, chemistry, or biology, any more than wave mechanics, chemical bonding, or laws of heredity are the direct subjects of religious inquiry. We cannot simply mesh all subjects together and still get the advances in particular fields which can come only through isolation and detachment. Furthermore, we said earlier that one reason why science and religion ought not to have factual conflicts is that they have a different content, i.e., refer to different aspects of the universe.

What we may hope for, then, is not a synthesis of subject matters but a blending of results. A better metaphor to use than that of chemical synthesis would be that of musical harmony, wherein each note retains its distinctiveness yet shares in a greater whole. If there is some ultimate validity in both science and religion, it is reasonable to suppose that they fit together in a unified pattern of thought. The characteristics of this pattern may not be determinable until it is reached, but some of the conditions for its achievement may perhaps be anticipated.

First, scientific explanations will not be regarded as completed apart from their significance in religious interpretation. To mention one example, if God is what religious theism conceives him to be, then the idea of God should be relevant to all phases of thought, including science. It would then be incredible for a science to look forward to the completion of its task without reference to the ultimate explanation of existence and value. William E. Hocking has shown one way in which the idea of God may be an integral part of psychological, sociological, and physical theory.[11] Conversely, certain scientific discoveries—for example, those concerning the cosmos, the evolutionary process, and history—may have a bearing on the particular conception of God which religion holds. The point is that in any synthesis truth will emerge through mutual interpenetration rather than scornful separation.

Second, the scope of different disciplines, whether scientific or religious, will become less rigidly fixed than now appears to be the case. For example, Henri Bergson, in his *Creative Evolution*,[12] has, by relating all of life to a fundamental life-force, both proposed a biological theory and laid the groundwork for a religious mysticism. His conclusions are open to question, but we must admit that it would be difficult to say whether the work is in biology or religion, for it is both. Likewise the understanding of personality, its structure, disorders, and needs, would be an understanding simultaneously psychological and religious. Other widening integrations may be expected, as truths from different fields are seen to coalesce.

Third, the gulf between fact and value will diminish if a synthesis is effected. The division between material facts, devoid of value and dealt with by science, and spiritual values, known by religion, will seem inadequate. The world of nature has spiritual meaning, and the world of spirit, at least for us, has material connections. We may, in a genuine synthesis, expect science to disclose the material conditions for spirituality, and religion to discover the spiritual significance of materiality.

SCIENCE AND RELIGION TODAY: A TRUCE OR A SETTLEMENT?

WILLIAM E. HOCKING

William E. Hocking (1873–) has been for many decades a prominent defender of idealist philosophy and liberal religion. Educated at Harvard, he studied also in Germany and then spent the greater part of his teaching career in the philosophy department at Harvard until his retirement. His books include The Meaning of God in Human Experience *(1912),* Human Nature and Its Remaking *(1918), and* Living Religions and a World Faith *(1940). In this selection, he inquires about the possibility of going beyond mere coexistence to a positive synthesis of scientific and religious ideas.*

Between science and religion there is today no corporate war. There are still a few scientific hot-heads who would like to put religion into the museum of antiquities: they are no longer representative. Whether there are any corresponding religious hot-heads who would care to suppress science or would conceive it possible to do so I doubt; I have never met one. There are those who gird at "science" in the large, meaning not science at all but an arrogant state of mind sometimes found in scientific men of an earlier vintage: this state of mind will soon be at a premium on account of rarity. No one is today calling for an Either-Or choice between two concerns both of which belong to everybody. We are all scientists by necessity; we are all, after some fashion, religious.

What then has become of that long run of hostilities, the so-called "Conflict between Science and Religion"? Most of it has gone into history, much of it into curious history, though its departing spasm is within our own memories. As a boy, I heard pulpit fulminations against Darwin.

From William Ernest Hocking, *Science and the Idea of God* (Chapel Hill: The University of North Carolina Press, 1944), pp. 3-10. Reprinted by permission.

My father, whose profession of medicine aligned him with science, yet banned Herbert Spencer from the family bookshelf. The line of debate was not the value of science on its own ground, but the capacity of science to reach a total picture of man and the universe, and to guide human life by that knowledge. This dispute is still with us but is seldom inflamed; it is relieved if not finally closed by a simple jurisdictional agreement. Science withdraws from making assertions about the whole of things, admits that its knowledge does not reach the whole, adding in parentheses a doubt whether "the whole" is a knowable object. Religion (together with philosophy) responds that it is just the whole of things which is—if I may put it that way—its special province, and agrees that it is futile to oppose science on its own ground since science is nothing but organized truth.

The idea of reaching agreement by establishing a separation of provinces is itself so inviting that it assuages tempers even before the boundary is clearly defined. It is hardly satisfactory to say, with a recent author, that "science has decided to stick to its last of building from part to whole, while religion builds from the whole to the part," for this would seem to ensure a collision somewhere in mid-journey. If religion is to have any foothold in human thought, there must be some definable region beyond the scope of science. And on the whole, science today is well disposed to join in an effort to define such a region. Witness the recent conferences on "Science, Philosophy and Religion," valuable if only for the fact of conference itself—remarkable, too, for the general absence of the old polemic bitterness.

Through such conferences it becomes evident that science has no unanimous voice as to what is beyond its own domain, present and future. Certainly it has no official voice. There is, however, a certain convergence of unofficial voices on two such ultra-scientific regions. First, the region commonly assigned to metaphysics, namely, whatever truth can be had either about the whole of things, as just mentioned, or about "the real" as distinct from the phenomenal. Second, the region of "values," that is to say, the estimation of goods and evils, of rights, duties, wrongs, of qualities of pleasure and pain, of beauties and uglinesses, utilities, wastes and detriments—all of these as bearing on a knowledge of the ends worth pursuing, the realm commonly assigned to ethics, aesthetics, and a side of economics. And since values arouse emotion both in anticipation and in enjoyment, this region will include all that side of language and logic which conveys emotion, the language of praise and blame, of epithet, poetry, exhortation, of hope and fear, love and hate, in brief the domain of "emotional meanings" which stands outside the domain of factual meanings proper to science. If ethics and asthetics founded on purpose and choice are still to be called "sciences," they are of a different order from the sciences of nature founded on causality which have the first right to the name. And religion makes its home in all these aspects of value, offers them a principle of order, declares what goods are most worth having and what are secondary or deceptive, proposes a valid way of life. Religion becomes the *arbiter of ends*, and thus the primary organizer of the practical life of man, an office not less important than that of science itself.

This proposed division of province, I repeat, is not affirmed by any corporate voice of science. I ought to note however that there is one voice crying in our time which has offered its services to science, and would be glad to be taken as official: this voice is "logical positivism." It began a quarter-century ago by denouncing both parts of our beyond-science territory, both totality-statements and value-statements, as "meaningless": the region beyond science is empty. This simple result was reached by an equally simple device: one had only to define "meaning" in such a way that totality-statements and value-statements could not possibly qualify—a political ingenuity introduced into supposedly serious thinking. Nothing was to be admitted as having "meaning" unless it brought you around to verifiable sense-data. The definition palpably begged the question, but many unwary minds were taken in the trap: metaphysics and religion, together with ethics, were neatly dismissed as nonsense, and humanity at a stroke was spared infinite fruitless discussion. Positivism thus made itself heir to the older and lingering anti-religious bias of Continental Europe.

But science has not as yet accepted this voice as its own. It perceives, I suspect, that in both these denials positivism was out of date at its birth. Positivism itself has begun to wake up to the old truth that men must live by their values, and to draw the logical conclusion that if (as it has been saying) value-judgments are meaningless, then human life is meaningless. This is uncomfortable, but there is no way out of it on the assumed premises. Fnding itself thus in the awkward position of identifying the valuable with the meaningless and the meaningful with the valueless, positivism today effects a strategic retreat by way of another definition, that of "importance": it allows that something may be "important" without being "scientifically meaningful." Under this clause, even religion is permitted to enter as "possibly important." But was it not about the middle of the nineteenth century when science inclined to describe its attitude toward metaphysics and the like as "agnostic"? And does not this imply that religion is "possibly important"? And is not the present effort to outline a province for religious thought a distinct stage ahead? As a leader of opinion, positivism slowly catches up with the led.

In point of fact, science is today concerned to see this task through. It not only admits, but insists, that science is not a complete guide to human living. This mood of humility is not unmingled with prudence; feeling the peril of our time, scientists also perceive the peril to science itself of being widely relied on for a sort of guidance it cannot give. Its proper business is to show the connections of events, so that men can use events as means to their ends. What these ends may be science does not specify; if it has ever led men to suppose that it can teach them what objects are worth pursuing, it is now eager to disavow any such capacity.

For its part, religion is equally careful to move out of any field that might bring it into conflict with science. It has become wary of making capital of the momentary dilemmas of science, or of staking out claims in science's unfinished work. Formerly religion was inclined to consider that every domain taken over by science as a field for impersonal causal law was so much territory subtracted from the scope of divine control. It therefore fought a loyal campaign of retreat, and made the most of any unexplained residues of Nature: the sources of life could not be explained; the mysterious origins of species; the marvelous fitness of the world for living beings; the emergence of human reason. Religion now realizes that it cannot live in temporary quarters from which it may be driven by the next scientific advance; nor can it subsist on the left-overs of uncompleted laboratory business.

This policy makes it hesitant in its claim to deal factually with "the whole of things," if this can be considered the ultimate goal of scientific description. Such a claim would seem to invite a conflict with science even if only at the Last Day! In some sense religion is obliged to deal with the whole; for anxiety about the whole in which he is placed is precisely what makes the human animal human, distinguishes him from the brute. The answer may be that religion is to deal with the whole as a realm of value rather than of fact. Such an understanding leaves it undisputed master in the field of ends, and sets it free to welcome the growing penetration of science into the problems of life, mind, and reason.

At the risk of troubling waters that are becoming serene, I fear I must denounce this division of labor. Peace on these terms has the character of a truce, not of a settlement. It means that in subscribing to the doctrine that "science is truth," which is correct, religion has also agreed that "truth is science," which is an overstatement: it means that religion has no truth of its own, a position which is intolerable.

Much contemporary religion bears the moral mark of an illegitimate surrender. It has abandoned at the behest of science first immortality, since for science there is no other world than this world, and mind and body are inseparable; then freedom, since science under the name of psychology takes over all of human nature into the natural system of causes and effects; and finally God as anything more than a name for our highest values. It was at first inclined to hand these three notions over to metaphysics; it has ended by abandoning metaphysics itself as a house built too near the crater of Vesuvius.

For a century and a half since Kant, first ethical then psychological and sociological interpretations of religion have been pressed to provide substitutes for the doctrinal elements of faith. Religious ideas become "postulates," that is to say, demands made on the world, launches of will, wills to believe. Or religion itself is a phenomenon of self-consciousness, a factor of social adjustment, a semi-beneficent illusion: we cannot say, "There is a God," but we can say, "Man is a praying animal"; scare him enough and he prays, revealing something "deep in subconsciousness" and therefore highly authentic. Of such anthropological verity is much contemporary religious thought constructed, science now holding the whip of a resigned authority. Religion shows gratification when the anchor of its drifting boat catches in a submerged tree!

Shall we be satisfied with this situation? To my mind this is less than peace by appeasement; it is peace by capitulation. So far as religion follows these paths, it yields that without which it cannot survive, and strengthens the current swing to a new dogmatism which confesses a desire to seem strong without being strong. Nothing can be won by falling back on Maginot Lines of Barthian pseudo-finality. In recognizing the capitulation, we gain nothing by forgetting that it is incidental to an advance. Religion is enriched by the abundance of relevant data, and new relationships brought to light by scientific enquiry. There can be no question of going back on what science has shown, nor on what it has contributed to religion. The question is solely, what is it that science has shown, and what is the truth which lies beyond that boundary?

AN ANALYSIS OF THE CONFLICT BETWEEN THEOLOGY AND SCIENCE[1]

BERNARD RAMM

Bernard L. Ramm (1916–) is one of the leaders in the rejuvenated movement of evangelical Protestantism. He studied at the University of Wisconsin, Eastern Baptist Theological Seminary, and the University of Southern California, and has taught theology at Bethel College and Seminary, Baylor University, and California Baptist Seminary. His books include Protestant Biblical Interpretation *(1956),* The Witness of the Spirit *(1959), and* Special Revelation and the Word of God *(1961). Here he analyzes the sources of conflict between science and theology and suggests ways of resolution.*

I. INTRODUCTION

That evangelicalism has not been in the good graces of science has been indicated in the previous chapter. The causes of such a condition are therefore an important consideration. Our task in this chapter is (i) to describe the tasks of theology and science, and (ii) to seek to understand how in the pursuit of these tasks theologians and scientists have come into conflict.

II. THE SPECIFIC TASKS OF SCIENCE AND THEOLOGY

To define the task of science is difficult because to define science itself is difficult. High school texts define science with an ease that we envy, but the task is not so simple in philosophy of science. The vexing problem

From Bernard Ramm, *The Christian View of Science and Scripture* (Grand Rapids: Wm. B. Eerdmans Publishing Company, 1954), pp. 45-58. Reprinted by permission.

[1] Studied historically by: A. D. White, *A History of the Warfare of Science with Theology* (1896), 2 vols.; D. O. Zöckler, *Geschichte der Beziehungen zwischen Theologie and Naturwissenschaft mit besonderer Rücksicht auf Schöpfungsgeschichte* (1879), 2 vols., and a corrective to White's history; J. Y. Simpson, *Landmarks in the Struggle Between Science and Religion* (1925); J. W. Draper, *The Conflict between Religion and Science* (1875); C. W. Shields, *The Final Philosophy* (1877).

of defining science is best seen when one tries to classify the sciences. The usual result is to identify science with all knowledge. By science we mean that approximate knowledge we possess of Nature and its phenomena, and this would include the pure sciences and the mixed sciences such as geology and astronomy (or if one prefers, the composite sciences). By extending our notion of science to include anything capable of a measure of systematic treatment and verification we would then include psychology, sociology, history and anthropology. If we were to identify the terms science and knowledge, then theology would be included. The scientist working in pure science thinks that all other types of knowledge are too loose to be classified as sciences, but the psychologist and sociologist do not readily acquiesce in this. However psychologists and sociologists usually draw the line to exclude theology, and this does not please the theologians. Any definition of science will be part arbitrary and conventional. We, therefore, in speaking of science mean to emphasize that body of knowledge dealing with the *structure* and *causal* or *functional relationships* of the *physical* and *space-time* aspects of the universe. Hence, our emphasis is on that which is *external* in contrast to the internal; on that which is *causal* or *determined* in contrast to that which is free or novel or spontaneous; on that which is *formal* in contrast to that which is *personal;* on that which is capable of *description by law* in contrast to that which is unique; and on that which is based on the *continuous* or *uniform* or *regular* in contrast to that which is novel, vertical, and occasional.

The definition of theology is almost as difficult as that of science, for there are those who wish either to annul religious knowledge or those who wish to make religious experience more fundamental than theology. Orthodox theologians insist that theological knowledge is valid knowledge, whereas liberals define theology as the science of religion. We define theology as the task of setting forth the claims of our knowledge of God, the verification of these claims, and the systematic and organic connections of our theological knowledge. Theological study has, however, two foci, one in experience and one in Scripture, and for this reason the study of theology has moral and spiritual considerations which the study of science does not have. Hence, there is an important subjective element in the study of theology as well as an objective element. Theology is a study by the regenerated heart and mind of (primarily but not exclusively) the Holy Bible to determine the system of truth it presents. Although in theology we believe we have objective and real knowledge, we believe that in large part it appears credible only to those who have had an inward experience of the grace of the Holy Spirit. The requirements for a scientist are such things as honesty, integrity, intelligence, patience, and fairness. There is no crucial experience which makes one a scientist. The requirements of a theologian include all those of a scientist and the additional spiritual ones. (The hyperorthodox frequently make the mistake of thinking that because they have the spiritual requirements they can treat with great disregard the scientific aspects of theological scholarship). In defining theology as our knowledge of God and of his relationships to creation we must add: *as carried on by a Christian man.*

It is, to speak as a theologian, the task of the scientist to explore the works or creation of God, and that of the theologian the speech of God in the Bible, Nature, and history. From the Christian perspective the true scientist should work in humility and reverence, believing that he is delving into the worship of God. Whatever theology brings forth from the scientific investigation of Nature comes at the end of the task and consists of the generalizations indicating how our knowledge of Nature dovetails with our theological knowledge. In the main, the task of science is the understanding of Nature; and the task of theology is the understanding of God. It is the thesis of this author that the two tasks and the two bodies of conclusions should exist in a state of harmony. The speech of God in Nature and in Scripture must accord.

III. WHY THEOLOGIANS
AND SCIENTISTS HAVE CONFLICTS

Ideally in their mutual pursuits the scientist and the theologian should supplement each other. Their efforts should merge into each other to form one harmonious continuum of reliable knowledge. But, much to the contrary, the relationship in many cases has been bitter and antagonistic. *Blame is on both sides.* The dogmatizing theologian has a blood-brother in the dogmatic materialist, and premature judgments in theology are akin to immature judgments in science. Out of the mistakes of both theologian and scientist has come the unfortunate history of their unfriendly relationship.

Mistakes peculiar to the theologian.

The first mistake peculiar to the theologian is that of attitude. He has been unsympathetic with science, or suspicious of it, or he fails to understand science. In this the theologian is to blame. If he is censorious of the scientist who makes amateurish remarks about theology, and wishes that the scientist would learn a little theology before he spoke, the scientist can also ask the theologian to learn a little science before he speaks. To view science as the work of scheming atheists, iconoclasts, or plotting infidels is not true to the facts nor felicitous of the spirit of the Christian theologian. Slurring the name of science, branding it all as devil inspired, chiding it unsympathetically, further aggravate the situation that is already bordering on the incurable.

The second mistake peculiar to the theologian is either (i) to identify a given world view with its science with the Bible or (ii) to derive too many empirical or specific data from the general assertions of Genesis 1. For example, the identification of the Aristotelian science with Christianity as occurred during the Middle Ages has done harm beyond any possible calculation. Much of the conflict between scientists and theologians was really between Aristotelianism and science, not Christianity and science. Theologians must be exceedingly careful to not identify Christianity with any perishable scientific world view.

Just as mistaken as identifying Christianity with Aristotelianism is the mistake of making the Bible speak too specifically on scientific matters. We have in Genesis 1 a broad, general sketch of creation. To try to prove minute points of geology, biology, botany or anthropology from it is therefore impossible and should not be attempted. When we try to do it, we force the record to speak in detail beyond which it is capable, and we are in danger of running into contradiction with the empirical facts established by the sciences. Few reliable conservative scholars today would state that we can positively identify the Hebrew word *kind* (Hebrew, *min;* LXX, *genos;* Vulgate, *genus* and *species*) with the modern scientific notion of *species*. None would certainly identify *min* with varieties. To attempt to identify *min* with species or varieties is making the record speak with a scientific particularity it does not possess. We judge it improper for the theologian to try to settle specific details about scientific matters by forcing the Bible to speak with a degree of definiteness its language does not possess.

Mistakes common to both theologians and scientists.

First, theologians and scientists may pronounce some scientific theory as final, and this can cause conflict. The theologian may presume a hypothesis to be a fact, and then have later developments in science demonstrate its falsity; the scientist may prematurely accept a hypothesis as true and find himself in conflict with the theologian. There have been no less than ten theories as to the origin of the solar system as listed in W. M. Smart's *The Origin of the Earth* (1951). Which is the true one? Which is the Biblical one? Premature judgment by either scientist or theologian may cause unnecessary friction. There are several schools of contemporary psychology, as there are of basic theory of acculturation in anthropology. "Denominationalism" afflicts science as well as the church, and for this reason both scientist and theologian must be careful of too easy an identification of any current school of scientific theory with the final truth.

Secondly, theologians and scientists must be keenly aware of the imperfections of human knowledge in both science and theology. Scientific theory is somewhat fluid under our feet. The history of atomic theory from 1885 to 1950 is so rapid it is almost breath-taking. Each removal of a past imperfection is a prophecy of a future imperfection. The same is the case with exegesis. Archaeology, philology, and history are constantly enriching our knowledge of the Old and New Testaments. With this enriched knowledge attends a more careful and accurate exegesis. Thus exegesis, to a certain extent, is in a state of flux.[2]

We can at this point take the advice of Pratt:

> The Book of Nature and the Word of God emanate from the same infallible Author, and therefore cannot be at variance. But man is a fallible interpreter, and by mistaking one or both of these Divine Records, he forces them too often into unnatural conflict.[3]

The third cause for conflict is misinterpretation of the Bible by scientist or theologian. If the scientist affirms that the Bible teaches creation at 4004 B.C. he needlessly makes science and Scripture conflict through misinterpretation. If the first step toward truth is the removal of error, the Ussher chronology should at this point be abandoned. If the scientist insists that the Bible teaches that the earth is flat, or the heavens solid, or that there are pillars supporting the sky, or that the entire solar system came to rest at Joshua's command, then through his own misinterpretation he brings the Bible into conflict with science.

If the theologian teaches that the earth is the center of the solar system, or that man first appeared on the earth at 4004 B.C., or that all the world was submerged under water at 4004 B.C. and had been for unknown millennia, he is misinterpreting Scripture and bringing Scripture into needless conflict with science. Both scientist and theologian must exercise unusual care in the interpretation of the Bible and it is just as mistaken to follow after improper interpretations of the Bible as it is to follow after unproved hypotheses in science.

Mistakes peculiar to scientists.

Just as there are certain mistakes that a theologian is susceptible to there are ones that the scientist is just as susceptible to in the relationship of theology to science. The first of these mistakes is to have an anti-

---

[2] Clay tablets from the ancient biblical lands have been the source of much new information—religious, political, and grammatical or linguistic. Even with reference to the famous virgin passage of Isaiah 7:14 there is information to be learned from the clay tablets. Cf. Cyrus H. Gordon, "Almah in Isaiah 7:14," *The Journal of Bible and Religion*, 21:106, April, 1953.

[3] J. H. Pratt, *Scripture and Science not at Variance* (1872), p. 8.

religious attitude. No system of knowledge can be learned without some sympathy or kindly feeling toward the system—something pointed out long ago by Augustine but never fully appreciated by educators nor epistemologists. Dogmatists study science as well as theology.

The evangelical indicates that man is a spiritual rebel and his spirit of rebellion is reflected in all his activities. Unsaved man opposes the doctrines of creation, sin, redemption, and eschatology. A man may be religious and yet antichristian. Opposition to Christianity at the level of science is in many instances simply localized or vocalized opposition to Christianity in general. Therefore antichristian man takes pleasure in making the gap between science and Christianity as wide as he can make it, and will heartlessly ridicule any efforts at reconciliation. In this instance, the gap between science and Christianity is in reality the gap between faith and unbelief.

However, Conservatives need to be careful that this is not exaggerated in their dealings with scientists. All science and all scientists cannot be dropped overboard on the sole grounds that they are not Christian. All of geology cannot be declared specious because geology has been developed principally by unsaved men. Truth is truth and facts are facts no matter who develops them. Man as a spiritual and intellectual rebel is part of the reason why there is tension between science and Christianity, but *it is not the entire reason.*

Putting the same truth positively we assert that the scientist's lack of faith incapacitates him from truly harmonizing science and Scripture. The evidence of Hebrews 11:3 cannot be controverted at this point ("Through faith we understand that the world came into being by the command of God, so that what is seen does not owe its existence to that which is visible," Weymouth). Nature as the creation of God can only be appreciated properly and interpreted correctly by the man of God, and the Bible as the Word of God is only so recognized by the man of God. Only the man of faith has the correct perspective and motivation to harmonize Scripture and science. Men without faith cannot but clash the gears.

However, the most drastic difference between science and evangelicalism arises from the usage of the scientific method and knowledge by the scientists. We must now examine why it is that scientists persist in creating a so-called scientific world view which clashes with the Biblical world view.

Science, narrowly conceived, is not partial to any philosophical system but forms a body of material which any philosophy must reckon with. Philosophers may claim that science is on their side or that their philosophy is constructed by the use of the scientific method and so lend the prestige of science to their philosophy. In either case science is made to serve metaphysics or philosophy. The materialist claims that science presents the same world view from empirical and experimental considerations that materialism presents from philosophical considerations. Similar use is made of science by pragmatism, naturalism, and positivism, all of which may be termed *scientisms*. All have in common the exaltation of the scientific method and scientific knowledge with reference to philosophical construction.

Obviously, if science and the scientific method be used to exclude the spiritual the Christian feels that the scientific method and scientific knowledge are abused. It is the Christian's obligation to show wherein is the type of reasoning employed which leads to scientisms.

1. The Christian philosopher indicates that all scientisms *over-simplify both the scientific method and the scope of reliable knowledge*. In reference to the over-simplification of the scientific method we mean that only certain aspects of the scientific method are emphasized and made important. The scientific method as usually listed in college textbooks in connection with the sciences is epistemologically disrespectful. What is presented is correct, but what is left unmentioned is as vital to the scientific method as what is mentioned. Included in the scientific methodology are: (i) requisite ethical norms on the part of the experimenter, e.g., honesty in reading his various meters, reporting variations, not fudging the evidence; (ii) the necessary integrity of the personal powers of the scientist, e.g., his memory, his sensory equipment, his judgment; (iii) the validity of the laws of logic as he manipulates his data; (iv) the necessity and validity of communication to other selves, for science is a community project and a social activity.[4] When the scientific method is usually discussed such notions as testability or intersubjectivity or experimentation are to the fore. This is a clear case of fudging, and it is only by such fudging that a plausible case can be made for scientisms. If we seek a grounding for (i) ethical norms, (ii) logical procedures, (iii) the integrity of personal powers, and (iv) the existence of other selves and our communication with them, in the same sense in which scientisms seek a grounding for experimentation, uniformity of nature, and sensory experience, we will discover that none of the scientisms can carry the burden. In the history of philosophy it will be discovered that philosophers can only find a locus for ethics, logical realism, selves, knowledge of other selves, in some sort of theistic system, and rightly so. Scientisms must admit that ethical norms, etc., are (i) operational procedures, or (ii) necessary assumptions

---

[4] J. H. Woodger, *Biological Principles* (1929), p. 228, lists the bare "fundamental types of judgments upon which all natural scientific knowledge rests, and which cannot be inferred from anything else." This is a very important and imposing list, and is the type of thing so many naive discussions of the scientific method omit. For metaphysics and epistemology these things which Woodger lists are exceedingly important no matter how much scientisms prefer to ignore them.

but devoid of any metaphysical standing, or (iii) conventions judged solely by their utility. The Christian philosopher insists that scientisms fudge at this point, and at the crucial point. With no possible justification one segment of the scientific method is given royal status (experimental, sensory, etc.) and the other segment (ethical norms, etc.) *just as important as the first* is written off as having no metaphysical importance. In a very clearly written essay Brightman has exposed this entire procedure, and shown that a *knowing, ethical, dependable, integrated, rational self is a necessary part of the scientific method.*[5]

If the scientific method is construed in terms far simpler than it actually is, obviously knowledge is also cut too short. Reliable knowledge must be enlarged as to include knowledge about ethics, logic, human personality and social communication. Such an enlarged notion of knowledge would permit theology its rightful place in the domain of reliable human knowledge.

2. The Christian indicts scientisms for their *reductionistic spirit.* Reductionism is the effort to explain the complex by the simple, and the higher by the lower. A typical reduction chain is as follows: what we call the mind is in reality a very complex set of nerve networks called the brain. These fibres are made up of complex organic compounds. These organic compounds can be resolved into their original chemical elements. *Ergo,* the brain is nothing but a highly complicated arrangement of several of the basic chemical elements. What is called mind turns out to be a complex grouping of matter. A typical reductionist statement, valuable for its simplicity and frankness is that of Russell:

> The evidence, though not conclusive, tends to show that everything distinctive of living matter can be reduced to chemistry, and therefore ultimately to physics. The fundamental laws governing living matter are, in all likelihood, the very same that govern the behavior of the hydrogen atom, namely, the laws of quantum mechanics.[6]

Then speaking directly of mental life he affirms:

> In the chain of events from sense organ to muscle, everything is determined by the laws of macroscopic physics.[7]

---

[5] E. S. Brightman, "The Presuppositions of Experiment," *The Personalist,* 19:136-143, 1938. In a subsequent issue Brightman was answered but in our judgment not refuted. Oman has also noted this. "The discovery of this order [in the universe] has been the achievement of minds which work by meaning and, therefore, not by mechanism or anything capable of quantitative measurement. The interests of freedom are the spring of the whole enterprise of science; upon free ideas and free experiments all its methods depend; and only for its uses by freedom has measurement or mechanism any value." John Oman, *The Natural and the Supernatural* (1931), p. 111.

[6] Bertrand Russell, *Human Knowledge* (1948), p. 33.

[7] *Ibid.,* p. 41.

Another form of reductionism is to say that religion is a disguised sex-response. Religion is thus reduced to physiology. Or, with reference to conscience, to call it the accumulated result of the countless "no's" we heard as children from parents and teachers, conscience is reduced to psychological conditioning. We have said "spirit of reductionism" for scientisms vary in their application of the reductionist principle. The materialists and positivists are the extreme reductionists. Naturalists have tried to avoid the reductionist's fallacy, but that they have is to be doubted.

The reductionist mentality is complex as it springs partly from the scientific ideal of simplicity, and partly from an anti-metaphysical or anti-religious mood. It amounts to depriving something of its own right and status. The Christian objects at this point. Mind, as we know it, functions in organisms, but if mind is equated with the brain the facts are misconstrued. Conscience may have numerous correlations with heredity, environment and physical elements of one's own body, but these modifications do not destroy its being and autonomy. In some instances religious feelings and sex feelings may merge or be confused, but that does not give us the right to discount all religion as disguised sex response.

The Christian philosopher urges at this point that *adequacy* is as much a guide as *simplicity* is, and that the reductionist in seeking simplicity ignores facts. Only when reductionism kills off a large measure of the fact-population can scientism make good its claims. But if we are fair to all experience, adequacy must be also reckoned with, and any procedure which sacrifices adequacy to simplicity is an abortive procedure.

3. The Christian philosopher indicts scientisms for their *irrational prejudice against teleological thinking.* By teleological thinking we mean that thinking which recognizes the validity of purpose, meaning, intelligence, wisdom and guidance as possible categories of the Real. Teleological thinking has always been associated with religious, spiritual, and idealistic thought. Scientisms have steadily ruled in favor of ateleological thought. They have unfairly tagged teleological thought as "sentimental" or "emotional" or "soft-headed" and prided ateleological thought as "factual" or "hard-headed" or "scientific."

We brand this prejudice against teleological thought as unjustifiable on the grounds that it is completely impossible of practice, and if completely impossible of practice it cannot be a true philosophical position. It is obvious psychological fact that people without will or purpose or motivation are already psychopathic (or shortly will be). It is common knowledge among anthropologists that uprooted primitive peoples suffer from melancholia and eventually die off. All normal psychological life is held together with purpose. The most ardent materialist or positivist is guided and motivated by purpose. The very fibre and glue of the philosophical activity itself is the purposive. Yet, in mental life scientisms must brand purpose as deceptive and of no metaphysical import. How is it possible that if all is materially or causally determined that such a deceptive item as purpose should be the very cement of healthy personality?

4. The Christian indicts scientisms for their *prejudice against the super-natural*. The problem of the supernatural is actually the problem of the conceivable or the inconceivable. Bett, in his work *The Reality of the Religious Life* (1949), ably argues that the entire concept of conceiv-ability is a slippery one. A vast array of modern attainments were all at one time declared inconceivable. When the history of things considered inconceivable is reviewed one shudders at ever uttering a statement, "it is inconceivable." That is to say, we are hardly in a position to dogmatize on inconceivability. Admittedly, *conceivability* does not prove actuality. But the deep-seated spirit of anti-supernaturalism among scientisms is built upon a theory of inconceivability which is not justifiable.

The categorical excluding of the very conceivability of the supernatural we consider a most improper procedure, and entirely untrue to what an examination of the concept of conceivability would warrant.

A *scientism* can be constructed only by its being partial and limited in its conduct of the philosophical quest. Combining abuses of the interpre-tation of the scientific method, and deep-seated prejudices in the inter-pretation of reality, scientisms created antichristian philosophies. The Christian philosopher affirms that a fair treatment of the scientific method, and a thorough appreciation of all the facts, lead not only to a fair and adequate appreciation of science and scientific methodology, but also to an appreciation of the Christian system of philosophy, and an appreciation of the Christian faith.

The main burden of this chapter then is simply this: *if the theologian and the scientist had been careful to stick to their respective duties, and to carefully learn the other side when they spoke of it there would have been no disharmony between them save that of the non-Christian heart in rebellion against God.* There would have been no stupid exegetical mis-takes of theologians, nor misunderstandings of the Bible by scientists. The theologian would not have needlessly stung the scientists, and the scientist would not have needlessly provoked the theologian. The issue between Christian and non-Christian would not have been a morass of blunder, mistake, and bigotry, but clearly that of belief or unbelief; faith or disobedience. *It is our purpose to show that there is nothing between the soul of a scientist and Jesus Christ save the disposition of the scientist himself.* We hope to show that whatever else is put between is put there improperly and that if the total facts are known its impropriety will be-come apparent. It is therefore not our purpose to coerce faith, but to remove the needless timber that men are wont to throw between themselves and the Savior.

SUGGESTED BOOKS

Burtt, Edwin A., *The Metaphysical Foundations of Modern Physical Science*, revised edition. London: Routledge & Kegan Paul, Ltd., 1932. An investigation of the philosophical assumptions which came to underlie the rise of modern science.

Dillenberger, John, *Protestant Thought and Natural Science*. Garden City, N.Y.: Doubleday & Company, Inc., 1960. Historical analyses of the problems and challenges resulting from the confrontation of Protestantism and science from the time of Copernicus to the present day.

Eddington, Arthur S., *Science and the Unseen World*. New York: The Macmillan Company, 1930. A lecture in which an outstanding astronomer and physicist maintains that both a scientific and a mystical outlook must be included in our world-view.

Mascall, E. L., *Christian Theology and Natural Science*. London: Longmans, Green & Co., Ltd., 1956. An endeavor at intellectual reconciliation of scientific and theological approaches to various specific issues of concern to both.

Needham, Joseph, ed., *Science, Religion and Reality*. New York: The Macmillan Company, 1925. Essays by Malinowski, Singer, Aliotta, Eddington, Needham, Oman, Wm. Brown, Webb, and Inge covering various aspects of the subject from different viewpoints.

Russell, Bertrand, *Religion and Science*. New York: Oxford University Press, 1935. A review of the conflict between religion and science during the last four hundred years by a well-known mathematician-philosopher who is a critic of all religion but not a naive eulogist of science.

Sullivan, J. W. N., *The Limitations of Science*. New York: The Viking Press, Inc., 1933. By surveying the history and the various fields of science the author indicates what science can and has achieved and what sorts of questions are not answered by it.

White, Edward A., *Science and Religion in American Thought*. Stanford: Stanford University Press, 1952. From Christian presuppositions the author investigates the impact of naturalism on religion from mid-nineteenth century to 1930 by analyzing representative thinkers.

V · RELIGIOUS LANGUAGE

One of the most intriguing problems in modern religious thought concerns religious language. The rise of this problem doubtless has many causes, not the least of which is the fact that the philosophical movement of language analysis has turned its attention from more formal, logical questions to the multiple uses which language has in specific realms of discourse, including religion. Widespread skepticism about religion and religious talk has also forced interpreters of religion to try to clarify what the use of religious language involves. Nor should we ignore, as a factor in the increased interest in this problem, the natural and continuing desire of religious communities themselves for self-clarification. In any case, the problem is one that must be confronted in any interpretation of religion which hopes to be relevant to contemporary thought.

THE PROBLEM STATED

In a general form, the problem of religious language is to discover the function or functions of religious discourse, that is, the use that language has when it is employed in a religious context. This very general way of putting the problem does not, however, bring out what is usually the principal concern of those who are engrossed in the problem. This concern—the concern which makes the problem religiously as well as linguistically interesting—may be brought out if we remark that religion almost always involves a conception of reality as being in some sense trans-human in character. Where this is not so, where religion refers only to human beings, religious discourse tends to be the same as moral discourse, with the possible exception that it suggests a greater intensity of feeling or conviction. It is the reference to trans-human religious reality that poses the specific problem regarding religious discourse. The problem is to indicate how ordinary language, which was born and bred for various uses in the world of men and natural objects, may nevertheless be used meaningfully to refer to trans-human religious reality. We may, therefore, state the problem of this chapter as follows: does language have a function or functions which enable it to refer meaningfully to trans-human religious reality; or, more simply, how do religious statements refer to religious reality? This is not the only question concerning religious language, but it is the one which goes to the heart of religion and the one which has received the greatest attention from writers on the subject.

It is not our purpose to analyze the nature of this problem in great detail. Suffice it to say that man's words, having a natural origin, are normally used to refer to familiar objects and to express familiar concepts, and for these uses he has familiar experiences and rules to determine when the words are used meaningfully. When we say, for example, that the cat is chasing the mouse, or that the angles of a triangle add up in degrees to two right angles, we know perfectly well, from familiar experiences, definitions, and rules, what the words mean and how to check to see whether they are being used correctly. But when ordinary words are used, as they are, to refer to a religious reality not considered one of the natural objects or abstract concepts of every-day experience, they are being used in some transferred sense. For example, if we say that all existence has a divine ground, or that God's love is like the father's love to his prodigal son in Jesus' parable, we are using ordinary words to refer beyond the range of ordinary objects to which they customarily apply. The word "ground" ordinarily refers to the earth beneath our feet, and the world "love" ordinarily refers to a human emotion. When such words are used in the transferred religious sense, are they still meaningful or do they carry us beyond the range of understandable usage? If they are meaningful, as religion believes them to be, in what way do they now refer? What explanation can be given to indicate that they have meaning and the sort of meaning they have? In what way do these ordinary words refer meaningfully to their religious object? This is the problem before us.

The problem of the meaning of religious statements must not be confused with another question, the question of truth or validity in religious statements. The failure to distinguish these two questions is the source of much confusion in the whole modern discussion of religious language. The one question is that of interpreting the kind of meaning religious statements have; the other question is that of ascertaining what reasons there are for believing particular religious statements to be true. We should not expect a theory of meaning to bear by itself the burden of proof or justification for religious beliefs. And yet this is just what some writers seem to expect. Having found no reasons, perhaps having had no experiences, on which to base religious belief, they expect the meaningfulness of religious statements to be explicated in such a way as to prove at the same time that certain religious statements are true. But language analysis itself is not the source of religious belief. Our problem then is this: if there are justifiable reasons for belief in a trans-human religious reality, in what way do religious propositions refer to that reality? We shall deal in the next chapter with the question of reasons for belief in God. Here we are concerned with the question of meaning.

So far we have spoken of religious language as if there were only one kind. But at least two types must be distinguished. One type is the language employed as part of religious acts or for direct religious instruction. This is religious language in the strict sense. The other type is theological language. It is language that is once-removed from immediate religious expression and is part of the attempt to give a reflective, explanatory account of the religious reality believed in. The language of prayer would be religious language in the strict sense, and the propositions of a theological textbook would be theological language. To name the distinction more sharply, we might call the two types devotional language and doctrinal language, provided we take these terms in broad enough senses to cover all the cases of religious language that are relevant. No doubt devotional language and doctrinal language always interpenetrate each other to some extent in actual use. But we shall occasionally find it helpful to have the distinction in mind.

One more point before we proceed: we have used the cumbersome term "trans-human religious reality" in order to make it clear that the problem we are considering is not confined to thinkers accepting the theistic conception of God. Others must face it also. In Part Two we shall be dealing specifically with personalistic theism and attendant problems. Here we are still in a somewhat wider context. It will sometimes be more convenient to speak of God rather than trans-human reality, but for this chapter the word God will be taken in the broadest sense in which it is used. It will be broad enough, for example, to cover the idea of God in the theology of Paul Tillich, who claims to have transcended theism; it will cover the Hindu conception of Brahman, or the Confucian conception of t'ien, and so on. Not all of these beliefs can be true. Our own point of view will be that theism is the most fitting completion of the kind of conclusion we shall reach regarding religious language. Nevertheless the problem is a common one.

A SHEAF OF ANSWERS

We shall now review a variety of proposed solutions to the problem at hand, keeping in mind two purposes for making the review. The first is to acquaint the reader with some of the contemporary thinking on the issue. Not all the answers that have been worked out can be given, and even those that have been must be dealt with very briefly. We may claim, however, that the principal and most representative kinds of answers will be included, although we shall not claim that any of them are treated as adequately as they deserve. But our purpose is not merely factual presentation. A further purpose is to consider the answers critically and to glean from them what may be valuable in a final understanding of how religious utterances can refer meaningfully to their object. With this purpose in mind, and with a recognized judgment made by the writer, we shall quite

frankly arrange the answers in an order which seems to us to move progressively toward the most satisfactory type of solution.

It may be helpful if the answers to be considered are listed at the outset,
so that the reader will know the direction in which we are to move. Our
question is, it will be recalled, to state in what way religious language
refers to trans-human religious reality. The answers we shall consider
reply to this question by saying: (1) nonsensically, (2) falsely, (3) convictionally, (4) mythologically, (5) ambiguously, (6) symbolically, (7)
literally, (8) analogically, and (9) parabolically.

NONSENSICALLY. One answer to the question is to say that the notion of
transferring words from the range of ordinary objects to trans-human
religious reality is without literal meaning, i.e., senseless. No meaning can
be attached to propositions that cannot be empirically confirmed or at
least translated into propositions permitting empirical confirmation. Observation of some sort is here the touchstone of literal meaning.

One interesting form of this view may be said to occur in the Renzai
sect of Zen Buddhism, with its use of questions, puzzles, and riddles
known as *koans*. If the Zen disciple takes these questions in their literal
meaning and tries by answering them to gain a rational comprehension
through propositions of ultimate existence, he has completely missed the
point and must be reprimanded by the Zen master. The point of the questions is to shock the pupil out of his usual rational categories and plunge
him into an intuitive grasp of the character of existence, *sunyata*, underlying ordinary experience. Both questions and answers are nonsensical if
taken as literal, rational meanings.[1]

The most systematic account of this view in the West, however, is
found in the school of thought known as logical positivism. Although
there have been different formulations of the main principle of this school,
the substance of it is the proposal that, aside from purely logical statements which get their meaning through formal definition, the only meaningful statements are those which have an empirical reference. "Empirical" here means "observable in some ordinary or scientific way." Since
statements about good and bad, right and wrong, reality and God, do not
have this reference to ordinary or scientific observation, they are meaningless or nonsensical.[2] They may have emotive or some other meaning,
but they have no literal sense.

One of the most successful strategies against logical positivism has been
to show that its own criterion of meaning is not subject to empirical confirmation and therefore comes down in the end to an arbitrary decision
not binding on rational thought. Equally important, however, in the context of religious interpretation, would be a reminder concerning two
simple facts. One is that religious communities for centuries have been

using language with trans-human reference in a way that is meaningful to them and with at least some intimation of what they are referring to. Whether they are also speaking truth or not is another question. But that they have been speaking with an objective reference in mind and under intelligible rules of usage is a fact of religious history. The other fact is that opponents as well as supporters of the belief in God have been debating the issue in an intelligible way for centuries. Thus, some have thought that the belief in God's reality is necessarily true; some have thought that it is probably true; some that it is probably false; and some that it is necessarily false. Obviously not all of these views can be right. But that thinkers converse at all is the stubborn fact which stands in the way of denying any meaning to trans-human religious reference in the discussion. The debate about God intends something meaningful, and both sides know it. We are left with the challenge, however, of making that meaning clearer.

FALSELY. A second answer is that, while religious statements may be literally meaningful, i.e., refer in their intention to trans-human religious reality, such statements are in fact false.[3] We cannot, in a discussion of meaning, treat the whole question of truth and verification of religious claims. This answer reminds us, however, that our theory of meaning is inseparable from the notion of truth and is valid only if there are independent reasons for affirming the truth of the religious beliefs we hold. In the next chapter, and also in Chapter XI, we shall adduce some of the principal reasons why various people attest that the belief in God is true. Theists find one or more of these reasons convincing and can proceed on that basis. But if someone else does not find them convincing, then the theory of meaning would have to stop in its tracks, except for those who might think that religious statements can be meaningfully related to a conception of reality without God. One might, for example, try to hold that religious statements are symbolical without committing himself to belief in God. We do not think that such a view is plausible. But at least we must recognize that our theory of meaning is closely related to our conception of truth and is not complete without it.

The point of the present answer, then, is this: if you say that religious statements are simply literal, and then go on to say that they are false, you have come to the end of the line in the theory of meaning. But this is not the view of religion itself, and so religious interpretation must proceed, for it thinks there are good reasons for saying that religious statements are not simply literal and false.

CONVICTIONALLY. Willem Zuurdeeg, in a unique and impressive work,[4] has developed a theory of religious language centering in the notion of convictional expression. Arguing that religious discourse is neither descriptive in character (or, in his term, indicative) nor yet emotive in essence, he maintains that it comprises a distinctive kind of language, convictional language. In great detail he compares convictional language with other types of languages, analyzes the convictional situation out of which convictional discourse comes, establishes a method of approach called situational analysis, and illustrates his thesis by treatments of specific religious outlooks and other world-views. Behind all this is the belief that a man *is* his convictions and when he speaks religiously he must be speaking from this convictional center and using his words to give expression to it.

Zuurdeeg's analysis illuminates the nature of religious language by showing how it differs from other languages and yet is meaningful discourse. We need not take issue with the analysis within its own province. It must be insisted upon, however, that religious language for believers in God has an indispensable objective reference, and to make this reference is part of the very function of the discourse. To avoid subjectivity there must be some literal, metaphysical reference in religious utterances. If they only point inward to convictions, even the convictions of a convictional community, it would seem that any question of truth or validity of convictions must be abandoned, for there would be no reference beyond the convictions to serve as a basis for their adequacy. For this reason religious discourse must intend a metaphysical dimension as well as a convictional one. Religious discourse certainly intends belief in the reality of its object. We must conclude, therefore, that convictional expression is only one component in the kind of religious discourse we are considering, namely, discourse about trans-human religious reality. We must also deal with the component which permits religious statements to be in some sense true as well as convictional.

MYTHOLOGICALLY. Myth has played a large role in the religion of the world. But a specific theory of meaning taking mythology as the root of religious language has been developed by Rudolf Bultmann. It is true that he is primarily concerned with what he judges to be the mythology of the New Testament,[5] but his thought clearly suggests a general theory of religious language—at least of much religious language of the past.

Bultmann's contention is that the Biblical writers, accepting a conception of the universe based on an outmoded astronomy and filled with supernatural beings, reflect this ancient cosmology in their accounts of history and God. Thus spiritual reality is described in terms of supernormal powers and beings having very anthropomorphic qualities and engaged in very anthropomorphic activities, and these powers and beings in turn are thought of as very much involved in the key events of Biblical history. The Biblical accounts of these happenings intend some trans-human religious reference, but they do so through stories and imagery of a thoroughly anthropomorphic character. These mythological elements can no longer be believed in a scientific view of the world; hence, there arises Bultmann's program for "demythologizing" the New Testament. That is, the myths must be restated in terms that will speak to human existence as it is lived out today.

Bultmann is widely regarded as having made too sweeping a judgment about mythology in the New Testament. Of more direct concern for our limited purpose, however, is the fact that, although mythology has appeared in religious discourse, it can hardly be thought of as exhaustive or as the most significant aspect of religious meaning. If we say that God is a spirit, for instance, or that God is love, we are hardly speaking mythologically. To be sure, such statements may have both literal and nonliteral elements when compared with a human reference, but to call them myths seems highly incongruous. Furthermore, the emphasis on changing traditional language into the latest modern concepts may obscure the question of the objective reference of religious language. The increase in popular modern appeal does not help in explaining how religious statements refer to their object.

AMBIGUOUSLY. Another view on the problem is that religious utterances are basically ambiguous, so that there can be no clear or uniform or specific meaning in them. Walter Kaufmann presents this view when he says that "many religious propositions, including almost all statements about God, are not reducible to any one meaning but [are] essentially ambiguous."[6]

One difficulty about such a view is that the concept of ambiguity may itself be ambiguous. William Empson has distinguished "seven types of ambiguity" in a book by that name. Kaufmann seems to mean by the concept simply the idea that for every interpretation of a religious proposition there is "an indefinite number of other possible interpretations." Now if this statement is literally (and not ambiguously) true, then it clearly follows that a religious proposition may mean anything to anybody, and this characteristic is part of its essence. No uniformly intelligible reference to objective religious reality can therefore be claimed for religious statements. Kaufmann accepts this result even to the point of maintaining that an unequivocal affirmation of the reality of God is unnecessary for significant religious assertions about God.[7]

This may be the way an existentialist philosopher feels in his encounters. But it surely does not reflect accurately the meaning of religious utterances to convictional communities for whom God is the main object of devotion. There is this truth in the view of ambiguity: namely, that there is generally more depth of meaning, devotional and theological, in religious statements than can be comprehended in a first or even a hundredth perusal. That is, spiritual growth is possible. But this is quite a different thing from saying that there is no unequivocal core of reference to an objective religious reality. The present view gives us an intimation of religious reality, but beclouded with so resplendent and rich a halo of subjective meanings that one cannot see, does not even care, whether religious discourse is talking about anything or not. Religious usage in convictional communities, on the other hand, intends something more than this private grandeur in its language about God.

SYMBOLICALLY. Paul Tillich has defended the theory that all statements about God are symbolical. That is, they are none of them literally true but are rather figures of speech which somehow stand for or point toward religious reality. Faced with the obvious difficulty of saying, on such a theory, what is being symbolized if there is no access to it apart from figurative symbols, Tillich approaches a basic nonsymbolic utterance by saying that God is simply being. That is, God is not a particular being, but being as such. This is the anchor point, and everything else that is said about God is figurative. In the latest of his formulations of this theory,[8] Tillich elaborates the definition of a symbol and treats more fully the problem of judging alternative symbols; but he remains steadfast in his basic interpretation. God may not be described by any attributes, qualities, activities, or personal traits unless these be taken as useful symbols, figurative speech, pointing to the ground of being, the unconditional, the ultimate, or, more simply, being itself.

There is a technical difficulty in this theory that still remains despite the attempt at a nonsymbolic anchor point. It is that the concept of being itself is indefinite and of no help in specifying what is symbolized if nothing more can be said about it literally. Being as such is so general a term that to use it for God is merely to substitute an all but empty concept for the term to be defined. One could, of course, embrace a simple pantheism in this way, but that is not Tillich's intention. Thus we are left with the view that all meaningful terms about God are symbolic, and there is no real anchor for interpreting their reference, for saying what they are about, or for selecting the more fitting symbols for religion.

But another consideration may be more important for us. Tillich's account probably corresponds very closely to the meaning of religious discourse as intended in the monistic form of Hinduism and in certain forms of Buddhism. There the intention is that no rational proposition can describe ultimate being and that religious speech, if used at all, is simply an aid in conveying the individual to an intuitive grasp of religious reality. Tillich holds, of course, that complete symbolism is the real meaning underlying Christian language also, even though this view runs counter to historic Christian devotion and theology. The historic intention of Christian language, as well as language of other theistic communities, has certainly been to say more about God in a nonfigurative sense than that God is sheer being. In particular, the intention has been to say that God is personal in a sense which is not entirely symbolic. It appears, then, that there must be a decision whether to go along with Tillich on the ground that personalistic theism has had its day and that day is over, or whether personalistic theism is still justified. The theory of meaning does not decide that issue. We thus come to a parting of the way, as we did in discussing the objects of faith. In that discussion we could all go a long way together, but finally the humanist went one way, the theist another. In the present case we can all acknowledge symbolism to a great extent; but finally the total symbolist goes one way, the personalistic theist another. The total symbolist gets off the train at the present stop; the personalistic theist must continue. Everyone with curiosity, however, may be interested in where the theist is going in his theory of meaning.

LITERALLY. In an interesting section entitled "The Literalness of Theism,"[9] Charles Hartshorne insists that language about God must, to be meaningful, be literal; in fact, the most literal of the senses pertaining to the words. For example, when we say that man is wise, we must immediately add qualifications, exceptions, reservations, but when we say that God is wise, we intend this plainly and literally without qualification. Man is wise—with qualifications; but God is wise—period. Man is socially aware—partially; but God is socially aware—period. Of course what Hartshorne has in mind here is metaphysical or theological speech about God and not the many forms of religious utterance that we have called collectively devotional discourse. The latter he would acknowledge to be often metaphorical and symbolical. But he can say that theology, understood as the "theory of the essence of deity" or the "pure theory of divinity," is literal or else it is a scandal.

With this proviso, namely, that devotional language must still be accounted for, we may judge that we have finally reached a solid truth, both in its own right and as a necessary anchor point for making acknowledged symbolism meaningful. I think there can be little doubt that the theological language used in theistic communities is intended to refer in some way literally to God as objective religious reality. Otherwise it would have in the end only a human dimension, which would be idolatry. We should prefer to say, however, that such language has a literal base or a core of literalness rather than that it is simply literal—period. For we do, after all, use the same words to apply to both God and man. A fuller theory must therefore explain both the literal and the nonliteral elements of the same language. Moreover, some theological words fit more readily than others into Hartshorne's refreshing analysis. For example, while words like "wise," "loving," and "socially aware" may be easily literal in relation to God, words like "creator," "immanent," and "self-revealing" may be more difficult. In the first group the words are applied to God in a pure, unqualified sense and to man in a diminished, qualified sense; but in the second group there seem to be more subtle differences than that.

ANALOGICALLY. One traditional way of accounting for the literal and nonliteral elements in religious language is known as the doctrine of analogy. It was developed in Scholastic theology but has also been re-stated in modern times.[10] It holds that when the same words are used to refer to both God and man, they are used not in a completely identical sense nor yet in completely different senses but in senses that are partly the same and partly different. This sameness-difference feature is the ana-logical use of terms.

Two types of analogy are recognized in the doctrine. In the first type words designate something which occurs primarily in God and in a sec-ondary way in man. For example, goodness and wisdom are found per-fectly in God but only imperfectly in man. This kind of analogy would account for Hartshorne's terms that apply literally to God and in a quali-fied sense to man. In the second type of analogy, where a series from per-fect to imperfect is not the main point of connection, the same terms are still said to apply to God and man alike, but this time not in a series but simply in respect to the kind of nature each has. For example, both God and man are said to be creators, and this means that there is some simi-larity involved, but that each creates in the way appropriate to the kind of nature each possesses. Both types are thought to be necessary in the doc-trine and to involve each other.[11]

The minimum truth in the doctrine of analogy is that it points to a fundamental feature presupposed in language used religiously, namely, the simultaneous resemblance and difference in the meaning of terms that are transferred from the human context to trans-human religious reality. Beyond this the doctrine has often involved metaphysical assumptions, e.g., fixed natures in things, some kind of exact proportionateness of be-ings, and the possibility of precise applications of the doctrine. This more technical, metaphysical form of the doctrine is much disputed, and many have questioned its soundness. But in the minimum sense just defined, it seems to have struck a basic element of religious meaning. That is, con-victional communities assume that when language is transferred from its ordinary human context to God, it is describing something quite differ-ent in kind but in a way always rooted in a similarity of meaning. Anal-ogy spells out that assumption.

PARABOLICALLY. Analogy cannot, however, be said to account for all forms of religious discourse, especially devotional language. Analogy seems to describe best the more formal theological utterances of religion. We can understand "God loves his creatures," for example, analogically; but, when the Psalmist speaks of God making him to lie down in green pastures, the words fit into analogy somewhat awkwardly. We can say that God loves man, and man loves man, analogically; but we do not say that God is made to lie down in green pastures, and man is made to lie down in green pastures, analogically. Here outright symbol and metaphor are predominant.

To account for this devotional language, and much theological speech as well, I. M. Crombie has employed the concept of parable in an extended sense.[12] Parables are stories which are highly metaphorical but which contain one central, literal point, one penetrating thrust, about the subject at hand. For example, the parable of the prodigal son depicts the love of God for his wayward creatures, and this is the one central thrust of the whole story. For Crombie, parabolic language is not confined to the ordinary narrative stories called parables. It is a common characteristic of other religious discourse as well. That is, in religious discourse words, including imagistic and metaphorical words, may be used in ways that are familiar in ordinary speech, but the whole, taken together, makes a single illuminating statement of truth about God.

> The point of the parable is that you do not suppose that there is any literal resemblance between the truth which is expressed and the story which expresses it, but you do suppose that if you accept the story, not as a true literal account, but as a faithful parable, you will not be misled as to the nature of the underlying reality.[13]

How do we know what is a faithful parable? How do we discriminate amid floods of parabolic language? Here we meet again the question of validity, which carries us beyond the problem of meaning. In answer to this question we shall for the moment simply register, without discussion, our agreement with Crombie that the basis for selecting valid parables comes partly from a natural theism and partly from the historic convictional community in which we share by responsible choice. And we shall interpret this point of view to mean, on the one hand, that some natural theology is valid, and, on the other hand, that some account must be given of revelation and its implications. Parts Two and Three of this work are devoted, respectively, to these two areas.

We must also add that parabolic language does not seem to cover all religious discourse. We have already asserted that analogy is a more fitting term for formal theological speech. In addition, some religious statements about God are—or at least are inseparable from—historical statements. An example would be the statement that God inspired the prophets. Here there is, to be sure, the use of analogy in the word "inspired"; but the real religious meaning of the statement consists in its believed historicity. In this statement the very religious meaning is an assertion of historical fact, though not empirical, sensory fact that could be observed. In other statements even empirical fact is involved, e.g., that Moses or Jesus were real historical persons. Such religio-historical statements are neither analogical nor parabolical.

CONCLUSION

Religious discourse is varied and complex both in composition and in intent. It would be hazardous to claim that one has accounted for all forms of religious discourse. But if we focus on the problem of how religious language refers to trans-human religious reality or God, and if we recognize that the question of validity is different from the question of meaning, we may say that the greater part of religious discourse is meaningful in the sense that it is governed by the following rules (not stated but nevertheless presupposed in actual religious discourse):

1. Religious discourse does not intend itself to be nonsensical or false, for then there would be no distinct religious meaning at all.

2. Religious language is primarily meaningful in a convictional situation, and such conviction usually arises from a natural theism or from within a convictional community.

3. Religious discourse is full of symbols and levels of meaning, not all of which are intended to be literal.

4. Religious language usually intends, however, a literal base as part of its essential meaning.

5. Much theological language and some devotional language gets its meaning through the use of analogy; that is, the words used apply to God and man analogically rather than equivocally or in an identical sense.

6. Much devotional discourse and some theological discourse employs language as a parable does, i.e., by expressing a single basal truth through a story, metaphor, or other familiar use of words.

7. Some religious statements are historical statements intending factual assertions.

NEW TESTAMENT AND MYTHOLOGY

The Mythological Element in the Message of the New Testament and the Problem of its Re-interpretation

RUDOLF BULTMANN

Rudolf Bultmann (1884–) is a German New Testament scholar who has been influenced by existentialism and has been engaged in translating New Testament thought into modern terms. He studied at Tübingen, Berlin, and Marburg, and then, after teaching briefly at Breslau and Giessen, he held a chair in New Testament at Marburg from 1921 to 1951. His works include Theology of the New Testament *(trans. 1951, 1955),* Jesus Christ and Mythology *(trans. 1958), and* Existence and Faith *(trans. 1960). The following selection is the first part of Bultmann's main essay in which he sets forth his conception of religious language as myth and the resultant need for demythologizing it.*

THE TASK OF DEMYTHOLOGIZING
THE NEW TESTAMENT PROCLAMATION

The Mythical View of the World
and the Mythical Event of Redemption

The cosmology of the New Testament is essentially mythical in character. The world is viewed as a three-storied structure, with the earth in the centre, the heaven above, and the underworld beneath. Heaven is the abode of God and of celestial beings—the angels. The underworld is hell, the place of torment. Even the earth is more than the scene of natural, everyday events, of the trivial round and common task. It is the scene of the supernatural activity of God and his angels on the one hand, and of Satan and his daemons on the other. These supernatural forces intervene in the course of nature and in all that men think and will do. Miracles are by no means rare. Man is not in control of his own life. Evil spirits may take possession of him. Satan may inspire him with

From Rudolf Bultmann, "New Testament and Mythology" in *Kerygma and Myth*, ed. Hans Werner Bartsch, trans. Reginald H. Fuller (London: S. P. C. K., 1953), pp. 1-16. Reprinted by permission of S. P. C. K. and the Seabury Press.

evil thoughts. Alternatively, God may inspire his thought and guide his purposes. He may grant him heavenly visions. He may allow him to hear his word of succour or demand. He may give him the supernatural power of his Spirit. History does not follow a smooth unbroken course; it is set in motion and controlled by these supernatural powers. This aeon is held in bondage by Satan, sin, and death (for "powers" is precisely what they are), and hastens towards its end. That end will come very soon, and will take the form of a cosmic catastrophe. It will be inaugurated by the "woes" of the last time. Then the Judge will come from heaven, the dead will rise, the last judgement will take place, and men will enter into eternal salvation or damnation.

This then is the mythical view of the world which the New Testament presupposes when it presents the event of redemption which is the subject of its preaching. It proclaims in the language of mythology that the last time has now come. "In the fulness of time" God sent forth his Son, a pre-existent divine Being, who appears on earth as a man.[1] He dies the death of a sinner[2] on the cross and makes atonement for the sins of men.[3] His resurrection marks the beginning of the cosmic catastrophe. Death, the consequence of Adam's sin, is abolished,[4] and the daemonic forces are deprived of their power.[5] The risen Christ is exalted to the right hand of God in heaven[6] and made "Lord" and "King."[7] He will come again on the clouds of heaven to complete the work of redemption, and the resurrection and judgement of men will follow.[8] Sin, suffering and death will then be finally abolished.[9] All this is to happen very soon; indeed, St. Paul thinks that he himself will live to see it.[10]

All who belong to Christ's Church and are joined to the Lord by Baptism and the Eucharist are certain of resurrection to salvation,[11] unless they forfeit it by unworthy behaviour. Christian believers already enjoy the first instalment of salvation, for the Spirit[12] is at work within them, bearing witness to their adoption as sons of God,[13] and guaranteeing their final resurrection.[14]

[1] Gal. 4. 4; Phil. 2. 6ff.; 2 Cor. 8. 9; John 1. 14, etc.
[2] 2 Cor. 5. 21; Rom. 8. 3.
[3] Rom. 3. 23-26; 4. 25; 8. 3; 2 Cor. 5. 14, 19; John 1. 29; 1 John 2. 2, etc.
[4] 1 Cor. 15. 21f.; Rom. 5. 12ff.
[5] 1 Cor. 2. 6; Col. 2. 15; Rev. 12. 7ff., etc.
[6] Acts 1. 6f.; 2. 33; Rom. 8. 34, etc.
[7] Phil. 2. 9-11; 1 Cor. 15. 25.
[8] 1 Cor. 15. 23f.; 50ff., etc.
[9] Rev. 21. 4, etc.
[10] 1 Thess. 4. 15ff.; 1 Cor. 15. 51f.; cf. Mark 9. 1.
[11] Rom. 5. 12ff.; 1 Cor. 15. 21ff.; 44b, ff.
[12] Ἀπαρχή: Rom. 8. 23, ἀρραβών: 2 Cor. 1. 22; 5. 5.
[13] Rom. 8. 15; Gal. 4. 6.
[14] Rom. 8. 11.

The Mythological View of the World Obsolete

All this is the language of mythology, and the origin of the various themes can be easily traced in the contemporary mythology of Jewish Apocalyptic and in the redemption myths of Gnosticism. To this extent *the kerygma is incredible to modern man, for he is convinced that the mythical view of the world is obsolete.* We are therefore bound to ask whether, when we preach the Gospel to-day, we expect our converts to accept not only the Gospel message, but also the mythical view of the world in which it is set. If not, does the New Testament embody a truth which is quite independent of its mythical setting? If it does, theology must undertake the task of stripping the Kerygma from its mythical framework, of "demythologizing" it.

Can Christian preaching expect modern man *to accept the mythical view of the world as true?* To do so would be both senseless and impossible. It would be senseless, because there is nothing specifically Christian in the mythical view of the world as such. It is simply the cosmology of a pre-scientific age. Again, it would be impossible, because no man can adopt a view of the world by his own volition—it is already determined for him by his place in history. Of course such a view is not absolutely unalterable, and the individual may even contribute to its change. But he can do so only when he is faced by a new set of facts so compelling as to make his previous view of the world untenable. He has then no alternative but to modify his view of the world or produce a new one. The discoveries of Copernicus and the atomic theory are instances of this, and so was romanticism, with its discovery that the human subject is richer and more complex than enlightenment or idealism had allowed, and nationalism, with its new realization of the importance of history and the tradition of peoples.

It may equally well happen that truths which a shallow enlightenment had failed to perceive are later rediscovered in ancient myths. Theologians are perfectly justified in asking whether this is not exactly what has happened with the New Testament. At the same time it is impossible to revive an obsolete view of the world by a mere fiat, and certainly not a mythical view. For all our thinking to-day is shaped for good or ill by modern science. A blind acceptance of the New Testament mythology would be irrational, and to press for its acceptance as an article of faith would be to reduce Christian faith to the level of a human achievement. Wilhelm Herrmann pointed this out many years ago, and one would have thought that his demonstration was conclusive. It would involve a sacrifice of the intellect which could have only one result—a curious form of schizophrenia and insincerity. It would mean accepting a view of the world in our faith and religion which we should deny in our everyday life. Modern thought as we have inherited it provides us with *a motive for criticizing the New Testament view of the world.*

Man's knowledge and mastery of the world have advanced to such an extent through science and technology that it is no longer possible for anyone seriously to hold the New Testament view of the world—in fact, there is hardly anyone who does. What meaning, for instance, can we attach to such phrases in the creed as "descended into hell" or "ascended into heaven"? We no longer believe in the three-storied universe which the creeds take for granted. The only honest way of reciting the creeds is to strip the mythological framework from the truth they en-shrine—that is, assuming that they contain any truth at all, which is just the question that theology has to ask. No one who is old enough to think for himself supposes that God lives in a local heaven. There is no longer any heaven in the traditional sense of the word. The same ap-plies to hell in the sense of a mythical underworld beneath our feet. And if this is so, we can no longer accept the story of Christ's descent into hell or his Ascension into heaven as literally true. We can no longer look for the return of the Son of Man on the clouds of heaven or hope that the faithful will meet him in the air (1 Thess. 4. 15ff.).

Now that the forces and the laws of nature have been discovered, we can no longer believe in *spirits, whether good or evil.* We know that the stars are physical bodies whose motions are controlled by the laws of the universe, and not daemonic beings which enslave mankind to their service. Any influence they may have over human life must be explicable in terms of the ordinary laws of nature; it cannot in any way be attributed to their malevolence. Sickness and the cure of disease are likewise at-tributable to natural causation; they are not the result of daemonic activity or of evil spells.[15] The *miracles of the New Testament* have ceased to be miraculous, and to defend their historicity by recourse to nervous disorders or hypnotic effects only serves to underline the fact. And if we are still left with certain physiological and psychological phenomena which we can only assign to mysterious and enigmatic causes,

---

[15] It may of course be argued that there are people alive to-day whose confidence in the traditional scientific view of the world has been shaken, and others who are primitive enough to qualify for an age of mythical thought. And there are also many varieties of superstition. But when belief in spirits and miracles has degenerated into superstition, it has become something entirely different from what it was when it was genuine faith. The various impressions and speculations which influence credulous people here and there are of little importance, nor does it matter to what extent cheap slogans have spread an atmosphere inimical to science. What matters is the world view which men imbibe from their environment, and it is science which deter-mines that view of the world through the school, the press, the wireless, the cinema, and all the other fruits of technical progress.

we are still assigning them to causes, and thus far are trying to make them scientifically intelligible. Even occultism pretends to be a science.

It is impossible to use electric light and the wireless and to avail ourselves of modern medical and surgical discoveries, and at the same time to believe in the New Testament world of daemons and spirits.[16] We may think we can manage it in our own lives, but to expect others to do so is to make the Christian faith unintelligible and unacceptable to the modern world.

The mythical eschatology is untenable for the simple reason that the parousia of Christ never took place as the New Testament expected. History did not come to an end, and, as every schoolboy knows, it will continue to run its course. Even if we believe that the world as we know it will come to an end in time, we expect the end to take the form of a natural catastrophe, not of a mythical event such as the New Testament expects. And if we explain the parousia in terms of modern scientific theory, we are applying criticism to the New Testament, albeit unconsciously.

But natural science is not the only challenge which the mythology of the New Testament has to face. There is the still more serious challenge presented by *modern man's understanding of himself.*

Modern man is confronted by a curious dilemma. He may regard himself as pure nature, or as pure spirit. In the latter case he distinguishes the essential part of his being from nature. In either case, however, *man is essentially a unity.* He bears the sole responsibility for his own feeling, thinking, and willing.[17] He is not, as the New Testament regards him, the victim of a strange dichotomy which exposes him to the interference of powers outside himself. If his exterior behaviour and his interior condition are in perfect harmony, it is something he has achieved himself, and if other people think their interior unity is torn asunder by daemonic or divine interference, he calls it schizophrenia.

Although biology and psychology recognize that man is a highly dependent being, that does not mean that he has been handed over to powers outside of and distinct from himself. This dependence is inseparable from human nature, and he needs only to understand it in order to recover his self-mastery and organize his life on a rational basis. If he regards himself as spirit, he knows that he is permanently conditioned by the physical, bodily part of his being, but he distinguishes his true self from it, and knows that he is independent and responsible for his mastery over nature.

---

[16] Cp. the observations of Paul Schütz on the decay of mythical religion in the East through the introduction of modern hygiene and medicine.

[17] Cp. Gerhardt Krüger, *Einsicht und Leidenshaft, Das Wesen des platonischen Denkens*, Frankfort, 1939, p. 11 f.

In either case he finds *what the New Testament has to say about the "Spirit"* (πνεῦμα) *and the sacraments utterly strange and incomprehensible.* Biological man cannot see how a supernatural entity like the πνεῦμα can penetrate within the close texture of his natural powers and set to work within him. Nor can the idealist understand how a πνεῦμα working like a natural power can touch and influence his mind and spirit. Conscious as he is of his own moral responsibility, he cannot conceive how baptism in water can convey a mysterious something which is henceforth the agent of all his decisions and actions. He cannot see how physical food can convey spiritual strength, and how the unworthy receiving of the Eucharist can result in physical sickness and death (1 Cor. 11. 30). The only possible explanation is that it is due to suggestion. He cannot understand how anyone can be baptized for the dead (1 Cor. 15. 29).

We need not examine in detail the various forms of modern *Weltanschauung*, whether idealist or naturalist. For the only criticism of the New Testament which is theologically relevant is that which arises *necessarily* out of the situation of modern man. The biological *Weltanschauung* does not, for instance, arise necessarily out of the contemporary situation. We are still free to adopt it or not as we choose. The only relevant question for the theologian is the basic assumption on which the adoption of a biological as of every other *Weltanschauung* rests, and that assumption is the view of the world which has been moulded by modern science and the modern conception of human nature as a self-subsistent unity immune from the interference of supernatural powers.

Again, the biblical doctrine that *death is the punishment of sin* is equally abhorrent to naturalism and idealism, since they both regard death as a simple and necessary process of nature. To the naturalist death is no problem at all, and to the idealist it is a problem for that very reason, for so far from arising out of man's essential spiritual being it actually destroys it. The idealist is faced with a paradox. On the one hand man is a spiritual being, and therefore essentially different from plants and animals, and on the other hand he is the prisoner of nature, whose birth, life, and death are just the same as those of the animals. Death may present him with a problem, but he cannot see how it can be a punishment for sin. Human beings are subject to death even before they have committed any sin. And to attribute human mortality to the fall of Adam is sheer nonsense, for guilt implies personal responsibility, and the idea of original sin as an inherited infection is sub-ethical, irrational, and absurd.

The same objections apply to *the doctrine of the atonement.* How can the guilt of one man be expiated by the death of another who is sinless—if indeed one may speak of a sinless man at all? What primitive notions of guilt and righteousness does this imply? And what primitive idea of God? The rationale of sacrifice in general may of course throw some light on the theory of the atonement, but even so, what a primitive mythology it is, that a divine Being should become incarnate, and atone for the sins of men through his own blood! Or again, one might adopt an analogy from the law courts, and explain the death of Christ as a transaction between God and man through which God's claims on man were satisfied. But that would make a sin a juridical matter; it would be no more than an external transgression of a commandment, and it would make nonsense of all our ethical standards. Moreover, if the Christ who died such a death was the pre-existent Son of God, what could death mean for him? Obviously very little, if he knew that he would rise again in three days!

The *resurrection of Jesus* is just as difficult, if it means an event whereby a supernatural power is released which can henceforth be appropriated through the sacraments. To the biologist such language is meaningless, for he does not regard death as a problem at all. The idealist would not object to the idea of a life immune from death, but he could not believe that such a life is made available by the resuscitation of a corpse. If that is the way God makes life available for man, his action is inextricably involved in a nature miracle. Such a notion he finds intolerable, for he can see God at work only in the life of the spirit (which is for him the only real life) and in the transformation of his personality. But, quite apart from the incredibility of such a miracle, he cannot see how an event like this could be the act of God, or how it could affect his own life.

Gnostic influence suggests that this Christ, who died and rose again, was not a mere human being but a God-man. His death and resurrection were not isolated facts which concerned him alone, but a cosmic event in which we are all involved.[18] It is only with effort that modern man can think himself back into such an intellectual atmosphere, and even then he could never accept it himself, because it regards man's essential being as nature and redemption as a process of nature. And as for the pre-existence of Christ, with its corollary of man's translation into a celestial realm of light, and the clothing of the human personality in heavenly robes and a spiritual body—all this is not only irrational but utterly meaningless. Why should salvation take this particular form? Why should this be the fulfilment of human life and the realization of man's true being?

---

18 Rom. 5. 12ff.; 1 Cor. 15. 21ff., 44b.

Not Selection or Subtraction

Does this drastic criticism of the New Testament mythology mean the complete elimination of the kerygma?

Whatever else may be true, we cannot save the kerygma by selecting some of its features and subtracting others, and thus reduce the amount of mythology in it. For instance, it is impossible to dismiss St. Paul's teaching about the unworthy reception of Holy Communion or about baptism for the dead, and yet cling to the belief that physical eating and drinking can have a spiritual effect. If we accept *one* idea, we must accept everything which the New Testament has to say about Baptism and Holy Communion, and it is just this one idea which we cannot accept.

It may of course be argued that some features of the New Testament mythology are given greater prominence than others: not all of them appear with the same regularity in the various books. There is for example only one occurrence of the legends of the Virgin birth and the Ascension; St. Paul and St. John appear to be totally unaware of them. But, even if we take them to be later accretions, it does not affect the mythical character of the event of redemption as a whole. And if we once start subtracting from the kerygma, where are we to draw the line? The mythical view of the world must be accepted or rejected in its entirety.

At this point absolute clarity and ruthless honesty are essential both for the academic theologian and for the parish priest. It is a duty they owe to themselves, to the Church they serve, and to those whom they seek to win for the Church. They must make it quite clear what their hearers are expected to accept and what they are not. At all costs the preacher must not leave his people in the dark about what he secretly eliminates, nor must he be in the dark about it himself. In Karl Barth's book *The Resurrection of the Dead* the cosmic eschatology in the sense of "chronologically final history" is eliminated in favour of what he intends to be a non-mythological "ultimate history". He is able to delude himself into thinking that this is exegesis of St. Paul and of the New Testament generally only because he gets rid of everything mythological in 1 Corinthians by subjecting it to an interpretation which does violence to its meaning. But that is an impossible procedure.

If the truth of the New Testament proclamation is to be preserved, the only way is to demythologize it. But our motive in so doing must not be to make the New Testament relevant to the modern world at all costs. The question is simply whether the New Testament message consists exclusively of mythology, or whether it actually demands the elimination of myth if it is to be understood as it is meant to be. This question is forced upon us from two sides. First there is the nature of myth in general, and then there is the New Testament itself.

The Nature of Myth

The real purpose of myth is not to present an objective picture of the world as it is, but to express man's understanding of himself in the world in which he lives. Myth should be interpreted not cosmologically, but anthropologically, or better still, existentially.[19] Myth speaks of the power or the powers which man supposes he experiences as the ground and limit of his world and of his own activity and suffering. He describes these powers in terms derived from the visible world, with its tangible objects and forces, and from human life, with its feelings, motives, and potentialities. He may, for instance, explain the origin of the world by speaking of a world egg or a world tree. Similarly he may account for the present state and order of the world by speaking of a primeval war between the gods. He speaks of the other world in terms of this world, and of the gods in terms derived from human life.[20]

Myth is an expression of man's conviction that the origin and purpose of the world in which he lives are to be sought not within it but beyond it—that it, beyond the realm of known and tangible reality—and that this realm is perpetually dominated and menaced by those mysterious powers which are its source and limit. Myth is also an expression of man's awareness that he is not lord of his own being. It expresses his sense of dependence not only within the visible world, but more especially on those forces which hold sway beyond the confines of the known. Finally, myth expresses man's belief that in this state of dependence he can be delivered from the forces within the visible world.

Thus myth contains elements which demand its own criticism—namely, its imagery with its apparent claim to objective validity. The real purpose of myth is to speak of a transcendent power which controls the world and man, but that purpose is impeded and obscured by the terms in which it is expressed.

Hence the importance of the New Testament mythology lies not in its imagery but in the understanding of existence which it enshrines.

---

[19] Cp. Gerhardt Krüger, *Einsicht und Leidenschaft*, esp. p. 17f., 56f.

[20] Myth is here used in the sense popularized by the "History of Religions" school. Mythology is the use of imagery to express the otherworldly in terms of this world and the divine in terms of human life, the other side in terms of this side. For instance, divine transcendence is expressed as spatial distance. It is a mode of expression which makes it easy to understand the cultus as an action in which material means are used to convey immaterial power. Myth is not used in that modern sense, according to which it is practically equivalent to ideology.

The real question is whether this understanding of existence is true. Faith claims that it is, and faith ought not to be tied down to the imagery of New Testament mythology.

The New Testament Itself

The New Testament itself invites this kind of criticism. Not only are there rough edges in its mythology, but some of its features are actually contradictory. For example, the death of Christ is sometimes a sacrifice and sometimes a cosmic event. Sometimes his person is interpreted as the Messiah and sometimes as the Second Adam. The kenosis of the pre-existent Son (Phil. 2. 6ff.) is incompatible with the miracle narratives as proofs of his messianic claims. The Virgin birth is inconsistent with the assertion of his pre-existence. The doctrine of the Creation is incompatible with the conception of the "rulers of this world" (1 Cor. 2. 6ff.), the "god of this world" (2 Cor. 4. 4) and the "elements of this world" στοιχεῖα τοῦ κόσμου, Gal. 4. 3). It is impossible to square the belief that the law was given by God with the theory that it come from the angels (Gal. 3. 19f.).

But the principal demand for the criticism of mythology comes from a curious contradiction which runs right through the New Testament. Sometimes we are told that human life is determined by cosmic forces, at others we are challenged to a decision. Side by side with the Pauline indicative stands the Pauline imperative. In short, man is sometimes regarded as a cosmic being, sometimes as an independent "I" for whom decision is a matter of life or death. Incidentally, this explains why so many sayings in the New Testament speak directly to modern man's condition while others remain enigmatic and obscure. Finally, attempts at demythologization are sometimes made even within the New Testament itself. But more will be said on this point later.

Previous Attempts at Demythologizing

How then is the mythology of the New Testament to be reinterpreted? This is not the first time that theologians have approached this task. Indeed, all we have said so far might have been said in much the same way thirty or forty years ago, and it is a sign of the bankruptcy of contemporary theology that it has been necessary to go all over the same ground again. The reason for this is not far to seek. The liberal theologians of the last century were working on the wrong lines. They threw away not only the mythology but also the kerygma itself. Were they right? Is that the treatment the New Testament itself required? That is the question we must face to-day. The last twenty years have witnessed a movement away from criticism and a return to a naïve acceptance of the kerygma. The danger both for theological scholarship and for the Church is that this uncritical resuscitation of the New Testament mythology may make the Gospel message unintelligible to the modern world. We cannot dismiss the critical labours of earlier generations without further ado. We must take them up and put them to constructive use. Failure to do so will mean that the old battles between orthodoxy and liberalism will have to be fought out all over again, that is assuming that there will be any Church or any theologians to fight them at all! Perhaps we may put it schematically like this: whereas the older liberals used criticism to *eliminate* the mythology of the New Testament, our task to-day is to use criticism to *interpret* it. Of course it may still be necessary to eliminate mythology here and there. But the criterion adopted must be taken not from modern thought, but from the understanding of human existence which the New Testament itself enshrines.[21]

To begin with, let us review some of these earlier attempts at demythologizing. We need only mention briefly the allegorical interpretation of the New Testament which has dogged the Church throughout its history. This method spiritualizes the mythical events so that they become symbols of processes going on in the soul. This is certainly the most comfortable way of avoiding the critical question. The literal meaning is allowed to stand and is dispensed with only for the individual believer, who can escape into the realm of the soul.

It was characteristic of the older liberal theologians that they regarded mythology as relative and temporary. Hence they thought they could safely eliminate it altogether, and retain only the broad, basic principles of religion and ethics. They distinguished between what they took to be the essence of religion and the temporary garb which it assumed. Listen to what Harnack has to say about the essence of Jesus' preaching of the Kingdom of God and its coming: "The kingdom has a triple meaning. Firstly, it is something supernatural, a gift from above, not a product of ordinary life. Secondly, it is a purely religious blessing, the inner link with the living God; thirdly, it is the most important experience that a man can have, that on which everything else depends; it permeates and dominates his whole existence, because sin is forgiven and misery banished." Note how completely the mythology is eliminated: "The kingdom of God comes by coming to the individual, by entering into his *soul* and laying hold of it."[22]

---

21 As an illustration of this critical re-interpretation of myth cf. Hans Jonas, *Augustin und das paulinische Freiheitsproblem*, 1930, pp. 66-76.
22 *What is Christianity?* Williams and Norgate, 1904, pp. 63-4 and 57.

It will be noticed how Harnack reduces the kerygma to a few basic principles of religion and ethics. Unfortunately this means that the *kerygma has ceased to be kerygma*: it is no longer the proclamation of the decisive act of God in Christ. For the liberals the great truths of religion and ethics are timeless and eternal, though it is only within human history that they are realized, and only in concrete historical processes that they are given clear expression. But the apprehension and acceptance of these principles does not depend on the knowledge and acceptance of the age in which they first took shape, or of the historical persons who first discovered them. We are all capable of verifying them in our own experience at whatever period we happen to live. History may be of academic interest, but never of paramount importance for religion.

But the New Testament speaks of an *event* through which God has wrought man's redemption. For it, Jesus is not primarily the teacher, who certainly had extremely important things to say and will always be honoured for saying them, but whose person in the last analysis is immaterial for those who have assimilated his teaching. On the contrary, his person is just what the New Testament proclaims as the decisive event of redemption. It speaks of this person in mythological terms, but does this mean that we can reject the kerygma altogether on the ground that it is nothing more than mythology? That is the question.

Next came the History of Religions school. Its representatives were the first to discover the extent to which the New Testament is permeated by mythology. The importance of the New Testament, they saw, lay not in its teaching about religion and ethics but in its actual religion and piety; in comparison with that all the dogma it contains, and therefore all the mythological imagery with its apparent objectivity, was of secondary importance or completely negligible. The essence of the New Testament lay in the religious life it portrayed; its high-watermark was the experience of mystical union with Christ, in whom God took symbolic form.

These critics grasped one important truth. Christian faith is not the same as religious idealism; the Christian life does not consist in developing the individual personality, in the improvement of society, or in making the world a better place. The Christian life means a turning away from the world, a detachment from it. But the critics of the History of Religions school failed to see that in the New Testament this detachment is essentially eschatological and not mystical. Religion for them was an expression of the human yearning to rise above the world and transcend it: it was the discovery of a supramundane sphere where the soul could detach itself from all earthly care and find its rest.

Hence the supreme manifestation of religion was to be found not in personal ethics or in social idealism but in the cultus regarded as an end in itself. This was just the kind of religious life portrayed in the New Testament, not only as a model and pattern, but as a challenge and inspiration. The New Testament was thus the abiding source of power which enabled man to realize the true life of religion, and Christ was the eternal symbol for the cultus of the Christian Church.[23] It will be noticed how the Church is here defined exclusively as a worshipping community, and this represents a great advance on the older liberalism. This school rediscovered the Church as a *religious* institution. For the idealist there was really no place for the Church at all. But did they succeed in recovering the meaning of the Ecclesia in the full, New Testament sense of the word? For in the New Testament the Ecclesia is invariably a phenomenon of salvation history and eschatology.

Moreover, if the History of Religions school is right, the kerygma has once more ceased to be kerygma. Like the liberals, they are silent about a decisive act of God in Christ proclaimed as the event of redemption. So we are still left with the question whether this event and the person of Jesus, both of which are described in the New Testament in mythological terms, are nothing more than mythology. Can the kerygma be interpreted apart from mythology? Can we recover the truth of the kerygma for men who do not think in mythological terms without forfeiting its character as kerygma?

An Existentialist Interpretation the Only Solution

The theological work which such an interpretation involves can be sketched only in the broadest outline and with only a few examples. We must avoid the impression that this is a light and easy task, as if all we have to do is to discover the right formula and finish the job on the spot. It is much more formidable than that. It cannot be done single-handed. It will tax the time and strength of a whole theological generation.

The mythology of the New Testament is in essence that of Jewish apocalyptic and the Gnostic redemption myths. A common feature of them both is their basic dualism, according to which the present world and its human inhabitants are under the control of daemonic, satanic powers, and stand in need of redemption. Man cannot achieve this redemption by his own efforts; it must come as a gift through a divine intervention. Both types of mythology speak of such an intervention: Jewish apocalyptic of an imminent world crisis in which this present

---

23 Cp., e.g., Troeltsch, *Die Bedeutung der Geschichtlichkeit Jesu für den Glauben*, Tübingen, 1911.

aeon will be brought to an end and the new aeon ushered in by the coming of the Messiah, and Gnosticism of a Son of God sent down from the realm of light, entering into this world in the guise of a man, and by his fate and teaching delivering the elect and opening up the way for their return to their heavenly home.

The meaning of these two types of mythology lies once more not in their imagery with its apparent objectivity but in the understanding of human existence which both are trying to express. In other words, they need to be interpreted existentially. A good example of such treatment is to be found in Hans Jonas's book on Gnosticism.[24]

Our task is to produce an existentialist interpretation of the dualistic mythology of the New Testament along similar lines. When, for instance, we read of daemonic powers ruling the world and holding mankind in bondage, does the understanding of human existence which underlies such language offer a solution to the riddle of human life which will be acceptable even to the non-mythological mind of to-day? Of course we must not take this to imply that the New Testament presents us with an anthropology like that which modern science can give us. It cannot be proved by logic or demonstrated by an appeal to factual evidence. Scientific anthropologies always take for granted a definite understanding of existence, which is invariably the consequence of a deliberate decision of the scientist, whether he makes it consciously or not. And that is why we have to discover whether the New Testament offers man an understanding of himself which will challenge him to a genuine existential decision.

---

[24] *Gnosis und spätantiker Geist*. I. *Die mythologische Gnosis*, 1934.

CONVICTIONAL
AND INDICATIVE LANGUAGE

WILLEM ZUURDEEG

Willem F. Zuurdeeg (1906–) is a Dutch thinker who has been keenly interested in the bearing of positivism and linguistic analysis on religious thought. He studied at Utrecht, Leyden, and Amsterdam and held a pastorate for a number of years in the Netherlands. He came to the United States shortly after World War II to teach briefly at Elmhurst College and since then has been at McCormick Theological Seminary as professor of philosophy of religion. The work from which the present selection is taken develops in a comprehensive manner the kind of approach found in an earlier work, The Consequences of the Vienna Circle Philosophy for Ethics *(1946). The following selection is an excerpt from Willem Zuurdeeg's provocative analysis of religious language as convictional language.*

A crucial issue for our whole approach is the relationship between convictional language and other languages. The other languages which lie within our range of interest are: indicative language, tautological language, and analytical language.

INDICATIVE, TAUTOLOGICAL, AND ANALYTICAL LANGUAGE

Indicative language is found (*a*) in a crude form in everyday language, (*b*) in a purified form in the language of empirical science. Scientific language begins by indicating things and observing them. It continues with description, comparison, and explanation. Another phase is the search for relationships and the attempt to place the phenomenon within its own system of relationships. Finally, scientific-indicative language returns to what is observable.

The purpose of this language is to know, not to evaluate, or to prescribe behavior. Because it refers to the visible, tangible world, which

From *An Analytical Philosophy of Religion* by Willem F. Zuurdeeg, pp. 44-47, 53-56. Copyright © 1958 by Abingdon Press. Reprinted by permission.

is a changing world, the "truth" of its statements is "relative," that is, dependent upon both the changing world and the specific position of the observer in space and time. This language, like convictional language, functions within a specific group. Indicative language, in its crude form of everyday language, is spoken by everybody belonging to the Western nations. In its refined form of scientific language, indicative language functions within the small groups of scientists, scholars, and technicians. Further discussion will be found in the last chapter.

Analytical language is the language of philosophy. It refers to the various languages spoken by human beings. One can argue that it is a part of indicative language, and indeed both have many traits in common. The difference is that analysis is not interested in facts but in meanings, namely, the meanings of the various languages in which human beings refer to facts, values, and "ideas." What has been said, in regard to indicative language, about understanding and not evaluating, and about relativity, holds true also for analytical language.

Tautological language is the language of logic and mathematics. The language of mathematics refers not to the tangible world but to mathematical ideas, such as the idea of a purely straight line. Its statements cannot be verified experimentally, but must be demonstrated to follow logically from the initial definition. Tautological statements do not add anything at all to the knowledge of the actual world; they develop the logical implications of the first definition. The truth of tautological statements is not relative but absolute, that is, independent of the changing world of the senses. If the statements are logically acceptable, they are completely true. The validity of tautological statements is, however, confined to the specific system built upon the original definition. As soon as a mathematician starts with another first definition, he arrives at a very different system of tautological statements, which, in their turn, are absolutely true.

CONVICTIONAL AND INDICATIVE
LANGUAGE IN THEIR RELATION TO "REALITY"

One of the most frequent misunderstandings about convictional language is the notion that it is arbitrary, outside the range of intelligent discussion. The people who make this objection place convictional language over against indicative language and claim that the latter is objective and public, whereas the first is subjective, and merely the expression of a personal preference. To be sure, it is not a simple matter to check the truth of convictional language. Before we enter into this, something else has to be said. In the above objection the suggestion is implied that indicative language refers to reality, whereas convictional language is a matter of fancy or imagination. Such a notion is not implied at all in the concept of convictional language as it is used in this book. Both convictional and indicative languages refer to "reality." Here lies a crucial problem. The assertion that both languages refer to "reality" does not imply any judgment on the part of the analytical philosopher about the nature of these "realities," for example, as to whether or not they are illusionary. It is not the analytical philosopher's business to decide whether the reality meant in a certain language is "really" there or not. The only thing he can do is to notice that if human beings speak either indicative or convictional language they refer to something which is "real" *for them.*

The "reality" meant is not the same in both cases. Anybody who speaks any convictional language has in mind all the reality there is, including the values and meanings involved. The modern scientist claims (in opposition to his predecessor of the nineteenth century) that his language does not refer to the "real" nature of the universe. He considers his theories as hypotheses which he uses to describe "facts," to explain them as fully as possible, and to predict future events. Some hypotheses may suffice to explain certain phenomena but not others. A different hypothesis has then to be introduced. In other words, theories are tools, instruments of explanation and prediction. They do not reveal anything to us about the "real nature" of "reality." Still, these theories have reality in mind, or better, a certain aspect of reality. That is to say that the scientist abstracts, from all other aspects of reality, those which are irrelevant for his work of prediction.

Likewise, a person who speaks convictional language has reality in mind, but in his case it is the totality of reality as he sees it in the light of his specific convictions. There is only one indicative language (we think of its purified form, science), but there are numerous convictional languages. These latter see reality in a different light. The philosopher has to abstain from attempts to declare that either science or a specific conviction discloses the "really Real."

THE HISTORICAL
CHARACTER OF THESE LANGUAGES

We may now turn to the relationship, not between indicative language and convictional language as such, but between the purified language of empirical science and some convictional languages of the Western civilization. Both are historical phenomena. We can say that the language of empirical science was emancipated from the Western convictional languages roughly around 1600. The fact that this emancipation was possible says something about these convictional languages. We will return to this issue later. Here we desire merely to emphasize the fact that this emancipation resulted in an enormous revolution. Up to that moment man had given account of things only in a convictional way. The empirical, indicative approach was not yet admitted as a valid, significant method with a right of its own. The planets had been considered as the spirits of the forefathers or as God's handiwork; the rainbow was a bridge to heaven, or the sign of the covenant between Yahweh and his people. From 1600 on, a new way of giving account arose. Planets are now considered as satellites of a sun, a rainbow as a prism effect of sunlight on raindrops. With a modicum of exaggeration we might say that now for the first time "things" appear. Water is now a thing, to be classified as H_2O, whereas it had been formerly the element of baptism, or the primeval ocean out of which life arises.

LANGUAGES AND SITUATIONS

The foregoing picture can be misleading if we interpret it to mean that indicative language has quite appropriately taken the place of convictional language. If we assume this (Comtean) position, we have left the realm of analytical discourse and entered that of a specific theology of history. As philosophers we are not allowed to evaluate this "emancipation" as though it meant a liberation from evil. We may employ this term only as a description of a historical process.

We will then notice that outside the domain of Western civilization, and within this domain before about 1600, one kind of language—namely, convictional language—was spoken almost exclusively, whereas in the modern Western world people speak various languages in different situations. People of this civilization may be said to deem it appropriate to speak scientific language in a laboratory and in a library, legal language in court, religious language in church and at a funeral, aesthetic language when discussing the value of a piece of sculpture, moral language in regard to the use of narcotics, etc. Thus there is a plurality of languages, each with its own approach, its own concern, it own kind of truth, each of them considered appropriate for its specific occasion.

.   .   .   .   .

CONVICTIONAL LANGUAGE
INFORMS INDICATIVE LANGUAGE

People possessed by strong convictions may often observe something which has indicative meaning and which had been overlooked. When Marx refers to class struggles, calls them necessary, and declares them an indispensable means to reach the good society, he speaks convictional language, yet he has also indicated something. Also, those present-day sociologists and economists who do not adhere to any form of Marxism at all admit that conflicts between groups of the population form a significant fact with which their science has to reckon. This fact was scarcely noticed before Marx formulated his convictional world view. Marx not only evoked convictional, theological thinking about the class struggle, but also opened the eyes of scholars to facts which had not been recognized earlier.

Many times men deeply moved by their convictions have stimulated scientific thinking. Freud's treatment of sex is highly convictional. Sex assumes in his "psychology" a cosmic, metaphysical status. Sex is the ruler of life, despised, repressed, veiled, but therefore the more powerful, the prime mover of arts, morals, civilization. And yet Freud has drawn attention to several undeniable facts, the importance of which is not denied by those who do not share his mythology at all.

It appears that people who are in the grip of convictions which are considerably different from the generally accepted beliefs can often open our eyes. For example, people moved by a powerful love, an intense hatred, or people living in other ages or different continents and who belong to confessional groups basically different from our group. The saying goes that love blinds, but sometimes love (or hatred, or other strong convictions) can sharpen our sight.

What is disclosed in this way has indicative meaning. We should not say that because Marx spoke of class struggle in a convictional way, modern sociological references to group conflicts are convictional also. The role of Marx's convictional language was heuristic. There is not an intrinsic but a heuristic relationship between Marx's conviction about class struggle and the modern scholar's indicative discussion of group conflicts. Marx's convictional speaking was the occasion for the rise of a fruitful indicative line of thought.

The service rendered by convictional to indicative language can be described as the blasting away of an obstruction, which prevented people from seeing clearly in an indicative way. This barrier is frequently of a convictional nature. In Marx's case the barrier consisted in people's conviction that the world has always known rich and poor and that therefore it meant a rebellion against God (or the World Order) to assume that society could be changed by human interference. In Freud's case the resistance against clear thinking derived from Enlightenment convictions about the basic rationality, goodness, and orderliness of "human nature."

The disclosing service rendered by convictional to indicative language effects a liberation. The thinking in many scientific fields (such as biology, psychology, economics, sociology, history of religions) is the result of an emancipation of indicative thinking from the power of convictional authorities and traditions. It has to be noticed that the process of emancipation is not a simple one. Many times the conviction which has destroyed an old obstruction immediately puts up a new one. Marx's conviction offers therefore a good example. This fact should warn us against the temptation to assume that the modern science of the twentieth century is completely free from such mental blocks. It is highly probable that future generations will wonder why we could not free ourselves from what they will consider obvious obstructions.

INDICATIVE ELEMENTS
IN CONVICTIONAL LANGUAGE

People sometimes object to the validity of the distinction between convictional and indicative language by remarking that convictional language also indicates facts—for instance, the language of Christian faith. They say that it is of the essence of the Christian faith to *know* certain things. First, this faith implies the claim to deal with historical persons, nations, and events: Moses, the prophets, the kings; Jesus of Nazareth; the disciples, the church, the reformers. All these and more are historical facts, which can be known. Second, this faith implies the claim that God is acting in history, that he is not merely a beautiful idea, but that the signs of his gracious activity can be seen and known in the actual world of history. Third, faith in God does not merely imply knowledge, it *is* knowledge of God. The believer knows more after his faith than before. He is certain, whereas before he was uncertain. Faith is trust, love, reverence, but these aspects are not different from knowledge, they are implied in it.

We begin our discussion with the third objection. The "knowing" which is spoken of here is different in kind from the knowledge of indicative language. It is an understanding which is guided by specific convictions. In order to keep our terminology clear we shall confine the use of "knowledge" and "cognitive" to indicative language. Sometimes theologians resent such procedure, apparently because they fear that this might arise out of a disdain for the Christian faith and a desire to set it aside as being not quite up to the level of respectable science. This is not necessarily the case. The knowledge expressed in indicative language is hypothetical, provisional, more or less probable, dependent upon verification, and impersonal. These characteristics do not at all apply to the understanding which is implied in the faith of a Christian, or in any other belief for that matter. Such an understanding is not *lower* than scientific knowledge, but different in character. Hence, we should not say that we can "know" God or any other nonempirical reality, that is, know in indicative language.

The answer to the second objection is basically the same, though we are not dealing here with nonempirical realities but with so-called historical facts. If one asserts, however, that a certain historical event is the result of God's work in history, one is speaking convictional language. The people who make such assertions do not mean something hypothetical, more or less probable. Therefore it is not indicative knowledge.

The problem seems to be different in the case of the first objection. Claims as to the historical existence of Moses, the prophets, and Jesus seem to be both indicative and indispensable elements of the Hebrew and the Christian faiths. Paul L. Holmer defends a particular thesis in this respect.[1] His discussion can be summed up as follows:

(1) Religious sentences are not "cognitive of trans-empirical realities."

(2) Some religious sentences are "cognitive of historical events."

(3) Religious sentences can be "the occasion for the cognition of . . . a new . . . mode of life."

(4) To consider sentences of type (2) and (3) to be true is not "the religious act of faith"; faith is the passionate becoming of a new man.

(5) To consider sentences of type (2) and (3) to be true is, however, "a necessary condition for religious faith."[2]

I agree with theses (1) and (4). In regard to the other theses the question has to be raised as to whether religious language about Moses or Jesus is ever indicative at all. Probably the answer has to be negative. Chap. V will treat more fully the claim that such language is "narrative," and that this is a kind of convictional language.

Here a few things can be pointed out: (*a*) In biblical times convictional and indicative languages were not distinguished as they are now. (*b*) When twentieth-century scholars look back upon the language of biblical times, they can distinguish between a convictional and an indicative aspect. (*c*) It appears to us that what biblical people were really interested in was what we would call the convictional element; the indicative element was held in the convictional framework. (*d*) The convictional language of biblical man had a specific form: it was a narrative. (*e*) It is doubtful that the statements which churches require their members to affirm can be called indicative statements. The requirement is probably the "repetition" of the old convictional narrative.

---

[1] "The Nature of Religious Propositions," *The Review of Religion*, March, 1955.
[2] *Ibid.*, pp. 148-49.

If it is denied that convictional language contains indicative elements, the question is raised as to whether this approach does not necessarily lead to the position that we as convictional people live in ivory towers. To a certain extent we have to accept this accusation. There are neither scientific nor philosophical proofs or arguments which can validate or invalidate any conviction. There is no public, objective court of reason which can decide who is wrong and who is right.

There is more to be said than this, however, Certainly communication takes place between people of different convictions, though this communication does not possess a scientific or philosophical character. We continually witness to each other. By means of our moral judgments, even more by means of our behavior, or better, by the way we are, and live, and meet persons and problems, we give testimonies as to what is our highest good. By living we "demonstrate" our most genuine convictions. By means of certain linguistic aspects of our living, we set forth our explicit views.

These demonstrations, both the implicit and the explicit, act as a challenge. They are invitations to other people to live, to think, to speak as we do. On the level of explicit communication the challenge can assume the form of an expression of the implications of the convictions held, and of a comparison with the presupposed implications of other views. Such a comparison never proves anything; the other person always needs to make an existential decision as to whether he will accept our challenge or not. The challenge on this level can take on all forms from an open attack of the other man's convictions, a condemnation on the basis of considering the view held by oneself as unquestionably true, to an entering into the other's view inspired by respect and made possible by empathy.

SUGGESTED BOOKS

Braithwaite, R. B., *An Empiricist's View of the Nature of Religious Belief.* Cambridge: Cambridge University Press, 1955. Argues that religious statements can be analyzed as moral assertions, i.e., declarations of intention concerning behavior.

Ferré, Frederick, *Language, Logic and God.* New York: Harper & Row, Publishers, 1961. "An introduction to contemporary linguistic philosophy as it bears on theological discourse."

Flew, Antony and Alasdair MacIntyre, eds., *New Essays in Philosophical Theology.* New York: The Macmillan Company, 1955. Essays by British analytic philosophers, some Christian and some non-Christian, on the linguistic aspects of religious subjects.

Langer, Suzanne K., *Philosophy in a New Key.* Cambridge: Harvard University Press, 1942. A study of symbolism and its importance in various kinds of human experience.

Martin, C. B., *Religious Belief*. Ithaca: Cornell University Press, 1959. By the methods of linguistic analysis the author claims to show that certain religious statements are either tautological or inconsistent.

Mascall, E. L., *Existence and Analogy*. London: Longmans, Green & Co., Ltd., 1949. A defense of an essentially Thomist doctrine of analogy by an Anglican theologian.

Moreau, Jules L., *Language and Religious Language*. Philadelphia: The Westminster Press, 1961. Historical and critical studies of theological language, especially the problem of translating it into meaningful terms in different ages.

Ramsey, Ian T., *Religious Language*. London: S.C.M. Press, Ltd., 1957. An attempt to show how contemporary language analysis can be of constructive use to theology in illuminating its claims and reforming its presentation.

PART TWO

PROBLEMS OF THEISTIC RELIGION

VI · THE REALITY OF GOD

Thus far we have discussed questions which are relevant to every religion. We now turn to a group of questions which can be discussed most profitably only in connection with theistic religion, i.e., religion based specifically on belief in God. The questions selected for treatment in Part Two are, first, the belief in God itself, and then the nature of man, the idea of immortal life, and prayer and worship. If our study up to this point can be called general religious interpretation, the present phase may be termed theistic interpretation.

The question of belief in God can be conveniently divided into the question of the reality of God, and the question of the nature of God. Which of these questions should be taken up first? A good case could be made out for either alternative. On the one hand, we could begin with the nature of God, for it seems that we must first know what kind of being we are talking about before we can say whether or not we accept its reality. On the other hand, we could begin with the existence of God, for the fundamental religious question seems to be whether we are actually confronted by God as a real being or whether the whole idea is an illusion. The second procedure appears to carry more weight. As long as we confine ourselves to the nature of God, without reference to actual existence, we are in the realm of possibility, and in this realm any number of conceptions of deity can easily be framed. Our reason and imagination are then let free to formulate a wide variety of speculative possibilities. The procedure is quite different, however, if we must chart our course by what we actually find true of existence. The conception of the nature of God which we then depict is one directed not by speculative possibility alone but by existence itself. For some philosophical purposes it may be useful to begin with the question of the nature of God, but for religious interpretation it seems better to begin with the question of existence, which is prior for the living of religion in actual life.

There appear to be three principal ways in which religious persons arrive at their mature views on the being of God. One way is by proofs alleged to demonstrate the existence of God. Another way is by accumulating evidence[1] suggesting the existence of God. And another way is by the experiences which come through the practice of religion. These approaches may be called, respectively, the rationalistic approach, the empirical approach, and the personal or existential approach. For analytical purposes, they can be put in the form of questions. (1) Can

151

the existence of God be proved? (2) What evidence is there that points to the reality of God? (3) How have men encountered the reality of God?

ON PROOFS OF GOD'S EXISTENCE

To offer a proof of the existence of God, if that is possible, is, strictly speaking, a task of philosophy of religion, and not of religious interpretation. The writer does not mean to intimate by this statement that he has a special proof up his sleeve which could be convincingly sprung on some other occasion, thus gaining for the moment the specious prestige of an accomplishment that could be achieved somewhere else. On the contrary, there seems to be a real difference in subject matter, or at least method, in the two cases. It must be recognized that the question of proving the existence of God might be crucial to some readers for passing from general religious questions to reflections on theistic religion. Anyone who cannot make this transition to theism on the basis of his own religious experience will want to drink deep of the perennial venture of philosophy for proofs.[2] As a matter of fact, the theist of personal experience will want to do this too, but for different reasons. He will be able to pass without hesitation from nontheistic religion to theistic investigations; but there is still much clarification and insight to be gained from the purely philosophical approach. In a word, then, we shall attempt no proof. If this comes as a disappointment to the reader, he can at least be reminded that there are a number of competent attempts that are accessible.[3] But while no proof is offered here, it is very much in the interest of religious interpretation that at least the significance and the nature of these proofs be properly understood.

The most obvious intention of proofs of the existence of God, whether of an older vintage, as in St. Anselm, St. Thomas, or Descartes, or of a newer flavor, as in F. R. Tennant or Charles Hartshorne, is to constrain the mind by rational demonstration to accept the conclusion. This being the intention, it is then up to every examiner of the argument to determine whether it is really sound or whether it contains some fallacy. In recent times, however, this rational significance of the proofs has been thought by many influential thinkers not to be their real significance at all. Either because they think Kant has conclusively refuted such arguments once for all,[4] or for some other reason, they interpret these arguments existentially rather than rationally. That is, they are not so much philosophical proofs as expressions of one's personal situation in life.[5] Some thinkers tend to regard them as expressions of man's dependence on the universe or his searching out for ultimate meaning in life. Others think of them as attempts to formulate and clarify the faith one has already accepted beforehand. In any case the function of the arguments is being analyzed anew.

Of course this raises the question of whether these arguments should be continued as matters of rational discourse. To this question it might be answered that these kinds of arguments, in addition to being helpful for self-clarification, are important for purposes of communication with other people. That is, a religious person might continue to use the arguments, even revise them, in order to approach people who reject theological beliefs and religious symbols, but who will still talk philosophy.

We should not minimize the important truth contained in this reconstruction. These arguments do spring from deep individual experiences. But neither should we confuse the origin of something with its validity. We cannot take a description of the original impulse to argumentation as a substitute for the consideration of the argument's merits as an argument. Furthermore, if the authors of these arguments were merely trying to express the states of their souls, or to clarify their own faith, it is doubtful whether they would have chosen so prosaic a way as philosophy for doing so. But, it may be replied, they did not know what they were doing. They thought they were giving rational proofs when they really were doing these other things. This is a precarious, self-refuting sort of reply. For by what logic do we select some of the great minds of the past as not knowing what they were doing, and exclude ourselves as latter-day critics from being in the same difficulty? Do our own contentions fall to the ground, then, for the same reason? That would be a peculiar way of establishing anything.

There is also a danger in using argumentation only for communication. If rational arguments have lost their significance as rational arguments, there is something suspect, even dishonest, in trying to win people over by specious intellectual devices. If the salt has lost its savor, this does not make it sugar. The only real alternatives left when rational argument is abandoned are silent mysticism or practical preaching. The more astute of the new interpreters have recognized this outcome frankly. But to many of us, this outcome surrenders a flowering capacity of human beings, their ability to reason with one another.

We see no alternative, therefore, to looking upon these traditional types of proof in their traditional significance, namely, as alleged rational demonstrations which deserve a fair hearing for the examination of their truth content. Neither philosophy nor religion gains by making an exclusively existentialist interpretation of these proofs. Philosophy does not, for it is thereby depleted of much of its rational significance. And religion does not, because the interpretation tends to suggest that philosophy and its arguments are all of a piece with religion.

From here it is a short step to saying that philosophy can be a substitute for religion, as indeed it has become for many of the existentialists. But when taken as religious expression, philosophy is a dry and dingy thing, not very likely to stir the heart and the emotions. If, however, it quickens the mind, which is its proper role, both philosophy and religion may benefit.

There is another important point to consider in connection with these proofs. Even if we grant that proofs of the existence of God are rational rather than existential, we cannot say that any proof, however strong it may be judged, gives complete certainty in its conclusion. This is so even if the argument is regarded as valid in itself and true in what it claims to show. This characteristic of proofs is often misunderstood, so that religion is affected adversely. That is, some people, expecting to find in philosophy a certification of religious beliefs which they could not find elsewhere, discover that philosophy cannot give such certainty, and so become even more disillusioned. Thus the theoretical uncertainty of philosophy spills over and affects the practical assurance of religion which might have been possible without it. It is therefore important, even from a religious point of view, that the nature of philosophical proof be correctly understood.

The common meaning of proof in logic and mathematics is an argument in which the conclusion follows validly from the premises or postulates. The actual truth of the conclusion is not shown; the main thing is that the argument hangs together logically. Thus, even if the conclusion is false, it could follow validly from the premises. But in science and philosophy, proof means an argument in which the conclusion not only follows validly from from the premises but is also shown reliably to be true. In this second meaning of proof, in order to show that your conclusion is true you must first show that your premises are true. Now in science, these premises, or laws, can be confirmed by actual observation, which is the scientist's method. But in philosophy—for example, in the case of arguments for the existence of God—you cannot do this. Here you can only establish your premises, upon which your conclusion is based, by looking with the eye of reason at various alternatives and deciding which of them seems most explanatory and most indispensable. Of course you could always prove your premises by using other arguments in which they are inferred as conclusions from other premises. But then these new premises would need the same treatment, until you finally ended up with ultimate premises which would have to be accepted without this kind of proof. Thus your ultimate premises cannot themselves be proved. To sum up, in the first meaning of proof, used in logic and mathematics, premises are simply taken for granted, whether true or false, and conclusions are drawn from them.

But in the second meaning of proof, used in philosophy, we must also be concerned with the truth of our premises. Yet, according to the very meaning of proof, our ultimate premises cannot themselves be proved. They must be accepted according to the criterion of what, all things considered, seems most reasonable to us.

Now this much being so, it is also fair to say that these ultimate premises cannot be absolutely final, beyond all dispute or intellectual modification. And if the premises of a proof are not absolutely final, not unmodifiably certain, neither will the conclusion be. Therefore, the most we could even hope for, theoretically, is a proof which seems more or less plausible. This limitation is inherent in the very nature of human proof and is rooted in human finiteness. Thus we should not expect from proofs of the existence of God, or from philosophy generally, what they cannot by their very nature yield. Humility in our expectations may help us to have a more appreciative understanding of the roles of both philosophy and religion in human life.

To summarize this section: A number of attempts at rational proof of God's existence have been made throughout the centuries. From one point of view these arguments can be seen as searchings of the human heart, ways of clarifying faith, or means of communicating religiously with others. But they must also be considered on their rational merits, as they were intended to be, and not sidestepped as irrelevant. Due to the nature of proof, however, these arguments cannot give certainty even if they are judged to be plausible. The most they can do is present lines of thought that may be more reasonable than others. This should be our attitude toward attempts at proof. The arguments themselves must be examined individually.

PROOF AND EVIDENCE

The second way of approaching the reality of God is the empirical way, in contrast with the rationalistic way. It is the approach based on inductive evidence rather than logical proof. The difference between the two is a formal one and may seem to be of no practical importance to religious persons for whom both are inferior in vitality to the third method, that of personal experience. But the first two approaches are important for the intellectual side of religion and therefore need to be examined. Some intention to the formal distinction mentioned is therefore relevant.

The difference between logical proof and inductive evidence is really a difference in the structure of their resulting arguments. The form of a logical proof can be put as follows: (1) If something is true in the world, e.g., that it is contingent, then God exists. (2) The world is contingent.

Therefore, (3) God does exist. Such an argument is always formally valid, for when you claim that if A is true then B is true, and then go ahead to assert that A really is true, you must of course conclude that B is really true also. Thus if your original premises are correct, you must conclude that God exists. But naturally your premises must first be shown to be true, as pointed out above.

Now in contrast to this type of argument, the form of argument based on inductive evidence can be put as follows: (1) If God exists, then such and such would be true in the world, e.g., the world would be orderly. (2) The world is orderly. Therefore, (3) God does exist. Such an argument is never formally valid, for when you claim that if A is true then B is true, and then go ahead to assert that B really is true, you are not necessarily required to say that A is really true also. This is so because, while B must always be true whenever A is true according to your first premise, A is not always forced to be true whenever B is true. Suppose we know, for instance, that if Jones wins the election an extra edition of the newspaper will be put out. Well, if later we discover that an extra edition of the newspaper has been put out, we cannot infer absolutely that Jones won the election, because an extra edition of the newspaper can come out for other reasons also. Thus we cannot say that the evidence brought forward in support of the last half of an "if-then" premise actually proves the first half of it, which in our case is also the conclusion that God exists. Such evidence does suggest that the conclusion is true; it does *confirm* it, but it does not *prove* it.[6] It is this kind of confirmation, then, that we are searching for when we look for evidence of the reality of God. We are looking for the kinds of actual things in our world that would be so if God does exist.

EVIDENCE FOR THE REALITY OF GOD

No originality is claimed in presenting the following evidences of God's existence. Indeed, most of them have been repeated in one form or another from time immemorial. The greatest intellectual concern today seems to be not so much to dispute the evidence but to raise the question of whether the hypothesis of God is the only one which can explain the facts. Thus there is a shift of emphasis from the evidence itself to a logical analysis of the relevant explanations. But that again is a task of philosophy. Religion itself is more concerned with the handiwork of God than with the hypothesis of God. Let us notice some of this religiously regarded handiwork, which, when logically regarded, constitutes evidence of the reality of God.[7]

The first pattern of evidence to be cited is the order and understandability of the world. The reasoning here would be: if God exists, then the world of his creation would exhibit orderliness and intelligibility;

the world does exhibit these characteristics; therefore, it is reasonable to suppose that the world points to God as a reality.

But is the world really so orderly and understandable? Much evidence to the contrary might be cited. We ourselves, in Chapter III, insisted that a strong element of faith in ultimate order is needed as we forge our way, scientifically and otherwise, into an unknown future. Yet these facts should not blind us to the great amount of regularity and intelligibility discovered in the past. Ordinary daily life itself attests repeatedly to this fact, and science has disclosed the operation of natural law in a way undreamed of in former eras. In short, the order of the world is not only a matter for faith concerning the future, but a reasonable conclusion concerning the past. And if order and intelligibility may be reasonably assumed as fundamental in our world, they may also be taken as evidence for God; for an orderly world tends to confirm the belief that it is the work of an orderly creator rather than not, and an intelligible world tends to confirm the belief that it is the product of intelligence rather than not.

A second source of confirmatory evidence is to be found in the very existence of human selves. The reasoning here might be summarized as follows: if God exists in anything like the usual conception of him, namely, as a living, creating being, then there would exist lesser personalities, who would be images or replicas of his nature. The actual world does contain lesser personalities; therefore, it is reasonable to suppose the existence of God as the source of these personalities. In this reasoning, the distinctiveness of human selfhood must be insisted upon, in fact argued for, in order for the evidence to hold up, for whenever human personality is interpreted in subpersonal or impersonal categories, a materialistic or some other nontheistic hypothesis is confirmed instead of the theistic one. This question of interpreting human selfhood involves a tremendous struggle, which is taking place in all areas of life the world over. The freedom, responsibility, uniqueness, and intrinsic worth of human selfhood are being challenged in many ways, subtle or overt. In this struggle theistic religion affirms unequivocally the uniqueness and irreducibility of the human self. It must unite with sympathetic secular thought to meet the counter-attacks on their own ground; but its own intuitions on this point are clear and explicit. It sees in the human self a spiritual reality whose freedom, creative power, and worth transcend the limits of any physical, social, or economic explanation. This being so, it concludes that such personalities have more probably gained their existence through the activity of a reality which is itself personal than through the activity of impersonal forces. Thus the very existence of persons tends to support belief in the real being of God.

Another source of confirmatory data is to be found in the phenomena called religious experiences. Here the reasoning would appear as follows: if God, as an object of worship and devotion, really exists, then existing individuals in the world would have multitudinous experiences in which he appears present and active to them. The actual world does include such experiences; therefore, we may suppose that God exists and is the real source of their experiences. Again, as in the case of the order and intelligibility of the world, and the case of the existence of persons, the distinctiveness of religious experiences must be defended against opposing analyses. But in this case religion is not so apt to get the independent aid of secular thought, since it is much more difficult to argue for the irreducibility of religious experiences without already assuming the theistic interpretation of the world. But, despite this difficulty, religious interpretation can still maintain consistently that the occurrence of constructive, transforming religious experiences does confirm the theistic hypothesis rather than another. A further problem in this line of reasoning is to ascertain what is meant by religious experience, for we cannot say that every experience that goes by the name religious is automatically a faithful indication of the reality of God. No doubt this problem will always be more easily solved by internal awareness than by external analysis. But granted the assumption that we can make a justifiable distinction between authentic and spurious religious experiences, based on their inherent luminosity and their subsequent fruits, we can then go on and maintain that the very occurrence of authentic religious experiences gives strong evidence for God's reality. The quantity and quality of these experiences of God in the world go very well with the theistic outlook, but such experiences are very difficult to fit into any other hypothesis. Some other hypothesis would have to interpret theistic religion, even at its finest, as pretty much of an illusion—so much of an illusion that educated people would obviously not wish to accept it, as many now do. Hence we may vouchsafe this evidence of religious experience as another way of confirming, though not proving, the central belief of theistic religion.

So much for the intellectual ways of approaching belief in God. Before turning to nonintellectual ways, we should add a word on the whole matter of using natural reason in this area.

Through the influence of Karl Barth and his followers, as well as through other influences, a great part of modern religious thought has come to believe that the unaided intellect, apart from revelation and faith, has no business offering arguments or evidence or God, since there is no possibility of reaching God in this way.[8] Theism will only give away its case if it tries to justify itself by the same rational categories and instruments already perfected with greater precision by the atheist. The technical way of stating this conclusion is to say that natural theology has been entirely abandoned by these thinkers in favor of revealed theology.

Our discussions in the chapters so far have been enough to suggest our opinion that in this controversy the best position is to recognize natural theology as a legitimate enterprise but also to admit that the most it can claim for its conclusions is a certain reasonableness and not the sort of demonstration that was claimed by earlier proponents.[9] To abdicate the employment of reasoning in theological matters is both an abandonment of our human nature and a shirking of our right, nay our duty, to converse with other minds. Moreover, when we employ reason we are not using the categories and instruments of the atheist but those of man. The total elimination of natural reason strikes the opposition, and even the friendly critic, as a kind of protective escapism instead of a positive position. Finally, it is a disappointing commendation for theism to leave the impression that, considered as faith, it is mandatory, but considered rationally, it doesn't make sense. Still, in all this we must not lose sight of the limitations to which human reasoning is subject.

HOW MEN HAVE ENCOUNTERED GOD

The third question posed earlier—How have men encountered the reality of God?—brings us to the nonintellectual mode of approach. We have already indicated that faith is the general term used to describe this mode of knowing. Faith in the present theistic context means the orientation or pattern of life based on willingness to live and act by the conviction of God's reality. Theists believe that in this faith God is somehow really known. But such faith is brought about in different media and then continues to have different emphases in different people's lives. It may be instructive to try to indicate some of these particular avenues by which people have been ushered into their faith and which may still be dominant in their religious experience afterwards. The problem here is to be psychologically true to actual life experiences and avoid a sentimental liberalism enamoured of a vague religiousness everywhere.

One obvious stimulus in the life of faith, and hence to the encountering of God, is the mediation afforded by other individuals. The religious qualities of other people often serve as a lure to the lonely, searching self. God is made a living option by his presence in the lives of others. Sometimes the stimulus may be no more than the simple declaration by another person of his belief in God. It was not just appeal to authority which prompted a student to say that if his mathematics professor believed in God, that was good enough for him. Not all influences of this sort are so naively stated. Yet it is true that there is a kind of magnetism surrounding firmly held convictions, especially if we feel they are the result of deep spiritual experience.

More powerful than simple testimony, however, are the living examples of other lives. The practiced spirituality of others draws us to them, and through them to God. Thus in the very midst of us, lives remind us that life is more than dust and lead us back to whence we came. Such persons may not be great in the world's estimation; generally they are not. If we happen to be associated with any of the spiritual leaders with whom man is from time to time blessed—leaders who spark a recrudescence in religious life or bring an old truth to new light—ours is the greater privilege.

Nor is this influence confined to our contemporaries. The nature of personality and of time are such that we can have vicarious contact with the religious personalities of the past as well as those of the present. Sometimes this kind of companionship seems more real than that with our immediate associates. The culmination of this kind of experience comes in the fellowship possible with the central personage of our religion. No general statement can be made at this point covering all religions, since the role of the central personage in them differs so radically. But we can say that space and time are no barriers to this most powerful of personal influences.

Another way to which people have testified of encountering God is through sharing in a convictional community. Participation in corporate experience has always been an awakening and intensifying fountain of religion. Through common work and worship, common expression of basic convictions, men come to feel the presence of divine activity in their corporate life. Usually this community will mean a church or other religious institution, in which case the experience of worship and prayer is the focal point of the relationship to God. But such community participation is not confined to formal religious institutions. It may occur in any experience involving like conviction. Thus the shared toil of daily life, the mutual support in personal crises, the solidarity in just causes, and the common devotion of pioneering groups may all inaugurate feelings of accord and sustenance which the participants find impossible to explain apart from the working of divine providence.

In addition to these directly personal influences of individuals and communities, there are other less personal but nonetheless vital contexts in which God is encountered. One of these is religious writing. Usually this will mean the sacred scripture accepted by one's convictional community. But other works have also been attested to as being instrumental for this purpose—confessionals, spiritual autobiographies, devotional classics, poetry, theological tracts. Notable conversions have been reported as having occurred in conjunction with the reading of powerful passages from scripture or elsewhere; and these sources continue to provide stimuli in the quieter life of faith that follows.

Other persons testify that they encounter God not so much in these previous ways as through nature. While we may readily grant that the experience of nature would not of itself lead to belief in God apart from a predisposition of faith, this does not alter the fact that God may be encountered through nature by the receptive mind. In addition to the order and intelligibility of nature, there appear to be two primary characteristics of nature which arouse religious experience. These are its mystery and its beauty. Mystery is felt in the feelings of awe and wonder that overwhelm us in the presence of nature, and these feelings do not, interestingly enough, disappear with the accumulation of knowledge. Beauty is felt to inhere in the intricate symmetries of individual objects and organisms, in the larger settings of natural occurrence, and even in the whole of nature. Through such experiences people have claimed that they were brought by nature to God, the infinite mystery.

Lastly, we shall mention one other class of experiences which are especially significant as approaches to God. These are experiences involving the unfolding of the self, its capacities, limitations, and relationships. In discovering their true self, men have also discovered God. Sometimes these experiences are intense feelings of anxiety, helplessness, despair, or dependence. Many are the accounts of people who reached the dregs of decadence or despair and who insist that they were renewed only when they were able to accept the power of faith in God. Sometimes the experiences may be of quite the opposite sort—joy, love, hope. Again, the moral experience of making choices may, through its apprehending of an objective moral order, lead to an awareness of the cosmic source of value. In many ways the self discovers itself, and in doing so traces its relation to the divine source of its being.

By all of these avenues and more, men have testified to an encounter with God. What we notice throughout all of these ways is the conviction of theistic religion, at least in its mature form, that God is known in and through the common events of life in the world. God is not encountered through peculiar visions, private voices, or magical meetings, but is mediated through the whole of life. The encounter with God is the encounter with life itself. There is, of course, the belief in special revelation which we shall take up in a later chapter. But what we have said here describes the ordinary life of man in his approach to God.

Because of the greater intimacy of these ways, those theologians are right who say that they are more persuasive than the intellectual ways, although we have argued that the latter are not to be slighted. Another conclusion to be drawn concerns the variety of contexts in which men have encountered God. There are those who would insist that there is no knowing of God apart from their own particular community, scripture, or doctrine. A more observant mind could not say this, and a more modest spirit would not place limits upon God in this way.

> When God reveals Himself to man, then a characteristic disturbance
> is set up in the human soul and in the life of our human society, and
> that disturbance is what we mean by religion. It is a disturbance of
> which we have all had some experience. Not one of us has been left
> alone by God.[10]

From the theistic point of view God is omnipresent and can therefore
be known in many situations.

GOD, AMBIGUITY, AND RELIGION

WALTER KAUFMANN

*Walter Kaufmann (1921–), an outspoken younger philosopher
and expert on Nietzsche, studied at Williams College and Harvard
University and has taught philosophy at Princeton since 1947. His
books include* Nietzsche *(1950),* From Shakespeare to Existentialism
(1959), and The Faith of a Heretic *(1961), as well as several edited
volumes. In this selection he argues that the existence of God cannot be proved, that the concept of God is essentially ambiguous,
and that religion is therefore a matter of loyalty and tradition.*

Can one prove God's existence? The major arguments for
God's existence fail to prove their point. Even if we grant their premises
and overlook fallacious reasoning, most of them are arguments for occult
powers and establish an overwhelming presumption in favor of the
existence of a great many such powers, of which not one resembles the
God of Moses, Jesus, or Mohammed. The ontological argument tries to
prove the existence of a perfect God but is fallacious. Kant, whose God
is similar to that of Judaism and Christianity, does not succeed in showing that reason demands his existence. The question remains: Can one
prove God's existence?

Yes, but this does not mean that God exists. The classical syllogism is:
All men are mortal; Socrates is a man; therefore Socrates is mortal. It
provides the recipe for proving with equal elegance that Socrates is
immortal: All men are immortal; Socrates is a man; therefore Socrates is
immortal.

By the same token, we can construct an indefinite number of proofs of

From: *Critique of Religion and Philosophy* by Walter Kaufmann, pp.
120-21, 124-30, 247-48. Copyright 1958 by Harper & Row, Publishers.
Used by permission of Harper & Row, Publishers, and Faber and Faber
Ltd.

God's existence. If Jesus was trustworthy, God exists; Jesus was trustworthy; therefore God exists. The construction of premises from which the existence of God will follow as a valid conclusion is a mere matter of ingenuity: valid proofs of God's existence are not hard to find. The crux is whether any such proof can be based on plausible premises. In that respect, the proof just offered is superior to the proofs of Thomas: millions would consent that both premises are plausible.

All valid proofs are if-then propositions: if the premises are true, then the conclusion must be true. When the argument is valid, those reluctant to admit the truth of the conclusion need only question the premises. Even where there are no other grounds for doubting the trustworthiness of any witness, the fact that he advocates a dubious belief is sufficient ground for asking whether he could not have been mistaken at least once.

In the case of Jesus, moreover, Albert Schweitzer and other New Testament scholars have long argued that he was mistaken about one of the most central tenets of his message; namely, that the world would come to an end before some of those who heard him would taste death. Schweitzer even argues that Jesus' ethic was designed only for the short interim before the end of our world and hence not only is inapplicable today but never was applicable.

Proofs which are based on *ad hoc* premises, made to measure for the conclusion, are even weaker. To give a crude example: If there is life, God must exist; there is life; therefore, God exists. Whoever is reluctant to accept the conclusion will question the major premise.

In the examples given so far, God appears in one of the premises. Can we prove God's existence with a valid argument in which God does not appear in any of the premises? Clearly, if God does not appear in any of the premises, he will not appear in the conclusion either: if he did, the argument would have to be invalid. But could we prove the existence of a being which has all of God's characteristics so that in effect we could prove God's existence, only without using the term "God"?

This question must be answered in the negative. The God of Judaism and Christianity is not one of a class of beings with a set of specifiable characteristics. Whatever can be proved to exist by means of arguments in which God does not figure in one of the premises is, from the Biblical point of view, a false god. Hypothetical functionaries can be proved like that, not God.

. . . . .

A functionary whose existence is implied not by *ad hoc* presuppositions, but by a scientific theory or by a metaphysic which did not assume this functionary to begin with, is a stopgap, likely to be dated by a future theory, and presumably not required even now by rival theories. But the God of Moses and of Jesus is no stopgap.

GOD AND AMBIGUITY. Propositions about God pose an important problem which is often overlooked: What do they mean? What does "God" mean?

The meaning of the word "God" is learned in large measure from the Bible, as is the meaning of "Methuselah" or "Moses"—or "paradise" or, to a lesser extent, "holy" or even "love." (See § 29.) We do not only permanently associate some words with particular Biblical sentences, passages, or stories, but the Bible is the world in which many of us—and many of our elders and hundreds of the writers whose works have formed our imagination and vocabulary—first encountered certain words, conceptions, and experiences.

Initially, we encounter God as a proper name. He is an individual whose character is manifested in his words and deeds. The character is complex, and as soon as we start abstracting traits from the many things he says and does we are in grave danger of falling into contradictions.

Even when we consider "God" as a proper name, certain differences between "God" and "Methuselah" or "Moses" are obvious. First, "God" occurs in so many more different contexts, in almost every book of the Bible, that the resulting complexity is many times, though not literally infinitely, greater than in the case of "Moses," not to speak of "Methuselah." Secondly, this appearance in widely different contexts and this relevance to radically divergent situations—to everything, in fact—becomes an essential feature of God.

Moreover, the character of God is not made manifest solely by what he says and does. He also appears, much more frequently and characteristically than anyone else, as the subject of direct address, as one to whom sacrifices are made or thanks given, and as the object of visions, love, or awe. To give an example: "hallelujah"—literally, "praise Yah (the Lord)" —is for most of us not so much a way of giving praise to someone whose existence is known independently as it is a shout of joy. We may associate it with the music of Handel or perhaps with the voice of Marian Anderson singing a spiritual. For some of us it may be nothing less than the ultimate expression of joyous emotion, of a triumph over sorrow, of release from care. Though we do not take it literally as meaning "praise the Lord," it enters into what "God" means to us.

Some emotions are intimately associated with, and most readily expressed in, phrases in which "God" appears in one way or another. The Bible and various hymns and benedictions inspired by it have given classical expression to any number of experiences—and raised our sights to all kinds of experiences which otherwise we might not know at all.

"God-fearing" denotes an attitude not fully conveyed by any paraphrase, and certainly not by any such literal rendering as "afraid of the deity." Or consider the priestly blessing: "The Lord bless thee and keep thee; the Lord make his face shine upon thee and be gracious unto thee; the Lord turn his face toward thee and give thee peace." What is meant is not that there is a character named God who has a face which, like the sun, he can let shine upon us. Indeed, it is not at all easy to say with precision what is meant, but again these words help to inform the meaning of "God."

We read Isaiah's account of the experience of his calling. He sees God on a throne surrounded by seraphim—probably, fiery serpents, not angels —with six wings. Is the Lord here still a character or, like the six-winged seraphim, part of a vision—the central element in an overpowering experience which can be represented only by using the most majestic terms: throne, holy, the whole earth, glory—and the Lord of hosts? We need not believe that one of the seraphim literally touched Isaiah's lips with a live coal, or that the Lord sat upon a throne surrounded by six-winged seraphim: surely, the writer had no such intention, but his vision has left a permanent mark on subsequent thought and feeling and the meaning of "God."

We may not know what to make of Isaiah's vision or the priestly blessing or the first chapter of Genesis, but our notion of God, whether we believe in him or not, is nourished by these sources; and when we read that a Hollywood star has said that God is "just a livin' doll" we hardly trust our eyes.

Now if we asked seriously whether this proposition about God is true or false, two kinds of answers could be given without broaching the problem of God's existence. In the first place, we can construe this statement precisely like a statement about Moses: we can ask whether it is in accordance with our literary reports. Asked whether Odysseus was phenomenally stupid, we could say No without committing ourselves regarding his historical existence.

Secondly, we can say that statements about God belong to a universe of discourse which has its own characteristic conventions—for example, the Jewish or the Christian religion—and we can then ask whether the proposition is in accordance with these conventions.

The two approaches, though they lead to the same verdict in the case at hand, are different: the conventions are not always in complete accord with the Bible. Pascal's familiar distinction between the God of Abraham, Isaac, and Jacob and the God of the philosophers needs to be supplemented with a similar distinction between the God of Scripture and the God of the creeds, the dogmas, and the theologians.

Asked if it is true that God loves man, one might say on the basis of Scripture, "Yes, but . . ." But if the universe of discourse is defined by the conventions of the Christian faith, the answer would be simply Yes, seeing that the proposition to be judged is itself one of these conventions.

To judge whether a proposition about God is true or false, we must know to what universe of discourse it belongs. "A bishop can move diagonally only" is true if the universe of discourse happens to be chess; not otherwise.

Much discourse about God is therefore meaningful and even verifiable in an important sense without implying that God does in fact exist. In some kinds of discourse statements about God are legitimately verified by references to the Bible, or found false because they are in conflict either with express assertions or with implications of some passages in Scripture. In other kinds of discourse statements about God are found to be true or false by referring back to the traditions of a religious community or a denomination. In both cases, disagreement may be frequent: in the case of Scripture, because different passages say different things and seem to have divergent implications; in the case of the traditions of denominations, because these traditions are not necessarily consistent and because different denominations disagree. For all that, there is an area of agreement, and some propositions about God would be considered true by almost everyone brought up against the background of the Bible, others false. All this is independent of the question whether God exists.

The question whether God exists is of a different nature. First of all, it is ambiguous in the sense that this question, too, might be asked without all reference to the question whether God *really* exists. What may be meant may be whether, according to the Bible or according to the traditions of some particular community, God exists. Answer: the Baalim and Ashtaroth do not exist, the Lord does.

In this context there is a legitimate sense in saying that God exists by definition. Without committing oneself to a scholastic metaphysic one might even say that in the Bible God is the most real being: this would be a trope, not altogether different from such colloquialisms as "Boy, does he ever exist!" Or "if he doesn't, who does?"

Interpreted at this level, the question whether God exists is comparable to the question whether Odysseus was cunning: what is asked about is an essential part of the conception. If the universe of discourse is Scripture, Judaism, or Christianity, "God exists" is true.

If we are asked whether Moses ever killed a man, the answer according to Exodus, and according to the denominations which accept this book as part of their canon of Scriptures, is: he did. But one could also ask whether Moses *really* killed a man. In that case, it would be assumed that there really was a historical character named Moses who in other respects was sufficiently similar to the character described in the Bible to warrant our identification of the two, and the question would be whether this particular incident, related in the second chapter of Exodus, was historically true or not. Asked whether Moses ever really existed, we could clearly say he did, if we were sure that all the statements made about him in Exodus, Leviticus, Numbers, and Deuteronomy were true. But if some of them were true and others were not true, the question might be difficult, if not impossible, to answer in one word. If there was a man who did all the deeds and said all the things ascribed to Moses, but his name was not Moses; or if there were two men, one who led his people out of Egypt and another who gave them their laws; or possibly many more than two, who during a period of two centuries had done some of the major deeds ascribed to Moses, while still other feats were done centuries later; then it would be impossible to say whether Moses ever really existed, unless we analyzed the question into several component queries.

The question whether God *really* exists offers the same difficulties as the question whether Moses really existed, but to a much higher degree. In the case of Moses, there is the name to hang on to: if a man by that name either led the Jews from Egypt or gave them at least some of their laws, we could say: yes, he did exist, but he did not do everything ascribed to him. And if a man named Moses performed both these feats—which is extremely probable (cf., e.g., Albright's essays)—we should have no hesitation whatever in affirming the historic existence of Moses even if some statements made about him in the Bible should be false. In the case of God, we have no name to hang on to, and he is credited with so much more than even Moses that *the question whether God really exists has no clear meaning.*

Furthermore, the word "exists" raises problems of its own. If it is meant in the same sense in which Moses might have existed, the sense in which chickens and chairs exist, most people would say that God does not "exist." The assertion of such spatial existence would immediately raise the question where, in what particular location, God could be found.

Those asserting God's existence have therefore often maintained that there are different modes of existence. This is a doubtful doctrine. It is said that not only material entities exist but also, as Plato claimed, mathematical objects, such as points, triangles, and numbers, as well as justice, love, and beauty. It is highly dubious whether anything is gained by speaking unidiomatically of the "existence" of such entities.

Even if it were legitimate to speak of different modes of existence, what could be meant by asking whether God "exists"? Saying that God exists in the same sense in which mathematical points exist would be hardly less atheistic than saying that his existence is comparable to that of unicorns. Those asserting the existence of God have sometimes recognized this difficulty and contended that God's mode of existence is unique, that he does not exist in the same sense in which anything else exists but in a sense peculiar to himself. Logically, however, this is no different from saying that God does *not* "exist."

One of the outstanding Protestant theologians of our time, Paul Tillich, admits as much when he says in an essay on "The Concept of God" that "the very term 'existence of God' is almost blasphemous" and that "every true theistic statement must be contradicted by an atheistic statement." And in the first volume of his *Systematic Theology* (237) Tillich writes: "It is as atheistic to affirm the existence of God as it is to deny it."

In spite of our ordinary way of speaking, which makes theism positive and atheism negative, the theist cannot say what he affirms; he can only deny the atheist's contention. The theist is not the man who affirms God's existence—on reflection, he admits that God does *not* "exist"—but the theist denies that God "exists" in the same sense in which unicorns exist.

It may seem that this extraordinary conclusion is incompatible with the way in which Tillich follows up the sentence quoted from his *Systematic Theology:* "God is being-itself, not *a* being." Tillich's affirmation suggests that theists affirm something after all, and that this affirmation is denied by atheists. But no atheist would deny the affirmation that "God is being-itself"; he would only say that in that case we might as well dispense with all reference to God and—like Heidegger, for example, to whom Tillich is exceedingly close—speak of "being." If Tillich really meant that "God is being-itself," he would not significantly disagree with atheists, except insofar as he was reluctant to give up the name of God and liked to use it redundantly for something for which we already have a perfectly good word. But Tillich, of course, does not really mean what he says here. Remember that "every true theistic statement must be contradicted by an atheistic statement." According to Tillich, "God is being-itself" is a true theistic statement; so we must add immediately that, of course, God is not really being-itself. Or perhaps we need not add it *immediately.*

In sum, terms applied to God do not mean what they generally mean. Those who say that God exists do not really mean that he "exists" in the same sense in which anything else exists. Those who say that God is being-itself, or a spirit, or love, do not mean these terms in any ordinary sense. But if terms applied to God do not mean what they generally mean, if they have a unique meaning when applied to God, then all such talk about God is conducted in a peculiar language with rules of its own.

In chess, "king" and "bishop" do not mean what they usually mean, but every term has a precise meaning, and the game would not be changed if we substituted "fool" for "bishop," as the French do, or "devil" for "king." But assertions about God depend entirely on their ambiguity: it is their apparent meaning, their surface sense, that counts 99 per cent of the time, and it is only under questioning that this is modified, and only under persistent attack is it withdrawn to the point where frequently no sense at all remains.

This is true not only of assertions about God. A world-famous Thomist says to an undergraduate who asks about the meaning of the new dogma about the assumption of the Virgin Mary: there has been an unfortunate movement in recent Catholicism that has depreciated the body, and by declaring that the Virgin's body was taken up to heaven we counter this ascetic tendency. A colleague asks: but if the body in the dogma is the physical body which asceticism depreciates, then it must take up space. Is heaven then to be understood spatially, and must a location in space be assigned to the body of the Virgin Mary? The Thomist replies: oh, no, there are all kinds of bodies, and the body of the Virgin that was assumed in heaven was not a spatial body.

To understand such peculiarities of theology, one must remember that theology, and indeed any systematic discussion of God, was born as a defensive maneuver. It is the product of a distinctive historic situation. Claims of a less sophisticated age have been exposed to rationalistic attack when theology appears to salvage the tradition. The word theology is encountered for the first time in Plato—at the point where he proposes to expurgate Homer's epics to rescue belief in the gods from the cynicism of the Greek enlightenment (*Republic*, 379). The theologian defends his religious heritage by sacrificing its plain exoteric meaning. He says to the atheist: you are quite right to deny what you deny, but I deny it, too; what you repudiate is indeed superstitious and wrong—but you are wrong, too.

The situation would be simple if the theologian rebuked the atheist for taking literally what ought to be read as poetry. But in that case the infidel might well reply: we are agreed; I like to read the Scriptures, too. The difference arises over the theologians' determined attempt to make univocal translations of essentially ambiguous propositions.

"God" is not a univocal term. The deeds and words of God; the visions, phrases, and relations into which God enters; and the thoughts and feelings about Him which are recorded in the Hebrew Scriptures add up to a conception overcharged with meaning. The God of Abraham, Isaac, and Jacob is not simply "being-itself." And now there have been added to this over-rich conception of the Hebrew Scriptures the sayings of Jesus and the stories of the Gospels, the theologies of the fourth evangelist and Paul, the ideas of the other authors of New Testament Epistles, the visions of the Revelation of St. John the Divine, and the vast lore, if not of the Talmud, Midrash, and the Jewish mystics, of the church fathers and the Christian mystics, the scholastics, and innumerable theologians and philosophers.

Seeing that "God" is so far from being a univocal term and that the terms applied to him by theologians are admittedly not intended to mean what they generally mean, it is no exaggeration if we conclude that *most statements about God are essentially ambiguous*. They cannot be called true or false. Interpretations of them which are true are usually ingenious or trivial or heretical—and often all three. The propositions themselves defy translation.

Religion and loyalty. Religious faith cannot be understood apart from faithfulness, fidelity, loyalty. It is loyalty that determines allegiance to Judaism, Christianity, Hinduism, or Buddhism. Acceptance of specific propositions as well as religious experience, whether mystic or prophetic, are secondary. What is primary is not a dedication to any humanistic ideal, but loyalty to a tradition and acceptance of its authority, at least up to a point.

Why are most believers so reluctant to specify the meaning of the religious propositions they cherish? There are at least three reasons. First, there is security in obscurity. Precision invites refutation.

Secondly, many religious propositions, including almost all statements about God, are not reducible to any one meaning but [are] essentially ambiguous. The believer feels that the original proposition is more profound than any translation he could ever hope to furnish: there is somehow more to it—namely, though he is not likely to think of it in these words, an indefinite number of other possible interpretations.

The third point is intimately connected with this ambiguity. The believer senses, however dimly, that previous generations, and even other believers today, associate widely different meanings with the same propositions. What determines his acceptance of religious propositions is not primarily their peculiar adequacy to his own intentions and ideas but a desire for continuity. As soon as a particular translation of a religious proposition is accepted as completely adequate, the continuity both with past generations and with one's own disappears.

Intellectually, the apparent agreement of believers is apt to be verbal rather than real. Many believers are far closer to many nonbelievers than they are to many of their fellow believers, provided we concentrate on what they really believe. But intellectual tenets are not the primary consideration when it comes to deciding to what community one wants to belong.

There is a close analogy between religion and marriage. We do not choose a person to live with by seeing with whom we can agree on the most propositions. A certain amount of agreement enters into the decision, but what is central is the will to stay together in spite of any disagreement.

There is a unity of will rather than intellectual agreement. The phrase "a unity of purpose" suggests itself, but "purpose" suggests a specifiable aim, and just this is usually lacking. Neither in marriage nor in religion are we likely to find any such specifiable aim; rather, the will to belong together, for better or for worse. Loyalty to a religion, too, may be rooted in love.

It is no accident that the moving words of Ruth in adopting a new religion are so often cited at weddings, even though she was not speaking to a man: "Whither thou goest, I will go; and where thou lodgest, I will lodge: thy people shall be my people, and thy God my God."

THE VALIDITY AND USEFULNESS OF NATURAL THEOLOGY

L. HAROLD DEWOLF

L. Harold DeWolf (1905–) studied at Nebraska Wesleyan University, Boston University, and the University of Nebraska. Before becoming professor of systematic theology at Boston University Divinity School, he had teaching experience at the University of Southern California, Garrett Biblical Institute, Wellesley College, and Old Umtali Theological Seminary in Southern Rhodesia. His books include The Religious Revolt against Reason *(1949),* A Theology of the Living Church *(1953), and* The Enduring Message of the Bible *(1960). Here he presents a defense of natural theology.*

By *natural theology* is here meant *the learning of some truth about God or about man's rightful destiny from considerations logically independent of the Biblical revelation and of a prior commitment to Christian faith.* For example, all five of Thomas Aquinas' famous philosophical arguments for God are exercises in natural theology. So also is F. R. Tennant's "wider teleological argument."[1] All ethical concepts of natural law, that is, moral law discoverable by philosophical method from broad considerations of reason and common human experience, are instances of natural theology.

Natural theology has a long and impressive history. It includes Socrates' belief in eternal unwritten laws; Plato's references to evidences of God's wisdom in the order of nature; Cicero's ridicule of the atheists' notion that a fortuitous "concourse of atoms" could have made this complex, mean-

From *The Case for Theology in Liberal Perspective* by L. Harold DeWolf, pp. 19-20, 31-36. Copyright 1959, W. L. Jenkins. The Westminster Press. By permission.

[1] See F. R. Tennant, *Philosophical Theology,* Vol. II, pp. 78-120. The University Press, Cambridge, England, 1928-1930.

ingful world; the highly developed thought about God and moral law in the writings of Seneca; the ethics of Epictetus grounded in his belief in the controlling providence of God; Plutarch's doctrine of the goodness, perfect justice, and love of God, and also his firm belief in human immortality assured by the love of God.[2] Among Christians, too, many have used natural theology in approach to the Biblical doctrine, in communication with non-Christians, or in other ways. Among them are such figures as Justin Martyr, Clement of Alexandria, Origen, Athanasius, Gregory of Nyssa, Augustine, Anselm, Thomas Aquinas, Duns Scotus, Raymond of Sabunde, John Calvin, Richard Hooker, Hugo Grotius, the Cambridge Platonists of the seventeenth century, Richard Baxter, John Locke, Joseph Butler, John Wesley, and many writers of more recent times.

Recently, however, the validity and usefulness of natural theology have been frequently challenged by influential Christian theologians. This negative attitude toward natural theology has raised one of the most conspicuous and important issues in current religious thought.

Sören Kierkegaard believed that the "infinite qualitative distinction" between time and eternity made quite impossible any crossing from man to God by the thought of man. Man can conjure up all kinds of human substitutes for God, but all of these are mere idols. The metaphysical task is for man simply impossible, as Socrates well knew. The only knowledge of God that is either possible for man or necessary to his salvation is the acceptance by faith of the supreme Paradox, the eternal God become man in time and crucified by men. This acceptance is not an act of the intellect, but is rather a passionate decision of the will. So runs Kierkegaard's thought.

. . . . .

POSITIVE USEFULNESS OF NATURAL THEOLOGY TO THE CHRISTIAN THEOLOGIAN

In defending his right to give the Gifford Lectures, despite his rejection of all natural theology, Barth makes the claim that natural theology soon becomes "arid and listless" when it is not in "conflict" with its "adversary" which stands in "clear antithesis" to it, namely, "the teaching of the Reformation."[3] He says this dependence of natural theology on opposition by a revealed theology that absolutely rejects it is "notorious,"[4] but he

---

[2] Further details, many other examples, and references to the sources are to be found in E. H. Gillett, *God in Human Thought*. Scribner, Armstrong and Company, 1874.

[3] Barth, *The Knowledge of God and the Service of God*, pp. 6-7, 9.

[4] *Ibid.*, p. 7.

does not cite a shred of evidence. Actually, the natural theology of the Stoics was ably constructed without such opposition and still retains sufficient vitality to exert considerable influence on the law and on international affairs as well as on philosophical and theological theory, especially through its concept of natural law. The natural theology of Thomas Aquinas and of many writers in the seventeenth, eighteenth, and nineteenth centuries flourished with the encouragement, rather than with the opposition, of most theologians with whom these writers were much concerned.

That natural theology is radically inadequate soil for the nurture of a living, redemptive faith would be cheerfully admitted, or rather emphatically asserted, by most of its Christian participants. But it is quite another thing to say that natural theology owes its vitality to opposition by theologians who attack it. This latter proposition is not only unsupported by the evidence but is disproved by the history of natural theology.

On the other hand, Christian theology needs the services of natural theology for several purposes. These can be given only brief statement here.

A part of the total task of Christian theology is to determine the kind of relations that subsist between Christian doctrines and all else that we know. The fulfillment of this purpose requires inevitably that questions of natural theology be raised, such as these: What evidences of God's existence and of his nature are to be found in the world? In what ways does man's need of God appear in human nature? A Christian theology that does not include the confronting of such questions has not yet taken seriously the effort to attain that wholeness of view required by the commandment to love God with all the mind. Barth, too, takes such questions seriously, but he argues that the answers to them would be wholly negative. The point is that such questions must be earnestly confronted, and if some positive lines of evidence are found to lead from man and the world to God, it is an obligation of the Christian theologian to explore these connections with care.

Natural theology serves to correct some of the errors produced by an exclusively Biblical or by Biblical and traditional theology. For example, Calvin was assisted by the natural theology of Cicero and others toward giving due emphasis to the first two chapters of Romans and putting in proper perspective Paul's other teachings, stressing our dependence on revelation and divine grace. On the other hand, Barth's own theology has in other ways obviously gained considerably over Calvin's by more recent developments based on presuppositions of natural theology. For example, Barth is not bound by any such rigid doctrine of Biblical inerrancy as restricted Calvin. This, of course, is due to the advances of textual and historical criticism. Barth takes these critical studies into account only spasmodically, yet they have given his use of the Bible much more flexibility than Calvin knew. But textual and historical criticism grew out of altogether secular literary and historical scholarship and are based on the assumption that there is continuity between the Biblical revelation and the rest of human history. Every time we use historical criticism in our study of the Bible, we are learning something about God's Word to man from historical knowledge gained from sources independent of the Biblical revelation. Biblical theology that makes use of historical criticism, then, implies the positive usefulness of natural theology.

To use another example, we may point out that the thought of the church has been stimulated, challenged, and modified for good, in recent times, by secular movements of thought. Reinhold Niebuhr, John C. Bennett, Walter G. Muelder, and other students of Christian social ethics have often pointed out examples of such contributions from non-Christian and even anti-Christian thought. To recognize such contributions is to imply acknowledgment of indebtedness to natural theology, for natural theology is the gaining of "truth about God or about man's rightful destiny from considerations logically independent of the Biblical revelation and of a prior commitment to the Christian faith."[5]

Natural theology provides a bridge for communication and intellectual co-operation of Christian theology with the natural and social sciences. Where Christian theology is taught as part of a university curriculum, it can scarcely participate in the common intellectual life of the university without accepting the services of natural theology. A department of Christian theology in which natural theology is opposed can issue pronouncements, and its members can as individuals participate in scientific activities. But can it participate in co-operative truth-seeking efforts with the sciences? Universities and our whole culture are already suffering badly from the disunity of intellectual fragmentation. Christian theology can be of important assistance in healing this condition, but only when it approaches other disciplines with a willingness to learn from them concerning its own subject matter, as well as to teach them important insights concerning their subject matter. To engage in this kind of co-operative intellectual task, with psychology, sociology, history, medical science, economics, political science, biology, and the physical sciences is to accept the services of natural theology.

In some aspects of human life, if the practical as well as the intellectual purposes of Christian theology are to be achieved, its participants must engage in certain common tasks with persons who stand outside the Christian faith. A common platform for such co-operation, for example, in the United Nations and its affiliated agencies is to be found in that division of natural theology concerned with natural law. The work of such

[5] Cf. definition above, p. 171.

men as Dr. Frederick Nolde suggests what can be done by men with Christian faith clarified by theological study and with willingness to enter wholeheartedly into discussion of current international issues on the basis of a humanly discoverable natural law. A Christian theology that includes the conviction that all natural theology must be rejected is cut off from effective participation in such important Christian ministries of conciliation and understanding.

In the communication of Christian faith—and Christian theology—to unbelievers, natural theology is so valuable as to be well-nigh indispensable. While studying and otherwise assisting theological education in Central and East Africa, in 1955-1956, the writer asked many articulate first-generation Christians what had motivated their turning from paganism to Christian faith. Invariably, an important part of the answer implied the truth of natural theology. These young Christians told me that the Christian message showed them clearly what they had long dimly understood—the kind of life they ought to live, with faith in the one supreme God. The Christian faith declared to them the God already dimly sensed but yet not well known, and enabled them to live a life in fulfillment of moral needs long felt but inarticulate and ineffectual. In evangelistic approach to communists in the United States, I have found a similar necessity to meet the unbeliever on a common ground of secular thought and universal human need. Philosophical criticism of Marxism and a positive arguing of natural theology must be used until the unbeliever is persuaded that it is reasonable to look for a solution of his most perplexing theoretical and practical problems in a theistic faith. Until he is so persuaded, all citations of Biblical and churchly authority only confirm him in his assurance that the Christian faith is an outmoded, prescientific superstition. Natural theology is no less valuable for the evangelistic Christian world mission today than when Justin Martyr wrote his apology or when Augustine was led through Platonism to Christ.

So valuable an ally deserves a better reputation with Christian theologians than Barth and some others would give it, unless better reasons can be adduced against it than have thus far come to light.

It is encouraging that in his later writing Barth has come nearer to conceptions of natural law by his doctrine of the "spheres and relations" (*Bereiche und Verhältnisse*) in which he says God as Creator has placed man to live "dutifully or undutifully" (*gehorsam oder ungehorsam*).[6] Moreover, Barth has learned to say that what God has commanded us in Christ is required of all men, and that the revealing work of Christ is not limited to those who have been reached by the church or by knowledge of the historical Jesus. In places such doctrines seem to bring Barth close to a teaching practically equivalent to doctrines of natural law and of

---

[6] Barth, *Kirchliche Dogmatik*, III, 4, p. 31.

natural theology, under other names and with dialectical modifications. However, such devious, subtle, and ambiguous expressions will not adequately counteract the influences set loose in theological thought by his earlier direct, clear, and sustained attacks on natural theology.

In many colleges and universities throughout the world various philosophies confront each other in vigorous opposition. Some teachers of philosophy interpret human experience in the terms of Marxian dialectical materialism. Some contend for other naturalistic philosophies without God. Others maintain that even to suggest that a divine purpose and power undergird this universe is to raise a nonsensical question. Countless students guided by such teachers of philosophy are convinced by them and so turn sadly from the church and from all consideration of the Christian faith. If there is no God, as their teachers have convinced them there is not, then obviously the Bible is simply false and its teachings outworn superstitions unworthy of serious consideration by honest and intelligent people.

At the same time, in other classrooms other philosophers are teaching that the world of nature and human nature cannot be explained in material terms and yet demands more unified and deeply meaningful explanation than the special sciences alone can give. Many of these philosophers proclaim the evidences of reason and purpose underlying the whole universe and so point their students toward God. In such classrooms Christian students find collateral confirmation of their Christian faith, and non-Christian students often begin thinking that religion may be, after all, a live option for honest people of the twentieth century. Some such students then turn to the church, listening eagerly to the gospel of Jesus Christ.

Such philosophical debates have been going on for many centuries. The incredible tragedy is that in our time many theologians have allied themselves with the philosophical foes of belief in God and hence of the Christian faith. Denouncing all philosophical approaches to God as idolatrous and presumptuous, they declare that man's reason is so corrupt that to our best thought, and hence to the best philosophy of which men are capable, atheism is the stronger contender. Nature and human nature, they say, appear to human reason as the mere products of blind force or chance, or else they say that the very questions about God are nonsensical until one has already accepted Jesus Christ by faith.

In short, the current theologians who renounce the possibility of natural theology are giving comfort to the deadliest enemies of the Christian faith to be found in the world today. These same theological foes of natural theology are deliberately undermining the prestige and increasing the difficulties of the best friends of the church and the Christian faith in the field of philosophy. The Christian philosopher finds himself confronted by able and dangerous contenders against all belief in God. While he wages this intellectual battle he now finds himself continually sniped at from behind by Christian theologians who would surrender on this field of battle at once, hoping to win on the church's home ground where the gospel is simply proclaimed, without argument for its truth. Unfortunately, most of the students who have, in the halls of philosophy, acknowledged the defeat of their belief in God consider that it would be dishonest for them now to take seriously the Christian proclamation. Consequently they will not be in church to hear it. The few who are will, for the most part, regard the whole teaching of the church as a nostalgic remnant of prescientific superstition.

All this is quite needless. Such men as Frederick R. Tennant, Edgar S. Brightman, William Ernest Hocking, Charles Hartshorne, and Peter A. Bertocci have demonstrated and are demonstrating that a philosophy pointing to God need ask no quarter in the great debate with philosophical atheism. In the minds of innumerable men and women such able philosophers are winning the debate and sending into the church eager listeners to the full gospel of Christ. The sad fact is that in this magnificent service to truth and to God they must fight against so many theologians, with their denunciations of the presumptuous pride of natural theology and their insistence that the Christian proclamation is in discontinuity with all that men rationally know or believe from other evidence.

SUGGESTED BOOKS

Baillie, John, *Our Knowledge of God*. New York: Charles Scribner's Sons, 1959. A new edition of a widely read book in which the author argues for direct knowledge of God, and the subservience of reason to belief, in the Augustinian tradition.

Heschel, Abraham J., *God in Search of Man*. New York: Meridian Books, Inc., 1959. A philosophy of Judaism based on three trails that lead to God: the world of things, the Bible, and sacred deeds, or worship, learning, and action.

Hocking, William E., *The Meaning of God in Human Experience*. New Haven: Yale University Press, 1912. An attempt to discover, albeit with assumptions drawn from philosophical idealism, how God is known in practical human life and thought.

Hume, David, *Dialogues Concerning Natural Religion*. New York: Hafner Publishing Company, 1948. A famous skeptical analysis of traditional rational arguments for theism.

Jones, Rufus, *Pathways to the Reality of God*. New York: The Macmillan Company, 1931. A leading Quaker and exponent of mysticism discusses many contexts of life through which men have come to know God.

Tennant, F. R., *Philosophical Theology*, 2 vols. Cambridge: Cambridge University Press, 1928, 1930. The first volume is a psychological and epistemological preparation for an extensive empirical argument for theism in the second volume.

Weigel, Gustave, S. J. and Arthur G. Madden, *Religion and the Knowledge of God.* Englewood Cliffs, N.J.: Prentice-Hall, Inc., 1961. A study of the epistemological problem of God and the possibility of natural theology from a Thomist point of view.

Wolf, William J., *Man's Knowledge of God.* Garden City, N.Y.: Doubleday & Company, Inc., 1955. An Episcopalian professor of theology discusses how God is found according to Christianity.

VII · THE NATURE OF GOD

It has been maintained that if belief in God is based on reason rather than faith, the result will be a conception of God that is quite depleted of the qualities regarded as most important for religion. There is a sharp difference, it is said, between the philosophical and the religious idea of God. If this assertion is made in such a way as to imply that the two conceptions are always irreconcilable, or that the use of reason is not valuable in the question of the existence of God, the assertion is an invidious one. But if it is only intended to point out that reason cannot by itself discover the nature of God in the religious sense, there is a significant truth in the claim. On this question we need to know not only the meaning of God to reason but also the meaning of God in religious experience.

In what follows we shall try to keep both of these criteria in mind, just as we did in the previous chapter. We shall begin by making some summary remarks on the linguistic problem concerning theistic belief, thus relating the earlier discussion of religious meaning to the present context. We shall then address ourselves to some of the familiar but difficult questions concerning the nature of God, both regarding his relation to the world and his intrinsic being. We shall conclude by considering the nature of God more particularly for his meaning in actual life, i.e., the meaning of God as a religious object. The length of treatment given to each of the questions is limited by space and therefore should not be taken to suggest that the questions are easily solved. They are not.

GOD AS PERSONAL

In Chapter V we dealt with the general theory of religious meaning. We need now to extend our conclusions briefly to theistic language, which must be used throughout the discussion of other theistic problems.

The main point of extension is that in theism the words, analogies, parables, and images that are used to describe God are drawn basically from the language about persons. This is not accidentally so, but comes from the explicit belief that God is personal. There have been various attempts to avoid this terminology on the ground that it is anthropomorphic, or else to permit it provided we say there is no truth in it, but only figures of speech. The result is a blurred conception which is made attractive for everyone because it can mean anything to anybody. Theism pales into any sort of positive response to life, which no one is likely to

179

challenge. In contrast to this we must admire the forthrightness of Sidney Hook when he says: "No matter how religion is reconstructed, there will always be a difference between the approach of a secular, rational, ethical humanism to the problems of man and society and the approach of religion. History cannot be disregarded so lightly."[1] This is what theistic religion believes also. And the fundamental difference is over the belief in God as personal. There is no use trying to blend inherently different world-views under a cloak of metaphors and devious assertions.

The theist must, however, try to vindicate his adoption of the language of personality. First a negative point can be made, and then two positive ones.

Negatively it can be pointed out that the linguistic problem is one that confronts every viewpoint which seeks to say something about reality, which seeks to go beyond the world of experience immediately felt in order to give some kind of explanation of the universe as a whole. That is, contrary to a common opinion, this is a problem facing not only the theistic world-view but other world-views as well. The theist is linguistically in no more of a peculiar position than other world-outlooks. When a materialist, for instance, speaks of omnipotent matter rolling on its relentless course,[2] he is taking matter to be in some sense an ultimate explanation of the world we know. But matter in this sense must mean something quite different from the matter we encounter in the ordinary physical objects around us. The matter of these physical objects is, as experienced, always individualized; it is caused by something else to exist in its present shape; and it is transitory. But matter as the ultimate explanation of things must be conceived quite differently: it must have some internal dynamism capable of generating the physical objects we know, including their laws of behavior; it must in some sense be the ground or sustainer of the world of experience; and presumably it is not transitory but permanent. To build up such a supreme conception of matter, words must be used which are drawn from the experience of material objects but which nevertheless refer to the matter of ultimate explanation. Since the problem is the same for the theist, the materialist has no initial advantage in sticking close to the world of ordinary objects.

On the positive side the first point is that theism adopts the language of personality because it believes this is the only way to account for all the phenomena, personal and nonpersonal, that we experience in the world. If you start with the idea of a conscious, purposeful God, you can account, through concepts like creation and creative will, for both the personal and the nonpersonal beings in the world. But if you begin only with the idea of impersonal force, it is difficult to see how consciousness, purpose, and value, all of them culminating in persons, can be fitted into your scheme. That is, we find in the world conscious, purposing, valuing beings as well as nonpersonal ones; but if your metaphysical vocabulary includes only impersonal items like force, matter, energy, even life, you are faced with the prospect of saying that personality and personal phenomena have arisen from that which is totally devoid of anything personal. For the theist that is too contradictory a notion to countenance.

The second point is that the language of personality has been found to be the most fitting language to correlate with the religious experience of theistic convictional communities. For Judaism and Christianity this would mean the religious experience of the Biblical tradition, which clearly conceives of God as personal. Such experience leads the convictional communities to affirm a living, concerned, purposeful God.

The rationale of the theistic use of language, then, is something like this: The basic assumption is that something about reality can be known and expressed. Without this starting point there would be sheer skepticism, which has difficulties of its own.[3] Then, since we must employ words from a human context to describe what is more than human, we must suppose that our accounts are partly literal and partly nonliteral. This feature of religious language is explained through the analogical and parabolical uses of words. Theism then goes on to the contention that the language of personality and personal life—consciousness, purpose, knowledge, goodness, love, creativeness—is the most instructive for describing the ultimate. This contention derives from the belief that God is, in a sense not entirely symbolical, a person.[4] Personalistic language is thought to explain more adequately the occurrence of the whole range of beings we know, and it also accords with the central experiences of theistic convictional communities.

With this background we can now proceed to some of the other questions concerning the nature of God.

GOD AND THE WORLD

One of these questions, which is fundamental both for its own sake and for its bearing on other questions, is that of the relation between God and the world. Here the term world means not just the physical universe but the entire cosmos, including persons, other living creatures, and physical entities. There are innumerable relations, of course, and our purpose will be limited to emphasizing some of the more significant ones.

One relation between God and the world which has great religious interest is that of dependence. According to theistic religion, the world is not self-generating or self-sustaining, but is dependent in its existence upon the will and power of God. This relation is expressed in the belief that God is the creator of the world. This belief does not necessarily mean, according to some theists, that God may not be, in some other sense, also dependent upon the world. But in the order of actual existence, God is not dependent for his existence on our world, whereas our world is dependent for its existence on God. That is, the relation is nonreciprocal. God is self-existent and self-sustaining, while the world is contingent, subject to disintegration, and in need of external sustenance for its continuing existence. For some thinkers this idea of dependence seems to be the basic meaning of creation. But for others the idea of coming into being through a free act of God is the fundamental aspect of creation. In any case the recognition of dependence is a common point of theism.

Closely connected with this relation of dependence is another, usually called the dual relation of transcendence and immanence. If the world is dependent for existence upon God, the characteristics of God must greatly transcend those of the world. But at the same time theistic religion conceives of God as containing the world within his compass, so that his being is in some way also present within the world as its support and energizing power. Thus there is a distinct difference in theism from both pantheism, which maintains that God and the world are one in substance, and from deism, which holds that God is entirely transcendent and removed from the inner processes of the world. Incidentally, we have a good example here of a case where language must be taken to have both a literal and a nonliteral element. For, unlike pantheism, theism conceives of God as "beyond" the world, and, unlike deism, it conceives of God as "within" the world; but both of these words usually have connotations of space, whereas this aspect of the physical world is not intended in the description of God. To state the main point again, the dual relation of transcendence and immanence allows of various refinements of interpretation; but in some sense theism gives a distinguishable meaning and prominence to both the "beyond-ness" and the "within-ness" of God.

Another relation of great interest is that of need. According to theistic religion the creatures of the world are in need of the activity of God in order to reach the perfection of their capacities. The religious significance of this relation is found in connection with human beings, who can be variously described as incomplete, unfulfilled, restless, and so forth, apart from a transforming experience of the divine being. Now in the case of the relation of dependence, we said that the relation is nonreciprocal; that is, God's existence does not depend on the world, but the world's existence does depend on God. Should we say the same thing in the case of need for fulfillment? In this relation also nonreciprocal, or is there some sense in which God may be said to need the world?

To use an analogy first, let us consider the artist. The experience of an artist is certainly incomplete with only the subjective component, the aim and feeling, of creating, without the objective expression, the formed material, which is the outcome of his creative urge. Another analogy might be the benevolent person, who has the potentiality for kindness, for good actions. If he never actualizes this potentiality, never does any good acts, he is incomplete in his benevolence. Yet he is not internally incomplete; rather he needs to exercise his benevolence toward other beings as fitting objects of his benevolent disposition. Thus both the artist and the benevolent person may be said to need their object in a certain sense. In a similar way, can we say that God needs the world as the fitting object of his creative will and his overflowing goodness?

We can arrive at the same conclusion by another consideration. We can hardly suppose, in theistic religion, that God is an indifferent, morally neutral being. We can only suppose, therefore, that he is, analogically, pleased with right decisions and sorrowful over wrong. That is, the adequacy or inadequacy of human choices makes a difference in the divine life. Thus it may be said that the perfection of the world enhances the content of divine happiness. This is not the fulfillment of a need in the ordinary human sense, i.e., the filling up of a lack, the completing of what is incomplete. It is, however, an appropriate fulfillment of the desire of God for perfection in his creatures.

To sum up, God creates not from subjective lack but from abundance of creative love. He is also enhanced in his divine experience by the perfection of his creatures. Thus we may conclude that in a somewhat strained sense God needs the world. But he needs it not subjectively, as we need him, but objectively, as the fitting expression of his creativity and as the fitting fulfillment of his will to perfection. That is, like an artist, he needs his object, the world, not from an inner deprivation but as the fitting outcome of inner abundance. We do not mean, of course, that he needs our particular world. Nor do we mean that the world and its creatures are as a matter of fact perfect.

We shall confine ourselves to mentioning these three relations—the nonreciprocal relation of the dependence of the world, the nonreciprocal relation of God's transcendence and immanence, and the quasi-reciprocal relation of need for fulfillment.

There is one other question on this topic that should be considered even in a brief treatment. That question is whether God should be thought of as a particular being, somewhat analogous to other particular beings, or whether he should be thought of as the power and ground of all particular beings, without being *a* being himself. Is God one being among other beings, or is God being itself? This question has been made prominent by Paul Tillich, who affirms the latter view.[5]

In answering this question we must distinguish between a quantitative and a qualitative answer. If there is no quantitative or numerical sense in which God is one being, *a* being, then his being presumably would be exhausted in that of other beings, and we would be thus tending toward pantheism, even though this might not be the intention. Now pantheism is a possible position, but it is not that of theistic religion. We must assume, therefore, that God is in some numerical sense *one* being, *a* being, with uniqueness of consciousness and purpose. But we must not conclude from this that he is a being like other beings that we encounter in the world of space and time. In this spatio-temporal sense, God is not one being among other beings. It is the nature of his being to be numerically distinct and unique, and yet to permeate and undergird the existence of other beings. In the purely quantitative sense, then, God is a being among other beings but not a being like other beings. Now in the qualitative sense we can say that God is "being itself." That is, when we ask what it means to *be*— what *being* is in the richest and fullest sense—we find the answer in the idea of God. God *is* in a full and perfect way, whereas we exist in an inadequate and imperfect way. God's being is the zenith of what it means to *be*. In this sense he is complete being, being without inadequacy, being itself.

POWER, KNOWLEDGE, AND GOODNESS

Another group of questions appears when we consider the internal nature of God. Probably the three characteristics most commonly discussed in this connection are God's power, knowledge, and goodness. Each of these characteristics gives rise to a special problem. First, is God's power unlimited or limited, infinite or finite? Second, would God's total knowledge of what happens interfere with man's being free in his actions? Third, can the goodness of God be reconciled with the evil in the world? Let us see what suggestions can be made on each of these questions.

POWER. There is a naive belief that the power of God means the capacity to do literally everything, no matter how impossible it may seem, and that the denial of this is irreligious. God must be literally infinite in power, it is said, or else it is not God we are speaking of. We may wonder, however, why sheer power, sheer overwhelming force, should have such a high religious value. But aside from this consideration, the belief is clearly untenable. It would mean, if taken literally, that God could do such things as cause something to exist and not exist at the same time, determine man's every action to the last detail and yet leave him free in every action, and change himself into a supremely evil being. Such a conception of infinite power is irrational and untrue to theistic religion. For God is perfect rationality and perfect goodness, never capable of violating these qualities.

At the other extreme there is a belief, not so naive perhaps, that God is a finite being, co-eternal with the world, and in the position of struggling with hostile forces in the world in order to bring about lawfulness and good.[6] The difficulty with this view is that it sounds too literally human; it does not reach the border area between literal language and analogical language, and consequently gives us a conception of God too similar to the human beings from whence the description comes. God seems to be too puny and human-like to be of high religious worth. Perhaps, then, the problem is misconceived when it is put in terms of a literally infinite or a literally finite God.

There may be a way out of the difficulty if we think of God not in terms of infinite or finite but simply in terms of what his nature is. Any being which is anything definite at all, including God, must have a characteristic nature. This means that God, like other beings, functions within his characteristic nature. We do not understand well this nature of God, but it seems quite plain that he cannot do contradictory things or act against his perfect goodness. There may also be other impossibilities characteristic of God's nature. In short, God acts within his nature, and he cannot act in keeping with natures that are foreign to his. If this is a limitation, it is not the sort often intended by the idea of a finite God; therefore, the term limitation is a very misleading one to use. Charles Hartshorne has distinguished two senses of the word "limitation."[7] One sense —the sense people usually have in mind—is that of a being which is bounded or restricted by a region of space or by some other being in space. The other meaning is that of a being acting according to its own inherent nature, remaining within the capacities of that nature, and not acting according to the nature of some other being which is not its own. God is limited in the second sense, if indeed that can be called a limitation. He is not limited in the first sense. That is, God need not be thought of as being forcefully limited by some other being, or as being restricted by anything outside his own nature.

KNOWLEDGE. The second problem, that concerning God's foreknowledge and man's freedom, may be stated simply. If God has total foreknowledge of human happenings, then is it not the case that there is only one way in which events can occur, namely the way he knows? If they occurred in another way, he would be mistaken, which is absurd. But if there is only one way in which the event can occur, how can there be genuine human freedom to choose between real possibilities? Now theistic religion has generally taken both the omniscience of God and the freedom of man as cardinal beliefs. A way must therefore be found to explain God's knowledge so as to preserve the reality of human freedom.

The usual solution to this problem is to say that the formulation of it in these terms involves an application of human concepts, which do not really apply to God. We ask whether God has foreknowledge of our future, and how we could then be free. But God's knowledge is not fore-knowledge of the future, because he has no future, no present, no past in our sense. God knows everything in a single eternal act, which is outside of time. Time is a human phenomenon; so the formulation of a problem in these terms in reference to God is simply irrelevant.[8]

It is always reassuring to know that there is really no problem when one is expressed. But somehow this problem continues to be meaningful. We know that there was a time in the past when we did not exist; yet God eternally knows what we shall do when, in our time, we do exist. How then can we be free? The question has meaning, and it should be dealt with and not dismissed. Moreover, would there not still be a question here apart from the time factor? That is, how can there be complete knowledge about what is the case and yet real human choices about what is the case? Again, we may wonder how God could have any knowledge of time if real time has no relevance or occurrence in his being. If God is totally removed from the world of time, would he not be lacking in knowledge—knowledge of what time actually is?

But if this solution to our problem does not satisfy us, the other extreme solution is not likely to either. The other extreme is that God has no knowledge of the future. The future is wide open, and God must simply wait to be informed about it through our actual choices and actions.[9] Such a conception gives us the human-like, finite being again whose resemblance to the God of theistic religion is quite remote.

Perhaps we can move toward a solution if we distinguish between what might be called actual knowledge and virtual knowledge. Actual knowledge would be the knowledge which God has of what is necessarily true and of what is actually accomplished already, while virtual knowledge would be the knowledge which God has of what has not yet happened. His virtual knowledge would be compatible with man's freedom, for while God's actual knowledge would be direct and necessary, his virtual knowledge of the future would be the result of his total purview of the possibilities open to man, plus his total knowledge of our characters and tendencies. Thus God knows the future not because it is part of an eternal, necessary truth, but because, in the living flow of time, he knows all possible futures and he also knows the lives of the human beings who choose them. It might be said that we have analogous knowledge in our own small stockpile, as when we know that an honest man who has proved himself will not cheat us. But of course we are sometimes mistaken, whereas God's knowledge, being complete, is not subject to our uncertainty and error. This virtual knowledge which God has of the future is like what, in human form, we should call the knowledge of reliable prediction based on exhaustive knowledge of the past. But again, our own knowledge of the future is smothered over with all sorts of extra assumptions and general ignorance, while God's knowledge would be free from these hindrances and hence perfectly certain. It is logically possible, one might have to say, for us to plunder our future away from God's envisionment of it. But this merely logical possibility is never an actual one, and hence never occurs, because of God's peculiar knowledge of the entire world. We may say that this is a logical conceivability only and not a real one, just as it is a logical but not a real possibility that a thoroughly honest man should cheat us. This kind of knowledge which God has, then, is complete, total, but does not constrain man to do what he does. Such virtual knowledge would, to repeat, refer only to God's knowledge of the future and not to the rest of his knowledge. Also we should not think of God as sitting down and working out inferences as we do. God's knowledge is immediate; but we cannot describe his knowledge except on the analogy of our own. So we must remember again that our language is analogical.

GOODNESS. The third question arises in connection with the goodness of God. The problem is to explain why, if God is good and also capable of removing evil, there is yet so much evil in the world. This is the famous problem of evil. Our discussion of this subject will be limited to a new classification of possible solutions to the problem, followed by a note or two of commentary.

Possible Solutions to the Problem of Evil

I. Nontheistic Solutions
　　1. Good and evil are subjective concepts; the universe itself is neutral. (Spinoza)
　　2. Evil is the ultimate principle of the universe. (Schopenhauer)
　　3. The real problem is to overcome evil, not theorize about it. (Dewey)
II. Theistic Solutions
　A. Solutions Calling for the Correction of Attitudes
　　4. Evil is unreal, resulting from misinterpretation of the world. (Christian Science)
　　5. There is no answer for man; the subject should be abandoned for more fruitful discussions. (Theodore M. Greene)
　B. Solutions Justifying God's Intentions
　　6. Evil is sent by a totally transcendent God whose holy power is beyond questioning. (Job in the end)
　　7. Evil is punishment for sin. (Job's friends)
　　8. Evil is sent as a test of faith. (Satan in the Job story)
　　9. Evil is provided as a contrast so that good will be appreciated more. (a popular lay view)

10. Evil is allowed as an obstacle making for moral growth. (Josiah Royce)
11. Evil serves some unknown purpose. (Aquinas, in part)
C. Solutions Placing the Source of Evil Outside God
12. Evil is the work of a devil. (Luther, C. S. Lewis)
13. Matter is the cause of evil. (Manichaeanism)
14. Evil must be possible if nature is to be governed by laws of orderly process. (F. R. Tennant)
15. Evil results from the fact that created beings must be finite. (William Temple)
16. Moral evil, at least, results from free human choices. (most theologians)
17. Delegated creativity in everything makes novelty possible, and with it, evil. (Whitehead, Berdyaev)

There are other distinctions that could be made to stretch the list even further, but it is at least representative of the more common types of solution that have been proposed. The three nontheistic solutions have been included for contrast and completeness.

The first thing to notice about all the theistic solutions is that they are not necessarily incompatible with one another. Many of them would at most cover only part of the problem. For example, some solutions are more pertinent to what is called moral evil, i.e., evil stemming from human action, and others to what is called natural evil, i.e., evil resulting from natural forces, whereas both types must be accounted for.

Another point to notice is that we should distinguish between philosophical solutions to the problem of evil, and consequential values derived from the fact of evil. For example, even if the assertion that excess evil is inflicted deliberately by God as a test of courage and faith is a questionable philosophical answer, it may nevertheless turn out that a certain evil would have a beneficial function in this regard. Thus we may find insights in many answers that we reject as the best theoretical answers.

In light of these considerations, most thinkers would doubtless find a combination of solutions necessary for the most coherent, comprehensive answer. For example, a reasonable approach might be found through a synthesis of the solutions numbered 10-11 and 14-17.

Finally it should be remarked that from the viewpoint of religion itself the problem of evil is not only a theoretical one but a practical one. Theism believes, through faith, that evil is a misuse of the good, and that the good is therefore more ultimate. It believes that the conditions of the world are such as to make growth into the good possible, despite evil. And it believes in the eventual triumph of good over evil because God's goodness is the pre-eminent fact of the universe. Meanwhile there is no attempt in theism to gloss over the stark fact of evil; at the same time there is that which can be gained from the suffering evil brings, and there is that about faith which finds in evil no permanent defeat.

GOD AS RELIGIOUS OBJECT

There are plausible differences of opinion within theistic religion, and even within a particular religion, on the sorts of questions we have just been considering. Moreover, one does not have to settle all the deeper philosophical questions about God in order to have a religious faith in God. Let us conclude, therefore, with a consideration of God as religious object. What is the religious significance when God is conceived analogically in a personalistic sense, i.e., as conscious, rational, feeling, willing, loving, concerned, judging, redeeming, and so forth?

There is religious significance, first of all, for our over-all outlook on the world. This conception of God means that the world is not underridden by a basic purposelessness and chance. There is a reason for things, and a reason in things. The diversity of the world is comprehended in a unity of purpose, and the catastrophes of the world are related to a unity of goodness. It means that the world has worth, and that each thing in it has worth. Nothing is lost in an oblivion of utter meaninglessness. The world is one in which significant values are realizable and conservable. The interrelation of God and the world intensifies this conception of over-all purpose and value permeating the world; for God is thought of as omnipresent in the world, maximizing his purposive, creating, valuing activity. Thus God is the ultimate guarantor that all is not vanity. This belief is the foundation of the religious attitude characteristic of theism.

Because God is regarded as absolute, purposive, righteous, and real, he is the supreme object of loyalty and devotion in theistic religion. Being infinite in goodness and compassion, he is revered and worshipped for his own sake. This worship is directed to God for his perfection and not to man for his contentment, and this is its religious significance. As a consequence, however, such worship has value significance for the worshipper. For example, God stands as the preventative against idolatry, i.e., making anything finite into an unqualified object of devotion. God also becomes the unifier of human values and the goal of man's activities. Thus the reverence of God for his own sake is inseparable from the reciprocal effects upon man and his values.

God in theistic religion also has significance because he is regarded essentially as moral personality. This means an inescapable relevance of religion to the conduct of life and to ethics, which have a religious base. God represents an uncompromising obligation toward living a good life and acting morally. This is described in religious language as the obligation to do the will of God. Adherents of theistic religion seek out, from the ways in which God reveals himself, what the will of God might be and how they might execute it. The determination of the content of theistic morality is a complex issue; but at least there is agreement that God represents an absolute demand for selfless living, even sacrifice, in opposition to self-glorification and self-indulgence.

God is also a moral judge according to theistic religion. When self-chosen disintegration is experienced, the self feels God's condemnation, not of itself, but of the corrupted features of its life. Divine will judges the self-will of man, and agony of spirit may result in man. But God is also the source of boundless moral power, the lure of goodness, from which the self can replenish its resources. Hence the paradox of theistic morality: when man acts morally, God's power is operative.

This last idea suggests next the consideration of the redeeming activity of God. In theistic religion the redemption of man is regarded as more than his capacity for moral living; it is the return of man from alienation to reconciliation with God. Theists differ in the ways they describe the respective roles of man and God in this process. Nevertheless the common belief is that God is the restorer and man the restored. Thus part of the religious significance of God is his own reconciling work—work that Hezekiah described by saying that "he hath both spoken unto me, and himself hath done it."[10]

The religious significance of God has its practical culmination in the day to day life of the individual, in the common life, as it has been called. The theist seeks to embody the likeness of God's love and justice in the living stream of personal and social relations. He seeks to make daily tasks reverential; he seeks to endue the secular with the sacred. Moments of intense mysticism, if they occur at all, are rare and on the whole are viewed as ultimate more in pantheistic religion than in theistic religion. In the latter, religious experience is not isolated from, the daily life of the individual but is a part of it. His calling, his vocation, is his means of giving expression to that experience. God as religious object gives meaning to vocation.

Through all its other ramifications, the religious meaning of God is the hope of fulfilled existence. This is a complex meaning which is not easy to characterize. As a minimum it means that our commitments and endeavors concerning reconciliation are not illusory or fruitless. The common life is often confused; the patterns of existence do not always make sense; the lurid blends of life's comedies and tragedies do not always yield a beautiful design. Yet one of the undying emotions in man is hope. God is the culminating object of this hope. Felt in a thousand ways, expressed in a thousand symbols, the hope for fulfillment finds its locus in God as its justification. This sort of hope is not a mere projected desire, for it is a consequence of belief in God and not its cause. Not that God is because we hope, but we hope because God is. Nor is it a mere private desire, for hope for self-fulfillment is integral with hope for the world's fulfillment. Thus God brings the world to that completion of destiny in which process we share by our ultimate commitments and endeavors. In a word, the hope and the anticipation of authentic existence are centered, for the theist, in God as both cause and goal, and this is the final meaning of God as religious object.

To summarize these points, God as religious object means that, because of what he is and not because of what we fancy him to be, God is the guarantor against meaninglessness in existence, the supreme object of human devotion, the unifier of human values, the inspirer of moral obligation, the breaker of self-will, the restorer of man to new life, the raiser of the common life from routine to service, the source of hope for fulfilled existence.

To see God in this light is religion's answer to the charge that he is an invented consoler, or, as many students are wont to say, a crutch, to give security to those who are not self-reliant. A crutch is something that is made up after a need is felt for some artificial support. Such a description does not correspond to the God of ethical theism. In the first place, to the great religious persons of history, such as the Hebrew prophets or Luther, God did not bring security in the usual sense but insecurity. God shatters man's complacency and contentment—although a by-product of man's response can be a deeper spiritual security. Secondly, theistic religion testifies that God often comes initially not to sooth man as he is but to judge his life and to demand reversal. God does not merely support man; he also convicts him and requires him to be himself. Finally, the kind of God which could be described as a crutch has always been rejected by thoughtful theists. They have no more interest in holding to such a conception than do the critics. God as religious object involves a far more profound conception than that.

THE TRANSCENDENCE OF THE IMMANENT

WILLIAM TEMPLE

William Temple (1881-1944) studied at Oxford and spent an active and distinguished career as an Anglican priest, bishop, archbishop, and Oxford lecturer, culminating in his appointment as Archbishop of Canterbury. His books include Christus Veritas *(1924),* Personal Religion and the Life of Fellowship *(1926), and* Christianity and Social Order *(1942). Here he presents the classical concept of God as eternal, unchangeable, independent of the world.*

Our argument has led us, provisionally at least, to the conclusion that the explanation of the world is to be sought in a Personal Reality, or to use the historic phrase, in a Living God.

But something remains to be said about the nature of His relation to the World and its Process. He is its explanation in such wise that it is dependent upon Him as He is not dependent upon it. Is it necessary, in order to be this, that He should be something more? We may readily agree that God's relation to the universe is not that of a carpenter to a box which he is making. He is not, in that sense, outside it and acting on it from without. He is Himself its life, its informing and vitalising principle. But in order to be that we have found that He must be Personal, and Personality always transcends its own self-expression. This does not necessarily mean that if we could apprehend the entire universe, spiritual and material, in all its extent of space and time, there would still quite certainly be something in God unexpressed in that panorama. It seems more natural to suppose that the Divine Artist has in His entire creation given complete expression to His mind and nature. But the contention that God is the explanation of the world because He is Person or Spirit does mean that if all else but God were abolished, God would still be Himself, whole and entire, capable of creating another world to take the place of the world which had gone out of existence. If God is Personal, He must express Himself; the Word was in the beginning with God; but His self-expression is not the self expressed; that remains always cause, never effect.

From William Temple, *Nature, Man and God* (London: Macmillan & Co., Ltd., 1934) pp. 265-70. Reprinted by permission of Mrs. Temple, St. Martin's Press Inc., The Macmillan Co. of Canada Ltd. and Macmillan & Co. Ltd.

Are we then to think of God as expressed in, or immanent in, His creation as a poet in his poems? That is an improvement on the analogy of the carpenter and his box. But it leaves God too external to the world. When I read Shakespeare's plays, I find there the thoughts of Shakespeare, not Shakespeare the "thinking living, acting man." When I hear my friend speak, or watch his action, I find there his living self. The principle that explains the process of the world must be no less intimately related to that process than a man to his conduct. In nature we find God; we do not only infer from Nature what God must be like, but when we see Nature truly, we see God self-manifested in and through it.[1] Yet the self-revelation so given is incomplete and inadequate. Personality can only reveal itself in persons. Consequently it is specially in Human Nature—in men and women—that we see God. But Human Nature is a thing self-confessedly defective; whether still struggling to its true self-realisation, or fallen from an "original righteousness," it can give but a fitful and distorted representation of the Personal Reality from whom it springs. If in the midst of the World-Process there should occur an instance of Human Nature free from all blemish or defect, there might be found there the perfect self-expression of God to those who share that Human Nature. So it might come, but not otherwise; and only if it so comes can the great hypothesis itself be secure.

Yet once more, if the Personal God thus indwells the world, and the world is thus rooted in Him, this involves that the process of the world is itself the medium of His personal action.[2] It is commonly assumed by those who use freely the terms Immanence and Transcendence that God as immanent is unchangeably constant, while God as transcendent possesses a reserve of resource whereby He can from time to time modify the constant course sustained by His immanent action. This seems to be a mere reflection of the wholly un-philosophic dichotomy of events into normal and miraculous. The naïve religious view is that God made the world and imposed laws upon it, which it invariably observes unless He intervenes to modify the operation of His own laws. From this naïve view springs the suggestion that it would better comport with the infinite Majesty of God that He should from the outset impose such laws as would never stand in need of modification. But if, as we have seen ground for holding, the World-Process is itself the medium of God's personal action, the whole situation is altered. There is nothing majestic about invariable constancy of personal action, which

---

[1] The parables of Christ strongly suggest such a view of the relation of Nature to God.

[2] "The world of nature cannot be understood by an intelligent theist otherwise than as the ever present working of a divine power."—A. S. Pringle-Pattison, *The Balfour Lectures on Realism*, 1933, p. 257.

remains unaltered whether the circumstances are the same or not; rather should it be called mulish. Constancy of purpose is a noble characteristic, but it shows itself, not in unalterable uniformity of conduct, but in perpetual self-adaptation, with an infinite delicacy of graduation, to different circumstances, so that, however these may vary, the one unchanging purpose is always served.

If we adopt this view, we shall have also to hold that no Law of Nature as discovered by physical science is ultimate. It is a general statement of that course of conduct in Nature which is sustained by the purposive action of God so long and so far as it will serve His purpose. No doubt it is true that the same cause will always produce the same effect in the same circumstances. Our contention is that an element in every actual cause, and indeed the determinant element, is the active purpose of God fulfilling itself with that perfect constancy which calls for an infinite graduation of adjustments in the process. Where any adjustment is so considerable as to attract notice it is called a miracle; but it is not a specimen of a special class, it is an illustration of the general character of the World-Process.

At the present time, as was remarked in the last lecture,[3] leading students of physical science are disputing about the question whether there is, for the purposes of their science, indeterminacy in the conduct of atoms; is the movement of *Quanta* physically indeterminate? Sir Arthur Eddington and Sir James Jeans say, Yes; Einstein, Planck, and Lord Rutherford say, No. But the theistic philosopher is not greatly interested, for in either case he will maintain that in the last resort there is no indeterminacy; in either case the universal determinant is the purpose of God.

Because He is the all-comprehending Mind, the course which He sustains in Nature is orderly; that it should be in any way capricious would imply such characteristics in God as are manifest defects or limitations when they appear in men. When there is no sufficient reason for variation, none will appear. And for the vastly greater part of Nature's course there is, so far as we can tell, no reason at all for variation, and much reason for uniformity. All purpose in finite creatures—and therefore all moral purpose—depends on the reliability of nature. We could make no plans if the rising of the sun to-morrow were not reasonably certain, or if there were serious risk of failure in the custom of gravitation. Moreover, it is good for us to be subject to the discipline of accident, so that even those occasions when we are tempted to think that Almighty Love must vary the course of nature to avert suffering from ourselves or our friends, are still illustrations of our ruling principle that the uniformity of nature is grounded in the purpose of God. But when

---

[3] See pp. 228-229 [in *Nature, Man and God*].

that purpose would be itself defeated by some anticipated occurrence, that occurrence is in fact impossible—as Christ suggested when he met the alarm of His disciples with the implication that the boat which carried the hope of the world could not sink.[4]

This is not popular doctrine in an age for which the metaphysics of every question is overshadowed by the physics, as in an earlier period the physics was by the metaphysics. Yet I am very sure that the conception of the Divine Personality is only tenable if it is taken in bitter earnest. And then it leads us to the conviction that the immanent principle of the World Process is a purposive Mind, guiding the movement of electrons and of galaxies by the requirements of its unchanging purpose, so that for the most part their course is constant, but the cause of their constancy is itself the cause of their variation when that serves the one purpose best.

Yet that which is found in the constancy and the adjustments alike—the immanent and self-adapting Spirit—is always the expression of the truly Personal Being whose self is thus manifested in successive partial disclosures. The immanent activity varies; but the transcendent Being is eternally self-subsistent and self-identical. God in the world acts now this way and now that as He carries to accomplishment His unchanging purpose. But God Himself, the root and ground of that unchanging purpose, eternally is. He is no more unchanging than He is changeable; for both of these express persistence through time. But God does not persist through time, for time itself is grounded in Him. He creates the world and guides it from phase to phase by His sustaining spirit active in and through it. But if He be no more than that sustaining spirit, we are back at the process which as a whole explains its parts but also as a whole is incapable of explanation. There is no need to fall back into that abyss if we are true to the principle of Personality. For a person is always somebody, so to speak, on his own account, over and above his activities. So too God is active in the world, and its process is His activity. Yet He is more than this; He is creator and therefore transcendent. Because He is, and is creative, He must create; therefore the universe is necessary to Him in the sense that He can only be Himself by creating it. But He is necessary to it, because it only exists by His fiat. God and the world are not correlative terms. God as immanent is correlative with the world; but that is not the whole nature of God. The more we study the activity of God immanent, the more we become aware of God transcendent. The Truth that strikes awe in the scientist is awful because it is His thought; the Beauty that holds spell-bound the artist is potent because it

---

[4] This is not, I think, an unfair paraphrase of Mark iv. 37. The astonishment of the disciples is that the storm ceased at His bidding—a minor matter. His astonishment was that they had any anxiety.

is His glory; the Goodness that pilots us to the assured apprehension of Reality can do this because it is His character; and the freedom whereby man is lifted above all other nature, even to the possibility of defying it, is fellowship with Him. "Heaven and earth are full of His glory"; but He is more and other than all that is in earth and heaven.

GOD AS SUPREME, YET INDEBTED TO ALL

CHARLES HARTSHORNE

Charles Hartshorne (1897–) studied at Harvard and later in Germany. He has taught philosophy at Harvard, the University of Chicago, and more recently at Emory University, and is considered a leading Whiteheadian philosopher. He is a co-editor of Philosophers Speak of God *(1953), and the author of* Man's Vision of God *(1941),* The Logic of Perfection *(1962), and other books. In the following selection he opposes the classical concept of God with his concept of God as temporal, changing in some respects, and relative to the world.*

RELIGIOUS MEANING OF ABSOLUTE

Why is it religiously significant that God be supposed absolute? The reason is at least suggested by the consideration that absoluteness is requisite for complete reliability. What is relative to conditions may fail us if the conditions happen to be unfavorable. Hence if there is to be anything that *cannot* fail, it must be nonrelative, absolute, in those respects to which "reliability" and "failure" have reference. But it is often not noted that this need not be every respect or aspect from which God's nature can be regarded. For there may be qualities in God whose relativity or variability would be neutral to his reliability. To say of a man that (as human affairs go) his reliability is established refers not to every quality of the man, but only to certain principles exhibited in his otherwise highly variable behavior. We do not mean that if something comes close to his eye he will not blink, or that if he is given bad-tasting food he will enjoy it as much as better fare. We mean that his fixed intention to act according to the requirements of the general welfare will not waver, and that his wisdom and skill in carrying out this aim will be con-

From Charles Hartshorne, *The Divine Relativity* (New Haven: Yale University press, 1948), pp. 22-34. Reprinted by permission.

stant. But in all this there is not only no implication that conditions will not have effect upon the man, but the very plain implication that they will have plenty of effect. Skill in one set of circumstances means one form of behavior, in another set another form, and the same is true of the intention to serve the general good. Of course, one may argue that complete fixity of good intention and complete constancy of skill imply every other sort of fixity as well. But this has never yet been definitely shown by careful, explicit reasoning, and anything less is inappropriate in as difficult a subject as we are dealing with. General hunches will not do.

A typically invalid argument in this connection is that unless God surveys at once the whole of time and thus is independent of change, he cannot be relied upon to arrange all events with due regard to their relations to all that has gone before and all that is to come after. This argument either rests on an equivocation or it destroys all religious meaning for the divine reliability. For, if it is meant in any clear sense, it implies that every event has been selected by deity as an element in the best of all possible worlds, the ideal total pattern of all time and all existence. But this ideal pattern includes all acts of sin and the most hideous suffering and catastrophe, all the tragedies of life. And what then becomes of the ideas of human responsibility and choice, and of the notion that some deeds ought not to have taken place? These are only the beginning of the absurdities into which the view thrusts us. To mitigate these absurdities theologians introduce various more or less subtle equivocations. Would they not do better to take a fresh start (as indeed many have done) and admit that we have no good religious reason for positing the notion of providence as an absolute contriving of all events according to a completely detailed plan embracing all time? The religious value of such a notion is more negative than positive. It is the mother of no end of chicanery (see the book of Job for some examples), of much deep feeling of injustice (the poor unfortunate being assured that God has deliberately contrived everything as exactly the best way events could transpire), and of philosophical quagmires of paradox and unmeaning verbiage. The properly constituted man does not want to "rely" upon God to arrange all things, including our decisions, in accordance with a plan of all events which fixes every least detail with reference to every other that ever has happened or ever "is to" happen. How many atheists must have been needlessly produced by insistence upon this arbitrary notion, which after all is invariably softened by qualifications surreptitiously introduced *ad hoc* when certain problems are stressed! We shall see later that the really usable meaning of divine reliability is quite different and is entirely compatible with a profound relativity of God to conditions and to change. For the present, I suggest that all we can assert to have obvious religious value is the faith that God is to be relied upon to do for the world all that ought to be done for it, and with as much survey of the future as there ought to be or as is ideally desirable, leaving for the members of the world community to do for themselves and each other all that they ought to be left to do. We cannot assume that what ought to be done for the world by deity is everything that ought to de done at all, leaving the creatures with nothing to do for themselves and for each other. Nor can we assume that the ideal survey of what for us at least constitutes the future is one which fully defines it in every detail, leaving no open alternatives of possibility. So far from being self-evidently of religious value, these assumptions, viewed in the light of history, seem clearly of extreme disvalue. Yet they are often either asserted, or not unequivocally denied or avoided, in the intemperate insistence upon the total absoluteness of deity.

GOD AS SOCIAL

We have also to remember that if there is religious value in the absoluteness of God, as requisite for his reliability, there is equally manifest religious value in another trait which seems unequivocally to imply relativity rather than absoluteness. This is the social or personal nature of God. What is a person if not a being qualified and conditioned by social relations, relations to other persons? And what is God if not the supreme case of personality? Those who deny this have yet to succeed in distinguishing their position from atheism, as Hume pointedly noted. Either God really does love all beings, that is, is related to them by a sympathetic union surpassing any human sympathy, or religion seems a vast fraud. The common query Can the Absolute or Perfect Being be personal or social? should really run In what sense, if any, can a social being be absolute or perfect? For God is conceived socially before he is conceived absolutely or as perfect. God is the highest ruler, judge, benefactor; he knows, loves, and assists man; he has made the world with the design of sharing his bliss with lesser beings. The world is a vast society governed by laws instituted by the divine monarch—the supreme personal power to whom all other persons are subject. These are all, more or less clearly, social conceptions —if you like, metaphors (though aimed, as we shall see, at a literal, intuited meaning) drawn from the social life of man. They constitute the universal, popular meaning of "God," in relation to which descriptions such as "absolute," "perfect," "immutable," "impassive," "simple," and the like, are technical refinements aimed at logical precision. They seek to define the somewhat vague ideas of *highest* ruler, *supreme* power, or *author of all*, himself without author or origin. "Immutable," for example, is an attempted definition of the superiority of deity with respect to death and degeneration, and also with respect to vacillation of will due to fear, or other weakness. Earthly rulers are all brought low by death; and their promises and protection and execution of justice must always be discounted somewhat in anticipation of the effect upon them of changing circumstances and the development of their own motives, the growth of good and evil in their own hearts. God is not under sentence of death, cannot decay; and his convenant abides, nor is his wisdom ever clouded by storms of blind passion, the effects of strong drink or of disease.

The future of theology depends, I suggest, above all upon the answer to this question: can technically precise terms be found which express the supremacy of God, among social beings, without contradicting his social character? To say, on the one hand, that God is love, to continue to use popular religious terms like Lord, divine will, obedience to God, and on the other to speak of an absolute, infinite, immutable, simple, impassive deity, is either a gigantic hoax of priestcraft, or it is done with the belief that the social connotations of the popular language are ultimately in harmony with these descriptions. Merely to speak of the "mysteriousness" of God is not sufficient. If he escapes all the resources of our language and analysis, why be so insistent upon the obviously quite human concepts, absolute, infinite, perfect, immutable? These too are our conceptions, our terms, fragments of the English or Latin languages. Perhaps after all it is not correct to say God is absolute. How shall we know, if the subject is utterly mysterious and beyond our powers?

THE SOCIAL NATURE OF EXISTENCE

The question Can a supreme being be social? is important not merely because men generally have meant by God a supreme social being. There are grounds for thinking that the popular religious emphasis is philosophically sound, that a supreme being must, for rational reasons, be conceived socially. Human nature is the supreme instance of nature in general, as known to us (apart from the "nature" of God himself), and moreover, it is the instance which in some respects at least is much more certainly and intimately known to us than any other. Human nature is social through and through. All our thought is some sort of conversation or dialogue or social transaction; when we have no one else to converse with, we converse, silently or even aloud, with ourselves. We love and hate and sympathize, not only in relation to others but in relation to our own past, future, or potential selves. Not only human beings stimulate such response, but animals, plants, mountains, ships, the moon, colors, sounds (think of groaning brakes, growling thunder, merry sunshine). One may say simply, all classes of concrete objects at least can be social objects for man. What would poetry be without personification, overt or implicit; what would art be without empathy, which is social response of a kind?

Now, further, not simply man, but all life whatsoever, has social structure. All organisms on the multicellular level are associations of cells. There is scarcely a line between societies and individuals formed by societies which reach a sufficient grade of integration. Cells themselves are associations of similar molecules and atoms. It becomes a question of how broadly one wishes to use terms where one says that the social begins, if indeed it ever begins, in the ascending scale of emergence. And the higher one goes in the scale the more obviously do the social aspects assume a primary role. Does this point to the conclusion that the supreme being is not social at all?

There are even more ultimate considerations. Logical analysis shows, according to such high authorities as Peirce and Whitehead, that the "social" in its most general sense is definable as the synthesis of all the universal categories. It is the union of absolute and relative, independent and dependent, freedom and order, individual and universal, quality and structure, and so on. A nonsocial conception is only arrived at by reducing some category to the zero case. Thus a mere "machine" is what a society would become if the element of routine interdependence should completely suppress the aspect of individual initiative or originality, or if quality (feeling) should vanish, leaving mere structure. And a wholly absolute and hence nonsocial deity is one to which the category of relation—without reference to which even "absolute" has no meaning—is denied application. Thus mechanism, materialism, and absolutism can all be viewed as special cases of the same error, the arbitrary reduction of one or more aspects of sociality to zero. A category so completely ultimate for thought and life as relation (or as felt quality) can, it seems, be assigned null value only in the case of "nonentity." Those who spoke of the wholly absolute deity as the great void perhaps spoke a little more truly than they intended.

The purpose of the foregoing discussion—whose implications could be fully set forth only in a treatise on metaphysics—is not to prove that all things, and therefore even God, must or can be conceived as social in nature; but only to show that the common antithesis between the personal or social deity of religion, and the impersonal or nonsocial supreme being of philosophy, is to be viewed with suspicion. Some of the greatest philosophies, from Plato to Whitehead, have held, with varying degrees of explicitness and consistency, that the social structure is the ultimate structure of all existence; and never has this idea been so explicitly and competently defended as during the last hundred years. Whitehead's supreme conception, for example, is that of a society of actual occasions, related one to another by the sympathetic bond of "feeling of feeling." Peirce's doctrine of agapism was similar. So was Fechner's "daylight view," And Fechner and Whitehead—in some passages, also Peirce—and many other recent thinkers, have held that deity is the supreme case of the social principle, rather than an exception to it.

SOCIAL DEITY AND CREATION

It may be thought that a socially conceived God could not be the creator. Can a member of a society create that society? Here we must remember the theological principle of "eminence." God, if social, is eminently or supremely so. On the other hand, that which in the eminent form is called divine creation, in a milder or ordinary form must be exhibited by lesser beings such as man. Man certainly is social. If then ordinary sociality is ordinarily creative, eminent sociality will be eminently creative, divinely creative. And ordinary sociality is, in a humble sense, creative. A man contributes creatively to the concrete actuality of his friends and enemies, and they to his. We *make* each other what we are, in greater or less degree.

The more important members of a society contribute more largely and vitally to the actuality of other members. The supreme member of a society would contribute most vitally and largely to the actuality of all. However, we shall be told, all this is not really "creation," since it presupposes a matter and at most adds a new form. In the first place, no one has proved or can possibly prove (against Peirce, Whitehead, et al.) that there is any "matter," apart from social terms and relations. Electrons and protons are, for all that anyone knows, simply the lowest actual levels of social existence. It may well be that a human mind is not sufficiently important in the world to call an electron into being where none was before. However, we do, by our thoughts and feelings, influence the formation of nerve cells (in the first years of life), and even more, of molecules in the nerves. This is not creation in the eminent sense, but it differs from this only as we might expect the ordinary to differ from the eminent. And the influence of our thought and feeling upon nerve cells and molecules is either a blind mystery, or it is a social influence, as Peirce and Whitehead, and before them (less clearly) Leibnitz, have pointed out.

That the human creator always has a given concrete actuality to work with does not of itself establish a difference between him and God, unless it be admitted as made out that there was a first moment of creation. For if not, then God, too, creates each stage of the world as successor to a preceding phase. Only a dubious interpretation of an obscure parable, the book of Genesis, stands between us and this view. What does distinguish God is that the preceding phase was itself created by God, so that he, unlike us, is never confronted by a world whose coming to be antedates his own entire existence. There is no presupposed "stuff" alien to

God's creative work; but rather everything that influences God has already been influenced by him, whereas we are influenced by events of the past with which we had nothing to do. This is one of the many ways in which eminence is to be preserved, without falling into the negations of classical theology.

ANALOGICAL CONCEPTS
AND METAPHYSICAL UNIQUENESS

It would be a misunderstanding of the social doctrine to accuse it of denying the radical difference between God and nondivine beings. Whitehead (and something similar might be said of Fechner) is so anxious that this difference should not be slurred over that he never, save once in conversation, has described God as a "society of occasions" (with "personal order") because, although that is what, in his system, God must be, it is equally clear that *this* society has a metaphysically unique status and character. By a metaphysically unique status and character I mean one whose distinctiveness can be defined through purely universal categories. It is impossible to define what is unique about my youngest brother in terms of categories alone. And if deity were conceived merely as very superior to man, this description might, for all we could know, apply to myriads of individuals somewhere in the universe. Besides, the description contains a nonmetaphysical term, man. But according to the view presented in this book, a purely metaphysical description applicable only to the one individual, God, is possible. Thus God is the *one individual conceivable a priori.* It is in this sense that concepts applied to him are analogical rather than simply univocal, in comparison to their other applications. For in all other cases, individual otherness is a mere specificity under more general characteristics—thus, my (not wholly definable) nuance of wisdom rather than yours. But in the case of deity, the most general conceptions, without anything more specific, suffice to "individuate" (though not, as we shall see, to particularize or concretize). The old dualities of creating and created, necessary and contingent, perfect and imperfect, expressed this metaphysical or a priori otherness of God. But, as generally stated, they did so in self-contradictory fashion. And it was not seen that, with respect to the category of relation, for example, a metaphysically unique status is definable in another way than through the simple denial of relativity. If the negative "nonrelatedness" is purely categorical, the positive "all-relatedness" is equally so. And we shall find that there is no logical reason why both may not apply to diverse aspects of deity. Then the metaphysical uniqueness would be a double one: no other being, in *any* aspect, could be either wholly relative or wholly nonrelative. Thus, while all beings have some measure of "absoluteness" or independence of relationships and some measure of "relativity," God, and only God, is in one aspect of his being strictly or maximally absolute, and in another aspect no less strictly or maximally relative. So both "relative" and "nonrelative" are analogical, not univocal, in application to deity. And since "social" is, in this reference, equivalent to the synthesis of independent and dependent, social also is analogical in its theological application. Accordingly, our doctrine does not "humanize" or anthropomorphize deity, but preserves a distinction that is completely metaphysical between deity and all else.

The distinction may be expressed under any category. For example, God is the only unconditionally "necessary" existent. What is unconditionally necessary in God, however, is not all of God, though it is unique to him. And in another aspect, God is not only possessed of accidents, but he is the sole being who possesses or could possibly possess all actual accidental being as his own actuality. Other beings are in no aspect strictly necessary, and in no aspect maximally accidental, but always and in all aspects something middling under both categories. In this middling character lies their "imperfection." The mediocre way in which they illustrate categories like possibility, necessity, relativity, independence, is their real otherness to the divine, not the mere fact that they do illustrate this or that category. Tradition put it otherwise, thus: "God is not subject to the category of relation, or of potentiality, or of passivity, etc."

To be sure, there are some apparent qualifications to be made of this historical account. There was said to be relation among the persons of the Trinity; and also God could be said to have "extrinsic potentiality," since his existence is the possibility of the world's existence. But these qualifications amount to little. "Relation" here is not the category of relativity in the basic or primary sense which is in question in this book. For that sense is the ability of a thing to express in its own nature those other things which, among alternatively possible or contingent things, happen to exist. (Persons of the Trinity, of course, are noncontingent.) This meaning of relation is, as we shall see, the fundamental one. Without it there could be no knowledge of what contingent things actually exist, and what possibilities of existence are unactualized. Moreover, necessity is a negative or at least an abstract conception. It may be defined as that whose nonexistence is not possible; or as that which, being common to all possibility (its least common denominator, or abstract identity), has no possible alternative. On the other hand, Peirce[1] has shown that the definition of the possible as the nonnecessary presupposes another and positive meaning, that of spontaneous variety, particularity. Extrinsic potentiality is also, like relation between exclusively necessary factors, a derivative or negative form

---

[1] See, in *Collected Papers*, especially Vols. I and VI, discussions of firstness, possibility, chance, variety, spontaneity.

of its category. Plato extrinsically "produced" Leibnitz, in that the actual coming to be of Leibnitz did not change or enrich the actuality of Plato. He who causes others to reach the promised land but himself remains outside—as the historical Plato remained outside the philosophy of Leibnitz (in the sense that he did not know or enjoy it)—exercises extrinsic potency, potency of producing but not of being. Alternative possible effects of such an agent cannot be regarded as deliberate deeds on his part. To decide this, when deciding that was possible, is to be in one state of decision when another was possible. In so far as Plato consciously chose the kind of successors he was to have, just so far his potency was intrinsic as well as extrinsic. And he was a human being, able to produce a human being's characteristic effects, only because he did exercise intrinsic potency. Conscious freedom is decision among alternative possibilities of intrinsic being. Plato chose the sort of influence he was to have by choosing what he was himself to be. This is all that can be meant by conscious choice. It may be that God has only to say, "Let there be light," and there is light. But God's saying "Let there be light" is a state of his being, and a nonnecessary state, for otherwise either we have a vicious regress, the "Let there be light" becoming something outside himself, so that he must have said Let such a saying be; or else the saying is his very essence, and then he could not possibly have failed to say "Let there be light," and the saying can have been no decision, no free act at all.

SUGGESTED BOOKS

Barth, Karl, *The Humanity of God*, trans. Thomas Wieser and John N. Thomas. Richmond, Va.: John Knox Press, 1960. Three recent essays developing Barth's conception of the immanence of God.

Brightman, Edgar S., *The Problem of God*. Nashville, Tenn.: Abingdon Press, 1930. A philosophical analysis by a leading personalist sympathetic to the idea of a finite God.

Collins, James, *God and Modern Philosophy*. Chicago: Henry Regnery Company, 1959. A study of recent conceptions of God by a prominent Catholic philosopher.

Ferré, Nels F. S., *The Christian Understanding of God*. New York: Harper & Row, Publishers, 1951. An interpretation which attempts to reflect faithfully both the Christian doctrine of transcendence and the emphasis on immanence made in process philosophy.

————, *Evil and the Christian Faith*. New York: Harper & Row, Publishers, 1947. An interpretation of the problem of evil by a Christian theologian who sees suffering as a clue to the meaning of life but does not claim a complete solution by reason alone.

Hartshorne, Charles and William L. Reese, eds., *Philosophers Speak of God*. Chicago: University of Chicago Press, 1953. An anthology illustrating the chief philosophical conceptions of deity, plus an evaluation by the editors based on their own classification of possible views.

Horton, Walter M., *God*. New York: Association Press, 1937. A little book designed to state in simple language the basic religious meaning of God.

Sontag, Frederick, *Divine Perfection*. New York: Harper & Row, Publishers, 1962. Historical analyses of "possible ideas of God" and an attempt at a "contemporary constructive effort."

VIII · THE RELIGIOUS NATURE OF MAN

Of all the human interests that have a possibility of uniting mankind in common endeavors, the interest in man himself is one of the greatest. From Easterner and Westerner, scientist and artist, theist and agnostic, and from many other quarters, interpretations pour. We are all human and in search of ourselves. Because of this breadth of interest, the quantity of insights about man's nature is perhaps larger than in the case of any other topic. Most of these interpretations are helpful and relevant in some respect, and if they err it is usually because of what they leave out rather than what they affirm. But the massive accumulation of insights also contains a danger. We may easily mistake the shallow for the deep, the accidental for the essential; we may lose man in voluminosity. There seems to be considerable merit, therefore, in attempting to rescue in concise form a portrait of man as a distinctive spiritual being. What is it that makes man significant from a religious point of view?

In this portrait we shall not be concerned with economic, sociological, psychological, and other interpretations of man that are relevant at other levels of significance. We shall be concerned with the nature of man in the light of the reality and nature of God. What, in a word, is the religious nature of man? This restriction does not mean that other aspects of man's being are not related to his religious significance. It means rather that without certain basic characteristics he would be on the plane of lesser, nonreligious beings where other modes of interpretation are more adequate. We seek to identify some of these characteristics.

PERSONALITY AND CREATURELINESS

Man is a personal being. This statement can be a cliché. Certainly it is a statement which often has little meaning. Yet if all of its import could be understood, it would give us the clues to the distinctiveness of man, and hence to the possibility of his being truly religious.

Being personal means that man has a conscious life. That is, he not only receives thousands of impressions, but he is cognizant of them and he reflects upon them. He brings them together, looks at their meaning, and sorts them out, selecting and rejecting, musing and planning. Again, he not only acts upon impulse; he also examines and modifies the impulses he acts upon. Being personal also means that man has reason, both theoretical and practical. It means that he can imagine and create things from the materials presented to him. It means that he has inner feelings, whether profound or superficial, kindly or cruel, tender or tough. It means also that he can enter into intersubjective experiences with other persons at a level whose meaning cannot be reduced to physical relationships. The conscious intimacy of intersubjective experience defies explanation by physical, economic, or other categories.

But all these things—conscious awareness, reflection, reasoning, imagining, feeling, intersubjective experience—do not touch the heart of what it means to be personal. Beyond all these, man has the capacity to meditate, deliberate, and choose. He is a decision-making creature. It is here that we penetrate most fully the depths of man's personality. By his own deliberate choice he can incline himself toward the fair or the foul, the noble or the base, God or mammon. And in this decision-making man discovers himself, that he has a self, or rather that he is a self. There is a personal center who deliberates, decides, chooses. Thus being personal means, amid many other things, being a self who deliberates and chooses its way through life.

Just as vividly felt as are these creative qualities of personality is another aspect of human life, attested to strongly by theistic religion, not to say common human feelings. Man knows that he did not give to himself his potentialities. He simply found himself possessing them. That is, he operates within prescribed limits which he did not himself determine. He is constantly being jarred into the realization that his life is circumscribed in certain ways, inscrutable to him perhaps, but none the less definite. He might like at times to have arranged things otherwise; but he does not arrange these things. In short, he has not only the power of human consciousness but the limits of it. He is not only the fact of personality but, in religious terms, the gift of personality. He is not only a creator; he is also a creature.

Being creaturely means that man is a recipient. He is placed in existence by God with personality and potentiality. What he gives is given from what he has originally received. In addition to this meaning of receiving, man is a social being who needs to receive social goods and services for the continuance of life in society. He also needs to receive the bounties of the nonhuman world, and in one sense these are prior since they are fundamental to survival. No one is self-sufficient at the physical and social planes for the maintenance of life, to say nothing of a full and varied life. Such receiving may arouse feelings of hostility, but they may also call out our feelings of appreciation and opportunity.

In realizing that he is a recipient, man realizes that he is dependent. Creatureliness means dependence. In addition to the dependence for our very existence, man is dependent upon God for continued sustenance and for salvation. Theistic religion sees man as ultimately dependent in all these ways upon the initiating activity and concern of God, without whom he would have neither existence nor continuing life nor hope of fulfillment.[1] Man does not survive by his own efforts but by divine power; he is not saved by himself but by divine love. Recognition of such dependence does not destroy the significance or the efficacy of human endeavor. It is rather an acknowledgment of the originating source of power for such endeavor.

These elements of creatureliness remind us of still another. Man has a certain position in the order of the world and an obligation to preserve it with dignity. He cannot act beyond his potential, and he must not fall below it. "Man is neither angel nor brute," says Pascal, "and the unfortunate thing is that he who would act the angel acts the brute."[2] Thus man is required to recognize, respect, and re-set when broken the due proportionateness which ideally exists between himself and other beings. In what ways and by what vocation man affirms his place in the world of creatures are not determined for him. But the fact of having a station in the scheme of things is a determined part of creatureliness, a fact to be accepted and an obligation to be fulfilled. Man has a place, but he must also find his place, in the universe. He cannot be more than a man, and he dare not be less than a man.

The idea that man is a personal creature is sometimes expressed by saying that he is the *imago dei*, the image of God. This doctrine should not be thought of as meaning that man alone bears any relation to God and that other, nonhuman beings do not. For if all things have a common origin in the source of all beings, then they all retain traces of that origin and reflect it in some way. Nevertheless, there seem to be unique reasons why man is singled out for special consideration as an *imago dei*. One of these reasons is that the most distinctive attributes of God are thought of as best describable through personal categories rather than through categories drawn from the nonhuman realm. Man is the image of God, in one sense, in that his consciousness, reason, will, and feeling are like the divine nature to some degree, and these characteristics are most fundamental in both instances. To be sure, we think of God through these personal categories because we have first experienced them in ourselves, but if both man and God are personal, we could hardly expect anything else. So the conception of God cannot be taken simply as a projection of human qualities. Having personal characteristics, man images God in another way, a more fundamental way from the religious point of view. This is through the affinity of the original goodness of man with that of the divine nature. Other beings reflect the perfection of God in their own way. But man can do so through right purposes, right thinking, right sympathies, right faith, and can thus mirror the divine nature more completely. Everyone knows that man does not show a great deal of this reflection in his present state. But theistic religion believes that this original goodness, with which we were created, is still the most fundamental part of us. No matter how much we have distorted it, it is still in us potentially, and it is somehow related to an original ideal for us in the mind of God. Because of this link with the goodness of God, which is somehow still in man despite the distortions, he has been given the presumptuous title of *imago dei*.

FREEDOM AND SINFULNESS

Man is a free being. It was inevitable that this be so if he were to be the kind of personality we have been portraying, for only a free being could mirror the true nature of God and worship him completely. This is something of a paradox, i.e., to speak of the inevitability of freedom. Yet it points to a basic fact of man's life as he experiences it. Man has been determined to be free. His destiny is freedom. He can act freely; but he *must act*. This paradox sets the whole tone of our life. I can or I cannot. Shall I or shall I not?

The inevitability of freedom shows man the heights of loyalty which are open to him as a human being, and also the depths of degradation to which he might descend. It shows him that he is inscribed within boundaries, but yet that he can rotate within those boundaries and even in some cases choose the boundaries he will acknowledge. It shows him that he is a conditioned being, but also that he is obligated, responsible, accountable. It shows him that he can do something about the oppressions in human life, or else sit idly by. But what it shows him above all is that if he tries to escape from his freedom, he loses his very self, for to be a self is to be free.[3]

Man is aware of his freedom in intimate, moment by moment experiences of decision, rather than as the object of a proof. Thus freedom is more certain as a moral and religious fact than as a metaphysical postulate. Yet man is concerned with the idea of freedom as well as with the fact of freedom. And so, in his philosophical mood, he likes to define the meaning of freedom, debate the reality of freedom, and try to understand how and where freedom operates. But these are explanations and explorations of the living fact. Of more interest for religious interpretation is the question of why man was created to be free. And the answer is, as suggested above, that a creature who worships God and moves toward his destiny through free, deliberate choice is a more capable worshipper and a more appreciative valuer than is an already fixed and formulated image. In this case the dust of the earth that can blow this way or that is more resplendent than an immovable model of clay.

The consideration of the purpose for freedom leads to a further paradox, namely, that according to theistic religion the greatest freedom is found when man gives himself up to the divine will.[4] This does not mean that man's basic freedom is abandoned. It only means that a certain sort of lower-level, directionless freedom is given up so that a higher, sustaining freedom may be found through devotion to that being in relation to whom perfect service is perfect freedom.

The freedom of man, in conjunction with his reflective consciousness, points to another characteristic of the religious nature of man, one that results from his freedom, namely, the capacity for self-transcendence.[5] This capacity is suggested in such common expressions as that which advises one to "rise above the situation." Rising above the situation is something man can do as a human being and something he cannot do as an animal being. It is an act of the spirit by which he can catapult himself beyond the present situation. He is not confined to what he has been, or to what he is now; he can become something more. The time he lives in, the space he fills, the achievements he has accomplished, the reverses he has encountered, the good and ill of present existence—all these can be superseded by new endeavor or contemplation. Even when conditions cannot be radically transformed, he can rise above them in newer perspectives; he can see them in a new light.

One consequence of the capacity for self-transcendence seems to be that man must grow if he is to be fully human. If he does not continue to transcend himself, he seems to relapse, decline, deteriorate. There appears to be no happy, static medium. So perhaps we can say that to be human is to transcend oneself as long as time permits. There seem to be no foreseeable limits in the movement of life as the self overcomes obstacles, supersedes achievements, becomes bored by contentment, and moves on again. Thus man can uncover more and more of the potentials in his selfhood and bring these into realization. The religious significance of this capacity for self-transcendence is that man can move toward more and more ultimate dimensions of commitment and concern, i.e., he can grow in spiritual life, provided his initial faith, which is the heart of religion, has channeled him in the right direction.

Of course, man as we know him does not generally transcend himself in ways that bring him closer to his divine source or conduce to the realization of his true self. He willfully steers himself away from this direction. In theological language this is saying that man is subject to sin. There appears to be more sympathy today than there was a short time ago for the use of this term. Certainly there is more recognition in modern theology of the dark reality to which the term sin points. The human disposition which is called sinfulness has generally been viewed by theistic religion as radical in character and as requiring radical remedy.

The idea of sin should not be defined in a way that absolves man of the responsibility for it, nor in a way that makes man the sole source of evil in the world. Thus the notion of original sin, when it means an inheritance from the past, is strangely irrelevant if it involves the subtle escape that sin is somehow something which is forced upon us and not something of our own choosing. Far more penetrating is Kierkegaard's explanation that sin is man's unwillingness to be himself before God.[6] There is no escape from the fact that it is I who reject the good, I who choose the wrong, I who hate my neighbor, I who perjure myself, I who separate myself from the power making for righteousness. Man willfully does that which he would not do.

At the same time we must recognize that sometimes the reason why man does not do as he ought lies beyond his own direct control. Evil sometimes occurs through us whether we will it or not. In such cases we may be overriden by the variable elements in nonhuman nature, or by the past choices of our society which visits its iniquity upon later generations. In either case the point is that man can be victimized as well as vile. Sin is not regarded by theistic religion as a total explanation of evil. Moreover, callous and cruel as sin can be, there is still the ideal self that would do otherwise. So even while man willfully does what he ought not to do, there is still that within him which would do otherwise.

Sinfulness, then, is man's self-chosen separation from God. And here is another paradox. Man wants to know himself, to do what he ought, to be himself before God; but he is prevented in this. Yet very often the obstacle turns out to be his own choosings, his own pride, his own cravings. Man is a willful obstacle to being himself before God. This, too, is man.

UNIQUENESS, WORTH, AND COMMUNITY

Another group of traits having religious import may be seen by concentrating on man's individuality. In saying that a man is existentially unique, we do not mean to say that he is unique in worth or in rights, for these he shares equally with all other men. Rather we refer to the individualness of personality itself.

Perhaps the only way we can come close to defining the meaning of uniqueness is to point ostensively to different persons and utter the singular pronouns, I or you or him or her. The very linguistic form "I," for instance, announces the fact of individuality. It has a different designation wherever it is used. This is one reason why it is so difficult to talk about "the self." There is no self in general but only the unique

I's which the term "self" brackets conceptually. Many things can be said about these many I's, but the I-ness of each is what cannot be universalized. The I in its uniqueness cannot be described; it can only be expressed.

Uniqueness as mirrored in linguistic forms is also evident in our use of proper names. The fact that one is called by a personal name signalizes the belief that as a person he is in some way individually unique. Even when different persons are identified by the same sounds or marks, the names in practice are different; for when confusion arises, the real name is "John Jones who . . ." or "John Jones with the. . . ." Thus our individuality forces our language to conform to it, so that the use of proper names reflects that individuality. But language is only a sign; is not the fact signified. So what does our uniqueness involve in fact?

It may not seem to suggest much regarding a person's uniqueness to say that he occupies a particular space with a certain set of spatial relations all his own. But there is an element of uniqueness here. And when we add that his body occupies this space, a body capable of expressing and perpetuating in an individual way his mental and spiritual interests, the fact of uniqueness through space is seen to be still more significant.[7] Every time he sits or stands or eats or writes or salutes or assumes a prayerful repose or does a thousand other things, he is demonstrating his spatiality and the unique way in which it stamps his personality into the world of fact. He alone can assume just this position with just this body, reflecting just this person in just this space.

The factor of time must of course be added to that of space. Though one lives in common time with others, allowing communication to be possible, there are nevertheless unique elements of temporal existence as well. One emerges at a specific time in history—a century, a year, a month, a day, a moment. Objectively considered, the moment contains many other events. But there is also a subjective uniqueness about it; it is the moment of one's own birth, one's own creation, one's newness in time. And the same is true of death. One will uniquely die in time. Moreover, one experiences throughout his lifetime certain moments in a unique way. He can even, through his freedom, help to shape some moments in a unique manner. Thus there is a qualitative dimension of time which is an integral part of personal history. It is this personalization, this intimate, absorbing, throbbing character of time which makes it an individualizing feature of one's existence.

We come right to the heart of the matter, however, not by dwelling on this or that aspect of man's uniqueness, but by pointing to the whole complex structure of an individual personality, which includes his original store of potential for becoming a real human being, the present accumulations which constitute his existence now, and his ideal self held up in an eternal vision by God. This particular potential for being human in just this way, this present state of his life, incorporating the past, and this particular goal which he should fulfill—all this is the person, and here is where uniqueness is most evident. All this constitutes one's personal history. And there is no duplication of personal histories. Each is unique.

We turn next to the consideration of man's worth and dignity as an individual, which theistic religion has always affirmed. There are probably many ways in which people have come to accept this doctrine. But we shall suggest that something like the following kind of experience is very often the existential basis for the doctrine as far as theistic religion is concerned.

The individual person has within himself one tendency which, if followed, would carry him into a vacuous, unproductive, useless kind of life. On the other hand, he has a tendency which can lead him into a life of genuine, individualized service. He knows that both of these possibilities are open to him because he feels tensions and tugs in both directions. But the outcome of this struggle presents us with a paradox, for when a person skids downward toward emptiness and fruitlessness, he does not feel that he can reasonably blame this on other people or on outward conditions. It is due for the most part to his own apathy and selfishness, to dissension in his inward ranks. When, on the other hand, he finds himself able to maintain a life of service and contribution, he does not feel that he can reasonably attribute this to his own cleverness, his own steadiness, his own goodness. It is more like doing something worthwhile in spite of himself. In short, the downward path seems to be of one's own doing, while the upward path seems to be due to resources not entirely one's own. Donald Baillie has called this the paradox of grace.[8] Now these extra resources drawing a person upward can only be, according to theistic religion, personal in character. And they can only be operative if the person is somehow being regarded as an object of worth. Thus religious persons feel that they are being valued. They not only value things themselves, but they in turn are valued by a supreme reality. And since they can see absolutely nothing within themselves that could justify them in believing that they are valued more than other persons, they must necessarily believe that all persons are valued alike. Thus all persons are seen to have unlimited worth, and therefore to be deserving of respect and dignity among men.

But no matter how individual persons have come to see the truth of the doctrine, theistic religion upholds the great doctrine of the worth of the individual, with its attendant implications of equality and of universal rights. This tenet, which is also a part of modern, democratic belief, is viewed by theistic religion as having a theological basis. Man as an

individual is a being of infinite worth in himself, having received his being and his worth by divine creation. He therefore deserves unlimited
respect, sure protection of his rights, and active promotion of his welfare. We may be grateful that this doctrine has become as established
as it has in secular society. But we may also wonder how long it can
endure if its religious basis is not reaffirmed. Another perennial difficulty
is that the doctrine may remain too abstract, not receiving the concrete
application to individuals and groups that is necessary to make it practically meaningful. Yet the fact that it has been a rallying call to so many
people suggests that even in religion abstractions have some place.

The last characteristic to be depicted is far from the least in significance. It is that man has the potentiality for entering into intimate, soul-
stirring dialogues with other persons like himself. Man is a being in community with other persons.[9] This assertion is not exactly the same as the
familiar statements that man is a social being, man is a political animal,
man could not get along without others, man needs his fellows, and so
forth. These things are all true; but they seem to be quite compatible
with a view which regards the individual as a relatively complete and
autonomous unit, requiring only certain external relationships with other
such units in order to insure protection and prosperity. When we say
that man is not only a social being but a being in community, we mean
that he is not only related to others externally as in a nation, but also
internally as in a drama. That is, man does not know himself, does not
become himself, until he penetrates and is penetrated by the inner life of
other persons. He himself does not become a real self until he enters
into spiritual dialogue with another self. Here there is not just a relationship for mutual advantage, not just an exchange of words and ideas.
There is interchange of mind, feeling, and will at the level of unmasked
openness. There is the meeting of self with self. Until we know appreciation, understanding, love, and affirmation in this life of personal dialogue, we do not become aware of the meaning of these concepts, or of
other selves, or of our own self. To be sure, the ideal life of community
is rare in practice; it is clouded over with masks and barriers, customs
and conventions, which we choose to erect. But the need for it and the
capacity for it appear to be basic in man. Perhaps we should say that we
are beings in community partially and potentially, but that the ideal has
been distorted and disfigured.

This community relationship between persons, which Buber calls the
I-thou relationship, may also be applied, with the appropriate changes,
to man's relationship to God, the supreme person. The ideal divine-
human relationship is also that of beings in community, persons in dialogue, and in this relationship, and not apart from it, man discovers the

depths of his being, the essential self he can become. Here the person-to-person character of authentic human existence reaches its final stage.[10]

RELIGIOUS POSSIBILITIES IN MAN

We have been enumerating and commenting upon a selected number of characteristics of man—those which make him a religious being. Let us now attempt, in a brief conclusion, to indicate what the religious import of these several characteristics is. How, in a word, do these traits make man a religious creature?

Being personal is the prerequisite for being religious at all. With personality come possibilities for concern, commitment, devotion, worship, which are religious possibilities. Being a created person means that man's very existence points to the divine ground behind his creatureliness. That is, his existence points to the ultimate object of religious interest and shows by that fact the right relationship to be sought in his religion. He should exalt God who should be exalted and not give priority to any false gods or his own pretensions. Also his creatureliness means that there is a role, a vocation, for him to fulfill in accordance with his finite status. The symbol of the image of God reminds us even more of man's divine origin, as well as of the possibilities for good that he possesses despite his manifest evil.

Freedom is, to speak metaphorically, the pivot of religious life. It is through its operation that man's religion rises and falls. If man were totally conditioned by outside forces, this would not necessarily mean the absence of all the satisfactions of religion. But only freedom can give religion its distinctive meaning and vitality and make it more than an instrument for self-satisfaction. Freedom is that by which man gives or withholds his commitments, helps or ignores his neighbors, accepts or rejects the challenge of true selfhood, responds to or remains indifferent to the divine will. Self-transcendence is the capacity for growth in spiritual life. It means that his present attainments or lack of attainments are not permanent; he has richer potentialities and can express deeper meanings in the relationships of his life. Of course he can also rocket himself to heights of power and pride if he is not governed by a good will. So self-transcendence shows us the potential horror as well as the glory of our religious situation. The sinfulness of man, resulting from his freedom and his capacity for self-transcendence, poses the predicament which religion must solve, or rather which God must solve working through man's religion. It is the state of soul to which religion speaks.

The religious aspect of uniqueness comes in the idea of a particular vocation, a peculiar place in society and the world, for each man to ennoble. In each man there awaits, to use the language of St. Paul, a different spiritual gift to be developed. Uniqueness also points to theistic religion's belief that there is something radically individual in the ultimate reconciliation it seeks, as contrasted with absorption into an impersonal absolute where all individuality is lost. The worth of the individual points, in one direction, to the personality of God, from whence value derives, and hence to the ultimate object of religious faith and duty. At the same time it is fundamental in human relations as a guide and directive. It shows the goal for the application of religion to social life. In a private sense the idea of individual worth can give incentive, stamina, and even joy to the individual, for it can generate the confidence that though he may seem to be nothing yet he is something, though he is unworthy yet he is worthy, though he is unacceptable yet he is accepted. Finally, the idea of man in personal community points to the goal of human life and to the true end which religion seeks. A community of free, creating, loving, worshipping, valuing, and valued persons, all in relation to God, remains the hope of theistic religion.

I AND THOU

MARTIN BUBER

Martin Buber (1878–) has been one of the century's most penetrating interpreters of Jewish religion and culture. He studied at Vienna, Berlin, Zurich, and Leipzig, and taught at Frankfurt until he was forced to leave Germany when Hitler came to power. Since 1933 he has been at Hebrew University in Jerusalem. His numerous writings include Between Man and Man *(1946),* Eclipse of God *(1952), and* Good and Evil *(1953). In the opening portion of his influential reflection on the self,* I and Thou, *he develops the idea that the uniqueness of the self consists in its life of dialogue—with things, with other persons, with the eternal Thou.*

To man the world is twofold, in accordance with his twofold attitude.

The attitude of man is twofold, in accordance with the twofold nature of the primary words which he speaks.

The primary words are not isolated words, but combined words.

From Martin Buber, *I and Thou,* trans. Ronald Gregor Smith (Edinburgh: T. & T. Clark, 1937), pp. 3-16. Reprinted by permission.

The one primary word is the combination *I-Thou*.

The other primary word is the combination *I-It;* wherein, without a change in the primary word, one of the words *He* and *She* can replace *It*.

Hence the *I* of man is also twofold.

For the *I* of the primary word *I-Thou* is a different *I* from that of the primary word *I-It*.

Primary words do not signify things, but they intimate relations.

Primary words do not describe something that might exist independently of them, but being spoken they bring about existence.

Primary words are spoken from the being.

If *Thou* is said, the *I* of the combination *I-Thou* is said along with it.

If *It* is said, the *I* of the combination *I-It* is said along with it.

The primary word *I-Thou* can only be spoken with the whole being.

The primary word *I-It* can never be spoken with the whole being.

There is no *I* taken in itself, but only the *I* of the primary word *I-Thou* and the *I* of the primary word *I-It*.

When a man says *I* he refers to one or other of these. The *I* to which he refers is present when he says *I*. Further, when he says *Thou* or *It*, the *I* of one of the two primary words is present.

The existence of *I* and the speaking of *I* are one and the same thing.

When a primary word is spoken the speaker enters the word and takes his stand in it.

The life of human beings is not passed in the sphere of transitive verbs alone. It does not exist in virtue of activities alone which have some *thing* for their object.

I perceive something. I am sensible of something. I imagine something. I will something. I feel something. I think something. The life of human beings does not consist of all this and the like alone.

This and the like together establish the realm of *It*.

But the realm of *Thou* has a different basis.

When *Thou* is spoken, the speaker has no thing for his object. For where there is a thing there is another thing. Every *It* is bounded by others; *It* exists only through being bounded by others. But when *Thou* is spoken, there is no thing. *Thou* has no bounds.

When *Thou* is spoken, the speaker has no *thing*; he has indeed nothing. But he takes his stand in relation.

It is said that man experiences his world. What does that mean?

Man travels over the surface of things and experiences them. He extracts knowledge about their constitution from them: he wins an experience from them. He experiences what belongs to the things.

But the world is not presented to man by experiences alone. These present him only with a world composed of *It* and *He* and *She* and *It* again.

I experience something.—If we add "inner" to "outer" experiences, nothing in the situation is changed. We are merely following the un-eternal division that springs from the lust of the human race to whittle away the secret of death. Inner things or outer things, what are they but things and things!

I experience something.—If we add "secret" to "open" experiences, nothing in the situation is changed. How self-confident is that wisdom which perceives a closed compartment in things, reserved for the initiate and manipulated only with the key. O secrecy without a secret! O accumulation of information! It, always It!

The man who experiences has no part in the world. For it is "in him" and not between him and the world that the experience arises.

The world has no part in the experience. It permits itself to be experienced, but has no concern in the matter. For it does nothing to the experience, and the experience does nothing to it.

As experience, the world belongs to the primary word *I-It*.
The primary word *I-Thou* establishes the world of relation.

The spheres in which the world of relation arises are three.

First, our life with nature. There the relation sways in gloom, beneath the level of speech. Creatures live and move over against us, but cannot come to us, and when we address them as *Thou*, our words cling to the threshold of speech.

Second, our life with men. There the relation is open and in the form of speech. We can give and accept the *Thou*.

Third, our life with intelligible forms. There the relation is clouded, yet it discloses itself; it does not use speech, yet begets it. We perceive no *Thou*, but none the less we feel we are addressed and we answer—forming, thinking, acting. We speak the primary word with our being, we cannot utter *Thou* with our lips.

But with what right do we draw what lies outside speech into relation with the world of the primary word?

In every sphere in its own way, through each process of becoming that is present to us we look out toward the fringe of the eternal *Thou*; in each we are aware of a breath from the eternal *Thou*; in each *Thou* we address the eternal *Thou*.

I consider a tree.
I can look on it as a picture: stiff column in a shock of light, or splash of green shot with the delicate blue and silver of the background.

I can perceive it as movement: flowing veins on clinging, pressing pith, suck of the roots, breathing of the leaves, ceaseless commerce with earth and air—and the obscure growth itself.

I can classify it in a species and study it as a type in its structure and mode of life.

I can subdue its actual presence and form so sternly that I recognize it only as an expression of law—of the laws in accordance with which a constant opposition of forces is continually adjusted, or of those in accordance with which the component substances mingle and separate.

I can dissipate it and perpetuate it in number, in pure numerical relation.

In all this the tree remains my object, occupies space and time, and has its nature and constitution.

It can, however, also come about, if I have both will and grace, that in considering the tree I become bound up in relation to it. The tree is now no longer *It*. I have been seized by the power of exclusiveness.

To effect this it is not necessary for me to give up any of the ways in which I consider the tree. There is nothing from which I would have to turn my eyes away in order to see, and no knowledge that I would have to forget. Rather is everything, picture and movement, species and type, law and number, indivisibly united in this event.

Everything belonging to the tree is in this: its form and structure, its colours and chemical composition, its intercourse with the elements and with the stars, are all present in a single whole.

The tree is no impression, no play of my imagination, no value depending on my mood; but it is bodied over against me and has to do with me, as I with it—only in a different way.

Let no attempt be made to sap the strength from the meaning of the relation: relation is mutual.

The tree will have a consciousness, then, similar to our own? Of that I have no experience. But do you wish, through seeming to succeed in it with yourself, once again to disintegrate that which cannot be disintegrated? I encounter no soul or dryad of the tree, but the tree itself.

If I face a human being as my *Thou*, and say the primary word *I-Thou* to him, he is not a thing among things, and does not consist of things.

This human being is not *He* or *She*, bounded from every other *He* and *She*, a specific point in space and time within the net of the world; nor is he a nature able to be experienced and described, a loose bundle of named qualities. But with no neighbour, and whole in himself, he is *Thou* and fills the heavens. This does not mean that nothing exists except himself. But all else lives in *his* light.

Just as the melody is not made up of notes nor the verse of words nor the statue of lines, but they must be tugged and dragged till their unity has been scattered into these many pieces, so with the man to whom I say *Thou*. I can take out from him the colour of his hair, or of his speech, or of his goodness. I must continually do this. But each time I do it he ceases to be *Thou*.

And just as prayer is not in time but time in prayer, sacrifice not in space but space in sacrifice, and to reverse the relation is to abolish the reality, so with the man to whom I say *Thou*. I do not meet with him at some time and place or other. I can set him in a particular time and place; I must continually do it: but I set only a *He* or a *She*, that is an *It*, no longer my *Thou*.

So long as the heaven of *Thou* is spread out over me the winds of causality cower at my heels, and the whirlpool of fate stays its course.

I do not experience the man to whom I say *Thou*. But I take my stand in relation to him, in the sanctity of the primary word. Only when I step out of it do I experience him once more. In the act of experience *Thou* is far away.

Even if the man to whom I say *Thou* is not aware of it in the midst of his experience, yet relation may exist. For *Thou* is more than *It* realises. No deception penetrates here; here is the cradle of the Real Life.

This is the eternal source of art: a man is faced by a form which desires to be made through him into a work. This form is no offspring of his soul, but is an appearance which steps up to it and demands of it the effective power. The man is concerned with an act of his being. If he carries it through, if he speaks the primary word out of his being to the form which appears, then the effective power streams out, and the work arises.

The act includes a sacrifice and a risk. This is the sacrifice: the endless possibility that is offered up on the altar of the form. For everything which just this moment in play ran through the perspective must be obliterated; nothing of that may penetrate the work. The exclusiveness of what is facing it demands that it be so. This is the risk: the primary word can only be spoken with the whole being. He who gives himself to it may withhold nothing of himself. The work does not suffer me, as do the tree and the man, to turn aside and relax in the world of *It*; but it commands. If I do not serve it aright it is broken, or it breaks me.

I can neither experience nor describe the form which meets me, but only body it forth. And yet I behold it, splendid in the radiance of what confronts me, clearer than all the clearness of the world which is experienced. I do not behold it as a thing among the "inner" things nor as an image of my "fancy," but as that which exists in the present. If test is made of its objectivity the form is certainly not "there." Yet what is actually so much present as it is? And the relation in which I stand to it is real, for it affects me, as I affect it.

To produce is to draw forth, to invent is to find, to shape is to discover. In bodying forth I disclose. I lead the form across—into the world of *It*. The work produced is a thing among things, able to be experienced and described as a sum of qualities. But from time to time it can face the receptive beholder in its whole embodied form.

—What, then, do we experience of *Thou?*
—Just nothing. For we do not experience it.
—What, then, do we know of *Thou?*
—Just everything. For we know nothing isolated about it any more.

The *Thou* meets me through grace—it is not found by seeking. But my speaking of the primary word to it is an act of my being, is indeed *the* act of my being.

The *Thou* meets me. But I step into direct relation with it. Hence the relation means being chosen and choosing, suffering and action in one; just as any action of the whole being, which means the suspension of all partial actions and consequently of all sensations of actions grounded only in their particular limitation, is bound to resemble suffering.

The primary word *I-Thou* can be spoken only with the whole being. Concentration and fusion into the whole being can never take place through my agency, nor can it ever take place without me. I become through my relation to the *Thou;* as I become *I*, I say *Thou.*

All real living is meeting.

The relation to the *Thou* is direct. No system of ideas, no foreknowledge, and no fancy intervene between *I* and *Thou*. The memory itself is transformed, as it plunges out of its isolation into the unity of the whole. No aim, no lust, and no anticipation intervene between *I* and *Thou*. Desire itself is transformed as it plunges out of its dream into the appearance. Every means is an obstacle. Only when every means has collapsed does the meeting come about.

In face of the directness of the relation everything indirect becomes irrelevant. It is also irrelevant if my *Thou* is already the *It* for other *I's* ("an object of general experience"), or can become so through the very accomplishment of this act of my being. For the real, though certainly swaying and swinging, boundary runs neither between experience and non-experience, nor between what is given and what is not given, nor yet between the world of being and the world of value; but cutting indifferently across all these provinces it lies between *Thou* and *It*, between the present and the object.

The present, and by that is meant not the point which indicates from time to time in our thought merely the conclusion of "finished" time, the mere appearance of a termination which is fixed and held, but the real, filled present, exists only in so far as actual presentness, meeting, and relation exist. The present arises only in virtue of the fact that the *Thou* becomes present.

The *I* of the primary word *I-It*, that is, the *I* faced by no *Thou*, but surrounded by a multitude of "contents," has no present, only the past. Put in another way, in so far as man rests satisfied with the things that he experiences and uses, he lives in the past, and his moment has no present content. He has nothing but objects. But objects subsist in time that has been.

The present is not fugitive and transient, but continually present and enduring. The object is not duration, but cessation, suspension, a breaking off and cutting clear and hardening, absence of relation and of present being.

True beings are lived in the present, the life of objects is in the past.

Appeal to a "world of ideas" as a third factor above this opposition will not do away with its essential twofold nature. For I speak of nothing else but the real man, of you and of me, of our life and of our world —not of an *I*, or a state of being, in itself alone. The real boundary for the actual man cuts right across the world of ideas as well.

To be sure, many a man who is satisfied with the experience and use of the world of things has raised over or about himself a structure of ideas, in which he finds refuge and repose from the oncome of nothingness. On the threshold he lays aside his inauspicious everyday dress, wraps himself in pure linen, and regales himself with the spectacle of primal being, or of necessary being; but his life has no part in it. To proclaim his ways may even fill him with well-being.

But the mankind of mere *It* that is imagined, postulated, and propagated by such a man has nothing in common with a living mankind where *Thou* may truly be spoken. The noblest fiction is a fetish, the loftiest fictitious sentiment is depraved. Ideas are no more enthroned above our heads than resident in them; they wander amongst us and accost us. The man who leaves the primary word unspoken is to be pitied; but the man who addresses instead these ideas with an abstraction or a password, as if it were their name, is contemptible.

In one of the three examples it is obvious that the direct relation includes an effect on what confronts me. In art the act of the being determines the situation in which the form becomes the work. Through the meeting that which confronts me is fulfilled, and enters the world of things, there to be endlessly active, endlessly to become *It*, but also endlessly to become *Thou* again, inspiring and blessing. It is "embodied"; its body emerges from the flow of the spaceless, timeless present on the shore of existence.

The significance of the effect is not so obvious in the relation with the *Thou* spoken to men. The act of the being which provides directness in this case is usually understood wrongly as being one of feeling. Feelings accompany the metaphysical and metapsychical fact of love, but they do not constitute it. The accompanying feelings can be of greatly different kinds. The feeling of Jesus for the demoniac differs from his feeling for the beloved disciple; but the love is the one love. Feelings are "entertained": love comes to pass. Feelings dwell in man; but man dwells in his love. That is no metaphor, but the actual truth. Love does not cling to the *I* in such a way as to have the *Thou* only for its "content," its object; but love is *between I* and *Thou*. The man who does not know this, with his very being know this, does not know love; even though he ascribes to it the feelings he lives through, experiences, enjoys, and expresses. Love ranges in its effect through the whole world. In the eyes of him who takes his stand in love, and gazes out of it, men are cut free from their entanglement in bustling activity. Good people and evil, wise and foolish, beautiful and ugly, become successively real to him; that is, set free they step forth in their singleness, and confront him as *Thou*. In a wonderful way, from time to time, exclusiveness arises—and so he can be effective, helping, healing, educating, rising up, saving. Love is responsibility of an *I* for a *Thou*. In this lies the likeness—impossible in any feeling whatsoever—of all who love, from the smallest to the greatest and from the blessedly protected man, whose life is rounded in that of a beloved being, to him who is all his life nailed to the cross of the world, and who ventures to bring himself to the dreadful point—to love *all men*.

Let the significance of the effect in the third example, that of the creature and our contemplation of it, remain sunk in mystery. Believe in the simple magic of life, in service in the universe, and the meaning of that waiting, that alertness, that "craning of the neck" in creatures will dawn upon you. Every word would falsify; but look! round about you beings live their life, and to whatever point you turn you come upon being.

Relation is mutual. My *Thou* affects me, as I affect it. We are moulded by our pupils and built up by our work. The "bad" man, lightly touched by the holy primary word, becomes one who reveals. How we are educated by children and by animals! We live our lives inscrutably included within the streaming mutual life of the universe.

—You speak of love as though it were the only relation between men. But properly speaking, can you take it even only as an example, since there is such a thing as hate?

—So long as love is "blind," that is, so long as it does not see a *whole* being, it is not truly under the sway of the primary word of relation. Hate is by nature blind. Only a part of a being can be hated. He who sees a whole being and is compelled to reject it is no longer in the kingdom of hate, but is in that of human restriction of the power to say *Thou*. He finds himself unable to say the primary word to the other human being confronting him. This word consistently involves an affirmation of the being addressed. He is therefore compelled to reject either the other or himself. At this barrier the entering on a relation recognises its relativity, and only simultaneously with this will the barrier be raised.

Yet the man who straightforwardly hates is nearer to relation than the man without hate and love.

MAN AS HE ACTUALLY IS

EMIL BRUNNER

H. Emil Brunner (1889–), a distinguished Swiss theologian, has been one of the leaders, along with Karl Barth, in the movement to formulate a reconstructed Protestant orthodoxy. He studied at Zurich and Berlin and then spent several years as a pastor. Beginning in 1924, he has had a long teaching career in theology at Zurich, although he took out two years in the early fifties to teach in Tokyo. His works include The Divine Imperative *(1932),* The Divine-Human Encounter *(1938), and* Christianity and Civilization *(1948-49). In the following selection man is seen as characterized simultaneously by wretchedness and yet nobility.*

THE NEW STATE OF THE PROBLEM

The real enigma of man is the conflict within his own nature, not the fact that he is composed of body and soul; the real problem does not lie in the fact that man is part of the world and is yet more than the world; the real problem is that the unity of all these elements—given by the Creation—has been lost, and that instead of complementing and aiding one another, they are in conflict with one another. Non-Christian

From *Man In Revolt* by Emil Brunner, pp. 168-87. Tr. Olive Wyon. Copyright 1947. By permission of the Westminster Press and Lutterworth Press. [Footnotes omitted except for Biblical references.]

anthropology tries to deal with this conflict in two ways: either by ascribing it to the constitutional conflict between sense and spirit, or it seeks to resolve the discord by suggesting that the difficulties are merely successive phases in a process of development, continuous stages in self-realization. The Christian doctrine takes this conflict seriously: man, by his own act of self-determination, contradicts the divine determination in the Creation. It is this duality which gives its particular imprint to human life as it actually is. Because man has been created in the image of God, and yet has himself defaced this image, his existence differs from all other forms of existence, as existence in conflict.

The traditional doctrine assigned the Original Creation and the Fall, on the one hand, and man's actual sinful state, on the other, to two different subjects—in the one case to Adam, and in the other to myself. This, as we have already seen, meant that it could give only a partial expression to the fact of the conflict in human nature. The result was that either human nature was regarded as uninjured, and man's apostasy from God was regarded as something external to human nature; or that the corruption of human nature was emphasized to such a degree that justice was not done to the fact of the distinctively "human" element. All that could then be done was to argue that this quality of "humanity" was due to "relics of the original image of God." When we renounce the historical view of the Creation and the Fall we are set free from this dilemma, and we are able once more to see the contradiction in man as an actual conflict. Man as sinner is in permanent revolt, in a rebellion (which he cannot now renounce by his own efforts) against his divine determination as intended in the Creation, and thus against the nature given him by God. The divine Creation still exists in man, not in the shape of "relics," but as the primal element in human nature, inevitably but continually being denied afresh.

Man is and remains one who has his nature and existence in the Word of God, and is therefore, and for this reason alone, responsible. He does not cease to be in the Word of God, called by God and summoned to responsibility. But through his contradiction his attitude to the God who calls him is perverted; hence also the call itself has been transformed from a call of generous love into that of a demanding and accusing law. The law as the really determinative element of human existence is the sign of both these facts: that the call of God does not cease, and that man's hearing is perverted. It is not the law that is perverted, and it is not the God who reveals Himself in the law who is perverted, an idol; but man's understanding of the law, and therefore his legalistic understanding of God and man, is perverted, and the God which he makes for himself is an idol. Luther reveals profound insight when he reduces the whole of paganism—including false Christianity—to the one common denominator:

legalistic religion. The God who is understood from a legalistic point of view is an idol, that is, a God with whom we ourselves can deal; and the legalistic understanding of man is, in its deepest sense, self-deification, since it seeks in man that which can only be found in God: the truly human possibility of life.

Hence there is nothing human which does not suggest the *Imago Dei*, and there is nothing human which does not indicate the perversion of human nature. Even now, on this side of the Fall, there is a *humanum* which distinguishes man from all other creatures known to us. But this specifically human element is not uncorrupted human nature, as is taught by the Roman Catholic Church; nor is it merely a "relic" of the original human nature, as is represented by the Reformers. It is rather the whole of human nature created in the image of God, but in a completely perverted form. The human element as form, as structure—namely, as responsible being—has remained; the human element as content, that is, as being in love, has been lost. Man does not cease to be "in the sight of" God; but he is in the sight of God as a perverted being, and therefore God also appears to be perverted to him.

Hence the temptation continually arises to regard this form of humanity in itself, and the idea of man which it contains, as the real nature of man, as is done by Idealism. The responsibility of man which is distinctive of him, which he cannot evade or throw off, is understood in such a way that the law is interpreted as the law of his nature and is thus made the basis of the idea of autonomous humanity. Instead of man asking himself whether he is fulfilling this law, he deludes himself into thinking that this law is "in him." He ascribes what is God's claim on him and God's witness against him, to himself as the witness of his nature, and in so doing he conceals his own reality. Responsibility becomes divinity; this is the humanistic misinterpretation of formal "humanity."

On the other hand, on account of the corruption of the original Creation there is the danger of depreciating or secularizing the specifically human element which has remained even in sinful man, that is, of forgetting that even fallen man is still always in the sight of God, and that even in sinful existence the "theological" nature of man, that is, the nature which is related to God, is manifested. When man as sinner is severed from his imperishable relation to the Word of God, he becomes a *truncus et lapis* which is absolutely passive under the Divine Word, like an object which bears the divine operation without any willed response of its own, as a stone bears the blows of the stone-mason. A false humanism therefore brings with it a false, de-humanizing view of man.

According to the true Scriptural doctrine it is precisely that in man which indicates his sin which also indicates his divinely created nature, because both are understood in their actual contradiction to one another, and not in a neutral quality of nature which has, so to say, become full of dross. Man is a rebel against his divine destiny; he is the steward who pretends to be the master of the vineyard and then kills his lord's messengers. He is the prodigal son who has demanded "the portion of goods that falleth to him" and now squanders it. Not only has he done all this in the past, but the revolution is still in full swing. The fatality of the Fall does not consist in the fact that man was once created by God, and now, some thousands of years later, is nothing but the heir of the sin of Adam; the fatality of the Fall consists rather in the fact that every human being, in his own person, and in union with the rest of humanity, every day renews this Fall afresh, and cannot help doing so, that he is in process of falling and cannot escape from it, that he cannot get back to his origin. Hence the fact that he has been created in the image of God as his origin, which he is always denying, is always present in the accusing law which man always knows, somehow or other, as truth and yet in practice denies. If man is to be understood as he really is, he must be seen in this actual contradiction, which is the real conflict.

The traditional anthropology of the Church contradicts, however, not merely the Bible but the actual experience of man. Not as though experience as such could show us the real man; we know that every empirical programme is derived from hidden axioms. But the doctrine and message of the Church must be such that experience cannot charge it with falsehood. We must not hide behind the paradoxical character of the ecclesiastical doctrine, accessible only to faith, in order to hold fast statements which ought not to be regarded as true because experience proves them to be false. The genuine paradoxes of the Bible never contradict the truth of experience, however little they themselves may be accessible to experience. The Bible does not postulate any other kind of man than the one known to us by experience; but it interprets the enigma presented by man as we know him from experience, the enigma which no system of philosophy or psychology can solve. The conflict in man comes out in definite phenomena, although the background of these phenomena, the conflict between the origin and the contradiction, between creation and sin, does not itself "appear," but can only be grasped by faith. In the following pages facts of this kind are treated from three points of view: as manifestations of the image of God in man, of sin, and of the conflict between the two.

THE TRACES OF THE IMAGE OF
GOD AND OF THE "GREATNESS OF MAN"

There must certainly be something distinctive in man in the fact that, without being absolutely mad, he can confuse himself with God. Fichte is certainly not an idle talker; nor is even the most amazing audacity of the teaching of the Vedanta with its identification: "*Atman* equals *Brahman*, I equal God," *sine fundamento in re*. It is precisely this apex of the "misunderstanding of reason with itself" which is at the same time the clearest manifestation of the fact that man has been created in the image of God, and that this original divine destiny is still present with him in the midst of his perversion. The most daring of all sins, that of self-deification, is only possible through the divine destiny of creation, which raises man above the whole of the rest of the created world. What indeed is sin as a whole save this misunderstanding of man's God-given freedom? And is not this a sign of his Divine Origin? Man alone is a spiritual subject, like God. As spirit, he stands over against the whole world as a being which is not of this world. This superiority to the world he experiences in his power of perception. He "has" the world only because he stands away from it, at a distance, because he is "over against" it. As the subject of all knowledge, he cannot be compared with anything there is to be known. How could he to whom all is made subject, to whom it was said: "all is thine, of all trees shalt thou eat," he who alone might name the creatures, not be exposed to the temptation to touch the tree in the midst of the garden and to confuse it with the other trees, to wish to be like God? This sinful confusion, by which the copy makes itself the original, is only possible because it *is* a copy. The original relation of man to God lives in every spiritual act—in the very fact that it is a spiritual act. The spiritual is spiritual through the relation to the absolute, infinite, unconditioned.

Why does man seek for truth? Not merely because the knowledge of truth is useful to him, but because the idea of unconditioned truth leaves him no peace. He is seeking for his lost home, although he does not know it. The absolute nature of this idea of Truth contains the absoluteness of the Word of the Creator. He seeks and he must seek "what it is that holds the world together at its heart," the deepest ground, the primal Cause, the connexion; and his perceptive spirit bows before the law of the true, before the demands of "absolute," "objective" Truth, before truth for truth's sake. So great is the power of this idea of pure truth that for its sake he will even sacrifice his life. Who will deny that in this search for truth there is something holy? This search for truth cannot be understood in terms of biological concepts of self-preservation or of the preservation of the species. The idea of the unconditioned, of validity, of truth-in-itself, cannot be grasped from any instinctive copy of actuality. It is not derived from anywhere except from the divine origin, the Primal Word, in which the spirit of man is based, even after he has fallen.

This, too, is the truth which lies in the Ontological Proof for the Existence of God. The idea of God which the human mind necessarily forms, can only be explained from God Himself, true as it is that this self-formed idea of God is not the living God but an "*Abgott*" (idol) and gives man occasion for self-deification. Because man has been created in the Word of God, even as a sinner he cannot escape from the idea of God. He cannot escape from it, indeed, even when he denies it. Even in his denial of God, namely in its claim to validity, there lives, unconsciously to himself, faith in unconditioned truth.

The actual man, not only when he is thinking, but also when he is creating, lives on his divine origin in the Word. When the beaver "creates" his house, he does not go further than is useful to him. Man, however, even in the sphere of mere technique and civilization, always transcends the boundary of that which is merely useful. He experiences and seeks in technique at the same time dominion over Nature, not merely the utilization and exploitation of her material treasures. He desires to prove himself, to show his superiority over nature, he desires to triumph over it. But his divinely-created nature comes out still more clearly in his own "creative" acts, in which he consciously and willingly goes far beyond the borders of mere utility. Art in its historical beginnings may have arisen out of technical, or magical motives, or out of motives connected with self-preservation: but in any case its nature is independent of interest in the preservation of life; it is the shaping of the beautiful for the sake of beauty. Man contrasts the imperfect world of actual experience, as he knows it, with a perfect existence, a heightened, intensified, ideal existence, freed from the contingent and accidental, the sight of which gives him a satisfaction which is wholly different from that of the experience of any reality in this world as it is. Art is always—whatever else it may be—the child of the longing for perfection. But perfection is an "idea" which does not spring out of any observation of the existing world. Rather this idea is an original standard by which we measure all that now exists. Plato's argument that the idea of Perfection—even if it were only the idea of the perfect circle—does not spring out of any perception, but that, on the contrary, it precedes all perception, and alone makes it possible, has never been controverted from that day to this. The Perfect is not an "intensification of the imperfect"; for the intensification of the imperfect would be only that which is still more imperfect. It is also no "abstraction," the "elimination of the imperfect"; for in order to eliminate the imperfect I must use the idea of Perfection as the rule for elimination. Only complete stupidity can entertain the idea that the Idea can be derived from the perception. But art lives on the Idea—not on that which is thought, but on that Perception which it inwardly beholds, and for which it longs. All genuine creativeness comes from such a vision and such a longing, and this vision and longing comes from the Original Creation in the Word.

When the first Greek philosophers felt impelled to describe the ground of all as the Logos they must still have been dimly aware of the connexion between reason and the Word, an awareness which was lost by later rationalism. The fact that man can speak, and that he must speak, that he has the power of speech, of the word, has always and rightly been regarded as the most characteristic token of humanity. Animals have no language; moreover, they are unable to hold in their minds truth which is independent of an object or situation accessible to sense-perception. Speech is the expression of reason, not merely of the intellect. But speech is far more than this; speech is the expression of the fact that human existence consists of the relation between one human being and another. The fact that even when we are "by ourselves" we cannot do without speech, and that something has only really been thought out when it has been formulated in speech, is a sign that human existence is not a solitary rational existence but that it is a common existence in which we impart to one another. Speech is reason-in-community. We may indeed turn the current phrase, speech is the means of reason (which is derived from the idea of rational autonomy with its lack of community), the other way round and say: reason is the means of speech. We have been created in order that we may have "something to say to one another." However that may be, among all the indications of the creation of man in the Word of God, speech is the plainest. It was not the "Deed" but the "Word" which was "in the beginning"; for God has not created a world which is without meaning and without community. In the Word He created the World: this is the basis for the truth that He created it in and for love. Speech is not to be understood from the point of view of reason; but both reason and speech should be understood from the point of view of the Word of God, as the two most powerful indications of a lost divine origin, in which we still live, though in a perverted manner. That is why God reveals Himself and our origin through the Incarnation of the Word, and this again through the proclamation of the Message: thus by means of human speech.

But it is not only speech which points to the fact that in his origin man is destined for community. We can certainly make the attempt—and it has been made often enough—to understand all forms of community-life from the point of view of instinct. But all these attempts break down on the facts. The elements which compose instinct are not adequate to explain friendship, marriage, the unity of a people, the consciousness of humanity. In all these existing facts an ideal element is coupled with that of instinct: the idea of community, the capacity for community, the willingness for, and the longing for, community. Give a human being all that he longs for, "pressed down and running over," and take community away from him; he will be the most miserable of creatures. Even in his flight from community man seeks community: in the cloister. Behind the formation of states, the loud, dominating theme of world history, the will to gather all men into community, of the most comprehensive and concentrated kind, is at work as the secret, impelling force. Man is not a ζῷον πολιτικόν, but *humanus*. No πόλις, no nation-state can satisfy him, because beyond these boundaries dwell human beings who also belong to him. In the ancient imperialist or pacifist dream of the one kingdom of humanity there lives the "remembrance" of an original paradisiacal unity of all mankind as the destiny of humanity.

The most direct evidence for this truth is the ethico-religious consciousness. No human community now exists, or ever has existed, which has not had its moral code; no community has ever existed in which—in spite of constant changes—the distinction between the ethically "good" and that which is merely conventional or "utilitarian" has not been a vital part of its consciousness. In spite of the doctrinaire assertions of theologians, it is a fact that the moral sense extends far beyond the circles affected by the Christian ethic, and has a profound influence. The sense of responsibility is the really primal human phenomenon, which is not wholly absent from anyone; sometimes it attains an immense power, or again an incredible delicacy. In its negative form, particularly, as the sense of guilt, as the bad conscience, it is a force which mocks at all rationalizing views and does not care a fig for theoretical denials. It is simply there, and witnesses against us—to our lost origin. For there is nothing more profoundly human than the sense of guilt; nothing in which the lost image of God manifests its presence more clearly. It is the sense of responsibility and its power which stamps the life of man with that "humanity" which reason, even that of the greatest genius, can never give it, and, indeed, of which it often robs it. It is not man's creative power expressed in varying degrees of genius, nor his play and his laughter which make the life of man "full of human dignity"—even Hell has its geniuses, and there is a devilish laughter and play—but only unity in love and loyalty. The most richly endowed and the freest spirit could also be quite inhuman; the devilish element is not checked by creativeness but by unity-in-responsibility. But this union and this unity does exist always and everywhere to an unexpected and astonishing degree. In it we are not confronted by the riddle but by the mystery of man. Fidelity, where all the advantage would be on the side of infidelity; this is the miracle of the water which flows uphill. This miracle does happen. Here "supernature" is revealed in the nature of man, of fallen, sinful man. Here, in the midst of apostasy and contradiction, its origin is revealed as a sacred presence.

And yet the sense of the Holy, the religious element, is at first of quite distinct origin, and its development is to a large extent independent of ethics. Why must human beings worship gods? All the positivist theories of religion—its derivation from fear, from the desire and need for an explanation, from wonder at that which is unintelligible and the like

—do not answer the question: Why does man acknowledge something holy, which, often against his own desire and advantage, he feels he must worship and serve? Modern theories of religion may throw a great deal of light upon the more detailed content and *raison d'être* of religion, but the original fact itself, the recognition of a sacred power before which man must bow in adoration, not because he gets anything out of it, but because he is inwardly overwhelmed by the Holy, because he feels he "must not" do otherwise—"must" and "must not" are fundamentally religious words—defies all explanations, just as its intellectual correlate, the idea of the Absolute, of the Unconditioned and the Perfect, cannot be derived from any finite content.

According to the present state of ethnography, there never have been, anywhere, peoples without religion. This does not mean that it would be impossible for sinful man to be without religion. There is indeed, alongside of religion, also atheism and agnosticism, to-day perhaps for the first time as a mass-phenomenon. But even in the denial of God there is an awareness of God, and the motives for the denial of God are often more religious than those of the particular empirical religion whose content is denied. The religious instinct also expresses itself, unfailingly, in the godless disposition: as an impulse to posit something—however absurd —as unconditioned and to worship it as divine.

In the history of religions the Holy is always, in some way or another, separated from the Good; divinity and humanity lie apart. It is the distinctive element of the Christian idea of God that, although these two are not one, they are revealed in one; the Revealer of perfect humanity is at the same time the Revealer of the true Divinity, the Holy is also the Good, because the Holy, God, is revealed as love, which as such is the Good. But even if this unity remained concealed from the religious consciousness outside the Bible, yet in all religions there exist fragments, crooked, defaced, but yet undeniable traces of this primal mystery in which man has his origin. For that "Word which was in the beginning" is also the "Light which lighteth every man coming into the world." Hence the history of religion, whatever else it may be, is also, and above all else: a witness—even if perverted—to the relation of man to God. It witnesses to the fact that man can never get away from God, but that, in the midst of his flight from God, he must always turn to Him again and again; and that man, even when in turning away from God he distorts the picture of his nature, even in this perverted nature still preserves a remembrance of his origin, which manifests itself effectively in him and in his life. This is the Biblical doctrine: that although man through his apostasy is "far" from God, God Himself is "not far from every one of us," but that "in Him we live and move and have our being."[1] "Because that which may be known of God is manifest in them; for God manifested

---
[1] Acts xvii. 27 ff.; xiv. 17 ff.

it unto them."[2] He has not left Himself without witness unto man. But that which He shows them they have "changed" into idols.[3]

Thus even the most horrible idol tells us something of the secret of the Holy, and the most abominable cultus tells us something of the fact that we have been created by God for God. Hence religion always produces, in spite of the nonmorality which it may contain, the sense of a holy bond and of a sacred unity, which makes life human. Therefore, to use the words of an unbeliever, religion, whatever it may be, is the soul of all human culture; and where it dies, there culture declines into mere civilization and technique (Spengler).

THE MANIFESTATIONS OF THE CONTRADICTION AND THE "MISERY OF MAN"

There is no stronger proof of the actuality and depth of that contradiction, which we called "primal sin," than the self-deification of man. Only rarely is this innermost tendency of our *cor incurvatum in se ipsum* consciously and openly manifested. The formula "God and I are one" designates a "summit" of mystical religiosity. It presupposes a complete severence from the concrete world of experience. For in this world of experience man is not given much opportunity to confuse himself with the Almighty. What man experiences primarily is his impotence and nothingness. The end of his Faustian way of knowledge is "and I see that we can know nothing" *ignoramus ignorabimus, docta ignorantia*, the despair of all knowledge—not merely of its attainment—scepticism.

What do we really know, if we do not know the whole? What is a knowledge that immediately changes itself into fresh problems? Is our progress in knowledge simply like the movement of people stranded on a moving ice-floe, who do not know whence it comes or whither it is going? Is it anything more than the aimless "progress" of the Wandering Jew?

Certainly, our knowledge is useful in the technical sphere; for it helps us to control and use the forces of nature. At least in the world of facts our knowledge helps us to find our way about in practical matters. But does this mean: to *know?* Do we know what an atom is, what matter or force is, time or space, life or impulse? It is true of course that knowledge is moving forward in *one* direction; once for all we have left behind us the view of the universe held in the ancient world. But where will the next century be? And does not all progress in knowledge also bring with it an increasing alienation from reality? Is not the very abstraction which makes things useful to us in the technical sphere also that which separates us from the intimacy of the knowledge of nature which is possessed by the primitive man, the artist, and the child? Does not the

[2] Rom. i. 19.
[3] Rom. i. 23.

simple human being know better what fire and water are than the scholar
who gives us the formula for it? And further, are not those who know
the most, most inclined to fall a prey to the completest scepticism, since
with every advance in knowledge the question "What *is* that which *is?*"
has only become more perplexing? "And I see . . . that we can know
nothing. . . ." Is not perhaps that very objectivity, which is the pride
of our knowledge, that which most thoroughly separates us from reality?
All our modern progress in knowledge has not brought us any nearer to
essential truth; indeed, it has only led us still further into the feeling that
we know nothing, that everything is dim and obscure, that we are
strangers in the universe. Ultimately does not an honest little sparrow
know more about the mystery of nature than we who are so clever? O
irony of *homo sapiens*, O the tragi-comedy of man, who confuses himself
with God!

But the *misère de l'homme* does not only become evident in the sphere
of knowledge. The creative human being has to-day brought things to
such a pass that he has learned to understand the story of the *Magician's
Apprentice* as his own. He falls into imminent danger through all the
serviceable spirits which he has created for himself; the thousandfold
strengthening of his sense-organs, of his hands and feet through technique, has not really made him richer; in any case, it has not made him
happier and freer. He has become the slave of his own machine. He must—
what irony—"serve" it (Haecker), must live for it; human life must be
adapted to its laws. While mankind has come a hundred times closer together, so far as space is concerned, inwardly, in the same degree, it has
become more remote and far more divided.

In the sphere of cultural, actual creation, this is less impressively felt;
but perhaps this is still more dangerous. The outcry, "the intellect the
enemy of the soul," is not a chance outburst; the flight into the primitive
is not merely a natural symptom of fatigue, but a deep despair of this
whole mental activity which we call education, art, culture. The intellectual, the bearer of culture, is somehow essentially an enemy of man,
because through a system of intellectual values or goods he conceals,
masters, or destroys the distinctively human element. Was Ferdinand
Ebner wrong when he described all this intellectuality as a mere "dream
of the intellect"? Do we not see again and again that somehow this
intellectuality makes people unfit for life? We long for simplicity, for
that which is wholly natural. But it seems as though man, and man alone,
were condemned never to find the simple and the natural. Every wild
rabbit can live his own rabbit-life quite naturally and fully; man cannot
do so, as a civilized being; from the very outset he is burdened with a
kind of insanity which makes all his attempts to be natural, and to enjoy
existence in a simple way, unsuccessful.

Whether we regard man as an individual or as a social being, it is all the same. Since history has been in existence this has been its theme: the contrast between individualism and collectivism, freedom and authority, independence and submission, the predatory man and the herd-man. Every movement which aims at helping the individual to attain his rights ends in libertinism and the dissolution of community—the Athenians knew quite well why they gave Socrates the cup of hemlock; and every reaction which tries to assert community, authority, order, the whole over against the caprice and the egoism of the individual, ends in oppression, violence, and dull stupidity. The movements for freedom, full of vitality at the outset, and splendid in their leaders, shatter community, and the movements for community, at first full of a deep sense of responsibility and of service, trample on the individual and his rights. It is not the observation of the processes of nature, but the contemplation of this tragic element in human history, which is the school of pessimism, of despair of man, and of his destiny.

Man has a *conscience*, which an optimistic Enlightenment declared to be the "Voice of God." What has not this conscience already commanded man to do! The blood-feud as well as the Inquisition, with its tortures and its burnings, anarchy as well as tyranny, cynical frankness as well as diplomatic lies, all appeal to this "Voice of God." Have there ever been greater tormentors of mankind than the conscientious, the moralists, the "Pharisees of the idea"? Instinctive sadism is simple compared with the cruelty of those who are doctrinaire, who sacrifice all human happiness, rights, freedom and heart to the idea, the principle, the "great cause." *Fiat justitia, pereat mundus!* The divine Moral Law within us—what arrogance, what an insane assumption of divinity has already arisen from this source! Which is worse: the chaos of lawlessness and immorality or the slavery of custom and the hostility to life of a rigid morality? Which is more terrible, the morally degraded, the "publican," or the morally "just," the "Pharisee"?

Humanity: the battlefield of demons; the human spirit: the arsenal of the instruments for the destruction of life. How impotent is human reason in construction, how almighty in destruction! With a few bombs man destroys in a few seconds the work of centuries, and no one knows whether the next war will sweep away, in a few days, the culture of thousands of years, for ever. It is not the animal instincts, but the mind of man which is the origin of all evil, the same mind which creates, builds, carries on research, strives, which seeks truth and loves righteousness, which longs after love and community; this same mind, this same "heart which glows with a sacred fire" is the fiery abyss whence issues all that is demonic and destructive.

The same mind which worships the divinity also flees from it. What is the history of religion itself but the story of the way in which man, who cannot get rid of God, tries to get off as easily as he can? This origin of the development of the religious imagination lies far behind all conscious motives. No one consciously tries to escape from the Lord God, the Living God, by his pantheistic idea of God; and yet this is the case. Religious symbols, and also the real formative forces of metaphysical thought, arise out of the unconscious. But the unconscious is not something to which man is helplessly exposed. The unconscious, also, is a sphere for which man is responsible—even though, like Original Sin, it may lie behind all that we have at our spiritual disposal, even though it may seem to us to be a kind of Fate.

Many and varied are the ways by which guilty man tries to evade the Divine Gaze. They are summed up in the history of religions, of their cults and mythologies. Its principle is the deification of the world, whether in the primitive imaginative form of pagan polytheism, or in the conceptually abstract form of pantheistic metaphysics; or it may take the opposite form: the banishment of God from the world, the impotent, dethroned, distant Divine Being, the fallen dynasty of the gods, the shadowy First Cause, the Creator-God of Deism, who "only pushes from without, Celestial bodies, driving them about"; and finally atheism, which says bluntly: "God is dead" (Nietzsche), which imagines that with its theoretical denial of God it has got rid of God for ever. It would be an undertaking of more than theoretical value to write a Christian mythology, or theory of idols, a doctrine of the formation of idols written from the point of view of faith in God. In the first chapter of the Epistle to the Romans Paul has sketched in the main features of such a Christian doctrine of the creation of idols. The idol arises through man's apostasy from the Creator and the transference of the homage which is His due to the creature. The motive for this apostasy and this false transference of homage is ingratitude and disobedience. It is so much easier for man to worship idols than to worship God. Even when the idol demands much from man, it does not demand the man himself; even where one offers all to the god, in so doing one does at least gain his favour. And again: where the god or the gods gain full power over man, man falls into demonic dependence which destroys responsibility. Even Pantheism and Deism, these more abstract and reflective forms of mythology, are also efforts to escape from the claim of God.

The idol has an infinite number of faces; it appears as one and as many, in personal or in wholly impersonal form, as a transcendental concept or even as something finite which, unawares, has been treated as infinite. But the idol is always a power to which man is enslaved, without being truly responsible to it—"carried away unto these dumb idols," says Paul—a power which binds without setting free, or which sets free without binding, which one cannot truly, in the sense of reverence, fear. The idol is always a secularized God and a deified world, a humanized God who is not truly human, or a deified man who is not truly divine. The idol is always as much like the devil as the true God; it is never both the Holy and the Merciful, the Absolute and the Personal, the Lord of All and the Good Shepherd who lays down His life for the sheep. The idol is always—and this describes his nature most fully: the godlessness of man projected into the unconditioned, whether this god is called Zeus or the All-Self, the All-One, Nothing; or else "Reason," "culture," "Man," "Humanity," "the ideal society" or anything else. As a mountain climber at evening may suddenly perceive his own figure reflected upon a sea of cloud beneath him, but enlarged and distorted, so the idol is my godless self projected on to the plane of the unconditioned, and distorted in the mist of my fanciful imagination. We can, indeed, truly say that man creates his idol in his own image. But there is one thing we must never forget: the fact that man is able to do this, and that he feels impelled to do so, he derives from God.

Single out any part of human life that you may choose, whatever you examine will always be a product of the original perversion, of the primal sin! But when you see sin you also see the image of God. Only where there is the *Imago Die* is there also *peccatum;* sin itself is a testimony to the divine origin of man. Even where man revolts against God in titanic rebellion, and with great daring and insolence "gets rid" of Him, or deifies himself, even there, behind the human perversion, the Divine image itself looks forth. Man could not be godless without God; he could not curse God if he were not first of all loved by God. The wrath of God under which the idolatrous, sinfully perverted man stands is simply the divine love, which has become a force opposed to him who has turned against God. The wrath of God is the love of God, in the form in which the man who has turned away from God and turned against God, experiences it, as indeed, thanks to the holiness of God, he must and ought to experience it.

SUGGESTED BOOKS

Buber, Martin, *Between Man and Man*, trans. Ronald Gregor Smith. Boston: The Beacon Press, 1955. A collection of five works extending and applying Buber's conception of the life of dialogue.

Calhoun, Robert L., *What is Man?* New York: Association Press, 1939. A short study of the common sense, scientific, philosophical, and religious portraits of man.

Cherbonnier, E. La B., *Hardness of Heart*. Garden City, N.Y.: Doubleday & Company, Inc., 1955. "This book attempts to correlate the Biblical understanding of sin with the facts of modern life."

Doniger, Simon, ed., *The Nature of Man.* New York: Harper & Row, Publishers, 1962. An anthology of essays by theologians and psychologists exploring many aspects of man's being.

Fromm, Erich, *Man for Himself.* New York: Holt, Rinehart and Winston, Inc., 1947. A study of humanistic ethics which contains a psychological analysis of modern man.

Macmurray, John, *The Self as Agent.* New York: Harper & Row, Publishers, 1957. Criticizes the traditional philosophical theory of the self as primarily knowing subject and defends a view of the self as active participant involved in personal relations.

Weiss, Paul, *Nature and Man.* New York: Holt, Rinehart and Winston, Inc., 1947. Argues that man illustrates universal characteristics of nature, especially freedom, and that therefore "man and his problems are one with the rest of nature."

IX · THE RELIGIOUS DESTINY
OF MAN

The question of man's destiny is one of the most challenging for religious interpretation. It is a fundamental one because it brings to a head both theoretical beliefs and practical aspirations. On the one hand, the question is a focal point for many of our philosophical and theological suppositions. On the other hand, what we believe about the ultimate end of man conditions how we act now to a greater extent than we often think. To illustrate these contentions we need only compare the beliefs of an Epicurean, a Hindu, and a New England Puritan, and their resultant modes of life.

In treating this problem we shall observe two restrictions. First, we shall observe the same limit that we did in the previous chapter on the nature of man. That is, we shall not be concerned with all things that might be said about the destiny of man, but only with those that are of direct religious import. We shall not, for example, be concerned with such questions as whether man's brain is destined to become any larger through evolution. The second restriction is that we shall not be discussing matters of political destiny on this earth—and we should now add outer space—i.e., international movements, etc. I do not wish to suggest that these aspects of man's destiny are without religious significance. But they are matters of religious ethics and the philosophy of history and are beyond the topic chosen for treatment under the present heading. We shall be concerned, in short, specifically with the idea of immortal life.

It should also be made clear that this discussion is not intended as a complete eschatology such as would be found, for example, in a system of Christian theology. We shall confine ourselves to what seem to us some foundation principles. The discussion may, if you like, be called preliminary to a fuller eschatological theory.

Some readers may hold that a discussion of immortal life is out of place from the start, on the ground that no one is in a position to inform us about existence beyond our temporal life. Why then discuss it? The answer comes readily: because immortal life has been an important belief in religion, because what we believe about it has a bearing on practical life, and because, precisely where we are limited in the realm of knowledge, we need to decide what we can reasonably and religiously accept on faith.

SELFHOOD

The first point which is of absolutely vital significance in this area—one without which the whole discussion of immortal life cannot meaningfully proceed—has to do with the concept of human selfhood. Stated negatively, the point is that, whatever we conceive the nature of the human self to be, the self cannot, from a theistic point of view, be regarded as exhaustible in the notion of the physical body. Stated positively, the self is a thinking, willing, history-making entity, with inner experiences of memory, feeling, and thought, evaluating, planning, and deciding, to which bodily processes are co-ordinate functions. To state this point in so bald a fashion is not by itself to assert belief in immortality. There are philosophers who believe that mental life is more characteristic of the self than physical functions are, but who do not believe in immortality. There are also thinkers who believe firmly in a providential God but not in an immortal life in any personal sense. But while the point does not itself assert immortality, it does assert a necessary condition for any kind of conception of personal immortality.

As soon as one accepts this view of selfhood as being partially transcendent, his path immediately bristles with the hosts and ghosts of philosophical questions that are raised. The genii of almost every philosophical problem come to haunt him. Merely to enumerate some of them is enough to force home the complexity of the view being maintained. What exactly is the self? Is it a kind of substance or is it a congeries of experiences? Is there direct evidence of its existence and nature, or is it only a postulated entity? Is the self essentially reason or mind, or is it something else? What is the relation between self, mind, and body? Do psychic factors and physical factors influence one another? What is their relationship? How is the brain related to mind and self? What is the significance of the fact that cortical areas concerned with self-awareness have to some extent been identified in the brain? What is the relation between mental experience and physical sensation? Do we have direct awareness of other selves, or are they only inferred entities? How can we vindicate our belief in the spiritual character of reality? These questions are enough to cause mild consternation to all but the most phlegmatic minds. Naturally we cannot hope to deal with them here. They are mentioned only to indicate that we must not be unaware of the many difficulties connected with the religious view we are accepting. These questions also show that religious interpretation needs, as suggested earlier, the assistance of philosophy.

A number of considerations, drawn from both empirical and rational sources, conspire to support the claim that psychic forces are irreducible to physical, that the self is partially transcendent over nature, or, in more traditional language, that the world of the spirit is no illusion. Many philosophers' books are filled with these considerations. From a religious perspective, however, the most telling evidence comes from the fact that inner experiences of commitment and meaning present themselves as forcibly and finally as do the stubborn facts of the external world. Not that a philosophical doctrine is revealed in such experiences: rather the experiences themselves bear the hallmarks of inexplicability by purely physiological causes. That is to say, the understanding of commitment can never come through the observation of brain activity or even of an entire behaving organism, but only through the concerned decisions and responses of one's inner self. The network of ideas contained in this assertion can be summarized by saying that there is subjective life as well as objective data, that subjectivity is as crucial as objectivity. By subjectivity is not meant that quality of being flighty, removed, and illusory which is sometimes attached to the term, but rather that of being passionately concerned, engrossed, and responsible. The way the term subjective is used in reference to student examinations is an analogy to the meaning here. A subjective examination does not mean one in which students can be irresponsible or disorganized, but simply one in which they are to bring themselves and their own thoughts into the answers. It is through an inner involvement that religion finds its heartbeat. Thus there is external history reported by a historian; but there is also the meaning of history in our subjective life. There is a visible institution described by a sociologist; but there is also the meaning of that institution emblazoned on the inner consciousness of a willing participant. There is a complicated organism analyzed by a biologist; but the same body is used by the self to advance or degrade the development of the self. Such considerations lead inevitably to the conclusion that the self is a unique and partly transcendent kind of entity.

Saying exactly what the self is is no simple project.[1] The various efforts of psychoanalysis, physiology, physics, and philosophy have produced significant changes in our thinking today. There seems to be much less of a tendency today to think of the self as an independent substance or substantial form conjoined to the body, and much more of a tendency to think of it as an integration of psychic forces or functions but with still a dominant center of consciousness. These forces or functions have been classified and subdivided in different ways. They would include the rational function, the emotional matrix, the capacity of will, the bodily processes, etc., and psychic factors more submerged or unknown. In this realm religion can be quite willing to look to all these other disciplines for insight. It is well to remember, however, that, even objectively considered, religion is in no worse ignorance than these other fields as to

the exact nature of the self. For there is no clear and agreed upon conception. And, on the subjective side, religion has the testimony of the
ages regarding something, however defined, of spiritual irreducibility in
the self. This double consideration makes belief in the uniqueness of
selfhood a reasonable tenet of religious faith.

DEATH

So much for the first step in a religious approach to the question of
immortal life. The second step has to do with the significance of death.
Death has a symbolic meaning of great significance in theistic religion, so
that an acute awareness of it is important for the religious person to grasp.
There are three aspects of death—almost three meanings of death—which
must be taken into account. All of them have deep religious import. One
of these is physical death; it is the expiration of the body to which all
human selves are subject. The second is what might be called moral
death; it refers to the annihilation or purgation of the sinful self which
is essential for any kind of perfected life. The third may be called spiritual
death; it refers to the possibility of final disintegration or extinction of
the entire self.
Physical death is, of course, a biological occurrence. At the scientific
level there is little to remark in it except for changing behavior patterns
of material elements. For theistic religion, however, physical death has
symbolic meaning in two ways. It is a powerful symbol of the finiteness
of man, and it dramatizes the creativity of God. The second of these
points probably needs most clarification, for, it might be asked, is not
death a sign rather of the impotence than of the creativity of God? This
would be true only if human purposes were identical with divine purposes, and if all the meaning of human life were obliterated at physical
death. Theistic religion holds that neither of these is really the case.
Death as a symbol of divine creativity comes about, then, in this wise:
Physical death means the end of the integration of the self as we know it.
We are space-bound, time-bound, body-bound creatures in this world. In
fact, some thinkers—even theistic thinkers—believe that our psychic life
is so bound up with our physical life that death must mean the end of
the whole self and that immortal life is inconceivable. Without going so
far, we must certainly say that the life of the self as we have experienced
it in this world comes to an end. This means that if there is any continuation or transformation of the self there must be at work something besides
the ordinary processes of survival in nature. There must be an act of
sustenance or transformation comparable, let us say, to the act of creating the self in the first place. In this way physical death comes to be in

theistic religion, as usually conceived at least, a reminder of the creativity and power of God.

The meaning of physical death as a symbol of human finiteness is more plain to us. Each man must succumb sooner or later to the contingencies of nature. We may try to avoid facing this fact, but there is no escape from it. All earthly endeavors and successes must come to an end for us. Snapped off then are the aspirations and ambitions, the pride and position, the vitality and virtue that have occupied our life so fully. Our living body turns into a limp corpse to take its place among the silent graves of the dead.[2] There is no need to dwell on this fact here. The only value would be that of repetition—as a learning device; for religion demands that we be fully aware of the reality of death. Art and meditation, however, are better vehicles for instilling this awareness than is an academic discourse. Death may be an awful prospect, but awful or not, religion bids us know it and accept it. For with the acceptance comes a full recognition of man's position of finiteness and dependence.

The idea of moral death may be regarded as a metaphor taken from the idea of physical death. Nevertheless it points to something of great religious significance. It is the notion of the elimination or destruction of the vicious, sinful component in us, i.e., the death of the old self in us. This is regarded as a prerequisite to the possibility of perfected selfhood or reconciliation. It is the negative requirement—that which must be rejected—as contrasted with the positive content of ideal selfhood. Such rejection may be an excruciating process, for it means giving up what may be most dear to us, namely, our own selfishness. In this sense we may have to give up some of our highest (but petty) values for the sake of a new self whose real value we never imagined. Moral death is thus a purgation process; it means killing the willful egoism and vicious self-centeredness to which we are subject.

The third meaning of death is what has been called spiritual death. It signifies the final disintegration or frustration of the self. Sometimes this is thought of as existence in hell, however that be conceived, and sometimes complete extinction of selfhood due to self-destructive choices. Unlike what we have called moral death, it is not regarded as a desirable thing, but rather as the climax of failure in living. It means ultimate failure in selfhood. It is something to be avoided by all efforts but yet a distinct possibility unless one follows a pattern of right choices. This spiritual death is related to moral death in the sense that, without the death of the selfish self, total disintegration may eventually follow. Only on such a foundation of purging away the self that refuses to be itself can a new self, the true self, be built. Thus looking forward to moral death may be painful but yet a hopeful prospect, because it reverses the tendency toward spiritual death and leads to purity of selfhood.

These three meanings of death come together in that only beyond life as we know it is their significance to be found. While it is not logically impossible that holiness be reached in this life, any more than it is logically impossible that a person continue to survive physically, as a matter of fact neither of these things occurs. Hence we must look beyond history for the final meaning and culmination of death. The significance of death lies beyond death.[3]

IMMORTAL LIFE

We come next to the third step in our interpretation. So far we have asserted the unique character of the self, and then the symbolic power of death by which it carries us beyond itself to find its meaning. Now in this third step we encounter directly the question of survival.

As soon as we mention the question of survival beyond death, quantitative images are most likely to pass before our minds—a long duration of time, a continuation in a horizontal line, a person just like ourselves living on and on into the distant future. Do I survive my body and live on endlessly? But this merely quantitative form of the question is, as often pointed out, of doubtful religious significance. It is possible to believe in immortality in this sense without having the idea raise any more religious issues than are already contained in present existence as we know it. Some of the Stoics, for instance, apparently held a belief in survival for a limited time after death before a final conflagration would end the whole world; but the problem of life and the solution to it, i.e., the religious quest, was already fully understandable in terms of current conditions of life. The short survival period beyond death added nothing to the religious side of Stoicism. The case does not seem to be markedly different if this quantitative survival is extended without end, until a kind of indefinite everlastingness puts a halt to our rational comprehension of such a linear movement forward. Many thinkers in the past have held this view of the soul—Plato being the most notable example. The very meaning of soul, according to this view, includes endless survival. Thus survival after death does not, in this view, contribute to the religious understanding of the self but is simply a natural feature of its being. In order to climax this point, one should mention that it is even possible to accept a doctrine of immortality in this quantitative sense without believing in God, and at least one thinker is known for this view.[4] We must conclude, therefore, that the question of mere survival is a philosophical question but not necessarily a religious one. It might even be argued that quantitative survival is a scientific question—one for which deciding evidence is not obtainable at present but in principle possible.

These remarks should be sufficient to indicate that mere survival—with the same round of activities of our present self going on and on forever—is not the human destiny theistic religion looks for. In religion, not quantity of time but quality of life is the thing. Thus, whenever or wherever or however it occurs, the religious destiny of man means, for the individual, a perfected life, a blessed life, eternal life in the New Testament sense; and for all of personality together, the perfected community, the "beloved community," the kingdom of God in the New Testament sense. The question, then, is not, "Will I survive my body?", but rather, "What kind of status should I look to as the culmination of human destiny?". Theistic religion is concerned with the quality of that which survives the death of the selfish, sinful self, and it has the boldness to assert in faith that the religious destiny just indicated is really in the making. This is the only kind of survival that is worth religious consideration.

All this is not to say that survival beyond physical death, which we have called quantitative survival, is irrelevant to religious destiny, or that it is opposed to it. Quite the contrary. The first complements the second in some indiscernible way. If the meaning of our history lies beyond history, if, in other words, the culmination of our destiny—blessedness—is not fully possible under present conditions (and it seems foolish, in the light of our knowledge of man and society, to say that it is), then there must be some sort of survival beyond physical death, and also beyond moral death. In this way quantitative survival supplements the idea of religious survival; but it is a derivative notion and not the primary question. Also there is no specification here of what such survival might involve or be like. There is only the firm conviction that the meaning and value of human selfhood will not be shipwrecked on the universe, that God will bring human destiny to its fulfillment, that what God has willed shall survive.

Here, then, we have the principal reason why theistic religion can accept wholeheartedly the belief in some sort of immortal life. The reason—as far as natural theology is concerned at least—is really an inference from the nature of God. Because God is what he is, a valuer of selves, their reality is not lost. Other arguments have been given in the history of philosophy, which even there are not worth a great deal—not merely because they touch only quantitative survival, but because they are not convincing in their own right.[5] From the viewpoint of religion, the most relevant consideration is always the purpose of God. It seems incredible that God, as personal, purposeful, and merciful, should will the meaning and value of selfhood to evaporate at death. Now some have maintained that this meaning and value can be preserved without any type of self-survival at all, and that the self, having contributed its life to the whole, can disappear contented in the assurance that its mark has been permanently left. For theistic religion generally, however, the fulfillment of purpose can only occur in consciousness, and therefore the worship of God, which is our purpose, and the blessed community, which is God's purpose for us, must involve real selves. This means that some remnant of the self, whatever that may be, scalded and scourged by temporal life, and finally transformed through the love of God, survives our inscrutible death. The cup of personal history runs over.

OTHER QUESTIONS

The self, while integral with the body, is nevertheless transcendent enough not to be definable in bodily terms alone. Death has a great symbolic meaning in pointing to the limitations of man and the creative power of God. Human destiny consists not in endless duration of the present self but in the transformation of the present self toward perfection, to which end the survival of some aspect of the self is an appropriate inference from the providence of God. These are the three steps we have made, the three theses that are of most religious significance in the question of immortality. The discussion might well end at this point, except that there are several other points of interest which are persistent and should at least be remarked upon briefly.

One of these points is the matter of heaven and hell in human destiny. What shall we think of these concepts which have played such a large part in so many religions? Certainly the term heaven, at its best, has been a helpful symbol in arousing commitments and actions concerning the goal of ultimate reconciliation with God, the state of perfected life, and in focusing confidence in the eventual triumph of God over the forces of evil. Some have not hesitated to think of heaven as quite a literal, physical place, where the righteous will go to live,[6] but others have preferred to keep the meaning symbolical. Thinking about heaven has also had, it must be admitted, an unfortunate connotation, namely, when it is viewed as a reward of happiness given out in exchange for performing certain good works during one's lifetime. The implication is that one should be good in order to bring about for oneself a heavenly reward. Such a crudely selfish motivation for moral endeavor is of inferior worth both in morality and in religion.

The idea of hell has also had symbolic significance in pointing to the depths of degradation into which man can fall when out of harmony with God. The speculative and controversial questions come, however, in connection with the idea of an actual hell beyond death. Some think of hell, as in the case of heaven, as a literal place, where condemned people reside and suffer; others prefer to say only that hell is a state of endless torment resulting from absence from God, i.e., permanent separation from God.

In both conceptions the difficulty is that of trying to square the idea of willed eternal punishment by God with the idea of infinite mercy in God, especially if the punishment is regarded as predestinated. As has often been pointed out, this doctrine of hell seems to assign to God a kind of cruelty greater in magnitude than that which characterizes man who is admittedly sinful. Still there are intelligent people and prominent groups who hold the belief, maintaining there is no inconsistency since the hell which is inflicted is somehow deliberately chosen by man in face of the opportunity for eternal life which is also open to him.

Those who reject this form of hell may hold that some lives are taken into eternal life upon death and that others become totally extinct. Another alternative[7] is to hold that, while some lives may be taken into eternal life upon death, others may continue in some form of existence until they too reach eternal life or else willfully place themselves beyond its attainment. It may also be held that, either upon death or eventually, God's mercy saves all, for all have a positive role in his ultimate purpose for man. This is the doctrine of universal salvation. In this case extinction or hell remain only as possibilities.

In the end no answer on this topic is likely to be entirely satisfactory to human reason. But, in summary, two principal questions continue to be debated and to be of importance for religious interpretation: (1) whether eternal torment can be permitted by infinite mercy, and (2) whether salvation is selective or universal.

A further question regarding immortal life has to do with the unity of self and body. Does immortal life mean disembodied spirits living on? This notion is not very plausible in its own right, and it is not typical of theistic religion. It may be helpful to point out that our body can be looked upon in two ways, physically and instrumentally. On the one hand it is an animated, unified grouping of physiological processes; but it is also an instrument for the expression of the self's thoughts and acts. Theistic religion, and certainly Christianity, has generally found it more plausible to hold that some body in the second sense, some agency of self-expression, must be integrated with the self in order for it to be an active entity. We do not know what this would involve beyond death when the present unity of self and body is destroyed. St. Paul refers to it as a spiritual body without attempting to elaborate.[8]

This is perhaps the place to comment on the distinction between immortality and resurrection. It is common nowadays for some theologians to set immortality in opposition to resurrection and to spurn the former in favor of the latter doctrine. In one sense there is a contradiction between the two, but not in every sense.

We began our discussion by speaking of immortality in its broadest sense, namely, any form of continuing status of the self beyond death.

We then went on to specify that for theistic religion the only kind of immortal life worth considering is a qualitatively transformed life, what the New Testament calls eternal life. Now if this is our meaning of immortal life, and if the doctrine of resurrection means that God provides a body for the self, fits it out, as it were, with a new body for its self-expression, then it is clear that immortality and resurrection do not contradict each other but rather supplement each other.[9] The one refers to the self's continuance in a transformed state, the other to its body or means of self-expression. It was common in medieval times, in fact, for thinkers to speak of both immortality and resurrection, depending on whether the context was primarily philosophical or theological, and not to think of them as opposed.

In one sense, however, there is a contradiction between immortality and resurrection. Sometimes immortality is taken to mean the specific belief that an entity called the soul is by its very nature endless, that it contains an inherent quality of being forever indestructible.[10] In contrast to this notion, resurrection denotes the belief that, just as the self was originally created, so any continuance beyond death is a divine act. Self and body being a unity, death puts an end to persons apart from divine action. As thus stated, there is an opposition between the doctrines. It is the opposition between automatic, natural survival, and continuance by supernatural power and intent. In this controversy Christianity and some other theistic religions have stood on the side of resurrection rather than immortality. They have rejected the notion that the soul is naturally endless and that it might survive without some form of body. A better way of stating this point, however, would be to say, not that immortality is opposed to resurrection, but that the idea of immortality in theistic religion is opposed to the Platonic idea of immortality since the former includes resurrection of self and body rather than natural survival of a soul.

Other questions persist. What of the connection between selfhood in immortal life and the self of present experience? The first images that come to mind may be those of remembering our past life in the same way that we remember it now—with its joys, sorrows, friends, foes, and so forth. Some would even have families reassembling. But if there is any truth in what we have suggested about death and destiny, such speculations are idle.

Is there no connection, then, between the newness of life which God actuates and the present life of the self? Perhaps we can get a vague suggestion from what we know of memory in our own lifetime. Quite apart from what psychoanalysis says, we know that we sometimes remember childhood experiences as strangely distant and remote, hardly real at all, yet somehow relevant to us. Again, we sometimes look at past experiences, especially those before important changes or conversions, as peculiarly isolated and removed from us now; we stare at them, analyze them, appraise them, as if they were foreign objects; yet we know they are related to us. Is there a vague analogy to be drawn from these memories? Could it be that immortal life includes, as present within consciousness, the removed yet strangely familiar meaning of temporal life?

And what of the character of immortal life? Can we say that it is primarily activity or primarily quiescent contemplation? But we have entered the region where thought surrenders to the silken sad uncertainties, and even imagination flickers. Far better, then, to taper off quietly, leaving to death the things that are not to be comprehended. We may visit the realm of speculation; but we must live in the realm of faith.

THE PROBLEM OF HUMAN IMMORTALITY

EDGAR S. BRIGHTMAN

Edgar Sheffield Brightman (1884-1953) was an able and prolific spokesman for the school of personalism in philosophy and religion. He studied at Brown University, Boston University, and also in Germany. After teaching at Brown, at Nebraska Wesleyan University, and at Wesleyan University, he spent the greater part of his career at Boston University. His books include Religious Values *(1925),* Moral Laws *(1933), and* Person and Reality *(published posthumously, 1957). In the following selection Brightman examines crucial arguments for and against immortality.*

CRUCIAL ARGUMENT AGAINST IMMORTALITY: PHYSIOLOGICAL PSYCHOLOGY

The only really strong argument against immortality is that based on a materialistic interpretation of physiological psychology. It runs somewhat as follows: consciousness is proved to depend on brain; if brain is injured, consciousness is injured, and the contents of consciousness are determined by bodily states or external stimuli which in turn are communicated to the brain. When the brain ceases to function, conscious-

From Edgar Sheffield Brightman, *A Philosophy of Religion* (New Jersey: Prentice-Hall, Inc., 1940), pp. 395-404. Reprinted by permission.

ness ceases; the death of the body destroys the cause of the "soul," and it is absurd to suppose an effect to continue after its cause has been destroyed. This argument is strong because it follows logically from its premises and because its premises seem to have the full support of empirical science. Corliss Lamont, in his searching investigation, *The Illusion of Immortality*, rests the case against belief chiefly on this argument, which he calls "monism in psychology," because it implies the indissoluble union of personality with body.[1] If personality is simply a function of body, lasting as long as body lasts and disintegrating as soon as body ceases to be body—that is, ceases to be living organism—then obviously there is no shred of truth in the belief in immortality.

We have here a crucial argument. No educated person can fail to be aware of it. Yet many educated persons are not convinced by it. Why? Is it merely because their emotions blind them to the evidence? Or is the argument after all not strictly crucial?

As the scholastics say, we must make a distinction here. There are points of view from which the physiological argument is crucial, and there are points of view from which it is not crucial, depending on one's metaphysical postulates. Let us consider some possible postulates and their consequences.

First, we might take positivism, a very popular view at the present time, as our postulate. It must be admitted that positivists at present are changing their views so often that positivism is a veritable Heraclitean river. Out of the stream we may rescue, perhaps arbitrarily, a definition of positivism, based on A. J. Ayer's discussions in *Language, Truth, and Logic*. From Ayer's book we gather that logical positivism is the view that there are two kinds of meaningful propositions, the logical and the empirical. Logical propositions are necessary because tautological, but give no information about the world. Empirical propositions are probable and refer only to sense experience.[2] From such premises it is both simple and necessary to infer, as Ayer does (177) that there is no meaning, no "factual content," in the proposition that there is a "transcendent" God or a future life. Physiological psychology rests on observations of sense data and is meaningful and verifiable; belief in immortality rests on no such observation and so is meaningless, or, as the positivists like to say, it is "nonsense."

Since the postulate of positivism is a fundamental rejection of all aspects of experience except sensation, it is plain why it does not convince most minds as a disproof of immortality. There are two reasons for rejecting the positivistic definition of meaning, as applied to immortality.

---

[1] Lamont, IOI, 109-110; cf. 99, 105-106, 112.
[2] See Ayer, LTL, Chap. I, esp. pp. 16, 19, 24, 31, Chap. II, p. 42, and Chap. IV entire.

The first is that immortality "is an hypothesis about our own future experience, and our understanding of what would verify it has no lack of clarity."[3] If any hypothesis about future experience is meaningful, statements about immortality have meaning. But the second reason for rejecting positivism is even more important. If all meaningful statements (except logical tautologies) must refer to sense experience, then all such statements as the following are meaningless: "I remember, I anticipate, I share a meaning with you, I experience values, I criticize my values, I seek for truth about values, we love truth, we worship." A postulate which requires us to consider meaningless experiences as universal as these reveals itself as arbitrary in the extreme. The empiricist who appeals to experience has no right to restrict his attention to specially favored parts of experience. If experiences of sense give us access to probable knowledge about certain aspects of the universe, it is at least possible that experiences of value and of personal unity and purpose may shed light on other aspects.

Positivism, however, is not the only postulate which, if true, would be fatal to belief in immortality. More important, more deeply rooted in the human spirit, is the postulate of materialism, which is the most ancient, the most instinctive, and the most perplexing "animal faith" of the race. Like positivism, materialism rests on the postulate that sensation is the gateway to knowledge. However, while the positivist limits his statements to what he can verify, the materialist goes far beyond the verifiable, for he declares that the universe consists, not of verifiable sensations, but of (essentially unexperienceable) material things and processes. Then he adds to his postulate the thesis that the only true *substance* or *cause* in the universe is material substance and its activities. By introducing such categories as substance and cause,[4] the materialist has on the one hand departed far from positivism; on he other, he has made a greater appeal to ordinary common sense.

---

[3] The quoted words are from the brilliant presidential address of Clarence I. Lewis, "Experience and Meaning," *Phil. Rev.*, 43 (1934), 143, which is a critique of one aspect of logical positivism. Moritz Schlick, in an article on "Meaning and Verification," *Phil. Rev.*, 45 (1936), 357 (reprinted in *Gesammelte Aufsätze*, 356), grants to Professor Lewis that "the hypothesis of immortality is an empirical statement which owes its meaning to its verifiability," but adds that "it has no meaning beyond the possibility of verification." If Schlick meant by "possibility" actual possibility, then he denied meaning not only to immortality but also to statements about the past or the interior of the earth. If he meant ideal possibility, the positivistic case against immortality as meaningful has collapsed.

[4] Reference to these categories makes it evident, if it was not already evident for other reasons, that philosophy of religion is a branch of metaphysics and that its problems are intertwined with metaphysical ones. No philosophy of religion can be complete in itself. A study of metaphysics should both precede and follow a study of philosophy of religion. Bowne's *Metaphysics* remains one of the most useful introductions to the field.

The bearing of materialism on belief in immortality is very clear. If materialism be true, then the material objects and processes investigated in physiological psychology are the real causal substances which produce consciousness. Once accept the materialistic postulate, and immortality is impossible. Our body causes our personal consciousness and when the body ceases to function, its effect will necessarily cease to be. We should notice, however, that the force of this reasoning derives not from the scientific observations of the physiological psychologist, but rather from the philosophical postulate which underlies the interpretation of those observations.

If materialism is true, there is no basis for immortality. But is the materialistic postulate really true? We have said that many educated persons were not convinced by the physiological-psychological argument against immortality; the chief logical reason for this is the unconvincingness of materialism. In several previous discussions in this book arguments against materialism have been presented. At the cost of some repetition, let us briefly review some of the chief difficulties of materialism. Materialism means that the universe is supposed to consist of nothing but physical substances and their causal activities. If we had no experiences other than sensations, this supposition might appear acceptable, were it not for the annoying empirical fact that sensations are not physical but mental in character. Yet, even in dealing with purely physical objects, materialism fails to account for the rational order of things, even for mechanistic regularities; the uniformity of law is an inexplicable coincidence, a sheer miracle, if each physical object is endowed with its law-abiding properties without any common cause. Thus theism (or personalism), which defines matter as the will of God in action (or at least as an effect of that will), accounts more consistently for the material facts than does materialism itself.

Further, the immediate empirical situation which contains all the facts that are to be explained is the field of consciousness. Materialism postulates that what is always experienced as conscious and immaterial must be explained by what is never conscious or immaterial. We can understand how motions can be explained by other motions, as in physics; but we cannot understand how motions of matter can produce consciousness. If we say that they do, and that's an end of it, we should ask ourselves how we are so sure that there is any unconscious, substantial, causal matter in the first place. If the postulate of materialism is a false dogma, then the mystery of the interaction of mind and body, although still inscrutable, becomes the more manageable mystery of the interaction of mind and mind. If materialism is false, the body may be itself part of the activity of the Cosmic Mind. If materialism is true, consciousness is a stranger in the universe and its intrusion must be accepted as a miracle; if theism or personalism be true, the facts of consciousness are clues to the nature of all reality.

The more closely we inspect conscious experience, the more difficulties emerge for materialism. We experience personal identity, unity, memory; materialism offers no account of these facts that explains their characteristic features. We experience purpose; materialism has to try to explain purpose away. We experience values and ideals; materialists also experience them and often are loyal to them, but their philosophy renders the very experience of ideal value unintelligible and offers no theory of obligation. In short, materialism, based as it is on an exclusive preference for sensations, cannot in the nature of the case give a coherent description of experience as a whole, and cannot even include sensations themselves in the domain of matter.

If the postulates of both positivism and materialism are questionable, it is clear why the argument against immortality based on physiological psychology is not truly crucial, even though it seems to be so. It is the strongest objection there is, but it is not decisive. While asserting the dependence of the mind on the body, and fully accepting all the facts of physiology, the philosopher may still inquire into the nature and the cosmic relations of the reality that appears as his body. If the body is viewed as materialistic postulates require, death is final. But if the body is interpreted on theistic postulates, the destiny of personal consciousness in the world will not be determined by the laws of matter but rather by the purpose and will of the God whose activity is very incompletely revealed in the object we call the human body.

No science can settle the question of immortality, not even physiological psychology. Neither can it be settled by intensity of hope or desire or faith. The ultimate question at stake includes but transcends science and religion; it is metaphysical.

CRUCIAL ARGUMENT FOR IMMORTALITY: THE GOODNESS OF GOD

Just as there is really only one vigorous argument against immortality (which reduces to the argument for a materialistic philosophy), so there is only one vigorous argument for immortality (which reduces to the argument for a theistic philosophy). If there is a God—a supreme, creative, cosmic person—then there is an infinitely good being committed to the eternal conservation of values.[5] That being is the controlling and directing power in all natural processes and is engaged in a process of imma-

---

[5] This argument is stated simply and effectively by Charles R. Brown in *Living Again* (Cambridge: Harvard University Press, 1922).

nent coöperation with all other persons. Since all true values are experiences of the fulfillment of ideal purposes by persons, the existence of values depends on the existence of persons. Value is personality at its best. God, the conserver of values, must be God, the conserver of persons.

We have found reason to regard God's power as finite; but there is no sufficient reason for supposing it to be so finite that he cannot conserve values. In a word, every argument for God, whether as absolute or as finite, is an argument for God's power to control his universe so as to achieve value; and every argument for God's goodness is an argument for his obligation to maintain persons in existence as intrinsic values that could not be lost without a total failure of God's good purpose. For if all persons were to perish with their bodily death, God would be in an unenviable position. He would either continue forever to create new persons, or he would give up the enterprise of creation. If he continued to create new persons, then he would be conducting a cosmic bonfire, with each new generation warmed by the burning of the previous one; God and man alike could look back on centuries of effort with no permanent results, no persons treated as ends in themselves, no life coming to full development. Or if he abandoned the enterprise of creation, then there would finally be no result at all from the entire race of personal beings except in God's memory; the eternal ideals would be as abstractly valid as they were before creation, a disappointed and frustrated God would remain—and all the intrinsic value of each person (except God) would be irretrievably lost. That the arguments for God are at the same time arguments for immortality is indicated by the fact that there has been only one well-known philosophical believer in immortality who denied theism, namely, J. M. E. McTaggart, and the correlative fact that substantially every theist has accepted immortality.

The arguments for God[6] are either directly based on the spiritual value and meaning of personality or else point to traits in objective nature which reveal personality at work there. On the other hand, no argument for immortality which leaves out the reference to God has any cogency; hence no argument that rests the case on any one intuition or fact carries weight.

The ordinary Christian believer doubtless bases his faith largely on the accounts of the resurrection of Jesus in the New Testament. Those accounts, however, cannot be regarded as conclusive, taken by themselves. Historical criticism shows that it is very difficult, if not impossible, to determine exactly what happened on the first Easter. The only historical certainty is that somehow the early disciples became convinced that Jesus was living. This conviction, however caused, does not constitute evidence

[6] See Chapter VII [in *A Philosophy of Religion*].

for immortality unless taken in connection with the total personality of Jesus, his faith, its grounds, and its influences. Only when interpreted in the light of a theistic world view does the resurrection story become validly symbolic of immortality.

Just as the argument from physiological psychology rested on materialistic postulates, so the argument from the goodness of God rests on theistic postulates. The initial data of materialistic (and positivistic) postulates are found in sense experience. The postulate of theism is that the real universe, to which our experience refers and in which it arises, must be conceived in such a way as to include and account for all the initial data, that is, the entire range of conscious experience: for sense data, and also for personal consciousness, reason, memory, purpose, freedom, and value—in short for all that materialism included and for all that it omitted in its postulation.

Does this mean that the theistic argument for immortality is truly crucial, whereas the materialistic argument against it was not? Let us be fully clear. It cannot be asserted on any empirical or rational basis that theism is the only possible view. Rigorous necessity cannot be ascribed to the proof. But it may justly be said that as between materialism and theism, the former accounts for a narrower range of the evidence and advances a postulate more remote from experience than does theism. Whereas materialism leaves the existence of consciousness and of spiritual life a mystery, theism shows it to be a rational expression of the nature of the universe. Thus materialism is an improbable inference from the total initial datum of experience, while theism is more probable, because more inclusive. "Matter" cannot be ultimate, because it is an hypothesis incoherent with experienced facts. God can be ultimate, because the concept of God is coherent with all the facts.

Rationally, then, faith in immortality is better grounded than is materialistic denial of that faith. Yet neither the argument from physiological psychology nor that from the goodness of God is crucial in the sense of being absolutely decisive. For the ultimately decisive information we must await the experience of death and what lies beyond it. Meanwhile, it would appear that doubts of immortality are to some extent emotional. "Animal faith," deriving from our bodily sensations is often emotionally more powerful than "moral faith," deriving from our ideal natures. But the thinker dare not allow emotional intensity, animal or moral, to weight any argument. In philosophy and in religious faith, as well as in practical life, there is a perpetual struggle of spirit to control the brute facts of The Given and to wrest meaning from them. Rational purpose has to test and guide emotion—a task of supreme difficulty. Spinoza rightly says, "All things excellent are as difficult as they are rare."

THE END OF HISTORY

REINHOLD NIEBUHR

Reinhold Niebuhr (1892–) has been one of America's most pene-trating analysts of the human situation and interpreters of man's life in history and society from the viewpoint of Christian ethics. He studied at Elmhurst College, Eden Theological Seminary, and Yale Divinity School. He served as a pastor in Detroit from 1915 to 1928 and then taught at Union Theological Seminary until his retirement in 1960. More recently he has been at Harvard. His many books include Moral Man and Immoral Society *(1932)*, An Interpretation of Christian Ethics *(1935), and* Faith and History *(1949). Here he expounds a theme which he himself has done much to make prominent, the concept of the end of history.*

Everything in human life and history moves towards an end. By reason of man's subjection to nature and finiteness this "end" is a point where that which exists ceases to be. It is *finis*. By reason of man's rational freedom the "end" has another meaning. It is the purpose and goal of his life and work. It is *telos*. This double connotation of end as both *finis* and *telos* expresses, in a sense, the whole character of human history and re-veals the fundamental problem of human existence. All things in history move towards both fulfillment and dissolution, towards the fuller embodi-ment of their essential character and towards death.

The problem is that the end as *finis* is a threat to the end as *telos*. Life is in peril of meaninglessness because *finis* is a seemingly abrupt and capri-cious termination of the development of life before it has reached its true end or *telos*. The Christian faith understands this aspect of the human situation. It shares an understanding of the tension between time and eter-nity with all other religions. But it asserts that it is not within man's power to solve the vexing problem of his subjection to, and partial freedom from, the flux of time. It holds, furthermore, that evil is introduced into history by the very effort of men to solve this problem by their own resources.

The evil thus introduced by the "false eternals" of human pride compli-cates the problem of historical fulfillment. The culmination of history must include not merely the divine completion of human incompleteness but a purging of human guilt and sin by divine judgment and mercy.

We have previously considered the implications of the revelation of God in Christ for the interpretation of history, and sought to establish that the Kingdom of God as it *has come* in Christ means a disclosure of the meaning of history but not the full realization of that meaning. That is anticipated in the Kingdom which *is to come*, that is, in the culmination of history. It must be remembered that a comprehension of the meaning of life and history from the standpoint of the Christian revelation includes an understanding of the contradictions to that meaning in which history is perennially involved.

Such an understanding by faith means that the world is in a sense already "overcome"; for none of the corruptions of history, its fanaticisms and conflicts, its imperial lusts and ambitions, its catastrophes and tragedies, can take the faithful completely unaware.[1] The light of revelation into the meaning of life illumines the darkness of history's self-contradictions, its fragmentary realizations of meaning and its premature and false completions. But obviously such a faith points to an *end* in which history's incompleteness and corruption is finally overcome. Thus history as we know it is regarded as an "interim" between the disclosure and the fulfillment of its meaning. Symbolically this is expressed in the New Testament in the hope that the suffering Messiah will "come again" with "power and great glory."[2] Men shall "see the Son of man sitting on the right hand of power, and coming in the clouds of heaven."[3]

THE NEW TESTAMENT IDEA OF THE END

This hope of the *parousia* in New Testament thought is sometimes dismissed as no more than a projection of those elements of Jewish apocalypse to which the first coming of Christ did not conform and for the satisfaction of which a "second coming" had to be invented. On the other hand they have frequently been taken literally and have thus confused the mind of the church. The symbol of the second coming of Christ can neither be taken literally nor dismissed as unimportant. It participates in the general characteristic of the Biblical symbols, which deal with the relation of time and eternity, and seek to point to the ultimate from the standpoint of the conditioned. If the symbol is taken literally the dialectical conception of time and eternity is falsified and the ultimate vindica-

---

[1] *Cf.* 1 Thess. 5:3-6. "For when they shall say, Peace and safety: then sudden destruction cometh upon them, as travail upon a woman with child. . . . But ye, brethren, are not in darkness, that *the day should overtake you* as a thief. Ye are all the children of light. . . . Therefore . . . let us watch and be sober."

[2] Mt. 24:30.

[3] Mt. 26:64 and Mk. 13:26.

tion of God over history is reduced to a point in history. The consequence of this falsification is expressed in the hope of a millennial age. In such a millennial age, just as in a utopian one, history is supposedly fulfilled despite the persisting conditions of finiteness. On the other hand if the symbol is dismissed as unimportant, as merely a picturesque or primitive way of apprehending the relation of the historical to the eternal, the Biblical dialectic is obscured in another direction. All theologies which do not take these symbols seriously will be discovered upon close analysis not to take history seriously either. They presuppose an eternity which annuls rather than fulfills the historical process.

The Biblical symbols cannot be taken literally because it is not possible for finite minds to comprehend that which transcends and fulfills history. The finite mind can only use symbols and pointers of the character of the eternal. These pointers must be taken seriously nevertheless because they express the self-transcendent character of historical existence and point to its eternal ground. The symbols which point towards the consummation from within the temporal flux cannot be exact in the scientific sense of the word. They are inexact even when they merely define the divine and eternal ground of history in terms of contrast to the temporal. They are even more difficult to understand when they seek to express the Biblical idea of an eternity involved in, and yet transcending, the temporal.

The *eschata* or "last things" in New Testament symbolism are described in three fundamental symbols: the return of Christ, the last judgment and the resurrection. They must be considered in order.

The Parousia

The idea of the return of the triumphant Christ dominates the other two symbols. The judgment and the resurrection are a part of the vindication of God in the return of Christ. To believe that the suffering Messiah will return at the end of history as a triumphant judge and redeemer is to express the faith that existence cannot ultimately defy its own norm. Love may have to live in history as suffering love because the power of sin makes a simple triumph of love impossible. But if this were the ultimate situation it would be necessary either to worship the power of sin as the final power in the world or to regard it as a kind of second God, not able to triumph, but also strong enough to avoid defeat.[1]

The vindication of Christ and his triumphant return is therefore an expression of faith in the sufficiency of God's sovereignty over the world and history, and in the final supremacy of love over all the forces of self-

---

[1] In Zoroastrianism, the only other historical religion beside Judaism and Christianity, this dualistic conclusion is actually drawn and history is conceived as an equal battle between the good and evil God. But even in Zoroastrianism the good God triumphs in the end.

love which defy, for the moment, the inclusive harmony of all things under the will of God.

This return of Christ stands at the "end" of history in such a way that it would sometimes appear to be a triumph in history and to mean a redeemed temporal-historical process. But according to other, and usually later, interpretations, the fulfillment of the historical process is also its end in the quantitative sense; and the redemption of history would appear to be its culmination also. This twofold aspect of the final vindication of Christ implies a refutation in Biblical faith of both utopianism and a too consistent otherworldliness. Against utopianism the Christian faith insists that the final consummation of history lies beyond the conditions of the temporal process. Against other-worldliness it asserts that the consummation fulfills rather than negates, the historical process. There is no way of expressing this dialectical concept without running the danger of its dissolution. The dissolution has, in fact, taken place again and again in Christian history. Those who believed in the simple fulfillment of history have been arrayed against those who believed that historical existence was robbed of its meaning in the final consummation. Both parties to the debate used Christian symbols to express their half-Christian convictions.

If we analyse the meaning of the two subordinate symbols of the "last judgment" and the resurrection it becomes clear that, according to Biblical faith, some aspects of history are refuted more positively while the meaning of historical existence as such is affirmed more unequivocally than in alternative conceptions.

The Last Judgment

The symbol of the last judgment[2] in New Testament eschatology contains three important facets of the Christian conception of life and history. The first is expressed in the idea that it is Christ who will be the judge of history. Christ as judge means that when the historical confronts the eternal it is judged by its own ideal possibility, and not by the contrast between the finite and the eternal character of God.[3] The judgment is

---

[2] Cf. Mt. 25:31 ff. "When the Son of man shall come in his glory, and all the holy angels with him, then shall he sit upon the throne of his glory: and before him shall be gathered all nations; and he shall separate them one from another, as a shepherd divideth his sheep from the goats."

II Cor. 5:10: "For we must all appear before the judgement seat of Christ; that every one may receive the things done in his body, according to that he hath done, whether it be good or bad."

[3] Augustine interprets the idea that we must be "made manifest before the judgment seat of Christ" as follows: "God the Father will in his personal presence judge no man, but He has given His judgment to His Son who shall show himself *as a man* to judge the world, even as he showed himself as a man to be judged of the world." *De civ. Dei*, Book XIX, ch. 27.

upon sin and not finiteness. This idea is in logical accord with the whole Biblical conception of life and history, according to which it is not the partial and particular character of human existence which is evil, but rather the self-love by which men disturb the harmony of creation as it would exist if all creatures obeyed the divine will.

The second facet in the symbol of the last judgment is its emphasis upon the distinction between good and evil in history. When history confronts God the differences between good and evil are not swallowed up in a distinctionless eternity. All historical realities are indeed ambiguous. Therefore no absolute distinction between good and evil in them is possible.[4] But this does not obviate the necessity and possibility of a *final* judgment upon good and evil. To be sure the righteous, standing before the last judgment, do not believe themselves to be righteous,[5] and their uneasy conscience proves the final problem of history to be that, before God, "no man living is justified." There is no solution for this final problem short of the divine mercy and the "forgiveness of sins." We have already noted the import of the Christian doctrine of the Atonement. It affirms that the ultimate mercy does not efface the distinctions between good and evil; for God cannot destroy evil except by taking it into and upon Himself. The very rigour with which all judgments in history culminate in a final judgment is thus an expression of meaningfulness of all historic conflicts between good and evil. Yet the necessity of a "final" judgment upon all other judgments is derived from the ambiguity of these conflicts.

The third facet in the symbol of the last judgment is to be found in its locus at the "end" of history. There is no achievement or partial realization in history, no fulfillment of meaning or achievement of virtue by which man can escape the final judgment. The idea of a "last" judgment expresses Christianity's refutation of all conceptions of history, according to which it is its own redeemer and is able by its process of growth and development, to emancipate man from the guilt and sin of his existence, and to free him from judgment.

Nothing expresses the insecurity and anxiety of human existence more profoundly than the fact that the fear of extinction and the fear of judgment are compounded in the fear of death. The fear of extinction is the fear of meaningless. When life is "cut off" before any obvious completion; when *finis* so capriciously frustrates the possibility of achieving *telos*, the very meaningfulness of life is called into question. But before faith can apprehend the divine mercy which completes our incompleteness and for-

---

[4] This is the point of the parable of the wheat and the tares, both of which must be allowed to grow until the harvest (final judgment) because they cannot always be distinguished from one another. Mt. 13:24-30.

[5] *Cf.* Vol I, Ch. II.

gives our sins it must confront the divine judge. In that confrontation it is not death but sin as the "sting of death" which is recognized as the real peril. For the ending of our life would not threaten us if we had not falsely made ourselves the centre of life's meaning.[6]

Literalistic conceptions of the allegedly everlasting fires of hell have frequently discredited the idea of a final judgment in the minds of modern Christians. But moral sentimentality in modern Christianity would have probably dissipated the significance of the idea of judgment, even if a literalistic orthodoxy had not seemed to justify the dissipation. It is unwise for Christians to claim any knowledge of either the furniture of heaven or the temperature of hell; or to be too certain about any details of the Kingdom of God in which history is consummated. But it is prudent to accept the testimony of the heart, which affirms the fear of judgment. The freedom of man, by which he both transcends and is creative in history, makes the fear of a judgment beyond all historical judgments inevitable. Many a court of opinion may dismiss us with a: "Well done, thou good and faithful servant"; but we will deceive ourselves if we believe such a judgment to be final. If men are fully aware, they will discern an accent of the fear of judgment in the fear of death. The fear of death arises merely from the ambiguity of finiteness and freedom which underlies all historical existence; but the fear of judgment is prompted by awareness of the mixture of sin and creativity which is the very substance of history.

The Resurrection

The idea of the resurrection of the body is a Biblical symbol in which modern minds take the greatest offense and which has long since been displaced in most modern versions of the Christian faith by the idea of the immortality of the soul. The latter idea is regarded as a more plausible expression of the hope of everlasting life. It is true of course that the idea of the resurrection transcends the limits of the conceivable; but it is not always appreciated that this is equally true of the idea of an immortal soul. The fact is that the unity of historical existence, despite its involvement in and transcendence over nature, makes it no more possible to con-

---

[6] In one of the profoundest of the later Jewish apocalypses, the Fourth Ezra, the fear of extinction is compared with the fear of judgment. Judgment is regarded as preferable to mere extinction because it is a part of the consummation of life: "Woe unto those who survive in those days! But much more woe unto those who do not survive. For they that do not survive must be sorrowful knowing, as they do, what things are reserved in the last days but not attaining unto them. But woe also unto them that survive, for this reason, that they must see great peril and many distresses even as these dreams do show. Yet it is *better to come into these things* incurring peril, than to *pass away as a cloud out of the world* and not see what shall happen in the last time." IV Ezra 13:15 ff.

ceive transcendent spirit, completely freed of the conditions of nature, than to conceive the conditions of nature transmuted into an eternal consummation. Either idea, as every other idea, which points to the consummation beyond history, is beyond logical conception. The hope of the resurrection nevertheless embodies the very genius of the Christian idea of the historical. On the one hand it implies that eternity will fulfill and not annul the richness and variety which the temporal process has elaborated. On the other it implies that the condition of finiteness and freedom, which lies at the basis of historical existence, is a problem for which there is no solution by any human power. Only God can solve this problem. From the human perspective it can only be solved by faith. All structures of meaning and realms of coherence, which human reason constructs, face the chasm of meaninglessness when men discover that the tangents of meaning transcend the limits of existence. Only faith has an answer for this problem. The Christian answer is faith in the God who is revealed in Christ and from whose love neither life nor death can separate us.

In this answer of faith the meaningfulness of history is the more certainly affirmed because the consummation of history as a human possibility is denied. The resurrection is not a human possibility in the sense that the immortality of the soul is thought to be so. All the plausible and implausible proofs for the immortality of the soul are efforts on the part of the human mind to master and to control the consummation of life. They all try to prove in one way or another that an eternal element in the nature of man is worthy and capable of survival beyond death. But every mystic or rational technique which seeks to extricate the eternal element tends to deny the meaningfulness of the historical unity of body and soul; and with it the meaningfulness of the whole historical process with its infinite elaborations of that unity.[7] The consummation of life in these terms does not mean the preservation of anything significant in either the individual or the collective life of man in history.

As against these conceptions of consummation in which man denies the significance of his life in history for the sake of affirming his ability to defy death by his own power, the Christian faith knows it to be impossible for man or for any of man's historical achievements to transcend the unity and tension between the natural and the eternal in human existence. Yet it affirms the eternal significance of this historical existence from the standpoint of faith in a God, who has the power to bring history to completion.

In the symbol of the resurrection of the body, the "body" is indicative of

---

[7] Professor John Baillie has called attention to the fact in his profound study of the Christian hope of everlasting life that the Platonic conception of immortality is but a more philosophical version of the primitive and animistic sense of a shadowy survival after death. Such a survival, according to Professor Baillie, may be convincing but not comforting. *And the Life Everlasting*, Ch. 4.

the contribution which nature makes to human individuality and to all historical realizations. We have previously noted that human individuality is the product of both the self-consciousness of spirit and the particularity of a finite natural organism.[8] In the same way every cultural and spiritual achievement, every social and political organization in history embodies both natural conditions and normative concepts which transcend and defy the particular and unique situation in which they develop. Climate and geographic limits, poverty and plenty, the survival impulse and sexual desires, and all natural conditions leave their indelible mark upon the spiritual constructions of history. Yet historical achievements transcend these limits in varying degrees of freedom. The doctrine of the immortality of the soul implies that eternal significance can be ascribed only to that element in the historical synthesis which transcends finite conditions. If this implication is followed to its logical conclusion nothing remains in eternity but an undifferentiated unity, free of all particularity and distinctions. We have previously observed how this conclusion is rigorously drawn, particularly in Buddhism and Neo-Platonism.

The doctrine of the resurrection of the body implies that eternal significance belongs to the whole unity of an historical realization in so far as it has brought all particularities into the harmony of the whole. Consummation is thus conceived not as absorption into the divine but as loving fellowship with God. Since such a perfect relation with God is not a human possibility it depends upon the mercy and power of God. Christian faith can only trust His mercy to deal with the recalcitrance of sin, even as it trusts His power to overcome the ambiguity of man's finiteness and freedom.

It is important to recognize that the rational difficulties which confront us in the doctrine of the resurrection are not all derived from literalistic corruptions of the doctrine; and they are, therefore, not all surmounted, if literalism is disavowed. Even if we do not believe that, "the earth will give back those that it treasured within it and Sheol will give back that which it had received and hell will return that which it owes"[9] we are still confronted with the formidable difficulty of asserting, what seems logically inconceivable, namely, that eternity will embody, and not annul, finiteness, or, in the words of Baron von Hügel, that the "total abidingness of God" will not destroy our "partial abidingness."

This rational difficulty partly explains the inconsistencies of Jewish apocalyptic writings, which furnished the background of New Testament conceptions. Sometimes they presented the consummation of history as something which occurred on this side of the "end of time." In that case the "resurrection of the just" was believed to usher in a millennial age

---

[8] Cf. Vol. I, Ch. III [Of *The Nature and Destiny of Man*].

[9] Similitudes of Enoch, 51:2.

upon this earth. Sometimes, particularly in the later apocalypses, the fulfillment and the end of history were conceived as coinciding; and all limitations of nature and time were believed to be transcended in the consummation.[10]

The second idea is of course more tenable than the first. But if the first had not preceded, and left its mark upon the second, the latter might well have had little to distinguish it from Greek conceptions of immortality. The whole Hebraic-Biblical conception of the unity of body and soul and of the meaningfulness of the historical process was bound to lead to this wrestling of the mind of later Judaism with this insoluble problem. New Testament thought wrestled with it too. St. Paul was convinced that "flesh and blood cannot inherit the kingdom of God; neither doth corruption inherit incorruption."[11] But this conviction did not drive him to the conclusion that everlasting life annuls all historical reality for which "the body" is the symbol. He believed rather that "it is sown a natural body and is raised a spiritual body" and that the consummation means not to "be unclothed, but clothed upon."[12] In that succinct phrase the Biblical hope of a consummation which will sublimate rather than annul the whole historical process is perfectly expressed. It is not possible to give a fuller or more plausible account of what is implied in the Christian hope of the fulfillment of life; and it is well to remember that the conditions of finiteness make a more explicit definition of the consummation impossible. It is therefore important to maintain a decent measure of restraint in expressing the Christian hope. Faith must admit "that it doth not yet appear what we shall be." But it is equally important not to confuse such restraint with uncertainty about the validity of the hope that "when he shall appear, we shall be like him; for we shall see him as he is."[13] The Christian hope of the consummation of life and history is less absurd than alternate doctrines which seek to comprehend and to effect the completion of life by some power or capacity inherent in man and his history. It is an integral part of the total Biblical conception of the meaning of life. Both the meaning and its fulfillment are ascribed to a centre and source beyond ourselves. We can participate in the fulfillment of the meaning only if we

---

[10] Edwyn R. Bevan observes: "As time went on, and the thought of the religious Jews became mature, it was largely realized that no Kingdom of God limited by the essential conditions of earthly life could satisfy the spirit of man." *The Hope of the World to Come*, p. 26.

R. H. Charles makes the same point, believing that eschatological thought gradually yielded to the conviction that "the earth, however purified is no fitting place for an eternal Messianic kingdom." *A Critical History of the Doctrine of the Future Life in Israel*, p. 220.

[11] I Cor. 15:50.

[12] II Cor. 5:4.

[13] I John 3:2.

do not seek too proudly to appropriate the meaning as our secure possession or to effect the fulfillment by our own power.

THE END AND THE MEANING OF HISTORY

If there are partial realizations of meaning in history, as well as corruptions and distortions, it ought to be possible to discern them from the vantage point of the true end. For this reason a Christian interpretation of human destiny requires one further view of the meaning of history in the light of what is believed about the character of the ultimate consummation. If the final consummation fulfills, rather than annuls, historical meaning, the real content of this meaning must be illumined by the light of faith. Furthermore it must be possible to gain some insight into the character of the sinful corruptions of meaning, particularly since they are mostly derived from the error of regarding partial realizations as the final fulfillment.

Such an examination of history in the light of the Christian interpretation of the end must begin with a distinction between two dimensions in the relation of eternity to time. Eternity stands over time on the one hand and at the end of time on the other. It stands over time in the sense that it is the ultimate source and power of all derived and dependent existence. It is not a separate order of existence. For this reason the traditional connotation of the concept, "supernatural," is erroneous. The eternal is the ground and source of the temporal. The divine consciousness gives meaning to the mere succession of natural events by comprehending them simultaneously, even as human consciousness gives meaning to segments of natural sequence by comprehending them simultaneously in memory and foresight.

Eternity stands at the end of time in the sense that the temporal process cannot be conceived without a *finis;* and eternity cannot be conceived as having a *finis.* Eternity outlasts time, though we know nothing about either an abrupt ending of the world or of the gradual dissipation of its natural energies. Our efforts to picture the relation in spatial terms always leads us astray and prompts us to project a particular point in future time which will also be the end of time. This effort to picture the end of time from inside the time process is the cause of most of the literalistic corruptions of the Christian conception.

The two dimensions of the relation of eternity to time result in two perspectives upon the meaning of history. From the one perspective we discern those qualities and meanings of history which seem to have absolute significance without reference to their relation to the continuum of history. An act of martyrdom or of perfect sacrifice may or may not have discernible historical consequences, and may be appreciated without reference to the consequences. It may "be recorded in heaven" without being obviously recorded on earth. There may also be a "final" judgment upon particular evils in history without waiting for a "last" judgment, *i.e.*, suspending judgment until all its historical consequences have been recorded. On the other hand a "final" judgment about any historical matter may be a judgment which seeks to comprehend a particular event, act or quality in history in the light of its consequences in history. It is not possible, of course, for finite minds to reach a vantage point from which they could deliver final judgment from either perspective. But their effort to do so is illustrative of the two dimensions of history in its relation to the eternal.[14]

In so far as the freedom of man to be creative in history implies a freedom over history itself, there are tangents of freedom which stand in direct relation to eternity. This dimension of history prompts, and would seem to justify, Leopold von Ranke's famous dictum[15] that each moment of time and history is equidistant from eternity. But the dictum is only partially justified, for it leaves the other dimension of history out of account. History is also a total process which requires understanding of its totality from some "last judgment."[16] In so far as every act and event, every personality and historical construction is immersed in an historical continuum it takes its meaning from the whole process. If we look at history only from "above" we obscure the meaning of its "self-surpassing growth." If we look at it only from a spatially symbolized end we obscure all the richness and variety which is expressed in its many parts.

SUGGESTED BOOKS

Berdyaev, Nicolas, *The Destiny of Man*, trans. Natalie Duddington. London: Geoffrey Bles, Ltd., 1937. A work on Christian ethics by a Russian

---

[14] It might be well to observe at this point that the synoptic symbol of "The Kingdom of God" is more "existential" than the Johannine and Greek conception of "eternal life." To place "eternity" and "time" in juxtaposition is to distinguish primarily between the flux of process and the principle which underlies the process. The juxtaposition of "Kingdom of God" and history implies a more religious and existential definition of the relationship. The sovereignty of God over all creaturely wills has the same two relations as eternity has to time. It is on the one hand the authority of the source of life over all life at any moment. It is on the other hand a sovereignty which is finally vindicated in "the end."

[15] *Cf. Ueber die Epochen der Neueren Geschichte.*

[16] Benedetto Croce seeks to do justice to the two dimensions of the historical in the words: "Every act stands altogether in relation to itself and altogether in relation to something else; it is both a point of repose and a stepping stone; and if it were not so it would be impossible to conceive the self-surpassing growth of history." *History as the Story of Liberty*, p. 90. An act cannot stand only in relation to itself. It must be related to some realm of meaning, but it can transcend the meaning of the historical process.

existentialist thinker who regards questions of eschatology as inseparable from ethics.

Bultmann, Rudolf, *The Presence of Eternity*. New York: Harper & Row, Publishers, 1957. Gifford lectures on history and eschatology, arguing that the meaning of history lies in the eschatological present experience of historical individuals.

Cohen, Morris R., *The Meaning of Human History*. La Salle, Ill.: The Open Court Publishing Company, 1947. A naturalistic philosopher discusses the philosophy of history and concludes that history is essentially tragic but not devoid of ethical value and opportunity.

Cullman, Oscar, *Immortality of the Soul or Resurrection of the Dead?* New York: The Macmillan Company, 1958. A contrast between Greek and early Christian concepts, concluding that early Christianity believed in resurrection of the dead as opposed to the Greek idea of immortality of the soul.

Du Noüy, Lecomte, *Human Destiny*. New York: Longmans, Green & Co., Inc., 1947. A biologist sees evolution as now transferred from the physical to the spiritual realm and as leading to a "glowing destiny of man" in the process.

Feifel, Herman, ed., *The Meaning of Death*. New York: McGraw-Hill Book Company, Inc., 1959. An anthology in which "philosophers, religionists, and scientists" discuss the problem of death "from varying bases."

Lamont, Corliss, *The Illusion of Immortality*. New York: G. P. Putnam's Sons, 1935. A humanistic criticism of the belief in immortality.

Niebuhr, Reinhold, *Beyond Tragedy*. New York: Charles Scribner's Sons, 1937. Essays on the Christian interpretation of history.

X · PRAYER AND WORSHIP

In this chapter we shall attempt to deal with some of the intellectual difficulties which attend the practice of prayer and worship. The most obvious of these is whether prayer is worthwhile at all. Many people can find meaning in some aspects of religion, such as faith, the sinfulness of man, and even immortal life, but seem to think prayer is based upon outright selfishness, groveling attitudes, or uncritical assumptions. They ask with Job: "What is the Almighty, that we should serve him? and what profit should we have, if we pray unto him?"[1] But there is no use arguing in the abstract whether prayer is worthwhile. Prayer, like immortal life, acquires significance only within the context of theistic religion. If theism is thought to be justified, then prayer will be seen as an important religious act. But if theism is not thought to be justified, then prayer will not be either—except perhaps in the sense of meditation, a sense quite different from that which it has in theistic religion.[2] Though we cannot profitably discuss the question in the abstract, we can at least try to see how theistic religion views the matter of prayer, and the related practice, worship.

SOME CHARACTERISTICS OF PRAYER

The best place to begin is to understand what religious theism conceives prayer to be. What characteristics are most descriptive of it, most essential in it? We shall note four such characteristics. These will not exhaust what all theists would want to say about the nature of prayer, nor what specific religions would want to say about it. But they will perhaps indicate enough of its nature to show why it is central in theistic religion and to offset the charge that it must consist in selfish or debasing attitudes.

The first description to be mentioned is that theism regards prayer as a response to divine action. It is not that man first decides to seek out God and then uses prayer as a possible device for this purpose. The belief is rather that God has first acted to reveal himself in history and personal life, and man responds to this initiative. One aspect of his response is prayer. The belief that God and not man is the true initiator of religious acts such as prayer is found abundantly in religious literature. The Psalmist, for example says: "Lord, thou hast heard the desire of the humble: thou wilt prepare their heart, thou wilt cause thine ear to hear."[3] This belief implies that men pray for the same generic reason that they create art and establish friendships, namely, because they are overcome by a powerful experience which they cannot artificially generate or manipulate. They do not just seek to pray: they find themselves praying. They do not just pray on behalf of themselves: they pray in spite of themselves.

What is the significance of this characteristic? It means that prayer is more devotion than demand, more consecration than calculation, more service than self-advancement.

A second characteristic is that prayer is an act of communing or converse with God. Prayer has been described simply as communion with God. More devotional accounts will speak of man's conversation with God, talking things over with God, lifting the heart to God, and so on. Beneath these figurative ways of speaking there is a simple yet fundamental point: if theism is really true, if God really exists as theism conceives him to exist, then it cannot be the case that God will run his own course and man his and never the twain shall meet. Rather there will be dramatic points of intersection, since both are personal and in search of the personal. Prayer is the name given to one form of that intersection, the form in which man gives conscientious expression to his own attitudes and needs in the light of divine capacities and intentions.

If prayer is an act of communing or converse with God, then the attempt to verbalize prayer is not the primary thing in it. The spiritual experience in it is primary. Words have an instrumental function of selection, clarification, directing attention, and corporate sharing. But Jesus warns specifically against confusing genuine prayer with verbal utterance: "And in praying do not heap up empty phrases as the Gentiles do; for they think that they will be heard for their many words."[4]

But this does not mean that prayer is to be thought of as a vague emotion, a misty contact, precious to the pious but beneath the dignity of mature reason. It involves an indispensable element of intellectual control and self-conscious direction. St. Paul placed careful stress on this point. "For," he writes, "if I pray in a tongue, my spirit prays but my mind is unfruitful. What am I to do? I will pray with the spirit and I will pray with the mind also. . . ."[5] Prayer is thus thought of as an act of communing with the whole self.

A third characteristic of prayer is that it is to a large extent adoration. Sometimes adoration is singled out as constituting a separate type of prayer. It is more appropriately regarded as an essential ingredient in all prayer. One often hears clergymen speak of prayers being "offered" to God. The significance of this is that prayer is not so much an instrument for obtaining human benefits as an expression of adoration offered to God. Thus not only does prayer have its inception in the initiating activity of God, but it also has its goal in him and the effecting of his will. The last phrase sums up a great deal, for prayer as adoration means that the purpose of it is not that of *affecting* but that of *effecting* the divine will.

A fourth characteristic of prayer is that it issues in renewed dedication on the part of the one who prays. Job was doubtless wrong in making his primary question that of "what profit should we have, if we pray unto him?". Prayer is not a matter of getting profit for oneself. But at least it can be said that one consequence of prayer is restoration of incentive, renewal of purpose. Among other things, prayer is dedication. This is indeed a profit received. But dedication means that the emphasis is not upon what one can get out of it but upon what one can give through it.

To enumerate these characteristics of prayer—that it is a response to divine action, that it is man's communing with God, that adoration is a central part of it, and that it issues in dedication—does not by itself dispel disturbing questions. But it may at least serve to indicate that for theistic religion prayer is not, in intention at least, the credulous little ritual it is sometimes pictured to be.

ASKING FOR THINGS

How does it happen, then, it may be wondered, that so many prayers involve asking for things? Does not this feature make prayer the self-centered instrument we said it was not, or, as one student put it, merely a sophisticated kind of "gimme!"?

The fact that theistic religion does consider asking for things in prayer to be justified is quite apparent. St. Paul says: "Have no anxiety about anything, but in everything by prayer and supplication with thanksgiving let your requests be made known to God."[6] Jesus is even more emphatic: "And whatever you ask in prayer, you will receive, if you have faith."[7] Why has this emphasis been so strong?

In answering this question the whole problem seems to be one of trying to discover useful analogies and instructive word sequences that will convey the intended meaning of asking and avoid improper meanings. We need to understand that the theological meaning of asking is not exactly the same as that to be found in the familiar request-response situations of daily life.

Let us consider, by way of illustration, a typical request-response situation. A child asks his father for a quarter. The father looks up in mild surprise, then asks what the quarter is wanted for. The child replies. Then the father begins to weigh the request. He considers how politely the request was made, whether the proposed use of the money is desirable, whether the child should work for the quarter, and so on. He then fishes in his pocket to see if he has the cash on hand, deliberates a little more, and is still undecided. The artless child performs at a strategic moment the useful art of persuasion, commonly known as coaxing. Finally the father hands over the coin, perhaps cheerfully, perhaps grudgingly.

This is a typical asking situation in ordinary life. But it is a bad analogy for the idea of prayer. In the first place, the father was not aware of his child's desire or need until the request was made. But God is not thought of as being informed in any way by the petitions of man. Jesus said that "your Father knows what you need before you ask him."[8] Nor is God thought of as undecided at the time of petition, nor as having to deliberate back and forth until he makes up his mind, nor as open to persuasion by arguments or appeals. Prayer is not a method of bending God's will which is otherwise adamant or uncongenial. God is thought of as ever constant in purpose, ever desirous of the true good of his creatures, ever searching for the fitting means to achieve that good. There is another point as well. The child may have asked his father for something which was beyond the father's capacity to give. But the asking which is considered appropriate in prayer is never a petition for the impossible or even a setting aside of the orderly processes of the world.

What can be said on the positive side? If asking does not mean informing the mind of God, transmuting the will of God, or changing the order of God, what does it involve?

Let us consider what may be a better analogy. A father wishes to send his son to college and to help him out with a substantial share of the financial obligations. The son is intelligent and is well-suited in most ways for greatly benefiting from the college experience. Everyone, including the son himself at bottom, knows that this would be a natural step for him and one by which he would probably find himself. But a certain rebelliousness prevents the son from accepting his father's offer. Consequently the son is somewhat at odds with himself, lacking in real motivation, not knowing what he wants to do in life. In the end, however, he swallows his pseudo-pride, accepts the offer, agrees to cooperate in the financial burden, and discovers some vocation in his college years.

In this situation the father is already aware of his son's need and is desirous of meeting it. Yet nothing can really be done unless the son is willing to ask for what is needed. This kind of asking is more akin to the asking of prayer. Such asking is the act by which man places himself within the divine compass and is willing to receive the good that is always being sought for him. In personal life there are some things which simply cannot be accomplished unless one is willing to receive them, willing to ask for them. Not even God can force the gifts of the spirit on one who is free to choose; one must decide to ask for them and accept them. That is why asking for things is considered justified. It is a matter of opening up the self to receive that good which is always available.

Asking in prayer, then, involves a yielding of the self. One writer summarizes: "The fundamental pattern of petition is the conscious offering of our needs and desires to God, allowing Him to purify and mature them, and then trusting Him totally with the results."[9] The language of prayer, therefore, really consists not of "gimme" words but of "giving" words. That is, paradoxical as it sounds, asking in prayer is a kind of giving, the giving of the self, with all of its needs, limitations, attitudes, aspirations, and weaknesses, into the power of love which is at the heart of the universe. Such giving makes it possible for a person then to receive whatever comes about in his life. In ordinary spoken prayers this asking is cast into the form of particular requests, pleas, petitions, appeals for blessing, and so on. This is considered appropriate for human clarification and emphasis. But the deeper meaning of asking gives meaning to the rest. Jesus prayed "Thy will be done" before he asked for daily bread.

PRAYER AND NATURAL LAW

But does prayer make any difference in the world, and if so, can this fact be reconciled with the reign of law?

First, then, is prayer efficacious in the world, or, in religious language, is it answered? We must first note an ambiguity in the latter way of putting the question. To ask whether prayer is answered might suggest that prayer is primarily a matter of asking for personal benefits, whereupon the worthwhileness of it is then judged on the basis of whether these specific benefits come about. But if that is not the fundamental meaning, as we have indicated, then prayer will be seen to be its own intrinsic value, its own reason for being. Nevertheless, when this ambiguity is clarified, persons of theistic persuasion still maintain that prayer does have great effects in the world, that it is answered. The Psalmist says: "O thou that hearest prayer, unto thee shall all flesh come."[10] And the Epistle of James declares: "The prayer of a righteous man has great power in its effects."[11] Theism does not maintain that the answering of prayer comes in the form of favors granted to favorites, or of willful violations of orderly processes in nature. Moreover, it does not equate the answering of prayer with the kinds of outcomes that human beings might have wished or even expected. God's ways are not man's ways. But to the actual fruitfulness of prayer, however that be interpreted, there is unlimited testimony among religious folk.

Now how does this belief in the efficacy of prayer square with the belief in natural law? Is there room for prayer in a world of orderly mechanism?

We have heard a great deal in this century about the changes which have come into physical theory and which represent a shift from the mechanistic view that prevailed for two centuries after Newton. Modern thought is filled with notions that the universe is no longer regarded as a rigid machine, that rigorous prediction has given way to statistical approximation, that the world may be organismic rather than mechanistic, that novelty is as primordial as determinism. In all this there is a point that is relevant and a point that is irrelevant to the theistic conception of prayer. The irrelevant point is that theism has never regarded its overall outlook as contingent upon the prevailing scientific view of the physical world. It has viewed prayer as efficacious regardless of how the physical world is designed. If the world is mechanistic, so be it. Theism can hold, as it sometimes did, that prayer is one causal agency built into the predetermined mechanical structure of things. But the relevant point is that it is more coherent to maintain that prayer is effective if the world is one in which creative novelty is possible and voluntary acts can help to shape the outcome of events. Without rigid mechanism it is easier to hold that prayer as a spiritual agency is interrelated with, and determinative of, physical occurrence. So on the whole theism has welcomed the new developments, not as essential to itself but as more compatible with its own basic intuitions.

Prayer need not be thought of as contravening natural law; it can be viewed as one factor which natural law must take into account. We shall have to say, therefore, that we do not know all there is to know about the ultimate laws of the universe, and that we do not know the exact relation between spirit and matter. Prayer would be incompatible only with a materialistic conception of nature. So the basic conflict is not between prayer and natural law but between theism and materialism. If you believe in theism, you may hold consistently that spiritual agencies and physical facts are interrelated. If you believe in materialism, there is no room for this possibility.

One consequence of the theistic outlook is that the same pattern of events is viewed from more than one perspective. Suppose, for example, that a person becomes gravely ill. Many despair of his surviving. But with great earnestness he prays for recovery in order to carry on some important work. In time he does recover. Now some doctors may give a purely physical explanation of the recovery. Others may appeal to psychosomatic explanations. But from the theistic point of view the recovery may very well be seen as an answer to prayer, i.e., as the action of God through the medium of the prayer. And these different perspectives on the situation are not incompatible. There can be, without conflict, physical, psychological, and theological levels of explanation for the same event. The point is that the same event has different meanings from different perspectives. So important is this principle in religious interpretation, as well as in other areas, that we ought perhaps to give it a name—the principle of multiple perspectives. It holds that the same event can be viewed compatibly with different meanings from more than one angle.[12] This does not mean, of course, that God contributes one portion of the event, say sixty per cent, and man contributes the other forty per cent, or vice versa. Rather the whole event, e.g., the recovery, has its physical basis; the whole event has relation to psychic factors; and the whole event has a spiritual interpretation.

One special difficulty concerning the efficacy of prayer is how a person's prayer for others, or intercessory prayer, is operative. We can readily understand how others might be influenced through a person's own actions on their behalf which are stimulated by prayer. We can also understand how others might be influenced by the fact of their knowing that someone is concerned enough about them to pray for them. And we could even give some meaning to direct interpersonal influence akin to telepathic communication. But religious theism does not confine itself to explanations by these mechanisms alone, none of which would necessarily require the reality of God. It holds that in some mysterious way God brings about effects in his own way through the medium of intercessory prayer. A theoretical basis for this belief might be found in the interrelatedness of all creatures, as envisaged, for example, in the philosophy of Leibniz or Whitehead. We are members one of another through our relation to God, and therefore mutual influence through him is possible. The practical reason for this arrangement, and the reason why God does not break in arbitrarily to pull us out of jams, may be found in the belief that there is a purpose for the whole taken as a whole as well as for individuals as individuals. Prayer for one another may provide opportunities and power by which God can effect a more meaningful corporate redemption than would be possible by piecemeal unilateral coercion.

In the end there can only be intimations rather than clear comprehension of spiritual laws. One reason for this is our imperfect practice of religion. St. Paul asserts flatly that "we do not know how to pray as we ought. . . ."[13] And if there is deficiency in the practice of something, we cannot expect an explanation which is necessarily geared to that practice as its resource to be free from defect either.

INFLUENCE UPON GOD

A further question of great theoretical interest is that of how prayer may be said to affect the divine life of God. This question comes about because of two fundamental, yet seemingly opposite, religious feelings. On the one hand, we feel that God is self-contained, perfect in every respect, eternally the same, not subject to change. Anything other than this would seem to present too human a view of God. From this point of view prayer cannot literally affect God in the sense in which one person can affect another person by his trust, praise, gratitude, and petitions. There is nothing we can add to God and no way in which we can influence him, since he is eternally perfect and ever immutable. On the other hand, we feel equally strongly that prayer is related to a deity who is concerned about man, one to whom it makes a real difference how and what men pray, one through whom results are actually wrought by prayer. From this point of view it would seem that God must be affected in some literal sense if prayer is what theism claims it to be, for a being who is eternally the same cannot by definition respond to and interact with the world.

Two solutions to this problem are common, one a more classical and the other a more modern type. Both seek to preserve the absoluteness of God and the efficacy of prayer.

The more classical solution holds that God is eternal, beyond influence from time, and that he experiences total knowledge and total happiness in a single, all-encompassing act. But included within that knowledge and that happiness is the fact that human beings glorify him and pray to him. Human prayer, therefore, has a part in the divine experience. Prayer is meaningful and effective, but not in the sense that it *changes* God in any way or *causes* his happiness as an antecedent event. That is, it is not true of God that at Time A he is incomplete in some respect, at Time B prayer is offered, and at Time C he is changed or fulfilled in some way. Such is the temporal pattern when human beings affect one another or when man interprets the influence of God upon himself. But in God all things, including our prayers, are eternally present in his experience. They have their effect, but in a formal sense, not in a temporal, causal sense. God creates and acts with these prayers eternally in mind. Thus God is absolute, and yet prayer is efficacious.

The more modern solution holds that the absoluteness of God does not require that he be thought of as beyond all relation to time or remote from influence by the world of creatures. Absoluteness consists rather in his supreme goodness, power, knowledge, and happiness. Thus God may be said to need his creatures—not, of course, in the sense in which they need him, but in the sense that they are the requisite products of his creative love if it is to be active. He therefore suffers with their shortcomings, exults with their devotion, responds to their religious acts, all in some rather literal way. Thus God is absolute in those respects in which it is religiously necessary to say that he is, and yet prayer is efficacious through a real, not just a formal, interaction between God and man.

In either of these views there are some respects in which prayer does not have effect upon God and some respects in which it does. We suggested earlier that prayer is not generally conceived of as influencing the knowledge, the goodness, or the orderliness of God. These are among the unchanging divine attributes. In what respects, then, can influence be said to occur? First, if God suffers and exults in interaction with human responses, then prayer would make a difference in the exact character of the divine happiness. Again, prayer might affect his specific purposes. That is, granted that the ultimate purposes of God are eternal and unchanging, theism may consistently hold that, to allow for human freedom, the specific ways of accomplishing those purposes are not predestined in detail. Thus his specific, local purposes may be affected by the character of human prayer. And from this it follows that his ways of action in the world will also be conditioned by prayer. "We know that in everything God works for good with those who love him, who are called according to his purpose."[14] But we must repeat that these modes of influence will be understood by the one theory in a merely formal sense and by the other theory in a more literal sense.

THE TRUE OFFICE OF WORSHIP

The experience of worship can be described with such terms as pure reverence, disinterested homage, devoted service, selfless acclaim to God and his goodness. Worship is a part of prayer, since adoration is essential in the latter. But prayer involves other sorts of elements as well, such as petition and intercession. In another sense worship is wider than prayer, since worship may include any activity, attitude, or thought consciously directed to the service of God.

The true office of worship is, in religious words, to glorify and magnify God. Specifically its true function is not that of obtaining peace of mind, happiness, or stability for the worshipper, even though in many cases these things may be by-products. In genuine worship man at last lays aside his preoccupation with his own status, his selfish desires, his personal advancement, in order to give complete adoration to God.

This point may be amplified by referring to the Westminster Confession, whose well-known statement of life's purpose many would accept. It says that the chief end of man is to know God and enjoy him forever. Leaving aside the consideration that some would like to have a mention of creative activity as well as of knowing and enjoying, the point we wish to bring out in connection with this statement is that one of the key words in it is the word "him." There is a common tendency to replace this word subconsciously with the word "oneself" and then take such a statement to mean that the chief end of man is to know God and enjoy oneself forever. Translated into earthly terms, the result of this replacement is a kind of theological hedonism, in which worship becomes an experience of self-satisfaction, religion an instrument for personal contentment, and God himself a mere concept to help out in the adjustments of life. But this is a perversion of the real meaning of worship in theistic religion, which is not the enjoyment of *oneself* but the knowing and enjoying of *him*.

This attitude of worship in theistic religion raises, however, a criticism that we shall take time to consider. It often appears to critics of theism that the idea of worship is inappropriate on two counts: it makes God into a monarch seeking flattery, and it robs man of his dignity and self-reliance. As for the first of these charges, it is argued that a God who would create persons merely to praise and adore him must be somewhat self-centered, egotistical, vain, that is to say, no God at all. How could we conceive of a God wanting people around just to sing his own praises and land his own virtues? Is not this a sheer desire for flattery and a very unbecoming trait? As for the second charge, it is argued that worship requires man to debase himself and to surrender his rightful pride and stature as a human being. Is not worship a groveling attitude in which man becomes a submissive, obsequious vassal?

This kind of criticism ignores what religious theism conceives God to be. He is no Aristotelian, statue-like deity, drawing everything to himself and giving nothing. His essential nature is that of limitless, searching, even suffering love. God is love, and worthy of worship on that account. Worship does not mean bowing down to the calls for flattery by a potentate whose nature is sheer, brute power; it is giving oneself over to the service of the only reality which is perfect and consistent in selfless, outgoing love. And since religious theism finds this love to be not an abstract principle nor a theoretical ideal but centered in the activity of a divine person, worship is directed through personal symbols to that divine person who is love.

Thinking of God in this way also deflects the charge that worship debases man's selfhood. God is not thought of as creating men to be servile footstools. Being love, he wills the good of his creatures for the creatures' sakes. He seeks not servility but emancipation, which is the only state in which true devotion can occur. Thus man will not serve God by choking his own potentialities, any more than a son will honor his father by staying home to become an indolent, compliant toady. God is worshipped not by debasing oneself but by becoming oneself, one's true self.

THE PRACTICE OF PRIVATE PRAYER

*"There is that near you which will guide you; O wait for it, and be
sure ye keep it."—Isaac Penington*

DOUGLAS STEERE

*Douglas V. Steere (1901–) studied at Michigan State College and
Harvard University and has spent his teaching career at Haverford
College. Although he is a professor of philosophy, his writings
have been mainly on themes of religious devotion, and reflect his
Quaker concern for inner contemplation. They include* On
Beginning from Within *(1943),* Doors into Life *(1948), and* Work
and Contemplation *(1957). In this excerpt he explains the nature
of prayer in a theistic sense.*

THE NATURE OF PRAYER

"Ostriches never fly; fowls fly, but heavily, low down, and
seldom; but eagles, doves, and swallows fly often, swiftly, and on high."
Once more Francis de Sales is contrasting the drowsy ones, the "good"
ones, and the devout ones. Of all the practices that serve to arouse this
spiritual nimbleness and swiftness and vivacity of devotion, none is so
central as the practice of private prayer. In fact, this practice is in itself
an act of devotion. For the great Christian men and women of prayer
have always looked upon prayer as a *response* to the ceaseless outpouring
love and concern with which God lays siege to every soul.

Prayer for them is a response to the prior love of God. Nearly a
thousand years ago Bernard of Clairvaux gave a matchless word on this
in a talk to his religious brotherhood: "Do you awake? Well, He too is
awake. If you rise in the nighttime, if you anticipate to your utmost
your earliest awaking, you will already find Him waking—you will
never anticipate His own awakeness. In such an intercourse you will
always be rash if you attribute any priority and predominant share to
yourself; for He loves both more than you, and before you love at all."

The prayer of devotion is a response, a reply, the only appropriate
reply that a man or a woman could make who had been made aware of
the love at the heart of things, the love that environed them, that rallied

From Douglas V. Steere, *Prayer and Worship* (New York: Association
Press, 1938), pp. 10-15, 27-35. Reprinted by permission.

them, that wearied out evil and indifference by its patient joy. To sense that is for a man to long to love back through every relationship that he touches. "I trow God offers himself to me as he does to the highest angel," Meister Eckhart, the great German mystic, cries out, "and were I as apt as he is, I should receive as he does." And in one of his later sermons Meister Eckhart went a step further and could say, of God's own delight in this outpouring of His love, "The joy and satisfaction of it are ineffable. It is like a horse turned loose in a lush meadow giving vent to his horse nature by galloping full tilt about the field; he enjoys it and it is his nature. And just in the same way God's joy and satisfaction in his likes finds vent in his pouring out his entire nature and his being into this likeness." With such a consciousness of the love of God, is it any wonder that in Eckhart's day, in the fourteenth century, we hear of an old woman who was seen coming along the streets of Strasbourg carrying a pail of water in one hand and a torch in the other? When asked what she was about, she answered that with the pail of water she was going to put out the flames of hell and with the torch she was going to burn up heaven, so that in the future men could love the dear Lord God for himself alone and not out of fear of hell or out of craving for reward.

Prayer then is simply a form of waking up out of the darkness in which our life has been spent in half-intentions, half-resolutions, half-creations, half-loyalties, and a becoming actively aware of the real character of that which we are and of that which we are over against. It is an opening of drowsy lids. It is a shaking off of grave-clothes. It is a dip into acid. It is a daring to "read the text of the universe in the original." "We should in ourselves learn and perceive who we are, how and what our life is, what God is and is doing in us, what he will have from us, and to what ends he will or will not use us," says John Tauler, a disciple of Eckhart's.

To know and to love God directly is to come to know what we are. All true Christian prayer also presupposes the further step, that there are things He will have from us and that some of our responses are true and authentic responses to His love and others are not. Prayer is an attempt to get ourselves into that active co-operation with God where we may discern what is authentic and be made ready to carry it out.

With our increased knowledge about the continuous reorganization of life that goes on in the depths of the unconscious, the impressive definition of prayer as *the soul's sincere desire* has appeared. In this sense the fearful man prays by his acts of withdrawal, of cringing, of brooding, of distrust; and the man of faith prays by his openness, freedom, readiness to take risks, trust of the future. Both pray by these acts even though they are not conscious of them as prayer. There is a large measure of truth in this interpretation. For many forms of prayer do send down into the unconscious: positive imagery, positive resolutions, positive incentives to action. And these forms of prayer would willingly recognize that these elements operate within the unconscious to aid, and to bring into fruition in the life of inward desire what is begun above the threshold of consciousness, what is intentionally and consciously sought after in prayer. Yet since this deep unconscious intention of the soul is able to be reached and affected by consciously directed intention, *prayer* in this sense becomes not merely *the soul's sincere desire*, but prayer is the process of intentionally turning the focus of the soul's sincere desire upon the active nature of the Divine Love and by every device within its power holding it there until it becomes engaged.

There is no fear here of the charge of autosuggestion in prayer that so haunted the last generation. It is freely admitted from the outset that large elements of prayer are and should be of that character. One wise writer has suggested recently that the very purpose of the active cultivation of the interior life is to transform the gifts of grace into an effective autosuggestion. All that is meant by this word autosuggestion, or self-suggestion, is that the suggestion is selected and presented by the person to himself. We have come to recognize that all that we know has been suggested to us either by our external or internal environment in the form of what is called heterosuggestion.

In entering prayer we have a perfect right to choose from this random mass of heterosuggestions some that we regard as more significant than others, and to dwell upon them. "Whatsoever things are true, whatsoever things are honest, whatsoever things are just, whatsoever things are pure, whatsoever things are lovely, whatsoever things are of good report; if there be any virtue, and if there be any praise, think on these things." Autosuggestion is no more than this act of dwelling upon selected aspects of experience. By the mere act of dwelling upon them we do not necessarily prove them to be true. Nor did we intend to. That matter of truth is both a prior and a subsequent matter of tests and interpretations to which either auto- or heterosuggestions must be submitted. These selected aspects of experience with which we may enter prayer are, however, only a threshold of past experience that we cross in order to engage with what is there. And they are subject to revision and to addition as the prayer brings its bearer to new levels of insight.

Prayer is often defined as *speech with God*. It may begin that way. But prayer of a high order rarely stops there. Real prayer is more nearly *work* with God. In Japan, a student of painting is not allowed to touch his brush to the canvas until he has spent hours moving first his body and then his brush in a synchronizing response to the curves of the mountain he would paint. This empathy, this *feeling into* the subject by the body and the limbs, is not unlike prayer. The swift and agile acts of devotion that follow are only the setting down on the canvas of daily life what is felt into and moved into and yielded to in prayer.

In prayer, what looks like passivity may conceal the most intense activity. It may in truth be "a rest most busy." Unless there be that coincidence of wills, which means that the human will is brought low, is tendered, is transformed, the New Testament is quite clear that its amazing promises of the power of prayer do not apply: "*If ye abide in me, and my words abide in you,* ye shall ask what ye will and it shall be done unto you." In the most real prayer of all there is wrought that refocusing of the life of the one who prays until he is brought to abide in the Divine love and the character of the Divine love to abide in him. Then and then only does the promise of extending that transforming power indefinitely really hold. At those moments a man comes to recognize the distinction between his praying and his being prayed in, and to realize that most of what has been described above is only *praying* and that what really matters is to be *prayed in*.

To the prayer of the woman who begged that the wicked Dean Inge might die, to the prayers for the preservation of his ecclesiastical property made by an official of a church that still held its buildings although it had lost its people, to the prayers of any army chaplain that the enemy be destroyed, to the prayers of a student on the matter of his life partner, for the confirmation of an accomplished decision that he had no intention of changing—to these prayers apply the piercing ray of this prescription: "*If ye abide in me and my words abide in you,* ye shall ask. . . ." By the light of this condition, the flesh of selfish lust and desire melts away and only the firm bony structure of the true willingness to cooperate with the Divine remains. Unless you are ready and willing to seek that kind of inner empathy and submit to that kind of inner renovation, it would be better not to play at praying.

. . . . .

As we bear in mind the intense spiritual action upon us of this Divine *field of force* when we open ourselves to it, we may expect to approach the matter of asking for specific things in prayer—of petitional prayer with a better hope of understanding it.

There are those who look upon any specific request in prayer as a sign that the one who makes it is still at an infantile level in prayer—that he still looks upon God as a kind of a glorified Santa Claus to whom he sends up his Christmas lists. To these persons, petition has no place in mature prayer. "When I pray for aught, my prayer goes for naught, when I pray for naught, I pray as I ought." They would commend to us Thomas Aquinas' single petition when visited in prayer, and asked what he desired as reward for his matchless writings in defense of God's cause: *"Naught but Thyself!"* Often they remind us that God knows our need before we utter it, and hence our petition is superfluous.

It is impossible for me to face these difficulties without a sense that they are not so real as they sound. Remembering always the wise New Testament condition to insure participation and distinguish prayer from magic—"If ye abide in me and my words abide in you, ye shall ask what ye will. . . ."—remembering Jesus' inclusion of the element of petition in the simple "Our Father" which he gave to the people, and remembering his own free use of petition in his prayers—our minds may be set somewhat at ease about being childlike enough to use it freely. It is not a question of adding to God's knowledge of our needs, nor is it a question of "changing God's mind" by our request. To bring a specific request into the silence and lay it before God is to enter more deeply into the "Spiritual Combat." What I request is a desire, or a longing or an aspiration that is a part of me—whether it be good or evil. If I did not raise it in prayer it would remain a part of me. If it was something below my best it might go on increasing until it gained control. If it was in keeping with my best and yet was never brought into prayer, it might lack that confirmation that would be the factor in its accomplishment.

If my life is to be lived as a friend of God, to be lived in response to the discerning love of God, how can I do other than to lay my desires and longing before Him for review and plead the case for them if I feel strongly about them? If I believe I love a girl, or if I am considering some undertaking whose success seems of great moment to me, where better could I take these matters than to prayer, where I may ask God to further them? That He will do so is another matter. I may beg with all my might for some outcome, and I may, after an hour, arise convinced that it is not to be, or that it must be in another form, or that I must wait, or that I must take this costly step in order for it to come about. It does not matter where or with what petitions we begin in prayer. *What is really important is where we end, where we are brought to in prayer.* The real question to ask of ourselves after prayer is: "Were you faithful? Did you yield?"

But what about prayers for rain? Those who ask this question usually set up a deep ditch between the *psychological* and the *physical* and insist that whereas prayer may affect the psychological, it may never cross the ditch to influence the physical. George Meredith insisted that we ought not to expect God to step in between us and the operation of His laws. In the healing of the sick, the boundaries of this ditch have changed somewhat since Meredith's time. Some physicians have begun to admit that what the patient believes profoundly affects his chances for physical recovery. This has not meant an abandonment of medical science. It has only been a recognition that body and mind are not enemies, but function as a whole, and that the structure of the "laws" that the human being responds to is broader than he, as a doctor, had formerly suspected. In fact the very status of physical laws is at no point so absolute or inexorable as Meredith and his generation believed it. Some of the ablest of scientists are willing to admit that science deals with reality in only one of several possible ways, each of which leave out something which could be known only by the adoption of a different approach.

We do not know that prayers for rain affect a power that supplies a factor left out by meteorological predictions. Neither do we know that this is not the case. In either event, it implies no abandonment of our active co-operation with our creative stem: the earth and the air—the conservation of moisture by the planting of forests, the plowing under of humus matter, the continuing to experiment with mechanical means of influencing the precipitation of moisture-laden clouds, the improvement of our techniques of irrigation. Prayer is only another form of this same intimate co-operation between us and the stem. If a group of people are suffering from a drought that threatens them with extinction and if they are people who hold up their every need in prayer, they can and should make no exception of this need. The boundaries of this ditch are yet to be established, and is there not the promise that if you abide in the life, "ye shall ask what ye will . . ."? There is, then, no absolute limit that can be placed upon petition. The only limit is man's need. But the prior condition must never be forgotten—the condition is to abide in Him and that His words shall abide in you. The condition is that you shall yield, that you shall respond, that you shall be faithful. Faith in God is set prior to faith in prayer, yet given this, you may begin at any point. And those old friends of prayer take their every need into prayer with great ease and confidence.

PRAYER OF INTERCESSION

Prayer for others is a form of petitional prayer that makes deep demands on the faith of an individualistic generation that has so largely lost its sense of inner community. Yet at no point do we touch the inner springs of prayer more vitally than here. For when we hold up the life of another before God, when we expose it to God's love, when we pray for its release from drowsiness, for the quickening of its inner health, for the power to throw off a destructive habit, for the restoration of its free and vital relationship with its fellows, for its strength to resist a temptation, for its courage to continue against sharp opposition—only then do we sense what it means to share in God's work, in His concern;

only then do the walls that separate us from others go down and we sense that we are at bottom all knit together in a great and intimate family. There is no greater intimacy with another than that which is built up through holding him up in prayer. The firm bond that existed between John Fredric Oberlin and his parish was laid each morning in the hour that he devoted to prayer for his individual parishioners. We are told that as they went past his house at this hour in the morning, they did so in quiet, for they knew what was happening there. Forbes Robinson's *Letters to His Friends* reveal his constant use of this form of prayer for his Cambridge associates. He remarks in one letter that if he would really reach some need in his friend's life, he would always prefer a half-hour's silent petition for him to an hour's conversation with him.

An unbeliever once mockingly begged Catherine of Sienna that she pray for his soul. She prayed by day and by night, and the power of renovation disarmed and brought him to his knees. I know of a Japanese girl whose father had found a whole chain of reverses too much for him to meet normally and who had taken the alcoholic short-cut. She prayed for him hour after hour until the time came when he yielded, gave up drink, committed his life to the center of Divine love he had experienced, and with the help and love of his devoted family he has continued in a new way of life.

It is not a question of changing God's mind or of exercising some magical influence or spell over the life of another. Before we begin to pray, we may know that the love of One who is actively concerned in awaking each life to its true center is already lapping at the shores of that life. We do not do it all. Such prayer is only co-operation with God's active love in besieging the life or new areas of the life of another, or of a situation. If you pray for something other than what is in keeping with that co-operation, you go against the grain, and if you remain in prayer and are sensitive, you will realize this and be drawn to revise it. As in all petitional prayer, he who really prays must be ready himself to yield.

You may pray for the release of some area of life in a friend and find that you are called upon to set right something in your own life that has acted as a stumbling block to him. You may pray that your friend be given courage to endure certain hardships and find that you are drawn to pack your bag and go and join him or that you are to give up your pocket money for the next month or even perhaps to give a fortnight or a month's salary to help along his cause. In intercessory prayer one seldom ends where he began.

During these active forms of work in the silence: in contrition, in purification, in simplification and refreshment, in petition, and in intercession, frequently if we are sensitive and listening, there come clear insights of things to be done. Often they come in that receptive silent waiting after we have opened our needs and where we do nothing but wait for direction. Again they may come during the day and push their way in between events that seem to bear no connection with them. These insights are precious and are to be heeded if we are to live in response to that which we feel in prayer. When they involve some real readjustments that may be costly to effect, the Quakers have called these *concerns*. They want a word for the tiny promptings, the gentle whispers that are equally as important and that may represent concerns in the forming.

"Prayer is incipient action," and these clues are the lines along which the molten freedom of the man in prayer are to be cast. *"Mind the light"* reads an inscription on a sundial. Come under holy obedience. Here is the unformed side of life's relationships—the letters to be written, the friends to be visited, the journey to be undertaken, the suffering to be met by food, or nursing care, or fellowship. Here is the social wrong to be resisted, the piece of interpretative work to be undertaken, the command to "rebuild my churches," the article to be written, the wrong to be forgiven, the grudge to be dropped, the relationship to be set right, the willingness to serve God in the interior court by clear honest thinking and the refusal to turn out shoddy work. Yet we need more than the intimations. We need spiritual staying power to carry them out. "Profession of truth, without the life and power, is but a slippery place, which men may easily slide from," wrote Isaac Penington. He commends his own practice of praying to be established in the power that will enable him to carry out these leadings. "I wait on Him for the strength to fulfill it." Here in the silence, as that power gathers, it is well to face the difficulty one will meet in carrying out this concern. Here in the silence it is well to see the only semi-inflammable character of the bridge you mean to burn; to face the inertia, the resistances, the amused smiles of friends; the coldness and want of understanding on the part of many who resent having their attention called to social injustice in which they are involved—the strangling doubts of your own later hours—doubts that led Theresa of Avila to say: "I see few people who have not too much sense for everything they have to do." These need to be met and overcome in the silence.

If we ignore these leadings, they poison future prayer. Katherine Mansfield wrote, "I went upstairs and tried to pray, but I could not, for I had done no work." And if they are ignored, they break the precious chain of influence that this act may have set going. You become a link in this chain when you begin to pray. If you fail, it must wait for another. "Were you faithful? Did you yield?"

There is nothing greater than this constant fidelity. "The world goes forward," wrote Harold Gray, who served a term in Leavenworth during the war for his conscientious objection, "because in the beginning one man or a few were true to the light they saw and by living by it enabled others to see." Holy obedience to the insights, the concerns that come, that persist, and that are in accord with co-operation with God's way of love is not only the active side of prayer, but is the only adequate preparation for future prayer.

There can be no complete prayer life that does not return to the point from which we began—the prayer that is a response to the outpouring love and concern with which God lays siege to every soul. When that reply to God is most direct of all, it is called *adoration*. Adoration is "loving back." For in the prayer of *adoration* we love God for himself, for his very being, for his radiant joy.

"Religion is adoration," was a favorite remark of that veteran of prayer, Friedrich von Hügel. "The most fundamental need, duty, honour, and happiness of men is not petition or even contrition, nor again, even thanksgiving . . . these three kinds of prayer which indeed must never disappear out of our spiritual lives, but *adoration*." Adoration is not alone a special stage in prayer, although it may be that, too. All the truest prayer is shot through with it and its mood is the background to all real contrition, petition, and intercession.

In adoration we enjoy God. We ask nothing except to be near Him. We want nothing except that we would like to give Him all. Out of this kind of prayer comes the cry "Holy! Holy! Holy!" In the school of adoration the soul learns why the approach to every other goal had left it restless.

WORSHIP AND WORK

ROBERT CALHOUN

Robert L. Calhoun (1896–) studied principally at Carleton College and at Yale and has spent his career at the latter institution teaching in the College, the Graduate School, and the Divinity School. He is one of the country's outstanding historians of philosophy and theology and is known to have several potential volumes in these areas which have not yet been published. His interest in religious vocation is seen in his God and the Common Life *(1935) and to a lesser extent in the little book,* What is Man? *(1939). In the following selection he interprets daily work as a divine calling.*

To regard daily work as in any vital sense divine calling is to use concepts that are full of obvious paradoxes. The tensions between egoistic drive and self-transcending devotion, narrow specialization and wholeness, habituated skill and readiness for change, what actually is and what ought to be—all these are characteristic of human work in any conceivable stage of development. It is a tangle of threads that refuse to be sorted out. In a way, these tensions and many more like them characterize all human living, which, as we have remarked, is ambivalent, unsimple, two-directional through and through. The ambiguities and paradoxes of work are not then different in kind from those of life itself. But it does not follow as self-evident that the turbulent, tangled, broken web of actual work—or of actual life at large, for that matter—deserves to be called religious, in the sense of service to God.

Our problem, of course, is not whether human work in all its aspects can be called religious. The whole foregoing argument rules out any such possibility. Our problem is whether everyday work, the work that is open to ordinary people under ordinary conditions, deserves at all to be called religious in any of its major aspects or modes. Granted that many people doing ordinary work are also religious people, is their piety to be found in their work or wholly apart from it? To this question, our whole argument is meant to answer emphatically: "In their work, no less than outside it." It remains to see whether this answer can be justified now in more specific terms.

From Robert L. Calhoun, *God and the Day's Work*, Reflection Books edition (New York: Association Press, 1957), pp. 98-108, 113-14. Reprinted by permission.

Perhaps the best approach is an indirect one. We have thought of religion throughout as "worship and devout work together." Instead of saying more about work just now, let us think for a moment about worship, in which the religious orientation of human life is most clearly evident.

A man worships, in the last analysis, not because he chooses to do so but because he cannot help it. Confronted by reality that seems to him divine—overwhelming in power or goodness, or both—a man has no option. He must bow down and pray.

He may first be driven to see and acknowledge his God by many sorts of impact. One is disaster. It may be individual frustration or great sorrow; it may be the ills and suffering of mankind, realized with fresh insight. Human powers and values at such a time seem nothing. The course of life appears no more than the fluttering fall of a dead leaf, tossed here and there by winds that are lifeless and cold. And yet, because the human spirit is not a dead thing, it seeks to rise above its trouble; and it is often met in its struggles by a Reality hitherto unknown or forgotten. The exact nature of that which grips men in extremity defies description. Yet there comes a sense, more certain than any argument can provide, of a final Being, more real than all the pain and disappointment and fear that press on every hand. It is not as though one had encountered a great wall and could go no further, for the Reality that one faces does more than halt the aimless straying. Man overwhelmed with evil is made to think again, to "repent," to recognize a primary root of the trouble in himself. Once he grapples with this fact and, in the ensuing struggle, attains a new orientation, there emerge for him new perspective and increased strength. He is "converted," turned about, made new, reborn. Although he cannot undo the evil that has been done, his life is set now in a new direction, his despair kindled into hope. In the extremity of failure or of suffering, man may thus be made to acknowledge that not as a result of his own efforts but, as it were, in spite of them, he is in the presence of God, to whom he finds himself in a new way committed.

So, too, with great success and the half-painful ecstasy of triumph and joy that attends it. These are "experiences of consummation" in which a man beholds the fruition of his plans and efforts. Intelligence and hard work have resulted in a thing of beauty, or at least in work well done, whether it be a symphony or a solid road. In such a situation the pure egoist, of course, will not worship. All the work and all the results, he presumes, are his alone; and by himself he stands in elated self-satisfaction. But a wiser man knows that many factors have made his success possible. He will see in his work, not merely the distinctive turn of his own hand, but the manifold influences of a thousand. The very intensity of his happiness makes him the more acutely aware of the organic interrelatedness of a multitude of factors in what he has helped to achieve. And above them all he will discern God, who gave him materials, created and maintained the conditions for his toil, and carried him forward to its completion. For him there will be a new venturesomeness, a desire to carry on, confident in the trust he holds in God's goodness. Worship, coming thus at the peak of successful attainment, issues again in wholehearted commitment.

We cannot hope to describe such experience. At best, words can only be reminders to those who already know something of it. One element in it is awe, noble fear, "*Ehrfurcht.*" Not base fear, for this is an impulse simply to flee. Not calm observation, in which dread is absent. Awe is rather the fascinated and purging dread of one who wishes to fly, but somehow is held and purified. The gentle Christ crucified between two thieves inspires noble fear. Brutal torture bids us run; unsullied goodness bids us stay. So gripped, we see more than a man hanging on a cross. We see God, moving dimly behind the scaffold, within and beyond the sorrow and the pain. We are aware, again, not of a wall that leaves us unable to move, but of a living Presence into whose hands we commit our lives. But not to rest. The creative touch of God's spirit in worship does not leave man quiescent; it calls him to active work. The God discovered is at work. Indeed, the very discovery is a result of His initiative in bringing men and the world back to himself. A world is in the making, and communion with God in worship sends man forth into the very heat of the task.

Yet, if we turn back from the high vision that comes in the best hours we know to the noise and smoke of our factories, the grinding toil of our farms and mines, the routine and the anxious maneuverings of our offices and board rooms, what warrant is there for seeking God in these? What possible ground have they in common with the worship that moves our life to its deepest springs, leaving it purged and renewed? The answer has been given in terms, partly of factors in the nature of work itself, partly of human dispositions that give some work a value not dependent simply on the details of what is being done. The whole answer may be put now into a somewhat different perspective.

Let us say that work can truly become vocation, surcharged with religious meaning, only when it awakens and sustains the love of the workman. To say this, is to risk derisive skepticism. For "love" has become a word for the sentimental and mealy-mouthed. Popular singers, starry-eyed nature worshippers, perennial adolescents, various sorts of softlings—these are the folk whose damp ecstasies have misted and melted a powerful word almost beyond recognition. Whether the word now can be made acceptable to men producing machinery and tilling the land is doubtful. Yet the experience for which it stands is vital to the human worth of any kind of work.

What we mean here is, first, a lusty, sensuous delight in things men see and handle, and in the seeing and handling of them: well-planed wood or a sweet-running engine, good soil or well-bred livestock. Such love of the things with which one works—materials, tools, books, plants, and animals—is the best solvent of the paradoxes that complicate the worker's living. It gives reality to the assurance that in the devotion of his life, a man will find it. Necessity and freedom cease to be at war for the worker who loves his job. Such love, too, is the best safeguard against shame or cynicism, despondency and aimless drift.

Love of things needs to go with a love of people that is no less vigorous and realistic. There is such a thing as honest devotion to a work project, a business enterprise, a material achievement, that exploits human beings almost without being aware of them. It is possible, indeed, for such devotion to an engrossing task to reach fanatical heights of self-sacrifice, at which a hard-driving chief is as ruthless to himself as to his subordinates and competitors. To prevent high-minded inhumanity of this sort from destroying the very well-being of persons from which work derives its first significance, the surest resource is full-blooded love for one's fellow men. The love of which most of us are capable is not divine compassion. Neither is it merely the wholesale, innocuous good will often presented as "Christian charity." Timid preachers have much to answer for, in their well-meant substitution of a decorous shadow for the vital, dangerous substance. The commandment to love one's neighbor as oneself calls for robust, delighted interest in other people. It implies a deep, warm satisfaction in working and being with them. There is no demand that they be idealized out of human semblance, their virtues magnified and their faults ignored. The demand is that they be squarely recognized as persons and neighbors, with all their faults and virtues; and that, as such, they be welcomed for what they are and what they can be.

Such love of things and people is dangerous because it continually imperils the established routines and value judgments of conventional living, because it lays open to grievous disappointments and injuries the one who thus commits himself instead of holding aloof, and because it can slip over into sensuality or idolatry. Nevertheless, it is what makes the difference between dutiful plodding and exuberant release of energy that brings satisfaction beyond every conscious wish. Under its influence, work takes on the most vital and wholesome characteristics of play, in which present rather than merely future satisfaction is sought and in which an easing of strain, an active relaxation and restoring of hard-driven powers, is found. When work itself is thus recreative, obviously the worker's vocational problem is happily solved. For him, work and worship go naturally together, without the confusion that can vitiate both.

· · · · ·

Divine vocation, then, takes shape in work. Divine vocation is a call also to worship. Man, whom we know best as a worker, we know also as capable of rising above his labor and above himself into a conscious meeting with God. In worship, however, man is never allowed to rest. The God he meets is at work. Indeed, his very meeting with God, however it may take place, is evidence of God's activity. As when a fast-turning stone is touched by steel there is a spark, a recoil, and a new edge on the steel, so from worship man can return to active life filled with a steady love that can remake his existence. Through the daily round of a particular challenging job, through socially responsible work, man can follow his true calling as God's co-worker.

SUGGESTED BOOKS

Barth, Karl, *Prayer*, trans. Sara F. Terrien. Philadelphia: The Westminster Press, 1952. Exposition of the catechisms of the Reformation on this subject, concentrating on the Lord's Prayer.

Butrick, George A., *Prayer*. New York and Nashville: Abingdon Press, 1942. A comprehensive study in four parts: Jesus and prayer, prayer and the world, personality and prayer, and the way of prayer.

Calhoun, Robert L., *God and the Common Life*. Hamden, Conn.: The Shoe String Press, 1935. An attempt to discover the meaning of God for, and the basis of value in, daily work and play.

Hayman, Eric, *Worship and the Common Life*. New York: The Macmillan Company, 1944. Worship and its relevance to modern life are discussed, with special emphasis on Quakerism.

Magee, John, *Reality and Prayer*. New York: Harper & Row, Publishers, 1957. A sensitive, informed discussion of both theoretical and practical questions concerning prayer.

Steinberg, Milton, *Basic Judaism*. New York: Harcourt, Brace and World, Inc., 1947. A lucid exposition of Jewish beliefs, ideals, and practices.

Underhill, Evelyn, *Mysticism*. New York: Meridian Books, Inc., 1955. A sympathetic psychological study of the mystical form of life and its meaning for theology.

———, *Worship*. New York: Harper & Row, Publishers, 1936. Theological, descriptive, and historical studies of the various types of Christian adoration.

PART THREE

INTERPRETING CHRISTIAN THOUGHT

XI · THE CONCEPT OF REVELATION

In the chapters that follow we will examine some of the prominent issues that arise in the attempt to understand correctly the nature of Christian belief and practice. Such issues are not of interest solely to Christians, for many non-Christians show interest in what Christians say, too. But the debate on these issues is centered primarily within the Christian community as part of its own effort to interpret and proclaim its own message aright.

We shall try to avoid in our discussion merely pommeling one party line against others, as if the addition of one more voice to one existing party would be of any general interest or would sway the balance in the modern theological controversies. Instead our concerns will be mainly (1) to interpret what is of distinctive emphasis in Christianity as a whole, i.e., what is Christian in the Christian religion, but still (2) to reflect some of the varying positions in Protestant thought on major issues. And, recognizing that to have no position is impossible, we shall occasionally take sides on the issues where this does not seem intrusive; but we shall assume that one may take sides on the issues themselves without following dogmatically the tenets of a particular school of thought.

To be specific, Protestant theology has been classified for more than a quarter of a century now into three camps, Liberalism, Fundamentalism, and Neo-orthodoxy. This classification will no longer do as a general classification, although it may still be useful on particular issues. For one thing, it does not cover all thinkers. In 1955 William Hordern could distinguish twice that number of emphases, including Orthodoxy, Fundamentalism, Liberalism, Neo-liberalism, Neo-orthodoxy, and Modern Orthodoxy.[1] He might now add the newer Evangelicalism which does not describe itself as Fundamentalist.[2] The threefold classification also obscures (as any classification does) the significant agreements among theologians of different persuasions, and overlooks the exploratory, developing character of most of the trends in theological thought. We would do well, therefore, to discuss issues rather than attack or defend supposedly fixed schools of thought.

We begin with the idea of revelation because of its foundational character as the medium of what Christians believe as truth.

REVELATION AS A CHRISTIAN CATEGORY

In Chapter I we suggested that revelation taken in the broadest sense of the word as any basic intuitive experience in which truth is believed to be found may be said to characterize any religion. In the Christian tradition the term has a much more specific meaning, although it is not entirely unrelated to the broader definition. The principal difference is seen when we focus on the fact that in Christianity the center of all faith and worship is the personal God known in the Bible and in Christ. One striking attribute of God as thus seen is that he and not man is the prime initiator of man's religion. He is the creator of the world and the director of history. He brings about the reconciliation of man. This means that revelation is the free, purposeful act of God in which he discloses that of himself which he chooses to disclose. It is not man's self-discovery; it is God's self-disclosure.

As long as we move within the broader, general definition, it is perfectly possible to interpret the revelatory experience as one in which man is the central protagonist, discovering and deciphering an aloof and passive deity. The experience, to be sure, is illuminating and surcharged with meaning; but God is virtually the remote observer of deism or the inviting statue of Aristotle, while man the hero figures out through his own ability more and more insights about the divine dimension of life. In fact religious history has sometimes been written in purely naturalistic terms as the slow but steady progress of man's own insights and discoveries.

Such a view has not been that of the Christian tradition. On the face of it, we may wonder how such a view was ever thought to be consistent with any conception of a personal God. If God is essentially personal, active, and loving, then it must be he who takes the lead in breaking through to man in man's history and individual life. "Revelation is the self-manifestation of God."[3]

This concept of revelation as God's self-disclosure is one conviction that differentiates monotheistic religions—in particular Christianity, Judaism, and Islam—from other religions in which a personal God is not the main focus. When the term revelation is used in these other religions, it is generally taken in the broader sense of any illuminating religious experience. When the Hindu Vedas are said to be revealed, for instance, this does not mean that they are the willed communication of a supreme personal God, but rather that they are the authoritative teaching of ancient inspired seers. What differentiates Christianity and Judaism from Islam is the belief that the most decisive of the revelatory acts of God have occurred within the Biblical tradition. And what differentiates Christianity from Judaism is the belief that the qualitative culmination of these acts is to be found in the person of Christ, so that he is the center of history and the standard for judgments of revelation.

Revelation as a Christian category, then, is a personal category. It is a person-to-person communication, a self-initiated manifestation of God made known to persons and through persons. It is not something calculated, planned, and then experienced by man, but may on the contrary come with suddenness and unexpected import; for this is the nature of personal disclosures. It may reach into man's ignorance and complacency with unsought, even unwanted, judgment, or it may thrust into his confusion and sinfulness with an unknown redemptive power; for such is the way personality can affect personality. Moreover, something of mystery always accompanies revelation, for in personal disclosures the person remains partly hidden as well as partly manifest. God is thus the unknown as well as the known. It is in these person-to-person relations that the Christian meaning of revelation is to be found.

THE SCOPE OF REVELATION

It is customary in Christian thought to distinguish between general revelation and special revelation. General revelation refers to the common understanding of God that might be acquired through nature, through history, or through religious experience anywhere and by anyone in the world. Special revelation, on the other hand, refers specifically to the saving events of the Biblical tradition and of Christ. The usual interpretation of this doctrine is that some understanding of God is possible to anyone at any time or place through general revelation, but that the redeeming activity of God is made fully manifest to man only through special revelation.

It is doubtless accurate to say that most Christians have held to a belief in general revelation in some way similar to the formulation just expressed. Some thinkers have been interpreted, however, as holding that there is no knowledge whatever of God, i.e., the true God, outside of the Biblical tradition. Aside from the fact that such a view would seem to limit the concern of God, the view has been criticized as not corresponding to the assumptions of the Biblical writers themselves, e.g., St. Paul.[4] It has also been criticized as not being a fitting explanation for the fact that many individual non-Christians seem to reach a religious sensitivity and a devotion to God which exceed the spirituality of individual Christians. The appropriate attitude for Christians, therefore, is not to deny a general revelation and claim that they have the only revelation, but to witness to what they believe to be the special revelation of God.

While there is much agreement on a doctrine of general revelation, there is often sharp difference as to what the significance of the doctrine is. For easy reference we may distinguish a negative view and a positive view. The negative view, usually associated with Orthodox Protestantism, stresses the limitations and sinfulness of man which the doctrine presupposes. That is, the fact that God is known incompletely and distortedly throughout the world is a testimony to the sinfulness of man by which he has corrupted his vision of God. General revelation thus points up the condemnation of man and the judgment of God upon him. This is the view developed by the conservative Dutch theologian, G. C. Berkouwer, who says, for example: "The message of the general revelation of God rings out the accusation (not the excuse) of man. . . ."[5] But this is also the view of the less conservative Emil Brunner.[6]

The positive view, associated with the followers of Thomas Aquinas in Roman Catholicism, but also present in the Protestant tradition, stresses the capabilities of man due to general revelation. That is, because God is nowhere absent from man's life, man can use his reason and experience to obtain knowledge, to develop humane morality, and to become aware of God even though he may not be familiar with the Christian revelation. General revelation thus makes possible certain attainments of man because of divine support.

So far these two views need not be regarded as contradictory. Each may be seen to emphasize a different truth. In the former view the point is that man by his own willful ignorance and sinfulness has often blurred a vision of God that might otherwise have been possible to him, and he is therefore in need of divine assistance. In the latter view the point is that man, despite himself, still retains some capacity for discovering meanings and making rational inferences. And these two points do not contradict each other but supplement each other.

A real contradiction arises, however, over whether natural theology, i.e., independent rational knowledge of God apart from revelation, is possible. The negative view denies this possibility and the positive view affirms it. In criticizing all rational knowledge of God, however, the negative view can hardly avoid undermining the validity of all reason and hence undercutting its own view, which uses reason a great deal to explain and recommend its own position. It is difficult to accept a bifurcation in which reason is permitted to be valid in the recommendation of one's own position, and in many other human endeavors, and then is charged with running totally amuck as far as any inferences about God are concerned. On the other side it must be recognized that, if one believes in the Christian conception of God, one must believe that no human undertaking occurs in complete isolation from God's activity. In fact, it is doubtful whether natural theologians ever meant to say that rational knowledge of God arises without any preliminary, implicit presentation by God of himself to man. The inquiry, like all human inquiries, begins with some intimation of its result. In this sense natural theology only makes explicit what is implicitly there in experience to be found. But the point is that God, through general revelation, has permitted himself to be knowable to some extent by rational inference apart from special revelation. Even the existentialist Pascal could say: "The conduct of God, who disposes all things kindly, is to put religion into the mind by reason, and into the heart by grace."[7] We conclude that natural or philosophical theology has a rightful place, though not as a rigorous science.

THE CONTENT OF REVELATION

We have discussed the meaning of revelation and the extent of revelation. We now come to the most difficult question, that of content. What is it that is revealed in revelation? Granted that revelation means the self-disclosure of God, what does God disclose in his revelation to man?

Three principal answers to this question can readily be distinguished in current religious thought. The first of these places the emphasis on some human value. What is disclosed in revelation is some insight, power, direction, or illumination. This view steers away from any suggestion that truth itself, or even God, is the content of revelation. The second view focuses its attention on words and statements as the content. That is, revelation consists essentially of true propositions communicated by God. This conception is referred to as propositional revelation. The third view maintains that the content of revelation is God himself. That is, what God reveals is not human value or informational propositions but his own person. This occurs in the events of personal life through divine-human encounters.

These differences concerning content bring with them differences in the way in which these three views tend to look upon the Biblical record regarded as a vehicle of revelation. The first view tends to see the scripture as an accumulation of human insights and discoveries, some of which may have been prompted directly by divine action. The second view considers the scripture to be composed of those very propositions believed to have been communicated from God. And the third view looks upon the scripture as the verbal record or interpretive report of the personal encounters which are believed to constitute the substance of revelation.

The first of these views does not wish to deny that God is active in history. What it does deny is that man's experience of God's activity enables him to know God with immediacy or to say that he has received truth directly in such experience. Religious experience is full of meaning, value, and illumination; but one does not contact God directly, and no knowledge is present except by reflective inference from the experience. In a discussion of revelation Professor DeWolf says that there is a sense in which all knowledge comes from God and yet all knowledge is mediated through us and our rational capacities.[8] No exception can be made in the case of religious experience or revelation. It follows that special revelation differs from general revelation only in the degree of illumination felt by man and not in the directness or immediacy with which God discloses himself to man.

The chief reason for the acceptance of this view has undoubtedly been the great disparity in the revelations that have been claimed in the world.[9] Because of the diversity, the disagreements, the contradictions, in what has been claimed by different people as revealed truth, one can only be suspicious of all claims to direct knowledge of God. Such claims tend to confuse intensity of feeling with immediacy of knowledge. All claims to revelation must therefore be subjected to critical examination where reason can judge upon their validity, sort out the elevating from the debasing kinds, and come up with what seems on the whole to be the most plausible and coherent version of religious truth. This truth is always an inference from, an interpretation of, religious experience according to the test of rational coherence.

This view has been criticized by both of the other views as leading, interestingly enough, to greater subjectivity rather than to greater objectivity. Because this view denies that the Biblical record and the person of Christ are objectively revelatory in themselves, its defenders are thrown back upon the inner feelings of religious followers as the source of religious truth. With all objective criteria gone, the beliefs which are allegedly reasoned out on the basis of rational coherence are in actuality merely the private opinions of the one who happens to be reasoning. This is borne out by the fact that these opinions, given out as rationally tested truths, are not accepted by all reasoners but only by those who have a predisposing faith in them in the first place. When the defenders of this view come out with Christian principles, they are being naïve if they think they are giving reasoned truths instead of expositions of their own faith. Furthermore, by making rational coherence the one and supreme test of religious truth, they are excluding arbitrarily the possibility that God may disclose himself as he wills and not in ways provable by man. They are confined to what their limiting criterion will permit; but the Biblical God is not.

The second view, the propositional theory, does not deny that revelation brings power and illumination to man. It also believes that in revelation God manifests himself, discloses his own being and nature as he chooses. But it insists that all this is ill-founded unless the truth of revelation is guaranteed, and this can be done only if God himself gives us infallible propositions. The point may be put in this way: man, being sinful, is in need of redemption, which ultimately can occur only through the saving power of God in Christ; but in order for man to surrender himself to the right thing he must be assured that what he commits himself to is truth rather than illusion. Man's own reasoning cannot guarantee such needful truth, cannot bring him to a saving knowledge. At best it can reach only tentative conclusions and hypotheses, and at worst it can plunge him into fatal error. Divine authenticity is needed. It is inconceivable, then, that God is the source of man's salvation and yet leaves him without the truth necessary for that purpose. Infallible propositions give to man the guaranteed truth he needs.

The concern of the propositional theory is thus focused on the necessity of true doctrine. This line of thought is brought out succinctly by Bernard Ramm in the following criticism of the opposition:

> On the same page in which revelation as "propositional" is sternly scouted, the necessity of sound doctrine is advocated. But how sound doctrine can be deduced from a non-propositional, encounterish revelation is not clearly presented.
>
> . . .
>
> If there is no information in revelation is not our encounter uninformed? Is it not strange alchemy which can transmute truths of revelation out of a truthless revelation?
>   Putting it directly, if divine revelation is truly revelation it must reach the human race in a substantial form. It must come as speech or language and bearing a rich conceptual booty with it. . . . The danger in contemporary theology is that in so reacting against propositional revelation it will bury the rights of truth.[10]

There is difference of opinion as to whether the propositional theory of revelation is historically the position maintained in the Bible itself and in early church tradition. Its defenders argue that it is and its opponents claim that it is not. No church council or creed set forth an official doctrine on this point. So the issue cannot be settled by appeal to historical authority alone apart from contemporary interpretation.

The propositional theory has been criticized on several grounds. Perhaps the chief of these is the criticism that infallible propositions of revelation are not self-evident to the human mind without individual interpretation, and there is no provision in the theory for showing us how the present-day interpretations of fallible men can certify what the infallible propositions mean, or even which ones they are. Unless this is done the theory does not avoid the subjective element which it seeks to purge from theology. To speak of infallible propositions which are not infallibly known is to make a merely technical, academic distinction which has no actual relevance for theology. Hordern states this criticism as follows:

> If there is to be inerrant revelation of propositions, the hearer would have to be as inerrant as the speaker. If man is not infallible, and seldom have Roman Catholics or fundamentalists claimed infallibility for the hearer, then it may be emotionally comforting to claim that God spoke without error, but it is meaningless to us men who are fallible hearers, for we can never know infallibly that we understand correctly the infallible revelation.[11]

Another criticism has been that the propositional theory leads to a barren intellectual analysis of the words of revelation rather than to an emphasis on the personal, saving power or revelation. The point in God's revealing himself is that he meets man in his misery and brings him into reconciliation with himself; but instead of this our attention is directed by the propositional theory to more and more belabored refinements of verbal exegesis. John Baillie says that "the deepest difficulty felt about the equation of revelation with communicated truths is that it offers us something less than personal encounter and personal communication . . . ."[12] Thus the extreme reaction to subjectivity in revelation may bring with it a loss in the personal meaning of revelation.

There is also a problem concerning the justification of the propositional theory which its defenders must face. If the justification is based upon appeal to the Bible regarded as infallible propositions, then it tends to be circular, assuming what is supposed to be justified. If, on the other hand, the justification is based on a rational defense, as in the passage from Ramm, then there appears to be the same sort of reliance on rational procedure which was rejected in favor of propositional revelation.

Thinkers like the ones just quoted, who do not accept either of the first two views, tend to speak of the content of revelation as being not human illumination or revealed propositions but God himself. In this third view it is believed that for revelation to be meaningful God must somehow be directly present to man in revelatory experience. At the same time it is recognized that God does not come to man through special voices, secret whisperings, or private conversations. It is therefore common to speak of God making himself known in and through the events of what would otherwise be man's ordinary life. Thus revelation means the events of history and personal experience in which God encounters man. Events of this type have occurred with special revelatory meaning in Biblical history, culminating in Christ. The Bible is the record of those events. Revelatory divine-human encounters may occur, however, in other times and places as well. In fact, if they do not, the Biblical tradition and Christianity will become dead. Thus revelatory experience continues, but it always has Christ and his teachings as the final standard. Finally, since revelation in this sense always involves a fallible human receiver as well as a divine communication, one should never make the mistake of speaking with divine authority or of supposing that he knows God fully.

This third type of view is criticized by the supporters of the first two views in ways that have already been anticipated. Spokesmen for the first view insist that the evidence does not sustain the notion of a direct revelation of God. In fact, the existence of conflicting interpretations suggests the opposite. They also see a certain danger in saying that God is directly known, for this opens the possibility of claiming divine sanction for what is really human interpretation. The proponents of the second view maintain that this last theory does not escape the confinement to subjective utterance any more than the first view does. They believe that divine-human encounters which do not leave a deposit of truths are merely private affairs which cannot be the basis of sound doctrine, so essential for Christian faith.

REMARKS ON THE CONTROVERSY

In considering these varying interpretations of the content of revelation we must neither minimize the existence of the controversy nor exaggerate the extent of the divergence. The differences are real, but they need not obscure more fundamental agreements.

The truth in the first view is that there always must be a human formulation of what is received as revealed if the content is to be generally meaningful. Revelation does not occur in a manner so objective that inactive minds can apprehend it. On the other hand, if truth or God is not somehow directly present in revelation, then the content of revelation becomes virtually equivalent to private philosophical inferences. Against this conclusion the charge that it leads to a subjectivist predicament is valid. Of course we cannot say that just because we need something more objective than private philosophical inferences, therefore we do have something more objective. One could insist that such inferences are all that we have, slender as they may be, and we must learn to live with this state of affairs. But the subjectivist view does not seem to correspond to Biblical teaching and Christian tradition, which have believed that there is something more to revelation than human insights. We need not simply appeal to tradition, however. The main argument against the first view is that any meaningful Christian conception of God must surely include his capacity to break through as he chooses into man's life, and in ways which private philosophies might not have expected.

Both of the other views seem to do more justice to the objective content of revelation, the one by claiming that we have in the Bible a written series of divinely authenticated statements, and the other by maintaining that we have in the Biblical record a witness to real divine-human encounters. Both hold that theology properly derives from this objective source rather than from private inferences.

The difficulties in the propositional theory which were cited earlier are indeed grave ones for its defenders to meet. In their defenses they often appear to their critics to be putting the cart before the horse: they appear to be saying that we need an absolute guarantee of doctrinal truth, and since the propositional theory is the only one that will give this, therefore the propositional theory must be correct. But the question is one of adopting a view that corresponds to revelatory experience, not one of adopting a theory that suits what fallible men think they must have.

And yet the need for truth in revelation remains, and perhaps in a more acute way for the critics of the propositional theory than for its defenders. It is no solution to this problem merely to point out that God is directly present in revelatory experience. For the meaning of such experience must be brought out, and this requires the use of propositions regarded as true. The church must uphold certain beliefs as true, must make claims to truth, in order to mean anything definite by Christianity at all. Thus no interpretation can abandon the concern for truth if it wishes to avoid total subjectivity.

It seems evident that if revelation is to be an intelligible notion at all, it must include both personal encounters and claims to truth, however they be explained. To this extent Ramm is right when he says: "Revelation is event *and* interpretation, encounter *and* truth, a Person *and* knowledge."[13] The propositional theory tends to place the logical order of these as truth first and encounter second. That is, God first reveals truths to man in the form of statements which are free from any human fallibility, and then man, by giving assent to these truths, can have a transforming, saving experience. The opposing interpretation believes the logical order to be the reverse. God first of all meets man in dynamic personal encounters with transforming power, and then man, reflecting on these events, draws out the truths they must imply, these truths never being free from human fallibility. There is a real difference here, as mentioned above, one that has been the source of much division in the past, one that is not easily reconciled. And yet the division often seems to be exaggerated, for both views are, after all, seeking to give adequate expression to the same twofold concern, the experience of revelation and the truth of revelation, neither of which can be abandoned by either view.

In addition to this last comment, the more significant agreements between the defenders and the opponents of the propositional theory should not be overlooked. The controversy over this one doctrine need not, and often does not, lead to differences over other beliefs. In point of fact, of course, other differences in belief are frequently associated with the divergence over propositional revelation. But there seems to be no necessity about this. For example, thinkers like Karl Barth and Emil Brunner, who reject propositional revelation, have stated other doctrines about God, man, and Christ which place them in considerable agreement with orthodox theologians on these points. Again, some defenders of propositional revelation have come out for natural theology in a way which places them in considerable agreement with liberal theologians on that point. In the end the decision concerning propositional revelation does not determine what the essence of Christian belief is. That work still remains on either conclusion.

THE STORY OF OUR LIFE

H. RICHARD NIEBUHR

H. Richard Niebuhr (1894-1962) was an eminent theologian, though perhaps not as well known to the public as his brother, Reinhold. He studied at Elmhurst College, Eden Theological Seminary, Washington University of St. Louis, and Yale Divinity School. After brief periods of teaching at the first two of these institutions, he assumed his position at the Yale Divinity School, being appointed later to a Sterling professorship in theology and Christian ethics. His books include Christ and Culture *(1951),* The Purpose of the Church and Its Ministry *(1956), and* Radical Monotheism and Western Culture *(1960). His interpretation of revelation as historically oriented illumination and memory is presented in the following selection.*

HISTORY AS LIVED AND AS SEEN

We may be helped toward a solution of the problem of history and faith by reflection upon the fact that the history to which we point when we speak of revelation is not the succession of events which an uninterested spectator can see from the outside but our own history. It is one thing to perceive from a safe distance the occurrences in a stranger's life and quite a different thing to ponder the path of one's own destiny, to deal with the why and whence and whither of one's own existence. Of a man who has been blind and who has come to see, two histories can be written. A scientific case history will describe what happened to his optic

From H. Richard Niebuhr, *The Meaning of Revelation* (New York: The Macmillan Company, 1941), pp. 59-77. Reprinted by permission.

nerve or to the crystalline lens, what technique the surgeon used or by what medicines a physician wrought the cure, through what stages of recovery the patient passed. An autobiography, on the other hand, may barely mention these things but it will tell what happened to a self that had lived in darkness and now saw again trees and the sunrise, children's faces and the eyes of a friend. Which of these histories can be a parable of revelation, the outer history or the inner one, the story of what happened to the cells of a body or the story of what happened to a self? When we speak of revelation in the Christian church we refer to *our* history, to the history of selves or to history as it is lived and apprehended from within.

The distinction between *our* history and events in impersonal time, or between history as lived and as contemplated from the outside may be illustrated by contrasting parallel descriptions of the same social event. Lincoln's Gettysburg Address begins with history: "Four-score and seven years ago our fathers brought forth upon this continent a new nation, conceived in liberty and dedicated to the proposition that all men are created free and equal." The same event is described in the *Cambridge Modern History* in the following fashion: "On July 4, 1776, Congress passed the resolution which made the colonies independent communities, issuing at the same time the well-known Declaration of Independence. If we regard the Declaration as the assertion of an abstract political theory, criticism and condemnation are easy. It sets out with a general proposition so vague as to be practically useless. The doctrine of the equality of men, unless it be qualified and conditioned by reference to special circumstance, is either a barren truism or a delusion."

The striking dissimilarity between these two accounts may be explained as being due merely to a difference of sentiment; the blind devotion of the patriot is opposed to the critical acumen and dispassionate judgment of the scientific historian. But the disparity goes deeper. The difference in sentiment is so profound because the beings about which the accounts speak differ greatly; the "Congress" is one thing, "our fathers" are almost another reality. The proposition that all men are created free and equal, to which the fathers dedicated their lives, their fortunes and their sacred honor, and which for their children is to be the object of a new devotion, seems to belong to a different order of ideas than that to which the vague and useless, barren truism or delusion belongs. Though these various terms point to the same ultimate realities the latter are seen in different aspects and apprehended in different contexts. Moreover it seems evident that the terms the external historian employs are not more truly descriptive of the things-in-themselves than those the statesman uses and that the former's understanding of what really happened is not more accurate than the latter's. In the one case the events of history are seen from the outside, in the other from the inside. Lincoln spoke of what had happened in *our* history, of what had made and formed us and to which we remain committed so long as we continue to exist as Americans; he spoke of purposes which lie in our enduring past and are therefore the purposes of our present life; he described the history of living beings and not data relating to dead things. It is a critical history but the criticism of its author is not directed toward the general propositions so much as to the human beings who measure themselves and are measured by means of those general propositions; criticism is moral, directed toward selves and their community. The other account abstracts from living selves with their resolutions and commitments, their hopes, and fears. It is not critical of men but of things; documents and propositions are its objects. The events it describes happened in impersonal time and are recorded less in the memories of persons than in books and monuments.

The example from American history may be duplicated in the history of every other community. Pericles' Funeral Oration appeals to memory and may be paralleled by many an external account of the rise of an empire "acquired by men who knew their duty . . . and who if they ever failed in an enterprise would not allow their virtues to be lost to their country, but freely gave their lives to her as the fairest offering they could present at her feast." Hosea's account of the childhood of Israel and the Psalmist's recall of what "we have heard and known and our fathers have told us" have their counterparts in ethnological descriptions of early Semitic tribal life. Shakespeare's invocations of memories clustering about "this royal throne of kings, this sceptred isle . . . this land of such dear souls, this dear, dear land," and Burke's reverential regard for a tradition in which the hand of God is visible may be matched by cool, aloof accounts of the rise of the British empire. The distinctions between the two types of history cannot be made by applying the value-judgment of true and false but must be made by reference to differences of perspective. There are true and false appeals to memory as well as true and false external descriptions but only uncritical dogmatism will affirm that truth is the prerogative of one of the points of view. Events may be regarded from the outside by a non-participating observer; then they belong to the history of things. They may be apprehended from within, as items in the destiny of persons and communities; then they belong to a life-time and must be interpreted in a context of persons with their resolutions and devotions.

The differences between the outer history of things and the inner history of selves which appear in these illustrations need to be analyzed in a little more detail in preparation for our effort to understand the relation of revelation to history. It appears, first of all, that the data of external history are all impersonal; they are ideas, interests, movements among things. Even when such history deals with human individuals it seeks to reduce them to impersonal parts. Jesus becomes, from this point of view, a complex of ideas about ethics and eschatology, of psychological and biological elements. Other persons are dealt with in the same manner. One may look for an efficient factor among such impersonal elements, though its determination involves the peril of forsaking the objective point of view, as when a Marxist historian chooses economic elements or an intellectualist regards ideas in the mind as the motivating forces in history. Internal history, on the other hand, is not a story of things in juxtaposition or succession; it is personal in character. Here the final data are not elusive atoms of matter or thought but equally elusive selves. In such history it is not the idea of the soul which Socrates thought and communicated that is important but rather the soul of Socrates, "all glorious within," the soul of the "most righteous man of the whole age." In external history we deal with objects; in internal history our concern is with subjects. In the former, to use Professor Alexander's distinction, our data are "-eds," what is believed, sensed, conceived; but in the latter what is given is always an "-ing," a knowing, a willing, a believing, a feeling. Or, as Martin Buber would put it, in external history all relations are between an "I" and an "it," while in the other they are relations between "I" and "Thou"; moreover the "I" in the "I-it" relation differs from the self in the "I-Thou" setting.

Speaking as critical idealists we might say that in external history all apprehension and interpretation of events must employ the category of individuality but in internal history it is the category of personality that must be used in perceiving and understanding whatever happens. In *our* history all events occur not to impersonal bodies but to selves in community with other selves and they must be so understood. After the fashion of critical idealism we may distinguish external history as a realm of the pure reason from internal history as a sphere of the pure practical reason, though it is evident that Kantian reason must be understood in far more historical fashion than was the case in the eighteenth century when neither pure nor practical reason were thought to be socially and historically conditioned.

We may employ the method of critical realism rather than of critical idealism in making our distinction between external and internal history. From the realistic point of view we are concerned in external history to abstract from all that is merely secondary, from subjective and partisan accounts of what happened; we seek to set forth the primary characteristics of each event as these may be defined by taking into account the reports of eye-witnesses, of contemporary documents and those "permanent possibilities of sensation," the enduring institutions, the constant movements of mind and will available to the experience of all percipients.

In internal history on the other hand we are not concerned with the primary and secondary elements of external historical perception but with "tertiary qualities," with values. These are not private and evanescent as the secondary elements are but common and verifiable in a community of selves; yet they are not objective in the sense in which the primary qualities of external perception are said to be objective. Critical realism, however, like critical idealism, is so strongly conditioned by its historic association with non-historically minded natural science and particularly with mathematics that its use in this realm of thinking about history requires a prior readjustment of all its concepts. It is enough to point out that the distinctions which appear in all critical philosophy as between knowledge of the external world and knowledge of the internal, which drive even the most dogmatic positivists to assert that ethics and religion belong to some other realm than that with which objective knowledge is concerned, must also be made in our understanding of history. There is a descriptive and there is a normative knowledge of history and neither type is reducible to the terms of the other.

The distinction may be made clearer by noting the differences in the conceptions of value, time and human association which are employed in the two contexts.

In external history value means valency or strength. The objective historian must measure the importance of an event or factor by the effect it has on other events or factors in the series. Though he is also a self, living in community, having a destiny, and so unable wholly to escape a moral point of view, as scientific historian he is bound to suppress his own value-judgments as much as possible. Not what is noblest in his sight but what is most effective needs to be treated most fully. So Alexander may have a larger place in his account than Socrates, though as a self the historian may elect to follow right to martyrdom rather than might to victory. Economic motives in the framing of the American Constitution may require far more attention than moral ideals, though the historian be one who has abjured the ownership of property for himself and may live a semi-monastic life. Looking upon events in the manner of an impartial spectator, he seeks to suppress every response of love or repugnance and to apply a more or less quantitative measure of strength in determining the importance of persons or events.

In internal history, however, value means worth for selves; whatever cannot be so valued is unimportant and may be dropped from memory. Here the death of Socrates, the birth of Lincoln, Peter's martyrdom, Luther's reform, Wesley's conversion, the landing of the Pilgrims, the granting of Magna Charta are events to be celebrated; this history calls for joy and sorrow, for days of rededication and of shriving, for tragic participation and for jubilees. The valuable here is that which bears on the destiny of selves; not what is strongest is most important but what is most relevant to the lives of "I's" and "Thou's." Value here means quality, not power; but the quality of valued things is one which only selves can apprehend. In this context we do not measure the worth of even our own desires by their strength but by their relevance to the destiny of the self.

As with value so with time. In our internal history time has a different feel and quality from that of the external time with which we deal as exoteric historians. The latter time resembles that of physics. Physics knows a plain man's time which has for him a valency like that of the "real" money of his province; it also knows a sophisticated time which is aware of its own relativity. So in external history there is the time of the naive chronicler with his acceptance of dynastic dates, his reckonings of years since creation, his A.D.'s and B.C.'s; or this history may think of time in the sophisticated way of a culture philosophy. But all these time-conceptions have one thing in common—they are all quantitative; all these times are numbered. Such time is always serial. In the series, past events are gone and future happenings are not yet. In internal history, on the other hand, our time is our duration. What is past is not gone; it abides in us as our memory; what is future is not non-existent but present in us as our potentiality. Time here is organic or it is social, so that past and future associate with each other in the present. Time in our history is not another dimension of the external space world in which we live, but a dimension of our life and of our community's being. We are not in this time but it is in us. It is not associated with space in a unity of space-time but it is inseparable from life in the continuity of life-time. We do not speak of it in precise numbers but say in poetic fashion with Lincoln, "four-score and seven years ago," meaning not eighty-seven but our re-membered past. In humbler fashion we correlate, as gossips do, the lives and deaths and wars of kings with shocks and joys in our own history. Such time is not a number but a living, a stream of consciousness, a flow of feeling, thought and will. It is not measurable by the hours and years of a planetary and solar rhythm; its ebb and flow, its pulsations and surges, its births and deaths and resurrections are incommensurable with lunar or atomic tides. If they are to be measured it must be done by a comparison with other inner alternations; in our history we do not correlate the death of the heart with the declining sun nor its rebirth with nature's spring but with a crucifixion of the son of God and with his rising to new life.

Human association also differs when regarded from the external or in-ternal points of view. The external knower must see societies as made up of atomic individuals related to each other by external bonds. Yet even the human individuals are depersonalized, since they are understood as complexes of psychological and biological factors. Society, to his view, is a vast and intricate organization of interests, drives or instincts, beliefs, customs, laws, constitutions, inventions, geographic and climatic data, in which a critical and diligent inquiry can discover some intelligible structures and moving patterns of relation. In internal history, on the other hand, society is a community of selves. Here we do not only live among other selves but they live in us and we in them. Relations here are not external but internal so that we are our relations and cannot be selves save as we are members of each other. When there is strife in this community there is strife and pain in us and when it is at peace we have peace in ourselves. Here social memory is not what is written in books and preserved in libraries, but what—not without the mediation of books and monuments, to be sure—is our own past, living in every self. When we become members of such a community of selves we adopt its past as our own and thereby are changed in our present existence. So immigrants and their children do, for whom Pilgrims become true fathers and the men of the Revolution their own liberators; so we do in the Christian community when the prophets of the Hebrews become our prophets and the Lord of the early disciples is acknowledged as our Lord. Not what is after the flesh—that is what is externally seen—but what is after the spirit—what has become a part of our own lives as selves—is the important thing in this internal view. In our history association means community, the participation of each living self in a common memory and common hope no less than in a common world of nature.

It may be said that to speak of history in this fashion is to try to think with poets rather than with scientists. That is what we mean, for poets think of persons, purposes and destinies. It is just their Jobs and Hamlets that are not dreamt of in philosophies which rule out from the company of true being whatever cannot be numbered or included in an impersonal pattern. Drama and epic set forth pattern too, but it is one of personal relations. Hence we may call internal history dramatic and its truth dramatic truth, though drama in this case does not mean fiction.

The relevance of this distinction between two histories to the subject of revelation must now have become apparent. When the evangelists of the New Testament and their successors pointed to history as the starting point of their faith and of their understanding of the world it was internal history that they indicated. They did not speak of events, as impersonally apprehended, but rather of what had happened to them in their community. They recalled the critical point in their own life-time when they became aware of themselves in a new way as they came to know the self on whom they were dependent. They turned to a past which was not gone but which endured in them as their memory, making them what they were. So for the later church, history was always the story of "our fathers," of "our Lord," and of the actions of "our God."

The inspiration of Christianity has been derived from history, it is true, but not from history as seen by a spectator; the constant reference is to subjective events, that is to events in the lives of subjects. What distinguishes such historic recall from the private histories of mystics is that it refers to communal events, remembered by a community and in a community. Subjectivity here is not equivalent to isolation, non-verifiability and ineffability; our history can be communicated and persons can refresh as well as criticize each other's memories of what has happened to them in the common life; on the basis of a common past they can think together about the common future.

Such history, to be sure, can only be confessed by the community, and in this sense it is esoteric. One cannot point to historic events in the lives of selves as though they were visible to any external point of view. Isaiah cannot say that in the year King Uzziah died God became visible in the temple nor Paul affirm that Jesus the Lord appears to travellers on the Damascus road. Neither will any concentration of attention on Isaiah and Paul, any detailed understanding of their historical situation, enable the observer to see what they saw. One must look with them and not at them to verify their visions, participate in their history rather than regard it if one would apprehend what they apprehended. The history of the inner life can only be confessed by selves who speak of what happened to them in the community of other selves.

FAITH IN OUR HISTORY

The distinction between history as known by the pure and as apprehended by the practical reason, though it raises difficulties that must be met, does assist us to understand how it is possible for the word "revelation" to point to history and yet point to God also. It cannot point to God, as we have noted, if the history to which it directs attention is the chain of events that an impersonal eye or mind apprehends. For such history, abstracting from human selves, must also abstract events from the divine self and, furthermore, while it may furnish motives for belief in the occurrence of certain happenings it does not invite trust in a living God.

The error frequently made in the Christian community which has been the occasion for the rise of many difficulties in understanding and propagating the historical faith has been the location of revelation in external history or in history as known from the non-participating point of view. So revelation has been identified with some miracle, whether this was the single act of a person or his whole life or the life of a community, such as Israel or the church. In this way certain events in external history were set apart as sacred, or a sacred history of one community has been opposed to the secular histories of other societies. Sacred events were inserted into a context otherwise secular and the continuity between the two types of events denied. It was denied that the events of holy history were subject to the same type of explanation which might be offered for secular happenings; that so-called secular events might have a sacred meaning for those who participated in them as selves was not thought possible.

Much so-called orthodoxy identified revelation with Scriptures and regarded the latter as wholly miraculous, the product of an inspiration which suspended the ordinary processes of human thought and guaranteed inerrancy. But to validate the Scriptural miracle another needed to be inserted into history since that which stands completely alone is an impenetrable mystery, no matter how much astonishment it calls forth. So miraculous Scriptures were related to miracles in the realm of nature, to a sun that stood still, a virgin-born child, to water turned by a word into wine. Furthermore the psychological miracle of prophecy as a supernatural foretelling of events, as though by second-sight, was introduced to validate the wonder of the Bible. The consequence of this method of argument was that two systems of reality on the same plane—a natural, historical, rational system and a supernatural, super-historical and super-rational system—were set beside each other. They were on the same plane, perceived by the same organs of sense and apprehended by the same minds, yet there was no real relation between them. Revelation took place within the supernatural and super-historical system; reason operated in the natural series of events. The distinction between the history in which revelation occurred and that in which there was no revelation was transferred to persons and things having history; there were natural and unnatural events, persons and groups. It was assumed that the differences between nature and super-nature were due not to the beholder's situation but to the things viewed while the point of view remained constant. Hence arose the conflict between history and faith. For sacred events in a secular context must be secularly apprehended and to demand of men that they should exempt certain events in the chain of perceived happenings from the application of the laws or principles with which they apprehend the others is to ask the impossible or to make everything unintelligible. How much the tendency to self-defensiveness and self-glorification in Christianity contributed to this effort to exempt the faith and its history from the judgments applicable to ordinary events it is not possible to say. But it must be noted that the consequence of the attempt to isolate sacred from secular history led not only to fruitless quarrels with natural and social science but also to internal conflict and inconsistency since it tended to substitute belief in the occurrence of miraculous events for faith in God and invited dispute about the relative importance of many wonders.

If the distinction between history as seen from without by a pure reason and from within by a practical reason, and if the denial of the exclusive validity of either view be allowed, we are enabled to understand not
only how faith and history may be associated but how in the nature of
the case they must be allied.

CONTEMPORARY
VIEWS OF REVELATION

JAMES I. PACKER

*James I. Packer (1926–) studied at Oxford and then taught for
several years at Tyndale Hall, Bristol, before returning to Oxford
as librarian of Latimer House (an Anglican study house). He is
the author of* "Fundamentalism" and the Word of God (*1958*) *and*
Evangelicalism and the Sovereignty of God (*1961*). *Here he gives
a conservative's argument for propositional revelation.*

CURRENT VIEWS OF
REVELATION AND SCRIPTURE

Before going further, however, it is worth pausing to see on
what grounds modern theology bases its rejection of the historic view that
Biblical revelation is propositional in character; for, though this rejection
has become almost a commonplace of modern discussion, and is, of course,
axiomatic for those who accept Schleiermacher's interpretation of Christianity, it is clearly not something that can just be taken for granted by
those who profess to reject his view.

J. K. S. Reid recognizes that "there is no a priori reason why the Bible
should not have this . . . character" (viz., that of being a corpus of divinely guaranteed truths) (*The Authority of Scripture*, London, Methuen,
1957, pp. 162 f.). But if that is so, the a posteriori arguments brought
against this view must be judged very far from decisive.

Archbishop Temple, in his much-quoted discussions of our subject
(*Nature, Man and God*, London, Macmillan, 1934, Lectures XII, XIII;
essay in *Revelation*, ed. Baillie and Martin, London, Faber, 1937), rejected this conception of Scripture on three counts: first, that little of

From James I. Packer, "Contemporary Views of Revelation," in *Revelation and the Bible*, ed. Carl F. H. Henry (Grand Rapids: Baker Book
House, 1958), pp. 95-104. Reprinted by permission.

it seems to consist of formal theological propositions; second, that little or none of it seems to have been produced by mechanical "dictation," or anything like it; third, that if we are to regard the Bible as a body of infallible doctrine we shall need an infallible human interpreter to tell us what it means; and "in whatever degree reliance upon such infallible direction comes in, spirituality goes out" (*Nature, Man and God*, p. 353). But, we reply, the first two points are irrelevant, and the third false. To assert propositional revelation involves no assertions or expectations a priori as to the literary categories to which the parts of Scripture will belong (only study of the text can tell us that); what is asserted is merely that all affirmations which Scripture is found to make, and all other statements which demonstrably embody scriptural teaching, are to be received as truths from God. Nor does this position involve any a priori assertions as to the psychology of inspiration, let alone the mechanical "dictation-theory," which no Protestant theologian seems ever to have held. ("Dictation" in old Protestant thought was a theological metaphor declaring the relation of the written words of Scripture to the divine intention, with no psychological implications whatever.) Temple's third point we deny; we look to Scripture itself to teach us the rules for its own interpretation, and to the Holy Spirit, the Church's only infallible teacher, to guide us into its meaning, and we measure all human pronouncements on Scripture by Scripture's own statements.

Others raise other objections to our view of the nature of Scripture. It is said, for instance, that modern study has proved that Scripture errs. But *proved* is quite the wrong word: the truth is, rather, that modern critical scholarship has allowed itself to assume that the presence of error in Scripture is a valid hypothesis, and to interpret the phenomena of Scripture in line with this assumption. However, the hypothesis has never in any case been shown to be necessary, nor is it clear how it could be; and the Biblical doctrine of Scripture would rule it out as invalid in principle. Again, it is held that to regard the Bible as written revelation is bibliolatry, diverting to Scripture honor due only to God. But the truth is rather that we honor God precisely by honoring Scripture as his written Word. Nor is there more substance in the claim that to assert the normative authority of Scripture is to inhibit the freedom of the Spirit, who is Lord of the Word; for the Spirit exercises his Lordship precisely in causing the Church to hear and reverence Scripture as the Word of God, as Calvin reminded the Anabaptist four centuries ago.

However, despite the inconclusiveness of the arguments for so doing and the Bible's self-testimony on the other side, modern theology finds its starting-point in a denial that Scripture, as such, is revealed truth. The generic character which this common denial imparts to the various modern views is clearly brought out by Daniel Day Williams in the following passage:

> In brief this is the new understanding of what revelation is. . . . Revelation as the "self-disclosure of God" is understood as the actual and personal meeting of man and God on the plane of history. Out of that meeting we develop our formulations of Christian truth in literal propositions. . . . Revelation is disclosure through personal encounter with God's work in his concrete action in history. It is never to be identified with any human words which we utter in response to the revelation. In *Nature, Man and God*, William Temple described revelation as "intercourse of mind and event, not the communication of doctrine distilled from that intercourse."

Doctrines, on this view, are not revelation, though they are formulated on the basis of revelation. As Temple put it elsewhere, "There is no such thing as revealed truth. . . . There are truths of revelation, that is to say, propositions which express the results of correct thinking concerning revelation; but they are not themselves directly revealed" (*Nature, Man and God*, p. 317). What this really means is that the historic Christian idea of revelation has been truncated; the old notion that one part of God's complex activity of giving us knowledge of himself is his teaching us truths about himself is hereby ruled out, and we are forbidden any more to read what is written in Scripture as though it were God who had written it. We are to regard Scripture as a human response and witness to revelation, but not in any sense revelation itself. After observing that nearly all theologians today take this view, Williams goes on, in the passage from which we have already quoted, to explain the significance of this change: "What it means," he writes, "is that Christian thought can be set free from the intolerable dogmatism which results from claiming that God's truth is identical with some human formulation of it" (scriptural no less than later creedal, apparently). "It gives freedom for critical re-examination of every Christian statement in the light of further experience, and in the light of a fresh encounter with the personal and historical act of God in Christ" (*Interpreting Theology 1918-1952*, London, S.C.M., 1953; *What Present-day Theologians are Thinking*, New York, Harper, 1952, p. 64 f., drawing on Temple, *op. cit.*, pp. 316 ff.).

Professor Williams' statement well sums up the modern approach, and its wording suggests at once the basic problem which this approach raises: namely, the problem of objectivity in our knowledge of God. What is the criterion whereby revelation is to be known? If there is no revealed truth, and the Bible is no more than human witness to revelation, fallible and faulty, as all things human are, what guarantee can we have that our apprehensions of revelation correspond to the reality of revelation itself? We are sinful men, and have no reason to doubt that our own thoughts about revelation are as fallible and faulty as any; by what standard, then, are we to test and correct them? Is there a standard, the use of which opens in principle a possibility of conforming our ideas of revelation to the real thing? Historic Christianity said yes: the Biblical presentation of, and pattern of thinking about, revelation-facts is such a standard. Modern theology, however, cannot say this; for the characteristic modern position really boils down to saying that the only standard we have for testing our own fallible judgments is our own fallible judgment. It tells us that what we study in Scripture is not revelation but the witness of faith to revelation; and that what as Christian students we have to do is critically to examine and assess the Biblical witness by the light, not of extra-biblical principles (that, it is agreed, would be illegitimate rationalism), but of the contents of revelation itself, which the Church by faith has some idea of already, and which it seeks to clarify to itself by this very study. Such, we are told, is the existential situation in which, and the basic motive for which, the Church studies Scripture. And the "critical re-examination of every Christian statement in the light of further experience" which is here in view is a reciprocal process of reconsidering and re-interpreting the faith of the Church and the faith of the Bible in terms of each other: not making either universally normative for the other, but evolving a series of working approximations which are offered as attempts to do justice to what seems essential and constitutive in both.

Theology pursued in this fashion is held to be "scientific," and that on two accounts. In the first place, it is said, theology is hereby established as the "science of faith," a strictly empirical discipline of analyzing the contents of Christian faith in its actual manifestations, in order to elucidate the nature of the relationship which faith is, and of the object to which it is a response. (Reference in these terms to the reality of the object of faith is thought to parry the charge that this is just Schleiermacher over again.) Then, in the second place, this theological method is held to vindicate its scientific character by the fact that, in interpreting and restating the faith of the Bible, it takes account of the "scientific" critical contention that the Biblical witness contains errors and untruths, both factual and theological—a contention which, no doubt, is generally regarded these days as part of the faith of the Church. But it is clear that theology, so conceived, is no more than a dexterous attempt to play off two brands of subjectivism against each other. On the one hand, the subject proposed for study is still the Church's witness to its own experience, as such, and the contents of Scripture are still treated simply as important material within this category. It is true that (at the prompting of critical reason) the *prima facie* character of this experience, as one of objective relationship with a sovereign living God, is now taken seriously, and that due respect is paid to the Church's conviction that the Biblically-recorded experience of prophets and apostles marks a limit outside which valid Christian experience is not found, but this does not affect the basic continuity between the modern approach and that of Schleiermacher. On the other hand, autonomous reason still acts as arbiter in the realm of theological methodology, following out only those principles of judgment which it can justify to itself as "scientific" on the basis of its own independent assessment of the real nature of Christianity. It is true that (out of regard for the distinctive character of Christian experience) this "scientific" method recognizes the uniqueness of Christianity, and resists all attempts to minimize it; and to this end it requires us to master the Biblical thought-forms, in terms of which this unique experience received its classical expression. But it does not require us to accept the Biblical view of their objective significance except insofar as our reason, judging independently, endorses that view; and in this respect it simply perpetuates the theological method of the Enlightenment. The effect of following the modern approach has naturally been to encourage a kind of Biblical double-talk, in which great play is made with Biblical terms, and Biblical categories are insisted on as the proper medium for voicing Christian faith, but these are then subjected to a rationalistic principle of interpretation which eliminates from them their basic Biblical meaning (e.g., a story such as that of the Fall is treated as *mythical*, significant and true as a symbol revealing the actual state of men today, but false if treated as the record of an objective historical happening). Thus theological currency has been debased, and a cloud of ambiguity now broods over much modern "biblicism." This, at least, is to the credit of Bultmann that, having pursued this approach so radically as to categorize the whole New Testament doctrine of redemption as mythical, he has seen, with a clearheadedness denied to many, that the most sensible thing to do next is to drop the mythology entirely and preach simply that brand of existentialism which, in his view, represents the New Testament's real "meaning."

It is clear that, "scientific" or not, this nicely balanced synthesis of two forms of subjectivism is not in any way a transcending of subjectivism. It leaves us still to speculate as to what the Biblical symbols and experiences mean, and what is the revelation which they reflect and to which they point. It leaves us, indeed, in a state of utter uncertainty; for, if it is true (as Scripture says, and modern theology mostly agrees) that men are sinful creatures, unable to know God without revelation, and prone habitually to pervert revelation when given, how can we have confidence that the Biblical witness, and the Church's experience, and our own ideas, are not all wrong? Why should we think that by a "scientific" amalgam of the three we shall get nearer to the reality of revelation than we were before? What trust can we put in our own ability to see behind the Biblical witness to revelation so surely that we can pick out its mistakes and correct them? Such questions did not trouble the subjectivist theologians of the eighteenth and nineteenth centuries, who assumed the infallibility of the human intellect and wholly overlooked the noetic effects of sin; but the mid-twentieth century, haunted by memories of shattered philosophies and exploded ideals, and bitterly aware of the power of propaganda and brain-washing, and the control that non-rational factors can have over our thinking, is tempted to despair of gaining objective knowledge of anything, and demands from the Church reasoned reassurance as to the accessibility of divine revelation to blind, bedevilled sinners. But such reassurance cannot in principle be given by those who on scriptural grounds acknowledge the reality of sin in the mind, and hence the bankruptcy of rationalism, and yet on rationalistic grounds jettison the notion of inscripturated divine truth. For unless at some point we have direct access to revelation normatively presented, by which we may test and correct our own fallible notions, we sinners will be left to drift on a sea of speculations and doubts forever. And when modern theology tells us that we can trust neither the Bible nor ourselves, it condemns us to this fate without hope of reprieve.

Modern theology is, indeed, fully aware of the scriptural and churchly conviction that revelation is objectively and normatively presented in and by the Biblical witness to it. In an attempt to do justice to this conviction while still holding Scripture to be no more than fallible human testimony, theologians focus attention on two "moments" in the divine self-revealing activity in which, they affirm, revelation does in fact confront us directly and authoritatively. These are, on the one hand, the sequence of historical events in which revelation was given, once for all, to its first witness; and, on the other, the repeated "encounter" in which the content of that original revelation is mediated to each successive generation of believers. Both "moments," of course, have a proper place in the Biblical concept of revelation; what is distinctive about the modern view is not its insistence on them, as such, but its attempt to do justice to them while dispensing with that which in fact links them together and is integral to the true notion of each—namely, the concept of infallible Scriptures, given as part of the historical revelatory process and conveying that which is mediated in the "encounter." Most modern statements make mention of both "moments" in combination (compare Williams' reference to "a fresh encounter with the personal and historical act of God in Christ"), but they vary in the emphasis given to each. Scholars whose main interest is in Biblical history, such as C. H. Dodd and H. Wheeler Robinson, naturally stress the first (cf. Dodd, *History and the Gospel*, London, Nisbet, 1938; and Robinson, *Inspiration and Revelation in the Old Testament*, London, Oxford University Press, 1946). Those chiefly concerned with systematic theology and apologetics, such as (reading from the right wing to the left) Karl Barth, Emil Brunner, H. Richard and Reinhold Niebuhr, Paul Tillich and Rudolph Bultmann, lay more stress on the second (cf. Barth, *Church Dogmatics* I. 1, 2: *The Doctrine of the Word of God*, Edinburgh, T. and T. Clark, 1936, 1956; Brunner, *The Divine-Human Encounter*, London, S.C.M., 1944; *Revelation and Reason*, London, S.C.M., 1947; H. Richard Niebuhr, *The Meaning of Revelation*, New York, 1941; Reinhold Niebuhr, *The Nature and Destiny of Man*, I, London, Nisbet, 1941; *Faith and History*, London, Nisbet, 1949; Tillich, *Systematic Theology*, I, London, Nisbet, 1953; Bultmann, "New Testament and Mythology," in *Kerygma and Myth*, ed. Bartsch, London, S.P.C.K., 1953). These theologians all agree that what is communicated in the "encounter" is that which was given once for all in Christ; where they differ is in their views as to the essential content of the primary revelation and the precise nature of the existential "encounter." A third group of more philosophically-minded theologians have devoted themselves to fixing and holding a balance between these two emphases: among them, the late Archbishop Temple, Alan Richardson and John Baillie (cf. Temple, *loc. cit.*; Richardson, *Christian Apologetics*, London, S.C.M., 1947; Baillie, *Our Knowledge of God*, London, Oxford University Press, 1939, and *op. cit.*).

Can the objective accessibility of revelation be vindicated in these terms? We think not. Consider first the idea that revelation, imperfectly mirrored in the Bible, is directly available in the historical events of which the Bible bears witness. Temple expounded this idea very clearly. He thought of revelation as God's disclosure of his mind and character in the "revealing situations" of redemptive history. At no stage does God give a full verbal explanation of what he is doing, but he enlightens prophetic spirits to discern it. (The notion somewhat suggests a divine charade, to be solved by the God-inspired guesswork of human spectators.) The Biblical authors were prophetic men, and made roughly the right deductions from what they observed; though their recounting and explaining of revelation is marred throughout by errors due to human frailty. Our task is critically to work over the records which they left, checking and where necessary correcting their representations; and the facts themselves, thus discerned, will speak their own proper meaning to us.

But (not to dwell on the arbitrary and unbiblical features of this view, and the fact that, if true, it would create a new authoritarianism, by making the expert historian final arbiter of the Church's faith) we must insist that, on this showing, so far from being able to use historical revelation as a norm, we can only have access to it at all through prior acceptance of another norm. For, as Alan Richardson points out, commenting on Temple, all our study of the past is decisively controlled by the principle of interpretation which we bring to it; that is, by our antecedent ideas as to the limits of possibility, the criteria of probability and the nature of historical "meaning" and explanation. In this case, if we do not already share the supernaturalism of the Biblical writers' faith about God and his work in his world, we shall be debarred from sharing their convictions as to what happened in redemptive history. So the revealing facts of history are only accessible to those who are already sure that Christianity is true. And how do we become sure of this? By faith, says Richardson. But what is faith? Receiving what God has said, on his authority, is the basic Biblical idea. But Richardson cannot say this, for he has already told us that until we have faith we are in no position to gather from the human records of Scripture what it is that God has said. He wishes (rightly) to correlate faith with spiritual illumination. But he cannot depict this illumination as an opening of blind eyes to see what objectively was always the case—that the Bible is God's Word written, and its teaching is his revealed truth; for to his mind this is not the case. He is therefore forced back to illuminism. He has to represent faith as a private revelation, a divine disclosure of new information not objectively accessible—namely, that what certain human writers said about God is in fact true. On his assumption that Scripture, as such, is no more than human witness, there is nothing else he can say. So we see that the idea of an objective presentation of revelation in history, when divorced from the idea of a divinely authoritative record, can only in principle be maintained on an illuministic basis. Before I can find revelation in history, I must first receive a private communication from God: and by what objective standard can anyone check this? There is no norm for testing private revelations. We are back in subjectivism with a vengeance.

At this point, however, appeal will be made to the concept of "personal encounter." This, as generally expounded, attempts to parry the charge of illuminism by the contention that God, in sovereign freedom, causes the Biblical word of man to become his word of personal address in the moment of revelation. Brunner has, perhaps, made more of this line of thought than anyone else. Basing it on an axiomatic refusal to equate the teaching of Scripture, as such, with the Word of God, he treats the concept of personal encounter as excluding that of propositional communication absolutely. God's Word in the encounter comes to me, not as information, but as demand, and faith is not mental assent, but the response of obedience. Truth becomes mine through the encounter; but this truth consists, not in any impersonal correspondence of my thoughts with God's facts, but in the personal correspondence of my decision with God's demand. "Truth" is that which happens in the response of faith, rather than anything that is said to evoke that response; "truth" is an event, correlative to the event of revelation which creates it. But this is a very difficult conception. If we are to take seriously Brunner's Pickwickian use of the word "truth," then his idea is one of a communion in which nothing is communicated save a command. God speaks only in the imperative, not at all in the indicative. But is it a recognizable statement of the Christian view of revelation to say that God tells us nothing about himself, but only issues orders? And what is the relation between the command given in the encounter and what is written in Scripture? Never one of identity, according to Brunner; Scripture is human witness proceeding from and pointing to communication in encounter; but not embodying its content; for that which is given in the encounter is ineffable, and no form of words can properly express it. So, where Augustine said: "What Thy Scripture says, that (only that, but all that) Thou dost say," Brunner says: "What Thy Scripture says, that is precisely *not* what Thou dost say." But how, in this case, can Brunner parry the charge of uncontrolled and uncontrollable mysticism? Nor would he be better off if he said that what is spoken by God in the encounter is the exact content of Scripture texts, that and no more; for then he would either have to abandon the idea that Scripture is throughout nothing but fallible and erring human testimony, or else to say that God speaks human error as his truth, which is either nonsense or blasphemy.

Has the objectivity of revelation been vindicated by this appeal to the "encounter"? Has anything yet been said to make intelligible the claim that, though we regard Scripture as no more than fallible human witness, we still have available an objective criterion, external to our own subjective impressions, by which our erring human ideas about revelation can be measured and tested? It seems not. By deserting Richardson for Brunner, we seem merely to have exchanged a doctrine of illuminism (private communication of something expressible) for one of mysticism (private communication of something inexpressible). The problem of objectivity is still not solved; and, we think, never can be on these terms.

LESSONS FROM THE CONTEMPORARY SITUATION

From this survey, sketchy as it is, we learn three things.

First, we see the essential kinship of the various modern views of revelation. They differ in detail, but all begin from the same starting-point and have the same aim: to restore essential Biblical dimensions to the older liberal position.

Second, we see the dilemmas in which modern theology hereby involves itself. "Post-liberal" thought turns out to be liberalism trying to assimilate into itself certain Biblical convictions which, once accepted actually spell its doom. The spectacle which it provides is that of liberalism destroying itself by poisoning its own system. For liberalism, as such, rests, as we saw, on a rationalistic approach to the Bible; and the acceptance of these new insights makes it as irrational in terms of rationalism as it always was unwarrantable in terms of Christianity to continue following such an approach. By recognizing the incomprehensibility of God and his sovereign freedom in revelation, while retaining its peculiar view of Scripture—by trying, that is, to find room for supra-rational factors on its own rationalistic basis—liberalism simply lapses from coherent rationalism into incoherent irrationalism. For the axiom of rationalism in all its forms is that man's mind is the measure of all things; what is real is rational, and only what is rational is real, so that in terms of rationalism the supra-rational is necessarily equated with the irrational and unreal. By allowing for the reality of God who in himself and in his works passes our comprehension, theological rationalism declares its own bankruptcy, and thereby forfeits its quondam claim to interpret and evaluate Scripture, with the rest of God's works, on rationalistic principles—a claim which it could only make on the assumption of its own intellectual solvency. It is simply self-contradictory for modern theology still to cling to the liberal concept of Scripture while professing to have substituted the Biblical for the liberal doctrine of God. And the fact that it continues to do the former cannot but create doubt as to whether it has really done the latter.

Again, by admitting the noetic effects of sin, and the natural incompetence of the human mind in spiritual things, without denying the liberal assumption that reason has both the right and the power to test and explode the Bible's view of its own character as revealed truth, modern theology is in effect telling us that now we know, not merely that we cannot trust Scripture, but also that we cannot trust ourselves; which combination of convictions, if taken seriously, will lead us straight to dogmatic skepticism. Thus, through trying to both have our cake and eat it, we shall be left with nothing to eat at all. Modern theology only obscures this situation, without remedying it, when it talks here of paradox and dialectical tension. The truth is that, by trying to hold these two self-contradictory positions together, modern theology has condemned itself to an endless sequence of arbitrary oscillations between affirming and denying the trustworthiness of human speculations and

Biblical assertions respectively. It could only in principle find stability in the skeptical conclusion that we can have no sure knowledge of God at all.

Thirdly, we see that the only way to avoid this conclusion is to return to the historic Christian doctrine of Scripture, the Bible's own view of itself, which this book is concerned to present. Only when we abandon the liberal view that Scripture is no more than fallible human witness, needing correction by us, and put in its place the Biblical conviction that Scripture is in its nature revealed truth in writing, an authoritative norm for human thought about God, can we in principle vindicate the Christian knowledge of God from the charge of being the incorrigibly arbitrary product of our own subjective fancy. Reconstructed liberalism, by calling attention to the reality of sin, has shown very clearly our need of an objective guarantee of the possibility of right and true thinking about God; but its conception of revelation through historical events and personal encounter with the speaking God ends, as we saw, in illuminism or mysticism, and is quite unable to provide us with such a guarantee. No guarantee can, in fact, be provided except by a return to the old paths—that is, by a renewed acknowledgment of, and submission to, the Bible as an infallible written revelation from God.

SUGGESTED BOOKS

Baillie, John, *The Idea of Revelation in Recent Thought*. New York: Columbia University Press, 1956. A series of lectures reviewing contemporary Protestant views of revelation.

Barth, Karl, *The Word of God and the Word of Man*, trans. Douglas Horton, Torchbooks edition. New York: Harper & Row, Publishers, 1957. An early influential work presenting Barth's view of revelation and its implications for the practical life of the church.

Berkouwer, G. C., *General Revelation*. Grand Rapids: Wm. B. Eerdmans Publishing Co., 1955. A Dutch Calvinist theologian gives an orthodox Protestant view of revelation.

Clark, Gordon H., *Religion, Reason, and Revelation*. Philadelphia: Presbyterian and Reformed Publishing Co., 1961. A philosopher with an evangelical outlook defends propositional revelation and examines several problems pertaining to this view.

Farmer, Herbert H., *Revelation and Religion*. New York: Harper & Row, Publishers, 1954. An interpretation of Christian revelation in the context of its relation to non-Christian religion.

Macintosh, D. C., *The Problem of Religious Knowledge*. New York: Harper & Row, Publishers, 1940. The approach of Protestant Liberalism to man's knowledge of God is represented in this book.

Richardson, Alan, *Christian Apologetics*. New York: Harper & Row, Publishers, 1947. A British theologian expounds a neo-orthodox view of revelation and other Christian doctrines.

Weigel, Gustave, S. J., *Catholic Theology in Dialogue*. New York: Harper & Row, Publishers, 1961. Lectures to non-Catholic audiences on theological themes of mutual interest, including the interpretation of revelation and scripture.

XII · INTERPRETING THE BIBLE

Though Christians differ about the precise meaning of revelation, they are agreed in accepting the Bible as the repository of the central historical revelations. In one way or another they turn to the Biblical record as authoritative for faith and conduct, although they also know that contemporary interpretation and application are necessary. We are therefore led from the concept of revelation as such to the Bible and its interpretation. Of all the facets of this complex subject that might be considered, we shall address ourselves here to the historical orientation of the Bible, to the problem of Biblical inspiration, and to the general character of Biblical teaching.

THE HISTORICAL
ORIENTATION OF BIBLICAL RELIGION

One of the prime requisites for understanding the Bible is the ability to think in concrete, historical terms and not simply in abstract, speculative terms. The Bible confronts us not with theories, not with religious exercises, but with historical events and their interpreted meaning. In order to indicate this emphasis the distinction is often made between historical and nonhistorical religions. The religion stemming from the Bible is historical rather than nonhistorical. That is to say, it sees history, both in its entirety and in certain of its constituent events, as integral to God's purpose and man's reconciliation. The very meaning of Biblical religion is found in, though not confined to, crucial historical events. This is in contrast with a nonhistorical religion such as Buddhism, where the beginning and the end of history are of little religious interest, where temporal existence is permanently subject to the wheel of life and death,[1] and where salvation proceeds not by discovering meaning in and through the events of history but by so seeing the temporal process in an experience of individual triumph that its awful recurrence and sorrow are overcome.

But what, more precisely, does this historical orientation of Biblical religion involve? We shall distinguish a universal, a particularistic, and a transcendent emphasis.[2]

The universal emphasis of the Bible is found in the belief that the life of mankind is a unitary process and in the corollaries which this belief entails. The human race as a whole, including all individual men, is seen as having its temporal beginning in a divine creation. Likewise the end of history, whether that be taken in a temporal or in a qualitative sense, pertains to all men alike. From beginning to end the story of man is one story. Therefore the only adequate history is universal history.

What this implies is not a unity of political development, nor a unified cultural diffusion, but a universality of relevance for Biblical ideas. If, for example, the Bible depicts pride, self-deceit, and idolatrous penchants in man, it does not locate these in one person or nation but dramatizes them as tendencies to which all men are subject. If it portrays the need for reconciliation, it shows a universal need in the life of man. If it points the way to how that need may be met, it proclaims a message relevant to all men. All this is so because, in the Biblical mode of thought, mankind is historically one in origin, need, tendency, and end.

But the historical orientation of the Bible is not brought out merely by the emphasis that man's history is a unit and that therefore the Biblical teaching is universally applicable. The really decisive point on this score comes with the particularistic emphasis, since history is made up of particular events. This emphasis means the conviction that particular historical events are the media through which ultimate meaning and truth are made known. That is, God has revealed himself through particular persons and happenings, and it is in this concrete way that the truth relevant for man generally is communicated. The history and the destiny of man are illuminated and put into focus by the significance of these events. What is universal is made known through the particular.[3] The series of historical events recounted and reflected upon in the Bible are thus the indispensable keystones in Biblical religion. The Bible does not give a list of timeless truths to contemplate but a description of historical encounters with God which show both God and man in actuality.

Both the universal and the particularistic emphases, however, derive their meaning from the transcendent aspect of the Biblical understanding of history. The transcendent emphasis means the emphasis upon the sovereignty of God in relation to the world. Thus the unity of man's history is accepted not because of empirical confirmation but through the faith that all men have their existence from a divine source. The destiny to which man may look is relevant to all men because it represents the divine purpose for human life. The belief that particular persons and occurrences have unique revelatory meaning for all men is based upon the faith that God is able to, and has actually chosen to, make himself and his will known in this way. Thus the whole life of man, its beginning and end, its good and evil, its despair and hope, points to a creation and purpose originating beyond the world yet partially manifested within it. Without this transcendent emphasis the other emphases would be difficult to maintain and indeed rather arbitrary. With it, however, the entire Biblical outlook on history falls into perspective. Human history has meaning by reference to its transcendent ground.

It is within this general perspective that the Biblical teaching is conveyed. But before going on to the character of that teaching we must consider the fundamental problem which arises concerning the inspiration of the Bible.

THE QUESTION OF INSPIRATION

The common Christian belief is that the Bible is a vehicle for communicating God's special revelation to man. The common way of expressing this belief is to say that the Bible is the inspired word of God. But in what sense is the Bible inspired? There has been no clearly revealed truth on this point, so Christian interpretations have differed widely.

One historic belief about inspiration is known as verbal inspiration, meaning that the very words of the Bible have been inspired by God, so that their truth is infallibly assured by divine action. This belief is simply the application to the Bible of the doctrine of propositional revelation discussed in the previous chapter. When verbal inspiration is thought to refer to the Bible in its totality, it is called plenary inspiration, although the two beliefs are not necessarily equivalent. Opposed to verbal inspiration is the belief that the words of the Bible form the human account of God's revelation to man rather than the very words of God. On this view the Bible is inspired in that it records God's real disclosures of himself to human persons. This belief does not go by a familiar name as does the first. But since a common element in it is that God reveals himself in personal encounters rather than in words and statements, it might well be called the belief in personal inspiration.

It is still frequently the case that these two schools of thought give only a passing, slighting reference to the other. The one side may merely say that verbal inspiration was a burden from which we have finally been liberated by modern Biblical criticism, while the other side says that "personal encounter" inspiration is a sign of modernistic, subjective negativism. The one side may think it is a waste of time to go over old ground and hash out the same issue repeatedly. Why not go ahead with newer research on one's own assumptions? The other side may think it is a waste of time to spend much effort refuting modernistic deviations. Why not go ahead with the proclamation of the historic Christian faith? Actually there is a great deal to be said for these attitudes. Though one cannot always condone the language in which the attitudes are expressed, something can be said for encouraging each side to proceed with the truth as it sees it and making its case rest upon its merits and not upon denunciations of the other point of view.

At the same time the division remains, and the Christian message is not so likely to be as effective as otherwise when springing from a divided house. In any case a serious student should, for the sake of general knowledge and of open-mindedness, delve into the issue. As a step in that direction we shall present some of the arguments that each side musters in its behalf. We cannot go into any detail at all, but must confine ourselves to some of the sorts of points that come up in colloquial discussions and in writings on the subject.

Arguments Offered For Verbal Inspiration

1. The principal claim made by defenders of verbal inspiration is undoubtedly the claim that this belief was held and taught by Jesus Christ, for example in Matthew 5:17-18.[4] If Christ is the incarnation of God, as Christians believe, then his teachings have genuine authority; and if he taught that the scriptures are verbally inspired, this doctrine is inescapable. That he did teach the doctrine is clearly shown, it is claimed, by the adherence he displayed toward the Hebrew scriptures and by his quoting of them as being final and authoritative. Furthermore, he commissioned the New Testament writers with their authority. So we are bound to accept his attitude and teaching.

2. It is also claimed that verbal inspiration was assumed and taught by the writers of both the Old and New Testaments.[5] For example, the pronouncement, "Thus saith the Lord," is a familiar one in the Old Testament. Likewise the Apostles, receiving their commission directly from Christ, believed that they were writing from divine authority and at times stated as much, as in 1 Timothy 3:16. Not that the citation of verses proves the point, for that would be a case of circular reasoning, i.e., assuming that the verses are verbally inspired in order to prove that they are. The point is rather that there is a long and uniform testimony to the doctrine of verbal inspiration within the Biblical tradition, and this testimony cannot be dismissed without distorting the Biblical record.

3. It is further maintained that verbal inspiration was the original teaching of the church and continued to be its teaching until recent times.[6] Here again is a long historic witness that cannot be dismissed. This contention can be amplified by pointing out that the so-called "higher criticism" of the Bible is a comparatively recent phenomenon, not the heritage of the church, but rather an accompaniment of doctrinal deviations from the church's teaching.

4. Sometimes the internal unity and harmony of the Bible are given as

evidence of verbal inspiration.[7] Such unity and harmony are so striking, it is said, that only direct verbal inspiration could account for them. For example, the fact of prophecy in the Old Testament being fulfilled in the New Testament, or the way in which the entire Bible points to Christ as its center, are said to indicate more than human authorship.

5. The last argument we shall mention is somewhat of a deductive one. If God is the source of man's salvation, and if to that end he has revealed himself in the Biblical record, then he would surely guarantee that that record would be available to man in a true, saving form.[8] It is inconsistent to think of God revealing himself through the Bible in the first place and then leaving its composition to the human foibles and historical contingencies to which ordinary literary productions are subject. He therefore reveals his word through divinely given words.

Arguments Offered For Personal Inspiration

1. It is often pointed out that only the original manuscript of the Bible could be regarded as verbally inspired, since the later ones that we possess show differences among themselves due to the processes of human transmission. But no original manuscript is extant; we have only the later copies. So verbal inspiration is quite irrelevant, for it cannot be applied in our actual work of interpreting what we have.[9]

2. Verbal inspiration is meaningless without an infallible interpreter of the infallible words. Protestantism makes no such claim to infallibility for itself, and therefore a Protestant doctrine of verbal inspiration is but a half-way house to Catholicism, which does.[10] If Catholic authority is rejected, verbal inspiration cannot stand. The result of verbal inspiration in Protestantism has been a dogmatic splintering up into denominations, each claiming to have the verbally inspired truth—a sad commentary on the unity in Christ which should prevail.

3. The presence of internal discrepancies and historical errors in the Bible makes the belief in verbal inspiration untenable.[11] Different accounts of the order of creation in Genesis 1 and 2, differences in the synoptic Gospels regarding the same incident, and divergent accounts of the resurrection stories are often cited as examples of internal discrepancies. Inaccuracies in the data presented in Chronicles, the misnaming of some of the rulers referred to in the Bible, and the difficulties in some of the genealogies may be pointed out as illustrations of historical errors. Such things suggest human composition.

4. The Biblical writers held to a pre-scientific, three-story picture of the universe, which often enters into their writing, and these elements cannot be regarded as verbally inspired.[12] This picture of the world is seen especially in the early portions of the Pentateuch; but it is also

present in later writings, for it was the common cosmology of the ancient world. Modern Christians must preserve the basic religious truths of the Bible despite the pre-scientific manner in which they were sometimes expressed.

5. The nature of the Biblical writing itself is much better understood as a human response than as divinely given words.[13] The narrative base, the tales and anecdotes, the detailed specifications in the Old Testament, the dry legal material, the poetry and song, the wisdom sayings, the lustful passages, the prophetic oracles, the epistles to very local problems, the acknowledgments of Christ's lordship by his followers, the preservation of his sayings, the interpretation of his life and work—all this is characteristic of a people preserving its memories and recording its experiences. It is difficult to see how a transcendent God would hit upon this body of material and these styles of writing for a didactic communication of verbal truths. On the other hand it is quite understandable that such a body of material and such styles would result from a people's conviction that its history was being directed by God's presence and therefore had to be preserved in all of its variant detail.

Counter-replies

Each side is of course ready with its rejoinders. The defenders of personal inspiration may reply that Jesus never said he believed in verbal inspiration but on the contrary did not hesitate upon occasion to supersede previous teachings; that the Biblical writers assume only some kind of divine inspiration but do not specify this to be verbal inspiration; that there was no creedal formulation by the church supporting verbal inspiration rather than some other conception of the inspiration of scripture; that the unity which does exist in the Bible is just as compatible with some other theory of inspiration; and that there may be a good reason why God would withhold rather than guarantee infallible words, namely, to discourage man from making infallible claims for himself and becoming idolatrous about the Bible.

The defenders of verbal inspiration may reply that if God inspired the original manuscript of the Bible he would surely see to it that, despite errors of transmission, all necessary truths and doctrines are preserved; that there is a legitimate distinction between an infallibly inspired book awaiting interpretation and an infallible interpreter, and one can hold to the former without claiming the latter; that all alleged discrepancies can be so interpreted as to remove the difficulty, or at least if they cannot be fully accounted for at present they are too trivial to interfere with the main tenet of verbal inspiration; that the Bible is not a book of science and therefore, even if some of the Biblical writers did hold some pre-scientific views, as we might expect, these views did not enter into their presentation of accurate historical and religious truth; and that God would surely reveal himself through a body of material and through styles of writing that are humanly oriented and relevant, and not through some remote and strange hieroglyphics.

THE SIGNIFICANCE OF THE CONTROVERSY

There can be little doubt that this issue is a divisive one. Some would say it is the basic source of the cleavages in Protestantism. This may be going too far, for we cannot ignore historical, sociological, and temperamental factors as causes of division. Nevertheless there are differences in outlook which do trace directly to the divergence concerning inspiration.

Those who support verbal inspiration are more insistent upon the factual accuracy of the Bible in its recording of historical data and miraculous happenings. They do not hold, and indeed could not, a totally literal view of everything in the Bible, and they are not necessarily committed to accepting the total inerrancy of every word now in the Bible. But in point of fact they do adopt a much more literalistic approach to the scripture than do their opponents, except where this approach is obviously out of place, as in the case of parables. Scholars accepting inspiration are likewise more insistent that the Biblical books are unities and were written by the authors whose names they bear, whereas scholars accepting personal inspiration feel much freer in proposing new theories when they think these are historically and textually more adequate explanations of the composition and authorship of the Biblical books. Again, verbal inspiration leads to a view which tends to look upon prophecy in the Bible as the prediction of later events, occurring either in subsequent Bible times or in future history, whereas personal inspiration leads to a view which tends to regard references in the Bible to other events as having taken place after those events, prophecy being a way of speaking out for God rather than a literal forecasting of future occurrences. All these differences together often lead to further characteristic contrasts in doctrine, e.g., concerning creation, the sin of man, Christology, and eschatology. So the issue is not an inconsequential dispute.

At the same time there are basic agreements in Christian belief and practice which are usually more significant than the differences. Furthermore, it is worth calling attention to the numbers of problems which the answer to the inspiration question does not settle and which would still remain even if there were no dispute over inspiration. Agreement on the question of inspiration would not, for example, have determined in the early church which of the many current books were to be selected as the inspired books belonging to the New Testament canon. It would not determine today which manuscript or combination of manuscripts is closest to the original version. It would not explain for us the exact meaning of key words in the Bible, upon which differences in interpretation often hinge. It would not tell us what doctrines are essential for the definition of Christianity. It would not even decide in many cases which of several alternative theories on certain doctrines is the most adequate one. It would not tell us which theological dogmas if any must be affirmed in order for one to be a Christian. It would not tell us how the Christian teachings ought to be applied in today's world, or which of the teachings are especially relevant today and which referred primarily to Biblical times.

In short, we could imagine people agreeing upon verbal inspiration or else upon personal inspiration and still being confronted by the same decisions concerning all these crucial questions, which would still have to be answered through Biblical understanding, reason, and conscience. This should warn us against making this issue the principal axe to grind. While the issue is significant, it is not the key to final truth and unity. Perhaps through an increasing recognition of this fact, namely, that the battleground upon which people focused their venom in the past is not necessarily decisive for the other major issues of interpretation and application, greater accord and more unified emphases may be reached.

This is not to say that the question of inspiration should not continue to be discussed. Provided the debate does not usurp time needed for more important problems, it is generally instructive for one to review the reasons for one's position and to reconsider these in the light of arguments for alternative positions. Yet today something more than this customary debate seems called for. We need to give attention not only to the arguments themselves that are offered for each position but to the "meta-question" of what constitutes a relevant argument or a good reason in this area. For example, it is commonly acknowledged today that merely quoting verses of scripture as proof of a theory of inspiration is not a sufficient argument, since the procedure tends to be circular, drawing for proof upon that which is the subject of the controversy. Again, merely to accuse the other side of impiety and straying from the true faith is not a very convincing reason for one's own view. What is needed, then, is a consideration of the kinds of statements that will count as good arguments, and then an attempt to follow through in the identification of those lines of thought which may help toward a resolution of the dispute. Surely this is to be preferred to the stony stalemate which is often the only result of the usual display of the familiar types

of arguments. Of course some may say that this dispute is like that between Protestantism and Catholicism, where there can be no resolution
unless one capitulates and acknowledges the other as the true form of the
church. But there is this difference, that within Protestantism nothing
prevents anyone from changing or modifying his view of inspiration
and still continuing to be Protestant. And herein lies some measure of
hope for newer ways of approach.

THE NATURE OF BIBLICAL TEACHING

Pedagogically there is no one way in which the Bible communicates
its message. Naturally no book communicates if it is not perused with
some care and receptiveness. But even when these are present in the
reader, a variety of communicational procedures is evident. Sometimes the
teaching is frankly didactic, as in the legal codes, the prophetic pronouncements, and the theological passages of Paul. Sometimes it is
confessional narrative, as in the historical books of the Old Testament
and the Gospels of the New. All these may be considered more direct
means of communication. But there are many instances of indirect teaching as well. The abundance of poetic utterance is perhaps the prime
example of this. The parables of Jesus with their piercing thrusts, sometimes obvious, sometimes hidden, are another. There is even a method
so indirect that it borders on obscurity, viz., the apocalyptic writing.

When we seek to understand the nature of Biblical teaching, therefore,
we must find it not in a distinctive or unified pedagogical method, nor
for that matter in the psychological attitudes of readers, but in the
content of what is taught. This involves knowing its historical context
and its universal message.

Historically speaking, the unifying element in all the methods of
teaching is the fact that they all flow out of, or are related to, a unified
religious community, the Hebrew "people of God" in the Old Testament, the primitive Christian church in the New. The Bible is communication through a historical community. In one way or another it
tells us historically of the life, times, temptations, sins, renewals, expectations, fulfillments, and faith of a people who believed that its career was
divinely created, covenanted, commissioned, and destined. Exactly why
this people was chosen as a revelatory community is something of a
mystery now as it was then. But any meaningful statement on this point
acknowledges God's mercy toward all men and not just his favoritism
toward one historical nation. A Jewish legend has it that the same opportunity was given by God to all nations, but only the Hebrews were
willing to accept the responsibility and the suffering involved. Ap-

parently there had to be not only a chosen people, but to some extent a choosing people, or at least an accepting people. At any rate the universal message is taught through writings which, diverse as they are, constitute a unified testimony of a people to God's action in its history.

The understanding of the historical character of the Biblical teaching leads to the understanding that the Bible is a proclamation, a confessional, a witnessing record to God's activity in history and what that means for man.[14] Thus there are some approaches to the Bible which are quite inadequate from the point of view of religious interpretation—approaches which concentrate, for example, on culling out the literary gems from among the dead stones, or noting moral signposts in a barbarous age, or making miraculous incidents the key issue of religious concern, or explaining Biblical history solely through cultural antecedents and contemporary borrowings. All these types of study are helpful at their own level of interpretation; but they do not contain the religious meaning of the Bible.

That meaning unfolds only when the Bible is viewed as a convictional narration of how God has acted in history in order to bring his people back to what they ought to be. This constitutes the second unifying element in the Biblical teaching, i.e., its universal message. Not only is the Bible the complex story of a people; it is the cumulative revelation of what God has done, is doing, and will do in order to accomplish his eternal purpose for man. Through the recorded memory of certain events, persons, and declarations, God's universal concern for mankind is revealed, with both the judgment and the mercy that this implies. God is conceived of as ever seeking to reconcile man to himself, and the Bible declares this truth.

But all is not sweetness and light. It is no simple success story about God. For equally prominent in the story is man and his ambiguous nature. And even more striking is man's deep-seated tendency to reject the good that is offered to him in favor of more immediate, more alluring attractions. The Bible presents a vivid portrayal of what Emil Brunner calls "man in revolt." This is not to say that man is shown without the capacity for repentance, for change of heart, for right choice, even for human mercy. The truth is that he is depicted as a very untidy mixture of good and evil. But when he is capable of the good, the interpretation is that this occurs not through his own unaided efforts but through his acceptance of the divine grace that is open to his choice.

Such, then, is what the Bible appears to be all about religiously—the predicament of man caused by his own choosing, his need for reconciliation, and the redeeming activity of God to effect this reconciliation. By universalization from the history of the Hebrew people and the early church, the nature and need of man as such are illuminated, and the immanent working of God in all men revealed. Our predicament is the same, our need the same, our solution the same, our opportunity the same. It is against the background of this over-all teaching, namely, the religious history of a people and the reconciling activity of God, that the other particular teachings need to be understood.

For Christians the culmination of this reconciling activity of God for man's reclamation has occurred in the person of Christ. In him there is both the supreme revelation of God and the perfect example for man. Thus for them the Biblical teaching is judged by this standard. So from a consideration of the Biblical teaching in general we are led naturally to a consideration of the doctrine of Christ.

THE BIBLE AS THE WORD OF GOD

BERNHARD ANDERSON

Bernhard W. Anderson (1916–) studied at the College of the Pacific, Pacific School of Religion, and Yale. He is a professor of Biblical theology and Dean of the Faculty at Drew Theological Seminary and has taught previously at Colgate-Rochester Divinity School, the University of North Carolina, and Colgate University. In addition to Rediscovering the Bible, *he has written* The Unfolding Drama of the Bible (1953) *and* Understanding the Old Testament (1957). *Here he reviews briefly recent attitudes toward the Bible and then offers an interpretation of it as the word of God, but not as infallibly inspired.*

The uniqueness of the Bible, however, cannot be understood adequately by treating it merely as a human book. The Bible was never designed to be read as great literature, sober history, naive philosophy, or primitive science. Men remembered stories, treasured traditions, and wrote in various forms of literature because of one inescapable conviction: they had been confronted by God in events which had taken place in their history. Though hidden from mortal sight in light unapproachable, the holy God had revealed himself to mankind. He had taken the

From Bernhard W. Anderson, *Rediscovering the Bible* (New York: Association Press, copyright 1951 by Haddam House, Inc.), pp. 9-19, 20-22. Reprinted by permission.

initiative to establish a relationship with his people. He had spoken his Word of judgment and of mercy. "In many and various ways God spoke of old to our fathers by the prophets; but in these last days he has spoken to us by a Son." These opening words of the Letter to the Hebrews strike the keynote of the Bible. It is this central conviction which gives the Bible, both Old and New Testaments, the status of sacred scripture in the Christian Church.

This faith is a stumbling block to the modern mind. It would be more honest, however, to reject the biblical claim outright than to insist that the message of God's revelation is peripheral and that these people actually meant to say something other than they seem to say. The Bible has suffered seriously from readers who, like the legendary highwayman of ancient Greece, have attempted to force its message into the Procrustean bed of modern ways of thinking. As a consequence, some people have dismissed the theology of the Bible as a poetic or mythical embellishment of men's maturing awareness of the distinction between right and wrong. Others have treated it as elementary philosophy, the first efforts of the Hebrews reflectively to understand Reality. These approaches to the meaning of human existence may be adequate outside the Bible. But the men of the Bible say something very different. It is their claim that God himself has spoken with a decisiveness, a once-for-all-ness. They do not tell us about searching for moral values, or attempting to reach a more satisfying philosophy by standing a bit taller on their intellectual tiptoes. Rather, they bear witness to their encounter with God in the midst of crucial events of history, their engagement with him in moments of historical crisis. And, above all, this revelation was not peripheral or incidental to their message; it was the vantage point from which they viewed everything else—politics, social injustice, and war; past, present, and future. They do not argue this faith; they proclaim it with confessional language: "Here I stand, I cannot do otherwise."

The subject matter of the Bible, then, is God's self-revelation to men. Because of this stupendous theme, traditional Christianity has described the Bible as the "Word of God" and has insisted upon the divine authorship of Scripture. Says a New Testament writer: "All Scripture is given by inspiration of God," that is, as the Greek word suggests, it is "God-breathed" or "filled with the breath of God" (II Timothy 3:16). However seriously one may take the human dimension of Scripture, he cannot easily disregard the central claim of the Bible itself to be the record and witness of revelatory events in which God has spoken. This is sacred scripture because the Holy Spirit breathes through the ancient words and reveals to men in every age the Word of truth.

What does it mean to say that the Bible is inspired? This is the heart of our problem. It is no easy task to deal with the Bible in such a manner that one does justice both to its humanity and its divine authorship. Much confusion has been brought about by those who would oversimplify the matter, either by emphasizing the human element in Scripture to the point of stultifying its divine authorship, or by emphasizing the divine character of the Bible to the point of ignoring that it is a human book. The major cleavage in the Protestant churches in America is no longer denominational, geographical, or even doctrinal. The line is drawn at the point of the authority of the Bible, and in general Protestants can be divided according to which side they take in the debate over biblical inspiration.

Many Protestants have adopted a position which has been labeled "liberalism." Instead of hiding their heads, ostrich-like, in the barren sands of the past, these Christians sincerely and devoutly have attempted to make the Bible speak relevantly to the modern situation. A Christian cannot believe one set of ideas on Sunday and then live by another set of assumptions the rest of the week. Such religious "schizophrenia" is intolerable, for the Christian faith jealously demands the allegiance of the whole man. Therefore, liberals sought to adjust the inherited faith to the bewildering modern world whose outlook had been defined by the achievements of science. It was their intention to remain loyal to the biblical faith, but to make this faith relevant by translating its truths into the language of the modern age. This point of view was championed brilliantly by Harry Emerson Fosdick, who popularized the phrase, "abiding experiences in changing categories," and insisted that biblical truth could be lifted out of the biblical framework of expression and reinterpreted in the categories of modern thought.[1]

Specifically, this meant reinterpreting the Bible in terms of the concept of evolution, a scientific hypothesis which originally was applied in the field of biology but which soon was transferred to other fields of investigation until it became the dominant philosophical point of view on the American scene. This outlook found theological expression in the toning down or outright rejection of supernaturalism in favor of the idea of divine immanence, that is, God's indwelling in man and nature. For instance, creation by supernatural fiat was reinterpreted to mean God's continuing creation, his immanence in the long evolutionary upthrust.

· · · · ·

Applied to religious knowledge, the evolutionary interpretation found expression in the idea of "progressive revelation." That is to say, God works immanently within the historical process, revealing his timeless

---

[1] See Fosdick's book, *The Modern Use of the Bible* (Macmillan, 1929), especially chap. 4.

truths up to man's ability to understand; on man's side, this progressive illumination yields increasing "discovery" or expanding "insight." The Bible allegedly gives evidence of such progress. The religion of Moses is said to be comparatively primitive. But under the influence of the prophetic "genius," crude and barbarous elements were gradually removed, until Jesus finally came as the great discoverer of God and the teacher of the loftiest ethical principles. Since all humanity is involved in the evolutionary process, it is no more surprising that religions outside the biblical tradition should arrive at the same insights than it is that both Russia and America, working independently, should unlock the secret of the atom. According to this view, the greatness of Jesus is that he saw what many others had seen, or could have seen, but by his forceful teaching and sacrificial death he helped men to take truth seriously.

This modern view of the Bible enabled Christians to keep their heads erect in a world where only fools or fanatics would dare to challenge the assured results of science. Of course, liberals were also children of their time, and therefore fell into the temptation of revising the Bible in accordance with their own presuppositions. Nevertheless, liberalism at its best was governed by the spirit of evangelical Christianity.[2] This is noticeable, for example, in one of the characteristic elements of the liberal attitude: devotion to truth. A critical principle lies at the heart of the liberal attitude, the fearless application of which is akin to the spirit of ancient prophets who challenged all human securities. Just as the Protestant Reformation broke upon the world in protest against a Church which had identified itself with God's Kingdom on earth, so liberalism emerged as a prophetic challenge to a decadent Protestantism that had prematurely congealed Christian truth into a static system of belief. According to liberalism, all conclusions must be judged by truth itself. This attitude, when applied to biblical study, has aided in our rediscovery of the Bible by enabling us to read it in the light of the circumstances in which it was written.

Moreover, Protestant liberalism was a healthy relief from the one-sided emphasis upon the salvation of the individual soul. Liberalism flowered in the "social gospel" movement, as ably represented by men like Walter Rauschenbusch. If the liberal's expectancy of building a Christian society on earth was too much under the influence of the faith of the Enlightenment, it was certainly akin to the this-worldly religion of the Bible according to which all of life must be brought under the sovereignty of God. Finally, liberalism at its best was motivated by a vivid and vital rediscovery of Christian experience. If, as Luther said,

---

[2] See H. P. Van Dusen's discussion of liberal theology in *The Vitality of the Christian Tradition*, ed. George Thomas (Harper, 1941), pp. 168-174.

"every Christian must do his own believing, just as he must do his own dying," then likewise each age must make its own discovery of Christ and express its faith in its unique way. Liberalism did this for the late nineteenth and early twentieth centuries. Indeed, future historians undoubtedly will appraise liberalism as one of the most dynamic movements in the history of Christianity.

Although liberalism was swept along by a powerful current of evangelical Christianity, the theology of liberalism came too much under the influence of the modern world-view. It is one thing to attempt to translate the biblical faith into categories which modern man can understand; it is quite another thing to adopt modern categories as ruling principles of interpretation. In attempting to bring Christianity up to date, liberals virtually capitulated to the prevailing world-view of the day, so much so that the dividing line between liberal Protestantism and secularism became increasingly dim. Reaction was inevitable.

The reaction came in the form of a movement known as fundamentalism. Beginning during the period 1910-20 on an organized interdenominational basis, it was led by conservative Protestants who felt that "modernists" were "throwing out the baby with the bath" in their streamlining of the Christian faith. The historian will point out precedents for this movement in the sterile orthodoxy which set in shortly after the outburst of the Protestant Reformation, and in the decadent Calvinism which persisted in America, especially in rural areas, throughout the eighteenth and nineteenth centuries. Fundamentalism as such, however, is a distinctly twentieth century phenomenon, and is properly regarded as essentially a reactionary protest against the excesses of the modernizing of the Bible. Precipitated by the crisis occasioned by the introduction of the theory of evolution, it was aimed at restoring and preserving the fundamentals of the Faith. The movement gained national and even international attention through the "heresy" investigation of Harry Emerson Fosdick in 1923, and the infamous Scopes "monkey" trial at Dayton, Tennessee, in 1925 where the anti-evolution case was championed eloquently by William Jennings Bryan. Even yet, fundamentalism is a powerful force in the American religious scene. Young people become familiar with crusading fundamentalism through the "Youth for Christ" movement or, on the college campus, through the "Inter-Varsity Fellowship."

The key "fundamental" of the faith, according to this group, is the inerrancy of Scripture. In the words of a representative statement, it is "an essential doctrine of the Word of God and our standards that the Holy Spirit did so inspire, guide, and move the writers of the Holy Scripture as to keep them from error." This means that the words of the Bible are the very words of God himself. The writers of the Bible were mere passive secretaries who mechanically transcribed the divine words, these words being the media for conveying the thoughts of the Infinite Intelligence who knows everything past, present, and future. Because God is literally the author of Holy Scripture, the whole Bible "from cover to cover" is held to be absolutely infallible. In popular practice fundamentalists have claimed infallibility for a particular version of the Bible: the King James Version of 1611! Apparent contradictions in Scripture, they say, are not real and are made to vanish by the magic of an interpretative method which weaves together texts from all over the Bible. It is supposedly a matter of faith for the Christian to take the Bible exactly for what it says. If the Bible says that the world was created in six days, that God made a woman out of Adam's rib, that Joshua commanded the sun to stand still, that Balaam's ass talked, or that Jesus turned water into wine, then these matters must be accepted as facts. Many young people have gone away to college burdened with the anxiety that it is a sin to question the literal accuracy of the biblical stories.

Fundamentalists argue that the doctrine of the inerrancy of Scripture is a Christian belief of long standing. It is quite true that both Protestantism and Roman Catholicism have spoken of the Bible in the highest terms. Calvin, for instance, referred to the Bible as the infallible Word of God, and described it by such phrases as "God's own voice," "dictated by the Holy Spirit," and so on. Moreover, a recent Vatican Council declared that the books of the Bible are sacred "not because, having been composed by human industry, they were afterward approved by her [the Church's] authority, nor merely because they contain revelation without error, but because having been written under the inspiration of the Holy Spirit, they have God for their author, and as such were handed down to the Church herself." But in neither case did insistence upon the divine authorship of Scripture carry with it a slavish devotion to the letter of the Scriptures or involve the belief that the Bible is the sole norm for everything under the sun.[3] It is a great mistake to identify fundamentalism with the thinking of men like Luther or Calvin. Unlike classical Christian orthodoxy, fundamentalism is slavishly bound to the literal text of the Bible, and manifests open hostility to anything which goes under the name of biblical criticism. The point bears repetition that fundamentalism is a twentieth-century reactionary movement.

To the credit of fundamentalism it should be said that these conservative Christians have been sincere and devout in their attempt to defend the fundamentals of Christianity behind a Maginot line of biblical literalism. As we have observed, liberalism tended to veer away from the main

---

[3] For a treatment of "The Reformer's Use of the Bible," see Paul Lehmann, *Theology Today*, October, 1946, pp. 328ff. For a recent Catholic statement giving limited encouragement to biblical criticism, see the encyclical letter of Pope Pius XII, *Divino Afflante Spiritu* (1943).

stream of evangelical Christianity and to become a "modernism" carried along by the current of secularism. Thus one may say that fundamentalists, in their dogmatic way, have been making a valid protest against a secularized Christianity which failed to remember Paul's advice: "Be not conformed to this world. . . ." The protest, however, has had little effect on the real frontiers of theological thinking. It is significant that the current theological revival, spoken of earlier, has not been led by fundamentalists but by liberal Protestants whose liberalism was deepened and chastened by involvement in the world crisis.[4]

The real strength of fundamentalism lies in its weaknesses. When the securities of life are threatened, men seek an authority which is visible and absolute. The Bible, therefore, came to be an Ark of salvation in which, like Noah and his family, the faithful could find refuge from the storms of agnosticism and change which were sweeping the world. Fundamentalism is really a form of bibliolatry, that is, it is a faith in the Bible itself, rather than faith in the God who speaks his Word through the Bible. Despite its high regard for the Bible, this movement offers men a false and—paradoxical though this may seem—an *unbiblical* authority.

Moreover, part of the appeal of fundamentalism lies in its reactionary social position. Too often the defense of the Bible has been allied curiously with a reactionary defense of the status quo. It is hardly accidental that frequently the fundamentalist leadership has been recruited from, and the financial support for the movement given by, successful businessmen who have been more concerned about "saving souls" for eternity than about redeeming society in the name of Jesus Christ. The biblical justification for this escape from social radicalism has been the "premillennial" hope, that is, the belief that Christ must come again before the millennium of justice and peace can be introduced; in the meantime, the evils of society must continue and even become worse.[5] The belief that "Jesus is coming soon"—as one reads on signs along our highways—produces evangelists, but does not inspire a "social gospel." If liberalism has capitulated to secularism, it is equally true that fundamentalism in its own way has made even more dangerous concessions to the status quo.

In summary, fundamentalism and liberalism are both partly right and partly wrong. Fundamentalists are right in insisting that the Bible on its own witness presents men with the Word of God. When liberals equate "progressive revelation" with "increasing discovery," the word revelation is virtually emptied of meaning. The reality has gone, leaving behind only the empty word, like the lingering grin after the disappearance of the

---

[4] See the series of articles by Charles Clayton Morrison, "Neo-Orthodoxy's Liberalism," in *The Christian Century*, June 7, 14, and 21, 1950.

[5] Fundamentalists base this belief on Revelation 20:2-3, which they interpret to mean that Christ must come to inaugurate the "thousand years" of peace.

Cheshire cat; for that which men can discover potentially—like the secret of the atom—is scarcely the traditional meaning of "revelation." If there is revelation, God must reveal to man what man in his blindness cannot or will not see. He must shed eternal light upon the mystery of life. He must offer a divine solution to an otherwise insoluble human problem. Fundamentalists are keen enough to see this. But unfortunately they make so much of the divine authorship of Scripture that the human element is virtually eliminated, the human secretary being only a mechanical or passive transmitter of God's revelation.

Liberalism, on the other hand, is right in emphasizing the humanity of Scripture—"the warp of human life on the loom of Scripture, across which the shuttle of the Spirit of God so constantly moved," as H. Wheeler Robinson has put it. Whatever the inspired content of the Bible is, "we have this treasure in a frail earthen vessel." If God speaks his Word, men must hear it and respond within the limitations of concrete historical situations. Since the men of the Bible were men and not God they inevitably used the language of their time to communicate their faith. These things liberalism emphasized and brilliantly verified by means of historical criticism. Unfortunately, however, the human element of Scripture was overemphasized, especially under the influence of the dominant evolutionary philosophy, with the result that "God" became little more than a force at work in the social process, leading men to the formulation of loftier ideas and sounder ethical insights. Thus the uniqueness of the biblical revelation was often discounted and the divine authorship of Scripture reduced to an empty figure of speech. As liberal scholars are now recognizing increasingly, the weakness of the liberalism of the past was not in the use of the method of historical criticism, but rather the fault lay in the dubious presuppositions about the nature of man and history which governed the use of the method.[6]

. . . . .

What do we mean when we speak of the Bible as the "Word of God"? Let us recognize at the outset that we are using the language of metaphor. When the prophets exclaimed "thus saith the Lord" they were not putting quotation marks around the actual words which had been spoken by God; and when they exhorted their countrymen to "hear the Word of the Lord" they did not refer to a Voice which was carried to them on the sound waves. Speaking and hearing are the ways in which persons become related to one another.[7] If my friend speaks to me and I hear his word, a

---

[6] See the essay by T. W. Manson, "The Failure of Liberalism to Interpret the Bible as the Word of God," in *The Interpretation of the Bible*, ed. C. W. Dugmore (London: Society for Promoting Christian Knowledge, 1944).

[7] C. H. Dodd has discussed this matter nicely in *The Bible Today* (Macmillan, 1947), pp. 104 ff. This book, based on a series of "open lectures" at the University of Cambridge, provides a readable and valuable introduction to the Bible.

bridge of communication is thrown out from his life to mine, with the result that a relationship exists between us. Analogously, the Word of God, when heard in a historical crisis, is the medium through which God enters into *relationship* with men. Thus it is proper to speak of God revealing himself by his Word—the word of the prophets of old, and Jesus Christ, "the Word made flesh."

According to the Bible, man encounters God in history. Sometimes we say that we are most aware of God as we behold the beauties of nature. So Wordsworth—that mystic lover of nature—has caught our poetic fancy:

> And I have felt
> A presence that disturbs me with the joy
> Of elevated thoughts; a sense sublime
> Of something far more deeply interfused,
> Whose dwelling is the light of setting suns,
> And the round ocean, and the living air,
> And the blue sky, and in the mind of men.

The men of the Bible testify that the heaven and earth declare the glory of God, but to them nature was not the *primary* sphere of God's revelation. They first heard God's Word in moments of historical crisis, in events which were experienced with a unique meaning. To be sure, the encounter with God often took place in a setting of nature. Moses heard the divine call in the severe grandeur and serene solitude of the desert of Sinai; Elijah was addressed by God in the silence which followed nature's tumultuous display of earthquake, wind, and fire; and Amos received the divine summons as he was tending his flocks in the rugged wilderness of Tekoa. But in each of these cases there was an acute awareness of the historical crisis in which Israel was involved at the moment. Thus the "Word of God" was essentially the interpretation of a historical crisis in which men were grasped by God's claim upon them. In order to communicate the discerned meaning of events, the writers of the Bible employed words, but words, of course, are only symbols for the conveyance of meaning. Therefore the biblical interpreter must go beyond the letter of Scripture to the meaning. He must seek "the Word behind the words," as someone has put it.

In the strict sense, then, it is inaccurate to speak of the Bible itself as the Word of God. Properly speaking, the Bible *contains* the Word of God. The subject matter of the Bible is God's approach to man in history, in particular the stream of Hebraic-Christian history which begins with the Exodus and culminates in the coming of Jesus Christ. Though this book is characterized by great diversity and variety, both in literary form and religious content, its internal unity is the drama of the working out of God's purpose in the events of Israel's history. As someone has said, this biblical history is His-Story, in which he reveals his judgment upon men's sin and his intention and power to recreate mankind. The plot has

God's purpose at the beginning, God's ultimate triumph at the conclusion, and—at the tragic and victorious climax—a Cross, the sign of God's omnipotent love. Because the Bible is both the record of these unique events and the witness to their divine meanings, it may be called the Word of God.

If we are to hear God's Word spoken through the Bible to our situation today, our first task is to put ourselves within the world of the Bible. No casual or superficial reading of Scripture can accomplish this. We must avail ourselves of the results of historical criticism and biblical theology so that we may imaginatively relive the actual historical situation in which an Amos or a Paul heard the high calling of God. We must, as it were, sit where these ancient people sat and learn to look at the human scene from their unique point of view. We must live with the Bible until it becomes part of us, just as the actor identifies himself with the role that he plays. It is then, perhaps, that the Holy Spirit, breathing through the ancient words of the sacred page, will lead us to know that the "Word of the Lord" spoken by the prophets and embodied in Jesus Christ is actually the deepest interpretation of our own life situation and our world crisis in the twentieth century.

INSPIRATION IN ORTHODOX THEOLOGY

EDWARD J. CARNELL

Edward J. Carnell (1919–) has acquired a long list of degrees—from Wheaton College, Westminster Theological Seminary, Harvard Divinity School, and Boston University. After teaching briefly at Gordon College and Gordon Divinity School, he went to Fuller Theological Seminary, where he has served both as president and as professor of ethics and philosophy of religion. His books include An Introduction to Christian Apologetics *(1948),* A Philosophy of the Christian Religion *(1952), and* Christian Commitment *(1957). In the following selection he gives an account of the meaning of inspiration according to Protestant orthodoxy.*

HIGHER CRITICISM

Orthodoxy welcomes any investigation that throws light on the literary and historical background of the Bible. "If the Scriptures have God as their author, it surely concerns us all the more on that account, to

From *The Case for Orthodox Theology* by Edward John Carnell, pp. 97-102, 110-11. Copyright 1959, W. L. Jenkins. The Westminster Press. By permission of The Westminster Press and Marshall, Morgan & Scott, Ltd.

have them submitted to the most searching critical scrutiny."[1] Again, "I do not believe . . . that any really devout student of the Bible desires to tie up honest inquiry on any question of author, origin, date, or mode of composition of the Biblical books, which does not involve clear contradiction of the Bible's own testimony on these subjects. By all means, if any traditional opinion can be shown by valid reasoning on sound data to be in error on such points, let it be corrected."[2]

After saying this, however, orthodoxy faces no small difficulty deciding where legitimate criticism begins and ends. Some exegetes say that Ecclesiastes was written by Solomon; others, that an unknown author spoke in the name of the king's son, in an effort to dignify his narrative. Some say that Isaiah had one author; others, that parts of the book were written by a school of prophets. And so it goes. A measure of Christian charity is needed at this point, though orthodoxy is rarely willing to give it.

An outsider may wonder how orthodoxy can repudiate destructive higher criticism and still claim to be honest before the facts. The mystery is easily cleared up. "Destructive criticism is great and vigorous; it is learned and acute; it may possibly have just cause for its open contempt for the learning, the acuteness, the argumentative force and literary ability of the defenders of the trustworthiness of the Bible. But it does not reckon sufficiently with one fact. It has the Bible itself against it, and the Bible is always with us. When this criticism has been forgotten, the Bible will still be read by men, and will still convey to men its own views of the course of the history by which the true religion has been given by God to man."[3]

THE PROBLEM OF TEXTUAL HARMONY

Not all of orthodoxy's difficulties trace to friction between Scripture, science, and destructive criticism. There are problems inherent in the Biblical text itself. And we do not refer to passages where the Hebrew or Greek is obscure; we refer to passages that are ostensibly clear. For example, Jude says, "It was of these also that Enoch in the seventh generation from Adam prophesied, saying 'Behold, the Lord came with his holy myriads.' " (Jude 14.) Jude credits Enoch, the seventh from Adam, while external evidence credits the apocryphal Book of Enoch. Of course, orthodoxy can always say that Jude knew by inspiration that the seventh

---

[1] Robert S. Candlish, *Reason and Revelation*, p. 43.
[2] James Orr, *The Bible Under Trial*, pp. 9-10. Marshall Brothers, London, 1907.
[3] B. B. Warfield, "Professor Henry Preserved Smith on Inspiration," *The Presbyterian and Reformed Review*, Vol. V (1894), pp. 652-653.

from Adam spoke the words that now appear in the Book of Enoch; but the explanation sounds suspiciously affected.

Orthodoxy has never arranged a perfect harmony of the Gospels. For example, Mark says that a staff *should* be taken, Matthew that a staff should *not* be taken. "He charged them to take nothing for their journey except a staff." (Mark 6:8.) "Take no gold, nor silver, nor copper in your belts, no bag for your journey, nor two tunics, nor sandals, nor a staff." (Matt. 10:9-10.) About all orthodoxy can say is that data or circumstances are kept back which, if known, would resolve the inconsistency. It should not be supposed, however, that the Synoptics are replete with difficulties. General harmony has been established.

Even the claims of Romans and Galatians can be embarrassed by scattered verses in the Bible. For example, Romans says that *faith* is the instrumental cause of justification. Yet, when Ananias advises Paul, he uses language that suggests that *baptism* is the instrumental cause: "And now why do you wait? Rise and be baptized, and wash away your sins, calling on his name" (Acts 22:16). Peter uses similar language: "Baptism, which corresponds to this [Noah's ark], now saves you, not as a removal of dirt from the body but as an appeal to God for a clear conscience" (I Peter 3:21).

It is extremely difficult, if not impossible, to coax all the Biblical data into neat harmony. But this want of precision in no way affects the substance of the Biblical system. The rules of hermeneutics see to that. Theology is drawn from those portions of Scripture which have theology in view; and theology is the norm by which everything else in Scripture is understood. Whenever a passage conflicts with the teaching of Romans and Galatians, either the mind has failed to grasp its meaning, or the passage falls under the concept of progressive revelation.

THE NATURE OF INSPIRATION

Although orthodoxy stoutly defends the doctrine of inspiration, it has never devised an official view of inspiration. At least two schools of thought vie for primacy. The first is known as the Princeton Theology, while the second received its classical expression in Great Britain.

The Princeton Theology was brought to fruition by the two giants of Presbyterianism, Charles Hodge and B. B. Warfield. Their labor is possibly the finest theological and apologetical thrust in the history of American orthodoxy. Few men have equaled—certainly none has surpassed—the acuteness of these scholars.

The Princeton Theology contends that inspiration communicates truth on divine authority. The Scriptural expression "it is written" means "God says it." And whatever God says, is true because he says it. *"Inspiration is that extraordinary, supernatural influence (or, passively, the result of it) exerted by the Holy Ghost on the writers of our Sacred Books, by which their words were rendered also the words of God, and, therefore, perfectly infallible."*[4]

The texts that teach plenary inspiration are legion. Their force, says Warfield, cannot be dodged. "The effort to explain away the Bible's witness to its plenary inspiration reminds one of a man standing safely in his laboratory and elaborately expounding . . . how every stone in an avalanche has a defined pathway and may easily be dodged by one of some presence of mind. We may fancy such an elaborate trifler's triumph as he would analyze the avalanche into its constituent stones, and demonstrate of stone after stone that its pathway is definite, limited, and may easily be avoided. But avalanches, unfortunately, do not come upon us, stone by stone, one at a time, courteously leaving us opportunity to withdraw from the pathway of each in turn: but all at once, in a roaring mass of destruction. Just so we may explain away a text or two which teach plenary inspiration . . . but these texts of ours, again, unfortunately, do not come upon us in this artificial isolation; neither are they few in number. There are scores, hundreds, of them: and they come bursting upon us in one solid mass."[5]

The second school of thought was headed by the gifted English polemicist, James Orr. The communication of *life*, not knowledge, is the goal of inspiration. "In the last resort, the proof of the inspiration of the Bible . . . is to be found in the life-giving effects which that message has produced, wherever its word of truth has gone. This is the truth in the argument for inspiration based on the witness of the Holy Spirit. The Bible has the qualities claimed for it as an inspired book. . . . It leads to God and to Christ; it gives light on the deepest problems of life, death, and eternity; it discovers the way of deliverance from sin; it makes men new creatures; it furnishes the man of God completely for every good work."[6] Orr is an outspoken critic of the Princeton Theology. "The older method was to prove first the inspiration . . . then through that establish the revelation. This view still finds an echo in the note sometimes heard—'If the inspiration of the Bible (commonly some *theory* of inspiration) be given up, what have we left to hold by?' It is urged, e.g., that unless we can demonstrate what is called the 'inerrancy' of the Biblical record, down

---

[4] Warfield, *The Inspiration and Authority of the Bible*, p. 420. [Reprinted by permission of Wm. B. Eerdmans Publishing Company.]

[5] *Ibid.*, pp. 119-120.

[6] Orr, *Revelation and Inspiration*, pp. 217-218. [Reprinted by permission of Wm. B. Eerdmans Publishing Company.]

even to its minutest details, the whole edifice of belief in revealed religion falls to the ground. This, on the face of it, is a most suicidal position for any defender of revelation to take up. It is certainly a much easier matter to prove the reality of a divine revelation in the history of Israel, or in Christ, than it is to prove the inerrant inspiration of every part of the record through which that revelation has come to us."[7]

Two things can be said about this cleavage in orthodoxy: *first*, each school of thought tries to be honest with what Scripture teaches; *secondly*, each school builds its case on what it believes is the chief emphasis in Scripture. Apparently some passages connect inspiration with truth on divine authority, while others connect it with power to communicate life in Christ. The Princeton Theology draws on the first body of verses: "If we are to occupy the attitude toward Scripture which Christ occupied, the simple 'It is written!' must have the same authority to us in matters of doctrinal truth, of practical duty, of historical fact and of verbal form that it had to him; and to us as truly as to him, the Scriptures must be incapable of being broken.[8] The English school draws on the verses that link inspiration with power to communicate life in Christ: "Inspiration, Paul says, confers on Scripture the properties of being 'profitable for teaching, for reproof, for correction, for instruction which is in righteousness'—of being able 'to make wise unto salvation through faith which is in Christ Jesus.' Of similar nature are the qualities ascribed in the psalms to the law of God—'restoring the soul,' 'making wise the simple,' 'rejoicing the heart,' 'enlightening the eyes,' etc."[9]

The cleavage in orthodoxy is partly a reflection of the Biblical text itself. The passages on inspiration are apparently too rich and variegated to be comprehended under the limitations of any single theory.

It should be observed, however, that both schools of orthodoxy agree that God made a covenant with Abraham, and that Jesus Christ is the blessing of this covenant. Orthodoxy does not consider inspiration an end in itself. Whether *truth* or *power* is stressed, the Bible illuminates our pathway to Jesus Christ.

. . . . .

CONCLUSION

Three terminal observations must be made. *First*, classical orthodoxy rests its doctrine of inspiration on the testimony of Christ and the apostles. A fair and honest effort is then made to harmonize this testimony with the

---

[7] *Ibid.*, pp. 197-198.

[8] B. B. Warfield, "Reviews of Recent Theological Literature," *The Presbyterian and Reformed Review*, Vol. IV (1893), p. 499.

[9] Orr, *Revelation and Inspiration*, p. 200.

inductive difficulties in the text. *But in no case is the doctrine of inspiration accommodated to the difficulties.* If orthodoxy were to tolerate such accommodation, it would forfeit the principle by which *any* Christian doctrine is established. This would banish theology to the wastelands of subjectivity.

Secondly, even if it could be shown that the Chronicles are not entirely compatible with other Old Testament histories, the doctrine of Biblical inerrancy would *not* be demolished. Orthodoxy would simply shift its conception of the thing signified. Just as the inspired author of Job gives an infallible account of what Eliphaz said, so the inspired author of Chronicles gives an infallible account of what was said in the public registers and genealogical lists. At first blush this may seem like a very desperate expedient, but it actually implies no more than a strained use of procedures already at work in orthodoxy. If Hodge and Warfield had honored this as a possibility, they might have avoided their lofty disregard for the inductive difficulties. And if Orr had done likewise, he might have avoided his perilous admission of historical errors in Scripture.

Orthodoxy could profitably spend more time examining the relation between *assertion* and the *thing signified.* For example, on what standard was Semitic history written? Does poetry communicate feeling or truth? Is recorded religious experience normative for believers in another economy? Orthodoxy works itself into excessive difficulties by artlessly defining the relation between assertion and the thing signified. Crass literalism is hardly a worthy answer to irresponsible allegorizing.

Thirdly, orthodoxy may never officially decide whether the Holy Spirit corrected the documents from which the Chronicler drew his information. But this irresolution does not affect the theology of the church, for Paul received his theology directly from Jesus Christ (Gal. 1:11-12). He did *not* draw on existing documents. And theology is the norm by which a Christian understands everything else in Scripture—including the Chronicles of Israel which drew on sources which may or may not have been corrected by the Holy Spirit. Orthodoxy's intramural debate on inspiration in no way disturbs the truth of the gospel, and to think that it does is cultic.

SUGGESTED BOOKS

Dodd, Charles H., *The Bible Today.* Cambridge: Cambridge University Press, 1946. Succinct, nontechnical lectures explaining recent historical criticism and theological interpretation of the Bible.

Fosdick, Harry E., *The Modern Use of the Bible.* New York: The Macmillan Company, 1924. A book often regarded as the epitome of the approach to the Bible characteristic of Protestant Liberalism.

Goodspeed, Edgar J., *How Came the Bible?* New York and Nashville: Abingdon Press, 1940. A historical study of the formation of the Bible and of its translations.

Harris, R. Laird, *Inspiration and Canonicity of the Bible.* Grand Rapids: Zondervan Publishing House, 1957. A defense of verbal inspiration and the authoritative authenticity of the Biblical books.

Keller, Werner, *The Bible as History*, trans. William Neil. New York: William Morrow and Company, 1956. A documentation of the historical accuracy of the Bible, written by a German journalist in the scientific field.

Reid, J. K. S., *The Authority of Scripture.* New York: Harper & Row, Publishers, 1957. A survey of past and present views on the question of Biblical authority.

Warfield, Benjamin B., *The Inspiration and Authority of the Bible.* Grand Rapids: Wm. B. Eerdmans Publishing Co., 1953. A re-issue of a conservative landmark, with a new introduction by Cornelius Van Til.

Wood, James D., *The Interpretation of the Bible.* London: Gerald Duckworth and Co., Ltd., 1958. A history of how the Bible has been interpreted from ancient times to the present.

XIII · INTERPRETING CHRIST

In this chapter we shall consider the most distinctive affirmation of Christianity, the belief in Christ. We shall follow a traditional distinction between the person of Christ and the work of Christ. Since the person of Christ involves a claim about both humanity and divinity, we have a threefold outline before us: first, considerations respecting the humanity of Christ; second, considerations regarding his divinity; and third, considerations pertaining to his significance, i.e., his accomplishment.

JESUS AS HUMAN

Martin Buber has said that Jews, who look upon Jesus as a brother, are able to understand him much better than Christians, who submit to him as Lord and Saviour.[1] Whether this is true or not is, of course, a point at issue between Judaism and Christianity. But regardless of that difference, the statement points up a truth which Christians themselves have always meant to affirm but have sometimes neglected, so that they are reminded of it by others. The truth is that there can be no satisfactory understanding of Jesus unless he is seen as a fully human being, a fellow sufferer, a brother to us all. Though the Christian claim has not confined itself to assertions about his humanity, the intention has always been to acknowledge his complete humanity, with the limitations, temptations, and uncertainties that that entails. He is a human brother.

The assertion that Jesus is fully human is a theological statement. But it has psychological significance as well, and this is perhaps what Buber is teaching us by his claim. That is, unless Jesus has a human appeal to people, unless he speaks to them as one person to another, unless he attracts by his human suffering and sacrifice, he may not attract at all. Certainly for people not reared in a Christian culture direct pronouncements about Christ's deity, about his supernatural mission, about his relation to Old Testament expectations, and so forth, tend to be looked upon as provincial Christian doctrines unless they can be seen as related somehow to the human appeal which Jesus has. The testimony is great that the first attraction is to Jesus as a model of manhood and to how he shows us what we ought to be, especially as this appeal may be reflected in the contacts with the personal lives of his followers. And this human appeal should not be surprising, for it has been a Christian teaching that without the revelation of God in a human person the understanding of God would be veiled in obscurity and speculation.

But we need not go outside Christian culture for examples. The writer recalls hearing a student declare that, despite an upbringing in one of the major churches in Christianity, no attraction to Jesus was felt until on one occasion in college a guest lecturer spoke about Jesus as showing the ideal of human love that we ought to manifest toward others. Before this the student had only been aware that people seemed to have a warm spot in their hearts for Jesus because of some remote feat he had performed. But Jesus became significant only when there was a human appeal established.

Of course we cannot set up any absolute psychological priority here, for there is plenty of evidence—from Skid Row conversions and the like—to show that what people respond to first is not Jesus as a human brother but Christ as a savior from their degradation. So the truth in Buber's statement must be considered in the light of other sorts of Christian experience.

Regardless of the psychological priority of Jesus' humanity or of his divinity, however, the theological statement remains that the church affirms the complete humanity of Jesus. This may seem like a mere unilluminating tautology to repeat in today's world, as if any person who was born into the human race, who was raised in a family, who grew from boyhood to manhood, and so on, as Jesus is described in the Gospels, could be really no human being at all. But there was a movement afoot in the early Christian centuries to deny Jesus' humanity, a movement that had to be condemned by the church, and this tendency is a perennial danger to which Christianity is subject. The ancient heresy, known as Docetism, looked upon Jesus as a God appearing or masquerading in human guise. Such a view did not at all correspond to the testimony of Jesus' disciples and the New Testament writers. Hence, paradoxical as it may sound to the modern mind, which has difficulty not with Jesus' humanity but with the notion that he was the incarnation of God, the earliest apologetic task of Christian writers was to preserve Jesus' full humanity in the official teaching of the church.

The perennial danger is that Christians may not do justice to Jesus in his humanity, even though they may intend to do so. There has been a frequent tendency, for example, to speak of Jesus as embodying a generalized or idealized humanity, an impersonal kind of human nature, rather than a real, individual, personal consciousness like other men's. Thus we can find Jesus' humanity described as "a human nature impersonal in the sense that it had no personality separate from the divine nature. . . ."[2] With such a formulation it is difficult to see how one could have a human nature at all if it is impersonal. It is also difficult to understand how one could really be human if he does not have a personality of his own that is separate in some sense, though not necessarily in all senses, from God's consciousness. Such formulations do preserve, however, an element which distinguishes the Christian from the secular view of Jesus' humanity. This element is the belief that Jesus was sinless, i.e., that though he was fully human his capacity for free choice was always in accord with, in fact one with, the divine will. This belief is perhaps one reason why the tendency arose to speak of an impersonal human nature or of a humanity with no separate personality. But the modern tendency is to consider this oneness as integral with a fully individual consciousness, a personal subject like that of other men.

There are other types of view which hold that Jesus' humanity exhausts the meaning that he has for modern man. This is of course the secular view of Jesus, which sees him at best as a helpful example of certain moral virtues and at worst as an impractical rabblerouser. It is also the view to be found in sympathetic non-Christian religions, which look upon Jesus as a great human teacher or sometimes a religious prophet in the tradition of divinely chosen men who from time to time awaken man to an awareness of God. But this humanistic view is also held by some who describe themselves as Christians. They believe it is a proper conception of Christianity to think of Jesus entirely in human terms—as a unique man, a divinely chosen man, possibly even a perfect man, but completely a man none the less.

This humanistic interpretation by some who describe themselves as Christians raises the question of whether such a conception is to be considered Christian or not, inasmuch as historical Christianity has affirmed the twofold nature of Christ. The answer to this question is partly linguistic and partly theoretical. If the term Christian is taken in the doctrinal sense as referring to the distinctive, traditional beliefs of the church, the humanistic view cannot be considered Christian. If, on the other hand, the term Christian is taken in the cultural sense as referring to anything that has its roots in Christian civilization and values, then this conception and the groups which hold it would be Christian. Unitarians, for instance, who take their main inspiration from the tradition initiated by the life and teachings of Jesus, are Christian in the cultural sense and not in the doctrinal sense. Sometimes the term Christendom is used for the cultural meaning and Christianity for the doctrinal emphasis. Organized bodies of churches such as the National Council of Churches rightly base themselves on a doctrinal definition of Christianity rather than an amorphous cultural definition, and therefore groups which deny the divinity of Christ are rightly excluded.

There is a third meaning of Christian which is relevant here. In this sense it designates what is ultimately true about Christ. Accordingly, that view is Christian which is closest to the real truth about Christ. Now in regard to this third meaning, the humanistic interpreters claim that theirs is the most accurate interpretation of Jesus and that therefore they are more Christian than traditional Christianity, which is charged with having an over-belief. But historical Christianity believes that Jesus really was a divine-human person, so that those who deny this belief are missing the essence of Christianity and are therefore Christian not in the ultimate meaning of the term but only in a cultural sense. Thus to interpret Christianity fully we must move on to consider the belief in Jesus' divinity—some of the reasons for it, and what in general it means.

"GOD WAS IN CHRIST"

Though statements differ about what it means to speak of Jesus' divinity, the common experience of Christians has been such that it requires them to affirm this tenet as well as that concerning his humanity. Christians have found in Jesus more than a human brother; they have found also the Christ of faith. St. Paul says that "even though we once regarded Christ from a human point of view, we regard him thus no longer."[3] This statement has a specific historical reference, indicating the difference between the attitude natural to the living companions of Jesus who knew him in the flesh and the attitude of later followers who knew him only as a spiritual presence in their lives. But the statement also symbolizes the experience of Christians generally who, having encountered spiritually the Jesus of history, find assertions of mere humanity inadequate and so "regard him thus no longer." Instead they find in Jesus something which they can only express by reference to the presence of God in that unique life.

But what is it in the encounter with the historical Jesus that has led to the belief that "God was in Christ"? What, in a word, are the reasons why Christians affirm this doctrine? Three reasons appear to be most prominent.

The first of these reasons is an appeal to certain statements of Jesus himself and to other statements in the New Testament. This is the appeal to authority, and many Christians prefer this method of vindication to any other. There are occasions in the Gospels in which Jesus claims divine sonship for himself, speaks of his oneness with the Father, and even acknowledges that he is the Christ who was expected. Such statements are taken as self-authenticating, disclosing directly the divine nature of the one who spoke them. Such assertions cannot be gainsaid without making Jesus into an impostor or a hypocrite.

Edward J. Carnell defends the method of authority by referring to what he calls the principle of a decent society.[4] This principle asserts that in any society based on ordinary human morality people accept a man's word unless there is sufficient reason not to do so. Now in the case of Jesus, not only is there no sufficient reason to deny his word, but on the contrary there is every reason to believe that he was upright and truthful, in fact the model of the highest human virtue. We can do no less, therefore, than apply to him the principle that we apply generally in society. And if he testifies to his divine sonship, to his oneness with the Father, as he does, then we are bound to accept his word and support his claim.

In other New Testament writings there are statements about Jesus' divinity also, and with the method of authority these are taken as further proof of the truth Jesus spoke. Thus the emphasis is placed squarely on authoritative Biblical assertions.

The second reason looks to the experience of the early church as the confirmatory clue concerning Jesus' divinity. This is the appeal to historical inference, and many Christians believe that this is historically and logically a more adequate method of vindication than the appeal to authoritative statements, in view of the difficulties which the latter approach poses. This second reason consists in saying that the belief in Jesus' divinity was and is an inescapable inference from the experience which the early Christians underwent. From the career of a humble carpenter in Galilee there arose a spiritual power which turned the ancient world upside down. Those who shared in the original experience of him and in the movement that followed attributed their inner transformation not to their own efforts but directly to the presence of Jesus in their lives. Though the disciples were disillusioned at the time of Jesus' death, they and the other early Christians soon began, through the impact of the resurrection appearances and other experiences of Christ, to see Jesus as the incarnation of God and to refer to him by a variety of terms indicating his divine relationship. Only thus could they interpet what had happened to them personally and explain the spiritual power that had come into the stream of human life. No exclusively human figure could have changed them in that way, could have regenerated their lives in that way, could have altered the cultural pattern in that way. No other inference than Jesus' divinity was adequate.[5]

We today are bound to follow that inference unless we think their experience was an illusion. If we share at all in the historical experience stemming from that early Christian tradition and continuing since, if we believe that the power operative in that experience is the ultimate power in the universe, then we must accept the interpretation which alone gave it meaning for them.

The third reason for the belief is the experience of regeneration and direction which contact with Christ effects in people's own lives. This is the appeal to personal experience, and for many Christians it is in the end the only method of vindication that can be decisive. It is because of the impact of Jesus in their own lives and thoughts that they conclude God himself has been made known to them and that a human example alone could not effect such a transformation or call forth such worship. This reason is expressed in the following quotation:

> Because in and through Jesus, God has been brought near; because in him men have felt themselves compelled to worship; because he has been the bringer of a kind and quality of "salvation" which has about it the note of ultimacy, the Church has felt itself obliged to say that no judgment about him is adequate which does not relate him directly and immediately with the ground of being, God himself.[6]

Thus this approach places the emphasis on inward experience rather than external considerations.

These three reasons need not be thought of as mutually exclusive; they may be regarded as complementary. The appeal to authority carries little weight by itself if there is no personal experience to suggest the validity of the authority. The same may be said for the appeal to historical inference. And the fact of regeneration would not by itself imply Jesus' divinity if this were contravened by historic experience or by the religious authority one accepts. Christians have therefore tried to give due place to each of the reasons. So the question is not one of exclusion but of priority, and about that there is some difference.

In addition to the apologetic problem of presenting the reasons for the belief, there is the theological problem of clarifying what it means to say that Jesus exemplified both an individual manhood and the true being of God. Sometimes there is a sentiment to remain with the practical religious conviction that Jesus was both human and divine and to minimize the theological task of explication, which is seen as a superfluous addition not contributory to Christian experience. But the task is a natural one; it is simply the mind of the church at work thinking through what it believes. It is also a necessary one, for a belief will hardly commend itself if it remains in irrationality, as it is likely to do if it is not continuously examined. Faith must seek understanding.

The best starting-point for the interpretation of the doctrine of Christ —at least one which represents a point of common agreement among Christians—is perhaps the statement of Paul that "God was in Christ, reconciling the world to himself."[7] The statement has two thoughts, indicating both the person and the work of Christ. The question here is what is meant by saying that God was in Christ.

In the early centuries of the church there was a great deal of exploration, interpretation, and speculation carried on in the attempt to state in what respects Jesus expressed humanity and in what ways he manifested divinity. The culmination of this work came in 451 when the Council of Chalcedon pronounced a formulation of the doctrine that became official in the church. It held that Christ was a unique union of two distinct metaphysical natures, a human nature and a divine nature, so that he was fully human in every respect and also completely divine in every respect. This formulation has been called the two nature theory. Actually it is not so much a theory in the modern sense of the word as an attempt through doctrinal statement to preserve without loss the twofold emphasis in Christian experience in relation to Jesus. The formulation was a convictional expression. There was no attempt to probe the rational subtleties involved in the doctrine. The union of the human and the divine was frankly recognized as a mystery which human reason cannot penetrate. Previous speculations which had tried to separate and localize the human capacities and the divine capacities of Jesus had led to gross compromises of one or both of the aspects in the Christian conviction. The Chalcedonian formula sought to restore and maintain both elements of the conviction in their totality.

It is in the light of this experience of the church that the two nature formulation must be understood. It was a repudiation of the many weird formulas that misread the original Christian experience. When isolated from this experience and examined by itself, the formulation certainly presents rational difficulties.[8] To mention but one example, how could it be that, in regard to the same epistemological objects, Jesus could be both omniscient with respect to his divinity and yet limited in knowledge with respect to his humanity? Such difficulties are not hard to multiply.

Because of these difficulties many theologians are trying to restate the doctrine of Christ in terms more meaningful to the modern mind. Believing that they are no more required to compromise their rationality than their Christology, they are seeking to express the doctrine in ways that will avoid the seeming contradictions latent in the earlier formulation. More particularly, they are pointing out that the ancient formulation of this doctrine, as well as of other doctrines such as the trinity, was couched in language borrowed from Greek metaphysical thought—language containing such words as substance, nature, hypostasis, and logos. Such terms are no longer as communicative in modern thought. Therefore these theologians believe that, without sacrificing the twofold experience of Jesus' humanity and divinity, the doctrine must be expressed in more communicative language.

If there is one common element in these more recent formulations, it is perhaps to be found in the concept of revelation. "God was in Christ" is interpreted to mean that Jesus, through his birth, life, death, and resurrection, is a unique disclosure to man of what deity is. The danger here is to suggest by this terminology that Jesus was a mere instrument, a vehicle, through whom God worked. But such is not the intention. The intention is rather to affirm that what was operative in Jesus' perfect life was God himself, and that only if there was an identity involved could Jesus be a unique revelation of deity. Thus the emphasis is placed not on a literal, formal fusion of two otherwise incompatible metaphysical natures in a single substance, but upon the oneness of Jesus' life, will, and purpose with God. The belief in a unique God-man unity is preserved, but in terms of a living, dynamic, perfect self-identification instead of a synthesis of different substances.

In this unique manifestation of God in Christ the personal character of God is disclosed. For example, while the expression of love does not exhaust what it means to say that God was in Christ, Christians believe that God's love was shown in Jesus and that such love is the ultimate character of God. The love which Jesus manifested is the very love of God which entered the world for man's regeneration and reconciliation. Other personal qualities, such as grace, forgiveness, and suffering, are also stressed, but these qualities are but partial descriptions of the total Christ-event. In the end the claim is simply that the one true personal God revealed himself, his own person, in this one perfect human life. Christ is thus the supreme revelatory event of history.

"RECONCILING THE WORLD TO HIMSELF"

The second part of Paul's statement refers to what God has accomplished in Christ. This accomplishment has two principal aspects—the reconciliation which God himself effected through Jesus, especially in his death on the cross, and the renewal of life that can occur in man as a result of this action. These are sometimes called the objective and the subjective aspects.

The traditional theological term for God's reconciliation of man to himself through the life and death of Christ is atonement. If this term is taken to imply a particular theory about God's action in Christ, namely, the substitutionary theory, as it has been called, then the term is misleading, for there is clearly a difference between the fact of God's action and particular theories of how it is to be interpreted. Actually a more meaningful term to modern ears might be Paul's own term, reconciliation. Sometimes for communication the word atonement has been divided by hyphens and made to read at-one-ment. Atonement then means that God restores a union, an at-one-ment, between man and God. Both Catholic and Protestant clergymen have been heard to employ this usage, so evidently it is not a localized cliché but an expression having genuine communicational use.

Regardless of the terminology, the central belief is that God through Christ has effected a reconciliation of man to himself, has overcome the estrangement between man and himself and made it possible for man to be brought into fellowship with himself. How this is done has been a matter for theological interpretation. It has been estimated that there are more than a dozen theories about this work of Christ. It has become common in many Protestant discussions to distinguish three principal theories

INTERPRETING CHRIST

that developed historically and to suggest that each has a lasting truth as
well as an inadequacy when taken by itself. These theories will be briefly
mentioned.[9]

The first theory has been called the ransom theory, or sometimes the
classical theory. In its crudest form it spoke of Jesus being offered as a
ransom, or sometimes as a bait, to the devil for the release of man who
was in his grip. But the devil, upon accepting the offer, was unable to
hold Christ in his grasp, as demonstrated by the resurrection, and so was
permanently defeated, man being freed in the process. This notion appears
to present a case of celestial bargaining, even chicanery, and has not persisted in its cruder form. Many theologians, however, see a lasting truth
in its intent, namely, that through Christ God has overcome the power of
evil. Evil is real, but it is not the ultimate power in the universe; that
power is sacrificial love, as displayed in Jesus' life and supremely in his
death. Evil is ultimately subject to the power of love. Not that evil has
been henceforth eliminated, but its power has been broken and its con-
quest assured.

The second theory is called the substitutionary theory. It was introduced by St. Anselm and developed further by the Protestant reformers.
It holds that man, having fallen from a state of grace through his own
sinfulness, needs to mollify God's judgment of wrath upon him before
he can be reconciled. But man himself, now in a state of sin, cannot do
this; therefore, God, through his infinite mercy, sends his own son into
the world as a mediator to accomplish this work. Christ is thus a substitute for man. His death on the cross satisfies God's justice, but since God
himself undertook the mediation, his love is also shown in a supreme sacrifice.

For many this theory appears to be too legalistic and penal in character,
presenting God as a judge exacting retribution from an innocent victim
in a cosmic trial, while individual men are not involved in the process except to give subsequent assent to the belief that it took place. To think of
God as first of all needing to appease himself instead of forgiving directly,
and then as undertaking to appease himself instead of drawing men directly into fellowship, seems to present a conception of God inferior to
that known in Christ. Nevertheless, the same critics may see in the theory
the truth that God voluntarily shares the guilt of man, takes the initiative
in forgiving man, suffers and sacrifices for the end of reconciliation.

The third theory, introduced by Abelard and proposed in various
forms since then, has been called the moral influence theory. It holds that
God manifested in Jesus a supreme example of humble sacrifice and forgiving love. Man is attracted back to God through the powerful influence
of this example, something which could not take place without a pure
and perfect model to follow. The objection to this type of theory has
been that it de-emphasizes the essential activity of God in the process of

reconciliation in favor of the human magnetism of Jesus and the natural ability of man to follow along. However, the theory does involve individual men in the process more directly than the other two theories do, and since it is they, after all, who are being reconciled to God, the theory has received considerable support.

In the end many Protestants prefer a selective, pluralistic interpretation rather than a single, exclusive theory. George Forell summarizes this position as follows:

> In summary, it should be said that for the Protestant faith there are many different elements in Christ's atoning work on the Cross which are all valid and complementary to each other. The Cross is *sacrifice*, in that it is God's sacrifice for the sake of man. The Cross is *punishment*, in that it reveals the seriousness of the offense against the divine law. It contains elements of *satisfaction*. In Paul's words: *Christ redeemed us from the curse of the law, having become a curse for us.* (*Galatians 3:13*) But the Cross is also *example*. Jesus said to His disciples, *If any man would come after me, let him deny himself and take up his cross and follow me.* (*Matthew 16:24*) And finally the Cross is *victory*. It is the sign of triumph over the forces that separate man from God. It demonstrates that suffering and death can, through the grace of God, become meaningful and lead to peace and joy and life.[10]

The other aspect of the accomplishment of Christ is the regeneration that can occur in man. The Christian belief is that acceptance of and participation in the grace and love manifested in Christ can lead to redemption or renewal of life. We shall distinguish a psychological, a moral, and a spiritual dimension of this renewal.

First, immersion in the spiritual power of Christ has a bearing, Christians believe, on the emotions and attitudes, the motives and adjustments, which today we label psychological. Living in his spirit can lead to integration of personality, to mental health, to the capacity to love and to work, and so forth. Superficial interpretations regard this as the only function of Christ, so that one is almost left with the impression that God sent Christ into the world in order to confirm modern views of human need and to give timely tips on happy living. But such distortions notwithstanding, many serious psychologists, even non-Christian ones, have found the life and spirit of Christ to be the qualitative example of what man needs for genuine psychological health.

Psychological renewal may be chronologically prior, but logically speaking it is for Christians a by-product of other depths of renewal. One of these is moral regeneration. Christ may transform man's perspective in life, provide him with a supreme standard for conduct, and bring him the capacity for love, humility, forgiveness, patience, fortitude, and justice. Not that Christians are necessarily better than other people in their behavior, for they may not be any more filled with the spirit of Christ than are many non-Christians. Rather the belief is that Christians know the standard and source of all moral regeneration, and they attribute whatever level of true morality they have reached to that source and not to themselves.

Byond the psychological and the moral is the dimension of the spiritual, which concerns the final state of the self. Christians believe that Christ has the power of carrying man beyond psychological adjustment and ethical goodness to ultimate fulfillment itself. This fulfillment is the eternal life, the salvation, which the New Testament teaches. It is the final union of man with God—not the union of impersonal absorption but the dynamic identification of distinct persons with the being of God. Christians believe that immersion in the spirit of Christ makes this union possible. Here is the state in which man's alienation is overcome, his guilt forgiven, his longings fulfilled, his old self made new. There is seldom the expectation or the claim that such renewal as this will occur under present temporal conditions; but there is the belief that something of the grace which it portends can be experienced even now.

THE SHOCKING ALTERNATIVE AND THE PERFECT PENITENT

C. S. LEWIS

Clive S. Lewis (1898–) is a man who uniquely combines work as a scholar and professor, creative ventures in fiction, and popular writing on religious themes. He studied and taught at Oxford and has been since 1954 a professor of medieval and Renaissance English at Cambridge. His religious books include The Problem of Pain *(1940),* The Screwtape Letters *(1942), and* Miracles *(1947).* Surprised by Joy *(1955) is an autobiographical sketch. In this selection he sharpens the distinction between orthodox and liberal conceptions of Christ and defends the former.*

THE SHOCKING ALTERNATIVE

Christians, then, believe that an evil power has made himself for the present the Prince of this World. And, of course, that raises problems. Is this state of affairs in accordance with God's will or not? If it is, He is

From *Mere Christianity* by C. S. Lewis, pp. 37-46. Copyright 1943, 1945, 1952 by The Macmillan Company, and used with their permission and also with the permission of Geoffrey Bles Ltd.

a strange God, you will say: and if it is not, how can anything happen contrary to the will of a being with absolute power?

But anyone who has been in authority knows how a thing can be in accordance with your will in one way and not in another. It may be quite sensible for a mother to say to the children, "I'm not going to go and make you tidy the schoolroom every night. You've got to learn to keep it tidy on your own." Then she goes up one night and finds the Teddy bear and the ink and the French Grammar all lying in the grate. That is against her will. She would prefer the children to be tidy. But on the other hand, it is her will which has left the children free to be untidy. The same thing arises in any regiment, or trade union, or school. You make a thing voluntary and then half the people do not do it. That is not what you willed, but your will has made it possible.

It is probably the same in the universe. God created things which had free will. That means creatures which can go either wrong or right. Some people think they can imagine a creature which was free but had no possibility of going wrong; I cannot. If a thing is free to be good it is also free to be bad. And free will is what has made evil possible. Why, then, did God give them free will? Because free will, though it makes evil possible, is also the only thing that makes possible any love or goodness or joy worth having. A world of automata—of creatures that worked like machines—would hardly be worth creating. The happiness which God designs for His higher creatures is the happiness of being freely, voluntarily united to Him and to each other in an ecstasy of love and delight compared with which the most rapturous love between a man and a woman on this earth is mere milk and water. And for that they must be free.

Of course God knew what would happen if they used their freedom the wrong way: apparently He thought it worth the risk. Perhaps we feel inclined to disagree with Him. But there is a difficulty about disagreeing with God. He is the source from which all your reasoning power comes: you could not be right and He wrong any more than a stream can rise higher than its own source. When you are arguing against Him you are arguing against the very power that makes you able to argue at all: it is like cutting off the branch you are sitting on. If God thinks this state of war in the universe a price worth paying for free will—that is, for making a live world in which creatures can do real good or harm and something of real importance can happen, instead of a toy world which only moves when He pulls the strings—then we may take it it is worth paying.

When we have understood about free will, we shall see how silly it is to ask, as somebody once asked me: "Why did God make a creature of such rotten stuff that it went wrong?" The better stuff a creature is made of—the cleverer and stronger and freer it is—then the better it will be if it goes right, but also the worse it will be if it goes wrong. A cow cannot be very good or very bad; a dog can be both better and worse; a child better and worse still; an ordinary man, still more so; a man of genius, still more so; a superhuman spirit best—or worst—of all.

How did the Dark Power go wrong? Here, no doubt, we ask a question to which human beings cannot give an answer with any certainty. A reasonable (and traditional) guess, based on our own experiences of going wrong, can, however, be offered. The moment you have a self at all, there is a possibility of putting yourself first—wanting to be the centre—wanting to be God, in fact. That was the sin of Satan: and that was the sin he taught the human race. Some people think the fall of man had something to do with sex, but that is a mistake. (The story in the Book of Genesis rather suggests that some corruption in our sexual nature followed the fall and was its result, not its cause.) What Satan put into the heads of our remote ancestors was the idea that they could "be like gods" —could set up on their own as if they had created themselves—be their own masters—invent some sort of happiness for themselves outside God, apart from God. And out of that hopeless attempt has come nearly all that we call human history—money, poverty, ambition, war, prostitution, classes, empires, slavery—the long terrible story of man trying to find something other than God which will make him happy.

The reason why it can never succeed is this. God made us: invented us as a man invents an engine. A car is made to run on gasoline, and it would not run properly on anything else. Now God designed the human machine to run on Himself. He Himself is the fuel our spirits were designed to burn, or the food our spirits were designed to feed on. There is no other. That is why it is just no good asking God to make us happy in our own way without bothering about religion. God cannot give us a happiness and peace apart from Himself, because it is not there. There is no such thing.

That is the key to history. Terrific energy is expended—civilisations are built up—excellent institutions devised; but each time something goes wrong. Some fatal flaw always brings the selfish and cruel people to the top and it all slides back into misery and ruin. In fact, the machine conks. It seems to start up all right and runs a few yards, and then it breaks down. They are trying to run it on the wrong juice. That is what Satan has done to us humans.

And what did God do? First of all He left us conscience, the sense of right and wrong: and all through history there have been people trying (some of them very hard) to obey it. None of them ever quite succeeded. Secondly, He sent the human race what I call good dreams: I mean those queer stories scattered all through the heathen religions about a god who dies and comes to life again and, by his death, has somehow given new life to men. Thirdly, He selected one particular people and spent several centuries hammering into their heads the sort of God He was—that there was only one of Him and that He cared about right conduct. Those people were the Jews, and the Old Testament gives an account of the hammering process.

Then comes the real shock. Among these Jews there suddenly turns up a man who goes about talking as if He was God. He claims to forgive sins. He says He has always existed. He says He is coming to judge the world at the end of time. Now let us get this clear. Among Pantheists, like the Indians, anyone might say that he was a part of God, or one with God: there would be nothing very odd about it. But this man, since He was a Jew, could not mean that kind of God. God, in their language, meant the Being outside the world Who had made it and was infinitely different from anything else. And when you have grasped that, you will see that what this man said was, quite simply, the most shocking thing that has ever been uttered by human lips.

One part of the claim tends to slip past us unnoticed because we have heard it so often that we no longer see what it amounts to. I mean the claim to forgive sins: any sins. Now unless the speaker is God, this is really so preposterous as to be comic. We can all understand how a man forgives offences against himself. You tread on my toe and I forgive you, you steal my money and I forgive you. But what should we make of a man, himself unrobbed and untrodden on, who announced that he forgave you for treading on other men's toes and stealing other men's money? Asinine fatuity is the kindest description we should give of his conduct. Yet this is what Jesus did. He told people that their sins were forgiven, and never waited to consult all the other people whom their sins had undoubtedly injured. He unhesitatingly behaved as if He was the party chiefly concerned, the person chiefly offended in all offences. This makes sense only if He really was the God whose laws are broken and whose love is wounded in every sin. In the mouth of any speaker who is not God, these words would imply what I can only regard as a silliness and conceit unrivalled by any other character in history.

Yet (and this is the strange, significant thing) even His enemies, when they read the Gospels, do not usually get the impression of silliness and conceit. Still less do unprejudiced readers. Christ says that He is "humble and meek" and we believe Him; not noticing that, if He were merely a man, humility and meekness are the very last characteristics we could attribute to some of His sayings.

I am trying here to prevent anyone saying the really foolish thing that people often say about Him: "I'm ready to accept Jesus as a great moral teacher, but I don't accept His claim to be God." That is the one thing we must not say. A man who was merely a man and said the sort of things

Jesus said would not be a great moral teacher. He would either be a lunatic—on a level with the man who says he is a poached egg—or else he would be the Devil of Hell. You must make your choice. Either this man was, and is, the Son of God: or else a madman or something worse. You can shut Him up for a fool, you can spit at Him and kill Him as a demon; or you can fall at His feet and call Him Lord and God. But let us not come with any patronising nonsense about His being a great human teacher. He has not left that open to us. He did not intend to.

THE PERFECT PENITENT

We are faced, then, with a frightening alternative. This man we are talking about either was (and is) just what He said or else a lunatic, or something worse. Now it seems to me obvious that He was neither a lunatic nor a fiend: and consequently, however strange or terrifying or unlikely it may seem, I have to accept the view that He was and is God. God has landed on this enemy-occupied world in human form.

And now, what was the purpose of it all? What did He come to do? Well, to teach, of course; but as soon as you look into the New Testament or any other Christian writing you will find they are constantly talking about something different—about His death and His coming to life again. It is obvious that Christians think the chief point of the story lies here. They think the main thing He came to earth to do was to suffer and be killed.

Now before I became a Christian I was under the impression that the first thing Christians had to believe was one particular theory as to what the point of this dying was. According to that theory God wanted to punish men for having deserted and joined the Great Rebel, but Christ volunteered to be punished instead, and so God let us off. Now I admit that even this theory does not seem to me quite so immoral and so silly as it used to; but that is not the point I want to make. What I came to see later on was that neither this theory nor any other is Christianity. The central Christian belief is that Christ's death has somehow put us right with God and given us a fresh start. Theories as to how it did this are another matter. A good many different theories have been held as to how it works; what all Christians are agreed on is that it does work. I will tell you what I think it is like. All sensible people know that if you are tired and hungry a meal will do you good. But the modern theory of nourishment—all about the vitamins and proteins—is a different thing. People ate their dinners and felt better long before the theory of vitamins was ever heard of: and if the theory of vitamins is some day abandoned they will go on eating their dinners just the same. Theories about Christ's death are not Christianity: they are explanations about how it works. Christians would not all agree as to how important these theories are. My own church—the Church of England—does not lay down any one of them as the right one. The Church of Rome goes a bit further. But I think they will all agree that the thing itself is infinitely more important than any explanations that theologians have produced. I think they would probably admit that no explanation will ever be quite adequate to the reality. But as I said in the preface to this book, I am only a layman, and at this point we are getting into deep water. I can only tell you, for what it is worth, how I, personally, look at the matter.

On my view the theories are not themselves the thing you are asked to accept. Many of you no doubt have read Jeans or Eddington. What they do when they want to explain the atom, or something of that sort, is to give you a description out of which you can make a mental picture. But then they warn you that this picture is not what the scientists actually believe. What the scientists believe is a mathematical formula. The pictures are there only to help you to understand the formula. They are not really true in the way the formula is; they do not give you the real thing, but only something more or less like it. They are only meant to help, and if they do not help you can drop them. The thing itself cannot be pictured, it can only be expressed mathematically. We are in the same boat here. We believe that the death of Christ is just that point in history at which something absolutely unimaginable from outside shows through into our own world. And if we cannot picture even the atoms of which our own world is built, of course we are not going to be able to picture this. Indeed, if we found that we could fully understand it, that very fact would show it was not what it professes to be—the inconceivable, the uncreated, the thing from beyond nature, striking down into nature like lightning. You may ask what good will it be to us if we do not understand it. But that is easily answered. A man can eat his dinner without understanding exactly how food nourishes him. A man can accept what Christ has done without knowing how it works: indeed, he certainly would not know how it works until he has accepted it.

We are told that Christ was killed for us, that His death has washed out our sins, and that by dying He disabled death itself. That is the formula. That is Christianity. That is what has to be believed. Any theories we build up as to how Christ's death did all this are, in my view, quite secondary: mere plans or diagrams to be left alone if they do not help us, and, even if they do help us, not to be confused with the thing itself. All the same, some of these theories are worth looking at.

The one most people have heard is the one I mentioned before—the one about our being let off because Christ had volunteered to bear a punishment instead of us. Now on the face of it that is a very silly theory. If

God was prepared to let us off, why on earth did He not do so? And what possible point could there be in punishing an innocent person instead? None at all that I can see, if you are thinking of punishment in the police-court sense. On the other hand, if you think of a debt, there is plenty of point in a person who has some assets paying it on behalf of someone who has not. Or if you take "paying the penalty," not in the sense of being punished, but in the more general sense of "standing the racket" or "footing the bill," then, of course, it is a matter of common experience that, when one person has got himself into a hole, the trouble of getting him out usually falls on a kind friend.

Now what was the sort of "hole" man had got himself into? He had tried to set up on his own, to behave as if he belonged to himself. In other words, fallen man is not simply an imperfect creature who needs improvement: he is a rebel who must lay down his arms. Laying down your arms, surrendering, saying you are sorry, realising that you have been on the wrong track and getting ready to start life over again from the ground floor—that is the only way out of a "hole." This process of surrender—this movement full speed astern—is what Christians call repentance. Now repentance is no fun at all. It is something much harder than merely eating humble pie. It means unlearning all the self-conceit and self-will that we have been training ourselves into for thousands of years. It means killing part of yourself, undergoing a kind of death. In fact, it needs a good man to repent. And here comes the catch. Only a bad person needs to repent: only a good person can repent perfectly. The worse you are the more you need it and the less you can do it. The only person who could do it perfectly would be a perfect person—and he would not need it.

Remember, this repentance, this willing submission to humiliation and a kind of death, is not something God demands of you before He will take you back and which He could let you off if He chose: it is simply a description of what going back to Him is like. If you ask God to take you back without it, you are really asking Him to let you go back without going back. It cannot happen. Very well, then, we must go through with it. But the same badness which makes us need it, makes us unable to do it. Can we do it if God helps us? Yes, but what do we mean when we talk of God helping us? We mean God putting into us a bit of Himself, so to speak. He lends us a little of His reasoning powers and that is how we think: He puts a little of His love into us and that is how we love one another. When you teach a child writing, you hold its hand while it forms the letters: that is, it forms the letters because you are forming them. We love and reason because God loves and reasons and holds our hand while we do it. Now if we had not fallen, that would be all plain sailing. But unfortunately we now need God's help in order to do something which God, in His own nature, never does at all—to surrender, to suffer, to submit, to die. Nothing in God's nature corresponds to this process at all. So that the one road for which we now need God's leadership most of all is a road God, in His own nature, has never walked. God can share only what He has: this thing, is His own nature, He has not.

But supposing God became a man—suppose our human nature which can suffer and die was amalgamated with God's nature in one person—then that person could help us. He could surrender His will, and suffer and die, because He was man; and He could do it perfectly because He was God. You and I can go through this process only if God does it in us; but God can do it only if He becomes man. Our attempts at this dying will succeed only if we men share in God's dying, just as our thinking can succeed only because it is a drop out of the ocean of His intelligence: but we cannot share God's dying unless God dies; and He cannot die except by being a man. That is the sense in which He pays our debt, and suffers for us what He Himself need not suffer at all.

I have heard some people complain that if Jesus was God as well as man, then His sufferings and death lose all value in their eyes, "because it must have been so easy for him." Others may (very rightly) rebuke the ingratitude and ungraciousness of this objection; what staggers me is the misunderstanding it betrays. In one sense, of course, those who make it are right. They have even understated their own case. The perfect submission, the perfect suffering, the perfect death were not only easier to Jesus because He was God, but were possible only because He was God. But surely that is a very odd reason for not accepting them? The teacher is able to form the letters for the child because the teacher is grown-up and knows how to write. That, of course, makes it easier for the teacher; and only because it is easier for him can he help the child. If it rejected him because "it's easy for grownups" and waited to learn writing from another child who could not write itself (and so had no "unfair" advantage), it would not get on very quickly. If I am drowning in a rapid river, a man who still has one foot on the bank may give me a hand which saves my life. Ought I to shout back (between my gasps) "No, it's not fair! You have an advantage! You're keeping one foot on the bank"? That advantage—call it "unfair" if you like—is the only reason why he can be of any use to me. To what will you look for help if you will not look to that which is stronger than yourself?

Such is my own way of looking at what Christians call the Atonement. But remember this is only one more picture. Do not mistake it for the thing itself: and if it does not help you, drop it.

SOME CONTEMPORARY
VIEWS ON THE DOCTRINE OF CHRIST

WILLIAM SPURRIER

William A. Spurrier (1916–) is chaplain and professor of theology at Wesleyan University. He studied at Williams College and Union Theological Seminary and taught at Amherst before going to Wesleyan. He is the author of Power for Action *(1948) and* Guide to the Good Life *(1956). In the reading that follows he tries to show that conservative and liberal conceptions of Christ are not as far apart as they often seem.*

One of the reasons many moderns do not believe in the classical (orthodox) Doctrine of Christ is probably the use of ancient theological language, which does not seem to fit in with modern knowledge. Hence, when the Creeds and Church theology describe the Divinity of Christ as the God-Man idea, "very God of very God," many tend to dismiss such terms and say, how could a man be both God and Man at the same time? Yet it is surprising how many people believe Jesus to be something special. Many protest quite vigorously that they hold to no "divinity of Jesus" dogma, but do believe that He was "the best man that ever lived," and that the world would be a far better place if all followed His teachings. Indeed, many contemporaries are quite ready to accept Jesus as a kind of model or pattern for creative living. Some people will refer to Jesus as "Master" or even "Lord," but still will not tolerate the Divinity idea or the Incarnation doctrine.

So today, both within Christianity and outside of the Church, there are thousands of people who regard Jesus as the supreme example for living yet who will brook no theory of Divinity or God-Man idea. Moreover, most of these people would call themselves "liberal" in their outlook and regard themselves as outside of the "conservative" or orthodox school of theology. Indeed, some orthodox Christians have tried to declare that these "liberals" are not Christians at all, that if one does not agree to the Doctrine of the Incarnation and God-Man, one cannot be a Christian. This kind of attack has confirmed the liberal suspicion that the Doctrine of the Divinity of Christ is old-fashioned, narrow, and ridiculous. And

Reprinted with the permission of Charles Scribner's Sons from *Guide to the Christian Faith*, pp. 219-227, by William A. Spurrier. Copyright 1952 Charles Scribner's Sons.

by way of reply, the liberal has usually insisted that he is still just as much of a Christian as his conservative brethren and perhaps more so because the liberal has an open mind and does not accept dogma placidly or uncritically. So even in our present time, there is still a controversy over the problem of Christ. Much of this controversy, as in the past, is unnecessary.

It is the opinion of this writer that the liberal and conservative are much nearer together than they think, that their differences stem largely from a too literal interpretation of their respective descriptions of Christ, and from a too hasty judgment of what the other really *means* by his statements. For example, when a person says that he does not believe Jesus to be divine, but that he believes Jesus to be the best man that ever lived and worthy of following, what is he saying? He has said and done several things. First, he has made a value judgment about Jesus. In saying Jesus is "the best man," he has some criterion or standard of value by which he has rated Jesus and other great men, and rated Jesus first. But what is this standard? How does one decide what is "best?" Best from what point of view? Jesus is best as teacher, idealist, liver of life, etc? But these terms do not really tell us much; for the issue is: How does one decide what kind of teacher, idealist, liver of life, is best? When one says "best," he must have some idea or conviction or faith of what is "best." Yet most liberals never think this value judgment through, they do not define or explain what their standard is, what "best" is. Second, when the liberal states that Jesus is worthy of emulation, one could ask the same question of why Jesus is worth following. And the answer would be the same as above: because He is best. But what is best? And so the circle is completed.

But more important, one could raise the question of whether it is wise for people to follow any *one* man. Is any man, however noble and good, worthy of being called "Master," worthy of being followed as closely as we are able? Is this not dangerously close to the dictatorship principle, idolatry of a man? If one is urged to follow only the teachings of Jesus, there is the danger that, like the teachings of any great man, some are good, but some are not so good. And who decides what are the good and the bad ones? From what point of view? Or, if one is urged to follow the person of Christ, there is the danger of slavish imitation which tends to destroy our own individual personalities. These are some of the logical difficulties of the liberal statements about Christ. But the fact remains that most thinking liberals are fully aware of these dangers and they are the first to say that these pitfalls are not what *they mean* when they make their statements. And the conservative critic often overlooks what liberals are trying to say.

Very well, what are the liberals trying to say? They are trying to avoid the pitfalls of the historical controversies about the nature of Christ. They do not want to get caught in the difficult position of having to defend the idea that if Christ was the God-Man, does He thereby have two natures —one human, one divine? And how could such a dual nature be possible? The liberal position, therefore, tries to avoid such obtuse arguments and to replace them by a more simple and effective explanation. Further, the liberal is trying to say that the life and teachings of Jesus are extraordinary and of inestimable value for mankind, and that, therefore, Jesus is worth following as a man, and that His teachings should be put into practice because they will work for the benefit of all. And where does God come into this, a conservative might ask? To which the liberal would reply, "God is in this all the way." That is to say, God worked through Jesus just as He works through all people. The wisdom of God is seen in all great men, prophets of all religions—Jesus, Socrates, and Buddha. Jesus has given us additional insight into the nature of life and how it may best be lived. And is this not enough? Is this not reasonable and understandable? Why should this simple truth be cluttered up with a lot of mumbo-jumbo and dialectic dogma? If the writer understands the main sentiment, such is the liberal position.

What can be said concerning this view? Sympathy and appreciation of this position have been stated, and its validity as against the conservative attack has been implied. But one or two comments should be made. First, this writer would say that what the liberal really *means* by his statement is not very far from what the conservative really *means* by his position. As far as the author can see, the liberal's practical relationship to Jesus is the same as that of the conservative. For the liberal in practice is devoted to Jesus, lives by His teachings, and tries to develop attitudes similar to those exhibited by Jesus. Thus, in a very real and practical sense, Jesus is the master of life for the liberal. At the same time, the practical relationship of the conservative is nearly identical. For the conservative, also, is devoted to Christ, tries to practice His teachings, and cultivate the inner attitudes of Christ. Here, too, Jesus is Master and Lord. Where the two differ is in their *theoretical* explanations of Christ. The liberal may tend to give a humanist description, the orthodox a divine explanation. Both are aware of the difficulties and pitfalls in the *other's* description, but both tend to overlook or minimize the difficulties in their own definition. And, of course, there are many types of liberal views and many types of othodox views.

In general, each school is the same, but they will vary in detail. Thus, there is always the argument as to whether one should say, "God *was* in Christ" or "God *worked through* Christ," or "Jesus was the Perfect Man but not Divine" or "I'm a humanist but I agree Jesus was the best man that ever lived." Now, for all practical purposes, this writer cannot really see much essential difference. For example, what is the difference between perfect and divine? Or, if all is merely human, then how does one say "best"—"best" according to what standard? Or, what is the precise difference between God working (acting) through Christ, and being *in* Christ? So far as the author can see, there is no essential or radical difference. And the more the writer sees active Christians who hold these slightly different theoretical definitions, the more convinced he is that in practice the result is the same, that in action, Jesus *means* the same and does the same for all.

Practically speaking, some liberals believe in the divinity of Christ but theoretically do not. That is to say, in following Jesus and trying to live as He did and by His teachings, they are accepting Him as a kind of God. For them, Jesus is their determiner of destiny, the guide or authority which shapes their lives. If Jesus is the "best," He is also the Highest, the most worthy to be emulated. And as noted earlier, God is generally defined as that which gives meaning to life, that to which one gives his loyalty or devotion, or that by which a man lives. Thus, when the liberal says he follows Jesus as best, or worthy, and believes the world should be guided by His teachings, he has, in practical effect, made Jesus divine. That is why the author would say that the modern liberal position believes in the practical divinity of Christ, but many liberals do not believe in the theoretical divinity of Christ, and if one had to choose between one position or the other, this writer would choose the liberal position. For we would all be far better off if people were practicing the divinity of Christ instead of believing in the theory of it without practicing it. Of course, the ideal is to hold to both and achieve harmony of thought and action.

The final comment on the liberal position is the criticism that in their attempt to avoid the difficulties of theoretical arguments, some liberals have not dug deeply into the weakness of their own theoretical groundwork. As was suggested earlier, the statements of Jesus as "best" does not solve some of the problems of knowledge. The liberal has not faced the difficulties of how one can make value judgments, what criteria are necessarily involved, and how one arrives at such standards. The liberal has *assumed* some set of values, some view of life, and has made judgments accordingly, but he has not examined how he arrived at such assumptions and whether they are valid or not, and whether they can be proved as valid, or are part of one's faith. This is the whole problem of epistemology (knowledge) and faith, and this is one of man's most complex and difficult problems. There are no simple answers or "self-evident truths" here. And should the liberal begin digging here, he would find himself in the company of the orthodox theologians who, at best, are at least trying to harmonize these theoretical problems with practical actions. Perhaps it is no accident that liberalism was strongest in America in a period when Americans displayed tremendous practical activity and tended to ignore theoretical problems.

The conservative or orthodox position should now be examined. It was said that this view is derived from the New Testament account of Jesus as being in some way the Incarnation or Revelation of God. The problem for the Church theologians was to explain and try to make this experience of the disciples intelligible and defensible to others, as well as to themselves. The problem was complicated by attacks from two sides. One attack (the Gnostics) tried to make Jesus out as wholly divine and to discard His humanity altogether. Another attack (in several forms—Arianism, Apollinarians, etc.) tried to discard the divine aspect and emphasize only the human. Thus, when one reads Christian theology as it defended itself against the Gnostics, it looks as though Christianity was over-emphasizing the human side, and when the Church was defending itself against Arianism, it appeared that Christianity was over-stressing the divine side. But a careful reading of each of the Church's statements in the light of the total Doctrine of Christ, will reveal that Christianity was trying to maintain both aspects. Thus, the orthodox view is in the extremely difficult position of dealing with a miracle. This is the only honest and frank word to use here.

There is no use pretending that the belief in Jesus as the God-Man is a simple rational idea, or that it can be proved by a direct appeal to pure, historical evidences. This is why the problem of evidences and the problem of knowledge was stressed early in the book. This is why it was emphasized that the decision about Christ is one that goes beyond scientific data, and inevitably is decided upon the basis of whatever evidence there is, interpreted by personal faith and from within Christianity. That God should invade time, space, and history at a particular period in the person of Jesus of Nazareth, is not an everyday occurrence; that people should, in terms of their experience and interpretations, come to believe that in some special way God was present in—incarnate in—Jesus, is not open to simple explanations. It is, therefore, unusual, extraordinary, miraculous, and there is no wisdom in trying to pass this off as something quite simple and obvious. Faced, then, with this mysterious yet overpowering event, theology is bound to explain it as best it can.

But any good theologian knows his own limitations and the limits of theology itself. This humble wisdom of the Church theologians resulted in several creeds, many "systems," and many controversies. Had there been no such humble insight, there would have been one creed, one system, and no arguments. For truth would have been captured, defined, explained and believed with no further debate. To be sure, there were less humble churchmen who assumed they had arrived at the total story, and who tried to enforce this assumption. But they were always challenged and were never completely successful. Protests and Reformations arose—and they always will and should if Christianity is to grow. Thus, in the history of Christian thought, there are several descriptions of the nature of Christ, but what seems to be common to all of them is the firm conviction that God was in Christ in a more complete and special way than in any other person in history.

As to just *how* God was in Christ, in *what* precise *way*, who can say with exact authority? This is why there will always be debate on questions such as these. If God was in Christ, does it mean that Jesus was without sin? What part of Jesus was man—His body? What part was God?—His spirit? What about the biological problem of two natures—what about free will and foreknowledge? What about Jesus' mistakes in prophecy, Virgin Birth? These and a host of similar questions are the result of honest minds trying to track down the full implications of the God-Man idea. As can be seen, these are enormously difficult questions filled with mystery. Most of them are so difficult and complex that they can probably never be answered or proved beyond a shadow of a doubt. The lazy mind will stop and wave all the questions aside and say that they are a waste of time. But to a rigorously searching mind, questions must always be examined and ordered, and thought must balance with action.

So in theology, the search goes on. What is important is that each answer, or set of answers, be asserted with reservations and humility. This has not always been the case, and people have been read out of Christianity because of disagreement over one of these secondary problems. This is the great danger of the orthodox position. In trying to preserve the faith, the conservative often tends to regard ancient creeds and statements as sacred and true just because they are the tradition. He tends to accept too literally early formulations, and to forget that these statements were designed to meet special problems of culture at a special time in history. The Church's answer to Arianism in the fourth century may not be the right answer to the mechanist of the nineteenth century. The conservative also tends to forget that the "saints" who helped make tradition were, nevertheless, human beings and that the "saints" were saints partly because they were the first to admit their limitations.

The conservative is much at fault for his hasty condemnation of modern liberalism. Part of this orthodox error is the facile judgment that because liberalism uses different language and symbols it must mean something radically different. This assumption is not necessarily true. As suggested above, what many liberals mean is the same as what conservatives really mean—at least in terms of living. That they are often apart in thought is probably true. And here both are to blame, for the liberal tends to ignore theoretical problems and the conservative tends to overemphasize them. The author cannot pretend to settle the dispute here nor be so foolish as to present *the* system upon which all can agree. There are differences; there will be; there ought to be, on many things. But the writer is suggesting here that in addition to the differences, indeed, at the source of the variances, lies a profound and common agreement—Christ.

SUGGESTED BOOKS

Aulén, Gustaf, *Christus Victor*, trans. A. G. Hebert. New York: The Macmillan Company, 1931. An historical study of the three main types of the idea of atonement.

Baillie, Donald M., *God Was in Christ*, revised edition. New York: Charles Scribner's Sons, 1948. A critique of several Christologies and a reformulation of the doctrine of incarnation in terms of the experience of grace.

Braden, Charles S., *Jesus Compared*. Englewood Cliffs, N.J.: Prentice-Hall, Inc., 1957. A comparison of Jesus and other founders of religions which seeks to be fair and objective, though the author acknowledges his Christian faith from the beginning.

Johnson, Robert C., *The Meaning of Christ*. Philadelphia: The Westminster Press, 1958. A short book attempting to state in simple language the religious meaning of the incarnation and related Christian teachings.

Kepler, Thomas S., ed., *Contemporary Thinking about Jesus*. New York and Nashville: Abingdon Press, 1944. Anthology of Biblical critics on the Gospel tradition, Jesus' relation to history, eschatology and ethics, and modern evaluations of Jesus.

Klausner, Joseph, *Jesus of Nazareth*. New York: The Macmillan Company, 1925. A life of Jesus and an estimate of him by a Jewish historian.

Pittenger, W. Norman, *The Word Incarnate*. New York: Harper & Row, Publishers, 1959. A formulation of the doctrine of Christ by a theologian sympathetic to the concepts of process philosophy.

Ricciotti, G., *The Life of Christ*, trans. Alba I. Zizzamia. Milwaukee: The Bruce Publishing Company, 1947. A Catholic account of Jesus' life.

XIV · THE CHURCH

The term church is not an unambiguous one as it is used in Christian parlance. It may mean a particular building, as when we speak about going to a church; it may mean a particular congregation of people, as when we speak of the local church or mention the church in Corinth; it may be used in reference to a denomination or branch of Christianity, as when we speak of the Methodist Church or the Roman Catholic Church; it may mean a national religion, as when we refer to the Swedish Church or the Church of England; it may mean the entire community of living Christians, as when we speak of the church today or the church in the world; it may mean the total body of Christians, past and present, as when we say that the Christian Church believes such and such a doctrine or describe the church as the body of Christ; it may occasionally be used to refer to all those who truly practice the spirit and teachings of Christ, regardless of whether they are Christians in name or not, as when one might speak of the latent church or perhaps the true church; finally, it may suggest all those who do or will experience eternal life, as in the older reference to a church triumphant in contrast with the present church militant.

Despite these various meanings there is a fairly definite connotation intended when the doctrine of the church is discussed. In this connotation it is customary for the term church to designate the whole community of Christians rather than any one branch, to include both the living and the dead, and to refer to the historical organization rather than life beyond history. The other meanings are derivatives or extensions of this general meaning. With this connotation in mind we may approach more readily the Christian idea of the church.

THE NATURE OF THE CHURCH

WHAT IS THE CHURCH? In trying to state what the church is it always becomes necessary to refer to two aspects or emphases in its life. The church exists on the one hand as a spiritual fellowship in Christ and on the other hand as an organized institution. The two are not entirely different or separate from each other, but are in fact complementary. The spiritual fellowship is made manifest through its organized expression, and the organized institution is relevant and justifiable only as the locus of a spiritual community. These two aspects may be brought together in a single definition if the church is defined as the spiritual community of all

377

professing Christians expressing their common belief in Christ in organized forms.

Consideration of this twofold emphasis makes it easier to understand the special place which the church has in Christianity. The church is generally regarded as being a more integral part of Christianity than is the religious institution in many other religions. Perhaps the main reason for this is that the church, in its role as a spiritual fellowship, is seen as an end in itself, a religious end, and not merely as a means to individual enlightenment. That is, Christianity seeks, though it is not fully realized, a harmonious spiritual community of persons activated by Christ, and this is the church. In this sense the church is part of the very thing Christianity seeks in the world as an end. To be Christian, therefore, is to be part of the church, i.e., this community of persons. Christianity then goes on to say that this spiritual fellowship would only be a latent hope apart from the church as an organized institution. While there might be some theoretical or mystical sense in which spiritual fellowship might occur apart from the organized institution, this is practically and humanly not an actual likelihood. Hence the organized institution is both the inevitable and the appropriate outcome of the concern for spiritual fellowship.

Certainly the organization alone would be pointless if it were totally barren of spiritual fellowship and manifested nothing of the spirit of Christ. In this sense the organized church is a means to the end. On the other hand, spiritual fellowship for human beings acquires substance only through concrete embodiment. Hence the two aspects are integral. And when the organized church becomes a true locus of spiritual fellowship among Christians, then it too is part of the end sought because it is the appropriate vehicle of that end. Being a Christian, therefore, means also participating in the organized church in order to actualize the spiritual fellowship which is sought. Of course we must hasten to add that participation in the organized church is not equivalent with church membership. Either one may conceivably occur without the other.

WHO FOUNDED THE CHURCH? Christians believe that the church is not merely a voluntary association of people who want to preserve their memory of Christ and strengthen their devotion to him. They think it cannot be explained by an exact analogy with other human organizations and societies. They believe, in short, that it is not a human contrivance but a human response to divine action. In that sense the church was divinely instituted. This does not mean that its particular teachings and pronouncements have divine authority: that is quite a different matter. It means rather that God intended the spiritual fellowship centering in Christ, just as he did the Hebrew community from which it emerged.

At one level, then, the question of who founded the church is a question which points to the divine source of all sacred history. The same God who creates the world and man, who reveals himself in revelatory events, who governs the whole of human history, and who manifests himself in the person of Christ, also wills the spiritual union of Christ's followers or, as Christians would say, the church. It cannot be plausibly held that God revealed the organizational pattern of the church or transferred divine authority to its human leaders. But divine sanction for its existence and purpose can be claimed as a matter of religious conviction.

At the strictly human level the question of who founded the church refers to whether Jesus himself instituted the church or whether his followers thought of it afterward and then brought it into being themselves. On this question historical Christianity has insisted that the former is the case, and this is part of what is meant by saying that the church is not just a voluntary human association. The belief is that Jesus gathered round him a fellowship of disciples and thought of them as the nucleus of the kind of spiritual community which God intended among men and in which the real presence of God was felt. The Lord's Supper symbolized the consecration of that fellowship. From this fellowship the organized church developed. Many would go further and say that Christ also gave specific instructions about the details of organization and the transmission of authority. But this is a matter of unverifiable conjecture and in any case is not necessary to the conviction that the church originated from Jesus' own teaching and practice.

The church, then, was instituted by Christ. But this doctrine should not be stated in such a way as to suggest that his followers were mere passive recipients and mechanical performers of ecclesiastical instructions. The organized church is, after all, a very human institution, even though it seeks to be a divinely informed human institution. There is no logical or religious reason why the church cannot be thought of as intended by God, as instituted by Christ, and yet as worked out historically by a mixture of human wisdom and ignorance. Christ founded the church; but there is much in the church which he did not found.

What Is Christ's Present Relation to the Church? Granted that the origin of the church is to be found in Jesus' own teaching and practice, what is his relation to the church now? Obviously he is not physically present as its leader and teacher. How then is his spiritual presence to be thought of?

St. Paul answers this question metaphorically when he declares that the church is the body of Christ, who is its head. God, he says, "has put all things under his feet and has made him the head over all things for the church, which is his body. . . ."[1] The body of church members is unified by the presence of Christ as its head and indwelling spirit. "For as in one body we have many members, and all the members do not have the same function, so we, though many, are one body in Christ, and individually members one of another."[2] The members must therefore "grow up in every way into him who is the head, into Christ, from whom the whole body, joined and knit together by every joint with which it is supplied, when each part is working properly, makes bodily growth and upbuilds itself in love."[3] This metaphorical language indicates that the church has its direction, indeed its very existence and life, only from Christ as its head.

In more theoretical terms, how is Christ spiritually present in the church? We cannot say that the life of the church simply *is*, in the sense of identity, the spirit of Christ. That would not correlate with some of the more unseemly facts in the church's history. It would also seem to rule out a needed right of criticism, for if the church is already what it ultimately seeks to be, then criticism is out of place. Yet Christians believe that Christ is not absent from the church's life and history either. The church must therefore be thought of as partially fulfilling, but also partially distorting, the spirit of Christ. Dostoyevsky's legend of the Grand Inquisitor in *The Brothers Karamazov* is a grim reminder of how the church might stray in its real mission. But the Christian conviction is that, despite the distortions to which it is always subject, the church is still the vehicle of Christ's spirit and his work in the world. Christ is spiritually present in the church, then, as its animating power, as potentially coextensive with its history, but as never fully identical with it due to human distortions.

It follows from this that the true church exists where Christ is present, and this is why people can speak of making the church be the Church—that is, making the church where Christ's spirit is partially present into one where it is fully present.

THE FUNCTION OF THE CHURCH

Is the Church Necessary? This question, so frequently on the minds of students as well as others, is really a group of questions. To answer it there must be a linguistic analysis of "necessary" in order to determine what it may mean in a given context. Is the church necessary? "Necessary" in what sense? A number of relevant senses emerge which might complete the meaning of the question: necessary for Christianity? necessary to attend? necessary to belong to? necessary for salvation? These meanings raise different questions.

First of all, is the church necessary to Christianity? If the remarks in the previous section are adequate to Christian thought, then there is a real sense in which it can be said that the church, regarded as a spiritual fellowship, *is* Christianity. If one says, in this sense of the term church, that he believes in Christianity but not in the church, it is like saying, "I believe in Christianity but not in the spiritual fellowship of Christians." But suppose one says he does not mean the church as a spiritual fellowship but rather the church as an organized institution; it is the latter he rejects, though he accepts Christian belief. This raises again the question of whether the two aspects are integral or unrelated. Historic Christianity holds that they are integral. Without concrete, tangible, expressed, corporate acts of worship, memory, and work in an objective, ongoing medium, would not a spiritual fellowship wither away, if indeed it could exist at all?

Now if the church is necessary for Christianity, then this fact would seem to imply the necessity that individual Christians participate in it also. There is no point in maintaining that the church is necessary to Christianity and then saying that it makes no difference whether or not Christians attend its activities and participate in its work. Can there really be a convictional community of persons if each is gazing at the stars by himself, or worshiping on his own ski slope, or even meditating on his own thoughts?

But is it necessary to belong to some church? Here it seems that everything depends on what is meant by belonging. Certainly the mere addition of names to church rolls may prove to be a very superficial way of belonging. The greatest demand as far as belonging is concerned would seem to be that of oneness with, and participation in, the life of the church. And this can normally best be done through membership in some church. Many have struggled with this question, and many have reached a conclusion similar to that of Jane Addams, whose statement of her decision to join a church is very instructive:

> Who was I, with my dreams of universal fellowship, that I did not identify myself with the institutional statement of this belief, as it stood in the little village in which I was born, and without which testimony in each remote hamlet of Christendom it would be so easy for the world to slip back into the doctrines of selection and aristocracy?[4]

But what shall we say, it may be asked, of the further doctrine that the church is necessary for salvation, or, in other words, that there is no salvation outside the church? Some Christians would not consider this an adequate formulation of their Christian belief on the ground that salvation is entirely dependent upon God's mercy and not upon references to the church. The doctrine, however, in some form or other, has been part of traditional Christianity. But even when it is held, the term church does not refer to the organized institution. Enrollment in the organized church is not the connotation of what is meant by the church as necessary for salvation. That would exclude arbitrarily those who lived before the organized church existed or who had no acquaintance with it. Rather the term church here refers to the invisible, spiritual fellowship of persons, and there is no way in which fallible man can determine the extent of this. In fact, the doctrine in question can be held consistently with a belief in universal salvation on the ground that no man can know with certainty that God will not ultimately bring all persons into the spiritual fellowship which is the church. But however that may be, the doctrine is really, if we may put it this way, a qualitative description of salvation rather than a quantitative calculation about human souls.

If the church is necessary in the senses suggested, then the primary function of the church would seem to be not that of doing certain things but that of being something, i.e., being a genuine spiritual community giving allegiance to God and united by the spiritual presence of Christ.

WHAT FUNCTIONS DOES THE CHURCH PERFORM? The church also carries out in action certain functions in order to become the sort of end it seeks to be. It conducts services of worship as the focal point of corporate religious devotion. It administers traditional sacraments which through the centuries have symbolized God's presence to man. It preaches and teaches the Christian message for purposes of edification, instruction, and incitement. It sponsors projects of service in order to meet the human needs of the church. It seeks creative channels through which spiritual fellowship might be engendered. It carries on missions for the enactment of Christian love and for the spread of the gospel.

Sometimes it is felt that certain functions, e.g., preaching and the sacraments, constitute the essence of the church. But it seems inappropriate to define the essence of the church in terms of one or more of its activities, or indeed to define it at all except in a Christological way, e.g., by saying that it exists wherever Christ is truly present.

MISSIONS

IS MISSIONARY ACTIVITY JUSTIFIED? In this age of tolerance, which often means indifference, and of sociability, which often means complacency, the question of whether missionary work is justifiable has come to the fore. In many modern minds there is the lurking feeling, if not the outright demand, that each person, group, tribe, or nation should be left alone with its own preferences and without any interference or proselytizing from any outside source. Usually the reference is to religious interference or proselytizing. It is not always recognized that political parties seeking followers, social organizations seeking members, and intellectual movements seeking supporters are engaged in their own sort of missionary activity, and that such activity may often be the way in which a society remains alert and alive instead of becoming dead and dormant. Where this is recognized the contention may be that religion is excluded from this right to seek converts. But this is sheer prejudice. There is no consistency in saying that people may seek political or philosophical converts but not religious ones.

Sometimes the contention appears to be that the right to seek followers pertains to life within a democratic nation and does not extend to other lands and peoples. The national border thus becomes the dividing line. It is clear, then, that we have to deal with the question of whether the promotion of missionary activity throughout the world is warranted.

One answer to this question may be made by saying that truth and value are not based upon or confined to national borders. If any group feels, therefore, that it has truth and value in its tradition, it has the right to attempt to further such truth and value so that others may experience the same enlightenment, provided the means used in this process are entirely moral and democratic ones. It is interesting to note that John Stuart Mill, no friend of Christianity, thought it quite justifiable for civilized society to exercise influence and even control over uncivilized peoples for this very reason.[5] But it might be argued that while such interference could be justified in the case of uncivilized peoples, the same does not hold when a country has reached a civilized state. Here we may affirm the conviction that as peoples become more civilized they also become more democratic and free; and then it may be reasoned that, just as frank interchange is healthy within a nation, so a world-wide democracy may be benefited by the common right of groups to propose for acceptance their beliefs and practices, provided this is done in open, legal, and honest ways. Most countries acknowledge this right, although in some instances there have been restrictions upon certain undesirable forms of missionary activity.

So far we have been dealing with missionary activity in respect of political and moral rights. But some would hold that, though missionary activity may be a right, nevertheless it ought not to be done. That is, it may be justifiable in the sense that one has a right to do it, but it is not justifiable in the sense that one ought to do it, just as one has a right to be unfriendly to others but ought not to be so. It is one of those things which may be done but is in poor moral taste. Respect others, it is said, and let them alone.

The Christian religion is a missionary religion because of a felt obligation. It considers that this interest is the opposite of poor moral taste because it seeks to further truth and love in the world. Some would derive the obligation solely by authority, referring to Christ's words when he told his disciples to go into all the world and preach the gospel.[6] Others would say it is the logical outcome of Christian experience which seeks to share what it has found. There are also differences concerning the specific goal at which missionary activity should aim.[7] But the belief in missions is commonly accepted.

Most of Christianity is also quite willing to admit that some types of missionary activity have been based on ignorance of local culture, condescending attitudes, and divisive factionalism. Nevertheless Christians believe that, despite these shortcomings, the missionary enterprise can be and has been, when based on appreciation of people, humility, and love, a vehicle by which God can bring new life to those who are materially and spiritually downtrodden. And they also believe that those who are led to know about Christ and to experience God's love will be grateful for the gospel which was brought to them. Indeed this would naturally be so if Christ has truly revealed God for all men. In other words, just as we individually are grateful for the aid, the education, and the spiritual insight which were brought to us by others, even though we may have resisted them at the time, so people everywhere may have the same experience. The Hawaiian Islands are a case in point. There are those who think the Christian missionaries had no business interfering with this leisurely, unlettered, placid people of the Pacific. But Hawaiian Christians themselves are more inclined to thank God that the Christian missionaries from New England helped to transform the aimless vacuity of the ancestral mode of life.

INFALLIBILITY

Is the Church Infallible? A judgment should now be made on the idea of an infallible church, for this is perhaps the crucial issue dividing Christianity, and one that cannot be avoided. The Roman Catholic Church claims infallibility for itself, and maintains that on matters of doctrine and morals it can, through the office of the Pope, speak with infallible authority. Other Christian churches do not make this claim, although some individual Protestants have been known to speak with comparable confidence and to sound very much as if they were invoking the doctrine of infallibility. What, from a Christian point of view, is wrong with such a doctrine, according to Christians who do not accept the idea?

Although the doctrine is seen as an affirmation of truth by those who hold it, it is seen as an instance of sinful pride, if not blasphemy, by those who do not. It attributes to man the perspective and power which can belong only to God. It is a case of thinking of a human institution and authority more highly than anything human ought to be.

Moreover, dissenters find no warrant at all in the Bible for the assumption of infallible institutional authority. In fact, the whole tenor of the Bible rings out in the opposite direction: man is constantly being condemned for usurping God's authority, for being idolatrous. Nor can the passage so often cited, Matt. 16:18-19, be used to justify an infallible church, let alone one specific organized church. The language is highly metaphorical and there is no reference to infallibility, the church at Rome, or a pope. Only a stretch of the imagination, or at least a previous disposition to twist the words into a justification of what is already believed, could read into the passage anything more than a generalized commission of the church.

Opponents of an infallible church cannot conceive how any human being could speak with absolute finality, especially on matters as controversial as faith and morals. Of course Catholicism does not maintain that infallibility resides in the Pope in virtue of his humanity, but only in virtue of his office, and then only when he speaks *ex cathedra*. But to non-Catholics this is a mere subterfuge, for the office can be filled only by a fallible human being. Moreover, he reaches the church office through the selection of other church officials who are human and fallible. It is inconceivable that anyone could, through the vote of other fallible human beings, gain the right to speak with infallibility where he did not have it before. Again, infallibility is not claimed for all fields but only for faith and morals. So another inconceivability is how a human being could be fully fallible in some areas of thought and yet avoid the influence of his fallible humanity in others.

CHURCH UNITY

Can the Church Be One? The division over infallibility means, as is generally acknowledged today, that complete unity among Christians is impossible. No total reconciliation is possible as long as Catholicism maintains, as it does, that non-Catholics are not part of the true church, and none is possible as long as non-Catholics insist, as they do, that the Roman claim is sinful pride and cannot be submitted to.

This division need not prevent other fruitful types of unity. There can be, for example, considerable agreement in matters of doctrine or belief. Certainly this has often been true historically.

> Protestants and Roman Catholics alike accepted the great ecumenical creeds, such as the Apostles' Creed, the Nicene Creed and the Athanasian Creed. They all held the doctrines of the Trinity and, except for the Socinians, the deity and resurrection of Christ, the Bible as a revelation from God, the fall of man, original sin and the need of a moral life for the Christian.[8]

There can also be a great amount of agreement in matters of ethics, both at the theoretical and at the practical plane, although there are some issues in this area which are often sources of division as well. There can be significant unity in the sense of active cooperation in many areas of mutual concern, such as projects of social action and associations of higher learning. There can be some self-discoveries made through acquaintance with the other group's point of view. In this connection non-Catholics seem to be studying with greater interest the thought of Catholic writers, and Catholics seem to be viewing more seriously certain non-Catholic emphases.[9] Lastly, there is the most important unity of all, devotion to the same God and to the person of Christ.

SHOULD NON-CATHOLICS UNITE? Meanwhile non-Catholic constituencies can search for such unity as is possible to them, without the overriding insistence by one of them that it is the only true church. How far such unity is possible and desirable is still an open question.

In an article just prior to the third meeting of the World Council of Churches in November 1961, Henry P. Van Dusen outlined four conceptions of church unity which have been advocated and which find support in different elements of Christianity.[10] The first of these is purely spiritual unity, consisting in the fact that all the churches share a common allegiance to Christ, and not involving any associational or functional fusion. The second is the unity of mutual recognition, where the aim is ultimately for each constituency to acknowledge every other constituency—its doctrines, practices, and sacraments—on a basis of complete equality with itself as an expression of Christian faith. The third is the unity of actual association, in fellowship and in cooperative action, which goes beyond the mere existence of mutual recognition to active interparticipation. The fourth is oganic or corporeal union, i.e., complete organizational merger. The first two conceptions involve unity within, or perhaps despite, a basically denominational structure of the church that would continue. The third conception is what Van Dusen calls "conciliar ecumenicity" because it would focus in councils and associations beyond the denominational level. The fourth is the notion of a single church organization, sometimes called a "superchurch."

Many Christians believe that one of the first two types of unity is not only all that is possible but all that is desirable. Only the denominations, they hold, can maintain the traditions, the doctrinal standards, and the appropriate size to be effective. Others would strive for full, ecumenical interparticipation among the churches, although some would be wary of making the World Council of Churches the center of this ecumenicity, lest it become a superchurch. Others look forward to total organizational union on the ground that any split within the church is regrettable. It is doubtful, however, whether this goal of complete organic merger is very prevalent in any large segment of non-Catholic Christianity. At least there are several ideals that would be placed far ahead of this organizational consideration, namely, the real presence of Christ in whatever structure the church takes, the preservation of the traditional Christian message, the mutual acceptance of one group by another concerning belief and practice, and an active interchange and sense of community. Compared with these ideals the matter of organizational oneness seems less significant, and there may be positive advantages in avoiding bigness of organization under any conditions. In any case the question of the unity of the church has become a foremost issue and will probably continue to be so.

THE FORM OF THE CHURCH

KARL BARTH

Karl Barth (1886–) is one of the foremost theologians of the twentieth century and is generally acknowledged as the pioneer and leader of the movement in Protestantism which came to be called Neo-orthodoxy. After studying at Berne, Berlin, Tübingen, and Marburg and spending a number of years as a pastor, he held a position in theology at Bonn until the rise of Nazism. He left for Basel, where he taught until his retirement in 1961. His major work is his Church Dogmatics *in many volumes. His numerous other books include* The Epistle to the Romans *(trans. 1933),* The Word of God and the Word of Man *(trans. 1928), and* Against the Stream *(trans. 1954). Here he writes of the church as a vehicle of the word of God.*

I

We have seen in our last lecture that the divine mystery of the church is not identical with her human form, but we must seek the divine mystery of the church in her human form; otherwise we shall never find it. This form is, however, decisively conditioned by the fact that churches are *individual* and therefore *many* in number. The one holy church exists as a form only in such individuality and plurality. Only when sought

From Karl Barth, *The Knowledge of God and the Service of God*, trans. J. L. M. Haire and Ian Henderson (London: Hodder & Stoughton Ltd., 1938), pp. 162–73. Reprinted by permission.

in these, can she be found. For this reason the New Testament itself speaks of the *Church*, in speaking of the *churches*, and in speaking of the *churches* speaks of course immediately and directly of the *Church* also. The *Church* in the New Testament is the church in Ephesus, the church in Corinth, the church in Rome side by side. Conversely the church in Ephesus, in Corinth and in Rome side by side are in each case the *Church*. What on the other hand is utterly foreign to the New Testament is the conception only too familiar to us of an all inclusive church, whether already organised, or to be organised, or merely as an ideal to which the individual churches would stand in the relation of component churches. And this conception, only too common among us, could hardly be justified from the nature of the thing itself. Jesus Christ is one and does not exist in component parts. And if the church is the form of His earthly human existence during the time between His Ascension and His Second Coming she too cannot exist in parts, but must exist as a whole wherever she exists. She is in that case always the church as a whole in this place and in that, but not the sum of these churches, as though the individual churches were individual numbers, nor is she the harmony of them as if they were individual notes or instruments forming an orchestra. Wherever a church considers herself as a part of the church alongside other parts and is not conscious in all seriousness of being in her individuality the whole church, she has not yet understood herself or taken herself seriously as the church, that is, as an assembly of people under one head Jesus Christ. An association, in view of the idea underlying it and in view of its task, can share with other associations, possessing the same idea and task, in the carrying out of these, so that one association gives more prominence and attention to one side of their common cause, while another attends similarly to another side. For example, a Young Men's Christian Association may have various sections for sport or reading or politics. The church, however, cannot share in Jesus Christ in her faith or in her work. Wherever she is the church she cannot but will and do everything, or else be no church at all.

The legitimate differences between churches can only be of a technical nature. They are conditioned by differences of time and place, by the fact that we, as children of our time, can in the nature of the case no longer worship God and hear His Word in outward fellowship with the Christians of the fourth century, conditioned too by the fact that the Christians in Aberdeen, for example, cannot in the nature of the case meet together in outward fellowship, as a rule, with those of Edinburgh, much less with those of Basel. But the assembly itself, as an assembly of Christians, is one and undivided, then as to-day, there as here, and is always the same and complete both there and here, then and now. If individual churches unite with one another for joint deliberation, joint speech and action, that, whether it occurs in the narrower confines of a district or country or in œcumenical dimensions, does not mean that the *church* should or could be created thereby for the first time. If the individual churches in their individuality are not already *the church*, then all the churches of the world could unite as closely as they please to form a great union without thereby becoming the church. All that can happen at such a union, be it great or small, is simply that the churches *bear witness to the church* before the world and among themselves, just so far as they are really the church in their own individual existence, i.e. just so far as each of them in her technical difference from the others is at the same time *the church*, and wishes to be nothing but the one complete church in her faith, in her own work and in her relation to other churches. All conferences and all unions—and there are many of them today—which do not take place on this basis are so much idle chatter and ado about nothing, which had far better be omitted, because it can only obscure the question of the true nature of the church. This question is put in all seriousness to every individual church and congregation as such and must always be answered by her as an individual church or congregation.

II

Because the church exists in a form manifest to men and therefore in time and in this world, she is nowhere exempted at any time from the possibility of a complete or partial falling away from her head, Jesus Christ, and consequently she is nowhere exempted at any time from the danger of losing her character as the church. She can be and can remain what she is as the church—the assembly founded, sustained and ordered by Jesus Christ. She can be held together and continue so through "the unity of the Spirit in the bond of peace, *one* body, *one* spirit, *one* hope based on the calling, *one* Lord, *one* faith, *one* baptism, *one* God and Father" (Eph. 4, 3), and this unity, thus described, means that she is the one church of Jesus Christ. But she can also lose this unity of hers in Jesus Christ wholly or in part. She can become a society, an institution, set up, protected and utilised by men on their own authority, a piece of work in which, under the title of the service of God, man is openly or secretly concerned with his own glory. This will probably show itself at once in tension and division within the church and in deviation of doctrine and life from the promise and the command, to which a church will hold, if she is *the* church. But this will not always show itself immediately. A church may maintain the external fellowship and tradition and orthodoxy in their entirety and yet cease to be a church. I do not know whether the fathers of the Scottish Confession saw this as clearly as we must see it.

But we must see and assert clearly, that the *church* is *always* threatened by the question whether she is the true or the false church, and that perhaps most of all when she thinks most confidently that she is the true church.

This fact brings a necessary unrest into the life of the church and of each church and also into the relation of individual churches to one another. Both the true and the false church exist. No church is ever exempted from the question, "*Am* I the true church?" And no church is exempted from submitting herself to the enquiry of the other churches, "*Art* thou the true church?" This distinction and this question is one which causes unrest and pain, but which may not be suppressed even for the sake of love or peace. We can have no peace with one another or only a hollow peace, where such peace is not our peace in Jesus Christ. Between the true and the false church there can be agreements of one kind or another, tolerance and the like, but not the peace which is our peace in Jesus Christ. It is therefore not merely folly, but downright treason—and this has shown itself more than once in the œcumenical movement—to designate the true and the false church (e.g. the Evangelical Church and the Roman Catholic Church) as parts of the one church of Jesus Christ, as discords which quite well admit of being united in one all-embracing concord to form a harmony. This may hold good when it is a matter of discords on both sides; false churches may meet together very well in such a higher unity, for all false churches do belong together and could form an excellent unity—and it is a point worthy of consideration, whether many a church conference and union has not prospered so well simply because it was a case of a false church that was able to reach a happy understanding and union with another false church. But discord and concord can only disturb and cancel each other. The true and the false church as such admit of no uniting, but are as incompatible as fire and water and woe to him who would deny that. He would thereby only prove that what he considers to be the true church and believes he could unite with other churches is itself the false church, or that he treats the true church as if it too were the false church—and it is just this which is treasonable in such a proceeding. For the true church lives on the truth and in the truth, and truth will not admit of fusion with its contrary, error. The antithesis between the true and the false church is therefore one which must not be ignored, but must be honestly recognised, and that precisely for the sake of love and peace properly understood. The antithesis must be overcome not through the victory of one party over another in a church, or through the victory of one church over another, but through the victory of the truth, through the restoration of the lordship of Jesus Christ in the church. This overcoming of error through the truth is the problem which is raised and must be answered in every age in every church and in the relation of

every church to every other. Where this problem did not exist, the church
would be eo ipso the false church.

III

The church is engaged in a struggle for *her true nature* as the church.
Each church is always faced with the question, does the one, true, holy
church exist in her? Does she herself exist as the true church, or is she
not perhaps something quite different? May she not be just a piece of
venerable tradition fostered by certain families or circles and belonging to
the place or land in which she exists? Or is she perhaps just one of the
instruments of power of society or of the ruling class in society? The
socialists and communists have said so at times. Or is she perhaps just a
harmless association to satisfy certain religious needs? Or may she be
actually just a shop, in which well-meant morality and "Weltanschauung"
of all kinds is offered for sale and disposed of? One feels at times that she
is just such a shop, where the wares are cheap and are therefore not held
in much honour.

No church exists that has not always to be facing the question whether
she is indeed the true church. This holds good both of a great national
church or even a world church (even though, like the Roman Church, it
were ever so strongly entrenched in its doctrine and orders) and of a sec-
tarian church (even if its life were ever so deep and animated). There is
no church therefore which has not to fight for her existence as the true
church. The true church exists in human form, in time, in the course of
history, and is therefore subject to the temptation to give up her true nature,
a temptation which can threaten her at every moment from without or
within (or from without *and* within) and which means for the church the
danger of becoming a false church. This temptation has to be resisted, and
woe to the church which will not resist.

But everything here depends on the resistance being the right resistance
(2 Tim. 2, 5). Where and when does that take place? Clearly we must
answer, in accordance with all that we have said about the real Christian
life, the ordinance governing it and the true Christian life and about the
mystery of the church, that this takes place wherever the Holy Spirit is at
work in the church. The work of the Holy Spirit is the founding, forming and sustaining of faith in Jesus Christ—a faith which consists in thank-
fulness and penitence, and which fulfills the law of God by love to God
and one's neighbour, and in which we are comforted by the fact that the
Son of God has intervened on our behalf. It is God's grace and God's
work when men are awakened and called to this faith and are sustained in
it. The true church exists where this takes place and only there. Stated in
terms of general principles, the church's struggle for her existence can

consist simply in the existence of faith and the working of the Holy Spirit in her. The true church exists at the place where this happens. Anything else which might be asserted here is beside the point. The Scottish Confession has enumerated some of the things which at the time of its composition were usually cited as evidence of the true church, and has affixed the necessary question marks. Here it is again speaking in opposition to Roman Catholicism. But there are also non-Catholic churches which would do well to pay attention at this point. In settling this question about the true church, the decisive factor is not the antiquity of the church, as the Confession says (e.g. Cain was older than Abel), nor is it the place (Jerusalem was the city of God and Christ was crucified in it), nor is it succession (for such a succession was to be found in the family of Aaron, which contained ultimately an Annas and a Caiaphas), nor are numbers decisive (the Scribes and Pharisees were more numerous than the disciples of Jesus). And we could continue ourselves—the decisive factor is not the intensity of the piety prevalent in the church (the Pharisees did not fall short in that respect and were Pharisees for all that), nor the beauty of the service (there was no lack of that in Bethel and yet God rejected it through the mouth of Amos), nor her works and sacrifice, nor her morality (it was precisely zeal for that which brought Christ to the Cross), nor the best theology (it never flourished so well as at the time of the destruction of Jerusalem). Why is all this not decisive? Why can a church possess all these advantages and still be a false church? Because all these are advantages according to our own standards, which themselves rest on estimates and valuations of such magnitudes and values as underlie our human judgment. But what makes a church true has nothing to do with any of these magnitudes and values. The true church is distinguished from the false only by the fact that in her Jesus Christ is *present in power*. The true church exists, shines out, fights against temptation and escapes the danger of becoming a false church only where, through the power of Jesus Christ Himself, men enquire about Him, i.e. where they do not care about anything else—success or outward safeguards or about expansion or virtues and wisdom, but about Him and Him alone. Where this question is a burning one, bringing unrest and longing and anger and love, there the true church lives. And there alone; for this alone is the question asked by faith.

IV

The distinction of the true from the false church is thus always a spiritual distinction, and only as such can it become manifest. This does not mean that the distinction remains invisible. But it does mean that it can only be made by God, and also can only be made visible by Him. It means that this distinction cannot be drawn by us, but can only be recognised by us in faith as one already made by God Himself. The Scottish Confession, like most Reformed Confessions, specifies three points at which this distinction made by God can be seen. Let a man ask, it says, where there is to be found true preaching of the Word of God as witnessed to by the prophets and apostles. Secondly, where are the sacraments as instituted by Jesus Christ rightly administered? Thirdly, where is to be found the ordinance of the church, which is required of us by the Word of God and which means the necessary crisis also among individual men within the church? Note that all these three points—these notae ecclesiae—are of a spiritual nature. All three say, the true church is to be seen where the Holy Spirit of God wills it. For God's Holy Spirit decides where there is true preaching, right administration of the sacraments and faithful accomplishment of this discipline and crisis. And *in what way* God's Holy Spirit decides in these matters, will be seen and known and recognised through faith and so through the Holy Spirit Himself. But God's Holy Spirit speaks and may be heard at the place where He has his dwelling and from which He comes to us, namely, in Jesus Christ as the Word of God. The Holy Spirit is not some unknown fluid which can mean different things at different times, nor is He a magic charm. He is the Spirit of Jesus Christ. What the Reformed Confession means by specifying these three points is that, when we enquire about the true church and consider preaching, the sacraments and the ordinance of the church, it is Jesus Christ Himself as the Word of God, who has to be the subject of our enquiry. We *can* enquire after Him, for He exists in concrete form, as witnessed to in the Bible, in the written word of prophets and apostles. And if we enquire after Him, we shall not remain unanswered. If we measure the life of the church by this standard, it will become clear to us *what* He has founded and sustained as His church and therefore as the true church. And it will also become clear what is the other church, the one that is not His, the false church or the "filthie synagogue" as the Confession calls it. It will become clear, that is, at these three points, whether the church, after whose true nature we are enquiring, is or is not a church *reformed* by Him, that is, a church which He has made subject to Himself. The true church, i.e. the reformed church, is always undergoing this reformation, the reformation, that is, of her preaching, her sacraments and her ordinance by the Word of God. The false church, that is always the unreformed church, was perhaps reformed four hundred years ago, only now to reveal the fact that she is afraid of allowing herself to be further reformed. Faith is necessary, that the church may again and again undergo this reformation by the Word of God, and thus let herself be distinguished as the true church from the false. And faith is necessary in order to see this distinction. What is divine will be done only by God. And that

God does what is divine will only be known through God revealing it. But when we have faith like a grain of mustard seed, then the church is undergoing reformation, and when we have faith like a grain of mustard seed we can see this reformation too, and with it the distinction of the true church from the false.

THEOLOGICAL REFLECTIONS
ON THE ECUMENICAL MOVEMENT

GUSTAVE WEIGEL

Gustave Weigel, S.J. (1906—) is a prominent American theologian and ecclesiologist. His degrees are from Woodstock College and the Università Gregoriana in Rome. He taught for many years at the Universidad Catolica de Chile and has been at Woodstock College and School of Divinity since 1948. He is the author of Faith and Understanding in America *(1959),* Catholic Theology in Dialogue *(1961), and other works, and a co-author of several other volumes. In the following selection he discusses the Catholic attitude toward church unity.*

Visser't Hooft finds that Catholic ecumenists fall into two classes, and paradoxically the same man may be of both classes in different phases of his thought.[1] Some Catholics take an "outsider's" view of the Council [World Council of Churches] considering it something strange and disturbing. Others are capable of taking an "insider's" view of it; for, though as Catholics they do not participate in the Council, yet they existentially feel its élan for unity, and they realize that this impulse is the Catholic urge they themselves possess.

The General Secretary of the Council has put his finger precisely on the Catholic ambivalence in curent ecumenical preoccupations. However, the ambivalence is not of the Catholic's making. Ecumenism, generically and abstractly, stands for a felt drive toward the reduction of all who

From Gustave Weigel, S.J., *A Catholic Primer on the Ecumenical Movement* (Westminster, Md.: The Newman Press, 1957), pp. 48-62. Reprinted by permission.

[1] W. A. Visser't Hooft, "Notes on Roman Catholic Writings concerning Ecumenism," Ecumenical Review 8 (1956), 191-97.

use the Christian name into a unity corresponding to the *una sancta* of the Nicene symbol. As a concrete label of our day, ecumenism usually refers to the World Council in its central and peripherical reality.

With regard to ecumenism in its abstract and generic sense, the Catholic feels no ambivalence whatsoever. He wholeheartedly desires the union of all Christians, and even non-Christians, in the *una sancta*. What is more, he has a perfectly clear concept of what that Church is. It is for him concretely the Catholic Church, visibly centered in the jurisdictional and doctrinal primacy of the Bishop of Rome. Hence, the Catholic spontaneously identifies the Church with the Catholic Church without further distinction, although he must frequently add the word "Roman" to avoid all equivocation. By his faith he holds that the one Church of Christ presently exists, essentially perfect, and it is exclusively the Catholic Church, whose visible Catholicity from the day of Peter's death to our own time implies Roman centrality. He inevitably feels as an expression of his own conviction the stirring words of Augustine:

> We must cling to the Christian religion and the fellowship of the Church which is catholic, and is called the Catholic Church not only by her own but by all her foes as well. Like it or not, even heretics and those fostered in schism call the Catholic Church by no other name than Catholic. The point is, they cannot be understood unless they specify her by that title which is the whole world's name for her.[2]
>
> There are many things which with absolute justice keep me in the bosom of the Catholic Church. There is the consensus of the nations and peoples. There is her prestige, miraculous by origin, nurtured by hope, heightened by love, rendered steadfast by antiquity. There is the succession of bishops, beginning with the See of the Apostle Peter to whom the risen Lord committed the shepherding of His sheep, and continuing down to our present episcopate. Finally, there is the very name, Catholic, which in spite of the presence of so many heretical groups, she alone has achieved—and not without cause. Although all heretics want to be called Catholics, yet when a stranger asks one of them where the Catholic Church gathers, he does not dare to point to his own basilica or dwelling.[3]
>
> We believe likewise in the holy Church—the Catholic Church, of course. It is true that heretics and schismatics call their congregations churches. But heretics, on the one hand, do violence to faith itself because they have false notions concerning God, and schismatics, on the other hand, break away from the loving brotherhood by their unjustified secession, even though they believe the same things we do. In consequence, neither heretics belong to the Catholic Church, because she loves God, nor schismatics, because she loves the neighbor.[4]

---

[2] *De vera religione* 7, 12 (PL 34, 128).
[3] *Contra epistulam Manichaei* 4, 5 (PL 42, 175).
[4] *De fide et symbolo* 10, 21 (PL 40, 193).

According to this faith the Catholic tries to live and act. He cannot do otherwise; here he stands; God help him. Amen.

The Catholic takes seriously the prayer of Christ "that all may be one." But he desires thereby the ever greater union of Catholics among themselves and the introduction of the "other sheep," Christ's by uncovenanted mercies, into the one fold, so that there will be but one fold and one shepherd. By Catholic faith every Catholic is intensely ecumenist.

However, when ecumenism is understood as the current phenomenon best observed in the World Council of Churches, then Catholic ambivalence begins to manifest itself. His own generic ecumenism logically draws the Catholic's attention to the reunion movement surging so mightily outside of his own Church. It gives him hope that his own ecumenical desires may be at least in part fulfilled. He need not see the World Council as something strange and disturbing; for the Instruction of the Holy Office did not hesitate to call it the fruit of the inspiration of grace. In consequence, the Catholic's love, good wishes, and prayers move toward the World Council. But here the ambivalence goes to work. He does not want the World Council to continue in definitive existence. He wants it to bring all of its churches into the Catholic Church. He considers the Council good and grace-inspired insofar as it will bring the "other sheep" into the fold of the one Shepherd, visibly represented by His one vicar. He does not at all consider it good if it will only serve to stabilize the alienation of the "other sheep."

This attitude is not ambivalent, given the Catholic's inevitable point of departure, but it seems highly ambivalent to one whose starting point is utterly different. Let us see the other point of view.

Ever since the split between Byzantium and Rome, efforts have been made to heal the breach. Three councils were held to bring the two churches together. As we know, there was no great degree of success in the endeavors, but all saw that reunion was a highly desirable thing. After the Western split of Christendom in the sixteenth century, plans for reunion were not lacking. Calvin himself looked for the union of the evangelical churches, but he could not persuade the Lutherans to accept his followers in communion, and the free-spirit evangelicals, misleadingly labeled Anabaptists, were not too keen for an over-all union. Leibniz later certainly dreamed of and worked for reunion.

Bishop Brent's pain and dismay at the sight of Christian division in our time was more dynamic than in others, but as events clearly showed, he was not alone in longing for union. The evils of division, the irrationality of it, the scandals resulting are all visible and saddening. Unity is the wish of Christ; unity is the demand of reason; unity is the goal of love.

Christians of the Reform tradition by and large do not claim that their churches are the Church of Christ. Calvin and Luther localized the congregations, leaving the question of the Church somewhat vague. Calvin's famous dictum that you cannot point to the Church with your finger indicates that the Church and the congregation must not be identified. You could belong to a congregation which was not Calvinist and yet belong to the Church, just as you could belong to a Calvinistic congregation without belonging to the Church. Calvin was willing to have intercommunion with Lutherans, even though Luther himself had rebuffed such advances. But in principle Luther could have united with the Swiss churches. That is why he could enter into conversation with them for this purpose. On the other hand, neither Lutherans nor Calvinists, and much less the "free spirits," could in principle unite with the Catholic Church. This was clear to all concerned in the problem. Ecclesiology was not a reflex discipline in those days—and it is only coming of age in our time. But there were ecclesiologies at work in all of the different groups then in existence. An implicit and unexpressed ecclesiology is not the absence of ecclesiology. It is a very dangerous theology, because it is assumed, half-unconscious, and thus never subject to analysis and criticism. The idea that Christian doctrine can prescind from ecclesiology is an idle fantasy. It is always present, because *ekklesia* is a key doctrine of the New Testament, which is recognized by all as an authentic and normative description of Christian faith.

Dr. Visser't Hooft complains because Catholics always see an ecclesiology in the World Council. He insists that it has none, though he admits that ecclesiological assumptions are in operation. I submit with all candor and humility that this is not an adequate analysis of the phenomenon. The Council is a fellowship of *churches* by definition. Its hope is to "manifest" the *una sancta* ever more genuinely. You cannot say *una sancta* meaningfully unless you understand the noun that necessarily goes with it, and that noun is *ecclesia*. How, then, can one adequately say that the World Council has no ecclesiology? Rather one should say, how can it not have one? Just because it is assumed and unformulated hardly makes it less dynamic or less operative.

Of course, Dr. Visser't Hooft is pointing to something easily verifiable and altogether true, namely, that given the many ecclesiologies of the member churches, the Council itself makes none of them its own. Moreover, it deliberately and consciously avoids the formulation and imposition of an ecclesiology. This is not a lack of courage nor a failure to see the high import of ecclesiology, but only the charitable urge to offend no one in order to keep all together in love and harmony. Let love operate, and ecclesiology will take care of itself. The Spirit alone can unite Christians, and the Spirit operates in and through love, which He infuses into the hearts of men.

There is much in this presentation of the facts which is true. As a call to collaboration it is highly moving. It stirs the best instincts embedded in Christian faith. The Catholic feels it. Even the "outsiders" experience the "insider" pull. But Christian faith demands that we examine the pull before we allow ourselves to be drawn by it.

In the fourth chapter of the First Epistle of John, where the primacy of love is inculcated, we also find a precautionary introduction:

> Beloved, do not believe every spirit, but test the spirits to see whether they are of God; for many false prophets have gone out into the world. . . . Little children, you are of God, and have overcome them; for he who is in you is greater than he who is in the world. They are of the world, therefore what they say is of the world, and the world listens to them. We are of God. Whoever knows God listens to us, and he who is not of God does not listen to us. By this we know the spirit of truth and the spirit of error.[5]

There is here an affirmation of the relevancy of the test of truth. Love is not to be identified with every upsurge of kindly feeling. The love Christians esteem so highly is the fruit of the Spirit who is the spirit of truth. If my feeling does not derive from this source, it is not the love of the gospel. True love is love in truth. Any other kind is not generative of the high goods enumerated in the thirteenth chapter of 1 Corinthians. In fact, it is quite capable of tragic destruction, as the Greek dramatists well showed.

Consequently, we must make some distinctions concerning the fruitfulness of the loving fellowship of all who claim the Christian name. If it is true love which kneads together the fellowship, it will begin in truth and enrich the vision of truth. If it be not love in truth, it will only obscure and mutilate truth. Lust is love. The will to possess is love. Calculated self-interest is a kind of love. Yet from these imperfect forms of love we need expect no lasting good. Not every kind of love is healthy; not every kind of love is creative. In a word, we must keep away from love rooted in delusion.

These are general ideas. They are not criticisms of the World Council. They only serve as a priori grounds for the criticism of a justification of the work and being of the Council by claiming it to be an exercise of love. In the light of our observations, such a justification cannot be ultimate; for it must ultimately show that the love at work in the Council is love in truth.

At this point the ambivalence is no longer on the Catholic side. It shows up crystal clear on the side of the non-Catholic ecumenists. I get the feeling that they are impatient of the question of truth and grow somewhat irritable when the question is raised. Of course we know they love the

---

[5] 1 Jn 4:1-6.

truth sincerely. Of course they want nothing but the truth. Of course they are searching for it and believe that man can find it. Theirs is not the stand of the sceptic or of the philosophic relativist. But truth is the word of God and "the word of God is living and active, sharper than the two-edged sword, piercing to the division of soul and spirit."[6] Whatever those words may mean, undoubtedly truth is divisive, but the Council wishes above all to be unitive. In consequence, it is unsure in its search for truth, torn by the hope that it will gradually be seen by all united, and by the fear that any heavy emphasis on it will break up the union.

One can easily object to all these reflections that they show beautifully the "outsider" mentality. If you shared the thrilling experience of harmonious collaboration and discussion, the exhilaration of common prayer, the transparent sincerity of intention in so many devout men and women, you would see at once that all your abstract difficulties are irrelevant. Because you have not felt all this, you can spin out your ivory-tower abstractions.

Is this answer really telling, or is it only avoiding the basic issue? Fortunately for the good of the Council itself, not all is sweetness and light at its meetings. There are deep conflicts which, because they are deep, are not always apparent on the surface. But they do manifest themselves at times in spite of the courtesy which is the soul of Council discussions. Sincerity, piety, devotion, and humble candor attract me to a man, but they are not proofs for the validity of the visions held by him, nor will they logically draw me to his beliefs any more than they will draw him to mine. When we do not agree, I am saddened, because I have learned to love my new friend, but I see that our oneness is going to be severely limited. If our disagreement is religious, our religious union will be thin. We shall be one in spite of it—but not in religious unity. And is not the World Council supposed to be a religious unity?

Human love, of course, can make me accept my friend's ideas. The long history of religious experience shows that, for love of man or maid, many a human being has left his or her previous religious faith. If the first faith was erroneous, its loss need not be regretted. If it was the truth, the man has rejected the revealing God—a fearful thing. Human love can produce either of the two changes.

Ah, but not love in the Spirit! Granted, but here again we must discern the spirits. It is moving to see so many workers of the Council give witness to the love they have encountered in their ecumenical work across denominational lines, and it is impressive to feel their conviction that the Spirit was at work. But their subjective estimate of what was going on carries no objective guaranty that they have judged the matter adequately. That the Spirit brought the ecumenists together was stated by the Instruc-

---

[6] Heb 4:12.

tion of the Holy Office. That the Spirit alone directs and guides the Council would be more than even ecumenists dare affirm.

In our time there is a reluctance to appeal to truth as normative for the affairs of men. This does not mean that our age as a whole is indifferent to truth or sceptical of man's capacity for achieving it. However, there is a widespread conviction that certain goods can be attained by bracketing the question of truth, at least in the initial endeavors. This mind seems to be shared by the champions of the Council.

When we deal with the problem of church unity, this methodological principle implicitly asserts that unity of doctrine is not necessary, at least in the beginning. Here we have an ecclesiology. If Descartes gave us the methodic doubt to get out of doubt, this ecclesiology could be described as methodic indifferentism in order to overcome indifferentism. It is difficult to see how Catholics are wrong when they find that indifferentism is the great danger of present non-Catholic ecumenism.

Moreover, even methodic indifferentism is impossible for a Catholic. As he sees it, Christianity always demanded orthodox doctrine as the first requisite of union. It is not altogether objective to point to the infant Church as if it allowed any type of doctrine. If the Pauline epistles because of their obscurity appear to give us a picture of doctrinal diversity among the first Christians, the Johannine tradition clearly denies that such a situation is possible. Judaizers and gnostics are certainly excluded from the *ekklesia* according to Johannine texts. Even Paul makes it clear that the doctrine he taught must be preserved. The resurrection of Christ, for example, simply cannot be denied. That there would be a wider variety of opinion in the early days is to be expected. It would take time for doctrinal uniformity to harden, but the principle of doctrinal uniformity was stressed from the beginning. It seems clear enough that the one faith demanded by Paul is not merely the identical Christ-surrender of all Christians but also the acceptance of the one doctrine.

It is here that we find an innocent blindness in so many non-Catholic ecumenists. They speak of the "rebuffs" of Rome, and this only means that Rome has consistently refused to take part in the non-Catholic ecumenical efforts. Those who speak of the "rebuffs" usually add with candor that there was no personal rejection, that every courtesy and good will was manifested to the persons who made overtures to the Catholics for collaboration.

The historical fact is that every living non-Catholic Christian community broke away from the Catholic Church. Some did it immediately; others split away from the churches which had previously done so. The Nestorians and Monophysites broke with the ecumenical Church, but there was no doubt where the ecumenical Church was. Constantinople represented the ecumene for the East and Rome represented it for the West. When Michael Caerularius in the eleventh century occasioned the definitive separation of Constantinople and Rome, there was no doubt in the mind of either East or West that the ecumenical Church was identified either with the Byzantine or with the Roman communion. For the Orient, Rome and the West were in heresy and therefore out of the Church; and for Rome, the "Greeks" were in schism and therefore out of the Church. The two sections were in perfect agreement that one or the other was the ecumenical church—not that both were. The Eastern Orthodox and the Catholics to this day maintain the same positions.

Today the Byzantine Orientals are in the Council. Whether they can consistently be there is a question for them to solve, but they are well aware of that question. Some of their delegates at Council meetings are uncomfortable and wonder if they should be there at all. Others believe that it is an admirable and charitable medium for giving witness to the truth which is fully contained exclusively in the Eastern Byzantine communities and which all others must accept in order to be truly in the Church of Christ. None has the intention of forming or entering a union which will be anything else than the Eastern Church as it is structured today. If Anglicans or others want intercommunion with the Byzantines, they must *first* as churches accept the dogmas of Byzantine belief. The question of valid succession and sacraments can be discussed only after that initial unity in *belief* is established.

When Orientals and Catholics hold dialogue, this point is so clear to both that there is never any ambiguity. Both know that what is called for by the other party in the dialogue is agreement on doctrine. One side is wrong and the other is right, and the side in the wrong must accept the right side before any reunion is possible. There never is the supposition that neither side is right and both are wrong, that neither is the Church but both are only defective phases of it. Neither do the Byzantines within the Council today believe that any church within the fellowship has any title, even partial, to the name of the Church of Christ except their own church. According to their theory, this is the Church into which the others must enter, and it visibly exists today without waiting for some future time for its manifestation.

Sometimes one doubts if non-Catholic ecumenists really know what they do when they invite the Catholic Church to enter into fellowship on the basis that they are somehow the Church of Christ. (Many non-Catholics do not want her invited!) Logically enough, Protestants insist on the validity of the action and fundamental positions of the Reformers in the sixteenth century. It is hard to see how they could be Protestants if they denied such validity. However, in affirming the position of the Reformers they must accept the consequences which the Reformers were courageous enough (as a Protestant would judge) or rash enough (as the Catholic thinks) to accept. The consequence was that they declared the Catholic Church to be an apostate church, and they in turn were considered heretical by the Catholic Church. The only logical thing for the Protestants is to ask the Catholic Church to become converted to Protestantism; for how can they ask an apostate church to enter into union with the Church of Christ without conversion? If the Catholics come to their union, some slight degree of conversion is already achieved. This is tantamount to suicide for the Catholic Church, and an invitation to suicide may be courteous in form but it is hardly gracious in substance.

This kind of reflection will strike non-Catholic ecumenists as being a mere exercise in logical subtleties. No one is asking the Catholic Church to change her views. But let us all come together and air our views. No more is being asked.

But there are assumptions at work in this seemingly reasonable stand. Non-Catholics know quite well what Catholics believe. There is no secret about it, because it is candidly and forthrightly stated over and over again. Bishop Stephen Charles Neill, a leading figure of the World Council, in a context somewhat different from ours, says:

> We are at a great advantage in dealing with our Roman Catholic friends, because we know exactly where we are with them, and if we are deluded, it is our own fault. . . . But I know exactly where I am with a Roman Catholic friend, and I do not regard him as uncharitable for holding a view to which, however untenable I may myself regard it as being, he is pledged as long as he remains a member of that Church.[7]

It seems to me that so many Protestants, with the best of good will, always hope that the Catholic Church has finally "come to her senses" and, if face can be saved, will retreat from her exclusivist position. This seems to them all that a reasonable man could do and they are handsomely prepared to recognize reasonableness in Catholics. They are too intelligent and too human to brand all Catholics as either fools or knaves. After all, Protestantism has relinquished so much of its characteristic stands and is willing to relinquish more. The Catholics certainly cannot be different. The tacit assumption is that all the churches have erred grievously, even in matters of substance. The tacit assumption is that the Church of Christ is an ideal which has never been actual in history, nor ever will be, though we can do much to approximate the ideal more closely. The tacit assumption is that all Christians belong to this Church of Christ, in spite of their defects, errors, and sins.

This is an ecclesiology. It is not a very satisfactory one, because it abounds in ambiguities of the most trying kind. Yet this ecclesiology must be accepted, at least for the sake of discussion, in order to enter the World

---

[7] *The Ministry of the Church,* ed. Bishop Stephen Neill (London and Edinburgh: Canterbury Press, 1947) p. 25.

Council. To say, therefore, that the Council has no ecclesiology is to refuse to reflect on the reality before us.

This ecclesiology, unrecognized though it be, cannot be accepted by a Catholic, not even as the starting point of discussion. The instructed Catholic, who knows that he can lose his grace of faith, can speculate on what would be his position in such an hypothetical event. The vast majority thinks that the only rational alternative to Catholicism is the complete rejection of Christianity. The average Catholic considers non-Catholic forms of Christianity either as rationally inconsistent or as not coherent with the facts of life and history. For him anything less than Catholicism is a *reductio ad absurdum* of Christianity, and the Council is, to say the least, prepared to accept something less than Catholicism.

I do not say these things to irritate non-Catholics. I pass over the question whether the Catholic conception is justified. I wish only to state that it is here as a palpable fact. The Catholic accepts as a fact that non-Catholics do not share his views, though it puzzles him. Is it too much to ask the non-Catholic to recognize the Catholic fact, puzzling though it may be?

SUGGESTED BOOKS

Adam, Karl, *The Spirit of Catholicism*, revised edition, trans. Dom Justin McCann, O.S.B. New York: The Macmillan Company, 1955. An eloquent apologetic stressing the centrality of Christ and the Church in all phases of Catholic religion.

Brown, Robert M., *The Significance of the Church*. Philadelphia: The Westminster Press, 1956. A short work in the Layman's Theological Library written in the new Protestant spirit which re-emphasizes the importance of the church.

Cairns, Earle E., *Christianity through the Centuries*, third edition. Grand Rapids: Zondervan Publishing House, 1958. A systematic, informative textbook on church history, generally objective except in its evangelical critique of the modern period.

Douglass, Truman B., *Why Go to Church?* New York: Harper & Row, Publishers, 1957. Broadcast talks giving a pastor's outlook on "some aspects of the Church's life in our time."

Jenkins, Daniel, *The Strangeness of the Church*. Garden City, N.Y.: Doubleday & Company, Inc., 1955. An interpretation of the church and its practices as part of the Christian Faith Series under the editorship of Reinhold Niebuhr.

Latourette, Kenneth S., *A History of Christianity*. New York: Harper & Row, Publishers, 1953. A comprehensive work on all phases of Christian history by an eminent church historian.

Niebuhr, H. Richard, *The Social Sources of Denominationalism*. New York: Holt, Reinhart and Winston, Inc., 1929. Investigation of the historical and social nature of church divisions, intended as a contribution to the ethical problem of disunity.

XV · CHRISTIAN BELIEFS

In Part Three we have discussed the foundations of Christian thought—revelation and the Bible, Christ, and the church. We have not yet brought together a summary of principal Christian beliefs. This is the purpose of the present chapter.

In undertaking this task it will not be our aim to try to present an entire condensed theology. Rather our aim will be to see in brief compass and in concentrated perspective what Christianity stands for. No synopsis like this could possibly substitute for a more extended exposition or include everything that everybody would consider vital. Also no claim to superiority for this particular synopsis needs to be made in order for it to serve its very limited function of concentrated focus.

The common ways in which interpreters attempt to communicate the basic Christian beliefs might be grouped under three categories. One of these is historical narration, that is, a recounting of what God has effected in Biblical history as Christians view it. Since Christianity is a historical religion, the emphasis is here placed upon the major revelatory events of history and the roles which God and man had in them. An example of this approach is found in the statement of faith prepared by the recently formed United Church of Christ.

A second way is that of informal discourse, in which the writer adopts one or more of a variety of tactics for his presentation, for example, comparing Christianity with other world-views, setting forth a Christian answer to the problems of modern life, or putting Christian ideas into colloquial language and every-day illustrations. C. S. Lewis provides an example of this kind of approach.

A third way is that of formal exposition, where a systematic, organized elaboration of doctrines is presented. This is the approach employed in systematic theology.

The procedure in this chapter falls naturally into the second of these types of presentation. Three tactics will be adopted. First, we shall ask what are the distinctive things about Christianity that are most appropriately included in a shorter definition of it. Next we shall relate Christian teaching to the general conception of religion discussed in Chapter I. Finally, we shall suggest a selected summary list of main emphases in Christian thought.

DEFINITIONS OF CHRISTIANITY

What is the *essence* of Christianity (to use a Greek term), or the *heart* of it (to use a Biblical term)? What is the core, of which theology is the elaboration? This is a proper question to consider because it directs our attention to the center rather than the periphery and because in practical contexts we are frequently required to refer to Christianity in quick and summary fashion.

We shall ask this question, imaginatively speaking, of four writers representing different traditions. The answers will be given in an order which, in the current theological parlance, would generally be regarded as moving from the more liberal to the more conservative dimensions of Christian thought.

Edgar S. Brightman maintains that the only general characterization of Christianity that is possible is the common allegiance of Christians to Jesus. "To be a Christian is not, primarily, to accept certain ideas, however true they may be; but, rather, it is to stand in actual relations to the life-stream of Christian history, a stream that flows from Jesus down to the present."[1] This view is arrived at from the assumption that the only way to tell what Christianity is is to say what is common to all of the diverse groups and traditions which historically have borne the designation of Christian. The result must be that the thinnest strand of similarity is taken as the definition, for that is the only common feature of all these groups. The wide compass of the definition is seen in the following statement: "The principle of this synthesis is that of following Jesus, yet freely interpreting his message, his doctrine, and his relevance to life, in loyalty to our best insights, whether they be Catholic or Protestant, theistic or humanistic."[2] Brightman goes on to list some *de facto* agreements which have historically accrued from following Jesus. These are largely personal qualities, such as faith in divine initiative, humility, and love of all persons.[3] These give more specific meaning to the idea of following Jesus; but they also suggest that Christianity is essentially ethics.

The chief difficulty in this answer is the assumption that Christianity must mean the lowest common denominator in all groups that wish for any reason to bear the title Christian. This is perhaps all right if what we want is a sociological or cultural definition rather than a religious one. But a more satisfactory theological approach must surely reflect what the main stream of Christianity has been, what the consensus of Christian thought through the centuries has emphasized. Brightman is right in claiming that any definition must be based on the historical actuality of Christianity and not on what the writer would prefer to have it mean. Yet it does not have to cover every deviation or aberration merely because the term Christian is retained by such individuals and groups. Also a definition should reflect, it would seem, not only what Jesus' followers thought but what Jesus himself taught. This can be denied only if Christianity is regarded as a later phenomenon not continuous with and not integral with the actual life and teaching of Jesus.

From these considerations we are led to suggest that a definition ought to include not only typical Christian attitudes and virtues but in addition some reference to the church and some elements characteristic of Christian belief. These factors are brought into a definition proposed by H. Richard Niebuhr, who specifically contrasts such a definition with the type of definition presented first.

> A Christian is ordinarily defined as "one who believes in Jesus Christ" or as "a follower of Jesus Christ." He might more adequately be described as one who counts himself as belonging to that community of men for whom Jesus Christ—his life, words, deeds, and destiny—is of supreme importance as the key to the understanding of themselves and their world, the main source of the knowledge of God and man, good and evil, the constant companion of the conscience, and the expected deliverer from evil.[4]

In the next definition the doctrinal element is even stronger, although the church is not directly mentioned. Arthur F. Holmes suggests that there are three basic beliefs that must be emphasized if Christianity is to be contrasted with some other world-view such as naturalism.[5] The first of these is the belief in God. Christianity is "clearly theistic." The second is the belief in Christ. Despite certain differences in interpretation Christianity is "rooted in the historic person and work of Jesus Christ." The third is a belief about man. It is the belief that man's peculiarly human endowments have come to him by divine action, more specifically from "divinely provided revelation and redemption." These emphases are concentrated in a short definition as follows: "Christianity may therefore be defined as that religion of revelation and redemption which centers in the divine person and historic work of Jesus Christ."[6]

When we turn to a Catholic spokesman we naturally find a greater emphasis on the church and the permanent embodiment of Christianity which that affords. Karl Adam writes:

> As the history of Christianity shows, it is a life, which manifesting its power first in the Person of Jesus delivered the souls of men from an earth-bound existence, created a new, supernatural community, and through it for all time by word and sacrament provides humanity with streams of truth and grace.[7]

There is also an emphasis on the thorough unity of the church which can be more easily maintained when the perplexing diversity of Protestantism is omitted from consideration as part of Christianity. "In reality Christianity is an intimate organic unity, a vital unity, which unfolds itself indeed to its fullness progressively, and yet in all the stages of its unfolding is a unity and a whole, the Christianity of Christ."[8]

For non-Catholics the identification of Christianity with the "supernatural community" of Roman Catholicism is much too narrow a conception. But we have also seen that a *de facto* cultural definition is too broad. Therefore it seems more appropriate that a definition stress the kinds of emphases expressed in the other two definitions. All in all, if we expect a definition to bring out the centrality of Christ, the spiritual community of the church, certain doctrinal references, and typical Christian virtues, and also to allow for considerable diversity of thought, the definition of Niebuhr is perhaps the most adequate of those mentioned. A variant might be that Christianity is the religion of the spiritual community centered in Christ, founded on him as divine revelation and means to reconciliation, and aspiring to his example of love and sacrifice. But we shall not proceed further with the attempt at refinement of a definition. Instead we shall turn directly to the next phase of our discussion.

CHRISTIANITY AND THE
GENERAL CONCEPTION OF RELIGION

It may be recalled that in Chapter I our definition of religion emphasized four points: the aim of reconciling an individual or a community with that objective reality, or in some cases an ideal value situation, which is considered to be of supreme worth; the practical commitments, in the form of beliefs and attitudes, which an individual or group has toward this aim; the endeavors and actions which result from these commitments and for this aim; and the fact that these commitments and endeavors are the most deeply gripping and most persistently governing in life, as signalized in the term ultimate. An attempt will now be made to relate Christianity to these general concepts, and to see how Christian thought regards Christianity as bringing to a culmination these religious tendencies of man. In doing this it must be repeated that there is no intention to show Christianity as an instance or subclass of a "religion in general." Religions are basically unique and are not adequately describable as equivalent flowerings of the same common core. It is possible, however, to note certain existential similarities that result in practice from universal human aspirations and thus to give a definition of religion. It is then possible to give the Christian way, or the Buddhist way, or the Islamic way, of interpreting such a definition, without suggesting that there is a subtle essence making all religions the same and without suggesting that all religions are equally true. It is in this more practical sense that we consider the question.

The reconciliation which Christianity seeks is that between the self and God and between the self and other persons. Both of these aspects of reconciliation are stressed in Jesus' familiar summary of the Jewish law. They should not, however, be thought of as separate experiences or as attainable in isolation from each other. From the Christian viewpoint the gulfs between man and man are not fully comprehended until they are interpreted through, and not fully surmounted until they are pervaded by, the meaning of reconciliation with God; and conversely, there is no real reconciliation with God if it is not carried over and made manifest in the relations between man and man. The hope is thus the reconciled community of all persons—each self with God and each self with every other.

What does this reconciliation really mean? It must be looked upon in the first place as a spiritual experience—an experience of person to person affirmation, an experience in which man feels himself receiving the love always extended to him by God and finds himself thereby able to return his own love and also have it spread out into all of his personal relationships. The heart of it is thus the mutual acceptance and affirmation expressive of compassion.

One of the distinctive Christian beliefs about this reconciliation is that, in the life of man as he now is, reconciliation is not an ordinary and natural thing to have happen. The reason is that man is his own greatest barrier to it. There are powerful urges to self-glorification, strong passions of selfishness, deep hates of oneself and others and God, not to mention more respectable conceits and contrivances, which prevent the occurrence of natural reconciliation. In fact, man does not accomplish it by his own efforts and will power at all. The reconciliation which is spontaneous acceptance and affirmation based on compassion is not gained by an act of moral will. The initiative is taken by God, who alone is consistent in reconciling love. Consequently, repentance on man's part and acceptance of forgiveness are needed for the experience of reconciliation to occur. Man is then liberated from pride and hate to become a new spiritual person. And the result is not, as is sometimes pictured, the abjectness of crumpled selfhood, but the capacity for creative endeavor based on spiritual strength and assurance. In such reconciliation man is able finally to be himself instead of a partial semblance of himself. Christianity believes, to be sure, that the union of man with God, and therefore the fulfillment of the self, is never wholly complete under present life conditions; but it also believes that a present experience of radical renewal can take place—call it "salvation," call it "realized eschatology," call it "the new being"—and that such experience can be a continuing channel of reconciling activity in the world.

One objection that is sometimes made against this outlook is that words like reconciliation and redemption are inappropriate to the goal of Christianity. They presuppose, it is said, a wide gulf, a yawning chasm, between man and God that must be bridged. But is there no place in Christianity for the once-born person as well as the twice-born, in William James's sense, for the person who has his religion all gaily and without trouble instead of with anguish and torment of soul? Must all Christians go through the tortured despair of an Augustine, a Luther, or a Kierkegaard? Is there no place for the religion of spontaneous feeling as in Goethe, or of natural harmony, as in Thoreau, who said he never quarreled with God?

An answer to this objection is that it neglects the distinction between the Christian doctrine of man and the psychology of individual temperament. The Christian view of man is that he is prone toward a self-willed alienation from God which results in human conceit on the one hand and disrupted human relations on the other. He who is unaware of the disharmony among men is unobservant, and he who has never quarreled with God probably does not have a God who can be quarreled with. But it is not a matter of how different people happen to feel about this circumstance of man's existence, or even whether they have any feeling about it at all. The alienation is still there to be overcome; the need is universal. That is, it is needful that all men know God and love him and their neighbor. Again, the experience of reconciliation may arise for some with more calm and contemplation, for others with more turbulence and anguish. Certainly there are few Christians (for good or for bad) that are as tormented as was Kierkegaard. But this psychological consideration does not alter the theological interpretation of man, his predicament and his need. Finally, if the experience of reconciliation issues in a cessation of turbulence, so that inward peace and harmony are felt, this psychological fact does not negate the theological statement of what is requisite for such "fruits of the spirit" to occur. In short, it is very misleading to take subjective states of feeling as the clues to Christian thought.

The most distinctively Christian emphasis in the interpretation of religion as reconciliation concerns, of course, the place which Christ has in the entire process. For Christians Christ is the means to reconciliation with God. As we have seen, there are different theories as to exactly how Christ makes operative this reconciliation; but the common conviction is that he does so. For this reason he has been called the mediator. This does not mean that Christ is an intermediary being between God and man. Nor does it mean that man cannot approach God directly but must turn aside to a third being first, namely, Christ. Rather Christ is thought of as God's own power of reconciliation in the world. Knowing Christ is believed to be the most direct and tangible way of knowing what God is like.

The Christian connotation of commitment involves Christ on the objective side and faith on the subjective side. But faith in Christ is not thought of as different from faith in God. Such commitment is ultimate for Christianity in the sense that it ought to be prior to all other concerns and in the sense that it gives illumination and perspective to all other concerns.

Christianity is also a religion in which action or endeavor is emphasized in order to sustain, cultivate, and extend the original faith, although in Protestantism this is interpreted not as a way of acquiring merit but ideally as a pure consequence of the original faith. The endeavors include private devotion, personal relations, public policy, and world outreach. In private devotion cultivation is sought through prayer, common worship, sacraments, the use of the Bible, and other ways characteristic of particular forms of Christianity. In personal relations the endeavor is to manifest toward other persons the same love which Jesus manifested of God. In public policy love is most adequately expressed through justice, and so Christianity has generally had a vital concern with basic social and political proposals. The endeavor of world outreach refers to the missionary function of the church. All of these endeavors may be thought of as part of or means to the final reconciliation which Christianity seeks.

MAIN EMPHASES IN CHRISTIAN THOUGHT

We now turn to our summary list of affirmations that have been dominant in Christian thought. The first problem in doing this is selecting the points that are most characteristic, and the second is stating the points so as not to be too broad or too narrow in covering actual Christianity. C. S. Lewis, in his familiar book, *The Case for Christianity*, emphasizes these beliefs as fundamental: that there is one God who is personal, good, and the creator of the world; that the world has been invaded by an evil power; that God came to man in Jesus; that Christ atoned for man's sin through his own perfect penitence; and that baptism, belief, and communion are the chief means of receiving the Christ-life.[9] Another popular treatment suggests these topics as basic: reason and faith, revelation, man, sin, God, Christ, resurrection, atonement, eternal life, and history.[10] A somewhat shorter sketch suggests these topics: revelation and reason; Biblical revelation; God; creation, man, and sin; Christ and the creeds; atonement; salvation by faith and new life in the spirit; and kingdom of God, history, and community.[11] A longer theological treatise follows this outline: the Christian concept of God, the God who acts, the victorious act of reconciliation, the broken and restored relationship with

God, the nature of the church, the constitutive factors of the church, the church in the present age, and the church in the light of the Christian hope.[12] These examples of outlines give some indication of the ground to be covered and also of the diversity in what is selected for emphasis.

The following sketch proceeds by giving a series of brief numbered points.

1. GOD. The beginning, center, and end of Christianity is God. Like religious theism generally, Christian thought holds that God is personal—conscious, purposeful, good, creating, free. It also generally holds to such metaphysical attributes of God as omnipotence, omniscience, omnipresence, eternity, unity, transcendence and immanence, although not always in the popular connotations of these words. But the abiding Christian concern is with the moral and religious qualities of God—righteousness, holiness, justice, love. Many symbols have been used to suggest these qualities. Amid all of these attributes, however, the peculiarly Christian emphasis is upon the belief that God is infinite compassion and that he takes the initiative in the reclamation of man, even to the point of breaking into human life in the person of Jesus.

2. REVELATION. Christianity believes that there is such a thing as personal impact of God upon man which constitutes a source of religious knowledge other than that of discursive reasoning. It believes that God is the initiator of such experience and that it is not simply man's insight. Man, however, must be the rational interpreter of such experience, and the truth which is derived from it cannot contradict our independent rational knowledge without one or the other being in need of modification. Thus revelation in no way minimizes either the theological or the independent use of reason, nor does reason by its nature exclude revelation. Revelation is generally held to be to some extent universal, but to be especially manifest in the Biblical tradition and Christ.

3. THE BIBLE. The Bible is the bearer of that aspect of revelation which is capable of being communicated through written words. It is seen as the written vehicle of the special revelation of God to man. It needs to be interpreted and appraised both scientifically and theologically in order for its religious meaning, its revelation, to become relevant; for its message, either for our life or for our understanding, is not grasped by a merely passive assent to its statements. It is the Bible itself, however, which is the object of such interpretation, and not man's feelings about it. The Bible is thus authoritative for Christian belief and practice, though Christians differ about what is involved in calling it an authority.

4. TRINITY. Christian thought emphasizes the belief that the person of God can be understood properly only if three aspects of his person are

distinguished and affirmed equally. These are symbolized as the Father, the Son, and the Holy Spirit. Many insist on the most literal meaning of this doctrine whereby it refers to three distinct metaphysical persons or personalities eternally present in God yet somehow still forming an unbroken unity. They are content to say that this is a mystery beyond human understanding. Others hold that the doctrine is intelligible only if it refers to three manifestations or functions of God—those of creator, redeemer, and sustainer of the world.

5. CREATION. Unlike the god of Aristotle or the Brahman of Shankara, God is conceived by Christianity as a personal, conscious, and free creator of the world of things, of life, and of man. This means that the world of finite things is radically dependent upon God for its existence in a sense which implies that God is not similarly dependent upon the world for his existence. It means also, more literally, that God is the creative power forming the world and man to be what they are. As far as the dimension of time is concerned, many insist that finite existence had a definite beginning point in time, and this beginning point is the moment when our world was made by God out of nothing, understanding this in as literal a sense as possible. Others, who cannot conceive of a beginning moment of time without any preceding moment, or of something coming literally out of nothing, prefer to say that creation means, essentially, the absolute dependence of all things on the creating and sustaining power of God, allowing for some speculation on the other points.

6. MAN. Christianity believes that man is both a spiritual and a natural being, and that while he may have some roots in the evolutionary past, this fact does not conflict with the belief that, in a religious sense, he is a special divine creation. Religiously, man possesses a unique soul, though this is not taken to dictate a particular analysis of what the soul involves at the strictly psychological or philosophical plane. In his religious origin man is a reflection of the divine nature, i.e., free personality. But he is also very much of an earthy creature, so much so that he is a psychophysical organism and not a disparate conjunction of a free-floating soul with a body. Thus man is never identical with, or part of, God, but always finite in relation to the infinite; yet he is also viewed as the image of God.

7. SIN. A doctrine of sin is characteristic of Christian thought about man. It refers to man's rejection of God and hence of his neighbor through self-will and pride. This tendency is generally conceived of as universal and radical—universal in that it pertains to all men, and radical in that it is not merely a surface accretion but goes to the root of man's nature. This does not mean that man is not originally good; in fact sin is viewed as

the corruption of an original good in favor of ill-conceived self-interest. The radical character of sin causes the basic religious problem of man, his need for reconciliation.

8. GRACE. Christianity does not believe that man is able to save himself, to effect his own reconciliation with God through his own meritorious efforts. Rather the infinite love of God for his creatures, called his grace, is needed, is available, is searching man out. Grace means that forgiveness for man's selfishness and pride is extended to him freely. It means also that when it is accepted through faith and gratitude, and not from a sense of deserving it for moral accomplishments, new power for living and reconciling action is possible. Man lives lovingly and justly when he himself has been made whole by love.

9. CHRIST. This love of God for man was demonstrated supremely, so Christians believe, in Christ, who is seen as the manifestation, the incarnation, of the very nature of God as love. Through Jesus' life, suffering, and triumph over death, God revealed decisively his reconciling love and certified that evil and despair are not ultimate in the world but can be and will be destroyed. Through Christ God provides the means for the redeeming of man from his unreconciled state. Christ, as the supreme instance of the divine word or *logos,* is thus the center of history and the key to its meaning and its destiny.

10. RESURRECTION. The resurrection of Christ is the central event in which the victory over death, evil, and despair is demonstrated. Christians differ about the extent to which the physical details in the resurrection stories are to be accepted. But there is general agreement that the resurrection appearances were no illusions and that they did in fact vindicate what God had revealed in Christ and did in fact lead to a new life of the spirit in Jesus' despairing followers. For this reason the resurrection is a crucial event for Christian faith.

11. RECONCILIATION. Christianity preaches the good news, the gospel, that reconciliation and new life are possible for man. Man does not have to remain without direction, hope, or wherewithal in the universe. For Christians the source of this reconciliation is God as revealed in Christ. And all men are called to this same source. Christ is seen simultaneously as making known what God is like, making the forgiving love of God open and operative in the world, and making it possible for man to overcome his pride or his self-abnegation or his ignorance and to accept the divine acceptance of him.

12. ETHICS. Through the acceptance of divine grace by faith, new spiritual life is possible. This experience, with Christ as its focal point, be-

comes the reservoir from which practical decisions and actions flow. The love which Christ showed becomes the model for personal relations. Love in public policy is expressed largely in endeavors toward justice and equality. The teachings of Jesus are taken as a basis for ethics; but there can be no mechanical application of these to modern times. Thus the emphasis is placed upon spiritual freedom stemming from loyalty to Christ rather than upon legalistic devotion to rules. Another virtue in Christian ethics is humility. Christians can claim no greater worth, rights, or moral superiority for themselves over other people.

13. THE CHURCH. The church has generally been seen as an essential part of Christianity. It is the organization and fellowship of all those who accept and seek to practice the faith centered in Christ. It is continuous with Jesus' own life and teaching and is the corporate locus for the cultivation and extension of his message. Protestants cannot, however, regard the church as infallible. It must, like all of life, come under the judgment of the one standard, that of Christ.

14. HISTORY. Christianity is a historical religion in that history as a whole has meaning and there are central historical events which are the clues to that meaning and the foundation of Christian faith. History is, religiously if not empirically, a unified human story which has its final meaning and culmination in a purpose beyond history. Thus actual empirical history is viewed neither as a meaningless repetitive cycle nor as a constant spiraling progress. It is rather an ambiguous series of failures and fulfillments as judged by the measure of Christ who reveals the qualitative character, though not the detail, of what ought to be. But Christianity also expects the end of history—not merely in a linear, chronological sense, but in the sense of its qualitative culmination, the fulfillment of what history is for.

15. ETERNAL LIFE. Not only history as a whole but each historical individual is thought of as having worth, meaning, and purpose. This purpose is eternal life—not in the sense that this should be the motive of his moral actions, but in the sense that this state is willed and purposed for him in the divine purpose. Eternal life is not merely a future prospect but rather a quality of existence which may be an anticipated present reality as well as a post-historical condition. Christianity believes, moreover, that God's concern for good, and power over death imply the retention of individual personality and not just abstract human values in the universe. Divided as to how describable the end of history can be, and as to possible states of existence in future life, Christian thought nevertheless agrees that present life is a crucial ground for decision concerning eternal life.

16. FINITUDE. A clear distinction is made in Christian thought between the finiteness of man and the infinity of God, the limitations of man and

the perfection of God. For Protestants this means that all things human are subject to fallibility, including statements of belief. There can be no final and immutable formulation of Christian thought. The church, its thought and its practice, is subject like everything else to divine judgment. This does not mean that truth is relative, that good and bad are purely subjective terms, or that man has no awareness of objective truth and goodness. It does mean that absolute intellectual certainty is unattainable, that humility is appropriate to intellectual discourse as well as moral character, and that Christian faith must always involve risk and venture as well as practical assurance.

THE TRUTHS CATHOLICS HOLD

RONALD KNOX

Ronald Knox (1888-1957) was a British priest, essayist, and detective story writer. Educated at Oxford, he converted from Anglicanism to Roman Catholicism in 1917 and later became Catholic chaplain at Oxford. His religious books include A Spiritual Aeneid *(1918),* The Mystery of the Kingdom *(1928), and* God and the Atom *(1945). In the following selection he gives a summary of basic Catholic beliefs.*

In this chapter I shall attempt no more than to give some outline of the main truths which Catholics believe as revealed truths. We could not have found them out for ourselves, by the unaided exercise of human reason; we believe them on the authority of Christ revealing; that is, because the Church to which he has bequeathed his teaching office gives us warrant for their assertion.

We believe, then, that within the unity of the Godhead there is a distinction of three Persons. The Eternal Father, himself the Fount of all being, is the First of these Persons. And we are taught to think of him as begetting, by an act of generation which lies altogether outside of time, a Son equal in glory with himself; or, if you will (so little justice can we do

From *The Belief of Catholics* by Ronald Knox, pp. 156-64, copyright 1927 Ronald Knox, published by Sheed & Ward, Inc., New York. With kind permission of Mr. Evelyn Waugh.

to such a mystery by any conceiving of ours), you may say that he gave utterance to a Word, the express Image of himself, a Word Timeless, Uncreated, Personal. And from these two Persons, Father and Son, proceeds a third Person, the Holy Spirit; the Love of the Father for the Son, the Love of the Son for the Father, is Personal too, and thus the Trinity is completed. The language in which this doctrine is defined does not (as far as we know) come down to us from our Lord himself; but it is the only language capable of safeguarding the beliefs of the earliest Christianity, as it expresses itself both within and outside of the sacred documents. The distinction between the Father, the Son, and the Holy Ghost would be unreal if it were less than Personal; their Unity would be unreal if it were less than substantial.

That anything should exist besides the Blessed Trinity is necessary neither to the Existence nor to the Happiness of the Godhead. But by a voluntary act God has (we can see for ourselves) brought a Creation into existence. We can see, or infer from what we see, parts at any rate of his material creation. But, since we know from the experience of our own soul-life that matter is not everything, it would be a ridiculously parochial assumption to suppose that there was not a vast invisible Creation as well —to suppose that our spirits are the only spirits which exist, God excepted. And in fact, Revelation assures us that angelic Beings, pure spirits not united to any material body, do exist—in what number, we have no means of imagining. Some of these spirits, by wilful rebellion against that service of God which was the purpose of their existence, have become confirmed in evil and merited God's eternal reprobation.

We now proceed to a doctrine which is the most paradoxical, perhaps the most improbable, in the whole of theology. It happens, however, to be a matter of daily experience. I mean the fact that God created a being in whom an immaterial spirit was united with a material body; a being, therefore, who should occupy a unique position of *liaison* between the two halves of Creation. The industrious quarrying of geologists has not made it clear whether there were once creatures, now extinct, which, without being human, approximated more nearly to our type than any of the brutes at present known to us. Still less have they produced any reason for supposing that the human race, as we now know it, is not a single species, but arose independently in various parts of the globe. The probabilities would in any case be against such an assumption. Revelation assures us that the whole human race is, as a matter of fact, descended from a single pair. It also tells us—what science could never prove, what our moral experience might suggest, but could never demonstrate—that this pair were created with natural gifts, and were endowed with supernatural graces, which they never bequeathed to their descendants. They were created (for example) in a state of innocence, their consciences not troubled by those suggestions of evil which now assail us. But a single fault, only less inexcusable than the fault of the rebel angels, reversed the destiny allotted to them and to their posterity. The supernatural endowments, once abused, were withdrawn thenceforward; and even our natural powers were mysteriously hampered by that duality of purpose which is our daily and humiliating experience.

The hope of eternal life was not denied to fallen man, but it was offered, now, only as the prize of a severe probation. And he must struggle against an internal enemy he found too strong for him, with only such crumbs of uncovenanted assistance as God's mercy might afford. It was not intended, in God's Providence, that this pitiful condition of things should endure as long as the world lasted. Man's fault had been foreseen, and with the fault the Remedy. God became Man in order that, dying, he might atone for our sins, and win us the graces normally necessary to the attainment of salvation.

The coming of our Lord was thus not merely a Revelation to illuminate our minds; it was also designed to rescue man from his impoverishment and his spiritual dangers. It was to win for us, not only those "actual" graces by which, since then as before, God has turned our hearts to himself, but "habitual" grace, the state of "justification," in which we are assured of God's friendship, are enabled, during our lifetime, to perform actions pleasing to him, and at our death, if we have persevered, to attain the felicity of heaven. To achieve such blessings for us, it was needful to make amends for the affront offered by the sin of our first parents to the outraged Justice of Almighty God. Although he could have accepted some lesser sacrifice, he determined to make atonement for us himself, and to make it in full measure by the perfect offering of Death.

The Second Person, then, of the Blessed Trinity became Man for our sakes. Without losing or laying aside the Divine Nature which is his by right, he united to his own Divine Person a second, human Nature, in which he was born, lived on earth, and died. Once more the stubborn tradition of the Church could not rest content until it had fortified itself within these safeguards of definition. To think of our Lord's Divine Nature as being annihilated, even temporarily, would be nonsense. A mere limitation of it, if that were thinkable, would not make it become truly human. To deny the reality of the human Nature would be false to all our evidence. Nothing less than a personal identity between the Eternal Word and Jesus of Nazareth would constitute a Divine Witness, or a Divine Victim. Every possible substitute for the received doctrine has been tried, and found wanting.

We believe that the circumstances of our Lord's coming into the world were marked by two miracles especially. In the first place, that she who was to be his Mother was endowed with that same gift of innocence which had been possessed and lost by our first parents; and that this freedom from the curse and the taint of "original sin" was bestowed upon her in the first instant of her Conception.[1] And we also believe that both in and after the Birth of our Lord she remained a pure Virgin. From her, nevertheless, our Lord took a true human Body, which was the receptacle of a true human Soul. And in this human Nature he lived and died and rose again; and at last ascended into heaven, where it still persists.

So much for his natural Body; he has also, as we believe, a supernatural Body, his Church. I am using metaphor here, in the sense which I explained at the beginning of the last chapter. In an ordinary way, when we speak of a collection of people as a "body" of people, we are using an unreal metaphor; we are speaking of a merely abstract solidarity as if it were a concrete thing. But when we speak of the Church as a supernatural Body, although we are still using metaphor, it is not an unreal metaphor; we mean that there is a real, not simply an ideal, solidarity between Christian people in virtue of their "incorporation" into Jesus Christ; and this metaphor of a "body" is the closest, the most apposite we can find. Thus the Church is not merely an institution outside ourselves or above ourselves; it is ourselves. We all know how the Englishman will rally to the appeal of his "country"; how he will lock his doors and hide his ledgers at the very mention of "the State." His prejudice against the Church is partly due to the impression that "the Church" is the spiritual analogue of "the State"; he thinks of it as a tyrannous, prying institution which is bent upon circumscribing his liberty. He does not reflect that "the Church" is also the analogue of a nation or country, but with a supernatural solidarity of its own which far transcends all merely racial ties. In this sublime creation of Providence, all that natural instinct of gregariousness which has given birth to the clan, the tribe, the nation, the party, the club, is pressed into a higher service and acquires a supernatural character. The Church is our Mother, in that her baptism gave us supernatural life; our Mistress, in that her teaching secures us from speculative error; but she is more than that: she is ourselves.

The life of grace which we live in the Church is engendered, nourished, and perfected in us by means of the Sacraments. I shall speak more of these in a later chapter; I only wish to indicate now what is the Catholic doctrine about their general character. I said in my last chapter, speaking of the "sacramentals" (holy water, blessed medals, etc.), that we regard these not as conveying grace in their own right, but as the occasions upon which God will see fit to accord us special graces, in answer to the

---

[1] It is perhaps worth observing that the doctrine of the Immaculate Conception means this and nothing else. On no subject is Protestant ignorance more inventive; Mr. Shaw, for example, in the preface of "Back to Methuselah," gravely credits us with the notion that our Lady was born of a virgin and not only she, but all her ancestresses.

prayers of his Church. Must we give the same account of the Sacraments themselves? If we do, we lessen their dignity; if we claim more for them, do we not lay ourselves open to the charge of "magic" which the rationalist levels at us?

We answer,[2] that the Sacraments themselves, with one noteworthy exception, do not "convey" grace in the sense in which a boat "conveys" its passengers, but in the sense in which a letter "conveys" information. The lines traced upon the paper do "convey" information, assuming the operation of the reader's intelligence. So the Sacraments "convey" grace, assuming that operation of Divine Power of which they are the covenanted instruments. I say the covenanted instruments; for here we do not merely trust that God will bestow grace in answer to the prayers of his Church; we know that God will bestow grace in fidelity to his own promises. As surely as God animates with a soul every child that begins to live, so surely he will implant first grace in every soul which receives baptism.

There is, as I have said, one exceptional Sacrament, the doctrine of which is not to be accounted for so easily. We believe that our Lord's human Body and Blood are actually present in the Host and in the Chalice. The explicitness of his own words has forbidden Catholics, in every age, to regard that Presence as conditioned in any way by the faith of the communicant or the worshipper. To say, or to imply, that the change effected by the words of consecration is only a change of significance is to rob our Lord's own words of their plain force. Yet it is a matter of experience that no change perceptible to the senses, whether of size, shape, colour, or texture is observable in the Sacred Elements. Are we to suppose, then, that our senses here delude us? We cannot willingly associate such deception with any work of God. It follows, then, that the *accidents* (the philosophical description of all that falls within the province of our senses) really remain unchanged. And from that it follows that the substance in which those accidents inhere must have been the thing changed; this is the last stronghold of reality. Transubstantiation is the only doctrine which will secure fidelity to tradition on one side, and the evidence of our senses on the other. The Mass, in which this momentous change is effected, is held by Catholics to be a true Sacrifice —the renewal of that Sacrifice made once for all on Calvary.

And here let it be observed, that the four most baffling mysteries of our religion—the Trinity in Unity, the Union of Natures in the Incarnation, the Real Presence in the Holy Eucharist, and the relation between Grace and Free Will—those four mysteries, over which controversy

---

[2] I am giving here one theological view, which is not the only view possible to Catholics.

has been most embittered throughout the centuries, lie there centred where human thought most fails us; they drive in their wedges (so to speak) at the weakest points in our human philosophy. Three Persons in one Substance, two Natures united in one Person—mysterious doctrine, assuredly; but is not the principle of individuation itself a mystery, over which philosophers have wrangled without attaining any measure of agreement? A change of substance which leaves the accidents unaffected —hard for us to imagine; but, then, whose imagination is not puzzled by the whole relation of universals to particulars? Grace all-powerful, yet the human will free—it sounds a paradox; yet is there not paradox already in the reaction of the free human will upon the motives which "determine" it? There is nothing inconceivable in doctrines such as those we have been citing; they are outside our experience, but not repugnant to thought. The imagination, however, naturally recoils from the contemplation of them, because their very terms plunge us into mystery.

I have mentioned the doctrine of actual grace; it would be beyond the scope of my present undertaking to expound the Catholic system, or rather systems, upon the point. It is enough to recall here that there are two notice-boards (as it were) to guide us, two general principles which secure us from misconceptions. On the one side, it is universally admitted, against the Pelagians, that nobody ever goes to heaven except through the free grace of perseverance. On the other side it is universally admitted, against the Calvinists, that nobody ever goes to hell except through his own fault.

The last paragraph reminds us of one department of Catholic theology which needs mention before this rude summary of its teaching is complete—I mean, its doctrine of the Last Things. We believe that the soul is judged immediately after its final separation from the body. If it is found to be outside God's friendship, it is condemned to eternal punishment, and a punishment which does not stop short with mere regrets, mere moral torments. If it is found in a state of grace, it is secure of its passage to heaven. But, for most of us, an expiation still remains to be made; nor do we achieve eternal happiness until we have paid the "debt" of suffering in which our sins, long ago forgiven, have involved us. It is for the lightening of this expiation that we pray when we offer our suffrages for the dead; it is for some remission of this debt, and not for any forgiveness of sins, that we hope when we try to gain an "indulgence." Beyond that lies the open vision of God, and such felicity as we may not dare to imagine. The justice of these, God's dealings, whether in general or in particular, will be fully revealed when this material order of creation ceases, and the bodies which are the connatural companions of our soul-life are restored from their corruption, a new creature in Jesus Christ.

THE MIND OF THE CHURCH

HUSTON SMITH

Huston C. Smith (1919–), after spending his first seventeen years in China, studied at Central College in Missouri, the University of California, and the University of Chicago. He has taught philosophy at the University of Denver, the University of Colorado, Washington University of St. Louis, and lately at the Massachusetts Institute of Technology. Besides his widely read The Religions of Man, *his publications include* The Purposes of Higher Education *(1955) and* The Search for America *(1959). Here he presents a historical exposition of some central doctrines of the church.*

The mind was not the first part of man to respond to Christ. As we have seen, experience came first—the experience of living in the actual presence of a life which drew from the disciples the conviction that if God were to take human form this is what he would be like. But though Christianity did not spring primarily from an act of the intellect, the mind soon found itself involved. This was inevitable. Religion always involves more than man's mind; nevertheless, being a response of his total self, the mind is never omitted. Once Christian experience had occurred, it was only a matter of time until the mind would seek to interpret this experience and Christian theology would be born. From then on the Church would be mind as well as heart.

Forced in this brief survey to choose, we shall confine ourselves to Christianity's three most distinctive tenets: the Incarnation, the Atonement, and the Trinity. From the very names of these doctrines it is apparent that our discussion must be theological, and before going further a word should be said about this discipline. Although our generation is witnessing a theological revival, the discipline is still a long way from her mediæval position as Queen of the Sciences. Modern man is more interested in ethics than in theology. Within Christianity this means that he appreciates the ethical teachings of Jesus more than the theological arguments of Paul. However little he may care to live by the Sermon on the Mount, he at least respects it. Doctrines like those we are about to discuss, on the other hand, he not only disbelieves but also finds tedi-

From Huston Smith, *The Religions of Man* (New York: Harper & Row, Publishers, 1958), pp. 285-93. Reprinted by permission.

ous or annoying. Even New Testament study in the first third of this century fell in step with this mood to the extent of trying to draw a sharp line between the "religion *of* Jesus" and "the religion *about* Jesus," between the forthright ethics of Jesus and the involved theology of Paul, between the human Jesus and the cosmic Christ, with strong insinuations that in each case the former was the nobler.

Notwithstanding the fact that even seminars can succumb to this view that the essence of religions is ethics, it is a fatal mistake; so much so, in fact, that it is scarcely too much to say that it can only arise as the result of a kind of religious blindness. For there are persons who are religiously blind just as there are those who can see nothing in painting. Such persons are not found only among skeptics and the unchurched; they number among the conventionally orthodox as well.

High religion always includes, of course, a summons to above-average morality, but it is a fatal blunder to assume that its eyes are fixed primarily on this summons. Its attention is on a vision which, almost incidentally and as a by-product sets morality in motion. A child growing up in a home has two questions. One of them is, How should I behave? The other, so much the more important that it may never be consciously asked, is, What will happen to me if I fall below my parents' expectations? What are the limits beyond which I will be rejected?

Theology is concerned with this second type of question. Its primary interest is not in how men should behave but in the character of the human situation. This being the more difficult question of the two, theology is often complicated and obscure. But the question with which it deals is basic. Moreover—and here is the paradox of the ethicist's neglect of it—the quality of man's morality depends on the answer he reaches regarding it.

When we apply these considerations to Christianity, we can understand why the New Testament did not close with the Four Gospels. These Gospels present Christ's teachings as to the way men should live. They show the perfection with which he himself exemplified this way. They are very, very great books. But they fail to tell us how we can act as Christ admonished. How can I become the kind of person who *can* take no thought for the morrow, turn the other cheek, and love without reserve?

This question was left for the other books of the New Testament to answer. We have already sketched the momentous sequence of experiences out of which they grew. Beginning with the disciples' conviction that Jesus was God and the direct experience of his love for them, they were brought to a radical realization that God loved them completely. The idea of God's love was not new, but in Christ's presence it ceased to be an idea and became a living reality. And the experience of its force was revolutionary. By loosing the strictures of guilt, fear, and self-centeredness, it enabled the disciples to love their neighbors to a degree of which they had never before been capable.

This brings us to the creeds, for these are attempts of the early Christian mind to understand conceptually the happening which had produced this change in their lives. The impact of Christ on their lives led simultaneously in two directions. Overtly it led to acts of loving kindness toward their fellow men; intellectually it led to the creeds.

We may begin with the doctrine of the Incarnation. Holding as it does that in Christ God assumed a human body, it affirms that Christ was God-Man, simultaneously both fully God and fully man. To say that such a contention is paradoxical seems a charitable way to put the matter—it looks more like a straight contradiction. If the doctrine held that Christ were half human and half divine or that he was divine in certain respects while being human in others, our minds would not balk. But such concessions are precisely what the creeds refuse to grant. In the words of the Creed of Chalcedon, Jesus Christ was "at once complete in Godhead and complete in manhood, truly God and truly man . . . of one essence with the Father as regards his Godhead, and at the same time of one essence with us as regards his manhood, in all respects like us, apart from sin."

The Church has always admitted that such assertions are anomalous to man's present understanding. The question is whether this is the last word on the matter. Actually we can ask the same question of science. There are so many findings in contemporary physics that refuse to be correlated in a single logical framework that Robert Oppenheimer has proposed a Law of Complementarity as the basic working concept in the field, meaning by this (in part) that opposing facts must be held in tension even where logically they are at odds if they can help account for phenomena observed. In more than one field, it seems, reality can be more subtle than man's logic at any given moment. Whenever we are forced to sacrifice either logic or evidence it would seem wise to stick with evidence, for this can lead to a wider logic whereas a rigid adherence to consistency can easily close the doors to ampler truth.

In suggesting that the early Christians were pressured by evidence into the logic-taxing assertion that Christ was both human and divine, we are of course speaking of religious evidence—intuitions of the soul concerning ultimate issues of existence. Such evidence cannot be presented with an obviousness that will compel assent, but if we try we can arrive at some intimation of the experimental leads the Christians were following. When in the year 325 the Emperor Constantine summoned the Council of Nicea to settle whether Christ was of the same substance as God or only of like substance, three hundred bishops and attendants came rushing in a frenzy of excitement from all over the empire, many of them with the eyeless sockets, disfigured faces, and twisted and paralyzed limbs they had gotten from Diocletian's persecution. Obviously more than mere words were at stake in such deliberations.

The Nicean decision that Christ was "of one substance with the Father" claimed both something about Jesus and something about God. Note first a claim it implied about Jesus. Among the many possible meanings the word "God" carries, none is more important than "that to which a man gives himself without reservation." In saying that Jesus was God, one thing the Church was saying is that his life provides the perfect model by which men may order their lives. Slavish imitation of details is, of course, never creative, but in proportion as Christ's love, his freedom, and the daily beauty of his life can find their authentic parallels in our own, these too approach the divine.

This much is obvious. But as we enter more deeply into the Incarnation we must be prepared for surprise. To begin with, we usually assume that its most startling claim concerns Jesus. That the son of a Jewish carpenter is to be identified with God—what could be more fantastic than this? Actually, however, the Greeks and Romans who heard the doctrine were more astounded by its other side; it was what the Incarnation asserted about God that they found disturbing. The thought that God might walk the earth in human form was not foreign to their thinking, but that he would voluntarily suffer for man's sake—this was the incredible part of the Christian claim. A God willing to proceed unmajestically, strength willing to become weakness, goodness good enough to be unmindful of its own repute, love plenteous enough to give and ask not for return—the revolutionary feature of the Christ-claim was not what it claimed for Jesus but what it claimed about God. This is why the early Christians seldom spoke of God without specifying that they were talking about "the God and Father of our Lord Jesus Christ." His relation to Christ had brought them a new understanding of his character. Christ was God's mirror; to know what God is like, the creeds were saying, look at him.

We would suppose that the difficult task confronting the Apostles would be to convince their listeners that Christ was God. Actually it proved to be harder to keep his humanity in view. So fast and completely did people accept his divinity that the first creed of the Church had to be directed almost entirely against the Marcion-sponsored, gnostic view that he was this only and not human as well.

> I believe in God the Father Almighty, Maker of heaven and earth; and in Jesus Christ our Lord, who was *conceived* by the Holy Ghost, *born* of the Virgin Mary, *suffered* under Pontius Pilate, was *crucified, dead*, and *buried*. . . .

How casually this Apostle's Creed touches on Christ's divinity! Even in the second century A.D. the point had no longer to be argued; it was assumed. The Creed's burden, carried by the words we have italicized, was to hammer home forever the fact that Christ was man as well. He *really* was born, it says; he really suffered, he really died and was buried. These incidents were not just make-believe, a sequence through which God merely gave the illusion of brushing with man's estate. Christ endured these experiences as fully as do we. He was "truly man."

It is not difficult to see why even at the cost of infinite logical awkwardness the Church insisted on Christ's humanity as well as his divinity. A bridge must touch both banks, and Christ was the bridge between God and man. To have said that Christ was man but not God would have been to deny that his life was fully *normative* and concede that other ways might be as good. To have said that he was God but not man would have been to deny that his example was fully *relevant;* it might be a realistic standard for God but not for men. To say that Christ was God is to say that the absolute love he embodied is the ultimate fact in the universe. To say that he was man as well is to insist that God's love is really love, being willing to assume the full conditions of humanity and to suffer. At each point the Christians could have relaxed their claims to relieve the strain on logic, but driven by what they had experienced, they refused to do so.

Turning to the doctrine of the Atonement, we find that its root meaning, of course, is reconciliation, the recovery of at-one-ment. Christians were convinced that Christ's life and death had effected an unparalleled *rapprochement* between God and man. In the words of Saint Paul, "God was in Christ reconciling the world unto himself." The Roman Catholic interpretation of this doctrine is couched in legal language. By voluntarily disobeying God's order not to eat of the forbidden fruit in Eden, Adam sinned. As his sin was directed squarely against God, it was of infinite proportion. Sins must be compensated for, otherwise God's justice is outraged. An infinite sin demands infinite recompense, and this could only be effected by God's vicarious assumption of our guilt and payment of the ultimate penalty it required, namely death.

Leading Protestant interpretations draw more on psychological than on legal concepts. All reconciliation presupposes an estrangement that has been overcome. In the Atonement this antecedent estrangement is between man and God, and its name is sin. It is with sin, therefore, that explication of the Atonement must begin.

Asked on his deathbed whether he had made his peace with God, Thoreau replied, "I didn't know we had quarreled." If there has been no quarrel, no reconciliation is needed; if there is no sin, no atonement is required. Christianity, however, maintains that sin is universal. In asserting this Protestant theology does not mean that everyone transgresses one or more of a bill of particulars, whether blue laws or the Ten Commandments. Kin to the word "sunder," sin in its Protestant interpretation means basically estrangement. By saying that all men are involved in it, this interpretation asserts that quite apart from any individual act of wrongdoing men are strangers to one another more than they should be. We are alienated from each other. We sense this alienation in the stab of jealousy rather than pleasure we feel in another's good fortune. We are tense in the presence of others, anxious as to the impression we shall make upon them. Our eyes are slits, narrowly squinting on ourselves instead of open to the scene of creation as a whole. We are lonely, and, as we look out upon the great unknown, immense, opaque, we are afraid, for we are alienated not only from other men but from the ground of our being which is God. All this is sin. Who can say when the human animal first fell from God's lap into this vast imbalance? The point is simply that it is here, around us, in us, through us, to the very core of our being.

The Christian view that all men are sinners is widely considered a morbid belief. Certainly it asserts a discrepancy between the actual and the ideal in man. But whether this admission is morbid depends on where the ideal is pegged. The New Testament writers who spoke of man's sin were not incompetent observers. The juices of life flowed as strongly in them as in anyone, and man's behavior struck them as embodying roughly the same proportions of good and bad others saw in it. But this, writes Paul Ramsay, "has been their misfortune, their burden and their ultimate hope: no longer to compare men with one another, or one day's deeds with another, but in all things to compare themselves first and secondly mankind in general with the glory of God and the image of perfect manhood seen in Jesus Christ."[1] In Christ the disciples had caught a new vision of what man might be, of the extent to which a love deeper than any they had known might pervade his whole life. John Wesley brings out the difference in the quality of this Christian love when, in saying that we should love our neighbor as he loves himself, he catches himself immediately and adds, "Nay, our Lord hath expressed it still more strongly, teaching us to love one another even as He hath loved us. 'As I have loved you, so love ye one another.' Now herein perceive we the love of God, in that he laid down his life for us."

Who will question that by this standard of love all men are found wanting, which is to say, are in sin, sundered from the life of love? In their encounter with Christ, however, the original Christians found this alienation removed. As we have seen, they felt close to God, loved by him, and loving him in return. As a consequence they found their fear, guilt,

---

[1] *Basic Christian Ethics* (New York: Charles Scribner's Sons, 1952), p. 291.

and selfishness—all of which are aspects of sin—overcome. And all this had been accomplished by Christ! Back of their theories as to why or how men were saved through Christ was the fact that they had experienced what it was like to *be* saved by him. The Church's theories of the Atonement likewise vary, but they too have sprung from the actual experience of life renewed by exposure to Christ.

The third crucial Christian concept is that of the Trinity. It holds that while God is fully one he is also three. The basis of this doctrine, like the two preceding ones, is contained in the New Testament. Jesus spoke of God. He also said, "The Father and I are one."[2] In addition he speaks of a third party in the Godhead: "I will ask the Father and he shall give you another Paraclete that he may abide with you for ever: the Spirit of Truth, . . . the Holy Ghost whom the Father will send in my name, he will teach you all things." In his final commission to the Apostles he collects these three persons of the Godhead into a single statement: "Go ye therefore into all the world, baptizing in the name of the Father, and of the Son, and of the Holy Ghost."

No concept of Christendom has enjoyed a greater reputation for obscurity than this. The Church itself has confessed it to be a mystery, true but beyond the reach of mind to fathom completely. Nevertheless, as nothing important in religion is entirely removed from human experience, here again it is possible to suggest by analogy something of what the doctrine involves. Some of the analogies that have been proposed are crudely physical (that water can retain its chemical identity while in the distinct states of ice, liquid, and steam); others are subtly psychological. Three that are closer to the latter variety may be mentioned.

Every instance of seeing is a real unity. Nevertheless three distinguishable aspects are involved: the object seen, the act of vision, and the mental interpretation. Similar triune patterns can be discovered in numerous other domains of human experience. Apparently the idea of three-in-one, whatever difficulties it may throw up for the understanding, is not foreign to our experience.

In the religious sphere man confronts God in three places, in the splendor and order of nature, in the historical person of Christ, and in the depth of his own heart. These are equally God; nevertheless they

---

[2] This does not contradict our earlier statement that we cannot derive from the Gospels a clear idea of who Jesus thought himself to be, for it remained for the Church to crystallize what these words mean. The vehement controversies in early Christendom concerning Christ's nature is clear proof that the meaning of his words is not unambiguous, to say nothing of whether he himself actually said all the things that are ascribed to him in the Gospels. A significant number of Christians believe that, as forty years intervened between his death and the first Gospel, some of his sayings represent convictions of the early church which were so fully believed that it became assumed that Jesus must have said them.

are distinct. They are, respectively, God the Father, God the Son, and God the Holy Spirit.

Dorothy Sayres' play, *The Zeal of Thy House*, proposes the analogy of the artist's creative act. First there is the Creative Idea, effortless and serene, beholding the entire work in an instance, a complete and timeless whole; this is the image of the Father. Next, not in time but in enumeration, there is the Creative Energy, working out the Idea in space and time with sweat and passion; this is the image of God incarnate, the Son, the Divine Word. Finally there is the Creative Power, the response the work elicits from the lively soul that perceives it; this is the image of the in-dwelling Spirit. "And these three are one, each equally in itself the whole work, whereof none can exist without other: and this is the image of the Trinity."

From the standpoint of Christian orthodoxy, it is important not to water down the Trinity by interpreting it as referring to three roles of a single person, as a man may simultaneously be a son, a husband, and a father. As the Athanasian Creed put the matter, "We worship one God in Trinity, and Trinity in Unity, neither confounding the persons nor dividing the Substance." Oneness is needed to insure simplicity and wholeness in man's devotion—there can be no compromise with monotheism. Distinctness is needed, from man's perspective, to do justice to the distinct ways in which this oneness comes to him. But before this, distinctness is required by the Godhead itself. For God is love, and love is meaningless except between persons. "The Godhead," writes a contemporary Roman Catholic theologian, "is a society of three divine persons, knowing and loving each other so entirely that not merely can none exist without the others, but in some mysterious way each *is* what the other is. In the deepest communion of man and woman, each desires to surrender so completely to the other as to be absorbed in that other. But in man, even the closest intimacy remains partial and incomplete. In the Godhead, the separate persons possess one nature. Each person remains himself, yet there is nothing of the divine essence that is not fully shared by each."[3]

SUGGESTED BOOKS

Aulén, Gustaf, *The Faith of the Christian Church*, second English edition, trans. Eric H. Wahlstrom. Philadelphia: The Muhlenberg Press, 1960. A widely used textbook in theology by a famous Swedish theologian.

Brunner, Emil, *Our Faith*, trans. John W. Rilling. New York: Charles Scribner's Sons, 1954. A compendium of Christian beliefs dedicated to the author's sons.

DeWolf, L. Harold, *A Theology of the Living Church*, second edition. New

---

[3] Thomas Corbishley, *Roman Catholicism* (London: Hutchinson House, 1950), pp. 40-41.

York: Harper & Row, Publishers, 1960. A textbook on Christian doctrine from a liberal perspective chastened by criticism of older liberalism.

Henry, Carl F. H., ed., *Contemporary Evangelical Thought*. New York: Harper & Row, Publishers, 1957. Papers by ten contributors discussing recent work by evangelical Protestant writers in various fields of religious study.

Hessert, Paul, *Introduction to Christianity*. Englewood Cliffs, N.J.: Prentice-Hall, Inc., 1958. A useful textbook on Christian doctrine based on the Bible conceived of as revelation but not as infallibly inspired.

Knox, Ronald A., *The Creed in Slow Motion*. New York: Sheed & Ward, 1949. A Catholic account of Christian doctrine, in a popular vein and following the Apostles' Creed.

Machen, J. Gresham, *Christianity and Liberalism*. New York: The Macmillan Company, 1923. An attack on liberalism by a leading Fundamentalist of the first half of the century.

Van Dusen, Henry P., ed., *The Christian Answer*. New York: Charles Scribner's Sons, 1945. Essays by Tillich, T. M. Greene, G. F. Thomas, E. E. Aubrey, and John Knox interpreting the Christian message for modern times.

Williams, Daniel D., *What Present-day Theologians are Thinking*, revised edition. New York: Harper & Row, Publishers, 1959. A survey for the layman of the recent theological renaissance and its varied thought on the issues of Biblical authority, ethics, Christ, and the church.

XVI · OTHER RELIGIONS

In this concluding chapter we shall deal with the problem of the relationship between Christianity and other religions. In recent years this problem has come increasingly to the foreground of Christian thought. This appears to be due mainly to the greater contacts with other into direct contact with people of other faiths. And on the other hand, modern transportation and communication have brought more Christians into direct contact with people of other faiths. And on the other hand, even when there is no first-hand acquaintance, the quantity of recent scholarly work on the world's religions has made it much more possible for people of one faith to have some understanding of other faiths. When we add to these facts the widespread concern about relativism today, it is not hard to see why this problem looms so large. More and more theologians are finding that they must deal with it.

The problem is a serious one because, as a problem in religion, it is not just about abstract differences, but about differences between people as well. This makes it a human problem as well as an intellectual one.

> The problem of religious diversity is a human problem, common to us all. It is becoming an incorporated, internal part of the fact of being a Christian that other intelligent, devout, and righteous men are Muslims, Hindus, Buddhists. . . . Every man is personally involved in all man's diversity. Man here is studying one of the most profound, one of the most perplexing, one of the potentially most explosive aspects of his own modern situation. We all are studying the fact that our human community is divided within itself religiously.[1]

To put the problem in this light means that there are more questions involved than might at first seem to be the case. It is not enough simply to set forth some abstractly possible relationships between Christianity and other religions and then pick one of them.[2] Such a procedure may confuse philosophical questions concerning truth content, historical questions concerning interpenetration, practical questions concerning tolerance and understanding, and theological questions concerning the presuppositions and aim of missions. In our approach we shall attempt to keep these several sorts of questions distinguished, recognizing however that they mutually involve one another.

TRUTH RELATIONSHIPS

Let us begin with the question of truth and bracket for the moment other considerations. The question is: how is the truth which Christians claim and confess related to the truth-claims of other religions? At this abstract level several alternatives can readily be seen.

One alternative is to hold that Christianity and other religions are all equally true. Or it might be held that they are all equally untrue because they are all completely symbolic. The first of these alternatives is like the view often attributed to Hindus; the second is like the view of many secular relativists. Neither alternative can be satisfactory to Christians. When beliefs conflict as notoriously as do religious beliefs, it is logically impossible to say that they are all equivalent in truth value. Moreover, Christians believe that in Christ there is the revealing source from which ultimate truth about God and the possibility of reconciliation and new life may be gained. This conviction rules out, for Christians, both of the alternatives mentioned so far.

Another alternative would be that the Christian doctrines are completely true and the doctrines of other religions are completely false. That is, Christianity has all the truth in religion and other faiths have none of it. Leaving aside the uncharitableness of this view, which of course is not the criterion in matters of truth, the view seems itself to be plainly false. For example, if the belief in a supreme, personal God is true, as Christians maintain, then since this belief is found in several religions there is obviously truth in those religions as well, even if we then go on and cite some differences in conception. The same point could be made with respect to other beliefs. In short, because of a certain degree of similarity in some beliefs held by both Christianity and other religions, it is not logically possible to say that Christianity has all the truth and other religions have none at all.

Still another alternative would be to make a distinction between higher and lower religion, or some similar distinction, and then to say that Christianity is an example of the higher type, other examples to be found in several other religions. This analysis has some merit for some purposes. But if it is taken as the entire answer to the question, then it really denies the uniqueness of Christ and the Christian revelation and is out of keeping with the meaning of historical Christianity.

If we cannot say that all religions are equally true or equally untrue, or that Christianity has all the truth and other faiths none, or that Christianity is one example among others of a higher religiosity, the only reasonable alternative is (and this has been the historic Christian view as well) that

Christian truth is the fulfillment or completion of the truth that is found in other religions. Thus if we think of some of the typical Christian beliefs discussed in Chapter XV, it may be said that some of these are held in a somewhat comparable way by other religions, some of them are held partially but not completely, some of them are held in an anticipatory form, and so forth. The truth to which Christians testify may then be viewed as bringing to a culmination these partial and incomplete apprehensions of religious truth to be found universally.

Some Christians, from a commendably zealous evangelical fervor for Christian doctrines, do not like the term fulfillment to describe the relation between Christianity and other religions. They think it suggests that all religions are going in the same direction, whereas some of them may be going in opposite directions, or that Christianity is only a little bit different from other religions, one rung higher on the same ladder, for instance. Such a view, they think, does not do justice to the uniqueness of the Christian revelation and the judgment which it brings on man's unrevealed natural religion.

But if we confine ourselves to the strictly logical consideration of propositional truth, it is difficult to see what other concept besides fulfillment or completion is possible, unless one tries to defend one of the implausible alternatives mentioned first. At the plane of logical analysis alone there seems to be, if one affirms Christian truth at all, no other acceptable view.

Perhaps an illustration will help to make the idea of logical fulfillment more clear. In working out his great synthesis of thought St. Thomas Aquinas drew heavily from the philosophy of Aristotle. Many of Aristotle's propositions he regarded as perfectly sound and others as showing usable insights. Nevertheless the Aristotelian system was reconstructed, added to, and superseded by St. Thomas in the light of Christian ideas. Thomistic philosophy can therefore be seen, in one of its aspects, as the fulfillment or logical completion of certain basic ideas in Aristotle. Thomists would say the same thing, in varying degrees, about the relation between Thomism and other philosophers before and after St. Thomas.

We are not, of course, defending Thomistic philosophy. But the illustration serves to suggest how Christian religious truth may be seen as fulfilling, logically speaking, the truths grasped in other religions. The truth relationship of fulfillment would not apply in the same way in detail to every religion, for there are some which are obviously closer to Christianity than others. But the general type of relationship could be said to be similar.

Perhaps the objection to the idea of fulfillment comes from confusing the logical concept of it with other sorts of fulfillment that might not apply. Let us therefore go beyond logical analysis, which, though necessary, is only a limited dimension of religious interpretation.

HISTORICAL AND EXISTENTIAL FULFILLMENT

Another meaning of fulfillment is that of historical culmination. It means bringing to actual fruition or empirical completion the aspirations and tendencies present in a historical movement.

In this sense the only religion of which Christianity could be said to be the direct fulfillment, from the Christian viewpoint, is Judaism, since Judaism is the historical tradition out of which Christianity grew. Jesus said that he came to fulfill the law and the prophets,[3] and this has been taken by Christians as one basis for saying that Christianity is the fulfillment of Judaism, or, more accurately, that Christ is the fulfillment of the Jewish hope. But in the same sense it sounds odd to say that Christianity is the historical fulfillment of Hinduism or Buddhism, with which it did not have anything like the historical connections that it had with Judaism. It sounds even more odd to say that Christianity is the historical fulfillment of Islam or Sikhism, which began long after Christianity was established.

Now it may be the case that, through the great amount of interchange among religions in modern times, historical developments could be such that both Christians and the adherents of some other religion would find it proper to say that Christianity is the historical fulfillment of that religion's aspirations. But this speculative possibility certainly does not justify one in saying that, in the same sense in which Christianity is seen as the historical fulfillment of Judaism, it is also the historical fulfillment of every other religion. And the reason is the difference in actual historical connections involved. The theological explanation for this difference is the Christian belief that the Jewish tradition was chosen by God as a special revealing tradition and a preparation for Christ.

There is, however, another meaning of fulfillment which makes it appropriate to speak of Christ as the fulfillment of man's religion generally. This may be called existential fulfillment. It means the fulfillment of man's basic need for reconciliation with God and his neighbor.

In this sense the Christian conviction is that God as revealed in Christ is the true fulfillment of man's need, the real source of his longed-for and much talked-of authentic existence. This being so, it is not the most fitting way of speaking to speak of existential fulfillment as a relationship between particular religions, i.e., the Christian religion and other religions. It is rather a relationship between God and man. The religion of Christianity testifies, sometimes faithfully, sometimes not, to that relationship. Thus if Christian belief is true, Christ, as the bringer of a new humanity, is the fulfillment of the spiritual needs of all men. Some of those men may be

in religions which help them toward this end, some of them may be in
religions which do not, and some of them may be in no religion at all. The
appeal however is to every man.

The reason why it is not fitting, in the sense of existential fulfillment, to
speak indiscriminately of Christianity as the fulfillment of other religions
is, as we have said, that such fulfillment is a God-man relationship and
not one between historical phenomena. But a secondary reason is that all
religions apparently are not moving in the same direction. Thus if a
religion is moving in antithesis to Christ and the practice of Christian love,
then Christianity comes not as a fulfillment but as a condemnation of that
tendency. Also when Christianity itself fails to live up to its Christian
faith, it is subject to the same judgment. The idea of fulfillment must be
counterbalanced by the idea of judgment, and Christian faith may represent either or both of these in relation to other religions and even in
relation to Christianity itself.

In actuality, then, no simple, uniform theory about Christianity as fulfillment or judgment of other religions is possible because of the plurality
of paths and interests that religions follow. We have suggested that all
religion arises from man's yearning for reconciliation. But in the concrete
existence of persons and cultures this aspiration develops into a wide
variety of forms. Thus religions may ask different questions, seek different
answers, and hence arrive at different principles and policies. While
Christianity asks, "How is man saved from sin?" Buddhism asks, "How
can one overcome the suffering in the world?" While Christianity is concerned with the meaning of the Cross, Confucianism is concerned with
bringing about harmony in social life. While a Christian pastor may
preach that divine grace is open to all, a Hindu yogi may prescribe
exercises for achieving one's own liberation from the wheel of rebirth.

What this means is that whether Christian faith is seen by Christians as
the existential fulfillment or as the judgment of other religions would
have to be decided not by a general rule but by careful attention to
similarities and differences in individual cases. Obviously Christianity and
Judaism are very close together—so much so that Reinhold Niebuhr has
maintained that Christian missions to Judaism are futile and should cease,
for Jews can find God sufficiently within their own Biblical tradition;[4]
and this despite the fact that Niebuhr believes Christian faith to be the
fulfillment of Judaism. In other cases the situation might be more ambiguous. In philosophical Taoism, for example, there is a reaching out for
an absolute principle in the universe, the Tao, and a turning away, in the
virtue of *wu-wei*, from self-salvation through meritorious action so that
the power of the Tao can flow in and through one's life. A Christian
might say that in one sense these aspirations are moving in the wrong
direction and must be so judged by Christian faith, but in another sense

they are moving in the right direction and are existentially fulfilled when the absolute principle is identified as the one personal God of the universe and the power for new life is identified as the grace of God as shown to man in Christ. And this would not be unlike St. Paul's attitude when he told the Athenians that the unknown god they worshipped was really the God of Biblical tradition.

In summary, God, whom Christians believe to have been revealed in Christ, in reconciling the world to himself is the true fulfillment of the spiritual needs of all men alike. In so far as Christianity is a faithful witness of this Christian faith, it is in varying degrees and ways both the fulfillment and the judgment of other religions. But it too is subject to the same criterion, the standard of Christ.

THE MEANING OF TOLERANCE

So far our discussion has been at a somewhat theoretical level. But there are also practical questions involved in the problem. One of these is the question of tolerance. Critics have argued that if Christianity claims a unique truth, as distinguished from claiming to be but one illustration of an identical truth common to all or at least many religions, there is no basis for tolerance in Christian thought. From the Orient comes this reaction: "The general impression which Christianity produces in the minds of the non-Christian and particularly the Easterner remains that of dogmatic religion with the faith and claim that Christ is the only Son of God."[5] Anyone who takes Christianity seriously must acknowledge the truth in this statement, although he might not be happy with such a formulation of it. But when this point is admitted, does it mean that Christianity must be dogmatic and without tolerance? Let us see.

Perhaps it would be best to begin with an account of what tolerance is, or rather what it should be. For Christians tolerance is part and parcel of the requirements of Christian love. But what, more specifically, does such love involve in this application as distinguished from other applications?

A good starting point is the meaning of tolerance in ordinary usage, that of permitting or allowing something, often called toleration. This is the notion which many people scorn as leading to a condescending attitude, a begrudging permission. They even dislike the term tolerance. But if we can overcome the language barrier, the idea involved is a fundamental one in genuine tolerance, even though it is negative and incomplete. To be permitted to think and speak freely, to be allowed to believe and act as one sees fit, to have the privilege of finding a way of life for oneself without interference—these are basic human rights, and where tolerance includes them we have gone a long way toward justice in society.

Still, from a Christian point of view, tolerance does include more than respectful noninterference. Perhaps we can see something more of what is included if we take note of a danger which might result from the limited connotation of tolerance as permission. The danger is that we might become so absorbed in respecting other people's right to have opinions that we lose interest in opinions themselves. We may champion the cause of free opinion and end up by not having a thought of our own. Even worse, we may come to think that any opinion is as good as any other, one principle as true as any other. John C. Bennett has stated this problem for Christians succinctly:

> The problem is this: how can we take seriously this attitude of openness to those who are outside the Christian circle without allowing our own commitment and the mission of the church to be undercut by a creeping relativism that may cause us to lose our sense of the claims of Christ or to accept complacently the religious *status quo* in the world?[6]

Because of this danger we should add as a second demand of tolerance the ceaseless endeavor to clarify and cultivate our own convictions. This is necessary for our own integrity and hence our very capacity to show love and tolerance. But it is also necessary in order that, knowing the meaning of conviction in our own lives, we may also know something of the meaning of conviction in other people's lives and thereby appreciate them better. Tolerance is on quicksand when it rests on vague, sentimental feelings about something that does not matter to us. Tolerance is best understood and best practiced when all the parties concerned have their own reasoned convictions and yet show the acceptance and respect due to everyone else.

A third requirement immediately suggests itself. What has been said so far might be practiced by a person who remained relatively aloof from other people's religions. But genuine tolerance demands a more positive, outgoing response. It involves not only permitting other opinions, not only thinking out our own convictions; it means also an active interest in learning about other people and their religious ideas and customs. It is with this searching, inquisitive desire to understand that we move definitely beyond negative tolerance. Moreover, there must be a willingness to consider other world-views seriously *as convictions* and to be receptive to the best cases presented for them. We do Christian faith little good by sealing it off in a safety deposit box to remain forever unchallenged by other living faiths. And even when our convictions, having been tried and tested, remain stable or are even strengthened by the interchange, there is still the demand of affirming such truth as we can in other religions, appreciating the insights and ways of saying things that we find acceptable, and benefiting wherever possible from their wisdom and lore.

Finally, it would seem that tolerance is one area where the golden rule does apply. We ought to show the same respect toward persons holding convictions opposed to ours as we expect from them. Or again, we ought to forgive those who offend us by being flippant about our convictions, just as we hope they would forgive us if we showed the same ill-humored tendency.

These are points that we would make in trying to spell out more explicitly the meaning of Christian love in the matter of tolerance. Now the question is whether there is a valid theological basis for this conception within Christian belief—or, in other words, whether Christian ethics is tolerant but Christian theology is narrow and intolerant.

EXCLUSION AND INCLUSION

We must begin by noting that every conviction has both an inclusive and an exclusive element. To believe anything definite at all is to include some affirmations in our acceptance and to exclude others. This is true of all convictions, not just Christian ones. For example, if a person believes that all religions are equally true, he may be including a great deal in his belief, but he is also excluding the conviction that one religion is the logical fulfillment of others. You can be all-inclusive in your thinking, including everything, only if you believe in nothing and stand for nothing.

What this polarity of inclusion and exclusion means is that we must give serious thought to exclusion as well as inclusion—not in a spirit of exclusiveness but as a matter of plain necessity. The problem of tolerance is often asked in terms of its application to inclusion alone: how can we include in our thought and action other people and their beliefs? But we need really to ask two questions: (1) how do we exclude other people and their beliefs where we must, and (2) how do we include other people and their beliefs where we can? We shall attempt to state some theological principles on each of these questions, and in so doing justify the practice of tolerance as defined above.

THE TOLERANCE OF EXCLUSION. The first Christian principle that is relevant to the tolerance of exclusion is the doctrine of God. According to Christian teaching, as expressed in I John 4:8, God is love. This means that the ultimate power in the universe is love. From this conviction Christians see that their attempt to reconcile opposition and conflict in the world must involve the same love. Thus is their obligation rooted in the doctrine of God. Jesus even enjoined his followers to love their enemies and do good to those who hated them. Christian exclusion must therefore be of a supremely moral character. There should be no room for condescension, narrow-mindedness, holier-than-thou attitudes, or hate. Other persons must always be affirmed, even if their beliefs and practices are not.

A second principle that is relevant is the doctrine of man's finitude. Since all human beings are finite and all human interpretations fallible, we can never take our own statements of what we hold as true to be final or adopt the attitude that we have nothing to learn from others. Christian exclusion must therefore be a self-critical exclusion. We cannot settle on fixed and irrevocable formulas for excluding other people and beliefs. Instead we must subject our policies to constant review, even if we decide after review not to change them. Furthermore, being finite and fallible, we ought in addition to being self-critical, to welcome external criticism from others. Our task is then to weigh this criticism and incorporate its truth wherever possible. Of course Christians will not surrender their convictions merely to accommodate criticism. It would be a weird kind of tolerance that would expect, for the sake of compatibility, a person to admit that his convictions are false when he believes them to be true and to assert that other people's convictions are true when he believes them to be false. He may admit that he might be wrong and that others might be right; but this is quite a different thing from surrendering convictions for the sake of accommodating criticism. But Christian exclusion does not stifle off criticism, but rather receives it graciously, weighs it with care, and utilizes it where possible. All this would seem to be required because of man's finitude.

A third principle that supports a highly ethical tolerance of exclusion is the Protestant doctrine of separation of church and state. Protestants, and some Catholics, justify in principle the permanent independence of state authority from ecclesiastical, and thereby found the right of private conviction on constitutional guarantees. This means that Christian exclusion involves a tolerance which does not depend solely on the moral goodness of individuals or the good auspices of a church hierarchy, both of which have been known to wane drastically in the heat of controversy and the desire for ascendency. Thus the love which is demanded in Christian exclusion is made more concrete by embodiment in the justice of democracy and law through which the right to differ is preserved.

Though exclusion is necessary, then, Christians must practice this, as required by these doctrines, with charity, with self-criticism and openness to external criticism, and with efforts toward democratic justice. But convictions also have an inclusive element that requires tolerance. How can Christians include other people and their beliefs?

THE TOLERANCE OF INCLUSION. One way in which other people and their convictions are included by Christians in tolerance is through the doctrine of creation. Christianity believes that all men are created equal in rights and in worth. It also believes that they are created equal in spiritual opportunity. That is, the religious fulfillment, the new life of the spirit, the salvation, that is open to any is open to all. The spiritual destiny which God envisions for human selfhood is relevant to all. Universal inclusion in this sense is quite compatible with the faith that Christ is a special revelation and that Christians have a special mission to perform.

Another principle under which Christianity includes other people and their religion is the doctrine of general revelation. God does not reveal himself only to a few selected people but to whoever is receptive. He makes himself known to non-Christians as well as to Christians. Though Christians believe that Christ is the central and unique revelation of God, this does not mean that revelation does not occur in some sense in other religions, nor does it abrogate the truths discoverable therefrom. If Christianity does not blandly say that all religions are the same, neither does it say that they are devoid of all truth. Truth is truth wherever it is found, and there are some truths, though not all, which can be found in many contexts. Wherever man is receptive, there God is always to some extent accessible and knowable.

Thirdly, the doctrine of Christ may be so interpreted as to have an inclusive aspect in relation to non-Christians and their convictions. Christ, as the second person of the Trinity, is not identical with the man Jesus but was incarnated in him. Being an eternal part of God's nature, Christ is not confined to any particular time or place. He can therefore be present in events and in the lives of persons outside the Christian tradition. Reinhold Niebuhr has spoken of a "hidden Christ" operative in human history at points not described explicitly as Christian.[7] Of course non-Christians would not explain these Christ-like actions and persons in Christian language; but it is a consistent extension of Christian thought to think of Christ and his spirit as not limited to Christian history alone.

Much of what has been said here about these principles governing Christian inclusion may be found in these summary words of Dean Bennett:

> Our final word of confession may be:
> The God who has come to us in Christ is the only God there is. He touches the hearts of men living under all of the religious systems. He is sometimes present in the "yes" that men say to the things which we affirm as Christians and he is sometimes present in the "no" that must be said to us when in our lives we hide the very truth that is given to us. He loves the whole world and the Christ whom he sent to save the world is the true light that enlightens every man.[8]

To summarize our discussion of tolerance: we began by suggesting a conception of Christian tolerance. We then saw that the practice of tolerance requires both an exclusion and an inclusion of other people and their convictions. So we have now indicated some theological doctrines which show how tolerance in both of its applications must be of a reconciling, ethical character. Briefly stated, in the tolerance of exclusion, the doctrines of God, of man's finitude, and of the separation of church and state require, respectively, love, humility, and justice toward those whom we exclude; and in the tolerance of inclusion the doctrines of creation, of general revelation, and of Christ, teach, respectively, the equality of all men before God, the openness of God to all men, and the possibility of Christ-like qualities outside the Christian religion. Our conclusion is that tolerance, as part of Christian charity and as specifically elaborated above, is justified theologically as well as on the basis of Christian ethics alone. There is no split between theological dogma and Christian love.

SOME IMPLICATIONS

We have discussed the theoretical relationship between Christianity and other religions in terms of logical, historical, and existential fulfillment, and the practical relationship in terms of the meaning and rationale of tolerance. It may be well in conclusion to touch briefly on several other questions which inevitably arise in connection with this problem.

One of these questions concerns the doctrine that there is no salvation outside the church, *extra ecclesia non salus*. Can this be reasonably maintained? It should be stated first of all that no Christian is able to pronounce final judgment on the destiny of any person or group. That is a relationship between man and God, not man and man. Furthermore, where the doctrine is accepted by Christians, the term church is certainly not restricted to the organized historical institution of Christianity, as if no one outside the organized church could be saved. Christians do not believe that the organized church is the exclusive vehicle of divine grace. What the doctrine generally means is that salvation signifies reconciliation with God through the spirit of Christ, and the church is the spiritual fellowship of such reconciled persons. It is the church in this sense that is necessary. Whether its ultimate composition is to be particular or universal is a further question, not decidable by man. But at least Christians believe that the new life that is possible through Christ is willed by God for all men alike.

Another question has to do with the empirical future of Christianity in relation to other religions. What should Christianity work toward in the light of the plurality of religons?

A number of answers to this question have been given. Perhaps the most famous classification of these is that of William E. Hocking, who found three main competing answers.[9] The first of these is radical displacement, where Christianity would totally supplant other religions because they are regarded as thoroughly false and harmful. The second is syncretism, where Christianity would blend with other religions into a world synthesis. The third is reconception, where each religion would remain unique but would reconceive itself so as to perfect its own potentialities.

As we think over these alternatives, none of them seems to be an especially happy choice from a Christian point of view. Reconception seems to come down to an intensification of the *status quo*. Syncretism would virtually eliminate the Christian claim about God, Christ, and man's reconciliation. Radical displacement is based on an unappreciative and faulty estimate of other religions. We should therefore turn back to what the Christian mission is. This mission is defined not by reference to world religions but by reference to existing persons. It is to bring all persons into reconciliation with God through the spirit of Christ. Wherever this happens a person will feel that his prior non-Christian religion has been displaced or fulfilled. And if this should happen generally, there would be a general displacement or fulfillment. In this sense Christianity works toward displacement, but it is not a displacement which denies or ignores the strengths and values in other religions. It is a displacement of logical and existential fulfillment rather than radical displacement.

Now when we ask specifically whether it is a Christian obligation to bring all people into the organized church, we are probably asking an academic question in view of the opposition to Christianity and the strength of other religions. In any case Christians are not obligated to do the impossible but only to witness to the truth that they have been given to believe. Employing the distinction between Evangelization and Christianization,[10] we may say that the obligation of missions is not the Christianization of the world but the evangelization of the world. That is, the aim is to make Christ known and to manifest his spirit.

Finally, it might be asked what all this implies for the individual Christian follower in his attitude toward other religions. One thing that may be said on this question is that the foregoing analysis suggests a twofold obligation, each side of which is made increasingly difficult in modern times through its tension with the other. The twofold obligation is greater conviction and greater openness. On the one hand, there is the obligation of maintaining the uniqueness and distinctiveness of the Christian faith. If one is going to accept Christianity at all, there is no use doing so in a watered-down form which does not correspond to historic tradition and which makes of it an easy-going ethics or a carbon copy of religiosity to be found almost anywhere. If it is the case that Christ is the reconciler of all men, the true light that enlightens every man, then this should be affirmed and its truth extended. On the other hand, there is the obligation of showing greater receptivity to other religions—to understand them, to learn from them, to incorporate their insights, to judge only from knowledge, to appreciate their values, to acknowledge their strengths, to affirm any propositions they hold that are equivalent to ours. With the ever-increasing contacts among religions little purpose is served either by haphazard convictions coupled with gushy openness or by adamant convictions coupled with belligerent broadsides. To couple firm conviction with appreciative openness may be as difficult a thing as it is rare. But there is this possibility also: that the two obligations, as necessary supplements to each other, may each be strengthened by their very tension.

THE MISSIONARY APPROACH

HENDRIK KRAEMER

Hendrik Kraemer (1888–) is a Dutch theologian much concerned with the practical and missionary aspects of Christian life. He studied at Leyden, Hamburg, Paris, and Cairo. He has taught at Leyden, Geneva, Union Theological Seminary, and Princeton Theological Seminary, and has spent much time in the Far East. His books include Religion and the Christian Faith *(1956),* A Theology of the Laity *(1959), and* World Cultures and World Religions *(1960). Here he presents the evangelical insistence upon the finality of Christian revelation and the complete opposition to any form of syncretism.*

In the preceding chapters we have seen in what kind of world Christianity is confronting the great non-Christian religions, and what are the different moods in which the missionary spirit of the Christian Church is trying to express itself. Further, the essential nature of Christianity, according to what we have called the prophetic religion of Biblical realism, has been outlined; and a sketch of the elementary forces and factors which condition the past and the present of the non-Christian religions has been given. Now we have reached the point where the proper subject of this book has to be discussed. As the satisfactory treatment of a problem is always dependent on the place and rank it occupies in the complex whole

From H. Kraemer, *The Christian Message in a Non-Christian World,* third edition (Grand Rapids: Kregel Publications, 1956), pp. 284-99. Reprinted by permission.

of problems to which it belongs, some stocktaking and drawing of conclusions is advisable in order to know where we stand.

The experience, then, of a hundred and fifty years of modern missions and of modern history in general, and of a hundred and fifty years of assiduous investigation into the huge complexes of spiritual life that are represented in the living non-Christian religions, has taught us some precious lessons which the missionary enterprise cannot afford to forget if it will be up-to-date in the deepest sense of this word.

The first lesson is this. The impression with which modern missions started their career, namely, that this universe of living non-Christian religions was adequately conceived by taking it to be a vast, degrading and decaying section of the spiritual life of mankind, steeped in darkness and error, has turned out to be utterly erroneous. The annals of modern missions testify to the natural vitality and tenacious strength as well as the inertia of these religions. They are the product of man's great efforts in the field of religion, and it must be affirmed with all possible clearness that the primitive apprehension of existence, from which the great naturalist religions sprang, has proved to be particularly creative both for good and ill in the matter of religion.

A very chastening and salutary lesson has also been that it is no longer possible to identify a so-called "Christian" civilization with Christianity. Empirical, historical Christianity, although its fundamental position is very different, has also to be viewed largely as a specimen of human effort in the field of religion, and therefore to be brought into line with the other religions as expressions of human spiritual life. The many striking similarities between historical Christianity and the other religions, evident in the startling correspondences in psychological experience and theological expression, are therefore not at all disquieting facts which need to be explained away, but the best evidences by which the unity of man as a religious being is demonstrated. Or to put it in other words, all the types of religion in the world and their variegated manifestations—the naturalist, the mystical, the moralist, etc.—have found their sublime and their more degraded expression in all religions, empirical Christianity included.

The significant difference between historical Christianity and the other religions lies in another direction than that of grade or richness of religious experience. Within the other religions the naturalist, the mystical, the moralist and other types and variations of religion are, to take only their most lofty embodiments, the development of apprehensions inherent in and fundamental to these religions; in historical Christianity they are always somehow misapprehensions of the prophetic religion of Biblical realism. The high and pure quality of religious and moral life that occurs in other religions as well as in historical Christianity is, we have now learnt, quite natural. It is evidence of the high capacity man has shown in the course of history in every branch of life, and consequently also in that of religion. The many appalling and abject phenomena in the non-Christian religions and also in historical Christianity are also quite natural, not, of course, in the sense of praiseworthy and unobjectionable, but in that of being the expression of the other side of man's double nature.

In this light it becomes clear that the two opposite attitudes customary in missionary circles are equally wrong and unrealistic. Some speak grudgingly or fault-findingly about the heights of the non-Christian religions and are inclined to lay all stress on their horrible depths. Others assiduously emphasize the heights of these religions but remain largely silent about the dark sides. Both, therefore, have a distorted view of these religions, not so much because they unduly vituperate or unduly praise them (although they certainly do so), but because they have a distorted view of man, whose nature is angelic and satanic. We must honestly recognize the angel as well as the demon in man, wherever we find him, in Christendom, in Hinduism, in China or anywhere else. All superiority-feeling is ridiculous from the standpoint of cultural history; and from the special religious standpoint implied in the Gospel which gives to a real believer in Christ the status of a forgiven sinner, it is in direct antagonism to the rudiments of essential Christianity.

Another lesson that modern missions must take very seriously in order not to foster misguided expectations or illusions, is the solid but never duly realized fact that these great non-Christian religions are to be understood in the first place as complex civilizations and social structures. This has enormous consequences for the way in which the modern missionary enterprise has to estimate the human possibilities and limitations of its peculiar modes of activity and appeal. All rash prophesying (such as has been so profusely practised in missionary publications) about the approaching destruction of such religions is naive.

In the first place social structures are often unusually tenacious, and, in the second place, the decline or the survival of such religions is, just because they are civilizations and social structures, more dependent on other (political, social, cultural) than purely religious factors. The term "religious" in connection with these religions is nearly always used in the specially "religious" sense of a life of conscious fellowship with God or of direct religious experience. It cannot be too often said that, when speaking in terms of life-systems, religion is a complex cultural, political and social entity, and the word "religious" therefore has primarily a social connotation. Modern missions, by principle and by necessity, work only through moral and religious persuasion and therefore they cannot and will not bring to bear upon the situation other influences than those that are strictly religious. The political, the social and the cultural factors, which stand largely outside the scope of missionary activity (although it is, of course, not without influence upon them), are therefore of greater significance for the negative or positive development of these religions as social institutions than the various instruments of missionary impact.

This alone is sufficient to demonstrate that the problem of the secularization of the East cannot, from the missionary point of view, be handled in the simple categories of rejection or approval. *If* the non-Christian religions are to be overthrown, as the phrase has it, it is not likely to happen as the result of the direct efforts of missions to replace these religions by Christianity, but as the outcome of a definite concatenation of these indirect factors, which is not in human hands. The highly important conclusion to which this leads is that Christianity's eventually becoming the dominant religion instead of the other religions cannot be represented as the simple result of the contest betwen truth and error, as was done so floridly in the militarist missionary rhetoric of the past, for the history of the disappearance of religions and their substitution by others teaches unambiguously that many political and cultural factors are of decisive importance in bringing this result about.

Further, the aim of all missionary work has therefore to be the clear and persevering witness in words and acts to Christian truth and life and the building up of living Christian communities, trustfully leaving to God what He will do with the work of His servants. This aim brings with it an enormous liberation of the mind from all agitated thinking and acting, and a purely religious attitude of lifting the eyes to the mountains whence help comes. Modern missions strive for a purely religious revolution through moral and religious persuasion. The modern world-situation which divorces religion from the other spheres of life expresses itself also in the principles of religious neutrality. This is a typically Christian product, because the peculiar sensitiveness that attaches to it derives from the fact that religion is assumed to be an inner conviction and not conformity to a standardized mode of group-life. Thus, Christianity will not find itself in the situation in which it was after Constantine and in the Middle Ages, when the overthrow of Roman-Greek paganism and the annihilation of the different forms of West European heathenism were mainly the result of political and cultural measures and revolutions, which aimed at the victory of Chrisitianity as a *social* phenomenon. Modern missions can never aim at this, because the concrete situation as well as the purely religious tenor of its activity excludes it. The modern missionary enterprise may therefore be compared to David, who in his combat with Goliath put aside the armour, the helmet and the sword of Saul, because he could "not move with these," and trusted to the "sling in his hand" (1 Sam. xvii. 39). The sling in its hand is the clear and persevering witness in words and acts to Christian truth and life and the building up of living Christian communities.

Still another lesson, far-reaching in its effect on the whole character and temperament of our missionary thinking, planning and expectation, is connected with the well-known fact that, through the witness and the activities of missions, the religious, moral and social outlook in the non-Christian world has to a considerable degree become permeated and leavened by "Christian" ideas, ideals and standards. In our description of the present condition of the non-Christian religions we have often had occasion to allude to this fact. Many ideas and motives that can historically be proved to be fruits from the tree of Christianity are incorporated in the modern expressions of the ancient religions. Christian modes of worship, or religious education, nurture and propaganda are freely used and assimilated. It is not exaggeration, or Christian self-complacency, but simply stating a fact to say that the process of purification and revivification which within the last hundred years has come over all great non-Christian religions is to a great extent due to the invigorating example of Christianity as represented by the missionary enterprise. The homage that in the modernization of the non-Christian religions is paid to the ethical and social note in religious life has been learnt from Christianity, rooted as it is in the prophetic religion of the Kingdom of holiness and righteousness, in the Kingdom of God. This *indirect* influence of Christian missions on the religious and on the whole social and cultural, and by virtue of that, even on the political, evolution of the modern East is really enormous. Latourette uses the term "mass modification" for this permeative process. Many people, inside and outside missionary circles, see in this indirect influence the greatest and most important result of the missionary enterprise. Even many friends of missions conceive this permeation to be either the kind of result with which missions ought gladly to be satisfied (only, if possible, in a still more accentuated form) or take it as an embryonic form of Christianity that will in the long run develop into a well-made, living body of functioning Christian life and conviction.

This appreciation of the process of permeation is, it seems, erroneous, because from the standpoint of theology and from that of daily experience with the non-Christian religions it is naive. It takes dreams, created by a noble type of humanistic idealism, as realities. Theologically speaking it is naive, because it tacitly assumes that conscious and exclusive loyalty to Christ and to what His life, His words and His work mean, is the natural outgrowth of idealistic attitudes and ideas. This tacit assumption is in glaring contradiction with the prophetic religion of Biblical realism which is (as has been shown) the "crisis" of all religions, philosophies, idealisms and world-views, none excepted. It is in no less glaring contrast with the actual facts as daily experience with the non-Christian religions presents them to us. Everyone who is familiar with conditions in the East knows that many non-Christian peoples have no objection whatever to recognizing Christ as one of the highest religious figures humanity has produced. To give Him an honourable place in the different pantheons does not meet with serious opposition. But to recognize Him and what He represents as the Lord of life, to whom supreme loyalty is due, is resolutely refused and rejected even by those who revere Him. Gandhi is a very clear example of this.

And what other reason than the inner conviction that He is *the* Truth and the sole One who is entitled to claim supreme loyalty from everyone, will induce anyone to risk the painful experiment of abandoning his ancestral religion with its many precious social and emotional bonds? This is especially true in the sphere of the naturalist religions that are by their syncretistic nature entirely bent on absorption, annexation and assimilation. By their relativism they have taught their adherents to give every religion and form of worship its "due" place, and have inculcated in them an aversion from making a definite, irrevocable choice. Moreover, a little sociological insight makes it evident that permeation, however valuable it may be culturally (and it certainly is), never can make this permeating religion the dominant moulder of religious and moral life. That is possible only when this religion is, *socially* speaking, the officially recognized and dominant spiritual force, or when it is, not a disembodied set of ideas and ideals that lend a definite colouring to the already existing apprehensions, but a clear-cut, self-conscious religious entity. Willoughby in his *The Soul of the Bantu* justly remarks that, despite all legitimate criticism of institutional Christianity, it is impossible to keep the essence of our religion alive unless it works through some human institution. Only if one of the alternatives mentioned above is realized in a civilization or in a people can one reasonably say that this religion is an established religion that has a really determinative influence in such a culture. In all other cases one can only speak of it as a more or less influential factor within a people and a civilization where a different religion or life-apprehension is the tacitly recognized spiritual authority.

On theological, on religious and on sociological grounds it is therefore vain and illegitimate to expect that the remarkable permeation of the East with ideals and ideas that are, historically speaking, derived from Christianity will naturally grow in the long run into a self-conscious Christian Church, for it is a mistake to conceive this permeative reality as an embryonic Christianity. One might even go further and state that it has, to a great extent, as experience teaches, rather the effect of stiffening the mind against religious change than of predisposing the mind in its favour. The great non-Christian religons have utilized the permeation of Christian ideas and ideals for their own internal and external strengthening. Movements such as the Brahmo Samaj have not proved stepping-stones to Christianity, as was originally expected. This stiffening reassertion in the process of assimilative change is quite natural. Religions all over the world are not pondering philosophers, who try disinterestedly to make out where truth lies; they are huge social bodies (comprising life-patterns, ideas, attitudes, volitions and strong emotions), that, as in the case of all social bodies, instinctively strive for self-assertion and self-perpetuation. Men like Gandhi, Tagore and Radhakrishnan, who evince each in his own peculiar way a strong permeation with ideals and ideas deriving from Christianity, are no "unbaptized Christians," as F. Heiler terms the two first-mentioned on account of the Christian elements in their thought-world, but have rather become invigorated Hindus by the process, with an unmistakable element of irritation in their attitude towards Christianity. There are elements in the concrete situations which make much of this curious blend of assimilation and irritation intelligible, but even if these elements did not exist, this blend is not at all strange when the peculiar character of Christianity, in the sense of Biblical realism, is kept in mind.

To *decide* for Christ and the world He stands for implies a break with one's religious past, whether this past is "Christian" in the qualified sense of the word or non-Christian. This break is something radically different from taking a sympathetic attitude towards His personality and teaching. It is even unfair and contradictory to call men like Gandhi and Tagore "unbaptized Christians" as Heiler does, because this interpretation of these two men by Heiler is given in order to accentuate the superb qualifications which Hinduism (in his opinion) possesses for forming a religious synthesis with Christianity. It suggests, however, the inferiority of Hinduism and the superiority of Christianity, and demonstrates that Heiler is still unconsciously haunted by the idea of superiority and inferiority in the relation of Christianity to the other religions. As a matter of fact, in the case of Gandhi and Tagore, however drastically their activist attitude towards life may differ from Hinduism as we know it, and however emancipated many of their leading ideas may be from dominant Hindu conceptions, the crucial fact is that they consciously keep to Hinduism as their recognized spiritual home, and even announce their new interpretation as being *for the sake of Hinduism*.

These few remarks about the mass-modification as caused by permeation are given in order to provide a warning against vain expectations and wrong missionary directives. They are not given to minimize the great importance of this cultural permeative process and the share missions had and have in it. This permeative process will go on in the future, probably to an even greater extent, and it is highly desirable that missions and the Christian Churches should continue to partake in it, not for the sake of permeation, but for the sake of revealing the true nature of the Christian

Church as a body that releases refreshing forces of light and life because of obedience to Christ and His Spirit.[1]

This discussion, as to how far the value of permeation goes, leads us on to another important conclusion from all that has been said in the preceding chapters. This conclusion is the more important because it furnishes the fundamental background for all thinking on adaptation and indigenization.

The conclusion we have in view is that the only valid motive and purpose of missions is and alone can be to call men and peoples to confront themselves with God's acts of revelation and salvation for man and the world as presented in Biblical realism, and to build up a community of those who have surrendered themselves to faith in and loving service of Jesus Christ. Why is this the only valid motive and purpose? Because only on the basis of this apostolic attitude and consciousness is the missionary enterprise really lastingly tenable and reasonable. All other motives and purposes may, according to circumstances, be of greater or less secondary importance and value, but if they take the place of this primary motive and purpose, mission work as such is no really tenable activity and must in the long run die from its lack of valid foundation.

All these other motives and purposes labour under an overt or covert relativistic subjectivism. To infuse Christian ideals and ideas into another people or religion or civilization and to do that in a sympathetic, generous spirit; to instill into the emerging world culture the blessings of an enlightened, free and reverent spirit; to seek with men everywhere a more adequate fulfillment of the "divine possibilities" of personal and social life; to strive after the spiritual unity of mankind—these are all very noble, altruistic and humane ideals, which have their own peculiar value and necessity, *provided they are kept in their place*. If they usurp the place of the apostolic motive, which is the alone valid and tenable one, they transform the Christian Church into a goodwill agency for the diffusion of refined and cultured idealism, which has lost all intrinsic relation with the central apostolic consciousness that we are to be witnesses to God and His revelational dealing with man and the world.

This, however, is not the only weak side of this standpoint. Another of its fatal weaknesses, though not always apparent on the surface, is that this subjectivist idealism can claim no right whatever to insist upon the value of its exertions in the face of other religions and civilizations. What will it answer if this foreign religious civilization says: I do not want your help and your permeations, despite all the nobility and charitableness of spirit in which you offer that help, for I have my own spiritual resources to draw upon and want to become saved according to my own fashion? There is, from the standpoint of secondary motives and purposes that

---

[1] In Chapter X, we will return to this subject.

have been falsely converted into primary ones, no valid answer to this argument.

There is no valid answer possible, not even if one takes the line that Jesus Christ is the only way by which men can reach a *satisfying* experience of God, or if one starts from the idea that the central concern of Christian missions is to be found in "the highest spiritual interests of mankind." Why not? Because—it is rather paradoxical to state this—these standpoints, that are born out of abhorrence of absolutist views and that seek the test of a religion not in an *a priori* certainty of its truth, but in the pragmatic demonstration of its worth, are themselves absolutisms. For, as *in their opinion* Jesus Christ provides men with the most satisfying experience of God, and missions are concerned with the good of "humanity," they think that they have the right to intrude upon the religious civilizations of the East. What will they answer if these civilizations and peoples say: "Our experience of God is as satisfying as yours. How do you know that yours is more satisfying? We have our own ideas about our highest spiritual interests." There is no answer from this standpoint because, although it is born of a deep and honest loyalty to Christ, it remains too subjectivistic.

The only valid and indestructible foundation of missions is the apostolic consciousness of joyful obedience to God's Will as manifested in the revelation in Christ, and our gratitude for this divine gift. All questions of superiority in the field of cultural achievement or psychological religious experience are irrelevant in this context. No pretensions whatever, derived from presumably superior ethical or religious or cultural elements, have anything to do with the apostolic claim and obligation of Christianity. Its only foundation is the objective and plain reality of God's revelation in Christ, and therefore, speaking fundamentally, it is quite immaterial whether the world asks for it or not. The only way to become wholly purged from all kinds of superiority-feeling is not the direct pursuit of a sympathetic or generous spirit towards other cultural experiences, however praiseworthy and valuable this may be, but the radically apostolic attitude; for this presupposes the not less radical humility that issues from the fact that all men of all civilizations (the "Christian" included) are, in the light of God's revelation, forlorn sinners and rebellious children of God.

"Orthodox" as well as "liberal" Christianity must therefore cease to try to effect the purification of the missionary atmosphere by quarrelling about the invalidity or validity of non-Christian religious experience and achievement; for the great significance of this experience and achievement is a solid fact. Orthodox and liberal Christians must both enter the purifying flames of the apostolic vision which confronts all civilizations and religions with God's revelation in Christ, and then discovers their common solidarity in forlornness and their being equally called to deliverance. In other words, in this case as in all other cases, our starting-point must be the dynamic theocentric world of Biblical realism, which is the direct antithesis to the static intellectualist conception of revelation so widely current, and also to the naive evolutionary conception of Christianity as a movement of growing truth. The only thing that being a Christian can mean is to make continuously renewed discoveries in the dynamic world of God's revelation and so grow gradually to the stature of full-grown men in Christ (cf. Eph. iv. 13).

In this light it is undeniable that the widely prevalent aversion to evangelization, to proselytism, to conversion, and the recommendation of "sharing religious experience" or of social service as the only valid missionary methods, are the offspring of a fundamental religious confusion. It is clear as daylight that once the cardinal fact is grasped that the apostolic theocentric apprehension is the only valid Christian apprehension, the Christian Church has not only the right but also the duty to take conversion and evangelization as prime necessities for mankind. To regard proselytizing, evangelization and conversion as "invading and violating the sacredness of personality" is built on a misinterpretation of religion as primarily the purveyor of psychological experience, which misinterpretation has lost all consciousness of the prophetic character of the Christian revelation. Nock in his *Conversion* explains very lucidly that the pagan religions in the Roman Empire did not really know the concept "conversion," because naturalist religions cannot conceive conversion in its real sense. The concept "conversion" occurs only in its intense and essential meaning in the realm of the prophetic religions. Jesus started His public career with the call to conversion, for the Kingdom cannot be grasped except through conversion. The concept of conversion in its essential meaning can only grow in the prophetic religion of the Christian revelation, because this is the sole religion that knows the absolute difference between good and evil. The inherent relativism of naturalist religions prevents them from having a radical conception of conversion.

The emphasis laid lately on "sharing religious experience" and on social service in substitution for evangelization as the most valid missionary approach, issues from the same religious confusion. "Sharing" labours under a conception of religion that takes it primarily as a psychological, cultural and immament value. Making social service the main and most legitimate missionary approach is the direct fruit of a pragmatist evaluation of religion. In both cases the real basis of missions and the prophetic and apostolic character of Christianity are destroyed, although in reality this destruction will remain concealed for a certain period. Or to put it in other words, in both cases the revelational basis of Christianity is implicitly, though often unconsciously, denied. The very urgent necessity that religion must find expression in the right quality of life—the thesis on which social service as the main missionary motive and approach is based, and which is in itself a right and indispensable proposition—never can wipe out the fact that in the field of religion we have only this alternative: either the paramount thing in a religion is that it conveys objective truth without which life has no real meaning, or its truth-quality is of secondary or minor importance and we remain forever caught in the chains of relativism, golden as they sometimes appear to be.

Evangelization, proselytism and conversion, then, belong to the core of the missionary enterprise. The real difficulties that exist in regard to these three concepts and attitudes in relation to the missionary approach are of quite a different order, and even apart from the fundamentally religious confusion we have treated already, make it intelligible why so much confusion and so much opposition have arisen around them. In the first place, the concrete forms in which the emphasis on and the occupation with evangelization, proselytism and conversion often exhibit themselves, in many cases make the impression of crude propaganda and intrusion upon the inner life of a fellow-man. A deal of what goes by the name of evangelization or proselytism or conversion is not to be identified with apostolic and prophetic obedience and witness, but often looks more like the mishandling of another man's spiritual life, although it springs from the conviction of missionary obligation. The protest of "liberal" Christians against this is often justified, for its attitude is often too oblivious of the radical humility and sensitivity that are included in the prophetic and apostolic consciousness of being pointers to God's revelation, just as the dread of evangelization felt by "liberal" Christians is often born of a complete, though unintentional, sacrifice of the revelational character of Christianity. A great deal of the "orthodox" missionary attitude needs as much purification and regeneration in the cleansing waters of Biblical realism as the "liberal" attitude does.

In the second place, another important reason why the problem of conversion and proselytism is so vehemently discussed at the present time is not at all religious in the strict sense of the word. It is a result of the fact that all over the world the great non-Christian religious systems, like many States, are in a stage of re-assertive consolidation that reveals itself in a hyperbolic sentiment of group-solidarity. We explained in the preceding chapter that Islam as a religion is this group-solidarity incarnate, and that this is the reason why it offers such a stubborn resistance to all missionary effort. With the great naturalist non-Christian religions the situation is somewhat different, but essentially the same. They also, as was pointed out in the fifth chapter, are religiously sanctioned group-solidarities.[2] Because of their naturalist character they do not understand the radical sense in which conversion is meant in Christianity. Moreover, in the modern deluge they are in a state of defensive consolidation and self-assertion, which intensifies the inherent tendency towards stressing the necessity of religious conformity as an expression of group-loyalty. This is the real background of the protest against conversion and proselytism which is so specially strong in India. That it is led by a man of such deep moral and religious sensitivity as Gandhi is one of the puzzling features of the situation in this puzzling country. Knowing this background the missionary enterprise need not be perturbed by it, but must strike its roots deeper in the apostolic prophetic soil of Biblical realism.

"Sharing religious experience" and "social service" are wrong and misleading as definitions of the real missionary motive and purpose; but as methods of approach and expression of the Christian mind they are valid and very valuable. Apart from the fundamental religious confusion that has been treated already there are other reasons which can account for the particular emphasis at present laid on these two attitudes. There is the haunting dread of all superiority-feeling; the delicate and justified desire to have real human contact on the footing of spiritual give and take; the partly-intelligible aversion from "dogmatic" religion and many forms of too one-sided stress on preaching, which is often in reality mere annoying interference. Another reason is the noble insistence on the necessity to demonstrate in practice that to be a Christian means a new quality of life, strengthened by the contemporary situation in which Christianity is tested as to its practical moral and social value. All these elements have co-operated in making the emphasis on sharing of religious experience and social service intelligible and partly justified. Every good missionary who knows something of the apostolic and prophetic temperament of Biblical realism knows about sharing religious experience, and even loves it; likewise he sees the great necessity of social service and will be devoted to it. To raise these methods of approach and expression of the Christian and missionary mind to the status of essential motive and purpose is a different matter. When to this is added the rejection of the validity of its apostolic and prophetic inspiration we have, fundamentally speaking, nothing else than the suicide of missions, though in practice they may continue for a certain period of time and even accomplish much work of noble quality.

---

[2] It ought to be said that the Christian Churches are always prone to succumb to the same danger.

THE PLURALITY OF RELIGIONS: BLEMISH OR BLESSING?

ARNOLD TOYNBEE

Arnold J. Toynbee (1889–), the noted British historian, studied at Oxford and at the British Archaeological School in Athens. Early in his career he taught at Oxford and held a number of government posts. But he spent the greater part of his career as Research Professor of International History at the University of London and as Director of Studies at the Royal Institute of International Affairs, retiring in 1955. He is best known for his ten-volume A Study of History. *Among his other works are* Civilization on Trial *(1948),* An Historian's Approach to Religion *(1956), and* Christianity Among the Religions of the World *(1957). In this selection he advocates the desirability of plurality of religions because of their complementary contributions to religious truth.*

One can imagine, for instance, a Buddhist submitting that it is in the context of Buddhist faith that the problem of suffering can be best understood—and not just understood, but grappled with and solved. It can be solved, I believe he would say, by the radical cure of plucking out all desire and casting it from one; and this, he would almost certainly go on to say, is not just an unpractical counsel of perfection. He would submit that a practicable way of attaining nirvana has been opened up for mankind by the Buddha's personal example and by the course of strenuous spiritual exercises that he has prescribed for other aspirants to this spiritual goal.

A Zoroastrian might submit that it is in the context of Zoroastrian faith that the goodness of God is best vindicated. Zoroastrianism, he would say, has not flinched from facing the problem of evil. It has recognized frankly that it is impossible to reconcile divine goodness with divine omnipotence, and it has held fast to its belief in God's goodness without seeking to evade the logical consequence—which is that God, being wholly good, cannot be all-powerful as well.

Conversely, a Hindu might submit that it is in the context of Hindu

From Arnold J. Toynbee, "The Plurality of Religions: Blemish or Blessing?" *Christianity and Crisis*, Vol. XXI, No. 16 (October 2, 1961), pp. 164-66. Reprinted by permission of Arnold J. Toynbee and *Christianity and Crisis*.

faith that the omnipotence of God is best vindicated. Like the Zoroastrian, the Hindu would say that his own religion has not flinched from facing the problem of evil. It has recognized frankly that it is impossible to reconcile divine omnipotence with divine goodness, and it has held fast to its belief in God's omnipotence without seeking to evade the logical consequence—which is, in Hinduism's view, that God, being omnipotent, must be the responsible author of the evil as well as of the good that is manifestly present in the Universe.

A Jew or a Muslim might submit that it is in the context of Jewish or Muslim faith that the oneness of God is best vindicated. It is vindicated here without equivocation. The Muslim might add that this unequivocal stand on the supreme issue of the oneness of God carries with it, as its corollary, a likewise unequivocal stand on the issue of the One God's human creatures' relations with each other. Islam is one of a number of religions that proclaim, in principle, the equality of all men and their consequent duty to treat each other as brothers, but a Muslim would probably claim that Muslims come the nearest to practicing what their religion preaches, and would go on to make the further claim that this is a direct consequence of the purity of Islamic monotheism.

A RECIPROCAL CONCESSION

I am unlikely to have succeeded in putting the positions of these non-Christian religions in exactly the form in which their own exponents would like to see them put; and I may not have singled out the points that are of the greatest importance in their eyes. I am venturing for a moment to act as their amateur spokesman in order to make a point of my own. My point is that, if a Christian asks non-Christians to accept the claim that certain important truths can be seen best in the context of Christian faith, he will think twice before refusing to make a reciprocal concession to similar claims when these are put forward on the other religions' behalf.

Let us assume that the adherents of the major religions agree with each other that each faith does provide the best context for seeing certain truths that they all consider to be important. This would lead to the conclusion that the different religions, between them, reveal a greater measure of spiritual truth and provide ampler means of salvation than can be found in any one of them, even at its widest gamut. This is not to say that all these religions are of equal spiritual value. Their gamuts may differ in range, and this perhaps greatly. There may be more truth and more salvation in some of them than in others. No doubt, each religion will appear to its own adherents to have the widest gamut of all. If it did not, they would have abandoned it and adopted another.

This natural and perhaps inevitable partiality towards one's own religion is also naturally and inevitably subjective. The adherents of the several religions are parties to their own respective cases and are consequently disqualified from passing judgment on the relative values of their own and the other faiths. They cannot transcend their own partiality and, therefore, cannot expect their neighbors to transcend theirs. This is not possible, and it also is not called for. All that is called for is a recognition, on all sides, that some truths are seen best, and that some means of salvation are found most effectively, in each of the religions and that, in this realm of spiritual values, no single religion has a monopoly.

If this conclusion were to be accepted as common ground, it would follow that the plurality of religions is not one of the blemishes of the universe but is, on the contrary, a boon for mankind. It is a boon because every one of the spiritual contributions made by the different religions has proved to be of spiritual value for some human beings, and indeed for large numbers of them. This means that if any one of these religions had never made its appearance, or if it were ever to become extinct, the means of illumination and the means of grace accessible to mankind would be, by that much, poorer than they are at present. This is not to say that some single one of the several existing religions may not be capable of providing this or that particular human soul with all the illumination and all the grace that this soul is capable of receiving.

While it is true that the gamut of each religion is limited, it is also true that the gamut of each soul is limited, too. But the gamuts of all souls are not identical with each other, any more than the gamuts of all religions are. There are different types of individual human character, and the plurality of religions is a boon in so far as it provides spiritual food for a range of types that cannot all find their food in any single religion, however wide this religion's gamut may be by comparison with the gamuts of others.

Innate differences of individual character are surely realities. They have been recognized and studied by a long series of investigators. Theophrastus was probably not the first of these, and Jung will surely not have been the last. It seems more likely that the study of human nature is still in its infancy. But perhaps it has already advanced far enough for us to be able to discern that every human being is something more than a standard sample of our common human nature and is, at the same time, something less than a completely unique personality. Besides being both of these things, he is also a representative of one out of a limited number of types of character. As far as we know, this fund of character-types is a common possession of the human race at all times and places. All the types are always to be met with in all races, civilizations, religions and nations. In the field of religion, this or that character-type will find its best spiritual food in something that is best given in this or that particular religious faith.

A WIDER RANGE OF CHOICE

Till quite recently, most people's religious allegiance has been imposed upon them, in advance, by a spiritually irrelevant accident. Most people have inherited, as a matter of course, the prevalent religion of the society into which they have happened to be born—and one's place and date of birth are the most arbitrary, as well as the most decisive, of all the accidents in life. One's inheritance of one's ancestral religion has normally been a matter of course because, so far, most human beings have lived in small insulated social and cultural compartments in which there has rarely been a local plurality of religions and, therefore, rarely an opportunity of choosing one's religion for oneself instead of inheriting it automatically from one's parents and teachers.

There have, however, been some exceptional social milieux—for instance the Persian, Roman, Chinese and other would-be world-states—in which a number of alternative religions have been at people's disposal to choose from. This situation, which has been exceptional hitherto, seems likely to become normal in our age, in which technology has succeeded in "annihilating distance." In this age of the airplane, telegraph, telephone, radio and television, the cultural heritage of every branch of the human race is coming to be accessible to every other branch.

In this new situation, every individual will have a greater opportunity than has normally been open to people in the past for choosing—when he reaches the age of discretion—the particular religion that seems to best meet his particular spiritual needs. These needs will vary according to the chooser's character-type and individual personality. Already within Western Christendom, it is becoming more and more usual for people who have been brought up as Roman Catholics, as Protestants of this or that denomination, as agnostics or as atheists to choose for themselves, when grown-up, some other religion or philosophy than the one in which they have happened to be reared.

It is already possible to foresee a time in which the range of choice will have been widened still further, and this not only in Western Christendom. One can foresee Western Christians choosing to become Eastern Christians, Muslims, Buddhists or Hindus, and can also foresee Eastern Christians and Buddhists and Hindus and Muslims choosing to become Protestants or Roman Catholics.

In taking account of this prospect, we have, of course, to bear in mind the truth that in the making of any choice the emotions, as well as the intellect, are always involved. Our emotions place practical limits on the range of choice that the intellect opens up in theory. One's feelings toward the religion in which one has been brought up as a child are bound to be different from one's feelings toward a religion that one deliberately adopts, as a substitute, at some later stage of life. If one clings to one's ancestral religion, the motive is unlikely to be simply an intellectual conviction that it has a higher spiritual value than another; an affection inspired by familiarity is also likely to weigh heavily in the balance. On the other hand, if one does wrench oneself away from one's ancestral religion, the emotional effort that this will demand is likely to transform affection into hostility. An ex-Roman Catholic, for instance, is notoriously apt to become not just a non-Catholic, but an anti-clerical. It is psychologically difficult to "get inside" a religion in which one has not been brought up as a child.

A religion that one has adopted in adult life out of intellectual conviction will not so easily win one's heart. On the other hand, if it does win it, this emotional tour de force is likely to inspire one with something of that zeal of the convert that animated, for example, St. Paul and St. Augustine. Not only does conversion have limiting conditions, but when, in spite of these, it is achieved, it brings with it new problems of its own. All the same, the possibility of choice between one's ancestral religion and a number of others is surely a spiritual boon for any human soul, considering how great the chances are that its ancestral religion will not happen to be the one that best meets its spiritual needs.

GOD'S DELIBERATE WORK

Judaism, Christianity and Islam hold in common an illogical belief. They believe that God is *both* wholly good *and* omnipotent. The illogicality of this belief is unacceptable to Hindus and to Zoroastrians. But the logical untenability of the Judaic religions' position does not necessarily put them out of court, for here we may be at the limits of the capacity of the human reason; and the reason cannot guarantee that there are not more things in heaven and earth than those that can be formulated in logical terms.

Suppose that Zoroastrianism and Hinduism agree, on this ground, to suspend their adverse logical verdict and to let the Judaic religions' illogical account of God's character pass as being non-disprovable in religion's trans-rational dimension of spiritual insight. This Judaic vision of what is God's nature seems bound to lead, if given the green light, to the conclusion that the plurality of religions has been the deliberate work of God's omnipotence acting under the inspiration of his goodness. God's goodness must mean mercy, compassion and love where he is dealing with his creatures; and this divine love, compassion and mercy must embrace all God's creatures without discrimination. God must care equally for all his human creatures in virtue of his goodness; and, if so, he must have used his omnipotence to provide for the spiritual illumination and salvation of human beings of every type of character. He must have provided for this at all times and places since man's pre-human ancestors were transfigured into human beings—transfigured, that is to say, into creatures that are spiritually capable, and also spiritually in need, of receiving light and of attaining salvation.

SUGGESTED BOOKS

Anderson, Gerald H., ed., *The Theology of the Christian Mission.* New York: McGraw-Hill Book Company, Inc., 1961. Essays on the Biblical basis, the history, and the theory of missions and the relation between Christianity and non-Christian religion.

Bouquet, A. C., *The Christian Faith and the Non-Christian Religions.* New York: Harper & Row, Publishers, 1958. Historical studies of the varying Christian views of non-Christian religion.

Ebersole, Mark C., *Christian Faith and Man's Religion.* New York: Thomas Y. Crowell Company, 1961. Analyses of Fromm, Bonhoeffer, Schleiermacher, Barth, and Niebuhr on the title topic.

Herberg, Will, *Protestant-Catholic-Jew.* Garden City, N.Y.: Doubleday & Company, Inc., 1955. A sociological study and theological critique of the changing pattern of religion in America.

Hocking, William E., *The Coming World Civilization.* New York: Harper & Row, Publishers, 1956. A newer statement of the author's advocacy of reconception within each religion rather than a synthesis of religions or a displacement of other religions by Christianity.

Kraemer, Hendrik, *World Cultures and World Religions.* Philadelphia: The Westminster Press, 1961. A study of the mutual impact of Eastern and Western religions and a declaration of the distinctiveness of Christianity in relation to Eastern thought.

Perry, Edmund, *The Gospel in Dispute.* Garden City, N.Y.: Doubleday & Company, Inc., 1958. A forthright assertion of the uniqueness of Christianity and the implications of this for the missionary contacts with rival missionary religions.

Schweitzer, Albert, *Christianity and the Religions of the World,* trans. Joanna Powers. London: George Allen & Unwin, Ltd., 1923. Argues that Christianity is superior to other world religions because of its essentially ethical character.

Toynbee, Arnold J., *Christianity among the Religions of the World.* New York: Charles Scribner's Sons, 1957. Four lectures presenting Toynbee's view of a plurality of acceptable religious paths.

FOOTNOTES

INTRODUCTION

1. C. J. Ducasse, *A Philosophical Scrutiny of Religion* (New York: The Ronald Press Company, 1953), pp. 13, 16.

2. Paul Tillich, *Systematic Theology* (Chicago: University of Chicago Press, 1951), I, 28.

3. Systematic theology is also called dogmatic theology, where "dogmatic" is simply the adjectival form of dogma, meaning doctrine, and does not refer to a dogmatic attitude in the emotional sense.

4. See, for example, the admirable book by Huston Smith, *The Religions of Man* (New York: Harper & Row, Publishers, 1958).

5. William Hordern, *A Layman's Guide to Protestant Theology* (New York: The Macmillan Co., 1955), chap. IX.

6. William Hordern, *The Case for a New Reformation Theology* (Philadelphia: The Westminster Press, 1959).

7. "Are there Tests of Revelation?" *Theology Today*, XII, No. 1 (April, 1955), 82-83. Most of the article is reprinted at the end of Chapter II.

8. This subject is discussed briefly in "The Culturally Conditioned Christian," *Religion in Life*, XXX, No. 2 (Spring, 1961), 279-84.

I. THE NATURE OF RELIGION

1. For a typical example see Bertrand Russell, *Why I am not a Christian, and Other Essays on Religion and Related Subjects*, ed. Paul Edwards (New York: Simon and Schuster, Inc., 1957).

2. A. C. Bouquet, *Comparative Religion*, fourth edition (London: Penguin Books, 1953), p. 15.

3. Bouquet, *Comparative Religion*.

4. *Webster's New International Dictionary of the English Language*, second edition, 1955.

5. A critique of some of these theories may be found in E. O. James, *History of Religions* (New York: Harper & Row, Publishers, 1957), chap. I.

6. Sigmund Freud, *The Future of an Illusion*, trans. W. D. Robson-Scott, Anchor Books edition (Garden City, N.Y.: Doubleday & Company, Inc., 1957), pp. 28-29. Reprinted by permission of Liveright Publishing Corporation.

7. See his article included at the end of this chapter.

8. *Literature and Dogma* (New York: The Macmillan Co., 1924), p. 18.

9. Some typical definitions are discussed by Winston L. King, *Introduction to Religion* (New York: Harper & Row, Publishers, 1954), chap. VI.

10. The kind of religion that seems to be based on feelings of natural harmony, rather than on responses to disrupted situations in need of mending, is still confronted by potential disruptions that must be avoided by ultimate commitments and endeavors concerning the existing reconciliation. Such religion is therefore covered by the definition.

11. This phrase of Prof. Tillich is a captivating one; but when taken by itself as a definition of religion it tends to suggest, despite Prof. Tillich's own disavowal, only one aspect of religion, the subjective.

12. In this connection the very title of one of Peter Bertocci's books is informative: *Religion as Creative Insecurity* (New York: Association Press, 1958).

II. TRUTH IN RELIGION

1. The value quality mentioned seems to attach more to the verb form of the word, *e.g.*, "I believe in him," than it does to the noun form, *e.g.*, "I stated a belief."

2. "Statement" and "proposition" are here used synonymously, although writers on logic would doubtless wish to distinguish them.

3. Those interested in studying the pragmatists' account of truth might begin with the initial presentation of it in William James, *Pragmatism* (New York: Longmans, Green & Co., Inc., 1907).

4. See Sören Kierkegaard, *Concluding Unscientific Postscript*, trans. David F. Swenson and Walter Lowrie (Princeton: Princeton University Press, 1941).

5. Sarvepalli Radhakrishnan, "Religion and Philosophy," *The Hibbert Journal*, Vol. 20 (1921), quoted in *The Examined Life*, ed. Troy Wilson Organ (Boston: Houghton Mifflin Company, 1956), 199-200.

6. John Baillie, *Our Knowledge of God* (New York: Charles Scribner's Sons, 1939), p. 16. Reprinted by permission of Charles Scribner's Sons, and Oxford University Press.

7. This task is called apologetics in traditional terminology. Those who would eliminate it are left with either irrationalism, which is absurd, or rational philosophy, which seldom concerns itself with particular religions and their particular tenets.

8. See Chapter IV for a fuller discussion of this topic.

III. FAITH

1. For a discussion of faith in the Middle Ages see the *Encyclopedia of Religion and Ethics*, ed. James Hastings (New York: Charles Scribner's Sons, 1912), V 690-91.

2. Erich Fromm, *Man for Himself* (New York: Holt, Rinehart & Winston, Inc., 1947), pp. 197-210.

3. Martin Buber, *Two Types of Faith*, trans. Norman P. Goldhawk (London: Routledge & Kegan Paul, Ltd., 1951).

4. For a criticism of the notion that faith is a factor in science see John Hick, *Faith and Knowledge* (Ithaca: Cornell University Press, 1957), pp. 66-69.

5. "Preface to St. Paul's Epistle to the Romans," trans. Charles E. Hay, in *Great Voices of the Reformation*, ed. Harry Emerson Fosdick (New York: Modern Library Inc., 1952), p. 122.

6. These four possibilities are elaborated by John A. Hutchison in *Faith, Reason, and Existence* (New York: Oxford University Press, 1956), pp. 93-99.

7. But for a view that gives faith the priority even in philosophy see Hutchison, *Faith, Reason, and Existence*, pp. 27-29.

8. For example, Jacques Maritain, *An Introduction to Philosophy*, trans. E. I. Watkin (New York: Sheed & Ward, n.d.), chap. VII.

9. For example, Peter A. Bertocci, *Introduction to the Philosophy of Religion* (Englewood Cliffs, N.J.: Prentice-Hall, Inc., 1951), pp. 92ff.

IV. RELIGION AND SCIENCE

1. Polykarp Kusch, "Scientists and Laymen," *The Key Reporter*, XXVI, No. 4 (Summer, 1961), 2. Copyright © 1961, The United Chapters of Phi Beta Kappa. Reprinted by permission.

2. A popular account of scientific method may be found in James B. Conant, *Science and Common Sense* (New Haven: Yale University Press, 1951), and a more technical discussion in Irving M. Copi, *Introduction to Logic*, second edition (New York: The Macmillan Co., 1961), Part Three.

3. A standard reference on this aspect of the subject is Andrew Dickson White, *A History of the Warfare of Science with Theology in Christendom*, 2 vols. (New York: Appleton-Century-Crofts, 1896).

4. Historical religions like Judaism and Christianity, however, which are based on the significance of certain historical events, obviously could not go all the way with this statement; for if these fundamental events could be shown not to have occurred, the character of the religion would be radically changed.

5. The reader may be interested in comparing a contemporary defense of miracles, such as that of C. S. Lewis in his *Miracles* (New York: The Macmillan Co., 1947), with a well-known skeptical analysis, *viz.*, David Hume, *An Inquiry Concerning Human Understanding* (New York: The Bobbs-Merrill Company, Inc.), chap. X.

6. See George Wald, "The Origin of Life," *Scientific American*, 191, No. 2 (August, 1954), 45. Also Leonard Engel, "The Race to Create Life," *Harper's Magazine*, 225, No. 1349 (October, 1962), 39-45.

7. Alfred North Whitehead, *Science and the Modern World*, Mentor Books edition (New York: The New American Library, 1948), Chap. XII.

8. John Dewey, *A Common Faith* (New Haven: Yale University Press, 1934), p. 1. Reprinted by permission.

9. Despite George A. Lundberg in *Can Science Save Us?* (New York: Longmans, Green & Co. Inc., 1947), who answers the title question in the affirmative.

10. For example, the appeal in the spring of 1957 by some two thousand scientists who signed a petition asking the government to stop the testing of nuclear bombs because of irradiation damage. See *Chemical and Engineering News*, 35, No. 24 (June 17, 1957), 42.

11. Wm. E. Hocking, *Science and the Idea of God* (Chapel Hill, N.C.: University of North Carolina Press, 1944), a selection from which is included at the end of this chapter.

12. Trans. Arthur Mitchell (New York: Modern Library Inc., 1944).

V. RELIGIOUS LANGUAGE

1. See D. T. Suzuki, *Zen Buddhism*, ed. William Barrett, Anchor Books edition (Garden City, N.Y.: Doubleday & Company, Inc., 1956), Chap. 6.

2. Alfred J. Ayer, *Language, Truth, and Logic* (New York: Dover Publications, Inc., n.d.), pp. 115-16.

3. For an argument that the belief is necessarily false see J. N. Findlay, "Can God's Existence be Disproved?" in *New Essays in Philosophical Theology*, eds. Antony Flew and Alasdair MacIntyre (New York: The Macmillan Co., 1955), pp. 47-56.

4. W. F. Zuurdeeg, *An Analytical Philosophy of Religion* (New York and Nashville: Abingdon Press, 1958), a selection from which appears at the end of this chapter.

5. "New Testament and Mythology," the first part of which is included in the readings for this chapter.

6. Walter A. Kaufmann, *Critique of Religion and Philosophy* (New York: Harper Row, Publishers, 1958), p. 247, included in the selection from this book at the end of Chapter VI.

7. Kaufmann, *Critique of Religion and Philosophy*, Sec. 66.

8. "The Religious Symbol" and "The Meaning and Justification of Religious Symbols," in *Religious Experience and Truth*, ed. Sidney Hook (New York: New York University Press, 1961), pp. 301-21 and 3-11, to be read in that order.

9. Charles C. Hartshorne, *The Divine Relativity* (New Haven: Yale University Press, 1948), pp. 36-40.

10. See, for example, E. L. Mascall, *Existence and Analogy* (London: Longmans, Green & Co. Inc., 1949).

11. The two types are called, respectively, analogy of attribution and analogy of proportionality.

12. "Theology and Falsification," in *New Essays in Philosophical Theology*, eds. Antony Flew and Alasdair MacIntyre (New York: The Macmillan Co., 1955), pp.

109-30; also "The Possibility of Theological Statements," in *Faith and Logic,* ed. Basil Mitchell (Boston: Beacon Press, 1957), pp. 31-83.

13. "The Possibility of Theological Statements," in *Faith and Logic,* p. 71. Reprinted by permission of Beacon Press and of George Allen & Unwin, Ltd.

VI. THE REALITY OF GOD

1. Strictly speaking, the premises of a deductive argument constitute evidence for the conclusion; but in this chapter it will be convenient to restrict the meaning of "evidence" to the narrower sense of inductive evidence, i.e., confirmatory facts.

2. For this purpose the student might begin with B. A. G. Fuller, *A History of Philosophy,* 2 vols., third edition revised by Sterling M. McMurrin (New York: Holt, Rinehart & Winston, Inc., 1955); or Frederick Copleston, S.J., *A History of Philosophy* (Westminster, Md.: The Newman Press, first vol. 1946, other dates for later vols.).

3. See, for example, Étienne Gilson, *The Philosophy of St. Thomas Aquinas,* trans. Edward Bullough (Cambridge: W. Heffer & Sons, Ltd., 1929), chaps. IV-V; or Samuel M. Thompson, *A Modern Philosophy of Religion* (Chicago: Henry Regnery Co., 1955), pp. 284ff.

4. Immanuel Kant, *Critique of Pure Reason,* trans. Norman Kemp Smith (New York: The Humanities Press, 1950), pp. 495-531.

5. For an example of such an interpretation see Erich Frank, *Philosophical Understanding and Religious Truth* (New York: Oxford University Press, 1945), chap. II.

6. It may be observed here that every scientific hypothesis is in the same position. While a given hypothesis may be very highly confirmed, even beyond reasonable doubt, other hypotheses can theoretically always be devised to account for the same facts. See Philipp Frank, *Philosophy of Science* (Englewood Cliffs, N.J.: Prentice-Hall, Inc., 1957), p. 16.

7. For a summary of the kinds of evidence usually appealed to in this connection see Horace T. Houf, *What Religion Is and Does,* rev. ed. (New York: Harper & Row, Publishers, 1945), chap. X.

8. See Karl Barth, *The Knowledge of God and the Service of God,* trans. J. L. M. Haire and Ian Henderson (London: Hodder and Stoughton, Ltd., 1938), Lecture I.

9. For example by Thomas Aquinas, *Summa Theologica,* Part I, Question 2.

10. Baillie, *Our Knowledge of God,* p. 3. Reprinted by permission.

VII. THE NATURE OF GOD

1. "The Atheism of Paul Tillich," in *Religious Experience and Truth,* ed. Sidney Hook (New York: New York University Press, 1961), p. 63. Reprinted by permission.

2. An allusion to Bertrand Russell, "A Free Man's Worship," reprinted in *Mysticism and Logic,* Anchor Books edition (Garden City, N.Y.: Doubleday & Company, Inc., 1957).

3. It is frequently pointed out, for example, that skepticism is self-contradictory if it maintains as an objective truth that no objective truth is possible.

4. I agree with William Hordern who makes this point at the end of some comments on Bultmann and Tillich in "Theology in Prospect," *The Journal of Bible and Religion,* XXVIII, No. 2 (April, 1960), 226.

5. *Systematic Theology* (Chicago: University of Chicago Press, 1951), I, 235ff.

6. See Edgar S. Brightman, *A Philosophy of Religion* (Englewood Cliffs, N.J.: Prentice-Hall, Inc., 1940), chaps, IX-X.

7. In a live discussion, Jan. 22, 1955.

8. This view is expounded by Boethius in the fifth book of *The Consolation of Philosophy*.

9. This theory is defended by Henri Bergson in his writings, especially *Creative Evolution* (New York: Modern Library, Inc., 1944).

10. Isa. 38:15.

VIII. THE RELIGIOUS NATURE OF MAN

1. Friedrich Schleiermacher took the feeling of dependence to be the very meaning of religion in his book, *The Christian Faith* (1821).

2. Blaise Pascal, *Pensées*, trans. W. F. Trotter (New York: E. P. Dutton & Co., Inc., 1908), VI, 358.

3. This theme has been developed with great penetration by Erich Fromm in his *Escape From Freedom* (New York: Holt, Rinehart & Winston, Inc., 1941).

4. See Donald M. Baillie, *The Theology of the Sacraments, and Other Papers* (New York: Charles Scribner's Sons, 1957), chap. III.

5. Reinhold Niebuhr has given a prominent place to this capacity for self-transcendence in his interpretation of the self in *The Self and the Dramas of History* (New York: Charles Scribner's Sons, 1955), Part I.

6. See *The Sickness Unto Death*, trans. Walter Lowrie, printed with *Fear and Trembling* in the Anchor Books edition (Garden City, N.Y.: Doubleday & Company, Inc., 1954), pp. 212f.

7. Gabriel Marcel has said that one's self *is* one's body, provided that this is not understood in a materialist sense. See *The Mystery of Being*, trans. G. S. Fraser, Gateway edition (Chicago: Henry Regnery Co., 1960), Vol. I, Lecture V.

8. Donald M. Baillie, *God Was in Christ*, revised edition (New York: Charles Scribner's Sons, 1948), chap. V.

9. The great classic on this theme to which most modern discussions are indebted is Martin Buber's *I and Thou*, [second edition (New York: Charles Scribner's Sons, 1958)] a selection from which appears at the end of this chapter.

10. Buber has even suggested that the I-thou relationship can be extended in some respects to the realm of nature and the realm of ideas.

IX. THE RELIGIOUS DESTINY OF MAN

1. For a brief account of some alternative conceptions of the self see Philip Wheelwright, *The Way of Philosophy*, rev. ed. (New York: The Odyssey Press, 1960), chap. VIII.

2. Karl Barth has given a vivid account of the meaning of physical death and burial in his *Dogmatics in Outline*, trans. G. T. Thompson, Torchbooks edition (New York: Harper & Row, Publishers, 1959), pp. 117-18.

3. For an interpretation of the meaning of death for the living see Douglas V. Steere, "Death's Illumination of Life," in *On Beginning from Within* (New York: Harper & Row, Publishers, 1943).

4. J. M. E. McTaggart, a recent British philosopher.

5. Edgar S. Brightman has examined a variety of weak arguments for and against immortality in the pages immediately preceding the ones comprising the selection at the end of this chapter, i.e., pp. 389-395.

6. See, for example, John Cogley, "What Is a Catholic?" in *A Guide to the Religions of America*, ed. Leo Rosten (New York: Simon and Schuster Inc., 1955), pp. 12, 14.

7. This alternative is apparently by-passed by Geddes MacGregor in his illuminating discussion in *Introduction to Religious Philosophy* (Boston: Houghton Mifflin Company, 1959), chap. 31.

8. I Cor. 15:44.
9. A useful article on this subject is that of James J. Heller, "The Resurrection of Man," *Theology Today*, XV, No. 2 (July, 1958), 217-29.
10. As in Plato's *Phaedo*.

X. PRAYER AND WORSHIP

1. Job 21:15.
2. It is interesting to note that amid Charles Hartshorne's departures from traditional Christianity he preserves prayer as one of its most valid features. See "A Philosopher's Assessment of Christianity," in *Religion and Culture*, ed. Walter Leibrecht (New York: Harper & Row, Publishers, 1959), pp. 178-79.
3. Ps. 10:17.
4. Matt. 6:7.
5. I Cor. 14:14-15.
6. Phil. 4:6.
7. Matt. 21:22.
8. Matt. 6:8.
9. John Magee, *Reality and Prayer* (New York: Harper & Row, Publishers, 1957), p. 125. Reprinted by permission.
10. Ps. 65:2.
11. James 5:16.
12. A now familiar illustration is given by H. Richard Niebuhr by comparing a scientific-historical description of the American Revolution with that of Lincoln in the Gettysburg Address. It is included in the selection at the end of Chapter XI.
13. Rom. 8:26.
14. Rom. 8:28.

XI. THE CONCEPT OF REVELATION

1. Hordern, *A Layman's Guide to Protestant Theology*.
2. See, for example, Edward J. Carnell, *The Case for Orthodox Theology* (Philadelphia: The Westminster Press, 1959), chap. VIII.
3. Emil Brunner, *Revelation and Reason*, trans. Olive Wyon (Philadelphia: The Westminster Press, 1946), p. 25.
4. Rom. 1:20.
5. "General and Special Divine Revelation," in *Revelation and the Bible*, ed. Carl F. H. Henry (Grand Rapids: Baker Book House, 1958), p. 22. Reprinted by permission.
6. *Op. cit.*, Chap. VI.
7. Pascal, *Pensées*, III, 185.
8. L. Harold DeWolf, *A Theology of the Living Church*, rev. ed. (New York: Harper & Row, Publishers, 1960), chap. 7.
9. See Bertocci, *Introduction to the Philosophy of Religion*, chap. 4.
10. *Special Revelation and the Word of God* (Grand Rapids: William B. Eerdmans Publishing Co., 1961), pp. 151, 152. Reprinted by permission.
11. Hordern, *The Case for a New Reformation Theology* (Philadelphia: The Westminster Press, 1959), pp. 59-60. Reprinted by permission.
12. John Baillie, *The Idea of Revelation in Recent Thought* (New York: Columbia University Press, 1956), p. 39. Reprinted by permission.
13. *Op. cit.*, p. 160. Italics original.

XII. INTERPRETING THE BIBLE

1. Junjirō Takakusu, *The Essentials of Buddhist Philosophy*, third edition, eds. Wing-Tsit Chan and Charles A. Moore (Honolulu: Office Appliance Co., Ltd., 1956), pp. 30-31.

2. This whole subject is discussed with great profundity by Reinhold Niebuhr in his *Faith and History* (New York: Charles Scribner's Sons, 1949).

3. This paradox has been called the scandal of particularity.

4. R. Laird Harris, *Inspiration and Canonicity of the Bible* (Grand Rapids: Zondervan Publishing House, 1957), pp. 46ff.

5. Harris, *Inspiration and Canonicity of the Bible*, pp. 61ff.

6. Geoffrey W. Bromily, "The Church Doctrine of Inspiration," in *Revelation and the Bible*, ed. Carl F. H. Henry (Grand Rapids: Baker Book House, 1958), p. 207ff.

7. Frank E. Gaebelein, "The Unity of the Bible," in *Revelation and the Bible*, pp. 391-95.

8. R. A. Finlayson, "Contemporary Ideas of Inspiration," in *Revelation and the Bible*, pp. 231-32.

9. J. E. McFadyen, "Inspiration," in *The Twentieth Century Bible Commentary* (New York: Harper & Row Publishers, 1932, 1955), pp. 9-10.

10. Hordern, *The Case for a New Reformation Theology*, p. 57.

11. Miller Burrows, *An Outline of Biblical Theology* (Philadelphia: The Westminster Press, 1946), pp. 24, 44-45.

12. Herbert H. Farmer, "The Bible: Its Significance and Authority," in *The Interpreter's Bible* (New York and Nashville: Abingdon Press, 1952), I, 26.

13. C. H. Dodd, *The Bible Today* (Cambridge: Cambridge University Press, 1946), pp. 12, 28, *passim*.

14. For books which take this approach in interpreting the Bible see the companion volumes: Bernard W. Anderson, *Understanding the Old Testament*, and Howard C. Kee and Franklin W. Young, *Understanding the New Testament* (Englewood Cliffs, N.J.: Prentice-Hall, Inc., 1957). For more conservative views on the questions of Biblical criticism involved see Edward J. Young, *An Introduction to the Old Testament* (Grand Rapids: Wm. B. Eerdmans Publishing Co., 1949), and Merrill C. Tenney, *New Testament Survey*, rev. ed. (Grand Rapids: Wm. B. Eerdmans Publishing Company, 1961).

XIII. INTERPRETING CHRIST

1. Ronald Gregor Smith, "The Religion of Martin Buber," *Theology Today*, XII, No. 2 (July, 1955), 208-9.

2. Emery H. Bancroft, *Christian Theology*, revised edition (Grand Rapids: Zondervan Publishing House, 1949), p. 53.

3. II Cor. 5:16.

4. Carnell, *The Case for Orthodox Theology*, pp. 82-83.

5. For an illustration of this approach see William A. Spurrier, *Guide to the Christian Faith* (New York: Charles Scribner's Sons, 1952), pp. 119ff.

6. W. Norman Pittenger, *The Word Incarnate* (New York: Harper & Row, Publishers, 1959), p. 129. Reprinted by permission.

7. II Cor. 5:19.

8. For a critique of this early form of the doctrine see John Baillie, *The Place of Jesus Christ in Modern Christianity* (New York: Charles Scribner's Sons, 1929), pp. 123-36.

9. A well-known work on this subject is that of Gustaf Aulén, *Christus Victor*, trans. A. G. Hebert (New York: The Macmillan Co., 1931).

10. *The Protestant Faith* (Englewood Cliffs, N.J.: Prentice-Hall, Inc., 1960), pp. 192-93. Italics original.

XIV. THE CHURCH

1. Eph. 1:22-23.
2. Rom. 12:4-5.
3. Eph. 4:15-16.
4. *Twenty Years at Hull-House* (New York: The Macmillan Co., 1910), p. 79. Reprinted by permission.
5. John Stuart Mill, *On Liberty* (New York: The Liberal Arts Press, 1956), p. 14.
6. Mark 16:15. Not contained in all mss.
7. See Gerald H. Anderson, ed., *The Theology of the Christian Mission* (New York: McGraw-Hill Book Company, Inc., 1961), and the review article, "A New Crisis in Foreign Missions?" *Christianity Today*, V, No. 15 (April 24, 1961), pp. 3-14.
8. Earle E. Cairns, *Christianity Through the Centuries*, third edition (Grand Rapids: Zondervan Publishing House, 1958), p. 384. Reprinted by permission.
9. See, for example, the sympathetic article by Gregory Baum, "Changes in Protestantism," in the Catholic magazine *Commonweal*, LXXII, No. 8 (May 20, 1960), 203-5.
10. "Conciliar Ecumenicity and Church Union," *Christianity and Crisis*, XXI, No. 18 (Oct. 30, 1961), 188.

XV. CHRISTIAN BELIEFS

1. "The Essence of Christianity," *The Crozer Quarterly* (April, 1941), in *Contemporary Thinking about Jesus*, ed. Thomas S. Kepler (New York and Nashville: Abingdon Press, 1944), 369.
2. Kepler, *Contemporary Thinking about Jesus*, p. 373.
3. Kepler, *Contemporary Thinking about Jesus*, pp. 373-78.
4. *Christ and Culture* (New York: Harper & Row, Publishers, 1951), p. 11, Reprinted by permission.
5. "Christianity and Naturalism," *Christianity Today*, III, No. 18 (June 8, 1959), 10.
6. Arthur Holmes, *Christianity and Philosophy* (Chicago: Inter-Varsity Press, 1960), p. 12. Reprinted by permission.
7. Karl Adam, *The Spirit of Catholicism*, rev. ed., trans. Dom Justin McCann (New York: The Macmillan Co., 1955), p. 67. Reprinted by permission.
8. Adam, *The Spirit of Catholicism*, p. 68.
9. C. S. Lewis, *Mere Christianity* (New York: The Macmillian Co., 1956), Book II.
10. William A. Spurrier, *Guide to the Christian Faith* (New York: Charles Scribner's Sons, 1952).
11. George F. Thomas, "Central Christian Affirmations," in *The Christian Answer*, ed. Henry P. Van Dusen (New York: Charles Scribner's Sons, 1945), pp. 91-135.
12. Gustaf Aulén, *The Faith of the Christian Church*, trans. Eric H. Wahlstrom, second English edition (Philadelphia: Muhlenberg Press, 1960).

XVI. OTHER RELIGIONS

1. Wilfred Cantwell Smith, "Comparative Religion: Whither—and Why?" in *The History of Religions*, eds. Mircea Eliade and Joseph M. Kitagawa (Chicago: University of Chicago Press, 1959), p. 55. Copyright 1959 by the University of Chicago. Reprinted by permission.
2. For a fine review of some of the classifications and views proposed on this problem see Hideo Hashimoto, "Christian Theology and the Challenge of Non-

Christian Religions," *The Journal of Bible and Religion*, XXVIII, No. 3 (July, 1960), 299-307.

3. Luke 6:27.

4. *Pious and Secular America* (New York: Charles Scribner's Sons, 1958), p. 108.

5. P. T. Raju, *An Extension Lecture on East and West in Philosophy*, quoted in W. H. Sheldon, "What Can Western Philosophy Contribute to Eastern?" *Philosophy East and West*, V, No. 4 (Jan., 1956), 302.

6. "Christ and Non-Christians," *Christianity and Crisis*, XXI, No. 8 (May 15, 1961), 74.

7. *The Nature and Destiny of Man* (New York: Charles Scribner's Sons, 1943), II, 109-110.

8. *Op. cit.*, p. 76.

9. *Living Religions and a World Faith* (New York: The Macmillan Co., 1940).

10. The distinction is made with a somewhat different connotation in the unsigned article, "A New Crisis in Foreign Missions?" *Christianity Today*, V, No. 15 (April 24, 1961), 11.

INDEX